CULTURAL
ANTHROPOLOGY

FOURTH EDITION

CULTURAL ANTHROPOLOGY

BARBARA MILLER

George Washington University

PEARSON

Boston   New York   San Francisco
Mexico City   Montreal   Toronto   London   Madrid   Munich   Paris
Hong Kong   Singapore   Tokyo   Cape Town   Sydney

Series Editor: *Dave Repetto*
Series Editorial Assistant: *Jack Cashman*
Marketing Manager: *Laura Lee Manley*
Production Supervisor: *Karen Mason*
Editorial Production Service: *Publishers' Design and Production Services, Inc.*
Composition Buyer: *Linda Cox*
Manufacturing Buyer: *Debbie Rossi*
Electronic Composition: *Publishers' Design and Production Services, Inc.*
Interior Design: *Anne Flanagan*
Photo Researchers: *Erin Curtis, Annie Pickert, and Naomi Rudov*
Cover Administrator: *Kristina Mose-Libon*

For related titles and support materials, visit our online catalog at www.ablongman.com.

Between the time website information is gathered and then published, it is not unusual for some sites to have closed. Also, the transcription of URLs can result in typographical errors. The publisher would appreciate notification where these errors occur so that they may be corrected in subsequent editions.

Library of Congress Cataloging-in-Publication Data

Miller, Barbara D.
    Cultural anthropology / Barbara D. Miller. — 4th ed.
        p. cm.
    Includes bibliographical references nad index.
    ISBN 0-205-48808-0
    1. Ethnology.   I. Title.

GN316.M49 2006
306—dc22

                                                            2006050831

Printed in the United States of America

10   9   8   7   6   5   4   3   [RRD-OH]   11   10   09   08

Brief Contents

Contents

■■■ I Introduction to Cultural Anthropology

1 Anthropology and the Study of Culture 2

2 Methods in Cultural Anthropology 32

▪▪▪ II Economic and Demographic Foundations

3 Economies and Their Modes of Production 62

4 Consumption and Exchange 90

5 Birth and Death 118

6 Personality and Identity over the Life Cycle 144

7 Disease, Illness,
and Healing   170

8 Kinship
and Domestic
Life   200

9 Social Groups and Social Stratification 232

10 Politics and Leadership 258

11 Social Order and Social Conflict   284

12 Communication 310

13 Religion 338

14 Expressive Culture 368

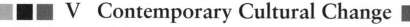

■■■ V Contemporary Cultural Change

15 People on the Move 396

16 People Defining Development 422

Boxed Features

Lessons Applied

Everyday Anthropology

Culturama

Critical Thinking

List of Maps

Preface

"I had no idea all those cultures were out there," said one of my students after taking my introductory cultural anthropology course. Another commented, "I'm a business major but I am going to keep the books from this course because they will help me in my career. I need to understand people."

Cultural anthropology opens up whole new worlds. Not just "out there," but here, there, and everywhere. The subject matter of cultural anthropology may seem distant, exotic, and "other"—jungle drumbeats and painted faces, for example. This book helps students to encounter those faraway cultures and to realize that their culture has its own versions of jungle drumbeats and painted faces. "Making the strange familiar" is essential learning in a globalizing world where cultural diversity may equal cultural survival for all of us. "Making the familiar strange" is a priceless revelation because it reduces the divide between "us" and the "other." "We" become an "other" through the insights of cultural anthropology.

To achieve this double goal, *Cultural Anthropology*, Fourth Edition, delivers information about the world's cultures and promotes critical thinking and reflective learning. This book is rich in global examples of cultural diversity and change. Students will find many points at which they can connect with the material and reflect on their own culture—for example, hairstyles, food symbolism, sleep deprivation, doctor–patient dialogues, the meaning of gestures, and racism.

The book's organization and pedagogical features help ensure student engagement. Knowing that it is impossible to place culture in a linear series of chapters in a totally satisfactory way, I have organized the material in five parts. Within the five parts, each chapter presents findings from the latest, cutting-edge research in cultural anthropology, explained in clear and engaging prose.

Highlights of Revised Chapter Contents

Part I, Introduction to Cultural Anthropology, includes two chapters that provide the foundation for the rest of the book. They describe what anthropology is and how cultural anthropologists do research. Samples of updates include:

- Chapter 1: Discrimination against Mexicana girls in middle schools of the U.S. Southwest
- Chapter 2: Being accused of spying when doing research in Damascus, Syria

Part II, Economic and Demographic Foundations, includes chapters that explain how people make a living and provide for their needs, how people reproduce and raise children, and how different cultures deal with the inevitabilities of illness, suffering, and death. Samples of updates include:

- Chapter 4: Globalization of the production and distribution of ecstasy
- Chapter 5: Illegal abortion and women's death in Brazil
- Chapter 7: Kinship and care of HIV/AIDS orphans in Africa

Part III, Social Organization, provides chapters about how people around the world organize themselves into groups based on kinship and other forms of affiliation, how they form political alliances, and how they deal with conflict and the need for order. Samples of updates include:

- Chapter 8: The "marriage crisis" among African American women in Syracuse, New York

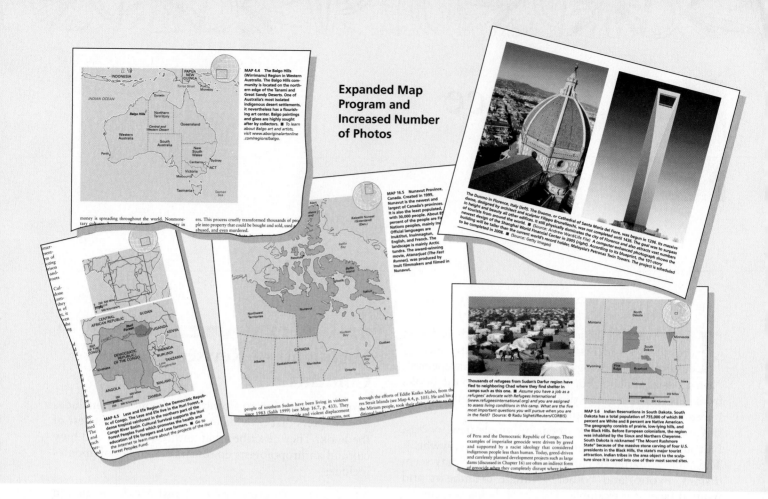

Expanded Map Program and Increased Number of Photos

MAP 4.4 The Balgo Hills (Wirrimanu) Region in Western Australia. The Balgo Hills community is located on the northern edge of the Tanami and Great Sandy Deserts. One of Australia's most isolated indigenous desert settlements, it nevertheless has a flourishing art center. Balgo paintings and glass are highly sought after by collectors. ■ To learn about Balgo art and artists, visit www.aboriginalartonline.com/regions/balgo.

MAP 16.5 Nunavut Province, Canada. Created in 1999, Nunavut is the newest and largest of Canada's provinces. It is also the least populated, with 30,000 people. About 85 percent of the people are First Nations peoples, mainly Inuit. Official languages are Inuktitut, Inuinnaqtun, English, and French. The landscape is mainly Arctic tundra. The award-winning movie, Atanarjuat (The Fast Runner), was produced by Inuit filmmakers and filmed in Nunavut.

The Duomo in Florence, Italy (left). The Duomo, or Cathedral of Santa Maria del Fiore, was begun in 1296. Its massive dome, designed by architect and sculptor Filippo Brunelleschi, was not completed until 1436. The goal was to surpass in height and beauty all other edifices. It still physically dominates the city of Florence and also attracts vast numbers of tourists from around the world. ■ (Source: Andrew Ward/Life File) A computer-enhanced photograph shows the newest design of the Shanghai World Financial Center in 2005 (right). According to its blueprint, the 101-story building will be taller than the current world's record holder, Malaysia's Petronas Twin Towers. The project is scheduled to be completed in 2008. ■ (Source: Getty Images)

MAP 4.5 Lese and Efe Region in the Democratic Republic of Congo. The Lese and Efe live in the northern part of the dense tropical rainforest in the Ituri Forest. Cultural Survival supports the Ituri Forest Peoples Fund which promotes the health and education of Efe foragers and Lese farmers. ■ Go to the Internet to learn more about the projects of the Ituri Forest Peoples Fund.

Thousands of refugees from Sudan's Darfur region have fled to neighboring Chad where they find shelter in camps such as this one. ■ Assume you have a job as a refugees' advocate with Refugees International (www.refugeesinternational.org) and you are assigned to assess living conditions in this camp. What are the five most important questions you will pursue when you are in the field? (Source: © Radu Sigheti/Reuters/CORBIS)

MAP 5.6 Indian Reservations in South Dakota. South Dakota has a total population of 755,000 of which 88 percent are White and 8 percent are Native American. The geography consists of prairie, low-lying hills, and the Black Hills. Before European colonialism, the region was inhabited by the Sioux and Northern Cheyenne. South Dakota is nicknamed "The Mount Rushmore State" because of the massive stone carving of four U.S. presidents in the Black Hills, the state's major tourist attraction. Indian tribes in the area object to the sculpture since it is carved into one of their most sacred sites.

- Chapter 9: Cell phone networking in Jamaica
- Chapter 10: Women political leaders

Part IV, Symbolic Systems, presents chapters on communication and language, religion, and expressive culture and art. Samples of updates include:

- Chapter 12: Endangered languages and language revitalization
- Chapter 13: Expanded material on Islam
- Chapter 14: Globalization and country music in Brazil

Part V, Contemporary Cultural Change, looks at two of the most important topics in contemporary cultural change: migration and international development. These chapters explicitly put culture into motion and show how people are both affected by larger structures, such as globalization or violence, and exercise agency in attempting to create meaningful lives. Samples of updates include:

- Chapter 15: Adopted children as involuntary migrants
- Chapter 16: Muslim women's nongovernmental organizations in Kazakhstan

New Features of the Fourth Edition

Expanded Map Program

All chapters contain several maps. Each map is carefully designed to enhance the text material and all are clearly labeled. Cross-references throughout the book to maps located elsewhere encourage students to flip forward and backward in the book. This process facilitates review and helps readers make connections across chapters about the cultural groups and topics discussed.

Increased Number of Photographs

Each chapter has more photographs than the previous edition. They are selected to reinforce the material being discussed or take it in a new direction. Captions for all photographs are clear and concise. Many contain a Thought Question to prompt class discussion or an idea for a research project.

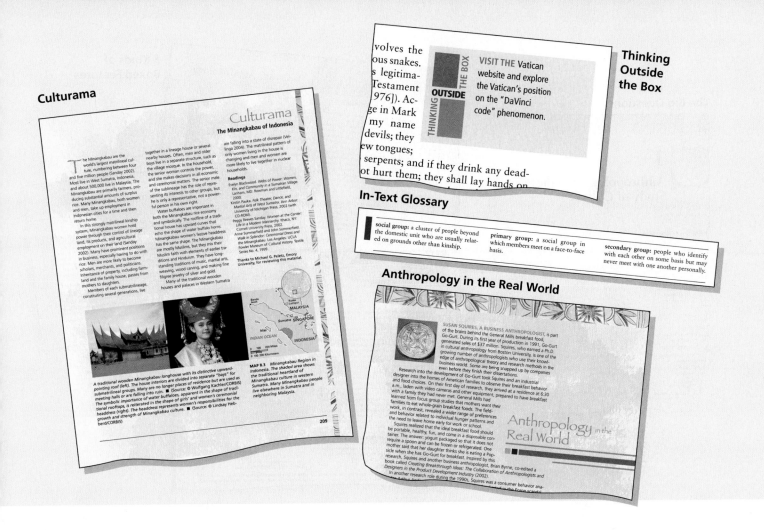

Culturama

All chapters include a one-page profile of a cultural group accompanied by a mini-panorama of two photographs and a map with captions. The summaries are brief, providing an enticing glimpse into the culture. At the end of each Culturama, a list of resources (readings, videos, and websites) offers avenues for those who want to learn more. A good class assignment would be for students to do some independent research on one or more of the cultures in the Culturamas, or they might choose a different culture and compose their own Culturama, with photographs (from Google.images, for example) and a map.

In-Text Glossary

Definitions for the Key Concepts are positioned on the bottom of the left page on the spread where the concept is first mentioned and defined. Key Concepts are also alphabetized in the Key Concepts list at the end of the chapter with page numbers included for easy cross-referencing. The end-of-the-book Glossary contains the complete list with definitions.

Thinking Outside the Box

Another new feature, Thinking Outside the Box, prompts readers to relate an issue to their own cultural experiences or suggests ideas for further research. Each chapter contains three or four of these features. For example:

- Chapter 5: In your microculture, is there a preference about the desired number of sons and daughters? Is there a preference for their birth order?

- Chapter 13: Visit the Vatican website and explore the Vatican's position on the "DaVinci code" phenomenon.

Anthropology in the Real World

Each of the book's five parts opens with a profile of an applied anthropologist, someone who uses his or her anthropology training in the "real world." Profiles include a business anthropologist, a medical anthropologist, a forensic anthropologist, a development anthropologist, and a federal relations anthropologist.

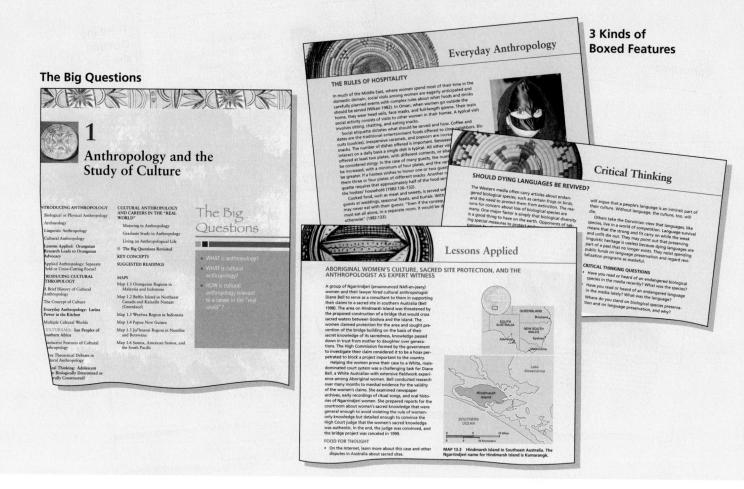

The Big Questions

1

Anthropology and the Study of Culture

INTRODUCING ANTHROPOLOGY
Biological or Physical Anthropology
Archaeology
Linguistic Anthropology
Cultural Anthropology
Lessons Applied: Orangutan Research Leads to Orangutan Advocacy
Applied Anthropology: Separate Field or Cross-Cutting Focus?
INTRODUCING CULTURAL ANTHROPOLOGY
A Brief History of Cultural Anthropology
The Concept of Culture
Everyday Anthropology: Latina Power in the Kitchen
Multiple Cultural Worlds
CULTURAMA: San Peoples of Southern Africa
Distinctive Features of Cultural Anthropology
Three Theoretical Debates in Cultural Anthropology
Critical Thinking: Adolescent Stress: Biologically Determined or Culturally Constructed?

CULTURAL ANTHROPOLOGY AND CAREERS IN THE "REAL WORLD"
Majoring in Anthropology
Graduate Study in Anthropology
Living an Anthropological Life
● The Big Questions Revisited
KEY CONCEPTS
SUGGESTED READINGS

MAPS
Map 1.1 Orangutan Regions in Malaysia and Indonesia
Map 1.2 Baffin Island in Northeast Canada and Kalaallit Nunaat (Greenland)
Map 1.3 Weyéwa Region in Indonesia
Map 1.4 Papua New Guinea
Map 1.5 Ju/'hoansi Region in Namibia and Botswana
Map 1.6 Samoa, American Samoa, and the South Pacific

The Big Questions

■ WHAT is anthropology?

■ WHAT is cultural anthropology?

■ HOW is cultural anthropology relevant to a career in the "real world"?

3 Kinds of Boxed Features

Everyday Anthropology

THE RULES OF HOSPITALITY

In much of the Middle East, where women spend most of their time in the domestic domain, social visits among women are eagerly anticipated and carefully planned events with complex rules about what foods and drinks should be served (Wikan 1982). In Oman, when women go outside the home, they wear head veils, face masks, and full-length gowns. Their main social activity consists of visits to other women in their homes. A typical visit involves sitting, chatting, and eating snacks.

Social etiquette dictates what should be served and how. Coffee and dates are the traditional entertainment foods offered to close neighbors. Biscuits (cookies), inexpensive caramels, and popcorn are increasingly offered snacks. The number of dishes offered is important. Between women who interact on a daily basis a single dish is typical. All other visits require at least two plates, with different contents, or else the hostess may be considered stingy. In the case of many guests, the number of plates must be increased, with a minimum of four plates, and the variety must be greater. If a hostess wishes to honor one or two guests, she serves them three or four plates of different snacks. Another rule of hospitality etiquette requires that approximately half of the food served be left over for the hostess' household (1982:130–132).

Cooked food, such as meat and sweets, is served when close friends are guests at weddings, seasonal feasts, and burials. When cooked food is served, guests may never eat with their guests: "Even if the consequence is that you must eat all alone, in a separate room, it would be disgraceful to do otherwise" (1982:133).

Critical Thinking

SHOULD DYING LANGUAGES BE REVIVED?

The Western media often carry articles about endangered biological species, such as certain frogs or birds, and the need to protect them from extinction. The reasons for concern about loss of biological species are many. One major factor is simply that biological diversity is a good thing to have on the earth. Opponents of taking special measures to protect endangered languages will argue that a people's language is an intrinsic part of their culture. Without language, the culture, too, will die.

Others take the Darwinian view that languages, like species, live in a world of competition. Language survival means that the strong and fit carry on while the weak and unfit die out. They may point out that preserving linguistic heritage is useless because dying languages are part of a past that no longer exists. They resist spending public funds on language preservation and regard revitalization programs as wasteful.

CRITICAL THINKING QUESTIONS
● Have you read or heard of an endangered biological species in the media recently? What was the species?
● Have you read or heard of an endangered language in the media lately? What was the language?
● Where do you stand on biological species preservation and on language preservation, and why?

Lessons Applied

ABORIGINAL WOMEN'S CULTURE, SACRED SITE PROTECTION, AND THE ANTHROPOLOGIST AS EXPERT WITNESS

A group of Ngarrindjeri (pronounced NAR-en-jeery) women and their lawyer hired cultural anthropologist Diane Bell to serve as a consultant to them in supporting their claims to a sacred site in southern Australia (Bell 1998). The area on Hindmarsh Island was threatened by the proposed construction of a bridge that would cross sacred waters between Goolwa and the island. The women claimed protection for the area and sought prevention of the bridge building on the basis of their secret knowledge of its sacredness, knowledge passed down in trust from mother to daughter over generations. The High Commission formed by the government to investigate their claim considered it to be a hoax perpetrated to block a project important to the country.

Helping the women prove their case to a White, male-dominated court system was a challenging task for Diane Bell, a White Australian with extensive fieldwork experience among Aboriginal women. Bell conducted research over many months to marshal evidence for the validity of the women's claims. She examined newspaper archives, early recordings of ritual songs, and oral histories of Ngarrindjeri women. She prepared reports for the courtroom about women's sacred knowledge that were general enough to avoid violating the rule of women-only knowledge but detailed enough to convince the High Court judge that the women's sacred knowledge was authentic. In the end, the judge was convinced, and the bridge project was canceled in 1999.

FOOD FOR THOUGHT
● On the Internet, learn more about this case and other disputes in Australia about sacred sites.

MAP 13.3 Hindmarsh Island in Southeast Australia. The Ngarrindjeri name for Hindmarsh Island is Kumarangk.

Continuing Features

Several continuing features make this textbook distinctive and effective.

The Big Questions

Three Big Questions are posed at the beginning of each chapter to alert readers to the chapter's overarching themes. They are carried through in the chapter outline as the three major headings. At the end of the chapter, The Big Questions Revisited provides a helpful review of the key points related to each Big Question.

Boxed Features

Everyday Anthropology boxes present cultural examples that connect to everyone's lives, in one way or another. For example:

■ Chapter 4: "The Rules of Hospitality." Readers can consider the material on Oman in relation to what they would serve to guests.

■ Chapter 8: "What's in a Name?" Naming children is meaningful in many ways. Readers will learn about gender differences in naming practices in the Hong Kong region and be prompted to ponder "what's in a name" in their own culture.

Critical Thinking boxes introduce an issue and show how it has been studied or analyzed from different anthropological perspectives. These boxes provide tie-ins to the major theoretical debates in cultural anthropology presented in Chapter 1. For example:

■ Chapter 1, "Adolescent Stress: Biologically Determined or Culturally Constructed?" This box presents the Mead-Freeman controversy about adolescence.

In other Critical Thinking boxes, readers are asked to reflect on received wisdom:

■ Chapter 3: "Was the Invention of Agriculture a Terrible Mistake?" This box discusses some of the down sides to the invention of agriculture, especially in terms of inequality. It prompts reflective learning.

■ Chapter 14: "Probing the Categories of Art." Critical thinking about one's own cultural categories is developed through this box that asks students to undertake a research project.

Lessons Applied boxes highlight how applied anthropologists work. Although students may appreciate the interesting material that cultural anthropology offers, they are still likely to ask, "Does this knowledge have any practical applications?" This fourth edition, even more than previous editions, shows the relevance of knowledge in cultural anthropology and the many ways it can be put into practice.

- Chapter 4: "Evaluating Indian Gaming in California." This box demonstrates the role of impact assessment.
- Chapter 13: "Aboriginal Women's Culture, Sacred Site Protection, and the Anthropologist as Expert Witness." This box explores the role of expert witness.
- Chapter 14: "A Strategy for the World Bank on Cultural Heritage." This box explores the role of influencing policy.

In addition to the boxed features that add depth and richness to the text, *Suggested Readings* are listed at the end of each chapter. Each selection has a brief annotation to guide students who may be looking for resources for a class project or report.

Commitment to Cultural Survival

In confirming our commitment to cultural survival, a portion of the royalties from sales of new copies of this book are donated by the author and the publisher to Cultural Survival. (See the Cultural Survival Mission Statement on the inside of the front cover of this book.) Cultural Survival helps support the preferred lifestyles and environmental context of indigenous people worldwide. Back issues of the journal, *Cultural Survival Quarterly*, are available on the Web at www.cs.org.

Cultural Anthropology for the Future

The excitement of cultural anthropology is undeniable, as is its relevance to important issues, global and local, from the spread of HIV/AIDs to conflict resolution in Sudan.

Knowledge of the world's cultures and how they are changing connects to all careers in this increasingly globalized world. The need to understand people (including ourselves) is critical to any endeavor in the short term and to the survival of humanity in the long run.

The study of the world's cultures is, admittedly, weighted down with some long words and analytical categories. But they are a small price to pay for bringing the world's peoples and cultures closer to you. If this book achieves my aspirations, anyone who reads it will live a life that is more culturally aware, enriched, and tolerant.

I take hope from the frequent emails my former students send me, telling me about how something they read in the newspaper, or something they saw in their travels, or an experience they had at a doctor's office, reminded them of the cultural anthropology class they took with me. Cultural anthropology makes connections.

Supplements

Along with this textbook come an array of supplements that will assist instructors in using the book and enriching the students' learning experience.

Instructor's Manual and Test Bank

An unusual feature of the Instructor's Manual and Test Bank is that it is written by the textbook author herself. In this manual, I include teaching tips and classroom exercises that I have used in many years of teaching cultural anthropology.

Computerized Test Bank

This computerized version of the test bank is available with Tamarack's easy-to-use TestGen software, which lets you prepare tests for printing as well as for network and online testing. Full editing capability exists for Windows and Macintosh.

Allyn & Bacon Interactive Video and User's Guide

This custom video covers a variety of topics, both national and global. The up-to-the-minute video segments are great to launch lectures, spark classroom discussion, and encourage critical thinking. The user's guide provides detailed descriptions of each video segment, specific tie-ins to the text, and suggested discussion questions and projects.

Allyn & Bacon Video Library

Qualified adopters may select from a wide variety of high-quality videos from such sources as Films for the Humanities and Sciences and Annenberg/CPB.

PowerPoint Presentation

The PowerPoint presentation for *Cultural Anthropology*, Fourth Edition, is substantially revised. It combines dozens of graphic and text images into teaching modules. Using either Macintosh or DOS/Windows, a professor can use the slides to create customized presentations for lectures. PowerPoint software is not required to use this program; a PowerPoint viewer is included to access the images.

Study Guide

The author-written Study Guide offers students a traditional format in which they can test their understanding of key material presented in the text through practice questions, key concept review, and other tools. The Study Guide has been completely updated, with the assistance of Miranda Horan, one of the author's M.A. students, to encompass all the new material in the fourth edition. It is available as a printed supplement that can be packaged free with the textbook or online at www.ablongman.com/miller4e.

The Anthropology Experience

This valuable multimedia resource for teaching and learning cultural anthropology includes a National Geographic video, an audio glossary, PowerPoint presentations, an illustrated supplementary cultural anthropology booklet, world-class anthropological photos in an accessible image bank, online activities, and more. Please visit www.ablongman.com/miller4e for more information on how to make use of these exciting media resources and how to make them available to your students.

Research Navigator for Anthropology

Research Navigator for Anthropology is a booklet designed to teach students how to conduct high-quality online research and to document it properly. It provides extensive help on the research process and an access code to four exclusive databases of reliable source material, including the EBSCO Academic Journal and Abstract Database, New York Times Search by Subject Archive, "Best of the Web" Link Library, and Financial Times Article Archive and Company Financials. Research Navigator helps students quickly and efficiently make the most of their research time. This resource is available free when packaged with the textbook.

Careers in Anthropology

This booklet by W. Richard Stephens contains biographies of anthropology professionals and helps answer the often-asked question, "What can I do with a degree in anthropology?" It provides information about career options targeted to typical students who are taking their first anthropology course. The biographies are organized by various fields and include discussions of what can be done with a B.A., M.A., Ph.D., or a combination of degrees.

The Blockbuster Approach: A Guide to Teaching Anthropology with Film

This supplement guides the instructor on how to integrate feature films into an introductory course successfully and offers hundreds of film suggestions for topics covered in *Cultural Anthropology*, Fourth Edition.

In Thanks

The breadth, depth, and quality of this fourth edition are the result of many people's ideas, comments, corrections, and care. Writing and revising a textbook can be a lonely endeavor: So much time is spent in front of a computer screen inputting new text, cutting text, and moving words around to make them more effective. On the other hand, I have never felt more connected with so many helpful people as I have with this revision. My heartfelt thanks go to everyone who, directly or indirectly, helped make this revision happen.

The cultural anthropologists who reviewed the fourth edition and offered their critiques and detailed suggestions shaped the revisions from start to finish. They are: Warren D. Anderson, Southeast Missouri State University; Monica L. Bellas, Cerritos College; Barbara Bonnekessen, University of Missouri–Kansas City; Dr. Lisa Pope Fischer, Santa Monica College; Pamela J. Ford, Mount San Jacinto College; Mary Kay Gilliland, Pima Community College; Nancy Gonlin, Bellevue Community College; Jeanne Humble, Bluegrass Community & Technical College; Ann Kingsolver, University of South Carolina; Martin F. Manalansan IV, University of Illinois; Jacquelyn Robinson, Albany State University; Harry Sanabria, University of Pittsburgh; Kathleen M. Saunders, Western Washington University; David Simmons, University of South Carolina; Kimberly Eison Simmons, University of South Carolina; Lori A. Stanley, Luther College; Jim Wilce, Northern Arizona University; and Peter Wogan, Willamette University. I tried my best, within a tight schedule, to take their invaluable comments into account. They pushed me hard and, in the process, taught me a lot.

Several other cultural anthropologists and one sociologist gave me careful critiques of the Culturamas. Their depth of expertise was crucial in helping me avoid errors, flesh out important details, enrich the list of resources, and provide updates on current changes. I think of these people as my "Culturama Angels." They are: Vincanne Adams, University of California at San Francisco: The Sherpas of Nepal; Myrdene Anderson, Purdue University: The Saami of Lapland, or Sapmi; Alison Brooks, George Washington University: San Peoples of Southern Africa; Linus Digim'rina, University of Papua New Guinea: The Trobriand Islanders of Papua New Guinea; Robert Foster, University of Rochester: The Trobriand Islanders of Papua New Guinea; Maris Boyd Gillette, Haverford University: Hui Muslims of Xi'an, China; Jennifer Kramer, University of British Columbia: The Kwakwa̲ka'wakw of Canada; Donald B. Kraybill, Elizabethtown College: The Old Order Amish of the United States and Canada;

Dorothy Hodgson, Rutgers University: The Maasai of Kenya and Tanzania; Diane E. King, Brown University and Washington State University: The Kurds of the Middle East; Beatriz Manz, University of California at Berkeley: The Maya of Guatemala; Madhusree Mukerjee, Independent Scholar and Activist: The Andaman Islanders of India; Michael G. Peletz, Emory University: The Minangkabau of Indonesia; David Z. Scheffel, Thompson Rivers University: The Roma of Eastern Europe; Jennie Smith-Pariola, Berry College: The Peyizan yo of Haiti; and Sita Venkateswar, Massey University: The Andaman Islanders of India. My email communications with these experts were always uplifting. Each one understood what I was trying to accomplish (the impossible!) in a one-page feature on an entire "culture," and they all helped me move toward achieving that goal. Several also contributed photographs that accompany the Culturamas, adding to the feature's richness and authenticity. Thank you all.

Abstracting key points from a book, even a journal article, and attempting to present them in a paragraph or two is a perilous activity. On this round of revisions, I consulted with some of the authors on whose work I had drawn, asking them to point out errors and misinterpretations. They sent me copies of their publications, pointed me to other experts, and gave me extremely important suggestions. They are: Abigail Adams, Central Connecticut State University: The "Break-Out" at VMI; Matthew Amster, Gettysburg College: Household change among the Kelabit; Alexander Dent, George Washington University: Country music in Brazil; Daniel Everett, Illinois State University: Pirahã language; Johannes Fabian, University of Amsterdam: The perils of translation; Lanita Jacobs-Huey, University of Southern California: Multisited fieldwork about African American hair and African American English; Susan Orpett Long, John Carroll University: Aging and the "good death" in Japan; Luisa Maffi, Terralingua: Endangered languages; Kimber Haddox McKay, University of Montana: Polyandry in the Himalayas; Tobias Hecht: Street children in Brazil; Laura Miller, University of Loyola, Chicago: Kogals of Japan; Kate Spilde Contreras, University of California at Riverside: Indian gaming in California; Anthony Stocks, University of Idaho: Indigenous territorial rights in South America; and Brian Craik, director of Federal Relations of the Grand Council of the Crees, took time to review my profile of him for the Anthropology in the Real World Feature.

The following people provided photographs that are new to this edition: Abigail Adams, Central Connecticut State University: Breaking Out at VMI; Matthew Amster, Gettysburg College: Kelabit longhouse and Kelabit nuclear house; Daniel Everett, Illinois State University: Pirahã scene; Maris Boyd Gillette, Haverford College: Hui women; Tobias Hecht and Isabel Balseiro, Harvey Mudd College: Brazilian street children; Lanita Jacobs-

Huey, University of Southern California: African American hair styling; Vickie Jensen, Westcoast Words: Alert Bay canoes and Hamatsa dance practice; Barry D. Kass, Orange County Community College, SUNY: Maasai woman; Stephen Lubkemann, George Washington University, and Richard A. Gould, Brown University: underwater archaeology; Deborah Pellow, Syracuse University: Hausa dowry goods; David Z. Scheffel, Thompson Rivers University: Romani school children and Roma housing in Svinia; Pankaj Sekhsaria: Jarawa woman and Jarawa on a boat; Patricia Tovar, Colombian Institute of Anthropology, ICANH, and Javeriana University in Bogatá: Colombian anthropology conference; Mark L. Weiss, National Science Foundation: biker in Washington, D.C.; and Rita Maddox: Japanese-American household shrine.

For the first edition, four anthropologists carefully reviewed multiple drafts of the book. I will always be grateful to them for their monumental contribution. They helped make this book what it is today: Elliot Fratkin, Pennsylvania State University; Maxine Margolis, University of Florida; Russell Reid, University of Louisville; and Robert Trotter II, University of Arizona.

The cultural anthropologists who served as reviewers for the second and third editions helped me move the book forward in many ways. They are: Jason Antrosio, Albion College; Diane Baxter, University of Oregon; Peter Brown, University of Wisconsin, Oshkosh; Howard Campbell, University of Texas, El Paso; (the late) Charles R. de Burlo, The University of Vermont; Elizabeth de la Portilla, University of Texas at San Antonio; William W. Donner, Kutztown University; Leslie Lischka, Linfield College; William M. Loker, California State University, Chico (his son took my class a few years ago!); Corey Pressman, Mt. Hood Community College; Ed Robbins, University of Wisconsin; G. Richard Scott, University of Nevada, Reno; Wesley Shumar, Drexel University; and Katrina Worley, Sierra College.

Many anthropologists and others have provided encouragement, suggestions, feedback, references, and photographs. They include Lila Abu-Lughod, Vincanne Adams, Catherine Allen, Joseph Alter, Donald Attwood, Christopher Baker, Nancy Benco, Marc Bermann, Alexia Bloch, Elson Boles, Lynne Bolles, John Bowen, Don Brenneis, Alison Brooks, Judith K. Brown, D. Glynn Cochrane, Jeffery Cohen, Carole Counihan, Liza Dalby, Loring Danforth, Patricia Delaney, Timothy Earle, Elliot Fratkin, Martin Fusi, David Gow, Curt Grimm, Richard Grinker, Daniel Gross, (the late) Marvin Harris, Cornelia Mayer Herzfeld, Michael Herzfeld, Barry Hewlett, Danny Hoffman, Michael Horowitz, (the late) Robert Humphrey, Anstice Justin, Laurel Kendall, David Kideckel, Stuart Kirsch, Dorinne Kondo, Conrad Kottak, Ruth Krulfeld, Joel Kuipers, Takie Lebra, David Lempert, Lamont Lindstrom, Samuel Martínez, Catherine McCoid, Leroy McDermott, Jerry Milanich, Kirin Narayan, Sarah

Nelson, Gananath Obeyesekere, Ellen Oxfeld, Hanna Papanek, Deborah Pellow, Gregory Possehl, David Price, Joanne Rappaport, Jennifer Robertson, Nicole Sault, Joel Savishinsky, Nancy Scheper-Hughes, Richard Shweder, Chunghee Soh, Martha Ward, James (Woody) Watson, Rubie Watson, Van Yasek, and Kevin Yelvington.

My students are a major source of inspiration. Many have offered updates, corrections, and ideas for new material. Nothing makes me happier than to see students get hooked on cultural anthropology and have it change their lives. I am deeply grateful to all my students who have gone on to live more anthropological lives. I welcome their emails from here, there, and everywhere about their accomplishments and insights. For this fourth edition, Stephen Blum, Dan Burd, Qaiser Khan, Wesley Lynah, and Julie Patel made specific suggestions that helped improve it. Two M.A. graduates of George Washington provided several photographs: Edward Keller III and Roshani Kothari.

For this edition, I was fortunate in working with a team of excellent people from start to finish. When we launched the fourth edition revision plan in 2005, Jennifer Jacobson was my editor at Allyn & Bacon in Boston. Her intelligence and verve were great assets. Her assistant, Liz DiMenno, was super. Both moved on to new positions with Allyn & Bacon. Dave Repetto took over as my anthropology editor in 2006. He is a high-energy leader with sharp insight and the gold-star ability to say "that's cool" and let us get on with our work. His new assistant, Jack Cashman, is holding up his part of the job just fine.

My development editor is Monica Ohlinger, head of Ohlinger Publishing Services in Columbus, Ohio. She heads her own business and has a growing number of excellent people working with her. It takes a lot of good communication between Monica and me to succeed. At some points, one phone meeting a week at 9:30 on Wednesday morning is not enough. And email? Lots of that, and always helpful. Monica led the entire process of this revision with great skill, intelligence, and enthusiasm. Her attention to both detail and the big picture helped tremendously as did her understanding of the entire publishing process. Even when the going was at its toughest, I looked forward to hearing the phone ring at 9:30 Wednesday morning, to the cheery voice saying, "Hi, it's Monica!"

Monica has built a strong team at Ohlinger Publishing Services. Erin Curtis did a great job with photo research. Brooke Wilson and Cortney White pulled together figures and permissions.

Once the draft chapters went into "production," I worked with Karen Mason at Allyn & Bacon in Boston. She dished chapters, maps, and figures, and made sure everything moved along according to the tight schedule. Lynda Griffiths was my copyeditor. She sent me packages of copyedited chapters at a pace I found difficult to match.

A major change in this edition is the substantially increased number and quality of maps. We have jumped from about one map per chapter to about five or six maps per chapter. Mary Swab, at Mapping Specialists in Madison, Wisconsin, did a superb job of understanding my "specs." She rendered beautiful and effective maps and responded to requests for revisions seemingly overnight. Her technical competence, speed, and intuition were critical in making the new map program work.

The Instructor's Manual, Study Guide, and PowerPoint slides are important assets for instructors. For the revisions and updating, I was ably assisted by Miranda Horan, an M.A. candidate in Anthropology and International Development at George Washington University.

Dispersed geographically as we are, everyone involved in the revision and production process shared the goal of taking the fourth edition to an even higher level in terms of currency, coverage, and relevance.

On a more personal note, I thank Bernard Wood for nudging me into using the Internet at home, something I had long resisted as an invasion of technology into my domestic life. It turned out to be essential for keeping on schedule.

I thank "the Millers"—my parents, siblings, aunts and uncles, and nieces and nephews—for their interest, support, and (my father's) comment about "all those long words." He's right. I am grateful to "the Heatons"—my former in-laws, including ex-husband, (late) parents-in-law, brothers- and sisters-in-law, and nieces and nephews—for their friendship and quippy comments about my book and other things.

I thank, especially, my son, Jack Heaton, for being a superb traveling companion on our trip around the world with the Semester at Sea Program in 1996, for his delicately effective comments about my (occasional) excesses in thinking, and for his continued psychological support and good company over lunch in Foggy Bottom throughout the long revision process. This book is dedicated to him.

Barbara Miller
Washington, DC

Prologue

The Importance of Commitment: A Note on the Cover Image

Michal Ronnen Safdie was born in Jerusalem in 1951. Her mother was a Holocaust survivor. She is the author of *The Western Wall* (1997), a book of photographs. Her work has been exhibited worldwide.

During her 2004 trip to Chad on the border with Darfur, Sudan, she documented the situation of the so-called "lucky ones," those who had survived the years of violence and genocide to face hunger, disease, and the uncertainties of life as displaced persons. Her focus is on human beings trying to rebuild their lives in the aftermath of terrible pain and struggle.

Safdie's images of people, mainly women and children, living in a refugee camp in Bahai Chad on the border with Darfur, bring the truth of violence and its consequences into plain view as well as the dignity and hope of a child. Her photographs do not allow us to forget.

The Importance of Names: A Note about This Book

Since the beginning of modern humanity, people have been naming each other, naming other groups, and naming features of the places they inhabit. People of earlier times often referred to themselves in terms that translate roughly into The People. As far as they were concerned, they were The People: the only people on earth.

Things are more complicated now. European colonialism, starting in the fifteenth century, launched centuries of rapid contact between Europeans of named continents, countries, and regions, and thousands of indigenous groups around the world. The Europeans named and described these groups in their European languages. The names were not those that the people used for themselves, or if they were, the transliteration into a European language altered local names into something very different from the original.

The Spanish explorers' naming of all the indigenous peoples of North America as Indians is a famous example of erroneous naming. When conquerors rename people and claim their territory, they simultaneously erase much of the indigenous people's identity and heritage.

The challenge of using the preferred names for people and places of the world faces us today. Until recently, indigenous peoples of the present-day United States preferred to be called Native Americans, rejecting the pejorative term Indian. Now, they are claiming and recasting the term Indian. In Canada, preferred terms are First Nations, Native Peoples, and Northern Peoples.

From small-scale groups to entire countries, people around the world are attempting to revive precolonial group names and place names. Bombay is now Mumbai. Group names and place names are frequently contested. Is someone Hispanic or Latino? Is it the Persian Gulf or the Arabian Gulf? Is it Greenland or Kalaallit Nunaat? Does it matter? The answer is yes, resoundingly, yes.

This book seeks to provide the most currently accepted names for people, places, objects, activities, and ideas. But by the time this page is printed, some names and how they are spelled in English will have changed. It is part of our job, as citizens of the world, to pay attention to names, to keep track of changes, and to respect the motivations behind them.

About the Author

BARBARA D. MILLER

Barbara Miller is Professor of Anthropology and International Affairs, and Director of the Culture in Global Affairs (CIGA) Research and Policy Program, at The George Washington University. She received her Ph.D. in anthropology from Syracuse University in 1978. Before coming to GW in 1994, she taught at the University of Rochester, SUNY Cortland, Ithaca College, Cornell University, and the University of Pittsburgh.

For thirty years, Barbara's research has focused mainly on gender-based inequalities in India, especially the nutritional and medical neglect of daughters in northern regions of the country. In addition, she has conducted research on culture and rural development in Bangladesh, on low-income household dynamics in Jamaica, and on Hindu adolescents in Pittsburgh. Her current interests include continued research on gender inequalities in health in South Asia, the role of cultural anthropology in informing policy issues, and cultural heritage and public policy, especially as related to women, children, and other disenfranchised groups. She teaches courses on introductory cultural anthropology, medical anthropology, development anthropology, culture and population, health and development in South Asia, and migration and mental health. In addition to many journal articles and book chapters, she has published

"Cultural anthropology is exciting because it CONNECTS with everything, from FOOD to ART. And it can help prevent or SOLVE world problems related to *social inequality* and injustice.*"*

several books: *The Endangered Sex: Neglect of Female Children in Rural North India,* 2nd ed. (Oxford University Press, 1997), an edited volume, *Sex and Gender Hierarchies* (Cambridge University Press, 1993), a co-edited volume with Alf Hiltebeitel, *Hair: Its Power and Meaning in Asian Cultures* (SUNY Press, 1998), and a text co-authored with Bernard Wood, *Anthropology* (Allyn & Bacon, 2006).

AFGH. = Afghanistan
ALB. = Albania
ARM. = Armenia
AUS. = Austria
AZER. = Azerbaijan
BANG. = Bangladesh
BEL. = Belgium
B & H. = Bosnia and Herzegovina
BUL. = Bulgaria
BURK. FASO = Burkina Faso
C. AFR. REP. = Central African Republic
CAM. = Cameroon
CRO. = Croatia
C. V. = Cape Verde
CYP. = Cyprus
CZE. = Czech Republic
DEM. REP. OF THE CONGO =
    Democratic Republic of the Congo
DEN. = Denmark
EQ. GUINEA = Equatorial Guinea
EST. = Estonia
GAM. = Gambia
G.-B. = Guinea-Bissau
GER. = Germany
GUI. = Guinea
HOND. = Honduras
HUN. = Hungary
ISR. = Israel
KAMP. = Kampuchea
KRYG. = Kyrgyzstan
LAT. = Latvia
LEB. = Lebanon
LITH. = Lithuania
LUX. = Luxembourg
MAC. = Macedonia
MOL. = Moldova
MON. = Montenegro
MYAN. = Myanmar
NETH. = Netherlands
POL. = Poland
ROM. = Romania
RUS. = Russia
SER. = Serbia
SLO. = Slovakia
SLOV. = Slovenia
SWITZ. = Switzerland
SYR. = Syria
TAJIK. = Tajikistan
THAI. = Thailand
TURK. = Turkmenistan
UZBEK. = Uzbekistan
U.A.E. = United Arab Emirates

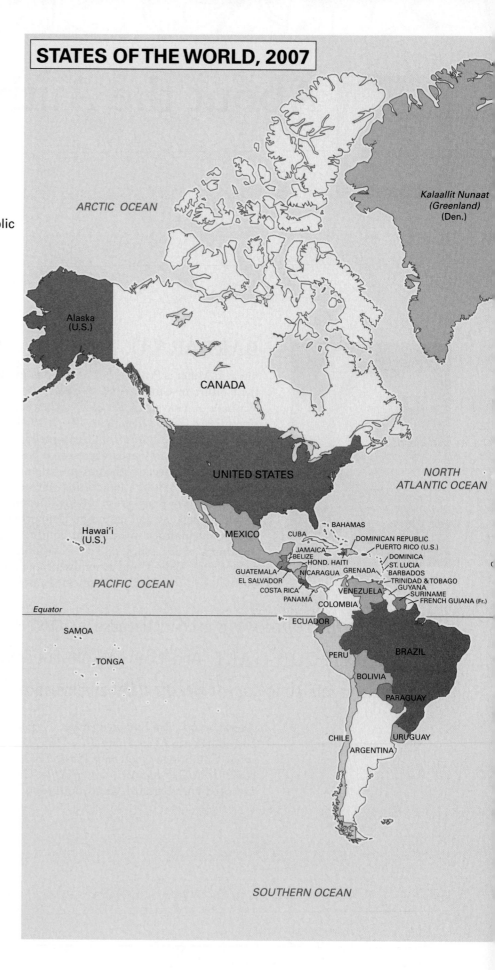

STATES OF THE WORLD, 2007

PART I Introduction to Cultural Anthropology

1 Anthropology and the Study of Culture

2 Methods in Cultural Anthropology

SUSAN SQUIRES, A BUSINESS ANTHROPOLOGIST, is part of the brains behind the General Mills breakfast food, Go-Gurt. During its first year of production in 1991, Go-Gurt generated sales of $37 million. Squires, who earned a Ph.D. in cultural anthropology from Boston University, is one of the growing number of anthropologists who use their knowledge of anthropological theory and research methods in the business world. Some are being snapped up by companies even before they finish their dissertations.

Research into the development of Go-Gurt took Squires and an industrial designer into the homes of American families to observe their breakfast behavior and food choices. On their first day of research, they arrived at a residence at 6:30 a.m., laden with video cameras and other equipment, prepared to have breakfast with a family they had never met. General Mills had learned from focus group studies that mothers want their families to eat whole-grain breakfast foods. The fieldwork, in contrast, revealed a wider range of preferences and behavior related to individual hunger patterns and the need to leave home early for work or school.

Squires realized that the ideal breakfast food should be portable, healthy, fun, and come in a disposable container. The answer: yogurt packaged so that it does not require a spoon and can be frozen or refrigerated. One mother said that her daughter thinks she is eating a Popsicle when she has Go-Gurt for breakfast. Inspired by this research, Squires and another business anthropologist, Brian Byrne, co-edited a book called *Creating Breakthrough Ideas: The Collaboration of Anthropologists and Designers in the Product Development Industry* (2002).

Anthropology in the Real World

In another research role during the 1990s, Squires was a consumer behavior analyst for Arthur Andersen, a leading accounting firm implicated in the Enron scandal. After the criminal activity at Enron was exposed, Squires and three other employees wrote a book analyzing the company's problems, *Inside Arthur Andersen: Shifting Values, Unexpected Consequences* (2003). The book discusses conflicts within the organization between a tradition of high ethical standards of accounting and the growing market demand for higher and higher profit levels.

Founding her own company takes Squires in a direction that builds on her previous ten years of experience. Tactics, LLC, provides ethnographic research for businesses, governments, and educational institutions in North America, Europe, and Asia. Squires defines her company's goal as "finding treasure" that is "buried in people's brains." So far, Tactics has created new products for telecommunication, the pharmaceutical industry, and computer software companies. It develops and evaluates business strategies, and advises on organizational management, employee training and performance, and customer satisfaction.

The work of Susan Squires demonstrates how theory and methods in cultural anthropology can benefit both the business world and the everyday lives of consumers. Two of the most valuable assets of cultural anthropology in the business world are, first, its holistic perspective, which looks at the larger context and reveals connections, and second, its attention to multiculturalism, which exposes differences in preferences, values, and behavior.

1

Anthropology and the Study of Culture

The Big Questions

- WHAT is anthropology?

- WHAT is cultural anthropology?

- HOW is cultural anthropology relevant to a career in the "real world"?

Folk dancers in Oaxaca, Southern Mexico. *(Source: Bob Krist/CORBIS)*

Old bones, *Jurassic Park,* cannibalism, hidden treasure, *Indiana Jones and the Temple of Doom.* The popular impression of anthropology is based mainly on movies and television shows that depict anthropologists as adventurers and heroes. Many anthropologists do have adventures and discover treasures such as ancient pottery, medicinal plants, and jade carvings. But most of their research is not glamorous. Some anthropologists spend years in difficult physical conditions searching for the earliest fossils of our ancestors. Others live among, and study firsthand, how people in Silicon Valley, California, work and organize family life in a setting permeated by modern technology. Some anthropologists conduct laboratory analyses of the contents of tooth enamel to reveal where an individual once lived. Others study designs on prehistoric pottery to learn what the symbols mean, or observe nonhuman primates such as chimpanzees or orangutans in the wild to learn how they live.

Anthropology is the study of humanity, including our prehistoric origins and contemporary human diversity. Compared to other disciplines that study humanity (such as history, psychology, economics, political science, and sociology), anthropology is broader in scope. Anthropology covers a much greater span of time than these disciplines and it encompasses a broader range of topics.

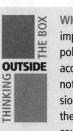

THINKING OUTSIDE THE BOX WHAT ARE your impressions of anthropology? How did you acquire them? Make notes of these impressions and review them at the end of the course.

Introducing Anthropology

The breadth of topics in anthropology matches its breadth in research methods, which range from scientific to humanistic. Some anthropologists consider anthropology to be a *science:* a form of inquiry that involves first the formulation of a hypothesis, or hunch, about the way things work and then observation or testing to see whether the hypothesis is correct. Other anthropologists pursue a *humanistic approach,* which is a subjective way of understanding humanity through the study of people's art, music, poetry, language, and other forms of symbolic expression. This approach avoids working from a pre-set hypothesis but instead seeks insight through culturally informed understanding.

No matter whether it is pursued from a more scientific or a more humanistic perspective, anthropology seeks to produce new knowledge, and this is its primary goal as an academic field of inquiry. But its findings are also relevant to significant real-world issues and therefore to the public at large. Anthropologists' research findings can influence government policy-makers, businesses, technology developers, healthcare providers, teachers, and the general public. You will learn more about these contributions in this chapter and throughout the book.

In North America, anthropology is divided into four fields (see Figure 1.1) that focus on separate, but connected, subject matter related to humanity:

- **Biological anthropology** (or physical anthropology): the study of humans as biological organisms, including their evolution and contemporary variation.
- **Archaeology** (or prehistory): the study of past human cultures through their material remains.
- **Linguistic anthropology:** the study of human communication, including its origins, history, and contemporary variation and change.
- **Cultural anthropology** (or social anthropology): the study of living peoples and their cultures, including variation and change. **Culture** refers to people's learned and shared behaviors and beliefs.

Some anthropologists argue that a fifth field, applied anthropology, should be added. **Applied anthropology** (also called practicing anthropology or practical anthropology) is the use of anthropological knowledge to prevent or solve problems or to shape and achieve policy goals. The author of this book takes the position that the application of knowledge, just like theory, is an integral part of each of the four fields and should be integrated within each of them.

Biological or Physical Anthropology

Biological anthropology encompasses three subfields. The first, *primatology,* is the study of the nonhuman members of the order of mammals called primates, which includes a wide range of animals from very small, nocturnal creatures to gorillas, the largest members. Primatologists study nonhuman primates in the wild and in captivity. They record and analyze how the animals spend

---

anthropology: the study of humanity, including our prehistoric origins and contemporary human diversity.
biological anthropology or **physical anthropology:** the study of humans as biological organisms, including their evolution and contemporary variation.
archaeology or **prehistory:** the study of

past human cultures through their material remains.
linguistic anthropology: the study of human communication, including its origins, history, and contemporary variation and change.
cultural anthropology or **social anthropology:** the study of living peoples and their

cultures, including variation and change.
culture: people's learned and shared behavior and beliefs.
applied anthropology or **practicing anthropology** or **practical anthropology:** the use of anthropological knowledge to prevent or solve problems or to shape and achieve policy goals.

A team of anthropologists and students discuss their research project on Silicon Valley culture. ■ *If you were given a grant to conduct anthropological research, where would you go and what would you study?* (Source: J. A. English-Lueck, Cofounder Silicon Valley Cultures Project)

their time, collect and share food, form social groups, rear offspring, develop leadership patterns, and experience conflict and conflict resolution. Primatologists are alarmed about the decline in numbers, and even extinction, of nonhuman primates. Many apply their knowledge to nonhuman primate conservation.

The second subfield is *paleoanthropology,* the study of human evolution on the basis of the fossil record. One

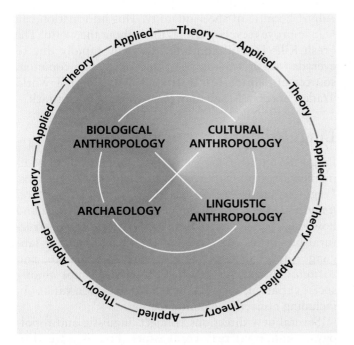

FIGURE 1.1   The Four Fields of Anthropology

important activity is the search for fossils to increase the amount and quality of the evidence related to the way human evolution occurred. Discoveries of new fossils provide "ah-hah!" moments and arresting photographs for the covers of popular magazines. A less glamorous but equally important activity in paleoanthropology is dating and classifying new fossils.

The third subfield is the study of *contemporary human biological variation.* Anthropologists working in this area define, measure, and seek to explain differences in the biological makeup and behavior of contemporary humans. In the past, biological anthropologists defined what they perceived as significant differences among modern humans as "racial" (quotation marks indicate that the meaning of this term is contested). Early anthropologists in the late nineteenth and early twentieth centuries used the term "race" to refer to social categories defined on the basis of skin color, hair texture, head shape, and facial features. These biological markers were supposedly associated with in-born ways of behaving and thinking. The controversial book, *The Bell Curve: Intelligence and Class Structure in American Life* (Herrnstein and Murray 1994), is an example of such thinking in the United States in its assertion that "race" determines intelligence and class position. In fact, DNA evidence clearly demonstrates that "races," defined on the basis of external physical features, are not scientifically valid categories; they lack internal consistency and they lack clear boundaries. Anthropologists do, however, recognize the reality of racism and that many people in many contexts worldwide discriminate against people on the basis of their imputed "race."

Maya people watch as forensic anthropologist Francisco de Leon conducts an exhumation of more than fifty bodies in a highland Guatemalan village in 1997. ■ *Are courses in forensic anthropology offered at your school?* (Source: AP/Wide World Photos)

Archaeology

Archaeology means, literally, the "study of the old," but "the old" is limited to human culture. Therefore, the time-depth of archaeology goes back only to the beginnings of *Homo sapiens* (around 200,000 years ago) or, more conservatively, to the earliest evidence of human-made tools (around 100,000 years ago). Archaeology encompasses two major areas: *prehistoric archaeology*, which concerns the human past before written records, and *historical archaeology*, which deals with the human past in societies that have written documents. Prehistoric archaeologists often identify themselves with broad geographic regions, studying, for example, Old World archaeology (Africa, Europe, and Asia) or New World archaeology (North, Central, and South America).

Another set of specialties within archaeology is based on the context in which the archaeology takes place. One such specialty is *underwater archaeology*, the study and preservation of submerged archaeological sites. Underwater archaeological sites may be from either prehistoric or historic times. Some prehistoric sites include early human settlements in parts of Europe, such as household sites discovered in Switzerland that were once near lakes but are now submerged.

Another specialty is *industrial archaeology*, which focuses on changes in material culture and society during and since the Industrial Revolution. Industrial archaeology is especially active in Great Britain, home of the Industrial Revolution. There, industrial archaeologists study such topics as the design of iron bridges, the growth and distribution of china potteries, miners' housing, and cotton mills. An important role of industrial archaeology is the conservation of industrial sites, which are more likely to be neglected or destroyed than are sites that have natural beauty or cultural glamour attached to them.

The archaeology of the recent past is another important research direction. An example is the "Garbage Project" conducted by archaeologists at the University of Arizona at Tucson (Rathje and Murphy 1992). The "Garbage Archaeologists" excavated part of the Fresh Kills landfill on Staten Island, near New York City. Its mass is estimated at 100 million tons and its volume at 2.9 billion cubic feet. Thus, it is one of the largest human-made structures in North America. Excavation of pop-top can tabs, disposable diapers, cosmetics containers, and telephone books reveals much about recent consumption patterns and how they affect the environment. One surprising finding is that the kinds of garbage people often blame for filling up landfills, such as fast-food packaging and disposable diapers, cause less serious problems than paper. Newspaper, especially, is a major culprit because of sheer quantity. This information can help improve recycling efforts throughout the world. The Fresh Kills landfill continues to grow rapidly due to everyday trash accumulation and other, less common, sources of debris, such as the remains from the World Trade Center in Manhattan following the 9/11 attack.

Linguistic Anthropology

Linguistic anthropology is devoted to the study of communication, mainly (but not exclusively) among humans. Linguistic anthropology has three subfields: *historical linguistics*, the study of language change over time and how languages are related; *descriptive linguistics* or structural linguistics, the study of how contemporary languages differ in terms of their formal structure; and *sociolinguistics*, the study of the relationships among social variation, social context, and linguistic variation, including nonverbal communication.

Several new directions connect linguistic anthropology to important real-world issues. First is a trend to study language in everyday use, or discourse, and how

Stephen Lubkemann is trained as both a cultural anthropologist and an underwater archaeologist. He is documenting the remains of the hull of DRTO-036, a vessel that wrecked in the Dry Tortugas in the mid-nineteenth century. It lies within Dry Tortugas National Park in the Florida Keys. ■ (Source: Photo by Richard Gould)

it relates to power structures at local, regional, and international levels (Duranti 1997a). In some contexts, powerful people speak more than less powerful people, whereas sometimes the more powerful people speak less. Power relations may also be expressed through intonation, word choice, and such nonverbal forms of communication as posture and dress. Second is increased attention to the role of information technology in communication, especially the Internet and cell phones. Third is attention to the increasingly rapid extinction of indigenous languages worldwide.

Cultural Anthropology

Cultural anthropology is the study of contemporary people and their cultures. It considers variations and similarities across cultures, and how cultures change over time. Cultural anthropologists learn about culture by spending extended periods of time living with the people they study (discussed in Chapter 2).

Since World War II, cultural anthropology has grown dramatically in North America. This growth has brought about the development of many specialties within the

Iron Bridge, England, is an important site of industrial archaeology. Considered the "birthplace of industry," the site includes the world's first iron bridge and remains of factories, furnaces, and canals. ■ *Take a virtual tour of the site by going to www .ironbridge.org.uk.* (Source: Barbara Miller and Bernard Wood)

Lessons Applied

ORANGUTAN RESEARCH LEADS TO ORANGUTAN ADVOCACY

Primatologist Biruté Galdikas (pronounced Beer-OO-tay GAL-dee-kas) first went to Indonesia to study orangutans in 1971 (Galdikas 1995). She soon became aware of the threat to the orangutans from local people who, as a way of making money, capture them for sale to zoos around the world. The poachers separate the young from their mothers, often killing the mothers in the process. Sometimes local police locate and reclaim the captured orphans. They try to return them to the rainforest, but the transition into an unknown niche is extremely difficult, and many do not survive.

Orangutan juveniles are highly dependent on their mothers, maintaining close bodily contact with them for at least two years and nursing until they are age 8. Because of this long period of orangutans' need for maternal contact, Galdikas set up her camp to serve as a way station for orphans, and she became the maternal figure. Her first "infant" was an orphaned orang, Sugito, who clung to her like its own mother for years.

The survival of orangutans on Borneo and Sumatra (their only habitats worldwide) is seriously endangered by massive commercial logging and illegal logging, population resettlement programs, plantations, and other pressures on the forests where the orangutans live.

Galdikas is focusing her efforts on Orangutan preservation. She says, "I feel like I'm viewing an animal holocaust and holocaust is not a word I use lightly. . . . The destruction of the tropical rainforest is accelerating daily" (Dreifus 2000:D3). Across all ranges, it is estimated that during the twentieth century the orangutan population experienced a huge decrease, from 315,000 in

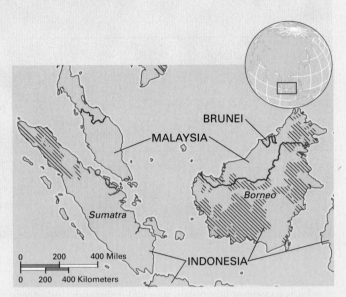

MAP 1.1 Orangutan Regions in Malaysia and Indonesia. Orangutans are the only great apes living outside Africa. Fossil evidence indicates that their habitats in the past extended throughout Southeast Asia and southern China. They are now limited to pockets of forest on the islands of Sumatra and Borneo.

1900 to 44,000 in 2000 (IUCN/SSC Conservation Breeding Specialist Group 2004). Aerial surveys (Ancrenaz et al. 2005) and DNA analysis of living orangutans (Goossens et al. 2006) confirm recent and dramatic declines that, if not halted, will lead to extinction in the next few decades.

---

field. Prominent areas of specialization include economic anthropology, political anthropology, medical anthropology, psychological anthropology, and development anthropology (the study of the effects and patterns of international development policies and plans in cross-cultural perspective). The rest of this book covers these and other topics.

Applied Anthropology: Separate Field or Cross-Cutting Focus?

In the United States, applied anthropology emerged during and after World War II. Its first concern was with liv-

ing peoples and their needs, which initially placed applied anthropology within the field of cultural anthropology. The number of anthropologists working in applied anthropology grew substantially in the later twentieth century. One reason for this growth was the decline in college and university teaching positions in anthropology since the late 1970s. This prompted anthropologists to explore jobs outside academia.

Given the expanded role of applied anthropology, many anthropologists feel that applied anthropology should be considered a fifth field. An alternative position is that the application of knowledge to solve problems, just like theory, should be part of each field (see Figure 1.1). This is the author's position, and therefore, many

Biruté Galdikas in Indonesia. She has been studying the orangutans for over three decades and is an active supporter of conservation of their habitat. ■ *Learn about her work and the status of wild orangutans by searching on the Web.* (Source: © Spooner/Redmond-Callow/Gamma Press)

Galdikas has studied orangutans longer than anyone else. She links her knowledge of and love for the orangutans with applied anthropology and advocacy on their behalf. Since the beginning of her fieldwork in Borneo, she has maintained and expanded the Camp Leakey field site and research center (named after her mentor, Lewis Leakey, who inspired her research on orangutans). In 1986, she cofounded the Orangutan Foundation International (OFI), which now has several chapters worldwide.

She has published scholarly articles and given public talks around the world on her research. Educating the public about the imminent danger to the orangutans is an important part of her activism. Galdikas and other orangutan experts are lobbying international institutions such as the World Bank to promote forest conservation as part of their loan agreements.

Camp Leakey employs many local people in diverse roles, including anti-poaching guards. The OFI sponsors study tours to Borneo for international students and opportunities for them to contribute to conservation efforts.

The success of Galdikas's activism depends on her deep knowledge of orangutans. Over the decades, she has filled thousands of notebooks with her observations of orangutan behavior, along with such details about their habitat as the fruiting times of different species of trees. A donor recently gave software and funding for staff to analyze the raw data (Hawn 2002). The findings will indicate how much territory is needed to support a viable orangutan population. In turn, these findings will facilitate conservation policy and planning.

FOOD FOR THOUGHT

- Some people claim that science should not be linked with advocacy because it will create biases in research. Others say that scientists have an obligation to use their knowledge for good causes. Where do you stand in this debate and why?

examples of applied anthropology appear throughout this book.

Applied anthropology is an important thread that weaves through the entire discipline of anthropology (Rylko-Bauer, Singer, and van Willigen 2006). For example, many archaeologists in the United States are employed in *cultural resource management (CRM)*, assessing the presence of possible archaeological remains before construction projects such as roads and buildings can proceed. Many biological anthropologists are employed as *forensic anthropologists*, participating in criminal investigations through laboratory work identifying bodily remains. Others work in the area of primate conservation (see Lessons Applied box). Applied linguis-

tic anthropologists consult with educational institutions about how to improve standardized tests for bilingual populations and conduct policy research for governments. Applied cultural anthropologists work in every domain of life, including education, health care, business, poverty reduction, and conflict prevention and resolution. Their many applied roles, from research and consulting to advocacy and activism, are highlighted in the Real World profiles at the beginning of each section of this book and in the Lessons Applied boxes in every chapter.

Many anthropologists are concerned that applied anthropologists should be addressing more directly and with greater force the negative effects of capitalist globalization, such as the increasing wealth gap between powerful, industrialized countries and less powerful, less industrialized countries (Hackenberg 2000). This challenge asks that anthropologists devote more attention to how their knowledge can be put to good uses. One anthropologist goes so far as to state, "Can anthropology in the 21st century be anything except applied anthropology?" (Cleveland 2000:373).

Introducing Cultural Anthropology

Cultural anthropology is devoted to studying human cultures worldwide, both their similarities and differences. Ultimately, cultural anthropology decenters us from our own cultures, teaching us to look at ourselves from the "outside" as somewhat "strange." Cultural anthropology makes "the strange familiar and the familiar strange" (Spiro 1990). A good example of making the familiar strange is the case of the Nacirema, a culture first described in 1956:

> They are a North American group living in the territory between the Canadian Cree, the Yaqui and the Tarahumare of Mexico, and the Carib and the Arawak of the Antilles. Little is known of their origin, though tradition states that they came from the east. According to Nacirema mythology, their nation was originated by a culture hero, Notgnihsaw, who is otherwise known for two great feats of strength—the throwing of a piece of wampum across the river Pa-To-Mac and the chopping down of a cherry tree in which the Spirit of Truth resided. (Miner 1965 [1956]:415)

The anthropologist goes on to describe the Nacirema's intense focus on the human body and their many private rituals. He provides a detailed account of a daily ritual performed within the home in a specially constructed shrine area:

> The focal point of the shrine is a box or chest which is built into the wall. In this chest are kept the many charms and magical potions without which no native believes he could live. These preparations are secured from a variety of specialized practitioners. The most powerful of these are the medicine men, whose assistance must be rewarded with substantial gifts. . . . Beneath the charm box is a small font. Each day every member of the family, in succession, enters the shrine room, bows his head before the charm-box, mingles different sorts of holy water in the

font, and proceeds with a brief rite of ablution. (1965: 415–416)

If you do not recognize this tribe, try spelling its name backwards. (*Note*: Please forgive Miner for his use of the masculine pronoun in describing Nacirema society in general; his writings are several decades old.)

This section provides a brief history of cultural anthropology and its theoretical foundations. It also includes discussion of the concept of culture; important cultural categories based on gender, "race" and ethnicity, and age; some distinctive features of cultural anthropology; and an overview of three major debates in cultural anthropology.

A Brief History of Cultural Anthropology

The distant origins of cultural anthropology go back to writers such as Herodotus (fifth century BCE, or Before the Common Era), Marco Polo (thirteenth to fourteenth centuries), and Ibn Khaldun (fourteenth century), who traveled extensively and wrote reports about cultures they encountered. More recent conceptual roots are found in writers of the French Enlightenment, such as philosopher Charles Montesquieu, who wrote in the first half of the eighteenth century. His book *The Spirit of the Laws*, published in 1748 [1949], discussed the temperament, appearance, and government of various people around the world. He explained cultural differences as due to the differing climates in which people lived (Barnard 2000:22ff). European colonial expansion prompted Enlightenment thinkers to question the accuracy of the biblical narrative of human origins. The Bible, for example, does not mention the existence of people in the New World.

In the latter half of the nineteenth century, the discovery of the principles of biological evolution by Charles Darwin and others had a major impact on anthropology by offering a scientific explanation for human origins and contemporary human variation. Biological evolution says that early forms evolve into later forms through the process of natural selection, whereby the most biologically fit organisms survive to reproduce while those that are less fit die out. Darwin's model is thus one of continuous progress of increasing fitness through struggle among competing organisms.

The most important founding figures of cultural anthropology of the late eighteenth and early nineteenth

---

functionalism: the theory that a culture is similar to a biological organism, in which parts work to support the operation and maintenance of the whole.
holism: the perspective in anthropology

that cultures are complex systems that cannot be fully understood without paying attention to their different components, including economics, social organization, and ideology.

cultural relativism: the perspective that each culture must be understood in terms of the values and ideas of that culture and should not be judged by the standards of another.

FIGURE 1.2   Key Figures in Cultural Anthropology

Late Nineteenth Century

Sir Edward Tylor	Armchair anthropology, first definition of culture
Sir James Frazer	Armchair anthropology, comparative study of religion
Lewis Henry Morgan	Insider's view, cultural evolution, comparative method

Early Twentieth Century

Bronislaw Malinowski	Functionalism, holism, participant observation
Franz Boas	Cultural relativism, historical particularism, advocacy
Margaret Mead	Personality and culture, cultural constructionism, public anthropology
Ruth Benedict	Personality and culture, national character studies
Zora Neale Hurston	Black culture, women's roles, ethnographic novels

Mid- and Late Twentieth Century and Early Twenty-First Century

Claude Lévi-Strauss	Symbolic analysis, French structuralism
Beatrice Medicine	Native American anthropology
Eleanor Leacock	Anthropology of colonialism and indigenous peoples
Marvin Harris	Cultural materialism, comparison, theory building
Mary Douglas	Symbolic anthropology
Michelle Rosaldo	Feminist anthropology
Clifford Geertz	Interpretive anthropology, thick description of local culture
Laura Nader	Legal anthropology, "studying up"
George Marcus	Critique of culture, critique of cultural anthropology
Gilbert Herdt	Gay anthropology
Nancy Scheper-Hughes	Critical medical anthropology
Leith Mullings	Anti-racist anthropology
Sally Engle Merry	Globalization and human rights

centuries include Sir Edward Tylor and Sir James Frazer in England and Lewis Henry Morgan in the United States (see Figure 1.2). Inspired by the concept of biological evolution, they developed a model of cultural evolution whereby all cultures evolve from lower to higher forms over time. This view placed non-Western peoples at a "primitive" stage and Euro-American culture as "civilization" and assumed that non-Western cultures would either catch up to the level of Western civilization or die out.

Polish-born Bronislaw Malinowski is a major figure of early cultural anthropology. In the first half of the twentieth century, he established a theoretical approach called **functionalism:** the view that a culture is similar to a biological organism, in which parts work to support the operation and maintenance of the whole. Religion and family organization, for example, contribute to the functioning of the whole culture. Functionalism is linked to the concept of **holism,** the view that one must study all aspects of a culture in order to understand the whole culture.

Franz Boas is considered the founder of North American cultural anthropology. Born in Germany and educated in physics and geography, he came to the United States in 1887 (Patterson 2001:46ff). He brought with him a skepticism toward Western science gained from a year's study with the Inuit, the indigenous people of Baffin Island (see Map 1.2). The Inuit experience taught him that people in different cultures have different perceptions of even basic physical substances, such as "water." Boas recognized the individuality and validity of different cultures. He introduced the now widely known concept of **cultural relativism,** or the view that each culture must be understood in terms of the values and ideas of that culture and not be judged by the standards of another. According to Boas, no culture is more advanced than another. His position thus contrasted markedly with that of the nineteenth-century cultural evolutionists.

In line with this thinking, Boas promoted the detailed study of individual cultures. He formulated the approach called *historical particularism,* or the view that individual cultures must be studied and described in their own terms and understood within their own historical context. In the Boasian tradition, generalizations about culture are invalid because they ignore the specific realities of individual cultures.

Boas helped to institutionalize North American anthropology as a discipline. While a professor at Columbia University, he trained many students who became prominent anthropologists. He founded several professional

Franz Boas is an important figure in the history of anthropology for many reasons, including his emphasis on a four-field approach and the principle of cultural relativism. ■ *Conduct research on Boas to learn about his life and contributions to anthropology.* (Source: © Bettmann/CORBIS)

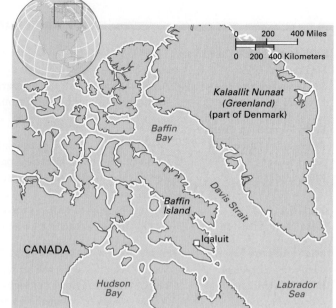

MAP 1.2 Baffin Island in Northeast Canada and Kalaallit Nunaat (Greenland). Baffin Island is the largest island in the Canadian Arctic. Iqaluit, a town of about 3,000 people, is the capital of the Nunavut territory. Kalaallit Nunaat, meaning The Human's Land, is the world's largest island and a self-governed Danish territory. Its population of 56,000 people is mainly of mixed descent between the indigenous Kalaallit (Inuit) and Danish people.

organizations, and he supported the development of anthropology museums. Boas was also engaged in debates about civil rights and social justice, and he carried out policy research related to these issues (Patterson 2001:48–50). His socially progressive philosophy sometimes embroiled him in controversy. One study, commissioned by President Theodore Roosevelt, was to examine the effects of the environment (in the sense of a person's location) on immigrants and their children. At this time, some leaders of the U.S. government were seeking justifications for limiting the numbers of immigrants. Boas and his research team measured the height, weight, head size, and other features of over 17,000 adults and children who had migrated to the United States. The researchers found substantial differences in the measurements of the older and younger generations. Boas concluded that body size and shape can change quickly in response to a different environment. The U.S. Immigration Commission, however, dismissed his findings, and Congress passed the Immigration Restriction Act in

1924. Through this study and many more, Boas left a legacy to anthropology that biology is not destiny and that no populations are innately inferior.

Margaret Mead, whose work is discussed in Chapter 6, was Boas's most famous student. She contributed to knowledge of South Pacific cultures, gender roles, and the impact of child-rearing practices on personality. Her scholarly works as well as her columns in popular magazines had wide influence on U.S. child-care patterns in the 1950s. Mead was thus an early *public anthropologist* who took seriously the importance of bringing cultural anthropology knowledge to the general public in order to create positive social change.

Following World War II, cultural anthropology in the United States expanded substantially in terms of the number of trained anthropologists and departments of anthropology in colleges and universities. Along with this growth came increased theoretical diversity. Several

---

cultural materialism: a theoretical position that takes material features of life, such as the environment, natural resources, and mode of production, as the bases for explaining social organization and ideology.

interpretive anthropology or **interpret-** ivism: the view that cultures can be understood by studying what people think about, their ideas, and the meanings that are important to them.

structurism: a theoretical position concerning human behavior and ideas that says "free choice" is an illusion since the choices themselves are determined by larger forces such as the economy, social and political organization, and ideological systems.

agency: the ability of humans to make choices and exercise free will.

---

anthropologists developed theories of culture based on environmental factors. They suggested that similar environments (for example, deserts or tropical rainforests or mountains) would predictably lead to the emergence of similar cultures. This approach pursued cross-cultural generalizations, and so it came into direct conflict with Boasian historical particularism (defined earlier). At the same time, French anthropologist Claude Lévi-Strauss was developing a quite different theoretical perspective, which became known as *French structuralism*. He maintained that the best way to understand a culture is to collect its myths and stories and analyze the underlying themes in them. (Later chapters in this book provide more details about the work of Lévi-Strauss.) French structuralism inspired the development of *symbolic anthropology*, or the study of culture as a system of meanings, which was especially prominent in the United States in the later part of the twentieth century.

In the 1960s, Marxist theory emerged in anthropology, stating the importance of people's access to the means of production. It inspired the emergence of a new theoretical school in the United States called **cultural materialism.** Cultural materialism is an approach to studying culture by emphasizing the material aspects of life, especially the natural environment and how people make a living. Also arising in the 1960s was the theoretical position referred to as **interpretive anthropology,** or intepretivism. This perspective developed from both U.S. symbolic anthropology and French structural anthropology. It says that understanding culture should focus on what people think about, their ideas, and the symbols and meanings that are important to them. These two positions will be discussed further later in this section.

Since the 1990s, two other theoretical directions have gained prominence. Both are influenced by *postmodernism*, an intellectual pursuit that asks whether modernity is truly progress and that questions such aspects of modernism as the scientific method, urbanization, technological change, and mass communication. The first theory is termed **structurism** (the author coined this term for lack of anything better), the view that powerful structures such as economics, politics, and media shape cultures and create entrenched systems of inequality and oppression. The second theory emphasizes human **agency,** or free will, and the power of individuals to create and change culture by acting against structures. These two contrasting positions also will be discussed later in this section.

Cultural anthropology continues to be rethought and refashioned. Over the past few decades, several new theoretical perspectives have transformed and enriched the field. *Feminist anthropology* is a perspective that emphasizes the need to study female roles and gender-based inequality. Starting in the 1970s, early feminist anthropologists realized that anthropology had largely bypassed women since its beginning. To address this gap, feminist anthropologists undertook research that explicitly focused on women and girls. A related area is *gay and lesbian anthropology,* or queer anthropology, a perspective that emphasizes the need to study gay people's cultures and discrimination based on sexual identity and preferences.

In North American anthropology, African American, Latino, and Native American anthropologists are increasing in number and visibility, yet anthropology in North America and Europe remains one of the "whitest" professions (Shanklin 2000). Leith Mullings outlines these steps for moving the discipline toward *anti-racist anthropology* (2005):

- Examine and recognize anthropology's history and implications with racism.
- Work to increase diversity in the discipline.
- Teach about racism in anthropology classes and textbooks.
- Treat the concept of culture within a political-economy framework.

Worldwide, non-Western anthropologists are contesting the dominance of Euro-American anthropology and offering new perspectives (Kuwayama 2004). In many cases, these anthropologists conduct *native anthropology,* or the study of one's own cultural group. Their work provides useful critiques of the historically Western, White, male discipline of anthropology.

THINKING OUTSIDE THE BOX

THIS BRIEF HISTORY of cultural anthropology describes early leaders who were mainly white, European or Euro-American, and male. Compare this pattern with the history of some other discipline you have studied. What are the similarities and differences?

The Concept of Culture

Although cultural anthropologists are united in the study of *culture,* the question of how to define it has been debated for decades. This section discusses definitions of culture today, characteristics of culture, and bases for cultural identity.

Definitions of Culture

Culture is the core concept in cultural anthropology, so it might seem likely that cultural anthropologists would agree about what it is. In the 1950s, an effort to collect definitions of culture produced 164 different ones (Kroeber and Kluckhohn 1952). Since then, no one has tried to count the number of definitions of culture used by anthropologists.

British anthropologist Sir Edward Tylor proposed the first definition in 1871. He stated, "Culture, or civilization . . . is that complex whole which includes knowledge, belief, art, law, morals, custom, and any other capabilities and habits acquired by man as a member of society" (Kroeber and Kluckhohn 1952:81). The phrase "that complex whole" has been the most durable feature of his definition. Two other features of Tylor's definition have not stood the test of time. First, most anthropologists now avoid using the word *man* to refer to all humans; instead, they use generic words such as *people* and *humans*. One may argue that the word *man* can be used generically according to its linguistic roots, but this usage can be ambiguous. Second, most anthropologists no longer equate culture with civilization. The word *civilization* implies a sense of "highness" versus noncivilized "lowness" and sets up a distinction placing "us" (people of the so-called civilized regions) in a superior position to "them."

In contemporary cultural anthropology, the cultural materialists and the interpretive anthropologists support two different definitions of culture. Cultural materialist Marvin Harris says, "A culture is the total socially acquired life-way or life-style of a group of people. It consists of the patterned repetitive ways of thinking, feeling, and acting that are characteristic of the members of a particular society or segment of society" (1975:144). In contrast, Clifford Geertz, speaking for the interpretivists, believes that culture consists of symbols, motivations, moods, and thoughts. This definition focuses on people's perceptions, thoughts, and ideas and does not include behavior as a part of culture. The definition of culture used in this book is that culture is learned and shared behavior and beliefs, and thus is broader than Geertz's definition.

Culture exists among all human beings. It is something that all humans have. Some anthropologists refer to this universal concept of culture as *Culture* with a capital *C*. Culture also exists in a more specific way. The term **microculture**, or local culture, refers to distinct patterns of learned and shared behavior and ideas found in local regions and among particular groups. Microcultures are based on ethnicity, gender, age, and more.

Characteristics of Culture

Understanding the complex concept of culture can be gained by looking at its characteristics. This section discusses some characteristics of culture.

Culture Is Not the Same as Nature The relationship between nature and culture is of great interest to cultural anthropologists in their quest to understand people's behavior and thinking. This book emphasizes the importance of culture (most of you will already have taken sev-

eral courses on biology, which emphasizes the importance of human nature). Obviously, culture and nature are intertwined and often difficult to separate in terms of their effects. For example, certain aspects of biology affect people's behavior and lifestyle, such as being HIV-positive. But it is impossible to predict how a person who is HIV-positive will fare in Culture A versus Culture B. Different cultural contexts shape matters such as labeling and negative stereotypes and access to care and support.

A good way to see how culture diverges from, and shapes, nature is to consider basic natural demands of life within different cultural contexts. The universal human functions that everyone must perform to stay alive are

- Eating
- Drinking
- Sleeping
- Eliminating

You may wonder about requirements for shelter and clothing. They vary, depending on the climate, so they are not included on this list. You may also wonder about sexual intercourse. It is not necessary for individual survival, so it is not included on this list, but it is discussed elsewhere in this book.

Given the primary importance of these four functions in supporting a human being's life, it seems logical that people would fulfill them in similar ways everywhere. But that is not the case.

Eating Culture shapes what people eat, how they eat, when they eat, and the meanings of food and eating. Culture also defines foods that are acceptable and unacceptable. In China, most people think that cheese is disgusting, but in France, most people love cheese. Throughout China, pork is a widely favored meat. The religions of Judaism and Islam, in contrast, forbid consumption of pork. In many cultures where gathering wild plant foods, hunting, and fishing are important, people value the freshness of food. They would consider a package of frozen food on a grocery store shelf as way past its time.

Perceptions of taste vary dramatically. Western researchers have defined four supposedly universal taste categories: sweet, sour, bitter, and salty. Cross-cultural research disproves these as universals. For example, the Weyéwa people of the highlands of Sumba, Indonesia (see Map 1.3), define seven categories of flavor: sour, sweet, salty, bitter, tart, bland, and pungent (Kuipers 1991).

How to eat is also an important aspect of food behavior. Rules about proper ways to eat are one of the first

---

microculture: a distinct pattern of learned and shared behavior and thinking found within larger cultures.

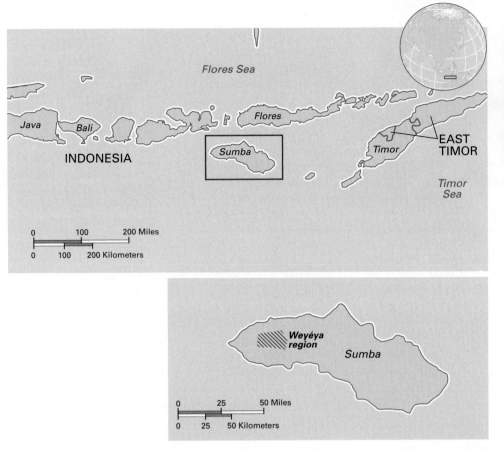

MAP 1.3   Weyéwa Region in Indonesia. Sumba, one of Indonesia's many islands, is seventy-five miles long. The Weyéwa people number about 85,000 and live in small settlements on grassy plateaus. They grow rice, maize, and millet, and raise water buffaloes and pigs.

things a person needs to learn when living in another culture. Dining rules in India require using only the right hand. The left hand is considered polluted because it is used for personal cleansing after elimination. A person's clean right hand is the preferred eating utensil. Silverware that has been touched by others, even though it has been washed, is considered unclean. In some cultures, it is important to eat only from one's own plate, whereas in others, eating from a shared central platter is considered proper.

Colombian anthropologist Patricia Tovar *(center)* at an anthropology conference in Colombia. In much of Central and South America, applied anthropology is an integral part of cultural anthropology.
■ (Source: Patricia Tovar)

Ethiopian women dining at an Ethiopian restaurant. The main meal consists of several meat and vegetable dishes, cooked with special spices and laid out on injera bread, a soft, flat bread that is torn into small pieces and used to wrap bite-sized bits of meat and vegetables. The entire meal can be eaten without utensils. ■ *How does this dining scene resemble or differ from a recent meal that you have had in a restaurant?* (Source: © Michael Newman/PhotoEdit)

Another area of cultural variation involves who is responsible for cooking and serving food. In many cultures, domestic cooking is women's responsibility, but cooking for public feasts is more often something that men do. Power issues may arise about who cooks what for whom (see Everyday Anthropology box).

Drinking Cross-cultural variations related to drinking are also complex. Every culture defines the appropriate substances to drink, when to drink and with whom, and the meanings of the beverages and drinking occasions. French culture allows for consumption of relatively large amounts of table wine with family meals, including lunch. In the United States, water is generally served and consumed during family meals. In India, water is served and consumed at the end of the meal. Around the world, different categories of people drink different beverages. In cultures where alcoholic beverages are consumed, men tend to consume more than women.

Culture often defines the meaning of particular drinks and the style of drinking and serving them. Social drinking—whether the beverage is coffee, beer, or vodka—creates and reinforces bonds. Beer-drinking rituals in U.S. college fraternities are a good example. In an ethnographic film entitled *Salamanders,* filmed at a large university in the northeastern United States, the fraternity brothers run to various "stations" in the fraternity house, downing a beer at each (Hornbein and Hornbein 1992). At one point, a brother chugs a beer, turns with a stagger toward the next station, falls flat on his face, and passes out. The movie documents another drinking ritual in which both young men and women at fraternity parties swallow live salamanders, sometimes two or three at a time, with large gulps of beer (this practice is now forbidden by law).

Sleeping Common sense might say that sleep is the one natural function that is not shaped by culture, because people tend to do it every twenty-four hours, everyone shuts their eyes to do it, everyone lies down to do it, and almost everyone sleeps at night. Going without sleep for an extended period would eventually lead to insanity and even death.

There are, however, many cultural aspects to sleep, including the question of who sleeps with whom, how much sleep a person should have, and sleep disorders. Across cultures, marked variation exists in rules about where infants and children should sleep: with the mother, with both parents, or by themselves in a separate room? Among indigenous peoples of the Amazon region of South America, mothers and babies share the same hammock for many months, and breastfeeding occurs whenever the baby is hungry.

Culture often shapes the amount of time a person sleeps. In rural India, women sleep fewer hours than men because they have to get up earlier to start the fire for the morning meal. In fast-track, corporate North America, "type A" males sleep relatively few hours and are proud of that fact—to sleep too much is to be a wimp. A new disorder in Japan, called *excessive daytime sleepiness* (EDS) (Doi and Minowa 2003), is especially common in Tokyo and other cities. Excessive sleepiness is correlated with more accidents on the job, more absenteeism, decreased productivity, deteriorated personal and professional relationships, and increased rates of illness and death. Women are almost twice as likely as men to experience EDS, and married women are especially vulnerable.

Eliminating Given its basic importance in cross-cultural experience, it is ironic that elimination receives little attention (in print) from anthropologists. Anyone who has traveled internationally knows that there is much to learn about elimination when in an unfamiliar context.

The first question is where to eliminate. Differences emerge in the degree to which elimination is a private act or can be done in more or less public areas. In many European cities, public options include street urinals for males but not for females. In most villages in India, houses do not have interior bathrooms. Instead, early in

THINKING OUTSIDE THE BOX

THINK ABOUT your everyday drinking patterns (no matter what the liquid) and then think about your drinking patterns on special occasions, including weekends, holidays, or special events such as weddings. What beverages do you consume, with whom, and what are the meanings and wider social implications involved?

LATINA POWER IN THE KITCHEN

Preparing food for someone else can mean many different things. For a chef, it can be a high-paying job and a source of high status. Within a family, cooking food for other members can be a sign of love and devotion. It may carry a message that love and devotion are expected in return.

Among Tejano migrant farm workers in the United States, preparing tamales is a symbol of women's commitment to their families and thus of the "good wife" (Williams 1984). The Tejanos are people of Mexican descent who live in Texas. Some of them move to Illinois in the summer, where they are employed as migrant workers.

For Tejanos, tamales are a central cultural identity marker. Tamales contain a rich inner mash of pig's head meat wrapped in corn husks. Making tamales is extremely time consuming and it is women's work. Typically, several women work together over a few days to do the necessary tasks: buying the pigs' heads, stripping the meat, preparing the stuffing, wrapping the stuffing with the corn husks, and baking or boiling the tamale.

Tamales symbolize and emphasize women's nurturance of their husbands. One elderly woman, at home in Texas for Christmas, made 200 tamales with her daughters-in-law, nieces, and goddaughter. They distributed the tamales to friends, relatives, and local taverns. The effort and expense involved were enormous. But for the women, it was worth it. Through their tamale making, they celebrate the holiday, build ties with people who they may need to call on for support, and maintain communication with tavern owners so they will watch over male kin who drink at their bars.

Tejano woman also use tamale making as a statement of domestic protest. A woman who is dissatisfied with her husband's behavior will refuse to make tamales; such refusal is a serious statement. The link between being a good wife and making tamales is strong. So, a husband can take his wife's unwillingness to make tamales as grounds for divorce. In fact, one young Tejano sued his wife for divorce in Illinois on the grounds that she refused to cook tamales for him (in addition to dancing with other men at fiestas). The judge refused to grant a divorce on such grounds. The Tejano community was

Tamales consist of fried meat and peppers in a cornmeal dough that is encased in cornhusks. ■ *What is a similarly important food item in your cultural world?* (Source: Philip Gould/CORBIS)

outraged and insisted that a proper wife should cook tamales for her husband.

FOOD FOR THOUGHT

- Provide an example from your microcultural experience about food being used as a way of expressing social solidarity or social protest.

the morning, groups of women and girls leave the house and head for a certain field where they squat and chat. Men go to a different area. Everyone carries, in their left hand, a small brass pot full of water with which they splash themselves clean. Think about the ecological advantages: this system adds fertilizer to the fields and leaves no paper litter. Westerners may consider the village practice unclean and unpleasant, but village-dwelling people in India would think that the Western system is unsanitary because using toilet paper does not clean one as well as water, and they would find the practice of sitting on a toilet less comfortable than squatting.

In many cultures, the products of elimination (urine and feces) are considered polluting and disgusting. Among some groups in Papua New Guinea (see Map 1.4), people take great care to bury or otherwise hide their fecal matter for fear that someone will find it and use it for magic against them. A negative assessment of the products of elimination is not universal, however. Among some Native American cultures of the Pacific Northwest region of Canada and the United States, urine, especially women's urine, was believed to have medicinal and cleansing properties and was considered the "water of life" (Furst 1989). In some death rituals, it was sprinkled over the corpse in the hope that it might rejuvenate the deceased. People stored urine in special wooden boxes for ritual use, including for a baby's first bath (the urine was mixed with water for this purpose).

Culture Is Based on Symbols

Our entire lives—from eating breakfast to greeting our friends, making money, creating art, and practicing religion—are based on and organized through symbols. A **symbol** is an object, word, or action with a culturally defined meaning that stands for something else with which it has no necessary or natural relationship. Symbols are arbitrary (bearing no necessary relationship to that which is symbolized), unpredictable, and diverse. Because symbols are arbitrary, it is impossible to predict how a particular culture will symbolize something. Although one might assume that people who are hungry would have an expression for hunger involving their stomach, no one could predict that in Hindi, the language of northern India, a colloquial expression for being hungry says that "rats are jumping in my stomach." The linguistic history of Barbara—the name of the author of this book—reveals that originally, in the Greek, it referred to people who were outsiders, "barbarians," and, by extension, uncivilized and savage. On top of that, the Greek term referred to such people as "bearded." The symbolic content of the American name Barbara does not immediately convey a sense of beardedness in its current context because symbolic meaning can change. It is through symbols that culture is shared, stored, and transmitted over time.

Culture Is Learned

Because culture is based on arbitrary symbols, it must be learned, in each context. Cultural learning begins from the moment of birth, if not before (some people think that an unborn baby takes in

In India, a white sari (women's garment) symbolizes widowhood. ■ *What might these women think about the Western custom of a bride wearing white?* (Source: Barbara Miller)

and stores information through sounds heard from the outside world). A large but unknown amount of people's cultural learning is unconscious, occurring as a normal part of life through observation. Schools, in contrast, are a formal way to learn culture. Not all cultures throughout history were exposed to formal schooling. Instead, children learned appropriate cultural patterns through guidance from elders and by observation and practice. Hearing stories and seeing performances of rituals and dramas are other long-standing forms of cultural learning.

Cultures Are Integrated

To state that cultures are internally integrated is to assert the principle of holism. Thus, studying only one or two aspects of culture provides understanding so limited that it is more likely to be misleading or wrong than more comprehensive approaches.

Consider what would happen if a researcher were to study intertribal warfare in highland Papua New Guinea (see Map 1.4) and focused only on the actual practice of warfare without examining other aspects of culture. A key feature of highland culture is the exchange of pigs at

---

symbol: an object, word, or action with culturally defined meaning that stands for something else; most symbols are arbitrary.

globalization: increased and intensified international ties related to the spread of

Western, especially United States, capitalism that affects all world cultures.

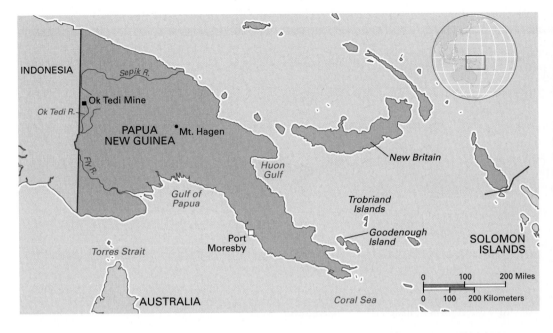

MAP 1.4 Papua New Guinea. The Independent State of Papua New Guinea gained its autonomy from Australia in 1975. Mostly mountainous with coastal lowlands, PNG is richly endowed with gold, copper, silver, natural gas, timber, oil, and fisheries. Its population is around 5,700,000. Port Moresby, the capital, has a high rate of HIV/AIDS infection among the working-age population.

political feasts. To become a political leader, a man must acquire many pigs. Pigs eat yams, which men grow, but pigs are cared for by women. This division of labor means that a man with more than one wife will be able to maintain more pigs and rise politically by giving more feasts. Such feasting enhances an aspiring leader's status and makes his guests indebted to him. With more followers attracted through feasting, a leader can gather forces and wage war on neighboring villages. Success in war brings gains in territory. So far, this example pays attention mainly to economics, politics, and marriage systems. But other aspects of culture are involved, too. Supernatural powers affect the success of warfare. Painting spears and shields with particular designs is believed to increase their power. At feasts and marriages, body decoration (including paint, shell ornaments, and elaborate feather headdresses) is an important expression of identity and status. Looking at warfare without attention to its wider cultural context yields an extremely narrow view.

Cultural integration is relevant to applied anthropologists interested in proposing ways to promote positive change. Years of experience show that introducing programs for change in one aspect of culture without considering their effects in other domains is often detrimental to the welfare and survival of a culture. For example, Western missionaries and colonialists in parts of Southeast Asia banned the practice of head-hunting. This practice was connected to many other aspects of the people's culture, including politics, religion, and psychology (a man's sense of identity as a man sometimes depended on the taking of a head). Stopping head-hunting might seem like a good thing, but its cessation had disastrous consequences for the cultures in which it was practiced.

Cultural Interaction and Change

Cultures interact with each other and change each other through contact. Trade networks, international development projects, telecommunications, education, migration, and tourism are just a few of the factors that affect cultural change through contact. **Globalization**, the process of intensified global interconnectedness and movement of goods, information, and people, is a major force of contemporary cultural change. It has gained momentum through recent technological change, especially the boom in information and communications technologies (Pieterse 2004).

Globalization does not spread evenly, and its interactions with and effects on local cultures vary substantially from positive change to cultural destruction and extinction. Four models of cultural interaction capture some of the variation (see Figure 1.3). The *clash of civilizations* argument says that the spread of Euro-American capitalism and lifeways throughout the world has created disenchantment, alienation, and resentment among other cultural systems. This model divides the world into the "West and the rest."

FIGURE 1.3 Four Models of Cultural Interaction

Clash of civilizations	Conflict model
McDonaldization	Takeover and homogenization model
Hybridization	Blending model
Localization	Local cultural remaking and transformation of global culture

FIGURE 1.4 Localization of Western Culture in Japan

Language

On average, Japanese speakers' language includes 10 percent loan words, most of which are from English, such as *hambaùgā shoppu* (hamburger joint) and *birru* (beer). Advertising uses many English loan words to generate catchy phrases that cannot be precisely translated: "Do you know me?" for American Express, "My life my gas" for the Tokyo Gas Company, and "My beautiful human life" for Shiseido cosmetics (Stanlaw 1992).

Public Bathing

A Japanese value on daily bathing, preferably in a *Sentō*, public bath, involves status, purity, cleanliness, and bonding through *hadaka no tsukiai*, noneroticized "naked bonding." In Tokyo now, about 70 percent of families have a private home bath and use public baths less frequently. The rise of home bathing is not associated with Westernization. Instead, the home bath is viewed as essentially Japanese, in spite of the Western-imported bathing products used (soap, towels). Along with the rise in home baths there has been a dramatic increase in the popularity of *onsen*, hot springs, as sites for family vacations and business meetings that convey a sense of Japanese identity (Clark 1992).

Shopping

Depāto, Western-style department stores that sell a variety of goods in one building, have played a major role in introducing Western goods into Japanese society by cleverly contextualizing them within Japanese customs. One such item is the diamond engagement ring, which has been promoted not as a sign of emotional love between the two engaged people but as part of *yuinōhin*, a series of gifts from the groom's household to the bride that symbolize a long and happy life together (Creighton 1992).

The *McDonaldization* model says that, under the powerful influence of U.S.-dominated corporate culture, the world is becoming culturally homogeneous. "Fast-food culture," with its principles of mass production, speed, standardization, and impersonal service, is taken to be at the center of this new global culture.

Hybridization is the third model. Also called *syncretism, creolization,* and *cultural crossover,* hybridization occurs when aspects of two or more cultures are mixed to form something new—a blend. In Japan, for instance, a grandmother might bow in gratitude to an automated banking machine. In the Amazon region and in the Arctic, indigenous people use satellite imagery to map and protect the boundaries of their ancestral lands.

A fourth pattern is **localization,** the transformation of global culture by local microcultures into something new. Consider the example of McDonald's restaurants. In many Asian settings, people resist the pattern of eating quickly and insist on leisurely family gatherings (Watson 1997). The McDonald's managers accommodate and alter the pace of service to allow for a slower turnover of tables. In Riyadh, Saudi Arabia, McDonald's provides separate areas for families and for "couples." Many other examples of cultural localization exist, throwing into question the notion that a form of Western "mono-culture" is taking over the entire world and erasing cultural diversity. In some contexts, Western culture is localized in ways that make it difficult for a Westerner to comprehend (see Figure 1.4).

Multiple Cultural Worlds

Many microcultures exist within larger cultures (see Figure 1.5). A particular individual is likely to be a member of several microcultures. Microcultures may overlap or may be related to each other hierarchically in terms of power, status, and rights.

The contrast between *difference* and *hierarchy* is important. People and groups can be considered different from each other on a particular criterion, but may or may not be unequal. For example, people with blue or brown eyes might be recognized as different, but this difference does not entail unequal treatment or status. In other instances, such differences do become the basis for inequality.

Class

Class is a category based on people's economic position in society, usually measured in terms of income or wealth and exhibited in terms of lifestyle. Class societies may be

FIGURE 1.5 Some Bases of Microcultures

Class	Gender and sexuality
"Race"	Age
Ethnicity and indigeneity	Institution

---

localization: the transformation of global culture by local cultures into something new.

class: a way of categorizing people on the basis of their economic position in society, usually measured in terms of income or wealth.

race: a classification of people into groups on the basis of supposedly homogeneous biological traits.

divided into upper, middle, and lower classes. Separate classes are, for example, the working class (people who trade their labor for wages) and the landowning class (people who own land on which they or others labor). Classes are related in a hierarchical system, with upper classes dominating lower classes. Class struggle, in the classic Marxist view, is inevitable as those at the top seek to maintain their position while those at the bottom seek to improve theirs. People at the bottom may attempt to improve their class position by gaining access to resources and by adopting aspects of upper-class symbolic behavior, such as speech, dress, and leisure and recreation.

Class is a recent social development in human history, extending back in time for only 10,000 years or more, and still not found in many local cultures. Among the few relatively undisturbed groups of indigenous peoples, everyone has equal wealth and sharing food and other resources among the group is expected.

"Race," Ethnicity, and Indigenous Peoples

Race refers to groups of people with supposedly homogenous biological traits. The term "race" is extremely complicated as it is used in diverse ways in different parts of the world and among different groups of people. Therefore, it makes sense to put the word in quotation marks in order to highlight its multiple meanings. In South Africa, as in the United States, "race" is mainly defined

A drawing of an Ainu (indigenous) person of Japan in a Chinese anthropology textbook published in 1918.

on the basis of skin color. In pre–twentieth-century China, body hair was the key biological basis for racial classification (Dikötter 1998). The "barbarian" races had more body hair than the "civilized" Chinese people. Chinese writers referred to bearded, male missionaries from Europe as "hairy barbarians." Into the twentieth century, some Chinese anthropologists divided humans into evolutionary stages on the basis of amounts of body hair.

Anthropological and other scientific research demonstrates that biological features do not explain or account for a person's behavior or lifestyle. Boas proved this point a century ago, and studies continue to pile up evidence. Rather than being a biological category, racial classifications are cultural constructions. They are often associated with discrimination against and cruelty toward those "races" considered less worthy by those in power. Examples are numerous. A notion of racial purity justified Hitler in his program of exterminating Jews and others who were not of the Aryan "race." Racial apartheid in South Africa denied citizenship, security, and a decent life to all those labeled "Black." In the United States, although racism is denied politically, it exists in many domains. African American political scientist Andrew Hacker states that race is the most important criterion of social difference in the United States (1992). In his book, *Two Nations: Black and White, Separate, Hostile, Unequal,* he writes that no one who is White in the United States can truly understand what it is like to be Black.

A view into the yard of a house of a low-income neighborhood of Kingston, Jamaica. ■ *Why do you think people in these neighborhoods prefer the term low-income to poor?* (Source: Barbara Miller)

Culturama

San Peoples of Southern Africa

San is a cluster name for many groups of southern Africa who speak related languages, all having glottal click sounds. Around 2,000 years ago, the San were the only people living in southern Africa, but today they are restricted to scattered locations throughout the region. European colonialists referred to San people as Bushmen, a derogatory term at the time but one that San people now prefer over what some locals call them. Some San also refer to themselves with the English language term First People.

For many centuries, the San supported themselves through collecting food such as roots and birds' eggs and by hunting eland, giraffe, and other animals. Now, pressure from African governments, farmers, ranchers, game reserves, diamond companies, and international tourism have greatly reduced the San's access to their ancestral land and their ability to survive. Some have been arrested for hunting on what they consider their land.

The Ju/'hoansi ("True People") are a subgroup of San who live in a region crossing the borders of Namibia, Botswana, and Angola and numbering between 10,000 and 15,000 people. As described by Richard Lee in the early 1960s, they were highly mobile food collectors and quite healthy (1979). Today, many have been forced from their homeland and live as poor, urban squatters or in government-built resettlement camps. Many work as farm laborers or in the international tourist industry, serving as guides and producing and selling crafts.

The specifics of their situation now depend on government policy toward indigenous foragers in the particular country where they live. Conditions are most difficult for them, at this time, in Botswana due to forced sedentarization.

Transnational advocacy organizations, including Working Group of Indigenous Minorities in Southern Africa (WIMSA) and First People of the Kalahari (FPK), are making progress in protecting the rights of San peoples. Recently, WIMSA waged an international legal case with a large pharmaceutical company and succeeded in ensuring that the San receive a portion of the profits from the commercial development of hoodia (*Hoodia gordonia*). Hoodia is extracted from a cactus indigenous to the Kalahari region. An effective appetite suppressant, it is now widely available in North America and on the Internet as diet pills.

Readings

Richard Katz, Megan Biesele, and Verna St. Denis. *Healing Makes Our Hearts Happy: Spirituality and Cultural Transformation among the Kalahari Ju/'hoansi*. Rochester, VT: Inner Traditions, 1997.

Sidsel Saugestad. *The Inconvenient Indigenous: Remote Area Development in Botswana, Donor Assistance, and the First People of the Kalahari*. Uppsala, Sweden: The Nordic Afrika Institute, 2001.

Marjorie Shostak. *Nisa: The Life and Times of a !Kung Woman*. Cambridge, MA: Harvard University Press, 1981.

Video

Bushmen of the Kalahari: A Bushman Story (National Geographic Videos, 1973).

Website

The Kalahari Peoples Fund, www.kalaharipeoples.org.

Thanks to Alison Brooks, George Washington University, for reviewing this material.

Richard Lee (left) asks Ju/'hoansi men about food plants of the Kalahari desert. This photograph was taken in 1968. Lee, and many other researchers affiliated with the Harvard Kalahari research project, learned to speak the Ju/'hoansi language and make glottal clicks using the upper part of the larynx. ■ (Source: Stan Washburn/AnthroPhoto) *San peoples have long consumed parts of the hoodia plant to suppress hunger and thirst when on long trips in the desert (right). Now they cultivate it for commercial use in a diet pill.* ■ (Source: Louise Gubb/CORBIS)

MAP 1.5 *Ju/'hoansi Region in Namibia and Botswana. Before country boundaries were drawn, the Ju/'hoansi freely ranged across their traditional territory (shaded area), depending on the seasonal availability of food and water. Now they must show a passport when crossing from one country to another.*

NAMIBIA

Ju/'hoansi region

BOTSWANA

SOUTH AFRICA

0   250   500 Miles

0   250   500 Kilometers

Ethnicity refers to a shared sense of identity among a group based on a heritage, language, or culture. Examples include African Americans and Italian Americans in the United States, the Croats of Eastern Europe, the Han of China, and the Hutu and Tutsi of Rwanda. This sense of identity is sometimes expressed through political movements to gain or protect group rights and recognition or more quietly stated in how one lives one's daily life. It can be a basis for social ranking, for claims to resources such as land or other property, and for social identity. Among many Native American groups in South and North America, ethnicity is an important basis of cultural revival.

Compared to the term "race," ethnicity appears to be a more neutral, less stigmatizing term. But it, too, has been, and still is, a basis for discrimination, segregation, and oppression. The "ethnic cleansing" campaigns conducted in the early 1990s by the Serbs against Muslims in the former Yugoslavia are an extreme case of ethnic discrimination. In China, Han ethnic domination over minority ethnic groups has been a reality for centuries. Han political repression of the Tibetan people prompted thousands of Tibetans to flee their homeland. Living in exile, they struggle to keep their ethnic heritage alive.

Indigenous peoples, following guidelines laid down by the United Nations, are defined as groups who have a long-standing connection with their home territory predating colonial or other societies that prevail in their territory (Sanders 1999). They are typically a numerical minority and often have lost the rights to their original territory. The United Nations distinguishes between indigenous peoples and *minority ethnic groups* such as the Roma, the Tamils of Sri Lanka, and African Americans. This distinction is more useful in some contexts than others (Maybury-Lewis 1997b). The San peoples of Southern Africa, and their several subgroups, are an important example of indigenous peoples whose way of life was dramatically affected by colonialism and now by globalization (see Culturama).

Gender

Gender refers to patterns of culturally constructed and learned behaviors and ideas attributed to males, females, or sometimes a blended or "third" gender. Gender can be contrasted to sex, which uses biological markers to define categories of male and female. Cultural anthropology shows that a person's biological makeup does not necessarily correspond to gender. Only a few tasks, such as nursing infants, are tied to biology.

Cross-culturally, gender differences vary from societies in which male and female roles and worlds are similar or overlapping to those in which genders are sharply differentiated. In much of rural Thailand (see Map 6.4, p. 163), males and females are about the same size, their clothing is similar, and their agricultural tasks are complementary and often interchangeable (Potter 1977). In contrast, among many groups in highland Papua New Guinea, extreme gender segregation exists in most aspects of life, including the kinds of food men and women eat (Meigs 1984). The men's house physically and symbolically separates the worlds of men and women. Men engage in rituals that purge them of female substances: nose or penis bleeding, vomiting, tongue scraping, sweating, and eye washing. Men possess sacred flutes, which they parade though the village from time to time. If women dare to look at the flutes, men traditionally had the right to kill them.

Age

The human life cycle, from birth to old age, takes people through cultural stages for which appropriate behavior and thinking must be learned anew. In many African herding societies, elaborate age categories for males define their roles and status as they move from being boys with few responsibilities and little status, to young men who are warriors and live apart from the rest of the group, to adult men who are allowed to marry, have children, and become respected elders. "The Hill," or the collective members of the United States Senate and the House of Representatives, is a highly age-graded microculture (Weatherford 1981). The Hill is a *gerontocracy* (a group ruled by senior members) in which the older politicians dominate younger politicians in terms of amount of time for speaking and how much attention a person's words receive. It may take a junior member between ten and twenty years to become as effective and powerful as a senior member.

Institutions

Institutions, or enduring group settings formed for a particular purpose, have their own characteristic microcultures. Institutions include hospitals, boarding schools and universities, and prisons. Anyone who has entered such an institution has experienced a feeling of strangeness. Until you gain familiarity with the often unwritten cultural rules, you may do things that offend or puzzle people, that fail to get you what you want, and that make you feel marginalized and insecure.

---

ethnicity: a shared sense of identity among a group based on a heritage, language, or culture.

indigenous peoples: groups who have a long-standing connection with their home territory that predates colonial or outside societies that prevail in that territory.

gender: culturally constructed and learned behaviors and ideas attributed to males, females, or blended genders.

Relationships of power and inequality exist within institutions and between different institutions. These relationships cut across those of other microcultures, such as gender. Schools, like hospitals and prisons, have their own institutional cultures. Anthropologists who study educational institutions show that schools often replicate and reinforce stereotypes, power relations, and inequalities of the wider society. A study of middle schools in the southwestern Rocky Mountain region of the United States found a situation in which teachers marginalized Mexican immigrant girls (Meador 2005). In this school, Mexican immigrant students are labeled as ESL (English as a second language) students because they are not fluent in English and take special courses designed to improve their English. So, from the start, language and labeling are problems for these students. In addition, the teachers' mental model of a "good student" is a student who is:

- Motivated to do well in school and gets good grades
- An athlete
- Popular and has good students as friends
- Comes from a stable family

It is impossible for Mexican immigrant children to conform to this image. Mexicana girls are especially disadvantaged because most are not interested in, or good at, sports. The few Mexicana girls who are motivated to try to get good grades are consistently overlooked by the teachers who instead call on students who are confident, bright, and popular, and who sit in front of the classroom and raise their hands eagerly.

Distinctive Features of Cultural Anthropology

Cultural anthropology has two distinct research goals and two distinct guiding concepts. Researchers and teachers in other disciplines have begun to adopt these goals and concepts in recent decades, so they are now found beyond cultural anthropology. Such cross-discipline contributions are something of which cultural anthropology can be proud.

Ethnography and Ethnology

Cultural anthropologists have two major goals in their study of culture. The first, **ethnography**, or "culture writing," is to provide an in-depth description of one culture. An ethnography provides firsthand, detailed information based on personal observation of a living culture for an extended period of time (Chapter 2 provides more details). An ethnography is usually a full-length book.

The second research goal of cultural anthropology is **ethnology**, or cross-cultural analysis, which is the study of a particular topic in more than one culture using ethnographic material. Ethnologists compare such topics as marriage forms, economic practices, religious beliefs, and child-rearing practices in order to discover patterns of similarity and variation and possible causes for them. For example, some ethnologists examine the amount of time caretakers spend with infants and how contact time may shape personality. Anthropologists also contribute ethnological insights to help improve public policy (Fox and Gingrich 2002). Taking a comparative or internationalist approach prompts a wide view of issues such as human rights, family organization, and religious beliefs and opens up more options for thinking about the quality of life today and in the future.

Ethnography and ethnology are mutually supportive. Ethnography provides rich, culturally specific insights. Ethnology, by looking beyond individual cases to wider patterns, provides a comparative view and raises new questions that prompt future ethnographic research and can provide policy insights.

Cultural Relativism

Most people grow up thinking that their culture is *the* way of life and that other ways of life are strange and inferior. Cultural anthropologists label this attitude **ethnocentrism**: judging other cultures by the standards of one's own culture rather than by the standards of other cultures. Ethnocentrism has fueled centuries of efforts to change "other" people in the world, sometimes through religious missionary work, sometimes in the form of colonial domination. European colonial expansion beginning in the fifteenth century was intended to extract wealth from the colonies. In addition to plundering their colonies, the Europeans imposed their "superior" culture on colonized peoples. British poet Rudyard Kipling famously stated that it was "the white man's burden" to spread British culture throughout the world. Many contemporary world powers hold similar attitudes, making and implementing foreign policy decisions that promote the adoption of their economic, political, and social systems.

The opposite of ethnocentrism is cultural relativism, the idea that each culture must be understood in terms of its own values and beliefs and not by the standards of another culture. Cultural relativism assumes that no culture is better than any other. How does a person gain a

---

ethnography: a firsthand, detailed description of a living culture, based on personal observation.

ethnology: the study of a particular topic in more than one culture using ethnographic material.

ethnocentrism: judging other cultures by the standards of one's own culture rather than by the standards of that particular culture.

sense of cultural relativism? The best way is to be able to spend substantial amounts of time living with people outside your own culture. Studying abroad and socially engaged travel help. More locally, you can experience aspects of other cultures by reading about them, learning about them in anthropology classes, doing Internet research, cooking and eating "foreign" foods, listening to "world music," reading novels by authors from other cultures, making friends who are "different" from you, and exploring the multicultural world on your campus.

One way that some anthropologists have interpreted cultural relativism is *absolute cultural relativism*, which says that whatever goes on in a particular culture must not be questioned or changed because it would be ethnocentric to question any behavior or idea anywhere. The position of absolute cultural relativism, however, can lead in dangerous directions. Consider the example of the Holocaust during World War II in which millions of Jews, Roma, and other minorities in much of Eastern and Western Europe were killed as part of the German Nazis' Aryan supremacy campaign. The absolute cultural relativist position becomes boxed in, logically, to saying that because the Holocaust was undertaken according to the values of the culture, outsiders have no business questioning it. Can anyone feel comfortable with such a position?

Critical cultural relativism offers an alternative view that poses questions about cultural practices and ideas in terms of who accepts them and why, and who they might be harming or helping. In terms of the Nazi Holocaust, a critical cultural relativist would ask, "Whose culture supported the values that killed millions of people on the grounds of racial purity?" Not the cultures of the Jews, Roma, and other victims. It was the culture of Aryan supremacists, who were just one group among many. In other words, the situation was far more complex than a simple absolute cultural relativist statement suggests. Rather, it was a case of *cultural imperialism*, in which one dominant group claimed supremacy over minority cultures and took actions in its own interests and at the expense of the subjugated cultures. Critical cultural relativism avoids the trap of adopting a homogenized view. It recognizes internal cultural differences and winners/losers, oppressors/victims. It pays attention to the interests of various power groups. Critical cultural relativism can be applied to illuminate recent and contemporary conflict situations, such as those in Yugoslavia, Rwanda, and Iraq.

Many cultural anthropologists seek to *critique* (which means to probe underlying power interests, not just to offer negative comments as in the general usage of the term criticism) the behavior and values of groups from the standpoint of some set of generally agreed-on human rights. But they recognize how difficult it is to generate a universal list of what all cultures view as good and right. As Claude Lévi-Strauss once commented, "No soci-

Native American dancers perform at the annual Gateway Pow Wow in Brooklyn, New York. ■ *Think of possible examples in your microculture of attempts to revitalize aspects of the culture.* (Source: © CRDPHOTO/CORBIS)

ety is perfect" (1968:385). While considering the "imperfections" of any and all cultures, cultural anthropologists, like people in general, should be open about their own positions and biases and try to view all cultures with an equally "critical" eye.

Valuing and Sustaining Diversity

Anthropologists value and are committed to maintaining cultural diversity throughout the world, as part of humanity's rich heritage. Thus, cultural anthropologists regret the decline and extinction of different cultures. Anthropologists contribute to the preservation of cultural diversity in many ways. Ethnography is one approach; the sheer act of describing cultures as they have existed, as they now exist, and as they change provides an archive of cultural heritage. Many cultural anthropologists have become activists in the area of cultural survival.

An organization called Cultural Survival has been helping indigenous peoples and ethnic minorities deal as equals in their interactions with outsiders. Cultural Survival's guiding principle is printed on the inside cover of this book. Cultural Survival sponsors programs to help indigenous peoples and ethnic minorities protect and manage natural resources, claim land rights, and diversify their means of livelihood.

Three Theoretical Debates in Cultural Anthropology

Each of the following three debates is concerned with cultural anthropology's basic questions about variations and similarities in how people behave and think and why people behave and think the way they do. Introduced briefly here, they will reappear throughout the book.

Critical Thinking

ADOLESCENT STRESS: BIOLOGICALLY DETERMINED OR CULTURALLY CONSTRUCTED?

Margaret Mead, one of the first trained anthropologists of North America, went to Samoa in 1925 to study child-rearing patterns and adolescent behavior. She sought to answer these questions (1961:24):

- Are the disturbances that vex adolescents in the United States due to the nature of adolescence itself or to the culture?
- Under different cultural conditions, does adolescence vary?

Mead observed and interviewed fifty adolescent girls of three different villages. Her conclusion, published in the famous book *Coming of Age in Samoa* (1961 [1928]), was that Samoan children grew up in a relaxed and happy atmosphere. As young adolescents, their transition to adulthood was sexually free and unrepressed. These findings had a major impact on thinking about child rearing in North America, prompting more relaxed forms of child rearing in the hope of raising less stressed adolescents.

In 1983, five years after Mead's death, Australian anthropologist Derek Freeman published a critique of Mead's work, saying that that her findings on adolescence were wrong. Freeman, a biological determinist, believes that adolescents everywhere are driven by hormonal changes that cause social and psychological upheavals. He pointed to two flaws in Mead's work. First, he says her fieldwork was inadequate because she spent a short time in the field (nine months) and had insufficient knowledge of the Samoan language. Second, he believes that her theoretical bias against biological determinism led her to overlook evidence that was contrary to her interests.

Freeman also marshals statistical evidence against Mead's position. He compares rates of adolescent delinquency in Samoa and England and finds that they are similar. In sum, he argues that sexual puritanism and social repression characterized Samoan adolescence and that adolescence is universally a difficult time.

Freeman's critique prompted a vigorous response from several cultural anthropologists in defense of Mead. One of these is Eleanor Leacock, an expert on how colonialism affects indigenous cultures. She claims that Freeman's position fails to take history into account: Mead's findings apply to Samoa of the 1920s, whereas Freeman's data are from the 1960s. By the 1960s, Samoan society had undergone radical cultural change because of World War II and intensive exposure to Western influences, including Christian missionaries. Free-

man's data, in Leacock's view, do not contradict Mead's findings because they are from a different period.

CRITICAL THINKING QUESTIONS

- Mead felt that finding one "negative case" (the absence of adolescent stress in Samoa) was sufficient to disprove the view that adolescent stress is a cultural universal. Do you agree that one negative case is sufficient?
- If an anthropologist found that a practice or pattern of behavior was universal, does that necessarily mean that it is biologically driven?

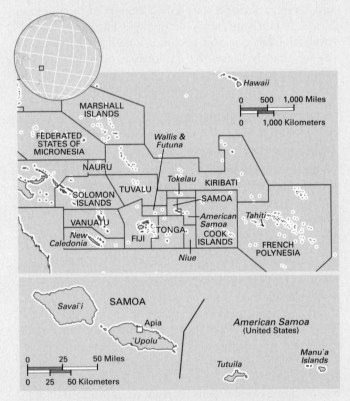

MAP 1.6 Samoa, American Samoa, and the South Pacific. Samoa, or the Independent State of Samoa, was known as German Samoa (1900–1919) and Western Samoa (1914–1997) until recognized by the United Nations as a sovereign country. Its population is around 177,000. American Samoa, or Amerika Samoa in Samoan English, is a territory of the United States with a population of about 57,000. During World War II, U.S. Marines in American Samoa outnumbered the local population and had a strong cultural influence. Unemployment rates are now high and the U.S. military is the largest employer.

Biological Determinism versus Cultural Constructionism

Biological determinism seeks to explain why people do and think what they do by considering biological factors such as people's genes and hormones. Thus, biological determinists search for the gene or hormone that might lead to behavior such as homicide, alcoholism, or adolescent stress (see Critical Thinking box). They examine cultural practices in terms of how these contribute to the "reproductive success of the species," or how they contribute to the gene pool of subsequent generations by boosting the number of surviving offspring produced in a particular population. Behaviors and ideas that have reproductive advantages are more likely than others to be passed on to future generations. Biological determinists, for example, have provided an explanation for why human males apparently have "better" spatial skills than females. They say that these differences are the result of evolutionary selection because males with "better" spatial skills would have an advantage in securing both food and mates. Males with "better" spatial skills impregnate more females and have more offspring with "better" spatial skills.

Cultural constructionism, in contrast, maintains that human behavior and ideas are best explained as products of culturally shaped learning. In terms of the example of "better" male spatial skills, cultural constructionists would provide evidence that such skills are passed on culturally through learning, not genes. They would say that parents and teachers socialize boys and girls differently in spatial skills and are more likely to promote learning of certain kinds of spatial skills among boys. Anthropologists who favor cultural construction and learning as an explanation for behaviors such as homicide and alcoholism point to childhood experiences and family roles as being more important than genes or hormones. Although most cultural anthropologists are cultural constructionists, many connect biology and culture in their work.

Interpretive Anthropology versus Cultural Materialism

As described earlier in the brief history of cultural anthropology, interpretive anthropology, or interpretivism, focuses on understanding culture by studying what people think about, their explanations of their lives, and the symbols that are important to them. For example, in understanding the eating habits of Hindus, interpretivists ask why Hindus do not eat beef. Hindus point to their religious beliefs according to which cows are sacred and it is a sin to kill and eat them. Interpretivists accept this explanation as sufficient.

Cultural materialism attempts to learn about culture by first examining the material aspects of life: the natural environment and how people make a living within particular environments. Cultural materialists believe that these basic facts of life shape culture, even though people may not realize it. They use a three-level model to explain culture. The bottom level is *infrastructure*, a term that refers to basic material factors such as natural resources, the economy, and population. According to this model, infrastructure tends to shape the other two domains of culture: *structure* (social organization, kinship, and political organization) and *superstructure* (ideas, values, and beliefs). This book's chapters are organized roughly in terms of these three categories, but with recognition that the layers are not neat and tidy but rather have interconnections.

A cultural materialist explanation for the taboo on killing cows and eating beef involves the fact that cattle in India play a more important role alive than dead or carved into steaks (Harris 1974). The many cattle wandering the streets of Indian cities and villages look useless to Westerners. But a closer analysis shows that the seemingly useless population of bovines serves many useful functions. Ambling along, they eat paper trash and other edible refuse. Their excrement is "brown gold," useful as fertilizer or, when mixed with straw and formed into dried patties, as cooking fuel. Most important, farmers use cattle to plow fields. Cultural materialists take into account Hindu beliefs about the sacred meaning of cattle, but they see its relationship to the material value of cattle, as symbolic protection keeping these extremely useful animals out of the meat factory.

The debate between interpretivism and cultural materialism has a long history in cultural anthropology. Its philosophical roots can be traced back to Plato, who said that the only reality is ideas and to Aristotle, who said that there is some sort of reality that we can learn about through observation. Some cultural anthropologists are strong interpretivists, whereas some are strong cultural materialists. Many combine the best of both views.

> **THINKING OUTSIDE THE BOX**
>
> IMAGINE THAT you are on a debating team. The issue is cars in the United States. Prepare to support both an interpretivist and cultural materialist position about how to understand why cars are so numerous in the United States.

---

biological determinism: a theory that explains human behavior and ideas mainly as a result of biological features such as genes and hormones.

cultural constructionism: a theory that explains human behavior and ideas as being mainly the results of learning.

Traffic in the city of Varanasi (Banaras), northern India *(top)*. Foreign visitors to India often comment that the presence of so many wandering cows is a sign of wastefulness and inefficiency. ■ (Source: © Jack Fields/CORBIS) **SUVs, trucks, and buses share the road in Los Angeles** *(bottom)*. SUVs are popular in the United States even though they are criticized by environmentalists for their poor gas mileage. ■ *If you were an energy policy-maker, what lessons would you draw from this pair of photographs?* (Source: AP/Wide World Photos)

Individual Agency versus Structurism

This debate concerns the question of how much individual will, or agency, affects the way people behave and think, compared with the power of forces, or "structures," that are beyond individual control. Western philosophical thought gives much emphasis to the role of agency, the ability of individuals to make choices and exercise free will. In contrast, structurism emphasizes that free choice is an illusion because choices are structured by larger forces such as the economy, social and political organization, and ideological systems.

A prime example is the study of poverty. Those who emphasize agency focus their research on how individuals attempt to act as agents, even in situations of extreme poverty, in order to change their situation as best they can. Structurists would emphasize that the poor are trapped by large and powerful forces. They would describe how the political economy and other forces pro-

vide little room for agency for those at the bottom. An increasing number of cultural anthropologists seek to blend a structural perspective with attention to agency.

Beyond the Debates: Holists at Heart

Cultural anthropologists often take different theoretical positions. Some apply their work while others stick to academic pursuits. But it is fair to say that cultural anthropologists are united in their interest in and care about humanity and its richly varied cultures.

Cultural Anthropology and Careers in the "Real World"

Some of you reading this book may take only one anthropology course to satisfy a requirement. Others may become interested in the subject matter and take a few more. Some will decide to major or minor in anthropology. Even just one course in anthropology can change your way of thinking about the world and your place in it. On top of that, it can add to your ability to get a job that values the kinds of thinking and skills that anthropology provides. Take a look at the inside of the back cover of this book for tips about how anthropology coursework can enhance your knowledge, skills, and résumé.

Majoring in Anthropology

An anthropology B.A. is a liberal arts degree. It is not, however, a professional degree, such as a business degree or a degree in physical therapy. It provides a solid education relevant to many career directions that are likely to require further study, such as law, criminal justice, medicine and health services, social services, education, humanitarian assistance, international development programs, and business. Students interested in pursuing a B.A. major in anthropology should know that anthropology is at least as useful as other liberal arts majors for either graduate study or a professional career.

Anthropology has several clear advantages over other liberal arts majors, and employers and graduate schools are increasingly recognizing these features. Cultural anthropology provides knowledge about the world's people and diversity. It offers insights about a variety of specialized research methods. Cross-cultural awareness and communication skills are valuable assets sought by business, government, health-care providers, and nongovernmental organizations.

The question students always ask is this: Is it possible to get a good job, especially one related to anthropology, with a B.A. in anthropology? The answer is yes, but it takes planning and hard work. Do the following: Gain expertise in at least one foreign language, study abroad, do service learning during your undergraduate years, and conduct an independent research project and write up the results as a professional report or conference paper. Package these skills on your résumé so that they appear relevant to employers. Do not give up. Good jobs are out there, and coursework and skills in anthropology are increasingly valued.

Anthropology can also be an excellent minor. It complements almost any other area of study by adding a cross-cultural perspective. For example, if you are majoring in music, courses about world music will greatly enrich your primary interest. The same applies to subjects such as interior design, psychology, criminal justice, international affairs, economics, political science, and more.

Graduate Study in Anthropology

Some of you may go on to pursue a master's degree (M.A.) or doctorate degree (Ph.D.) in anthropology. If you do, here is some advice. Be passionate about your interest but also be aware that full-time jobs as a professor or as a professional anthropologist are not easy to get. To expand possibilities of a good job, it is wise to consider combining a professional skill with your degree program in anthropology, such as a law degree, an M.A. degree in project management, a Master's of Public Health (M.P.H.), a certificate in disaster relief, or participation in a training program in conflict prevention and resolution.

Useful skills will make your anthropology degree more powerful. In biological anthropology, it may be coursework in anatomy that helps you get a job working in a forensics lab or teaching anatomy in a medical school. In archaeology, it may be your experience on a summer dig that helps you get a job with a firm in your home state that investigates building sites before construction begins to check for the presence of fossils or artifacts. In cultural anthropology, cross-cultural experiences or knowledge of a foreign language may get you a position with an international aid organization. In linguistic anthropology, your knowledge of bilingualism means that you can help design a more effective program for teaching English to refugees.

Living an Anthropological Life

Studying cultural anthropology makes for smart people and people with breadth and flexibility. In North America, college graduates are likely to change careers (not just jobs, but careers) several times in their lives. You never know where you are going to end up working, or in what endeavor. So it pays to be broadly informed about the world. Cultural anthropology will help you to ask original and important questions about the world's people and their relationships with one another and to provide original and important answers. It will enrich your daily life by increasing your exposure to the world's cultures. When you pick up a newspaper, you will find several articles that connect with what you have learned in your anthropology classes. You will be able to view your own everyday life as culturally constructed in interesting and meaningful ways.

The Big Questions Revisited

WHAT is anthropology?

Anthropology is an academic discipline, like history or economics. It comprises four interrelated fields in its attempt to explore all facets of humanity from its origins through the present. Biological or physical anthropology is the study of humans as biological organisms, including their evolution and contemporary variation. Archaeology is the study of past human cultures through their material remains. Linguistic anthropology is the study of human communication, including its origins, history, and contemporary variation and change. Cultural anthropology is the study of living peoples and their cultures, including variation and change. Culture refers to people's learned and shared behaviors and beliefs.

Each field makes both theoretical and applied contributions. The perspective of this book is that applied anthropology, just like theoretical anthropology, should be an integrated and important part of all four fields, rather than a separate, fifth field. Examples of applied anthropology in the four fields include forensic anthropology, nonhuman primate conservation, assisting in literacy programs for refugees, and advising businesses about people's preferences.

WHAT is cultural anthropology?

Cultural anthropology is the field within general anthropology that focuses on the study of contemporary human culture—that is, on learned and shared ways of behaving and thinking. It has several distinctive features that set it apart from the other fields of general anthropology and from other academic disciplines. Its two basic goals are ethnography and ethnology. Cultural relativism, attributed to Franz Boas, is a guiding principle that other disciplines have widely adopted. Cultural anthropology values and works to sustain cultural diversity.

Culture is the key concept of cultural anthropology. Some anthropologists define culture as learned and shared behavior and ideas, whereas others equate culture with ideas alone and exclude behavior as a part of culture. Besides the tricky area of defining culture, it is possible to point to characteristics of culture. Culture is related to nature but is not the same as nature; it is based on symbols and it is learned. Cultures are integrated within themselves. They also interact with other cultures and change. Several models of cultural interaction involve varying degrees of conflict, blending, and resistance. People participate in cultures of different levels, including local microcultures shaped by such factors as class, "race"/ethnicity/indigeneity, gender, age, and institutions.

Cultural anthropology has a rich history of theoretical approaches and changing topical focuses. Three important and enduring theoretical debates are biological determinism versus cultural constructivism, interpretive anthropology versus cultural materialism, and individual agency versus structurism. Each, in its own way, attempts to understand and explain why people behave and think the way they do and to account for differences and similarities across cultures.

HOW is cultural anthropology relevant to a career in the "real world"?

Taking just one course in cultural anthropology expands awareness of the diversity of the world's cultures and the importance of cross-cultural understanding. Employers in many fields—such as public health, humanitarian aid, law enforcement, business, and education—increasingly value a degree in cultural anthropology. In today's diverse and connected world, being culturally informed and culturally sensitive is essential.

Graduate degrees in cultural anthropology, either at the M.A. or Ph.D. level, are even more likely to lead to professional positions that directly use your anthropological education and skills. Combining graduate coursework in anthropology with a professional degree, such as a master's degree in public health or public administration, or a law degree, is a successful route to a meaningful career outside academia.

KEY CONCEPTS

agency, p. 13
anthropology, p. 4
applied anthropology (or practicing anthropology or practical anthropology), p. 4
archaeology (or prehistory), p. 4
biological anthropology (or physical anthropology), p. 4
biological determinism, p. 27
class, p. 20
cultural anthropology (or social anthropology), p. 4

cultural constructionism, p. 27
cultural materialism, p. 13
cultural relativism, p. 11
culture, p. 4
ethnicity, p. 23
ethnocentrism, p. 24
ethnography, p. 24
ethnology, p. 24
functionalism, p. 11
gender, p. 23
globalization, p. 19

holism, p. 11
indigenous peoples, p. 23
interpretivism, or interpretive anthropology, p. 13
linguistic anthropology, p. 4
localization, p. 20
microculture, p. 14
race, p. 21
structurism, p. 13
symbol, p. 18

SUGGESTED READINGS

Thomas J. Barfield, ed. *The Dictionary of Anthropology*. Malden, MA: Blackwell Publishing, 1997. This reference work contains hundreds of brief essays on concepts in anthropology, such as evolution, myth, functionalism, and applied anthropology, and on important anthropologists.

Stanley R. Barrett, *Anthropology: A Student's Guide to Theory and Method*. Toronto: University of Toronto Press, 2000. This book organizes the theoretical history of cultural anthropology into three phases and summarizes trends in each. The author discusses how to do research in cultural anthropology.

Catherine Besterman and Hugh Gusterson, eds. *Why America's Top Pundits Are Wrong: Anthropologists Talk Back*. Berkeley: University of California Press, 2005. Twelve anthropologists provide anthropologically informed critiques of such popular commentators as Thomas Friedman, Samuel Huntington, Robert Kaplan, and Dinesh D'Souza. Topics include globalization, ethnic violence, social justice, and the biological roots of behavior.

Mario Blaser, Harvey A. Feit, and Glenn McRae, eds. *In the Way of Development: Indigenous Peoples, Life Projects and Globalization*. New York: Zed Books, in association with the International Development Research Centre, 2004. Twenty chapters contributed by indigenous leaders, social activists, and cultural anthropologists address indigenous peoples' responses to capitalism and indigenous ideas about future change that is positive for them and for the environment.

Merryl Wyn Davies and Piero, *Introducing Anthropology*. Cambridge: Icon Books, 2002. This book offers insights on key thinkers, developments, and arguments in anthropology. Each page is illustrated with cartoon-like drawings that make for lively reading.

Roberto J. González, ed. *Anthropologists in the Public Sphere: Speaking Out on War, Peace, and American Power*. Austin: University of Texas Press, 2004. This collection includes over fifty op-eds that cultural anthropologists have published starting with one by Franz Boas in 1919. Most are recent and many address the post-9/11 situation and U.S. military operations.

Marvin Harris. *Our Kind: Who We Are, Where We Came From and Where We Are Going*. New York: HarperCollins, 1989. This book contains 100 essays on topics in anthropology's four fields, including early human evolution, toolmaking, Neanderthals, food preferences, sex, sexism, politics, animal sacrifice, and thoughts on the survival of humanity.

Ira E. Harrison and Faye V. Harrison, eds. *African-American Pioneers in Anthropology*. Chicago: University of Illinois Press, 1999. This collection of intellectual biographies highlights the contributions of thirteen African American anthropologists to the development of cultural anthropology in the United States.

Takami Kuwayama, ed. *Native Anthropology: The Japanese Challenge to Western Academic Hegemony*. Melbourne: Trans Pacific Press, 2004. The chapters in this book discuss various topics in Japanese anthropology, including "native anthropology," the marginalization of Asian anthropologists, folklore studies, and how U.S. anthropology textbooks present Japan.

James H. McDonald, ed. *The Applied Anthropology Reader*. Boston: Allyn and Bacon, 2002. This collection of over fifty brief essays explores topics in applied cultural anthropology, including ethics, methods, urban settings, health, international development, the environment, education, and business.

R. Bruce Morrison and C. Roderick Wilson, eds. *Native Peoples: The Canadian Experience*, 3rd ed. Oxford, Ontario: Oxford University Press, 2004. This sourcebook on Northern Peoples contains twenty-six chapters with sections divided by region. Chapters about various cultural groups provide historical context and updates on the current situation.

Thomas C. Patterson. *A Social History of Anthropology in the United States*. New York: Berg, 2001. This history of anthropology in the United States emphasizes the social and political context of the discipline and how that context shaped theories and methods.

Richard J. Perry. *Five Key Concepts in Anthropological Thinking*. Upper Saddle River, NJ: Prentice-Hall, 2003. The five key concepts are evolution, culture, structure, function, and relativism. The author raises thought-provoking questions about anthropology as being Eurocentric and about the appropriation of the culture concept beyond anthropology.

David H. Price. *Threatening Anthropology: McCarthyism and the FBI's Surveillance of Activist Anthropologists*. Durham, NC: Duke University Press, 2004. This book documents the political repression of anthropologists in the United States during the McCarthy era, focusing on the persecution of several anthropologists. The last chapter is a reminder that political oppression and censorship did not end after the McCarthy era.

Pat Shipman. *The Evolution of Racism: Human Differences and the Use and Abuse of Science*. Cambridge, MA: Harvard University Press, 1994. This book offers a history of the "race" concept in Western thought from Darwin to contemporary DNA studies. The author addresses thorny issues such as racism in the United States and Nazi Germany's use of Darwinism.

2
Methods in Cultural Anthropology

The Big Questions

- HOW do cultural anthropologists conduct research on culture?

- WHAT does fieldwork involve?

- WHAT are some important issues in cultural anthropology research today?

During his fieldwork among the Hare Indians in Northwest Canada, anthropologist Joel Savishinsky holds a 25-pound lake trout. His dog team is resting behind him. *(Source: © Joel Savishinsky)*

This chapter is about how cultural anthropologists do research. The first section describes the evolution of methods in cultural anthropology since the late nineteenth century. The second section covers the steps involved in a research project. The chapter concludes by addressing two urgent topics in cultural anthropology research. Throughout the chapter, you might consider the similarities and differences between research in cultural anthropology and research in other disciplines such as biology, psychology, political science, economics, and history.

Changing Research Methods in Cultural Anthropology

Today's methods in cultural anthropology are different in several ways from those used during the nineteenth century. Most cultural anthropologists now gather data by doing **fieldwork**, going to the *field*, which is wherever people and cultures are, to learn about culture through direct observation (Robson 1993). They also use a variety of specialized research techniques discussed in this section.

From the Armchair to the Field

The term *armchair anthropology* refers to how early cultural anthropologists conducted research by sitting and reading about other cultures. They read reports written by travelers, missionaries, and explorers but never visited those places or had any kind of direct experience with the people. Sir Edward Tylor, who proposed the first definition of culture in 1871, as noted in Chapter 1, was an armchair anthropologist. Sir James Frazer, another famous founding figure of anthropology, was also an armchair anthropologist. He wrote *The Golden Bough* (1978 [1890]), a multivolume collection of myths, rituals, and symbols that he compiled from his wide reading.

In the late nineteenth and early twentieth centuries, anthropologists hired by European colonial governments moved a step closer to learning directly about the people of other cultures. They traveled to colonized countries in Africa and Asia where they lived near, but not with, the people they were studying. This approach is called *verandah anthropology* because, typically, the anthropologist would send out for "natives" to come to his

Ethnographic research in the early twentieth century often involved photography. The girl shown here wears the skull of her deceased sister. Indigenous people of the Andamans revere the bones of their dead relatives and would not want them to be taken away, studied, or displayed in a museum. ■ (Source: A. R. Radcliffe-Brown, *The Andaman Islanders.* Cambridge: Cambridge University Press, 1964 [1922])

verandah for interviewing (verandah anthropologists, like armchair anthropologists, were men). A classic example of verandah anthropology is A. R. Radcliffe-Brown's book, *The Andaman Islanders* (1964 [1922]) (see Culturama, Chapter 3, p. 70). At time of Radcliffe-Brown's research on Great (now South) Andaman Island at the turn of the twentieth century, the indigenous population had been decimated by diseases brought in by the British colonizers and by the effects of direct colonial violence. Radcliffe-Brown's assignment was to do *salvage anthropology,* to collect what data he could from the remaining people in order to document their language, social life, and religious beliefs.

A bit earlier, in the United States during the mid-nineteenth century, Lewis Henry Morgan had taken steps toward learning about people through direct observation. A lawyer, Morgan lived in Rochester, New York, near the Iroquois territory. He became well acquainted with many of the Iroquois, staying with them for several two-week periods (Tooker 1992). These experiences provided Morgan with important insights into their everyday lives and formed the basis of his book, *The League of the Iroquois* (1851). This book helped change the prevailing

fieldwork: research in the field, which is any place where people and culture are found.

participant observation: basic fieldwork method in cultural anthropology that involves living in a culture for a long period of time while gathering data.

multisited research: fieldwork conducted in more than one location in order to understand the behaviors and ideas of dispersed members of a culture or the relationships among different levels such as state policy and local culture.

Euro-American perception of the Iroquois, and other Native American tribes, as "dangerous savages." It showed that Iroquois behavior and beliefs make sense if an outsider is willing to spend time learning about them through direct experience.

Participant Observation

A major turning point in how cultural anthropologists do research occurred in the early twentieth century, during World War I. It laid the foundation for the current cornerstone method in cultural anthropology: fieldwork combined with participant observation. **Participant observation** is a research method for learning about culture that involves living in a culture for an extended period while gathering data.

The "father" of participant observation is Bronislaw Malinowski. He adopted an innovative approach to learning about culture in the Trobriand Islands in the South Pacific during World War I (see Culturama, p. 39). "For two years, he set his tent in their midst, learned their language, participated as much as he could in their daily life, expeditions, and festivals, and took everything down in his notebooks" (Sperber 1985:4). As established by Malinowski, the key elements of participant observation are:

- Living with the people
- Learning the language
- Participating in their everyday life

By living with the people of the Trobriand Islands, Malinowski could learn about their culture in context, rather than through secondhand reports. By learning the local language, Malinowski could talk with the people without the use of interpreters.

The benefits of this new approach are evident in Malinowski's many writings about the Trobriand Islanders, including his most famous book, *Argonauts of the Western Pacific* (1961 [1922]). When the war ended, Malinowski returned to Europe and established the tradition of participant observation in the new university programs for training anthropologists.

In this early phase of fieldwork and participant observation, a primary goal was to record as much as possible of a people's language, songs, rituals, and social life because many cultures were disappearing. Most early cultural anthropologists did fieldwork in small, relatively isolated cultures. They thought they could study everything about such cultures; those were the days of holism (defined in Chapter 1). Typically, the anthropologist (a White man) would go off with his notebooks to collect data on a standardized list of topics including economics, family life, politics, religion, language, art and crafts, and more.

Lanita Jacobs-Huey's fieldsites include hairstyling competitions throughout the United States and London, England. Here, a judge evaluates the work of a student stylist at the Afro Hair & Beauty Show in London, England. ■ (Source: Lanita Jacobs-Huey)

Today, few if any such seemingly isolated cultures remain. Cultural anthropologists have now devised new research methods so that they can study larger-scale cultures, global–local connections, and cultural change. One methodological innovation of the late twentieth century is especially important in addressing these new issues: **multisited research,** which is fieldwork conducted on a topic in more than one location (Marcus 1995). While especially helpful in studying migrant populations in both their place of origin and their new location (Chapter 15), multisited research is useful for studying many topics.

Lanita Jacobs-Huey conducted multisited fieldwork in order to learn about the language and culture of hairstyles among English-speaking African American women (2002). She chose a range of sites throughout the United States and in London, England, in order to explore the many facets of this far-from-simple topic: beauty salons, regional and international hair expos and training seminars, Bible study meetings of a nonprofit group of Christian cosmetologists, standup comedy clubs, a computer-mediated discussion about the politics of Black hair, and a cosmetology school in Charleston, South Carolina.

Doing Fieldwork in Cultural Anthropology

Conducting fieldwork in cultural anthropology can be exciting, frustrating, scary, boring, and sometimes dangerous. One thing is true: Fieldwork, as an intensive and long period of cultural interaction, transforms the lives of everyone involved. This section explores the stages of a fieldwork research project, starting with the initial planning and ending with the analysis and presentation of the findings.

Beginning the Fieldwork Process

Before going to the field, the prospective researcher must select a research topic and prepare for the fieldwork itself. These steps are critical to the success of the project.

Project Selection

Finding a topic for a research project is a basic first step. The topic should be important and feasible. Cultural anthropologists often find a topic to research by carrying out a *literature review,* or reading what others have already written. Conducting a literature review often exposes a gap in previous research. For example, cultural anthropologists realized during the 1970s that anthropological research had bypassed women and girls, and this is how feminist anthropology began (B. Miller 1993).

Notable events sometimes inspire a research topic. The HIV/AIDS epidemic and its rapid spread continue to prompt research. The recent rise in the numbers of international migrants and refugees is another pressing area for study. The fall of state socialism in Russia and Eastern Europe shifted attention to that region; it also meant that cultural anthropologists could conduct fieldwork in previously closed countries. Conflicts in Ireland, Rwanda, the former Yugoslavia, Sudan, and other places spur cultural anthropologists to ask what keeps states together and what makes them fall apart (Harris 1992) and to contribute to their knowledge about conflict prevention and postconflict resolution (Lubkemann 2005).

Some cultural anthropologists find a focus for their research by choosing a particular material item, such as sugar (Mintz 1985), cars (D. Miller 2001), beef (Caplan 2000), money (Foster 2002), shea butter (Chalfin 2004), wedding dresses (Foster and Johnson 2003), coca (Allen 2002), and cocaine (Taussig 2004). The material items provide a focus for understanding the social relations

Visitors walk past a giant Coca Cola logo at a slogan launch party in Shanghai, China. The market leader in ready-to-drink soft drinks in China, Coca Cola brought pop stars to the party to entertain guests and promote its new slogan: "No Compromise on Real Refreshment, Coca Cola!" ■ *Go to the Internet to learn about Coca Cola's global market and its leading competitors.* (Source: Qilai Shen/epa/epa/CORBIS)

surrounding their production and trade and what they mean in terms of people's changing identities.

Another fruitful avenue for research is a *restudy,* fieldwork conducted in a previously researched community. Many decades of previous research provide a baseline of information on which later studies can build. It makes sense to examine changes that have occurred or to look at the culture from a new angle. For her doctoral dissertation research, Annette Weiner (1976) decided to go to the Trobriand Islands, following in the footsteps of Malinowski, to learn what people's lives were like over fifty years after his fieldwork. What she discovered prompted her to alter her original research plans (see Critical Thinking box and Culturama).

Even luck can lead to a research topic. Spanish anthropologist María Cátedra (1992) stumbled on an important issue during exploratory fieldwork in rural northern Spain (see Map 2.5, p. 51). A suicide occurred in a village in the mountains near where she was staying. The local people did not consider the suicide remarkable or strange. In fact, the area had a high rate of suicide. Later she went back and did long-term research on the social dynamics of suicide in this area (some of her findings appear later in this chapter).

---

informed consent: an aspect of fieldwork ethics requiring that the researcher inform the research participants of the intent, scope, and possible effects of the study and seek their consent to be in the study.

Preparing for the Field

After defining the research topic, it is important to secure funding in order to carry out the research. Academic anthropologists can apply for funding from a variety of sources, governmental and nongovernmental. Several sources of funding are also available for advanced graduate students. Undergraduate students have a more difficult time finding grants to support fieldwork, but many succeed.

Related to the funding question is whether it is appropriate for an anthropologist to conduct research while employed in the research setting. Employment provides financial support for the research, but it raises some problems. A basic dilemma, discussed later in the chapter, is the ethical principle that anthropologists cannot do "undercover" research. If you are working in a factory, for example, while studying what goes on in the factory, you must get people's permission for your study, something that is not always easy. More positively, a work role can help gain people's trust and respect. A British graduate student, Adam Kaul, worked as a bartender in a tourist town in Ireland (2004). This position greatly enriched his experience. It placed him at the center of the village, and people respected him as a hard-working person.

If the project involves international travel, the host government may require a visa and an application for permission to conduct research. These formalities may take a long time and may even be impossible to obtain. The government of India, for example, is highly restrictive about research by foreigners. Research permission for "sensitive" topics such as tribal people, border areas, and family planning is unlikely to be granted. China's restrictions against U.S. anthropologists doing research were lifted only in the past twenty years or so, but it is still not easy to get permission to do fieldwork and participant observation.

Some research topics are more sensitive than others are (Lee and Renzetti 1993). Sexual behavior is a potentially sensitive research issue, more from the point of view of research participants than from the host governments. Typically, it is even more difficult to research homosexuality than heterosexuality, because of mainstream norms, laws, and social stigma (see Everyday Anthropology box).

Many countries now also require that researchers follow official guidelines for *protection of human subjects*. In the United States, since the 1990s, universities and other institutions that support or conduct research with living people must establish *institutional review boards (IRBs)* to monitor all research related to living humans to make sure it conforms to ethical principles. IRB guidelines follow a medical model related to the need to protect people who participate as "subjects" in medical research. Normally, IRBs require informed consent, in writing, of the research participants. **Informed consent** is an aspect of research ethics requiring that the researcher inform the research participants of the intent, scope, and possible effects of the study and seek their agreement to be in the study. Obtaining such consent of research participants is reasonable and feasible in many anthropological research projects. Often, however, written consent is not reasonable or feasible, especially in oral-based cultures where most people are not literate. Fortunately, IRBs are gaining more experience with nonclinical research and the contexts in which many cultural anthropologists do research. It is now possible to request a waiver of informed written consent and informed oral consent instead. Because IRB guidelines do change, it is a good idea to check your institution's website for the latest policy.

Depending on the project location, preparation for the field may involve buying specialized equipment, such as a tent, warm clothing, waterproof clothing, and sturdy boots. For example, fieldwork in Siberia requires a sleeping bag adequate for nighttime temperatures below 220° Fahrenheit. Health preparations may require immunization against contagious diseases such as yellow fever. For research in a remote area, a well-stocked medical kit and basic first-aid training are essential. Research equipment and supplies are another important aspect of preparation. Cameras, video recorders, tape recorders, and laptop computers are now basic field equipment. Unlike the traditional paper notebook and pen, though, these machines require batteries and other inputs.

If a researcher is unfamiliar with the local language, intensive language training before going to the field is critical. Even with language training in advance, cultural anthropologists often find that they cannot communicate in the local version of the standardized language they studied in a classroom. Therefore, many fieldworkers rely on help from a local interpreter throughout their study or, at least, in its early stages.

Working in the Field

Fieldwork in cultural anthropology is a difficult and long process that involves the researcher coming to terms with an unfamiliar culture. The anthropologist attempts to learn the language of the people, live as they do, understand their lives, and be a friend. Before embarking on those activities, the project needs a site (or sites) and the anthropologist needs a place to live.

Critical Thinking

SHELLS AND SKIRTS IN THE TROBRIAND ISLANDS

A lasting contribution of Bronislaw Malinowski's ethnography, *Argonauts of the Western Pacific* (1961 [1922]), is its detailed examination of the **kula,** a trading network linking many islands in the region in which men have long-standing partnerships for the exchange of everyday goods such as food as well as highly valued necklaces and armlets.

More than half a century later, Annette Weiner (1976) traveled to the Trobriand Islands to study woodcarving. She settled in a village less than a mile from where Malinowski had done his research. She immediately began making startling observations: "On my first day in the village, I saw women performing a mortuary [death] ceremony in which they distributed thousands of bundles of strips of dried banana leaves and hundreds of beautifully decorated fibrous skirts" (xvii).

Nowhere in Malinowski's voluminous writings did these women's activities appear. Weiner was intrigued and decided to change her research project to investigate women's goods, exchange patterns, and prestige. Men, as Malinowski showed, exchange shells, yams, and pigs. Women, as Weiner learned, exchange bundles of banana leaves and intricately made skirts. Power and prestige derive from both exchange networks.

Reading Malinowski alone informs us about the world of men's status systems and describes them in isolation from half of the islands' population: women. Weiner's book, *Women of Value, Men of Renown* (1976), provides an account of women's trading and prestige activities as well as how they are linked to those of men. Building on the work of her predecessor, Weiner shows how a full

Bronislaw Malinowski during his fieldwork in the Trobriand Islands, 1915–1918. ■ *What are some of the differences between what his field research revealed about men's lives in the Trobriand Islands and what a "verandah anthropologist" would have learned?* (Source: Pearson Education)

understanding of one domain requires knowledge of the other.

CRITICAL THINKING QUESTIONS

- How is it possible that Malinowski overlooked women's exchange patterns?

- Do the findings of Annette Weiner simply provide another one-sided view?

- What might a cultural anthropologist discover in the Trobriand Islands now?

Site Selection

A research *site* is the place where the research takes place, and sometimes a project involves more than one site. The researcher often has a basic idea of the area where the fieldwork will occur—for example, a *favela* (shantytown) in Rio de Janeiro, a village in Scotland, or a factory in Malaysia. It is often impossible to know, in advance, exactly where the project will be located.

Selecting a research site depends on many factors. It may be necessary to find a large village, if the project involves class differences in work patterns, or to find a clinic, if the study concerns health-care behavior. It may be difficult to find a village, neighborhood, or institution in which the people welcome the researcher and the project. Often, housing shortages mean that even the most welcoming community cannot provide space for an anthropologist.

Here is an example in which a combination of factors came together in a positive way. Jennifer Robertson was seeking a research site in Japan for a study of urban population change. She selected Kodaira, a suburb of Tokyo

---

kula: a trading network linking many of the Trobriand Islands in which men have long-standing partnerships for the exchange of everyday goods such as food as well as highly valued necklaces and armlets.

The Trobriand Islanders of Papua New Guinea

The Trobriand Islands are named after eighteenth-century French explorer Denis de Trobriand. They include twenty-two flat coral atolls east of the island of New Guinea. The indigenous Trobriand population lives on four main islands. Kiriwina is by far the most populated, with about 28,000 people (digim'Rina, personal communication 2006). The Papua New Guinea (PNG) district office and an airstrip are located on Kiriwina at Losuia.

The islands were first colonized by Great Britain and then ceded to Australia in 1904 (Lawton 1987; Weiner 1988). The British attempted to stop local warfare and change many other aspects of Trobriand culture. Christian missionaries introduced the game of cricket as a substitute for warfare (see Chapter 14 for further discussion). In 1943, allied troops landed as part of their Pacific operations. In 1975, the islands became part of the state of Papua New Guinea.

Island-to-island cultural differences exist. Even within one island, people may speak different dialects, although everyone speaks a version of the language called Kilivila (Weiner 1988). The

Trobrianders grow much of their own food, including root crops such as yams, sweet potatoes, and taro; beans and squash; and bananas, breadfruit, coconuts, and betel nut. Pigs are the main animal raised for food and as prestige items. In the later part of the twentieth century, Trobrianders were increasingly dependent on money sent to them by relatives working elsewhere in PNG. Current development projects are encouraging people to plant more fruit trees, such as mango (digim'Rina 2005).

Kinship emphasizes the female line, meaning that mothers and daughters form the core of co-residential groups. Fathers, while not co-residential, are nonetheless important family members and spend as much time at child care as women do (Weiner 1988). Fathers of political status give their babies and children, both boys and girls, highly valued shell earrings and necklaces to wear. Mothers give daughters prized red skirts. Trobriand children attend Western-style schools on the islands, and many go to mainland PNG and beyond for further studies.

Today, elders worry that young people do nothing but dream about "money" and fail to care for the heritage of their ancestors. Another concern is that the coral reefs are being endangered by commercial overfishing.

Readings

Shirley F. Campbell. *The Art of Kula*. New York: Berg, 2002.

Bronislaw Malinowski. *Argonauts of the Western Pacific*. New York: E. P. Dutton & Co. 1961 [1922].

Linus S. digim'Rina. "Food Security through Traditions: Replanting Trees and Wise Practices." *People and Culture in Oceania*, *20*, 13–36, 2005.

Annette B. Weiner. *The Trobrianders of Papua New Guinea*. New York: Holt, Rinehart and Winston, 1988.

Video

The Trobriand Islanders of Papua New Guinea (Disappearing World, 1990).

Website

Promotion of Indigenous Wise Practices: Food Security, Trobriand Islands, Milne Bay Province, Papua New Guinea. www.unesco .org

Thanks to Linus S. Digim'Rina, University of Papua New Guinea, and Robert Foster, University of Rochester, for reviewing this material.

Trobriand men's coveted trade goods include this shell necklace and armlet (left). ■ (Source: Irven Devore/AnthroPhoto) A Trobriand girl wears a valued skirt at a dance in honor of the ancestors on Kiriwina Island. She and other female participants coat their skin with coconut oil and herbs and wear decorative flowers (right). ■ (Source: © Albrecht G. Schaefer/CORBIS)

MAP 2.1 *Trobriand Islands of Papua New Guinea. Also known as the Kiriwina Islands, these islands are an archipelago of coral atolls lying off the eastern coast of the island of New Guinea.*

Everyday Anthropology

TALKING ABOUT SEX

It is likely that all cultures define certain topics as out of bounds for public discussion within the group or for discussion with an outsider. Sex, as in sexual intercourse, is a frequently avoided area. Heterosexual societies are likely to limit talk about homosexuality even more. How does and can an anthropologist learn about sexuality, especially homosexuality? This box provides insights into how a U.S. anthropologist stumbled into learning about homosexuality in Brazil.

Richard Parker went to Brazil to study the historical and political aspects of *carnaval,* a popular public celebration that occurs at the beginning of the Christian period of Lent (1991). Parker became aware of how closely linked the celebration is to sexual symbolism and sexuality, both heterosexual and homosexual, and he realized how important these topics are to understanding Brazilian culture in general. As his research continued, he gained the trust of heterosexuals and gay men and lesbians. The quality of his personal relationships with his more than thirty participants was the key factor in the success of the study.

It may seem surprising, but Parker's research focus on sexual culture had a positive effect on his study by creating rapport through a shared sense of breaking the rules of social decorum. This kind of rapport would not develop from study of a less sensitive topic, such as employment or family life. Parker found that his research participants

> often seemed to take a certain pleasure in being part of a project which seemed to break the rules of proper decorum . . . while they often resisted, understandably, speaking too directly about their own sexual lives, they seemed to enjoy (and, at times, to take a positive delight in) the opportunity to speak freely about the question of sex more generally (1991:177).

A participant in *carnaval* (Brazilian spelling) in Rio de Janeiro, Brazil. This springtime celebration is an occasion of heightened merriment and display of sexuality. ■ *Think of a special event, or events, in your microcultural experience in which fun and sexuality are expressed in an "out of bounds" way. What are the characteristics of this special event?* (Source: © AFP/CORBIS)

Parker's rapport with his research participants is evident in the rich data that he collected on such topics as masturbation, oral sex, and anal sex. One lesson about fieldwork is that the sheer sensitivity of a topic does not always prevent its study. The researcher, however, has to be sensitive, too.

FOOD FOR THOUGHT

- How would you feel about discussing sexual behavior in your microculture with an anthropologist from Brazil?

(see Map 2.2), because of advice from a Japanese colleague. It had available housing and offered a good fit with her research interests. By happy coincidence, she was also familiar with the area:

> I spent my childhood and early teens in Kodaira [but] my personal past did not directly influence my selection of Kodaira as a fieldsite and home. . . . That I wound up living in my old neighborhood in Kodaira was determined

more by the availability of a suitable apartment than by a nostalgic curiosity about my childhood haunts. As it turned out, I could not have landed at a better place at a better time. (1991:6)

Gaining Rapport

Rapport is a trusting relationship between the researcher and the study population. In the early stages of research,

---

rapport: a trusting relationship between the researcher and the study population.

Jennifer Robertson (*far left*) celebrates the publication of her book, *Native and Newcomer* (1991), with several administrators from Kodaira City Hall. This informal gathering at a local restaurant followed a formal ceremony at the City Hall, where Robertson presented her book to the mayor of Kodaira, an event covered by city and regional newspapers. ■ *What cultural features are noteworthy about this gathering?* (Source: Jennifer Robertson)

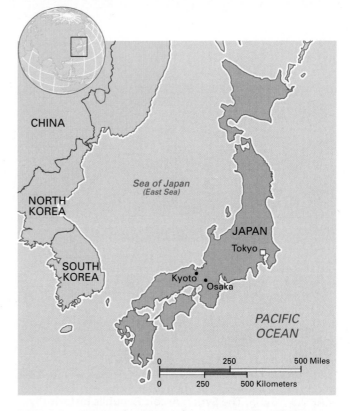

MAP 2.2   Japan. The State of Japan, or Nihon-koku or Nippon-koku, encompasses over 3,000 islands, most of which are mountainous. Its population is nearly 129 million. Greater Tokyo, with over 30 million residents, is the largest metropolitan area in the world. Japan has the world's second largest economy.

the primary goal is to establish rapport—probably first with key leaders or decision makers in the community who may serve as *gatekeepers* (people who formally or informally control access to the group or community). Gaining rapport involves trust on the part of the study population, and their trust depends on how the researcher presents herself or himself. In many cultures, people have difficulty understanding why a person would come to study them, because they do not know about universities and research and cultural anthropology. They may provide their own explanations based on previous experience with outsiders whose goals differed from those of cultural anthropologists, such as tax collectors, family planning promoters, and law-enforcement officials.

Many publications document problems related to how anthropologists present themselves in the field and how people understand who the anthropologist is and why he or she is there. Stories about *false role assignments* can be humorous. During his 1970s fieldwork in northwest Pakistan, Richard Kurin reports that in the first stage of his research, the villagers thought he was an international spy from America, Russia, India, or China (1980). Over time, he convinced them that he was not a spy. So what was he? The villagers came up with several roles for Kurin. First, they speculated that he was a teacher of English because he was tutoring one of the village boys.

Second, they guessed that he must be a doctor because he gave people aspirin. Third, they thought he might be a lawyer who could help them in local disputes because he could read court orders. Last, they decided he was a descendant of a local clan because of the similarity of his last name and that of an ancestral king. For Richard Kurin, the last of these was best of all, being a true "Karan."

Being labeled a spy is still a serious issue for anthropologists. Many people worldwide have no concept of what a cultural anthropologist is and why a person would want to, or be able to, spend a year or more living with them and learning about their everyday lives. Christa Salamandra, a Western-trained doctoral student in anthropology, went to Damascus, Syria (see Map 2.3), for her dissertation research (2004). Damascus is a city with a long history and is increasingly cosmopolitan. Damascenes, however, have little exposure to anthropology. Syria has no university with a department of anthropology, and there are no Syrian anthropologists. Salamandra's research interests in popular culture (movies, cafés, and fashion) perplexed the Damascenese, who decided she must be a foreign spy. One person said to her, "Your question is CIA, not academic" (2004:5).

Another situation of an assumed spying role arose in North Carolina, even though the anthropologist, Mary

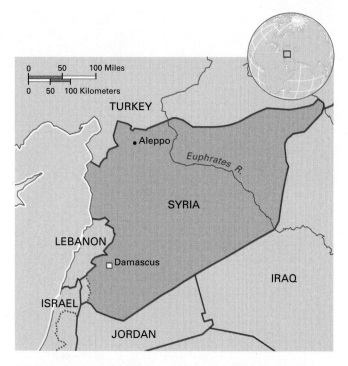

MAP 2.3 Syria. The Syrian Arabic Republic historically included the present-day territories of Lebanon, Israel, the Palestinian Territories, and parts of Jordan, but not the Jazira region in Syria's northeast. Its population is 19 million people. Syria's capital city, Damascus, with a population of 3 million people, is one of the oldest, continually occupied cities in the world.

Anglin, shared citizenship with the people (2002). During her fieldwork in a mica-processing factory in the western part of the state, some people thought she was an industrial spy. Anglin came from the northeastern United States, so she was not a "southerner." Worse than that, she had no kin connections in the region and no "family" (she was single). The Irish-Scottish residents of the area did not quickly welcome her, but she managed to get the factory owner to let her spend time in the factory as a participant-observer. Several of the women factory workers befriended her, but many of the local people continued to be suspicious. At one point, a rumor circulated that Anglin was an industrial spy, intent on learning about mica processing in order to sell the information to competitors. The rumor died down, but the factory owner later banned her from entering the factory.

Gift Giving and Exchange

Giving gifts to people involved in the research can help the project proceed, but gifts should be culturally and ethically appropriate. Learning the local rules of exchange is important (see Figure 2.1).

Matthews Hamabata, a Japanese American who did fieldwork in Japan, learned about the complexities of gift giving among Japanese business families (1990). He developed a close relationship with one family, the Itoos, and helped their daughter apply for admission to universities in the United States. When the applications were completed, Mrs. Itoo invited him to an expensive restaurant to celebrate. After the dinner, she handed him a small, carefully wrapped package, expressing her embarrassment at the inadequacy of her gift in relation to all that he had done for her daughter. When he returned home, he opened the gift. It was a box of chocolates. Upon opening the box, he discovered 50,000 yen (about U.S. $250). Hamabata felt insulted: "Who do the Itoos think they are? They can't buy me or my services!" (1990:21–22). He asked some Japanese friends what he should do. They told him that the gift signaled the Itoos' wish to have a long-standing relationship and that returning the money to the Itoos would be an insult. They advised him to give a return gift later on, in order to maintain the relationship. His gift should leave him ahead by about 25,000 yen, given his status as an anthropologist in relation to the Itoos' status as a rich business family. This strategy worked and the relationship between Hamabata and the Itoos remained intact.

Microcultures and Fieldwork

Class, race, gender, and age all affect how the local people will perceive and welcome an anthropologist. Some examples illustrate how microcultures influence rapport and affect the research in other ways.

Class In most fieldwork situations, the anthropologist is more wealthy and powerful than the people studied. This difference is obvious to the people. They know that the anthropologist must have spent hundreds or thousands of dollars to travel to the research site. They see the anthropologist's expensive equipment (camera, tape

THINKING OUTSIDE THE BOX

RECALL A SITUATION in which either you did not know what would be an appropriate gift to give someone (in terms of quality, cost, or some other factor) or you were faced with some other puzzling situation related to gift exchange. What were the cultural meanings underlying the situation?

FIGURE 2.1 Cultural Issues Related to Gift Giving in the Field

- What an appropriate or an inappropriate gift is
- How to deliver a gift
- How to behave as a gift giver
- How to behave when receiving a gift
- If and how to give a follow-up gift

recorder, video recorder, even a vehicle) and valuable material goods (stainless steel knives, cigarettes, flashlights, canned food, and medicines).

Laura Nader urged that anthropologists should also "study up" by doing research among powerful people such as members of the business elite, political leaders, and government officials (1972). As one example of this approach, research on the high-fashion industry of Japan placed the anthropologist, Dorinne Kondo, in touch with members of the Japanese elite—influential people capable of taking her to court if they felt she wrote something defamatory about them (1997). "Studying up" has contributed to awareness of the need, in all fieldwork situations, for recognition of the anthropologist's accountability to the people being studied.

"Race"/Ethnicity   For most of its history, cultural anthropology has been dominated by Euro-American White researchers who study "other" cultures that are mainly non-White and non-Euro-American. The effects of "Whiteness" on role assignments range from the anthropologist being considered a god or ancestor spirit to being reviled as a representative of a colonialist past or neo-colonialist present. While doing research in a village in Jamaica called Haversham, Tony Whitehead learned how "race" and status interact (1986). Whitehead is an African American and from a low-income family. Being of a similar "race" and class as the rural Jamaicans with whom he was doing research, he assumed he would quickly build rapport because of a shared heritage. The people of Haversham, however, have a complex status system that relegated Whitehead to a position that he did not predict, as he explains:

> I was shocked when the people of Haversham began talking to me and referring to me as a "big," "brown," "pretty-talking" man. "Big" was not a reference to my weight but to my higher social status as they perceived it, and "brown" referred not only to my skin color but also to my higher social status. . . . More embarrassing than bothersome were the references to how "pretty" I talked, a comment on my Standard English speech pattern. . . . Frequently mothers told me that their children were going to school so that they could learn to talk as pretty as I did. (1986:214–215)

This experience prompted Whitehead to ponder the complexities of "race" and status cross-culturally.

Similarly, for Lanita Jacobs-Huey, in her research on African American women's hair culture, being an African American did not automatically gain her acceptance (2002). Hairstyle is a sensitive subject related to African American identity. For example, in one part of her research, she attempted to establish rapport with Internet-based participants. Before the women would take her into their confidence, they wanted to know how she styled her hair.

Liza Dalby in formal geisha dress. ■ *Besides learning to dress correctly, what other cultural skills did Liza Dalby probably have to learn?* (Source: Liza Dalby)

Gender   If a female researcher is young and unmarried, she is likely to face more difficulties than a young unmarried man or an older woman, married or single, because people in most cultures consider a young unmarried female on her own as extremely unusual. Rules of gender segregation may dictate that a young unmarried woman should not move about freely without a male escort, attend certain events, or be in certain places. A woman researcher who studied a community of gay men in the United States says:

> I was able to do fieldwork in those parts of the setting dedicated to sociability and leisure—bars, parties, family gatherings. I was not, however, able to observe in those parts of the setting dedicated to sexuality—even quasipublic settings such as homosexual bath houses. . . . Thus my portrait of the gay community is only a partial one, bounded by the social roles assigned to females within the male homosexual world. (Warren 1988:18)

Gender segregation may also prevent male researchers from gaining access to a full range of activities. Liza Dalby, a White American, lived with the geishas of Kyoto, Japan, and trained to be a geisha (1998). This research would have been impossible for a man to do.

Age   Typically, anthropologists are adults, and this fact may make it easier for them to gain rapport with people their age than with children or the aged. Although some children and adolescents welcome the participation of a

Tobias Hecht plays a game with some of the street children in his study in Rio de Janeiro, Brazil. ■ (Source: Isabel Balseiro)

friendly adult in their daily lives and respond to questions openly, others are more reserved. Margaret Mead once commented, "Ideally, a three-generation family, including children highly trained to understand what they experience, would be the best way to study a culture" (1986:321). She recognized that this ideal would not be possible or practical, and that the best a fieldworker could do was to be imaginative and flexible in order to gain rapport with members of different age categories. This challenge may require learning and using age-specific language. A team of anthropologists studying sexuality among U.S. adolescents discovered that using age-appropriate language made it easier to establish rapport:

> In our experience, when asking an adolescent, especially a younger adolescent, a sensitive question such as "Have you ever had sexual intercourse?" the child spends far too much time in awe of the word "intercourse," investigating its meaning, and giggling at this clinical term. It is better for the researcher to ask simply, "Have you ever had sex?" (Weber, Miracle, and Skehan 1994:44)

Other Factors A researcher's role is affected by even more factors than those just discussed, including religion, dress, and personality. Being the same religion as the residents of a Jewish home for the aged in California helped a Jewish anthropologist establish rapport (Myerhoff 1978). This positive engagement is evident in a conversation between the anthropologist (A) and a woman named Basha (B):

> B: "So, what brings you here?"
> A: "I'm from the University of Southern California. I'm looking for a place to study how older Jews live in the city." At the word *university,* Basha moved closer and nodded approvingly. "Are you Jewish?" she asked.
> A: "Yes, I am."
> B: "Are you married?" she persisted.
> A: "Yes."
> B: "You got children?"
> A: "Yes, two boys, four and eight," I answered.
> B: "Are you teaching them to be Jews?" (1978:14)

culture shock: persistent feelings of uneasiness, loneliness, and anxiety that often occur when a person has shifted from one culture to a different one.

deductive approach (to research): a research method that involves posing a research question or hypothesis, gathering the empirical data related to the question, and then assessing the findings in relation to the original hypothesis.

inductive approach (to research): a research approach that avoids hypothesis formation in advance of the research and instead takes its lead from the culture being studied.

quantitative data: research that emphasizes gathering and analyzing numeric information and using tables and charts when presenting results.

qualitative data: research that emphasizes generating descriptive information.

etic: an analytical framework used by outside analysts in studying culture.

emic: what insiders do and perceive about their culture, their perceptions of reality, and their explanations for why they do what they do.

The anthropologist was warmly accepted, and her plan for one year of research grew into a long-standing relationship. In contrast, being Jewish posed a potential problem in another context (Freedman 1986). Diane Freedman conducted research in rural Romania in the 1980s. Given the pervasiveness of anti-Semitism there, she was reluctant to tell the villagers that she was Jewish and also reluctant to lie. Early in her stay, she attended the village church. The priest asked what her religion was. She opted for honesty and found, to her relief, that being Jewish had no negative effects on her research.

Culture Shock

Culture shock consists of persistent feelings of uneasiness, loneliness, and anxiety that often occur when a person has shifted from one culture to a different one. The more different the two cultures are, the more severe the shock is likely to be. Culture shock happens to many cultural anthropologists, no matter how much they have tried to prepare themselves for fieldwork. It also happens to students who study abroad, Peace Corps volunteers, and anyone who spends a significant amount of time living and participating in another culture.

Culture shock can range from problems with food to the language barrier. Food differences were a major problem in adjustment for a Chinese anthropologist who came to the United States (Shu-Min 1993). American food never gave him a "full" feeling. A U.S. anthropologist who went to Pohnpei, an island in the Federated States of Micronesia (see Map 1.6, p. 26), found that language caused her the most serious adjustment problems (Ward 1989). She reports on the frustration she felt: ["Even dogs understood more than I did. . . . [I will never] forget the agony of stepping on a woman's toes. Instead of asking for forgiveness, I blurted out, "His canoe is blue" (14).

A frequent psychological aspect of culture shock is the feeling of reduced competence as a cultural actor. At home, the anthropologist is highly competent, carrying out everyday tasks such as shopping, talking with people, and mailing a package without thinking. In a new culture, the simplest tasks are difficult, and one's sense of self-efficacy is undermined. In extreme cases, an anthropologist may have to abandon a project because of an inability to adapt to the fieldwork situation. For most, however, culture shock is a temporary affliction that subsides as the person becomes more familiar with the new culture.

Reverse culture shock may occur on coming home. A U.S. anthropologist describes his feelings on returning to San Francisco after a year of fieldwork in a village in India:

> We could not understand why people were so distant and hard to reach, or why they talked and moved so quickly. We were a little frightened at the sight of so many white faces and we could not understand why no one stared at us, brushed against us, or admired our baby. (Beals 1980:119)

THINK OF AN OCCASION on which you experienced culture shock, even if as the result of a brief cross-cultural encounter. How did you feel? How did you cope? What did you learn from the experience?

Fieldwork Techniques

The goal of fieldwork is to collect *data*, or information, about the research topic. In cultural anthropology, variations exist about what kinds of data to emphasize and the best ways to collect data.

Deductive and Inductive Research Approaches

A **deductive approach** is a form of research that starts from a research question or *hypothesis*, and then involves collecting data related to the question through observation, interviews, and other methods. An **inductive approach** is a form of research that proceeds without a hypothesis and involves gathering data through unstructured, informal observation, conversation, and other methods. Deductive methods are more likely to collect **quantitative data**, or numeric information, such as the amount of land in relation to the population or numbers of people with particular health problems. The inductive approach in cultural anthropology tends to avoid quantitative data and emphasizes **qualitative data**, or nonnumeric information, such as recordings of myths, conversations, and filming of events. Most anthropologists, however, operate somewhere between these two extremes, combining deductive and inductive approaches and quantitative and qualitative data.

Cultural anthropologists have labels for data collected in each approach. **Etic** (pronounced like the last two syllables of *phonetic*) refers to data collected according to the researcher's questions and categories, with the goal of being able to test a hypothesis (see Figure 2.2). In contrast, **emic** (pronounced like the last two syllables of *phonemic*) refers to data collected that reflect what insiders say and understand about their culture, and insiders' categories of thinking. Cultural materialists (review Chapter 1) are more likely to collect etic data, whereas interpretivists are more likely to collect emic data. Again, however, most cultural anthropologists collect both types of data.

Participant Observation

Most cultural anthropologists will tell you that participant observation is essential in order to learn about a culture. The phrase *participant observation* includes two

FIGURE 2.2 Two Research
Approaches in Cultural
Anthropology

Research Approach	Process	Data
Deductive (Etic)	Hypothesis followed by data collection	Quantitative data for hypothesis testing
Inductive (Emic)	No hypothesis, data collection follows from participants' lead	Qualitative data for descriptive insights

processes: *participating,* or being part of the people's lives, while carefully *observing.* These two activities may sound simple, but they are actually quite complex.

Being a participant means that the researcher adopts the lifestyle of the people being studied, living in the same kind of housing, eating similar food, wearing similar clothing, learning the language, and participating in the daily round of activities and in special events. The rationale is that participation over a long period improves the quality of the data. The more time the researcher spends living among the people, the more likely it is that the people will live their "normal" lives. In this way, the researcher is able to overcome the **Hawthorne effect**, a research bias that occurs when participants change their behavior to conform to the perceived expectations of the researcher. The Hawthorne effect was discovered in the 1930s during a study of an industrial plant in the United States. During the study, research participants altered their behavior in ways they thought would please the researcher.

An anthropologist cannot be everywhere, participate in everything, and observe everyone, so choices are involved in where to be and what to observe. As mentioned earlier, gender, age, and other microcultural factors may limit the anthropologist's participation in certain domains or activities. The sheer need for sleep may mean that the anthropologist misses something important that happens at night, such as a ritual or a moonlight hunting expedition.

Although participant observation is often equated with the casual term "hanging out," in fact, it means constant choices about where to be on a particular day at a particular time, what one observes, with whom, and what, by default, one misses. Depending on the research topic, participant observation may focus on who lives with whom, who interacts with whom in public, who are leaders and who are followers, what work people do, how people organize themselves for different activities,

rituals, arguments, festivals, funerals, and far more.

Talking with People

Common sense tells you that participating and observing are important, but what about talking to people and asking questions, such as, "What is going on here?" "What does that mean?" "Why are you doing that?" The process of talking to people and asking them questions is such an important third component of participant observation that the method should actually be called *participant observation and talking,* or perhaps the snappier phrase *inquisitive observation* (Bestor 2004). Cultural anthropologists use a variety of data-collection techniques that rely on talking with people, from informal, casual, and unplanned conversations to more formal methods.

An **interview** is a technique for gathering verbal data through questions or guided conversation. It is more purposeful than a casual conversation. An interview may involve only two people, the interviewer and the interviewee, or several people in what are called *group interviews* or *focus groups.* Cultural anthropologists use varying interview styles and formats, depending on the kinds of information they seek, the amount of time they have, and their language skills. The least structured type of interview is an *open-ended interview,* in which the respondent (interviewee) takes the lead in setting the direction of the conversation, topics to be covered, and the amount of time devoted to a particular topic. The interviewer does not interrupt or provide prompting questions. In this way, the researcher discovers what themes are important to the person.

A **questionnaire** is a formal research instrument containing a pre-set series of questions that the anthropolo-

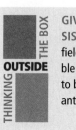

THINKING OUTSIDE THE BOX

GIVEN THE EMPHASIS on observation in fieldwork, is it possible for a blind person to become a cultural anthropologist?

Hawthorne effect: research bias due to participants changing their behavior to conform to expectations of the researcher.
interview: a research technique that involves gathering of verbal data through questions or guided conversation between at least two people.
questionnaire: a formal research instrument containing a pre-set series of questions that the anthropologist asks in a face-to-face setting, by mail, or by email.

gist asks in a face-to-face setting, or by mail or email. Cultural anthropologists who use questionnaires favor a face-to-face setting. Like interviews, questionnaires vary in the degree to which the questions are *structured* (close-ended) or *unstructured* (open-ended). Structured questions limit the range of possible responses—for example, by asking research participants to rate their positions on a particular issue as "very positive," "positive," "negative," "very negative," or "no opinion." Unstructured interviews generate more emic responses.

When designing a questionnaire, the researcher should have enough familiarity with the study population to be able to design questions that make cultural sense (Fitchen 1990). Researchers who take a ready-made questionnaire to the field with them should ask another researcher who knows the field area to review it in advance to see whether it makes cultural sense. Further revisions may be required in the field to make the questionnaire fit local conditions. A *pilot study* using the questionnaire among a small number of people in the research area can expose areas that need further revision.

Combining Observation and Talking

A combination of observation of what people actually do with verbal data about what people say they do and think is essential for a well-rounded view of a culture (Sanjek 2000). People may say that they do something or believe something, but their behavior may differ from what they say. For example, people may say that sons and daughters inherit equal shares of family property when the parents die. Research into what really happens may reveal that daughters do not inherit equal shares. Similarly, an anthropologist might learn from people and their laws that discrimination on the basis of skin color is illegal. Research on people's behavior might reveal clear examples of discrimination. It is important for an anthropologist to learn about both what people say and what happens. Both are "true" aspects of culture.

Specialized Methods

Cultural anthropologists also use a variety of more specific research methods. The choice depends on the anthropologist's research goals.

Life History A *life history* is a qualitative, in-depth description of an individual's life as narrated to the researcher. Anthropologists differ in their views about the value of the life history as a method in cultural anthropology. Early in the twentieth century, Franz Boas rejected this method as unscientific because research participants might lie or exaggerate (Peacock and Holland 1993). Others disagree, saying that a life history reveals rich information on individuals and how they think, no matter how "distorted" their reports are. For example, some anthropologists have questioned the accuracy of

Marjorie Shostak (*right*) interviewing Nisa during fieldwork among the Ju/'hoansi in 1975. ■ *What would you tell an anthropologist about your life?* (Source: © Mel Konner/AnthroPhoto)

parts of *Nisa: The Life and Times of a !Kung Woman* (Shostak 1981), probably the most widely read life history in anthropology. It is a book-length story of a Ju/'hoansi woman of the Kalahari desert of southern Africa (review Culturama box in Chapter 1, p. 22). Presented in Nisa's voice, it includes rich details about her childhood and several marriages. The value of the narrative is not so much whether it is all "true" or not; rather, the value is that we learn from Nisa what she wants to tell us, her cultural construction of her experiences. That counts as "data" in cultural anthropology, for it is "truly" what she reported to Marjorie Shostak.

In the early days of life history research, anthropologists tried to choose an individual who was somehow typical, average, or representative. It is not possible, however, to find one person who is representative of an entire culture in the scientific sense. Instead, anthropologists now seek individuals who occupy particularly interesting social niches. For example, Gananath Obeyesekere (pronounced Oh-baya-SEKa-ra) wrote a book called *Medusa's Hair: An Essay on Personal Symbols and Religious Experience* (1981), which presents the life histories of four Sri Lankan people, three women and one man. Each became a Hindu religious devotee and ascetic, distinguished by their thickly matted hair, twisted into coils like a snake. Their snaky hair is permanently matted and impossible to comb. According to the devotees, a deity is present in their matted hair. Analyzing the four life histories, Obeyesekere suggests that all four people had suffered deep psychological afflictions, including sexual anxieties. Their matted hair symbolizes their suffering and provides them with a special status as holy, thus

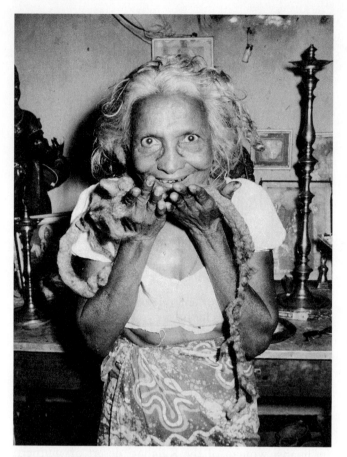

This Sri Lankan woman, whose life story Gananath Obeyesekere analyzed, is a priestess to a deity. She stands in the shrine room of her house, holding her matted, snaky hair. ■ *How do hairstyles in your culture express a person's religion, marital status, or sexuality?* (Source: Gananath Obeyesekere)

style of presentation, and the women were reluctant to adopt it (Young 1983). Marjorie Shostak, in contrast, found a willing and extremely expressive narrator in Nisa (1981).

Time Allocation Study A *time allocation study* is a quantitative method that collects data on how people spend their time each day on particular activities. This method relies on standard time units as the basic matrix and then labeling or coding the activities that occur within certain time segments (Gross 1984). Activity codes must be adapted to fit local contexts. For example, activity codes for various kinds of work would not be useful in a time allocation study in a retirement home. Data can be collected through observation that may be continuous, at fixed intervals (for instance, every forty-eight hours), or on a random basis. Continuous observation is extremely time consuming and means that the number of people observed is limited. Spot observations help increase the number of observations but may inadvertently miss important activities. Another option for data collection is to ask people to keep daily time logs or diaries.

Texts Many cultural anthropologists collect *textual material*, a category that includes written or oral stories, myths, plays, sayings, speeches, jokes, and transcriptions of people's everyday conversations. In the early twentieth century, Franz Boas collected thousands of pages of texts from Native American groups of the Northwest Coast of Canada, including myths, songs, speeches, and accounts of how to perform rituals. These collections provide valuable records of cultures that have changed since the time of his fieldwork. Surviving tribal members have consulted them in order to recover forgotten aspects of their culture.

Archival and Historical Sources Many cultural anthropologists who work in cultures with a written history gain important insights about the present from records of the past preserved in archives maintained in institutions such as libraries, churches, and museums. Ann Stoler pioneered the use of archival resources in understanding the present in her study of Dutch colonialism in Java (1985, 1989) (see Map 1.3, p. 15). Her archival research exposed details about colonial policies, the culture of the colonizers, and relationships with indigenous Javanese people.

National archives in London, Paris, and Amsterdam, to name just a few places, contain records of colonial contact and relations. Regional and local archives contain information about land ownership, agricultural produc-

beyond the rules of married life and conjugal sexual relations.

Life histories of several people in a similar situation can reveal both individual experiences and shared patterns. James Freeman's book, *Hearts of Sorrow* (1989), is an example of this approach with attention to refugees. It presents short "cuts" from several life stories of Vietnamese refugees living in southern California. These "cuts" portray a range of adaptive individual experiences and the overarching theme of sadness of all the refugees about the loss of their homeland.

The ability of people to present a story of their lives varies, depending on the cultural context. An attempt to gather life histories from women on Goodenough Island, Papua New Guinea (see Map 1.4, p. 19), was difficult because telling one's life story is a masculine

triangulation: research technique that involves obtaining information on a particular topic from more than one person or perspective.

tion, religious practices, and political activities. Parish churches throughout Europe keep detailed family histories extending back hundreds of years. Land-holding records and family registers are sources of historic cultural data in Japan and China.

Important information about the past can also come from fieldwork among living people through an approach called the *anthropology of memory*. Anthropologists collect information about what people remember as well as gaps in their memory, revealing how culture shapes memories and how memories shape their culture. Jennifer Robertson's (1991) research about neighborhood people's memories of life in Kodaira, Japan, before the influx of immigrants is an example of this kind of research. She used both interview data and archival data.

Multiple Research Methods and Team Projects

Most cultural anthropologists use several different methods for their research because just one would not provide all the varieties of data necessary to understand a given topic. For example, consider what interviews with people in 100 households would provide in terms of breadth of coverage, and then add what you could learn from life histories collected from a subset of five men and five women to provide depth.

Another way to add richness is the use of **triangulation,** a technique that involves seeking information on a particular topic from more than one angle or perspective (Robson 1993:290). Asking only one person provides information from only that person's viewpoint. Asking two people about the same thing doubles the information and often reveals that perspectives differ. The researcher may then want to check other sources, such as written records or newspaper reports, for additional perspectives (see Lessons Applied box).

Anthropologists, with their in-depth insights about real people and real people's lives, are increasingly taking part in multidisciplinary research projects, especially projects with an applied focus. Such teamwork strengthens the research by adding more perspectives and methods.

Recording Culture

How does an anthropologist keep track of all the information collected in the field and record it for future analysis? As with everything else about fieldwork, things have changed since the early times when a notebook and typewriter were the major recording tools. Yet there is continuity: Taking notes is still the trademark method of recording data for a cultural anthropologist.

Field Notes

Field notes include daily logs, personal journals, descriptions of events, and notes about those notes. Ideally, researchers should write up their field notes each day.

A multidisciplinary team comprising anthropologists, engineers, and agricultural experts from the United States and Sudan meet to discuss a resettlement project.
■ *Do some Internet research on Sudan and its varied cultures.* (Source: Michael Horowitz)

Otherwise, a backlog accumulates of daily "scratch notes," or rough jottings made on a small pad or note cards (Sanjek 1990a:95–99). Trying to capture, in the fullest way possible, the events of even a single day is a monumental task and can result in dozens of pages of handwritten or typed field notes. Laptop computers now enable anthropologists to enter many of their daily observations directly into the computer.

Tape Recording, Photography, and Videos

Tape recorders are a major aid to fieldwork. Their use may raise problems, however, such as research participants' suspicions about a machine that can capture their voices, and the ethical issue of protecting the identity of people whose voices are preserved on tape. María Cátedra reports on her use of tape recording during her research in the Asturias region of rural Spain (see Map 2.5, p. 51):

> At first the existence of the "apparatus," as they called it, was part wonder and part suspect. Many had never seen one before and were fascinated to hear their own voice, but all were worried about what I would do with the tapes. . . . I tried to solve the problem by explaining what I would do with the tapes: I would use them to record correctly what people told me, since my memory was not good enough and I could not take notes quickly enough. . . . One event helped people to accept my integrity in regard to the "apparatus." In the second *braña* [small settlement] I visited, people asked me to play back what the people of the first *braña* had told me, especially some songs sung by a group of men. At first I was going to do it, but then I instinctively refused because I did not have the first people's permission. . . . My stand was quickly known in the first *braña* and commented on with approval. (1992:21–22)

MULTIPLE METHODS IN A NEEDS ASSESSMENT STUDY IN CANADA

The United Way of Canada, a philanthropic agency, wanted to find out what the highest priorities were for their funding operations in Saskatoon, a city located in Canada's southern prairie (Ervin et al. 1991). Alexander Ervin put together a team of faculty and student researchers from the University of Saskatchewan's Department of Anthropology and Archaeology to respond to the United Way's request. At the time of the study in 1990, the city's population was about 200,000. The economy is based on agriculture, mining, forestry, and some manufacturing with an unemployment rate of 10 percent. In recent years, the city's population had grown substantially, including more First Nation (indigenous) people. Unemployment rates were among the highest in Canada and income levels the lowest. Food banks and soup kitchens were increasingly important for the many unemployed people.

Members of the team decided that they needed data about perceived needs of the people of Saskatoon, including the unemployed and poor as well as employed professionals, including people who worked for the sponsoring agency, the United Way. Data collection included several activities:

- Reviewing available written reports relevant to Saskatoon's needs
- Analyzing economic and social indicators
- Conducting 135 interviews with key people from community agencies
- Organizing three public forums bringing together city residents and United Way Board members
- Interviewing United Way agency executive directors

Information from these data-gathering activities provided breadth and depth about community needs and opinions as well as agency priorities and interests.

The research team produced a report that included a list of over 200 identified needs. It organized this extensive list into seventeen sectors, including general health, mental health, the senior population, First Nations issues, racism and discrimination, and immigrant and refugee resettlement. One of the most pressing community needs involves eliminating hunger, especially among children. The report recommended the provision of more food banks and attention to preventive health care for children. Another high priority is improving access to public transportation for economically disadvantaged people and for the elderly. The research revealed the need for better communication among nonprofit organizations in the city that seek to improve living standards.

The report suggested that the United Way take a stronger role in being an advocate for disadvantaged people rather than focusing on fund-raising.

FOOD FOR THOUGHT

- Conducting a community needs assessment requires a different research approach from traditional fieldwork in cultural anthropology. What are some of the pros and cons of such applied research?

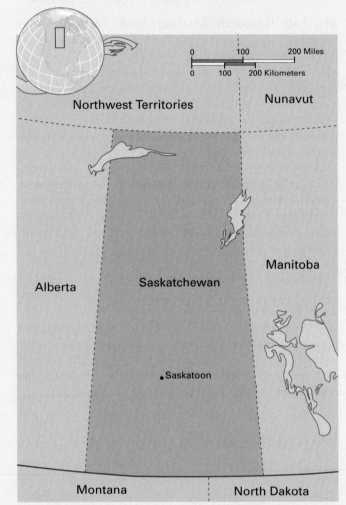

MAP 2.4 Saskatoon, South-Central Canada. The city of Saskatoon is the largest city in the Saskatchewan province with a population of over 200,000. After an economic slump in the 1980s and 1990s, it launched several new industrial parks in 2005. Corporate headquarters of industries involved in uranium and potash are located in Saskatoon. Food processing and information technology are important sources of employment.

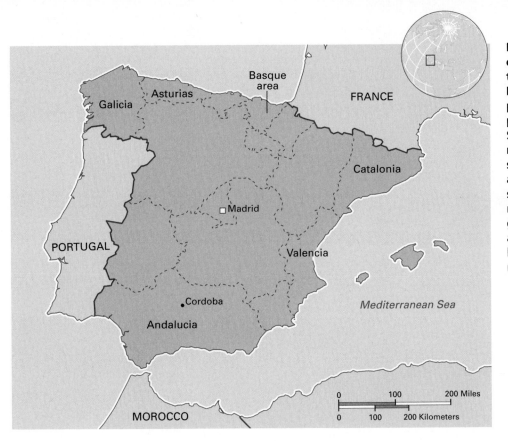

MAP 2.5 Spain. The Kingdom of Spain is the largest of the three countries occupying the Iberian Peninsula. The geography is dominated by high plateaus and mountain ranges. Spain's population exceeds 40 million. Spain's administrative structure is complex, including autonomous communities, such as Andalusia and Catalonia, and provinces. The central government is granting more autonomy to some of the localities, including the Basque region.

In order to be useful for analysis, tape recordings have to be transcribed (typed up), either partially or completely. Each hour of recorded talk takes between five and eight hours to transcribe.

Like tape recordings, photographs or videos capture more detail than scratch notes. Any researcher who has watched people performing a ritual, taken scratch notes, and then tried to reconstruct the details of the ritual later on will know how much of the sequencing and related activity is lost to memory within just a few hours. Reviewing photographs or a video recording of the ritual provides a surprising amount of forgotten, or missed, material. There is, however, a tradeoff. If you are using a camera or video recorder, you cannot take notes at the same time.

Kirsten Hastrup describes her use of photography in recording the annual ram exhibition in Iceland (see Map 2.6) that celebrates the successful herding in of the sheep from mountain pastures. This event is exclusively for men, but they allowed her to attend:

The smell was intense, the light somewhat dim and the room full of indiscernible sounds from some 120 rams and about 40 men. A committee went from one ram to the next noting their impressions of the animal, in terms of its general beauty, the size of the horns and so forth. Measurements were made all over but the decisive measure (made by hand) was the size and weight of the ram's testicles. The air was loaded with sex and I realized that the exhibition was literally and metaphorically a competition

of sexual potence. . . . I heard endless sexual jokes and very private remarks. The bursts of laughter followed by side-glances at me conveyed an implicit question of whether I understood what was going on. I did. (1992:9)

Hastrup took many photographs. After they were developed, she was disappointed by how little of the totality of the event they conveyed.

Data Analysis

During the research process, an anthropologist collects a vast amount of data in many forms. How does he or she put the data into a meaningful form? In data analysis, as with data collection, two basic varieties exist: qualitative (prose-based description) and quantitative (numeric presentation).

Analyzing Qualitative Data

Qualitative data include descriptive field notes, narratives, myths and stories, songs and sagas, and more. Few guidelines exist for undertaking a qualitative analysis of qualitative data. One procedure is to search for themes, or patterns. This approach involves exploring the data, or "playing" with the data, either "by hand" or with the use of a computer. Jennifer Robertson's analysis of her Kodaira data was inspired by writer Gertrude Stein's (1948) approach to writing "portraits" of individuals, such as Picasso. Robertson says that Stein was a superb ethnographer who was able to illuminate the "bottom

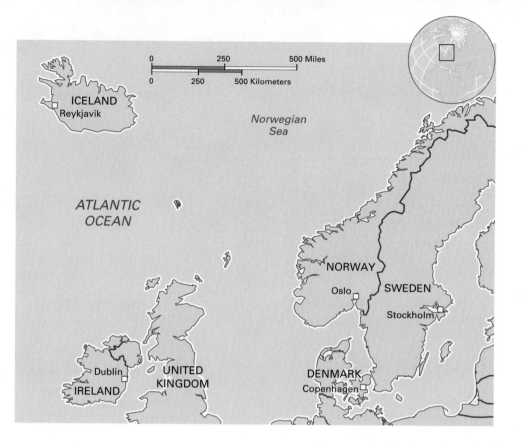

MAP 2.6 Iceland. The Republic of Iceland has a population of 300,000. A volcanic island, Iceland is the fifth richest country in the world, according to GDP (gross domestic product) per capita. It has a high quality of life and ranked second in the 2005 United Nations Human Development Index. Iceland's economy is based in exporting fish and fish products, technology, and tourism.

nature" of her subjects and their worlds through a process that Stein referred to as "condensation." To do this, "she scrutinized her subjects until, over time, there emerged for her a repeating pattern of their words and actions. Her literary portraits . . . were condensations of her subjects' repeatings" (Robertson 1991:1). Like Stein, Robertson reflected on all that she had experienced and learned in Kodaira, beginning with the years when she lived there as a child. Emerging from all this was the dominant theme, *furusato,* which literally means "old village." References to furusato appear frequently in people's accounts of the past, conveying a sense of nostalgia for a more "real" past.

Many qualitative anthropologists use computers to help sort for such *tropes* (key themes). Computer scanning of data offers the ability to search vast quantities of data more quickly and perhaps accurately than with the human eye. The range of software available for such data management—for example, ETHNO and The Ethnograph—is expanding. Of course, the quality of the results depends on, first, careful and complete inputting of the data and, second, an intelligent coding scheme that will tell the computer what it should be scanning for in the data.

The presentation of qualitative data relies on people's own words—their stories, explanations, and conversations. Lila Abu-Lughod presented Egyptian Bedu women's words in her book, *Writing Women's Worlds* (1993). She offers a light authorial framework that organizes the stories into thematic clusters such as marriage, production, and honor. Although Abu-Lughod provides an intro-

duction to the narratives, she offers no conclusion, thereby prompting readers to think for themselves about the meanings of the stories and what they say about Egyptian Bedu women's life.

Some anthropologists question the value of such artistic, interpretive approaches because they lack scientific verifiability. Too much depends, they say, on the individual selection process of the anthropologist, and interpretation often depends on a small number of cases. Interpretive anthropologists respond that verifiability, in the scientific sense, is not their goal and is not a worthwhile goal for cultural anthropology. Instead, they seek to provide a plausibly attractive interpretation, or a fresh understanding, that offers detail and richness.

THINKING OUTSIDE THE BOX

HAVE YOU EVER had the experience of taking photographs of a place, event, or people and then being terribly disappointed because the results did not capture the essence of your experience? What was missing from the photographs? (Do not include discussion of photographs that turned out badly due to technical reasons.)

Analyzing Quantitative Data

Analysis of quantitative, or numeric, data can proceed in several directions. Some of the more sophisticated methods require knowledge of statistics, and many require the use of a computer and a software package that can perform statistical computations. The author's research on low-income household budgets in Jamaica involved the use of computer analysis, first, to divide the sample households into three income groups (lower, medium, and higher). Second, the computer then calculated percentages of expenditures in the three categories of goods and groups of goods, such as food, housing, and transportation (see Figure 2.3). The number of households was quite small (120), and the analysis could have been done "by hand," but using the computer made the analysis proceed more quickly and more accurately.

Representing Culture

Ethnography, or descriptive writing about a culture (defined in Chapter 1), is the main way that cultural anthropologists present their findings about culture. In the early phase of cultural anthropology, in the first half of the twentieth century, ethnographers wrote about "exotic" cultures located far from their homes in Europe and North America. Two classic ethnographies of this period are A. R. Radcliffe-Brown's *The Andaman Islanders* (1964 [1922]), a study of indigenous people living on several islands off the coast of Burma (see Culturama, p. 70), and Bronislaw Malinowski's *Argonauts of the Western Pacific* (1961 [1922]), concerning men's trade networks linking several islands in the South Pacific (see Culturama, this chapter).

The early ethnographers tended to treat a particular local group or village as a unit unto itself with clear boundaries. Since the 1980s onward, ethnographies have changed in several ways:

■ Ethnographers now treat local cultures as embedded within regional and global structures and forces. For example, Carolyn Sargent studied medical care and childbirth among the Bariba people of Benin, West Africa (1989). She gathered interview data on people's traditional medical beliefs and practices and on their experiences with an urban hospital's obstetrics facility that employed more Westernized medical care. In her book, *Maternity, Medicine, and Power,* she interweaves attention to the clinical setting, women's beliefs about how to be a proper Bariba woman—they must not express pain during delivery—and power struggles between practitioners of Westernized medicine and traditional Bariba medicine.

■ Ethnographers focus on one topic of interest and avoid a more holistic approach. Edward Fischer's book, *Cultural Logics and Global Economics: Maya Identity in Thought and Practice* (2001), takes the topic of Maya political activism in Guatemala as its focus, setting it within the context of changing economic structures, family life, and individual action.

■ Ethnographers often are situated in Western, industrialized cultures. Philippe Bourgois's research in East Harlem in New York City for his book, *In Search of Respect: Selling Crack in El Barrio* (1995), explores how people in one neighborhood cope with poverty and dangerous living conditions. This topic resembles something that a sociologist might study, but a cultural anthropologist will provide rich details about the everyday perspectives and experiences of the people.

FIGURE 2.3   Mean Weekly Expenditure Shares (Percentage) in Eleven Categories by Urban and Rural Expenditure Groups, Jamaica, 1983–1984

Item	Urban				Rural			
	Group 1	Group 2	Group 3	Total	Group 1	Group 2	Group 3	Total
Number of Households	26	25	16	67	32	30	16	78
Food	60.5	51.6	50.1	54.7	74.1	62.3	55.7	65.8
Alcohol	0.2	0.4	1.5	0.6	0.5	1.1	1.0	0.8
Tobacco	0.8	0.9	0.9	0.9	1.1	1.7	1.2	1.4
Dry Goods	9.7	8.1	8.3	8.7	8.8	10.2	14.3	10.5
Housing	7.3	11.7	10.3	9.7	3.4	5.7	3.9	4.4
Fuel	5.4	6.0	5.0	5.6	3.7	3.9	4.1	3.9
Transportation	7.4	8.2	12.4	8.9	3.0	5.3	7.6	4.9
Health	0.3	0.6	0.7	0.5	1.5	1.4	1.7	1.5
Education	3.5	2.8	3.1	3.2	1.2	2.1	3.0	1.9
Entertainment	0.1	0.9	1.1	0.6	0.0	0.1	0.3	0.2
Other	5.2	8.3	6.9	6.8	2.1	6.0	6.9	4.6
Total*	100.4	99.5	100.3	100.2	99.4	99.8	99.7	99.9

*Totals may not add up to 100 due to rounding.

Source: From "Social Patterns of Food Expenditure Among Low-Income Jamaicans" by Barbara D. Miller in *Papers and Recommendations of the Workshop on Food and Nutrition Security in Jamaica in the 1980s and Beyond,* ed. by Kenneth A. Leslie and Lloyd B. Rankine, 1987.

Urgent Issues in Cultural Anthropology Research

This section considers two urgent issues in cultural anthropology research: fieldwork ethics and safety during fieldwork.

Ethics and Collaborative Research

Anthropology was one of the first disciplines to devise and adopt a code of ethics. Two events in the 1950s and 1960s prompted cultural anthropologists to reconsider their role in research in relation to the sponsors of their research and to the people with whom they were studying. The first was *Project Camelot* of the 1950s—a plan of the U.S. government to influence political leadership in South America in order to strengthen U.S. interests (Horowitz 1967). The U.S. government employed several anthropologists to collect information on political leaders and events, without revealing their purpose, and then report about their findings. It is still unclear whether all the anthropologists involved were completely aware of the political use of their research.

The second major event was the Vietnam War (or the American War, as people in Vietnam refer to it). This war brought to the forefront questions about government interests in ethnographic information, the role of anthropologists during wartime, and the protection of the people with whom anthropologists conduct research. Two bitterly opposed positions emerged within anthropology. On one side was the view that all Americans as citizens should support the U.S. military effort in Vietnam. People on this side said that any anthropologist who had information that could help subvert communism should provide it to the U.S. government. The other position stated that an anthropologist's responsibility is first and always to protect the people being studied, a responsibility that takes priority over politics. These anthropologists opposed the war and saw the people of South Vietnam as victims of Western imperialism. They uncovered cases in which anthropologists submitted information about people's political affiliations to the U.S. government, with the result being military actions and death of the people exposed by the research.

This period was the most divisive in the history of U.S. anthropology. It led, in 1971, to the adoption by the American Anthropological Association (AAA) of a code of ethics (see Figure 2.4). The AAA code of ethics states that an anthropologist's primary responsibility is to ensure the safety of the people participating in the research. A related principle is that cultural anthropology does not condone covert or "undercover" research. All anthropologists should inform potential research participants about the purposes and scope of the study.

Collaborative Research

A new direction in methods explicitly seeks to involve members of the study population in collaborative research—from data collection to analysis and presentation. **Collaborative research** is an approach to learning about culture that involves the anthropologist working with members of the study population as partners and teammates rather than researcher and "subject." This strategy, from the start, forces reconsideration of how anthropologists refer to the people being studied, especially the long-standing term *informant*. The term sounds hauntingly and negatively related to espionage or war, and implies a passive role on handing over information to someone else. As noted earlier in this chapter, IRBs use the term *human subject*, which cultural anthropologists reject for similar reasons. Some cultural anthropologists now use the term *consultant*, which implies work for hire. Perhaps the least objectionable term is *research participant*.

Luke Eric Lassiter is a pioneer in collaborative methods, first in research with Native Americans and later with African Americans (2004). During his doctoral studies at the University of North Carolina at Chapel Hill, he explored ways to conduct his dissertation research as a collaborative project. He developed a close working relationship with about a dozen Kiowa people in Oklahoma who were especially helpful to him in understanding and writing about Kiowa songs. They insisted that Lassiter's book should not be just another academic dissertation but should be for "normal" people. In response to this advice, Lassiter wrote for an audience that included both his professors at the university and the Kiowa people. Beyond learning came the benefits of sharing, as Lassiter says: "A collaborative ethnography opens up the possibility that ethnography can matter for people beyond the academy. This was brought home to me most powerfully when a sixteen-year-old Kiowa singer revealed to me that *The Power of Kiowa Song* was the first book he had actually read from cover to cover" (2004:8).

Lassiter's next project was even more widely collaborative. He involved his anthropology students in ethnographic collaboration with members of the African American community of Muncie, Indiana. This project resulted in a book with shared authorship (2004).

Cultural anthropologists are working to find better ways to share the benefits of research with the people and

---

collaborative research: an approach to learning about culture that involves anthropologists working with members of the study population as partners and teammates rather than as researchers and "subjects."

Research

1. Primary ethical obligations are to the people, species, and materials they study and to the people with whom they work. These obligations can supersede the goal of seeking new knowledge:

   • Avoid harm or wrong, understanding that the development of knowledge can lead to change, which may be positive or negative for the people or animals worked with or studied.

   • Respect the well-being of humans and nonhuman primates.

   • Work for the long-term conservation of the archaeological, fossil, and historical records.

   • Consult actively with the affected individuals or group(s), with the goal of establishing a working relationship that can be beneficial to all parties involved.

2. Ensure that anthropological research does not harm the dignity or privacy of the people with whom they conduct research, or harm the safety, well-being, and survival of animals with which they work.

3. Determine in advance whether human research participants wish to remain anonymous or receive recognition. Informed consent of persons being studied must be obtained in advance. Informed consent does not necessarily imply or require a written or signed form, but involves the quality of consent that is provided on the basis of a clear understanding of possible effects of participation in the research.

4. Recognize their obligations to individuals, groups, and host institutions that participated in or otherwise facilitated the research.

Responsibility to Scholarship and Science

1. Anticipate possible ethical dilemmas and raise these issues in their research proposals.

2. Assume responsibility for the integrity and reputation of the discipline and abide by general moral rules of science:

   • Do not deceive.

   • Do not knowingly misrepresent.

   • Do not prevent reporting of misconduct.

   • Do not obstruct the research of others.

3. Preserve opportunities for future fieldworkers.

4. Use findings in an appropriate fashion and, whenever possible, disseminate findings to the scientific and scholarly community.

5. Consider all reasonable requests for access to data and ensure preservation of data for posterity.

Responsibility to the Public

1. Make findings appropriately available to sponsors, students, decision-makers, and other nonanthropologists and ensure that such information is well understood and properly utilized.

2. It is possible to move to a position of advocacy, but this is an individual decision rather than an ethical responsibility.

Teaching

1. Do not discriminate on the basis of sex, marital status, "race," social class, political convictions, disability, religion, ethnic background, national origin, sexual orientation, age, or other criteria irrelevant to academic performance.

2. Strive to improve teaching, availability, counseling, and helping students obtain professional placement.

3. Impress upon students the ethical challenges in every phase of anthropological work.

4. Publicly acknowledge student assistance in research and preparation of work and compensate students justly for their participation in all professional activities.

5. Avoid sexual liaisons with students for whose education they are in any way responsible.

Application

1. Follow the same ethical guidelines in all anthropological work, be open with funders, and make carefully considered decisions about what types of work in which to be involved.

2. Be honest with employers about qualifications, capabilities, and aims and do not accept conditions contrary to professional ethics.

3. Be alert to dangers of compromising anthropological ethics and understand that contributions to public or private sector actions and policies may include both proactive participation and noncooperation, depending on circumstances.

Note: The AAA code does not dictate behavior or include sanctions. It is designed to promote discussion and provide general guidelines for ethically responsible decisions.

Source: Adapted from www.aanet.org by permission of the American Anthropological Association from the Code of Ethics of the American Anthropological Association, approved June 1998.

places we study (see Figure 2.5). Research methods in cultural anthropology have come a long way from the armchair to new strategies for nonhierarchical research. More progress lies ahead, however, in democratizing anthropology and making everyone a "barefoot anthropologist."

Safety in the Field

Fieldwork can involve serious physical and psychological risks to the researcher and to members of his or her family. The image of "the anthropologist as hero" has muffled, to a large degree, both the physical dangers and the psychological risks of fieldwork.

Dangers from the physical environment are often serious and can be fatal. In the 1980s, the slippery paths of the highland Philippines claimed the life of Michelle Zimbalist Rosaldo, a major figure in late twentieth-century cultural anthropology (review Figure 1.2, p. 11). Also, disease is a recurrent problem. Many anthropologists have contracted infectious diseases that have chronic effects or may be fatal.

Social violence figures prominently in some recent research experiences. During the five years that Philippe Bourgois lived in East Harlem, New York, he witnessed the following: a shooting outside his window, a bombing and machine-gunning of a numbers joint, a shoot-out and police car chase in front of the pizza parlor where he was eating, the aftermath of a fire-bombing of a heroin house, a dozen serious fights, and "almost daily exposure to broken-down human beings, some of them in fits of crack-induced paranoia, some suffering from delirium

The collaborative research team led by Luke Eric Lassiter includes Muncie community members as well as students and faculty from Ball State University. ■ *If you were asked to participate on the team, what would be your response and why?* (Source: © Danny Gawlowski)

tremens, and others in unidentifiable pathological fits of screaming and shouting insults to all around them" (1995:32). He was rough-handled by the police several times because they did not believe that he was "just a professor" doing research. He was once mugged for the sum of $8. Although his research placed him in danger, it also enabled him to gain an understanding, from the inside, of everyday violence in the lives of desperately poor and addicted people.

Anthropological research increasingly involves danger from public violence, such as political mobs or actual battles. This kind of research requires skills and judgment

---

FIGURE 2.5 Strategies for Community Collaboration in Anthropological Fieldwork

Communication and partnership
Community participation in problem setting
Communication with local organizations and councils
Interviews and oral histories
Work updates
Openness about problems
Shared ownership of findings
Shared authorship

Employment and training
Full-time employment of local people
Basic training
Formal training

Public presentation
Reports written in plain language

Periodic temporary exhibits
Photographic and video archive
Establishing a website
Making international connections

Education resources
Site visits
Children's books
Artifact database
Genealogy, oral history database

Community-controlled enterprises
Management of exhibits, learning center, or local museum
Publication royalties
Spin-off products such as t-shirts, project logo

Source: Abstract, "Transforming Archaeology through Practice: Strategies for Collaborative Archaeology and the Community Archaeology Project at Quesir, Egypt" by Moser et al., *World Archaeology*, vol. 34 (2002), pp. 220–248. www.tandf.co.uk.

that anthropology classes or research methods books do not typically address (Nordstrom 1997; Kovats-Bernat 2002). A new area, *war zone anthropology*, or research conducted within zones of violent conflict, can provide important insights into topics such as the militarization of civilian lives, civilian protection, the cultural dynamics of military personnel, and the prospects for postconflict reconstruction (Hoffman 2003; Hoffman and Lubkemann 2005). Anthropologists doing research in war zones require special training and experience in how to behave and survive. Previous experience in conflict zones as workers in international aid organizations or the military is helpful.

What about fieldwork danger in supposedly normal situations? After more than twenty years of fieldwork in the Kalahari desert, southern Africa, Nancy Howell (1990) suddenly had to confront the issue of danger in the field when one of her teenage sons was killed and another injured in a truck accident in Botswana while with their father, Richard Lee, who was doing fieldwork there at the time. In the months following the accident, she heard from many anthropologist friends who shared stories about other fieldwork accidents. Howell contacted the American Anthropological Association (AAA) to see what advice it provides about fieldwork safety. The answer, she learned, was not much. The AAA responded with financial support for her to undertake a detailed inquiry into fieldwork hazards in anthropology. Howell drew a sample of 311 anthropologists listed as employed in the AAA's Guide to Departments. She sent them a questionnaire asking for information on gender, age, work status, health status, and work habits in the field; and she asked for information on health problems and other hazards they had experienced. She received 236 completed questionnaires, a high response rate indicating strong interest in the study. She found regional variation

The food ration queue at an emergency clinic near Buedu, Sierra Leone. While conducting his dissertation research in war-torn Sierra Leone in 2001, Danny Hoffman combined traditional fieldwork techniques such as participant observation and interviews. But he also had to be alert to sudden danger and other risks specific to research during war. He believes anthropologists must be willing to take such risks in order to provide essential knowledge about the complex causes and consequences of war that are overlooked by war correspondents writing for the media. ■ *Do you agree or disagree with this position?* (Source: © Danny Hoffman)

in risk and danger. The highest rates were in Africa, followed by India, the Asia/Pacific region, and Latin America. Howell provides recommendations about how anthropologists can prepare themselves more effectively for preventing and dealing with fieldwork risks (see Figure 2.6). They include increasing risk awareness, training in basic medical care, and learning about fieldwork safety in anthropology classes.

FIGURE 2.6
Recommendations for Improving Fieldwork Safety

General
Raise awareness of the dangers of fieldwork:
• Overcome the tradition of denial of problems.
• Share information on risks and strategies for risk reduction more widely.

For fieldworkers
Anticipate potential risks at the chosen site.
Obtain appropriate medical training.
Locate medical care facilities in the country and region.

For colleges and universities
Train anthropology students in fieldwork safety.
Ensure that university policies on safety extend to fieldwork situations.

Source: Adapted with permission of the American Anthropological Association from Nancy Howell, *Surviving Fieldwork: A Report of the Advisory Panel on Health and Safety in Fieldwork*, American Anthropological Association, 1990.

The Big Questions Revisited

HOW do cultural anthropologists conduct research on culture?

Cultural anthropologists conduct research by doing fieldwork and using participant observation. In the nineteenth century, early cultural anthropologists conducted what we now call armchair anthropology, meaning that they learned about other cultures by reading reports written by explorers and other nontrained observers. The next stage was verandah anthropology, in which an anthropologist went to the field but did not live with the people. Instead, the anthropologist would interview a few members of the study population where the anthropologist lived, typically on his verandah. Fieldwork and participant observation became the cornerstones of cultural anthropology research only after Malinowski's innovations in the Trobriand Islands during World War I. His approach emphasized the value of living for an extended period in the field, participating in the daily activities of the people, and learning the local language. These features are still the hallmarks of research in cultural anthropology today. New techniques continue to develop to respond to changing times. One of the most important is multisited research in which the anthropologist studies a topic at more than one location.

WHAT does fieldwork involve?

Research in cultural anthropology involves several stages. The first is to have a research topic. A good topic is timely, important, and feasible. Ideas for topics can come from literature review, restudies, current events and pressing issues, and even sheer luck. Once in the field, the first steps include site selection, gaining rapport, and dealing with culture shock. Microcultures affect how the anthropologist will gain rapport and will shape access of the anthropologist to particular cultural domains. Participating appropriately in the culture involves learning local forms of gift giving and other exchanges to express gratitude for people's hospitality, time, and trust.

Specific research techniques may emphasize gathering quantitative or qualitative data. Cultural materialists tend to focus on quantitative data, whereas interpretivists gather qualitative data. When in the field, anthropologists take daily notes, often by hand but now also using a computer. Several other methods of documenting culture include photography, audio recording, and video recording. The anthropologist's theoretical orientation and research goals affect the approach to data analysis and presentation. Quantitative data may involve statistical analysis and presentation in graphs or tables. The presentation of qualitative data is more likely to be descriptive.

WHAT are some important issues in cultural anthropology research today?

Questions of ethics have been paramount to anthropologists since the 1950s. In 1971, U.S. anthropologists adopted a set of ethical guidelines for research to address their concern about what role, if any, anthropologists should play in research that might harm the people being studied. The first rule listed in the AAA code of ethics states that an anthropologist's primary responsibility is to maintain the safety of the people involved. Thus, anthropologists should never engage in covert research and should always explain their purpose to the people in the study and preserve the anonymity of the location and of individuals. Collaborative research is a recent development that responds to ethical concerns by pursuing research that involves the participants as partners rather than as subjects.

Safety during fieldwork is another urgent issue. Danger to anthropologists can come from physical sources such as infectious diseases and from social sources such as political violence. A survey of anthropologists in the 1980s produced several recommendations about increasing safety during fieldwork: raising awareness of possible risks, providing training in basic medical care, and teaching about fieldwork safety in anthropology classes.

KEY CONCEPTS

collaborative research, p. 54
culture shock, p. 45
deductive approach (to research), p. 45
emic, p. 45
etic, p. 45
fieldwork, p. 34

Hawthorne effect, p. 46
inductive approach (to research), p. 45
informed consent, p. 37
interview, p. 46
kula, p. 38
multisited research, p. 35

participant observation, p. 35
qualitative data, p. 45
quantitative data, p. 45
questionnaire, p. 46
rapport, p. 40
triangulation, p. 49

SUGGESTED READINGS

Michael V. Angrosino. *Projects in Ethnographic Research.* Long Grove, IL: Waveland Press, 2005. This brief manual provides students with ideas about what doing research in anthropology is like. It discusses the fundamental stages of three projects with insights about how students can conduct their own research.

H. Russell Bernard. *Research Methods in Cultural Anthropology: Qualitative and Quantitative Approaches,* 3rd ed. Newbury Park, CA: Sage Publications, 2002. This is a sourcebook of anthropological research methods providing information about how to design a research project, methods of data collection, and data analysis and presentation.

Sidney C. H. Cheung. *On the South China Track: Perspectives on Anthropological Research and Teaching.* Hong Kong: Hong Kong Institute of Asia-Pacific Studies, 1998. Thirteen chapters explore aspects of anthropological research and teaching in Chinese cultures, including Hong Kong, China, Taiwan, and Singapore.

Robin Patric Clair, ed. *Expressions of Ethnography: Novel Approaches to Qualitative Methods.* Albany: State University of New York Press, 2003. The chapters explore different genres for representing cultural experiences, including novels, poetry, and plays to present subject matter such as personal recovery after the 9/11 attack on the United States, surviving child abuse, and coping with an eating disorder.

Kathleen M. DeWalt and Billie R. DeWalt. *Participant Observation: A Guide for Fieldworkers.* New York: AltaMira Press, 2002. This book is a comprehensive guide to doing participant observation.

Alexander Ervin. *Applied Anthropology: Tools and Perspectives for Contemporary Practice.* Boston: Allyn and Bacon, 2005. Chapters discuss links between anthropology and policy, the history of applied anthropology, ethics, and specialized methods.

Carolyn Fluehr-Lobban. *Ethics and the Profession of Anthropology: A Dialogue for Ethically Conscious Practice,* 2nd ed. Philadelphia: University of Pennsylvania Press, 2003. The chapters address topics such as covert research, indigenous people's cultural rights, informed consent, and ethics in researching culture in cyberspace.

Peggy Golde, ed. *Women in the Field: Anthropological Experiences.* 2nd ed. Berkeley: University of California Press, 1986. The chapters discuss, for example, Margaret Mead's fieldwork in the Pacific, Laura Nader's fieldwork in Mexico and Lebanon, Ernestine Friedl's fieldwork in Greece, and Jean Briggs's fieldwork among the Inuit of the Canadian Arctic.

Bruce Grindal and Frank Salamone, eds. *Bridges to Humanity: Narratives on Anthropology and Friendship.* Prospect Heights, IL: Waveland Press, 1995. The chapters explore the "humanistic" dimension of fieldwork, in which the anthropologist reflects on friendships established in the field and what happens after the anthropologist leaves.

Tobias Hecht. *At Home in the Street: Street Children of Northeast Brazil.* New York: Cambridge University Press, 1988. Innovative research methods reveal much about the lives of Brazilian street children from their perspective.

Joy Hendry. *An Anthropologist in Japan: Glimpses of Life in the Field.* London: Routledge, 1999. This book describes the author's original research design, how the focus changed, and how she reached unanticipated conclusions.

Choong Soon Kim. *One Anthropologist, Two Worlds: Three Decades of Reflexive Fieldwork in North America and Asia.* Knoxville: University of Tennessee Press, 2002. The author reflects on his fieldwork, conducted over thirty years, on Japanese industry in the American South and, in Korea, on families displaced by the war and partition.

Luke Eric Lassiter. *The Chicago Guide to Collaborative Ethnography.* Chicago: University of Chicago Press, 2005. This handbook for doing collaborative anthropology also includes historical and theoretical perspectives on collaborative anthropology, exposing its roots in feminist, humanist, and critical anthropology.

Luke Eric Lassiter, Hurley Goodall, Elizabeth Campbell, and Michelle Natasya Johnson, eds. *The Other Side of Middletown: Exploring Muncie's African American Community.* New York: AltaMira Press, 2004. In the 1920s, Robert and Helen Lynd published a classic ethnography of "Middletown," a pseudonym for Muncie, Indiana. Decades later, a team of Ball State University anthropology faculty and students and members of Muncie's African American population collaborated to write an ethnography about "the other side" of Muncie. An accompanying DVD documents the project.

Lisa Lefler and Frederic W. Gleach, eds. *Southern Indians and Anthropologists: Culture, Politics, and Identity.* Athens: University of Georgia Press, 2002. Case studies include Powhatan identity, gender in Cherokee, ritual speech among the Yuchi, and adolescent substance abuse among the Choctaw.

Carolyn Nordstrom and Antonius C. G. M. Robben, eds. *Fieldwork under Fire: Contemporary Studies of Violence and Survival.* Berkeley: University of California Press, 1995. The chapters discuss fieldwork experiences in Palestine, China, Sri Lanka, the United States, Croatia, Guatemala, and Ireland.

Sarah Pink, *Doing Visual Ethnography: Images, Media and Representation in Research.* Thousand Oaks, CA: Sage Publications, 2001. The author considers a wide variety of topics in visual ethnography, including the role of subjectivity, the usefulness of visual methods, ethics, photography, video, and electronic texts.

Tom Ric with Mette Louise Berg, eds. *Future Fields,* special issue of the online journal, *Anthropology Matters,* Volume 6, No. 2, 2004. This issue includes eleven articles that address a range of methodological issues that cultural anthropologists are facing today, including emotional, financial, and ethical challenges as well as how to cope in situations of physical danger. The journal is accessible at no charge at www.anthropologymatters.com.

PART II
Economic and Demographic Foundations

LARA TABAC, MEDICAL ANTHROPOLOGIST, works at the New York City Department of Health and Mental Hygiene, along with another cultural anthropologist and 6,000 other employees. Her responsibilities with the DOHMH's Epidemiology Services require that she collect qualitative information from New Yorkers about how certain health issues affect their lives.

Tabac describes her job as an "unusual joint venture of words and numbers." She explains that the department is traditionally highly quantitative; it uses statistics to determine health-action agendas. The numbers "tell how many, but they do not tell why. In order to be responsive to the health needs of New Yorkers, the DOHMH needs to know why. This is where I come in."

Formal anthropological training reinforced and shaped Tabac's natural tendency to observe and ask questions. She now puts these skills and interests to work by listening to and talking with people who are affected by various health initiatives.

"I do a lot of listening on a wide range of topics, and I need only a MetroCard to reach far-flung and eclectic neighborhoods peopled with individuals who share their health dilemmas and life struggles with me, as well as their suggestions for improving the services and programs that will ultimately affect them."

One project that Tabac has been working on analyzes the sexual behaviors of men who have sex with men. Noting an increase in recent years of syphilis cases in this population, the DOHMH believes that the safe-sex message has lost its urgency. Tabac is consequently trying to determine what situations affect whether individuals in this group use condoms and for what reasons they do or do not do so.

To gather qualitative information about the issue, Tabac has spent many hours in Internet chat rooms and conducting open-ended, face-to-face interviews. "As a technique, interviewing is crucial for gaining a deep understanding of sensitive issues. . . . People tend to be more honest when they don't feel as though they are going to be judged by their peers." She notes that every interview for this project has been valuable.

Another project she has collaborated on involves interviewing injection drug users about unsafe injection practices, which often cause HIV, and other sexually transmitted diseases. Many public health experts believed that if people know how to protect themselves, they will do so, and considerable effort was put into educating individuals at risk. But recent research has disproved this assumption. Tabac's assignment was to discover when and why this assumption fails and to create alternative programs that might have more success in encouraging individuals to protect themselves from infectious disease.

Tabac finds her job with the DOHMH challenging and socially relevant. She took it because she wanted to contribute to improving the quality of people's lives. She has not been disappointed.

Anthropology in the Real World

3
Economies and Their Modes of Production

The Big Questions

- WHAT is the scope of economic anthropology?
- WHAT are the characteristics of the five major modes of production?
- WHAT are some directions of change in the five modes of production?

A woman pounding millet in Agadez in Niger, West Africa. Wild millet, a kind of grass, was first domesticated in Africa. Millet is now, after sorghum, the second most important food grain in Africa. It is typically combined with meat and vegetables in a stew, and it is also used for brewing beer. *(Source: © Charles Cecil)*

During the many thousands of years of human prehistory, people made their living by collecting food and other necessities from nature. All group members had equal access to life-sustaining resources. Most people throughout the world now live in economies much different from this description.

Economic anthropology is the subfield of cultural anthropology that studies economic systems cross-culturally. The term *economic system* includes three areas: *production,* or making goods or money; *consumption,* or using up goods or money; and *exchange,* or the transfer of goods or money between people or institutions (see Figure 3.1). This chapter first lays out the basic objectives of economic anthropology. Next, it turns to the subject of production and introduces the concept of **mode of production,** or the dominant way of making a living in a culture. Ethnographic examples illustrate each of five major modes of production. The chapter's last section discusses a case of economic change in each mode of production.

FIGURE 3.1 Three Components of Economic Systems

Production	Making goods or money
Consumption	Using up goods or money
Exchange	Transfer of goods or money

Culture and Economies

Economic anthropology differs from the discipline of economics in several ways. First, the subject matter of economic anthropology is much wider. It covers the entire range of ways that people make a living, not just modern capitalism. Second, economic anthropologists' methods are different. They often collect qualitative data and quantitative data, as discussed in Chapter 2, and they rely on fieldwork and participant observation rather than analyzing "canned" statistical datasets or census information. Third, economic anthropologists believe that it is important to gather emic data in order to understand people's own concepts and categories related to making a living, rather than simply applying Western concepts and categories. If you have taken an economics course, try to recall how much you learned about people from various world cultures. Several years ago, the author of this book presented a conference paper based on research in Jamaica on low-income household budgets. The commentator for the session was Gary Becker, Nobel–prize-winning economist. Instead of being critical about my small sample size and my simple statistical analysis (from an economist's perspective), he expressed enthusiasm about how anthropologists go out and collect their own data and know something about the people.

In spite of these differences between economics and economic anthropology, some shared territory also exists. Researchers in both disciplines are interested in production, consumption, and exchange. Some economists do learn a foreign language and some try to learn about economic behavior and thought by conducting fieldwork. Some economic anthropologists analyze large, quantitative datasets. Also, some economists and some economic anthropologists are working together on research and policy issues.

Many years of ethnographic research on economic systems has produced a rich set of knowledge on diverse ways of making a living. Anthropologists attempt to organize all this information by sorting it into categories, called modes. This chapter focuses on modes of production, and Chapter 4 covers modes of consumption and exchange.

Creating Typologies: Modes of Production

Categorizing a certain society as having a particular mode of production implies an emphasis on that type of production; it does not mean that it is the only kind of production undertaken. In a given society, some people will be involved in the prevailing mode of production while others will not. Also, a particular individual may be involved in more than one kind of production—for example, a person could be both a farmer and a herder. Another point to keep in mind is that the five modes of production, in reality, blend with and overlap each other. Therefore, it is possible that some cultures do not fit well within any one mode. Real life is always more complicated than the categories researchers create.

The modes of production are discussed in order of their historical appearance in the human record (see Figure 3.2). This continuum does not mean that a particular mode of production evolves into the one following it—for example, foragers do not necessarily transform into horticulturalists, and so on—across the continuum. Nor does this ordering imply a judgment

---

mode of production: the dominant pattern of making a living in a culture.

about the sophistication or superiority of more recent modes of production. Figure 3.2 is not a model of "progress" from left to right. The oldest system involves complex and detailed knowledge about the environment that a contemporary city dweller would find difficult to learn quickly enough to ensure survival.

Globalization and the World Economy

Although economic anthropologists focus on local economic systems, they are increasingly involved in researching how global and local systems are linked. The spread of Western capitalism in recent centuries has had, and continues to have, massive effects on other modes of production that it meets.

The intensification of global trade in the past few decades has created a global division of labor, or *world economy,* in which countries compete unequally for a share of the wealth (Wallerstein 1979). In this view, the modern world economy is stratified into three major areas: *core,* periphery, and semiperiphery. *Core areas* monopolize the most profitable activities, such as the high-tech service, manufacturing, and financial activities. They have the strongest governments, which play a dominating role in the affairs of other countries. *Peripheral areas* are relegated to the least profitable activities, including production of raw materials, foodstuffs, and labor-intensive goods, and they must import high-tech goods and services from the core. They tend to have weak governments and are dominated, either directly or indirectly, by core states. *Semiperipheral areas* stand in the middle.

According to this model, economic benefits are highly unequal across regions, with core areas profiting most.

Monterrey, Mexico, is the second-most important city in Mexico after the capital. Because of its strong steel industry, it is called "the Pittsburgh of Mexico." It has several major beer breweries and is home to the Mexican Baseball Hall of Fame. The city center has monuments of both Spanish colonialism and cosmopolitan modernity. ■ (Source: Barbara Miller and Bernard Wood).

FIGURE 3.2   Modes of Production

Foraging	Horticulture	Pastoralism	Agriculture	Industrialism/Informatics

Reason for Production
Production for use
  Consumption level: low
  Exchange: sharing-based
				Reason for Production
				Production for profit
				Consumption level: high
				Exchange: market-based

Division of Labor Family-based Overlapping gender roles				**Division of Labor** Class-based High degree of occupational specialization
Property Relations Egalitarian and collective				**Property Relations** Stratified and private
Resource Use Extensive and temporary				**Resource Use** Intensive and expanding
Sustainability High degree				**Sustainability** Low degree

A Ju/'hoansi traditional shelter. ■ (Source: © Irven DeVore/AnthroPhoto)

Core states have about 20 percent of the world's population and control 80 percent of the world's wealth (and they create 80 percent of world's pollution). Politically, the core continues to increase its economic power and political influence through international organizations such as the World Trade Organization (WTO) and regional arrangements such as the North American Free Trade Agreement (NAFTA). The last section of this chapter returns to the topic of economic globalization and cultural change.

Modes of Production

While reading this section, please bear in mind that most anthropologists are uneasy about typologies because they often do not reflect the complexity of life in any particular context. The main purpose of the categories is to help you organize all the ethnographic information presented in this book.

Foraging

Foraging is based on using food that is available in nature, provided by gathering, fishing, or hunting. It is the oldest way of making a living, a strategy that humans share with our nonhuman primate relatives. Although foraging supported humanity as the main economic strategy since our beginnings, it is in danger of extinction.

Only around 250,000 people support themselves predominantly from foraging now. Most contemporary foragers live in what are considered marginal areas, such as deserts, tropical rainforests, and the circumpolar region. These areas, however, often contain material resources that are in high demand in core areas, such as oil, diamonds, gold, and expensive tourist destinations.

Foragers collect food items available in nature. Depending on the environmental context, foragers' food sources include nuts, berries and other fruits, and surface-growing vegetables such as melons, roots, honey, insects, and eggs. They trap and hunt a wide variety of birds, fish, and animals. Successful foraging requires sophisticated knowledge of the natural environment and seasonal changes in it. Most critical is knowledge about the location of water sources and of various foods, how to follow animal tracks, how to judge the weather, and how to avoid predators. This unwritten knowledge is passed down over the generations.

Foragers rely on a diverse set of tools used for gathering, transporting, and processing wild foods. Tools include digging sticks for removing roots from the ground and for penetrating the holes dug by animals in order to get the animals out, bows and arrows, spears, nets, and knives. Baskets are important for carrying food. For processing raw materials into edible food, foragers use stones to mash, grind, and pound. Meat can be dried in the sun or over fire, and fire is used for cooking either by boiling or by roasting. These activities involve few nonrenewable fuel sources beyond wood or other com-

---

foraging: collecting food that is available in nature, by gathering, fishing, or hunting.

extensive strategy: a form of production involving temporary use of large areas of land and a high degree of spatial mobility.

	Temperate-Region Foragers	Circumpolar-Region Foragers
Diet	Wide variety of nuts, tubers, fruits, small animals, and occasional large game	Large marine and terrestrial animals
Gender division of labor in food Procurement	Men and women forage; men hunt large game	Men hunt and fish
Shelter	Casual construction, nonpermanent, little maintenance	Time-intensive construction and maintenance, some permanent

FIGURE 3.3 Temperate and Circumpolar Foraging Systems Compared

bustible substances for cooking. Foraging is an **extensive strategy,** a mode of production requiring access to large areas of land and unrestricted population movement. Cultural anthropologists distinguish two major varieties of foraging that are related to different environmental contexts: *temperate-climate foraging* and *circumpolar foraging* (see Figure 3.3).

The Ju/'hoansi people of southern Africa, as studied in the early 1960s, moved several times during a year, depending on the seasonal availability of water sources (review Culturama, Chapter 1, p. 22). Each cluster of families would regularly return to "their" territory, reconstructing or completely rebuilding their shelters with sticks for frames and leaf or thatch coverings. Shelters are sometimes attached to two or three small trees or bushes for support. The amount of time involved in gathering and processing food and constructing shelters is modest.

In contrast to foragers of temperate climates, those living in the circumpolar regions of North America, Europe, and Asia must devote more time and energy to obtaining food and providing shelter. The specialized technology of circumpolar peoples includes spears, nets, and knives, as well as sleds and the use of domesticated animals to pull them. Dogs or other animals used to pull sleds are an important aspect of circumpolar peoples' technology and social identity (see Everyday Anthropology box). Considerable amounts of labor are needed to construct and maintain igloos or log houses. Protective clothing, including coats, gloves, and boots, is another feature of circumpolar foraging that is time intensive in terms of making and maintaining.

Division of Labor

Among foraging peoples, a *division of labor,* or occupational specialization (assigning particular tasks to particular individuals), depends mainly on gender and age. Among temperate foraging cultures, a minimal gender-based division of labor exists. Temperate foragers get most of their everyday food by gathering roots, berries, grubs, small birds and animals, and fish, and both men and women collect these basic foods. Hunting large animals, however, tends to involve only men, who go off together in small groups on long-range expeditions. Large game provides a small and irregular part of the diets of temperate-climate foragers. In circumpolar groups, in contrast, hunting large animals (including seals, whales, and bears) and capturing large fish provide a significant part of the diet, require more time and labor, are dangerous activities, and tend to involve only men. Among circumpolar foragers, therefore, the gender division of labor is marked.

The issue of large game hunting connects to a long-standing theoretical debate in anthropology. Many anthropologists support a *Man the Hunter model* for explaining how humans evolved in prehistory (Lee 1979; Stanford 1999). This model says that early humans relied heavily on animal meat in their diets; that men were responsible for providing the meat, which explains men's high status in many societies relative to women; and that the need to hunt in groups formed the basis for social life, including the evolution of verbal language. This model gives much importance to meat and masculinity in explaining key features of humanity. Some of the scientific evidence used to support the model comes from fossils and stone tools. Some anthropologists also use examples of living foraging cultures as analogies, or models, for what prehistoric life may have been like.

Comparative studies of foragers around the world, however, indicate that substantial male involvement in hunting large game is not universal. In fact, it appears to be a minority pattern found in resource-limited environments (Hiatt 1970). The implication of this finding is that men's hunting of large game may be a recent adaptation of foragers to increasing resource scarcity and thus was not necessarily common throughout human prehistory.

Early feminist anthropologists in the 1970s critiqued the Man the Hunter model as male biased. Their research suggested an alternate view called the *Woman the*

THE IMPORTANCE OF DOGS

Dogs were the first domesticated animal, with evidence of their domestication from sites in eastern Europe and Russia, dating to around 18,000 years ago. In spite of their long-standing importance to humans around the world, few cultural anthropologists have focused their attention on humans and their dogs. One of the rare ethnographies to do so provides insights about the economic, social, and psychological importance of dogs among a group of circumpolar foragers.

Under 100 Hare Indians constitute the community of Colville Lake in Canada's Northwest Territories (Savishinsky 1974). They live by hunting, trapping, and fishing in one of the harshest environments in the world. Joel Savishinsky went to Colville Lake with the intention of studying stress, tension, and anxiety among this isolated group and how people cope. Environmental stress factors include extremely cold temperatures, long and severe winters, extended periods of isolation, hazardous travel conditions along with the constant need for mobility during the harshest periods of the year, and sometimes food scarcity. Social and psychological stress factors also exist, including contact with White fur traders and missionaries.

Savishinsky discovered the importance of dogs to the Hare people early in his research:

Later in the year when I obtained my own dogteam, I enjoyed much greater freedom of movement, and was able to camp with many people whom I had previously not been able to keep up with. Altogether I travelled close to 600 miles by dogsled between mid-

Hare Indian children use their family's sled to haul drinking water to their village. ■ *What tasks are children responsible for in a microculture that you know?* (Source: Joel Savishinsky)

October and early June. This constant contact with dogs, and the necessity of learning how to drive, train and handle them, led to my recognition of the

Gatherer model (Slocum 1975). It is based on evidence that most food in most foraging groups in temperate regions comes from gathering, which is mainly women's work. Among the free-ranging Ju/'hoansi, for example, women's gathering provided 75 to 80 percent of people's food, with men's hunting providing the rest, on an irregular basis. To complicate matters further, in some foraging societies, women hunt. Among the Agta of eastern Luzon, the Philippines (see Map 7.1, p. 174), a group of women go hunting while other women stay at the camp caring for the small children (Estioko-Griffin 1986). Most cultural anthropologists now agree that the Man

the Hunter model should be abandoned. The Man the Hunter model, however, lives on in much popular thinking, perpetuated through textbook images and museum displays of prehistoric peoples which depict men hunting and carrying dead animals while women carry babies or squat in front a fire, cooking (Gifford-Gonzalez 1993).

Age is a basis for task allocation in all modes of production, including foraging. Young boys and girls help collect food. Elderly people tend to stay at the camp area where they are often responsible for caring for children who are too young to go with their parents to collect food.

use rights: a system of property relations in which a person or group has socially recognized priority in access to particular resources such as gathering, hunting, and fishing areas and water holes.

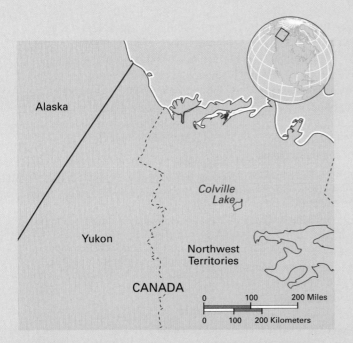

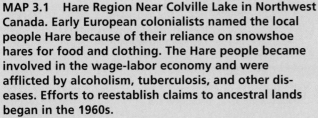

MAP 3.1 Hare Region Near Colville Lake in Northwest Canada. Early European colonialists named the local people Hare because of their reliance on snowshoe hares for food and clothing. The Hare people became involved in the wage-labor economy and were afflicted by alcoholism, tuberculosis, and other diseases. Efforts to reestablish claims to ancestral lands began in the 1960s.

social and psychological, as well as the ecological, significance of these animals in the lives of the people. (1974:xx)

Among the fourteen households, there are a total of 224 dogs. Some households have as many as four teams, with an average of 6 dogs per team, corresponding to people's estimation that 6 dogs are required for travel. More than being economically useful, dogs play a significant role in people's emotional lives. They are a frequent topic of conversation: "Members of the community constantly compare and comment on the care, condition, and growth of one another's animals, noting special qualities of size, strength, color, speed, and alertness" (1974:169). Emotional displays, uncommon among the Hare, are significant between people and their dogs:

> The affectionate and concerned treatment of young animals is participated in by people of all ages, and the nature of the relationship bears a striking resemblance to the way in which people treat young children. Pups and infants are, in essence, the only recipients of unreserved positive affect in the band's social life, all other relationships being tinged with varying degrees of restraint and/or negativism. (1974:169–170)

FOOD FOR THOUGHT

- Think of another culture (perhaps yours) in which dogs or some other domesticated animals are a focus of intense human interest. How do people and the animals in question interact? Are there age and gender differences in human relationships with domesticated animals?

Property Relations

The concept of *private property*, in the sense of owning something that can be sold to someone else, does not exist in foraging societies. Instead, the term **use rights** is more appropriate. It means that a person or group has socially recognized priority in access to particular resources such as gathering areas, hunting and fishing areas, and water holes. This access is willingly shared with others by permission. Among the Ju/'hoansi, family groups control access to particular water holes and the territory surrounding them (Lee 1979:58–60). Visiting groups are welcome and will be given food and water. In turn, the host group, at another time, will visit other camps and be offered hospitality there. In India's

Andaman Islands (see Culturama), each family group controls a known offshore area for fishing. Sharing access to these resources is expected but only if permission has been requested and granted. Encroaching on someone else's area without permission is a serious misdemeanor and is likely to result in violence. In foraging groups, use rights are invested in the group and are passed down equally to all children in the group.

**OUTSIDE THE BOX
THINKING**

THE ROLE OF RED MEAT in the diet of early human ancestors is a vigorously debated topic in anthropology. Some researchers say that eating red meat spurred the evolution of larger brains and the emergence of human culture such as language and toolmaking. If true, does this hypothesis necessarily support the Man the Hunter model of human evolution?

Culturama

The Andaman Islanders of India

The Andaman Islands are a string of islands in the Bay of Bengal that belong to India. For unknown numbers of centuries, many of the islands were inhabited by people who fished, gathered, and hunted for their livelihood. During the eighteenth century, when European countries were expanding trade routes to the Far East, the Andaman Islands were of major strategic importance as a stopping place.

At the time of the first, small settlements of the British in the late eighteenth century, the total indigenous population was estimated at between 6,000 and 8,000 (Miller 1997). Today, over 400,000 people live on the islands, mostly migrants from the Indian mainland. The total number of indigenous people is about 400. British colonialism brought contagious diseases and increased death from violence among disrupted Andaman groups and between the Andaman people and the British.

There are now four surviving clusters of indigenous Andamanese. The smallest group, just a few dozen people, consists of the remnants of the so-called Great Andamanese people. They live on a small island near Port Blair, the capital, in what is essentially a reservation area. Several groups of Great Andamanese people formerly lived throughout North and Middle Andaman Islands, but no indigenous people inhabit these islands now. The so-called Jarawa, numbering perhaps 200, live in a reserved area on the southwest portion of South Andaman. Currently, no outsider knows their language or what name they use for themselves. *Jarawa* is a term that the Great Andamanese people use for them. The Onge, around 100 in number, live in one corner of Little Andaman Island. Another 100 people or so live on North Sentinel Island. Outsiders call them the "Sentinelese." No one has established communication with them, and almost no one from the outside has gotten closer than arrow-range of their shore.

The 2005 tsunami disrupted much of the Andaman Island topography, particularly areas that had been cleared of mangroves and other trees. As far as anyone knows, none of the indigenous people died as a direct result of the tsunami, though many of the immigrant settlers did (Mukerjee 2005). The future of the indigenous people is more endangered by culture, in the form of immigration and development, than from nature.

Readings

Madhusree Mukerjee. *The Land of Naked People: Encounters with Stone Age People*. New York: Houghton Mifflin, 2003. www.samarmagazine.org/archive/article.

A. R. Radcliffe-Brown. *The Andaman Islanders: A Study in Social Anthropology*. New York: The Free Press. 1964 [1922].

Sita Venkateswar. "The Andaman Islanders." *Cultural Survival*, 280 (5), 82–88, 1999.

Website

www.andaman.org.

Thanks to Madhusree Mukerjee, independent scholar and activist, and Sita Venkateswar, Massey University, for reviewing this material.

A Jarawa woman receives a handout from a passenger bus driver on the Andaman Trunk Road (ATR) (left). Part of the ATR passes through the Jarawa reservation on South Andaman Island. ■ (Source: Pankaj Sekhsaria) Government officials from Pt. Blair make periodic visits by boat to the Jarawa area to attempt to build Jarawa trust (right). This landmark incident, of getting some Jarawa to board a government boat, occurred in 1998. The Jarawa occupy land that is rich in resources such as ancient hardwood trees. Rumors are that the administration wants to remove the Jarawa from their territory and exploit it for logging, tourism, and other commercial interests. ■ (Source: Pankaj Sekhsaria)

Map 3.2 *Andaman Islands of India. The 576 islands are geologically part of Myanmar and Southeast Asia. The British Empire controlled them until India's independence in 1947.*

ANDAMAN ISLANDS

North Andaman

Middle Andaman

South Andaman

North Sentinel Island

Port Blair

Little Andaman

0   50   100 Miles

0   50   100 Kilometers

Foraging as a Sustainable System

When untouched by outside influences and with abundant land available, foraging systems are sustainable, which means that crucial resources are regenerated over time in balance with the demand that the population makes on them. North Sentinel Island, one island in the Andaman Islands, provides a clear case because its inhabitants have lived in a "closed" system. So far, the few hundred indigenous people live in almost complete isolation from the rest of the world, other than the occasional helicopter flying overhead and the occasional attempt by outsiders to land on their territory.

One reason for the sustainability of foraging is that foragers' needs are modest. Anthropologists have typified the foraging lifestyle as the *original affluent society* because needs are satisfied with minimal labor efforts. This term is used metaphorically to remind people living in contemporary consumer cultures that foraging is not a pathetic, inadequate way to make a living, contrary to most ethnocentric thinking. In the 1960s, when the Ju/'hoansi people were still foragers, their major food source was mongongo nuts. At that time, these nuts were so abundant that there was never a shortage (Howell 1986). In addition, hundreds of species of edible plants and animals were available, with seasonal variations. The Ju/'hoansi were slender and often complained of hunger throughout the year. Their thinness may be an adaptation to seasonal fluctuations in food supply. Rather than maximizing food intake during times of plenty, they minimize it. Mealtime is not an occasion for stuffing oneself. Ju/'hoansi culture taught that it is good to have a hungry stomach, even when food is plentiful.

Because foragers' needs for goods are not great, minimal labor efforts are required to satisfy them. Foragers typically work fewer hours a week than the average employed North American. In traditional (undisturbed) foraging societies, the people spend as few as five hours a week collecting food and making and repairing tools. They have much time for storytelling, playing games, and resting. Foragers also traditionally enjoyed good health. During the early 1960s, the age structure and health status of the Ju/'hoansi compared well with people in the United States of around 1900 (Lee 1979: 47–48). They had few infectious diseases or degenerative diseases (related to aging such as arthritis).

Horticulture

Both horticulture and pastoralism are recent modes of production, having emerged only as recently as 12,000 years ago in the Middle East and then later in Africa,

Cassava, also called manioc, is a root crop grown extensively in western Africa. This man displays a cassava plant grown in Niger. Cassava and millet are the staple foods for many West Africans. ■ *Do research to find some West African recipes that include cassava or millet.* (Source: © Charles O. Cecil)

Asia, Europe, and the Western Hemisphere. Both of these modes of production depend on the *domestication* of plants and animals—that is, the process by which human selection causes genetic changes in plants and animals and leads to their greater control by humans in terms of their location and their reproduction.

Horticulture is a mode of production based on cultivating domesticated plants in gardens using hand tools. Garden crops are often supplemented by foraging and by trading with pastoralists for animal products. Horticulture is still practiced by many thousands of people throughout the world. Prominent horticultural regions are found in sub-Saharan Africa, South Asia, Southeast Asia and the Pacific, Central America, South America, and the Caribbean islands. Major horticultural crops include yams, corn, beans, grains such as millet and sorghum, and several types of roots, all of which are rich in protein, minerals, and vitamins.

Horticulture involves the use of handheld tools, such as digging sticks, hoes, and carrying baskets. Rain is the sole source of moisture. Horticulture requires rotation of garden plots in order for them to regenerate. Thus, another term for horticulture is *shifting cultivation.* Average plot sizes are less than 1 acre, and 2.5 acres can support a family of five to eight members for a year. Yields can support semipermanent villages of 200 to 250 people. Overall population density per square mile is low

---

horticulture: a mode of production based on growing domesticated crops in gardens using simple hand tools.

FIGURE 3.4   Five Stages in Horticulture

Clearing: A section of the forest is cleared, partially or completely, by cutting down trees and brush and then setting the area on fire to burn off other growth. The fire creates a layer of ash that is rich fertilizer. The term *slash and burn cultivation* refers to this stage of clearing.

Planting: People use digging sticks to loosen the soil. They place seeds though the broadcasting method (scattering the seeds by hand) or place slips of plants by hand into the loose soil.

Weeding: Horticulture involves little weeding because the ash cover and shady growing conditions keep weed growth down.

Harvesting: This phase requires substantial labor to cut or dig crops and carry them to the residential area.

Fallowing: Depending on the soil and the crop grown, the land must be left unused for a specified number of years so that it regains its fertility.

because horticulture, like foraging, is an extensive strategy. Horticulture is more labor intensive than foraging because of the energy required for plot preparation and food processing. Anthropologists distinguish five phases in the horticultural cycle (see Figure 3.4).

Surpluses in food supply are possible in horticulture. These surpluses enable trade relationships and can lead to greater wealth for some people. In the past, horticulture has been the foundation for complex and rich civilizations, such as the Maya civilization of Mexico and Central America of between 200 and 900 CE (Current Era).

Division of Labor

Gender and age are the key factors structuring the division of labor, with men's and women's work roles often being clearly differentiated. Most commonly, men clear the garden area while both men and women plant and tend the staple food crops. This pattern exists in Papua New Guinea, much of Southeast Asia, and parts of West and East Africa. Food processing involves women often working in small groups while men more typically form small groups for hunting and fishing for supplementary

food. Among horticultural groups in rural Malawi, in southern Africa, women are responsible for food crops and men are responsible for hunting game animals (Morris 1998). A common pattern among horticulturalists is for women to grow the staple food crops while men grow the "prestige foods" used in ritual feasts. In these contexts, men have higher public status than women.

Two unusual horticultural cases involve extremes in terms of gender roles and status. The first involves the precontact Iroquois of central New York State (Brown 1975) (see Map 3.3). Iroquois women cultivated maize, the most important food crop, and they controlled its distribution. This control meant that they were able to decide whether the men would go to war, because a war effort depended on the supply of maize to support it. A contrasting example is that of the Yanomami of the Venezuelan Amazon (see Map 3.4) (Chagnon 1992). Yanomami men clear the fields and tend and harvest the crops. They also do much of the cooking for ritual feasts. Yanomami women, though, are not idle. They play an important role in providing the staple food that comes from manioc, a starchy root crop that requires substantial processing work—it has to be soaked for a long time to remove toxins and then scraped into a mealy consistency. Among the Yanomami, however, men are the dominant decision makers and have more social power than Yanomami women do.

Anthropologists cannot explain the origins of different divisions of labor in horticulture, but the differences have implications for men's and women's status (Sanday 1973). Cross-cultural analysis of many horticultural societies shows that women's contribution to food production is a necessary but not sufficient basis for women's high status. In other words, if women do not contribute to producing food, their status will be low. If they do contribute, their status may, or may not, be high. The critical factor appears to be control over the distribution of what is produced, especially public distribution beyond the family. Slavery is a clear example of how a major role in production does not bring high status because slaves have no control over the product and its distribution.

Children do more productive work in horticultural societies than in any other mode of production (Whiting and Whiting 1975). *The Six Cultures Study* is a research project that examined children's behavior in horticultural, farming, and industrial settings. Children among a horticultural group, the Gusii of western Kenya, performed the most tasks at the youngest ages. Gusii boys and girls care for siblings, collect fuel, and carry water. Among the Gusii and in other horticultural societies, children do so many tasks because adults, especially

---

pastoralism: a mode of production based on keeping domesticated animal herds and using their products, such as meat and milk, for most of the diet.

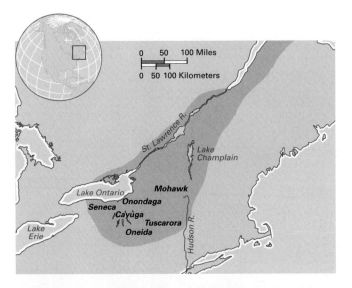

MAP 3.3 Precolonial Iroquois Region. At the time of the arrival of the European colonialists, the Haudenosaunee, or People of the Longhouse, extended over a wide area. The Mohawk stood guard over the eastern door of the confederacy's symbolic long house, and the Seneca guarded the western door. Six nations worked out a peace treaty among them and established a democracy. A great orator named Hiawatha promoted the plan throughout the tribes, and a Mohawk woman was the first to approve it.

women, are busy working in the fields and markets. Children's work in the domestic domain fulfills what would be adult roles in other economic systems.

Property Relations

Private property, as something that an individual can own and sell, is not characteristic of horticultural societies. Use rights are typically important, although they are more clearly defined and formalized than among foragers. By clearing and planting an area of land, a family puts a claim on it and its crops. The production of surplus goods allows the possibility of social inequality in access to goods and resources. Rules about sharing within the larger group decline in importance as some people gain higher status.

Horticulture as a Sustainable System

Fallowing is crucial in maintaining the viability of horticulture. Fallowing allows the plot to recover lost nutrients and improves soil quality by allowing the growth of weeds whose root systems keep the soil loose. The benefits of a well-managed system of shifting cultivation are clear as are the two major constraints involved: the time required for fallowing and the need for access to large amounts of

land so that some land is in use while other land is fallowed. Using a given plot for too many seasons or reducing fallowing time quickly results in depletion of soil nutrients, decreased crop production, and soil erosion. The following conditions are linked with such harmful practices and their negative consequences (Blaikie 1985):

- Pressure on access to land as a consequence of encroachment by outsiders such as loggers, miners, farmers, ranchers, tourists; creating conservation areas; and development projects such as dams
- Government policies that force horticulturalists to increase production for cash in order to pay taxes
- Interest of horticulturalists in increasing production for cash in order to buy manufactured commodities
- Pressure on land from internal population growth when outmigration is not an option

The last factor, population growth, is often blamed as the sole culprit for soil degradation and erosion in horticultural contexts, but often it is not involved at all. Ethnographic studies indicate, instead, that the major threats to horticultural sustainability worldwide are external factors.

Pastoralism

Pastoralism is a mode of production based on domesticated animal herds and the use of their products, such as meat and milk, for 50 percent or more of the diet.

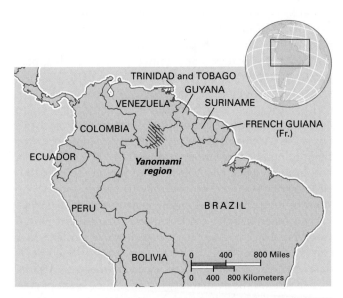

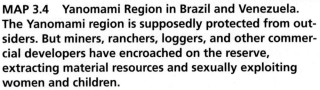

MAP 3.4 Yanomami Region in Brazil and Venezuela. The Yanomami region is supposedly protected from outsiders. But miners, ranchers, loggers, and other commercial developers have encroached on the reserve, extracting material resources and sexually exploiting women and children.

Pastoralism has long existed in the Middle East, Africa, Europe, and Central Asia, especially where rainfall is limited and unpredictable. In the Western Hemisphere, the only indigenous pastoralist system in existence before the arrival of the Spanish in the fifteenth century was in the Andean region; it was based on domesticated llamas (Barfield 2001). Sheep, goats, horses, and cattle became prominent after the Spanish conquest. Many Native American groups in the southwestern United States still rely on herding animals.

Pastoralists are associated with a limited number of animals. Worldwide, the six most popular species are sheep, goats, cattle, horses, donkeys, and camels. Three others have more restricted distribution: yaks at high altitudes in Asia, reindeer in northern sub-Arctic regions, and llamas in highland South America. Many pastoralists keep dogs for protection and for help with herding. Pastoralism can succeed in a variety of environments, depending on the animal involved. For example, reindeer herding is done in the circumpolar regions of Europe and Asia, and cattle and goat herding is common in India and Africa.

In terms of food, pastoralism provides primarily milk and milk products with occasional slaughtering of animals for meat. Thus, pastoralists typically form trade links with foragers, horticulturalists, or farmers in order to obtain food and other goods that they cannot produce themselves. Prominent trade items are food grains and manufactured items, such as cooking pots, for which they offer milk, animals, hides, and other animal products. Pastoralism may seem to resemble contemporary large-scale ranching, but, in fact, ranches resemble modern industry more than traditional pastoralism (Fratkin, Galvin, and Roth 1994; Loker 1993). The primary purpose of ranching is to provide meat for sale, whereas pastoralism provides many animal products. Also, pastoralism involves the movement of animals to pasture, whereas ranching moves the fodder to the animals.

Like foraging and horticulture, pastoralism is an extensive strategy. A common problem for all pastoralists is the continued need for fresh pasture and water for their animals. Herds must move or else the grazing area will become depleted. A distinction within the pastoralist category is based on whether the herds move over short or long distances (Fratkin, Galvin, and Roth 1994).

The Nuer people, cattle herders of southern Sudan (see Map 16.7, p. 443), are short-distance herders. In a classic ethnography, E. E. Evans-Pritchard (1965 [1947]) describes the Nuer as they were in the late 1930s. Depending on the availability of water, they spent part of the year in settled villages and part in temporary camps. Cattle and cows provided food for the Nuer from their milk, meat, and blood (the Nuer, and other East African pastoralists, extract blood from the cow's neck, which they drink). They also furnished hides, horn, and other materials for everyday use. They were the medium of

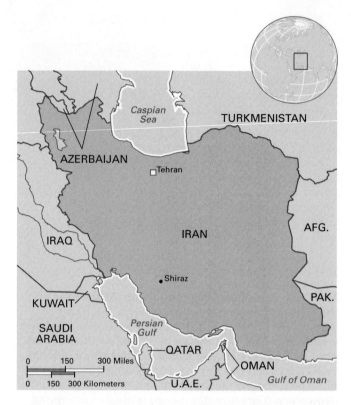

MAP 3.5 Iran. The Islamic Republic of Iran is one of the world's most mountainous countries. Its economy is based on oil, family farming, and small-scale trading. Iran is OPEC's second-largest oil producer and has the second-largest natural gas reserves in the world after Russia. The population of Iran is over 68 million. Its urban population is one of the fastest-growing worldwide. The official language is Persian (Farsi) and Shi'a Islam is the official state religion.

exchange for marriage and payment of fines. The importance of cattle in Nuer life is reflected in the Nuer's detailed vocabulary for cattle, which elaborates on their colors and markings.

Another group of short-distance herders are the Suri people of southern Ethiopia (Abbink 2003). As with the Nuer, cattle are an integral part of life. The Suri name their cattle, decorate them, apply ashes to them to protect them against biting insects, use various medicines for cattle illnesses, know animals' descent lines for several generations, and sing songs to and about them. African cattle herders sell their cattle with great reluctance since one's wealth and social identity depends on herd size and quality. The Suri are well known in the region for their cattle's excellent condition. Boys are each given a young bull, the most prized animal, to care for as they grow up. If a boy's bull should die, he will be overcome with grief and avoid eating its meat (which would be considered cannibalism) or the meat from any other animal with a similar color or name.

The Qashqa'i of Iran are long-distance herders of sheep and camels (Beck 1986). Iran offers a varied and rich natural resource base that supports pastoralism, agriculture, and large urban centers, including the capital city of Shiraz (see Map 3.5). The pastoralism of the Qashqa'i involves seasonal migration to remote pastures separated by about 300 miles. The vast distances make the Qashqa'i vulnerable to raids and create the need for negotiation with village leaders along the route for permission to cross their land. In order to deal with this vulnerability, the Qashqa'i developed linkages across several tribes that can be mobilized, temporarily, to create a large political unit under one leader. The Qashqa'i are an example of a pastoralist system in which political organization is highly developed.

Division of Labor

Families and clusters of related families are the basic unit of production. Gender and age are, again, key factors in the allocation of work. In many pastoralist cultures, gender roles are clearly divided. Men are in charge of herding—moving the animals from place to place. Women are responsible for processing the herd's products, especially the milk. A cultural emphasis on masculinity characterizes many herding populations. Reindeer herding among the Saami of Finland is closely connected to male identity to the extent that the definition of being a man is to be a reindeer herder (Pelto 1973) (see Culturama, Chapter 16, p. 434). In contrast, women are the herders among the Navajo of the American Southwest. Navajo men's major work role is crafting silver jewelry.

The size of the animal involved is sometimes, but not always, related to the gender division of herding. Girls and women are often herders of smaller animals, perhaps because smaller animals need to graze less widely and can be kept penned near the house. Boys and men tend the animals that are pastured farther away. Children play important roles in tending herds. Among the cattle-herding groups of Eastern Africa, for example, parents want to have many children to help out with the herds.

Property Relations

The most important forms of property among pastoralists are, by far, animals, followed by housing (such as tents or yerts) and domestic goods (rugs and cooking ware). Depending on the group, ownership of animals is inherited through males, most commonly, or, less frequently, through females, as among the Navajo. A concept of private property exists for animals, which the family head may trade for other goods. A family's housing materials are also their own. Use rights, however, regulate pasture land and migratory routes, and these rights tend to be informally regulated through an oral tradition.

Among the Ariaal, herders of northern Kenya, men are in charge of herding camels. ■ *Why do you think an adult man is in charge of these baby camels?* (Source: Elliott Fratkin)

Girls are in charge of herding water buffaloes to the Ganges River, at Varanasi, India, for watering. ■ (Source: Barbara Miller)

Pastoralism as a Sustainable System

Pastoralists have developed sustainable cultures in extremely varied environments, from the relative lushness of Iran to the more depleted situation of Mongolia. Pastoralism can be a highly successful and sustainable economic system that functions in complementarity with other economic systems. The Mongolian empire, one of the world's most powerful empires, was based on herding animals, along with pillaging. As with foraging and horticulture, however, when outside forces squeeze the space available for population movements, overexploitation of the environment results. A major external constraint on pastoralism is the goal of many governments to *sedentarize* (settle down) pastoralists. States want pastoralists to stay in one place so that the people

PRESERVING INDIGENOUS KNOWLEDGE ABOUT FARMING THROUGH DATABANKS

In 1992, the United Nations Conference on Environment and Development, held in Rio de Janeiro, first promoted global awareness of the complementary relationships between indigenous knowledge (IK) about the environment and biodiversity (Warren 2001). Scholars had long recognized the links (Scott 1998), but its official recognition in 1992 led to action directed at preserving and promoting IK in order to prevent loss of biodiversity. Cultural anthropologists have documented IK about agriculture in matters such as emic classification of soil types, what kinds of foods grow best in what contexts, how to mix crop plantings effectively, and how to prevent pests from destroying crops. Studies also reveal that indigenous knowledge varies microculturally. Men know some things, women know other things, the young and old have different kinds of IK, as do members of different economic niches within the same cultural area. All these varying "knowledges" need to be documented as part of indigenous cultural/agricultural heritage because they have local specificity and validity that outside systems often lack.

An effort is now underway to link universities and agricultural research laboratories worldwide in order to support IK data collection and documentation. Over thirty IK resource centers exist, housing computerized databases of case studies and ethnographic reports. Coordination among the centers is leading to improved guidelines and recommendations about data recording, archiving, and sharing. All of these practices are aimed at both preserving the knowledge for the future and providing wider access to it. Although the primary goal of the project is to support biodiversity, it will have the effect of supporting cultural diversity as well.

For examples of the Global Network of Indigenous Knowledge Resource Centers, visit this website: www.nuffic.nl/ik-pages/ikww/index.html.

FOOD FOR THOUGHT

- This global information network will clearly help inform agricultural policy-makers, but how will it benefit the people whose knowledge is being recorded and preserved in the databanks?

---

will be easier to keep track of and tax. States do not like pastoralists to move across state lines, as they have done long before state boundaries were created.

Agriculture

Agriculture is a mode of production that involves growing crops on permanent plots with the use of plowing, irrigation, and fertilizer; it is also called *farming*. In contrast to foraging, horticulture, and pastoralism, agriculture is an **intensive strategy**. Intensification involves the use of techniques that allow the same plot of land to be used repeatedly without losing its fertility. Crucial inputs include substantial amounts of labor for weeding, use of natural and chemical fertilizers, and control of water supply. The earliest agricultural systems are documented from the time of the Neolithic period, beginning around

12,000 years ago in the Fertile Crescent region in present-day Iraq. Agricultural systems now exist worldwide, on all continents except Antarctica.

Agriculture relies on the use of domesticated animals for plowing, transportation, and organic fertilizer either in the form of manure or composted materials. It is highly dependent on artificial water sources such as irrigation channels or terracing the land. Like the modes of production already discussed, agriculture involves complex knowledge about the environment, plants, and animals, including soil types, precipitation patterns, plant varieties, and pest management. Anthropologists refer to this knowledge as **indigenous knowledge (IK)** to distinguish it from Western, scientific knowledge. Long-standing agricultural traditions are now being increasingly displaced by methods introduced from the outside, and so the world's stock of indigenous knowledge is declining

---

agriculture: a mode of production that involves growing crops with the use of plowing, irrigation, and fertilizer.
intensive strategy: a form of production that involves continuous use of the same land and resources.

indigenous knowledge: local knowledge about the environment, including plants, animals, and resources.
family farming (formerly termed *peasant agriculture*): a form of agriculture in

which farmers produce mainly to support themselves but also produce goods for sale in the market system.

FIGURE 3.5 Characteristics of Three Forms of Agriculture

	Family Farming	Industrial Capital Agriculture	Industrial Collectivized Agriculture
Labor Inputs	Kin-based	Hired, impersonal	Communal
Capital Inputs	Low–Moderate	High	Moderate–High
Sustainability	High	Low	Low–Moderate

rapidly. In many cases, it has become completely lost, along with the cultures and languages associated with it. Many applied anthropologists are actively involved in recording indigenous knowledge as a resource for the future (see Lessons Applied box).

Occupational specialization increases in agricultural societies. Instead of people repairing their own tools and weapons, some people take on this work as a full-time job and no longer grow their own food, trading their skills for food with farmers. Other specializations that emerge as full-time occupations are political leaders, religious leaders or priests, healers, artisans, potters, musicians, and traders. Three major types of agriculture (see Figure 3.5) are discussed next.

Family Farming

One variety of agriculture is **family farming** (formerly termed *peasant agriculture*) in which production is geared to support the family and to produce goods for sale. Thus, family farming is always part of a larger market economic system (E. Wolf 1966). Today, more than one billion people, or about one-sixth of the world's population, make their living from family farming. Found throughout the world, family farming is more common in countries such as Mexico, India, Poland, and Italy than in more indus-

trialized countries. Family farmers exhibit much cross-cultural variety. They may be full-time or part-time farmers; they may be more or less closely linked to urban markets; and they may be poor and indebted or wealthy and powerful. Major activities in family farming include plowing, planting seeds and cuttings, weeding, caring for irrigation systems and terracing, harvesting crops, and processing and storing crops.

Division of Labor The family is the basic unit of production, and gender and age are important in organizing work. Most family farming societies have a marked gender-based division of labor. Cross-cultural analysis of gender roles in forty-six cultures reveals that men perform the "bulk" of the labor in over three-fourths of the sample (Michaelson and Goldschmidt 1971). Anthropologists have proposed various theories to explain why productive work on so many family farms is male dominated (see Figure 3.6). The remaining one-fourth of the sample includes cultures in which men's and women's roles are balanced and cultures in which women play the dominant role. These three variations on the gender division of labor in family farming are the subject of much anthropological research.

In farming systems where men play the major role in agriculture, women are likely to work in or near the

---

FIGURE 3.6 Three Hypotheses to Explain Male Dominance in the Gender Division of Labor in Family Farming

Men and Plowing Hypothesis

This hypothesis is based on the importance of plowing fields in preparation for planting and on the fact that plowing is almost exclusively a male task (Goody 1976). Some anthropologists say that men plow because they are stronger than women and have the advantage of greater aerobic capacity. In southern India, for example, weather patterns require that plowing be accomplished in a very narrow time period (Maclachlan 1983). Assigning the task to the physically stronger gender ensures that the work is done more quickly and is thus an adaptive cultural strategy because it increases the chances for a good crop.

Women and Child Care Hypothesis

This hypothesis says that women are not involved in plowing and other agricultural field labor as much as men because such tasks are incompatible with child care (J. K. Brown 1970).

Women and Food Processing Hypothesis

This hypothesis notes that agriculture increases the demand for labor within and near the house (Ember 1983). Winnowing, husking, grinding, and cooking agricultural products are extremely labor-intensive processes. Linked to women's primary roles in child care and increased fertility in farm families, these labor demands restrict women to the household domain.

Family farming in highland Ecuador. A man plows while women in the family follow, planting seed potatoes. ■ (Source: © Jeremy Horner/ CORBIS)

home, processing food, maintaining the household, and caring for children (Ember 1983). This division of labor results in the **public/private dichotomy** in family farm societies, in which men are more involved with the outside, public world and women are more involved in the domestic domain. In this variety of family farming, men work more hours per week than in foraging, horticultural, and pastoralist systems. Women's work hours, in contrast, are as high as they are in horticultural and pastoralist systems.

In family farms in the United States, men typically have the main responsibility for daily farm operations; women's participation ranges from equal to minimal (Barlett 1989:271–273). Women do run farms in the United States, but generally only when they are divorced or widowed. Women are usually responsible for managing the domestic domain. On average, women's daily work hours are 25 percent more than those of men. A trend is for family farm women to take salaried jobs off the farm to help support the farm.

Balanced work roles between men and women in family farming frequently involve a pattern in which men do the agricultural work and women do marketing. This gender division of labor is common among highland indigenous groups of Central and South America. For example, among the Zapotec Indians of Mexico's southern state of Oaxaca (pronounced wah-HAKA), men grow maize, the staple crop, and cash crops such as

bananas, mangoes, coconuts, and sesame (Chiñas 1992) (see Map 5.4, p. 128). Zapotec women sell produce in the town markets, and they make tortillas, which they sell from their houses. The family thus derives its income from the labor of both men and women working interdependently. Male status and female status are quite equal in such contexts.

Family farms in which females play the major role in production are called *female farming systems*. They are found mainly in southern India and Southeast Asia where *wet rice agriculture* is practiced. This is a highly labor-intensive way of growing rice that involves starting the seedlings in nurseries and transplanting them to flooded fields. Men are responsible for plowing the fields using teams of water buffaloes. Women own land and make decisions about planting and harvesting. Women's labor is the backbone of this type of farming. Standing calf-deep in muddy water, they transplant rice seedlings, weed, and harvest the rice. Why women predominate in wet rice agriculture is an intriguing question but impossible to answer. Its consequences for women's status, however, are clear. In female farming systems, women have relatively high status. They own land, play a central

---

public/private dichotomy: gender division in society that emerged with agriculture, whereby men are more involved with the nondomestic domain and women are more involved in activities in or near the home.

industrial capital agriculture: a form of agriculture that is capital-intensive, substituting machinery and purchased inputs for human and animal labor.

industrial collectivized agriculture: a form of industrialized agriculture that involves state control of land, technology, and goods produced.

This farmer works near a highly urbanized area of Kyoto, in Japan, where farming combines elements of industrial mechanization with intensive labor. ■ *Which features fit with industrialized agriculture and which do not?* (Source: Barbara Miller)

role in household decision making, and have substantial personal autonomy (Stivens et al. 1994).

Children's roles in agricultural societies range from prominent to minor, depending on the context (Whiting and Whiting 1975). The *Six Cultures Study,* mentioned earlier in the chapter, found lower rates of child labor in agricultural villages in North India and Mexico compared to those among the horticultural Gusii in Kenya. In many agricultural contexts, however, children's labor participation is high. In two Asian villages, one in Java (see Map 1.3, p. 15) and one in Nepal (see Map 7.5, p. 193), an important task of children, even as young as 6 to 8 years old, is tending the farm animals (Nag, White, and Peet 1978). In both villages, children spend more time caring for animals than adults do. Girls age 6 to 8 spend more time than adults in child care, and girls work more hours each day than boys. Some Javanese children in the 6- to 8-year-old group work for wages. Children in the United States are not formally employed in farm work, but many family farms rely on children's contributions on weekends and during summer vacations. Amish farm families rely to a significant extent on contributions from all family members (see Culturama, Chapter 5, p. 122).

Property Relations   Family farmers make substantial investments in land, such as clearing, terracing, and fencing, and these investments are linked to the development of firmly defined and protected property rights. Rights to land can be acquired and sold. Formalized, often written, guidelines exist about inheritance of land and transfer of rights to land through marriage. Social institutions such as law and police exist to protect private property rights.

In family farming systems where male labor and decision making predominate, women and girls tend to be excluded from land rights and other forms of property control. Conversely, in female farming systems, inheritance rules regulate the transmission of property rights more often through females. Class distinctions are more rigid, and there are greater gaps between those who have access to resources and those who do not.

Industrial Agriculture

Industrial capital agriculture produces crops through capital-intensive means, using machinery and inputs such as processed fertilizers instead of human and animal labor (Barlett 1989:253). It is practiced more often in the United States, Canada, Germany, Russia, and Japan and is increasingly being adopted in developing countries such as India, Brazil, and even in socialist countries such as China.

Industrial agriculture has brought with it the *corporate farm,* a huge agricultural enterprise that produces goods solely for sale and are owned and operated by companies entirely reliant on hired labor. Industrial agriculture has major social effects (see Figure 3.7).

Much of the labor demand in industrial agriculture is seasonal, creating an ebb and flow of workers, depending on the task and time of year. Large ranches hire seasonal cowboys for round-ups and fence mending. Crop harvesting is another high-demand point. Leo Chavez studied the lives of undocumented (illegal) migrant laborers from Central America who work in the huge tomato, strawberry, and avocado fields owned by corporate farms in southern California (1992). Many of the migrants are Maya people from Oaxaca, Mexico (see Map 5.4, p. 128). They cross the border illegally in order to find work to support their families. In the San Diego area of southern California, they live temporarily in shantytowns, or camps. Here is what a men's camp is like on Sunday when they do not go to work in the fields:

> On Sundays, the campsites take on a community-like appearance. Men bathe, and wash their clothes, hanging them on trees and bushes, or on lines strung between the trees. Some men play soccer and basketball, using a hoop someone has rigged up. Others sit on old crates or treestumps as they relax, talk, and drink beer. Sometimes the men talk about fights from the night before. With little else to do, nowhere to go, and few outsiders to talk to, the men often drink beer to pass the time on Saturday nights and Sundays. Loneliness and boredom plague them during nonworking hours. (1992:65)

Industrial Collectivized Agriculture   Industrial collectivized agriculture is a form of industrialized agriculture that involves nonprivate control of land, technology, and goods produced. Mao Tse-tung undertook a massive effort to establish collective production in China. Collectivism's basic goal was to provide for greater economic

FIGURE 3.7 Three Features of Industrial Agriculture and Their Social Effects

- Increased use of complex technology (including machinery, chemicals, and genetic research) on new plant and animal varieties.

  Social effects: This feature results in displacement of small landholders and field laborers. For example, replacing mules and horses with tractors for plowing in the U.S. South during the 1930s led to the eviction of small-scale sharecroppers from the land because the landowners could cultivate larger units. Similarly, the invention of mechanical cotton pickers displaced field laborers.

- Increased use of capital (wealth used in the production of more wealth) in the form of money or property.

  Social effects: The high ratio of capital to labor enables farmers to increase production but reduces flexibility. If a farmer invests in an expensive machine to harvest soybeans and then the price of soybeans drops, the farmer cannot simply switch from soybeans to a more profitable crop. Capitalization creates opportunities and risks for farmers. It is most risky for smaller farms, which cannot absorb losses easily.

- Increased use of energy (primarily gasoline to run the machinery and nitrates for fertilizer) to grow crops. This input of energy often exceeds the calories of food energy yielded in the harvest. Calculations of how many calories of energy are used to produce a calorie of food in industrial agricultural systems reveal that some 2.5 calories of fossil fuel are invested to harvest 1 calorie of food—and more than 6 calories are invested when processing, packaging, and transport are taken into account.

  Social effects: This energy-heavy mode of production creates farmers' dependence on the global market of energy supplies.

Source: Adapted from "Industrial Agriculture" by Peggy F. Barlett in *Economic Anthropology,* ed. by Stuart Plattner. Copyright © 1989. Published by Stanford University Press.

equality and a greater sense of group welfare than is possible under competitive capitalism. A variety of collective agriculture arrangements have been used, with varying degrees of success, in Russia, Eastern Europe, China, Tanzania, Ethiopia, and Nicaragua.

Cultural anthropology studies of collectivized agriculture are rare. This section presents findings from research conducted in Romania, specifically its Olt Land region, which comprises about sixty-five villages and a high degree of social homogeneity (Kideckel 1993) (see Map 3.6). David Kideckel conducted fieldwork in two periods: first in 1974, during a period of optimism for

socialism, and later in 1990, after the revolution that brought socialism's end.

Romanian socialism was established during the period of Soviet Union control. Romania had the most centralized state planning system in all of Eastern Europe (Kideckel 1993). The state oversaw nearly every aspect of society, from university enrollments to the production of steel and tractors. Romanian agriculture was organized into two categories: state farms and collective farms. By the early 1960s, about 30 percent of the land was in state farms, 60 percent in collectives, and 10 percent privately held. Workers on state farms were paid wages and received a small garden for their own use. Organized like a rural factory, the state farm provided services such as child-care facilities and shopping centers. Collective farms, in contrast, were ostensibly owned and controlled by their members, who pooled land, labor, and resources. Their earnings were determined by total farm production, and their wages tended to be lower than those of state farm workers. Collective farm workers were entitled to a "use plot" of the collective land.

In spite of the socialist rhetoric proclaiming equality among all workers, economic distinctions existed between men and women, and men had higher status. Women were relegated to agricultural and reproductive labor, whereas rural men moved into industry. Although women were the mainstay of collective farm labor, they were underrepresented among the leadership. Nevertheless, women's increased involvement in wage earning, compared to earlier times, and their roles in cultivating household use plots strengthened their influence in the household and the community.

After the revolution of 1989, the policy of returning land to private ownership had mixed results. State farms gave up land reluctantly. Many collective farmers thought that privatized farming was not worth the effort and risk

Migrant workers picking broccoli in Salinas, California.
■ *Compare how labor in corporate agriculture is organized to that on a collective farm under Romanian socialism.* (Source: © Morton Beebe/CORBIS)

MAP 3.6   Olt Region in Romania. The Olt region, or Olt Land, is near the Olt River in central Romania. Romania's geography comprises mountainous, hilly, and lowland terrains. Its population is over 22 million. Romania is the most economically developed country of southeastern Europe with strong agricultural and industrial sectors. The official language is Romanian and the major religion is Romanian Orthodox Christianity.

Members of this Romanian collective farm work team are sorting potatoes in 1975. Teams were composed of close friends, relations, and neighbors. ■ *How does this form of organization contribute to productivity?* (Source: David Kideckel)

because they were accustomed to shorter working days and shared risk. Some younger people welcomed the idea of private farming but lacked the necessary knowledge to succeed. With Romania's likely membership in the EU, agriculture in the country may go through yet another transition.

The Sustainability of Agriculture

Agriculture requires more in the way of labor inputs, technology, and the use of nonrenewable natural resources than the economic systems discussed earlier. The ever-increasing spread of corporate agriculture worldwide is now displacing other long-standing practices and resulting in the destruction of important habitats and cultural heritage sites in its search for land, water, and energy sources. Intensive agriculture is not a sustainable system. Furthermore, it is undermining the sustainability of foraging, horticulture, and pastoralism. For many years, anthropologists have pointed to the high costs of agriculture to the environment and to humanity (see Critical Thinking box).

Industrialism and the Information Age

Industrialism/informatics is the production of goods and services through mass employment in business and commercial operations and through the creation, manipulation, management, and transfer of information through electronic media. In industrial capitalism, the form of capitalism found in most industrialized nations, most

goods are produced not to meet basic needs but to satisfy consumer demands for nonessential goods. Employment in agriculture decreases while jobs in manufacturing and the service sector increase. In some industrialized countries, the number of manufacturing jobs is declining, with more people being employed in service occupations and in the growing area of information processing such as computer programming, data processing, and communications. Cybersystems and virtual economies are continuing to spread worldwide.

An important distinction exists between the **formal sector**, which is salaried or wage-based work registered in official statistics, and the **informal sector**, which includes work that is outside the formal sector, not officially registered, and sometimes illegal. If you have done babysitting and were paid cash that was not formally recorded by your employer (for tax-deduction purposes) or by you (for income tax purposes), then you have participated in the informal sector. Informal sector activities that are illegal are referred to as being part of the *underground economy*, a huge and uncounted part of global and local economies worldwide.

The Formal Sector

The formal sector includes a wide variety of occupations, ranging from stable and lucrative jobs to unstable or part-time and less lucrative jobs (Calhoun, Light, and Keller 1994). Cultural anthropologists have focused on small-scale workplaces, especially factories.

In one factory study, a team of cultural anthropologists and university graduate students studied the role of ethnicity in social relationships in a Miami clothing factory (Grenier et al. 1992). The clothing plant, a sub-

Critical Thinking

WAS THE INVENTION OF AGRICULTURE A TERRIBLE MISTAKE?

Most Euro-Americans have a "progressivist" view that agriculture is a major advance in cultural evolution because it brought with it so many things that Westerners admire: cities, centers of learning and art, powerful state governments, and monumental architecture:

> Just count our advantages. We enjoy the most abundant and varied foods, the best tools, and material goods, some of the longest and healthiest lives, in history. . . . From the progressivist perspective on which I was brought up, to ask "Why did almost all our hunter–gatherer ancestors adopt agriculture?" is silly. Of course they adopted it because agriculture is an efficient way to get more food for less work. (Diamond 1994 [1987]:106)

Another claim about the advantage of agriculture is that it allows more leisure time, so art could flourish.

On the other hand, many scholars raise serious questions about the advantages of agriculture. These "revisionists" argue that agriculture may be "the worst mistake in the history of the human race," "a catastrophe from which we have never recovered" (Diamond 1994 [1987]:105–106). Some of the "costs" of agriculture include social inequality; disease; despotism; and destruction of the environment from soil exhaustion and chemical poisoning, water pollution, dams and river diversions, and air pollution from tractors, transportation, and processing plants.

With agriculture, life did improve for many people, but not for all. Elites emerged with distinct advantages, but the gap between the haves and the have-nots increased. Health improved for the elites, but not for the landless poor and laboring classes. With the vast surpluses of food created by agricultural production, elaborate state systems developed with new forms of power exercised over the common people.

CRITICAL THINKING QUESTIONS

- What is your definition of "the good life"?
- What are the benefits and costs of achieving the good life among, say, the Ju/'hoansi compared to your vision of the good life in your microculture?
- Who gets to live the good life in each type of economy?

sidiary of the largest U.S. clothing manufacturer, employs about 250 operators, mainly women. The majority of employees are Cuban women who, fleeing from the Castro regime, immigrated to Miami many years ago. As these employees have begun to retire, they are being replaced by new immigrants from Central America as well as Haitians and African Americans.

The workers are organized into a union, but members of the different ethnic groups have more solidarity with each other than with people in the union. Interethnic rivalry exists around the issue of management's treatment of members of different groups. Many non-Cuban workers claim that management favors Cuban employees. Some supervisors and managers expressed ethnic stereotypes, but not always consistent ones: "Depending on whom one listens to, Haitians are either too slow or too fast; Cubans may talk too much or be extraordinarily dedicated workers" (1992:75). Managers see ethnic-based competition and lack of cooperation as a key problem that they attempt to deal with in various ways. For example, management banned workers from playing personal radios and installed a system of piped-in music by a radio station that supposedly alternates between "American" and "Latino" songs.

The Informal Sector

Studying the informal sector presents unusual challenges. People who work in the informal sector are unlikely to be clustered in one location such as a factory. Some informal sector workers are involved in illegal activities, which limits their willingness to be studied. On the other hand,

---

industrialism/informatics: a mode of production in which goods are produced through mass employment in business and commercial operations and through the creation and movement of information through electronic media.

formal sector: salaried or wage-based work registered in official statistics.

informal sector: work that is outside the formal sector, not officially registered, and sometimes illegal.

some research advantages exist. Compared to a CEO of a multinational corporation, people involved in the informal economy may have more time to share with an anthropologist. This is not always the case, however, since many informal sector workers are involved in more than one enterprise in an attempt to make ends meet, as well as being responsible for child care.

Informal economies also operate at the global level, including the illegal trafficking of people and goods. The illegal drug industry links informal economies at the global level to the local level. Neither international drug dealers nor street sellers pay income tax on their profits, and their earnings are not part of the official gross national product (GNP) of any nation. Currently, the drug traffic from Central and South American into North America is a multibillion-dollar business. Most of the supply moves through Mexico (see Map 5.4, p. 128). Fieldwork in a small, rural town in Mexico's central highlands shows how the legal and illegal economies related to drug trafficking are intertwined (McDonald 2005). This ethnography of the local *narcoeconomy,* or an economy based on the production and sale of addictive drugs, reports: "None of this could happen without deep interconnections between drug traffickers, and networks of well-placed politicians, civil servants, and security forces of various kinds" (2005:115).

What effects does the narcoeconomy have on local life in central Mexico? This ordinary town became a site of extraordinary inequalities: new, opulent houses for some, high-end clothing stores, a cyber-café, and a day spa. New farmers, willing to participate in the narcoeconomy, are moving in and gaining legitimacy in the community. These farmers are typically young men who come from local farm families and have worked in U.S. drug trafficking networks. They are hard working and interested in promoting local economic development. Through their experiences in the United States, they gained business skills and they understand the importance of networking. The positive features of this situation, however, are part of an economic system that is illegal.

In many parts of the world, sex work, like the narcoeconomy, is illegal. In the United States, it is legal only in the state of Nevada, where income from sex work is taxable. In Thailand (see Map 6.4, p. 163), laws about sex work are complicated (Jeffrey 2002). It is illegal to sell sex, but not to buy it. Recent legal reforms, however, pertain to the age of the sex seller and involve a prison sentence for anyone having sex with someone 15 years of age or younger.

Nevertheless, child sex work in Thailand is an increasingly important part of the economy. The number of child sex workers under 16 years old is estimated to be about one-third of the total prostitute labor force (Petras and Wongchaisuwan 1993). The increased fear of HIV/AIDS among men who seek commercial sex leads to

A street vendor in Kingston, Jamaica. In many modernizing countries, city planners are taking steps to make street vending illegal on the grounds that such informal stands are unsightly. ■ *If you were the mayor of Kingston, what position would you take on the street vending issue?* (Source: Barbara Miller)

the demand for ever-younger sex workers who are assumed to be less likely to be carriers of the virus. Recruitment of children as young as 6 years old began in the 1990s.

How do children become involved in commercial sex work? Family poverty is a major part of the answer in Thailand. Low and declining incomes in rural northern Thailand continue to prompt parents to send children into sex work. Within the context of severe and increasing poverty in northern Thailand, however, a village-based study provides further details about how culture shapes family decisions about sending daughters into sex work (Rende Taylor 2005). In northern Thailand generally, and in the study village, daughters are valued members of the family. Along with their value come obligations to the family. From an early age, the eldest daughter is expected to assume major household responsibilities, including care of her younger siblings. The youngest daughter will inherit the house and, with it, the obligation to care for her aging parents. Middle daughters are the ones most likely to be sent outside to earn an income, often in commercial sex work. Parents are more concerned about the welfare of the family than about a daughter's involvement in commercial sex work. They say, "The problem here isn't that our daughter sells her body . . . it's that we have no food to eat" (2005:416).

The views and voices of the children themselves are also important (Montgomery 2001). Research in a small slum community on the edge of a tourist town, frequented mainly by Europeans, reveals that the children reject the view of child prostitutes as mere victims, a view promoted by international organizations concerned with child welfare and rights. They believe the work they do is moral because it is done in support of their family. The child sex workers and their pimps, also children, exercise some choice in deciding which clients to accept and which to reject. These insights do not deny the fact that the child sex workers are exploited and often seriously harmed. They do however, provide a fuller picture by showing how the children define their work as related to family obligations, and how they seek to protect themselves within a context of limited options.

This study, and other research on child labor worldwide, raises important questions about what childhood is, what a good childhood is, and what child rights are and should be (Panter-Brick and Smith 2000). The voices and views of the children must be heard. But scholars and activists must look beyond the children's emic worlds to the global, macroeconomic structures that generate and support the people who pay for sex with children and the poverty in the communities that send children into sex work. So far, the author of this book has not seen a study of the people who seek commercial sex.

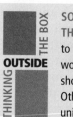

Changing Modes of Production

This section looks at changes that have occurred recently in the five modes of production. Contemporary economic globalization is the latest of many outside forces exerted on local economies. Most notably, European colonialism, starting in the fifteenth century, had dramatic effects on indigenous people's production, mainly through the introduction of cash crops such as tea, coffee, and cotton; co-optation and control of local labor through slavery, indentureship, and hire; and taking over land for colonial plantations and other enterprises.

As noted at the beginning of this chapter, the spread of Western capitalism in recent times continues to have far-reaching effects on the local economies with which it comes in contact. In the later part of the twentieth century, major economic growth in Asia, the demise of socialism in the former Soviet Union, and the increasing economic power of the United States throughout the world have combined to move everyone, everywhere into the global economy. The term *global economy* refers to the interconnectedness of all aspects of international, transnational, national, and local economies: raw materials, labor supply, transportation, finance, and marketing (Robins 1996).

This interconnectedness is characterized by its instantaneity. Electronic forms of communication mean, more than ever, that when a core economic center sneezes, the rest of the world will catch a cold. Social scientists vigorously debate the effects of economic globalization on poverty and inequality (Ravaillon 2003). Economists, relying on country-level figures about changing income levels and distribution, often take the view that economic

globalization is beneficial, overall, because it increases economic growth. Cultural anthropologists, who work with local-level data and a more "on the ground" view, tend to emphasize the negative effects of capitalist expansion into noncapitalist settings (Blim 2000). They point to three major transformations:

THINKING OUTSIDE THE BOX SOME PEOPLE THINK that in order to protect child sex workers, the children should be unionized. Others argue that unionization conveys a message of acceptance of this role for children. Where do you stand on this issue and why?

- Recruitment of former foragers, horticulturalists, pastoralists, and family farmers to work in low levels of the industrialism/informatics sector and their exploitation in that setting
- Dispossession of local people of their land and other resource bases and substantial growth in the numbers of unemployed, displaced people
- Increases in export commodity production in periphery regions in response to the demands of a global market

Examples exist of some foraging-horticultural groups choosing to become involved in the global economy on their own terms (Godoy et al. 2005). Far more often, however, these cultures have been destroyed by the intrusion of Western economic interests, their local knowledge has been lost, and the people have become demoralized, distressed, ill, and suicidal. The following examples illustrate ways that small-scale cultures have dealt with Western capitalism and globalization.

Foragers: The Tiwi of Northern Australia

The Tiwi live on two islands off the north coast of Australia (see Map 3.7) (Hart, Pilling, and Goodale 1988). As foragers, the Tiwi gathered food, especially vegetables (such as yams), nuts, grubs, small lizards, and fish. Women provided the bulk of the daily diet with their gathered vegetables and nuts that they ground and cooked into porridge. Men sometimes hunted kangaroos, wild fowl, and other game such as goanna (large lizards). Vegetables, nuts, and fish were abundant year round. The Tiwi lived a more comfortable life than Aboriginal groups of the mainland, where the environment was less hospitable.

The Tiwi have long been in contact with foreign influences, beginning in the 1600s with the arrival of the Portuguese, who were attracted to the islands as a source of iron. Later, in 1897, an Australian buffalo hunter named Joe Cooper came to the islands and kidnapped two native women to train as mainland guides. Cooper and his group greatly changed the Tiwi by introducing a desire for Western goods, especially tobacco. Later, Japanese

art, especially carving and painting, is widely recognized in Australia and internationally. Tiwi are active in public affairs and politics, including the aboriginal rights movement. Another major factor of change is international tourism, a force that the Tiwi are managing with dignity and awareness. One Tiwi commented that tourism may mean that "white people too will learn to live with and survive in the country" (Hart, Pilling, and Goodale 1988:144–145).

Horticulturalists: The Mundurucu of the Brazilian Amazon

Outside economic and political factors have major effects on horticultural societies. The rubber industry's impact on indigenous peoples of the Amazon ranges from maintenance of many aspects of traditional life to the complete loss of traditional lifeways. Like the Tiwi, the Mundurucu have experienced neither cultural preservation nor complete loss (Murphy and Murphy 1985). After the arrival of Brazilians, who were commercial rubber producers in the Amazon in the late nineteenth century, many Indians began to work for the Brazilians as latex tappers. For over a century, Mundurucu men combined their horticultural tasks with seasonal work collecting latex in the rubber area. Marked cultural change occurred when many Mundurucu people opted to leave their traditional villages, migrating to live in the rubber area year-round.

In the traditional villages, men live in a separate structure at one side of the village. Husbands visit wives and children in their houses. In the rubber settlement, husbands and wives live together in their own houses, and there is no separate men's house. In the traditional villages, women's communal work groups share water-carrying tasks. Such groups do not exist in the rubber settlement villages. Husbands in the new villages have taken on the task of carrying the water, so men work harder than they did in the traditional village. Although women in the settlement area work more hours per day than men, they believe that life is better because they like living in the same house with their husbands.

Pastoralists: The Herders of Mongolia

In the early 1990s, cultural anthropologist Melvyn Goldstein and biological anthropologist Cynthia Beall (1994) gained permission to do fieldwork among herders in Mongolia, a landlocked and mountainous country located between Russia and China (see Map 13.6, p. 360). The Mongolian rural economy has long been, and still is, heavily dependent on animal herds. The "big five" animals are sheep, goats, yaks, horses, and camels. Sheep and goats provide meat and clothing and some milk, yaks are most important for dairy products because they give milk all year, and horses and camels provide trans-

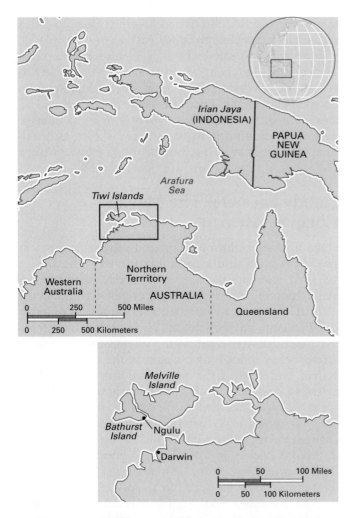

MAP 3.7 Tiwi Region in Northern Australia. The Tiwi Islands consist of Bathurst and Melville Islands. The total number of Tiwi is about 2,500 people. Most Tiwi live on Bathurst Island. In 2001, the Tiwi Islands Local Government Area was established, launching a new era of local government with statutory authority.

traders arrived and offered Tiwi men manufactured goods in return for Tiwi women. In the early 1900s, the French established a Catholic mission on one island. The mission disapproved of the traditional Tiwi marriage pattern of polygamy (multiple spouses, in this case a man having more than one wife) and promoted monogamy (one husband and one wife) instead. The year 1942 brought World War II to the Tiwi as the Japanese bombed and strafed a U.S. airstrip. Military bases were prominent on the islands. Tiwi dependency on Western manufactured goods increased.

Tiwi residence patterns changed substantially in the later part of the twentieth century. The Tiwi have become settled villagers living in houses built of corrugated iron sheets. Tiwi men now play football (soccer) and water polo and engage in competitive javelin throwing. Tiwi

Aboriginal artist Eymard Tungatalum retouches a traditional Tiwi carving in an art gallery in Australia's Northern Territory. Tungatalum's carvings, along with songs and poems, are an important part of the Aboriginal people's efforts to revive their culture. ■ (Source: © Reuters/Megan Lewis/Archive Photos)

portation. Goldstein and Beall wanted to study the effects of the transformation from a socialist, collectivized economy to a capitalist, market system.

Starting in the 1950s, the (then) USSR ruled Mongolia and sought to transform it into an agricultural and industrial state. The government established urban centers, and the urban population began to grow while the rural population declined. The state provided all social services such as health and education. There was no homelessness or unemployment.

The official policy regarding pastoralism was to ban private ownership and collectivize herds. The transition was difficult. Collectivization resulted in a 30 percent reduction of livestock, as owners chose to slaughter animals rather than collectivize them (Barfield 1993). Subsequently, state policy was altered to allow herders to control some animals as their own. By the early 1990s, the government's main policy was *privatization*, a process of transferring collective ownership and provision of goods and services to a system of private ownership. Collective ownership of herds was abandoned, and family-organized production was reinstated.

Goldstein and Beall selected a remote region for their research: the Moost district in the Altai Mountain area in the southeastern part of the country, which is 99.9 percent pasture (1994). At the time, the area contained about 4,000 people and 115,000 head of livestock. Goldstein and Beall set up their tent and were immediately welcomed by an invitation to have milk-tea, a hot drink made of tea, water, milk, butter, and salt. During their stay, they spoke with many of the herders, participated in their festivals, and learned about people's perceptions of economic change. The people had to adjust, first, to the dramatic restructuring of their economy from private

family herding to collectivized herding. Then, in just a few decades, they had to adjust back to private herding.

Privatization created serious problems for the herders. Their standard of living declined markedly in the 1990s. Goods such as flour, sugar, candy, and cooking oil were no longer available. Prices for meat fluctuated widely, making it difficult for them to know how to manage their herd size efficiently. Social services such as health care and schools were less available and of lower quality.

Family Farmers: The Maya of Chiapas, Mexico

Some applied anthropologists and other development specialists have said that family farmers who live in "closed" communities are "risk averse" because they avoid adopting innovations such as new techniques for cultivation, new seed varieties, and new forms of fertilizer. Economic anthropologists demonstrate, in contrast, that such risk-averse behavior may make sense. Family farmers have intimate knowledge of the environmental systems within which they work, and they are capable of assessing costs and benefits of innovations. Both perspectives emphasize the farmers' agency as decision makers who thoughtfully determine whether they should change in certain directions or not.

Frank Cancian, in 1960, studied production among the Maya of Zinacantán, located in the Chiapas region of Mexico's far south (see Map 5.4, p. 128). He returned in 1983 to conduct a restudy and thus learned of changes that had taken place in the intervening twenty years (1989). At the time of his first research, most Zinacantecos were family farmers, making a living by growing corn and selling some of their crops in a nearby city. They were largely independent of outside forces in terms of their own food supply. The community was closely knit, its social boundaries defined by people's commitment to community roles and ceremonies. Twenty years later, both the local economy and the social system had changed, reflecting the much greater effects of the world economy on the region.

The major direct cause of change was a large increase in public spending by the government in the 1970s. This spending supported the construction of roads, dams, schools, and housing throughout the Chiapas region. The government also sponsored outreach programs to promote agricultural change, mainly crop diversification and ways to increase production. Another important factor was the oil boom in northern Chiapas and Tabasco province, which brought unprecedented amounts of cash into the local economy.

By the early 1980s, 40 percent of the households had no land at all and planted no corn. Most people had become involved in wage work, and unemployment, rather than a bad farming season, was the major threat

Even the most remote areas of Mongolia are now connected to the wider world through satellite dishes.
■ (Source: © Adrian Arbib/CORBIS)

to food security. Wage work included the new opportunities in road construction, government jobs, transportation (of people, food goods, and flowers), and full-time trading in urban markets reachable by the new roads.

This story, in its general outlines, is similar to that of many family farmers throughout the world, especially in developing countries. It involves transformation from production mainly for own use to production mainly for sale within a cash economy geared toward making a profit. Overall, the area became more prosperous, more monetized, and more dependent on the outside economy. A second characteristic is the dislocation of farm owners from their land and their recruitment in the wage labor force. Many self-employed farmers sold their land and entered the wage economy. Another trend is increasing social inequality. Many Zinacantecos raised their incomes substantially during this period, but many others did not. Those who had the ability to buy a truck and take advantage of the new opportunities for urban trade created by the roads were the ones who became rich. Households with the least access to cash were left behind, and these households were characteristically headed by single women.

Industrialists: Factory Workers in Ohio

Increased mechanization is a major aspect of change in industry worldwide, and it has marked effects on labor demand and household income of workers. Unemployment and manufacturing declines in America's Rust Belt are well-known trends in industrial lifeways. Gregory Pappas studied unemployment in Barberton, a working-class Ohio town (1989). A tire company that had been the town's major employer closed in 1980, eliminating 1,200 jobs. Pappas lived in Barberton for a year, interviewing many people. He also sent a questionnaire to over 600 displaced workers for further information.

Pappas learned how unemployed workers cope either by migrating or by finding new ways to spend their time in Barberton. The unemployed factory workers of Barberton are faced with having to construct a new identity for themselves: "For factory workers the place of employment is crucial; their identities are bound up in a particular place, and plant shutdowns compromise their ability to understand themselves" (1989:83). As one unemployed man commented, "I don't know who I am anymore." In this context of decline, levels of stress and mental disorder have increased for many people.

Global Capitalism: Taiwanese Industrialists in South Africa

In South Africa during the 1990s, after the dismantling of apartheid, political leaders adopted a Western-style, capitalist economic policy (Hart 2002). One step toward expanding production and trade was to forge links with Taiwanese businesses in hopes of transferring to South Africa the Asian economic "miracle." Several Taiwanese industries were established outside major urban areas. Although there is no simple explanation for the so-called Asian economic miracle, one component was family-based production in which power structures based on age and gender ensure compliance among workers.

Taiwanese managers tried to use such a hierarchical family system in South Africa in order to ensure a smoothly functioning labor force. Research in Taiwanese knitwear factories in KwaZulu-Natal province, western South Africa (see Map 9.5, p. 247), reveal substantial worker resentment against the Taiwanese managers. Women workers were especially vocal. Taiwanese patterns of communicating with women workers by using an idiom of family did not work with the South Africans. The women said they felt as though they were being treated like animals. The Taiwanese industrialists were separated from the workers by a wide racial, economic, and social divide. Imposing hierarchical family metaphors failed to create a cooperative workforce in South Africa. Many of the Taiwanese industrialists found themselves a focal point of local political conflict. In one town, a Chinese welcome monument was removed.

Although Karl Marx predicted that capitalism would wither away, it has not yet done so. In its latest aspect, global incorporation, its effects are ever more powerfully felt in localities worldwide. Marx would be interested to observe how the Tiwi are developing international tourism, how the Maya people in Chiapas took up road construction for cash, and how Taiwanese knitwear manufacturers in KwaZulu-Natal encountered problems in cross-cultural labor management. He would perhaps be amused to see how, at the same time, cultural anthropologists are trying to document and understand these changes.

The Big Questions Revisited

WHAT is the scope of economic anthropology?

Economic anthropology is the study of production, consumption, and exchange cross-culturally. Economic anthropologists classify cross-cultural data on production, or ways of making a living, into five modes: foraging, horticulture, pastoralism, agriculture, and industrialism/informatics.

The current world system economy is increasingly competitive and unequal, placing some countries in the core where their strong governments protect and expand their economic interests. Some countries are in the semiperiphery, and many are in the periphery. Economic anthropologists mainly study local economic practices and beliefs but they increasingly realize that they must also study regional and global factors that affect local economies.

WHAT are the characteristics of the five major modes of production?

Foraging relies on collecting food that is available in nature. In foraging societies, the division of labor is based on gender and age, with temperate foragers having more gender overlap in tasks than circumpolar foragers. All group members have equal rights to resources. Foraging has long-term sustainability when not affected by outside pressure.

Horticulture and pastoralism are extensive strategies that depend on domesticated plants (horticulture) and animals (pastoralism). Horticulture requires fallowing, and pastoralism requires the constant movement of animals to fresh pastures. The division of labor varies, including situations in which men do more productive work, those where women do more work, and those in which workloads are shared between men and women. Use rights are the prominent form of property relations. Both have long-term sustainability when not affected by encroachments.

Family farming systems produce crops for their own use and for sale in the market. Most family farming systems involve more male labor in the fields and more female labor in the domestic domain. Socialist states cre-ated a form of labor organization for farming through the collective. Agriculture's sustainability is limited by the need to replenish the land.

In industrialism/informatics, the division of labor is highly differentiated by class, gender, and age. Widespread unemployment is found in many industrial economies. In capitalist societies, private property is the dominant pattern. Socialist societies have attempted to distribute property among all people, but most attempts have not been successful. Industrialism/informatics lacks sustainability.

WHAT are some directions of change in the five modes of production?

Foragers are being incorporated into settled economies as their access to land is constricted by outside forces and as governments force them to sedentarize. Many former foraging people now work as farm laborers and in other jobs of low status in the mainstream cash economy. Others are advocating for the revitalization of their culture in the new global economy, producing art for sale on the world market, developing cultural tourism opportunities for outsiders, or gaining a share in profits related to commercialization of their indigenous knowledge.

Horticulture and pastoralism are under great pressure from the competing economic forms of agriculture and industrialism. Many former horticulturalists have migrated to plantations or urban areas and become part of the cash economy. States have pressured pastoralists to settle down or (in communist systems) to become collectivized and then (with the decline of communism) decollectivized. Family farms are declining worldwide in number as corporate farms increase. The labor supply has changed from being family based to including a high proportion of migrant laborers. Along with industrialism, the Information Age has emerged with its emphasis on economic processes that involve virtual workplaces and the movement of information, created the new, combined mode of production called industrialism/informatics.

Capitalism increasingly involves international investments and location of production sites in countries where wages are low. Such situations implicate culture in complex ways, including managerial issues and cross-cultural communication.

KEY CONCEPTS

agriculture, p. 76
extensive strategy, p. 67
family farming, p. 77
foraging, p. 66
formal sector, p. 81
horticulture, p. 71

indigenous knowledge, p. 76
industrial capital agriculture, p. 79
industrial collectivized agriculture, p. 79
industrialism/informatics, p. 81
informal sector, p. 81

intensive strategy, p. 76
mode of production, p. 64
pastoralism, p. 73
public/private dichotomy, p. 78
use right, p. 69

SUGGESTED READINGS

Anne Allison. *Nightwork: Sexuality, Pleasure and Corporate Masculinity in a Tokyo Hostess Club.* Chicago: University of Chicago Press, 1994. Based on the author's participant observation, this book explores what it is like to work as a hostess in a club that caters to corporate male employees and discusses how that microculture is linked to men's corporate work culture.

Mary K. Anglin. *Women, Power and Dissent in the Hills of Carolina.* Urbana: University of Illinois Press, 2002. This book addresses class, gender, and race issues within a focus on women workers in a mica processing factory in the Blue Ridge Mountains of North Carolina.

Michael Blim. *Equality and Economy: The Global Challenge.* New York: AltaMira Press, 2005. The author examines the relationships between global capitalism and social inequality at three levels: households, states, and international.

Jans Dahl. *Saqqaq: An Inuit Hunting Community in the Modern World.* Toronto: University of Toronto Press, 2000. This ethnography of the Saqqaq, people of eastern Greenland, is based on fieldwork carried out at several times since 1980 in order to provide a diachronic perspective.

Daniel Dohan. *The Price of Poverty: Money, Work, and Culture in the Mexican American Barrio.* Berkeley: University of California Press, 2003. This ethnography explores poverty among Mexican Americans in two neighborhoods in California: undocumented immigrants in San Jose who work mainly in the Silicon Valley and urban Chicanos of Los Angeles.

J. A. English-Lueck. *Cultures@SiliconValley.* Stanford: Stanford University Press, 2002. A team of professors and anthropology students at San Jose State University have been conducting research for over a decade in Silicon Valley, and this book is the result of that work. The focus is on describing what life is like for people in a "technology-saturated" environment, from working to shopping to family life.

Elliot Fratkin. *Ariaal Pastoralists of Kenya: Surviving Drought and Development in Africa's Arid Lands.* Boston: Allyn and Bacon, 1998. Several phases of ethnographic research among the Ariaal people of northern Kenya, beginning in the 1970s, provide insights about pastoralism and changes it is undergoing in the area. The book also discusses social organization and family life.

Carla Freeman. *High Tech and High Heels in the Global Economy: Women, Work, and Pink-Collar Identities in the Caribbean.* Durham, NC: Duke University Press, 2000. This study examines the effects of globalization in the context of "informatics," or information-based work, in Barbados. The workers are women. Although their time in the factory is highly regimented, they express agency in terms of their self-definition as "professionals" in comparison to other factory workers.

Cori Hayden. *When Nature Goes Public: The Making and Umaking of Bioprospecting in Mexico.* Princeton NJ: Princeton University Press, 2003. An ethnography of global connections and complexity, this book examines relationships between pharmaceutical companies seeking new drug products and their relations with indigenous and local peoples.

David Uru Iyam. *The Broken Hoe: Cultural Reconfiguration in Biase Southeast Nigeria.* Chicago: University of Chicago Press, 1995. Based on fieldwork among the Biase people by an anthropologist who is a member of a Biase group, this book examines changes since the 1970s in farming, fishing, and trade as well as related issues of environmental deterioration and population growth.

Heather Montgomery. *Modern Babylon? Prostituting Children in Thailand.* New York: Bergahn Books, 2001. The author conducted fieldwork in a tourist community in Thailand where many parents commit their children to prostitution. She sought to gain a view of this system from the perspective of the children and the parents.

Brian Morris. *The Power of Animals: An Ethnography.* New York: Berg, 1998. In Malawi, southeastern Africa, men's roles in animal hunting and women's roles in farming are crucial to understanding wider aspects of Malawian culture, including diet and food preparation, marriage and kinship, gender relations, and attitudes about nature.

Katherine S. Newman. *Falling from Grace: The Experience of Downward Mobility in the American Middle Class.* New York: The Free Press, 1988. This book provides ethnographic research on downwardly mobile people of New Jersey as a "special tribe," with attention to loss of employment by corporate managers and blue-collar workers and the effects of downward mobility on middle-class family life.

Richard H. Robbins. *Global Problems and the Culture of Capitalism.* Boston: Longman, 1999. Robbins critiques the role of capitalism and global economic growth in creating and sustaining many world problems, such as poverty, disease, hunger, violence, and environmental destruction. The last section includes case studies.

Deborah Sick. *Farmers of the Golden Bean: Costa Rican Households and the Global Coffee Economy.* Dekalb: Northern Illinois University Press, 1999. This book is about coffee-producing households in Costa Rica and the difficulties that coffee farmers face as a consequence of unpredictable global forces.

Michael K. Steinberg, Joseph J. Hobbs, and Kent Mathewson, eds. *Dangerous Harvest: Drug Plants and the Transformation of Indigenous Landscapes.* New York: Oxford University Press, 2004. The chapters in this book address opium and the people of Laos, opium production in Afghanistan and Pakistan, struggles over coca in Bolivia, marijuana growing by the Maya, use of kava in the Pacific, and policy questions.

4

Consumption and Exchange

The Big Questions

- WHAT is consumption in cross-cultural perspective?

- WHAT is exchange in cross-cultural perspective?

- HOW are consumption and exchange changing?

A scene at the annual camel fair in Pushkar, in Rajasthan, India. Every year, 200,000 people gather to trade and admire camels and other animals. Herding people set up camp and are joined by food vendors, carousel operators, and tourists. Camel races and cattle beauty contests are high points. (*Source: © Brian A. Vikander/CORBIS*)

Imagine that it is the late eighteenth century and you are a member of the Kwakwaka'wakw (pronounced: KWA kwuh kyuh' wakw) of British Columbia in Canada's Pacific Northwest region (see Culturama near the end of this chapter, p. 114). You and your tribal group are invited to a **potlatch,** a feast in which the host lavishes the guests with abundant quantities of the best food and many gifts (Suttles 1991). The most honorable foods are fish oil, high-bush cranberries, and seal meat, and they will be served in ceremonial wooden bowls. Gifts include embroidered blankets, household articles such as carved wooden boxes and woven mats, canoes, and items of food. The more the chief gives, the higher his status rises and the more his guests are indebted to him. Later, when it is the guests' turn to hold a potlatch, they will give away as much as, or more than, their host did.

The Pacific Northwest region is rich in fish, game, berries, and nuts, among other foods. Nonetheless, given regional climatic variation, food supplies were often uneven, with some groups each year having surpluses while others faced scarcity. The potlatch system helped to smooth out these variations: Groups with a surplus would sponsor a potlatch and those experiencing a leaner year were guests. In this way, potlatching established a *social safety net* across a wide area of the Northwest.

This brief sketch of potlatching shows the linkages among the three economic processes of production, consumption, and exchange (review Figure 3.1, p. 64). Potlatches are related to production, are opportunities for consumption, and involve exchange. Chapter 3 began the discussion of economic systems with the subject of production. This chapter provides cross-cultural examples of the other two components of economic systems:

- **Mode of consumption:** the dominant way, in a culture, of using up goods and services.
- **Mode of exchange:** the dominant way, in a culture, of transferring goods, services, and other items between and among people and groups.

The chapter's last section provides examples of contemporary change in consumption and exchange.

![decorative band]

Culture and Consumption

This section examines the concept of consumption, cross-cultural patterns of consumption budgets, consumption

inequalities, and two theoretical positions on *food taboos* (forbidden food).

What Is Consumption?

Consumption has two senses: First, it is a person's "intake" in terms of eating or other ways of using things; second, it is "output" in terms of spending or using resources to obtain those things. Thus, for example, "intake" is eating a sandwich; "output" is spending money at the store to buy a sandwich. Both activities fit within the term of consumption.

People consume many things. Food, beverages, clothing, and shelter are the most basic consumption needs in most cultures. People also may acquire tools, weapons, means of transportation, computers, books and other items of communication, art and other luxury goods, and energy for heating and cooling their residence. In noncash economies, such as foragers, people "spend" time or labor in order to provide for their needs. In money-based economies, such as industrialized contexts today, most consumption depends on having cash or some virtual form of money.

Modes of Consumption

In categorizing modes of consumption, it makes sense to consider two contrasting modes, with mixed modes in the middle (see Figure 4.1). They are based on the relationship between *demand* (what people want) and *supply* (the resources available to satisfy demand):

- **Minimalism:** a mode of consumption characterized by few and finite (limited) consumer demands and an adequate and sustainable means to achieve them. It is most characteristic of free-ranging foragers but is also found to some degree among horticulturalists and pastoralists.
- **Consumerism:** a mode of consumption in which people's demands are many and infinite, and the means of satisfying them are never sufficient, thus driving colonialism, globalization, and other forms of expansionism. Consumerism is the distinguishing feature of industrial/informatic cultures. Globalization is spreading consumerism throughout the world.

The social organization and meaning of consumption varies cross-culturally. As noted in Chapter 3, foragers

---

potlatch: a grand feast in which guests are invited to eat and to receive gifts from the hosts.
mode of consumption: the dominant pattern, in a culture, of using things up or spending resources in order to satisfy demands.

mode of exchange: the dominant pattern, in a culture, of transferring goods, services, and other items between and among people and groups.
minimalism: a mode of consumption that emphasizes simplicity, is characterized by few and finite (limited) consumer

demands, and involves an adequate and sustainable means to achieve them.
consumerism: a mode of consumption in which people's demands are many and infinite and the means of satisfying them are insufficient and become depleted in the effort to satisfy these demands.

FIGURE 4.1 Modes of Production, Consumption, and Exchange

Foraging	Horticulture	Pastoralism	Agriculture	Industrialism/Informatics
Mode of Consumption Minimalism Finite needs				**Mode of Consumption** Consumerism Infinite needs
Social Organization of Consumption Equality/sharing Personalized products are consumed				**Social Organization of Consumption** Class-based inequality Depersonalized products are consumed
Primary Budgetary Fund Basic needs				**Primary Budgetary Fund** Rent/taxes, luxuries
Mode of Exchange Balanced exchange				**Mode of Exchange** Market exchange
Social Organization of Exchange Small groups, face-to-face				**Social Organization of Exchange** Anonymous market transactions
Primary Category of Exchange The gift				**Primary Category of Exchange** The sale

are generally egalitarian, whereas social inequality characterizes most agricultural and industrialism/informatics societies. Among foragers, sharing within the group is the norm, and everyone has equal access to all resources. Among the Ju/'hoansi (review Culturama in Chapter 1, p. 22): "Even though only a fraction of the able-bodied foragers go out each day, the day's return of meat and gathered foods are divided in such a way that every member of the camp receives an equitable share" (Lee 1979:118). Among the Hadza of northern Tanzania, people prize meat and eagerly anticipate the arrival of a hunting group with large game to share. The man who brings home large game will abide by unwritten rules of sharing and give 90 percent or more of the meat to

Well-stocked and brightly lit candy shops are a prominent part of urban nightlife in Valencia, Spain. Sugarcane was introduced into Spain by the Arabs. Later, the Spanish established the first sugarcane plantations on Madeira and the Canary Islands using enslaved laborers from Africa. ■ *Log your food and drink consumption every day for a week and assess the role that sugar plays in the results.* (Source: Barbara Miller and Bernard Wood)

Seoul, capital of the Republic of Korea. The demand for electricity in urban centers worldwide has prompted construction of many large dams to generate power. Food must be shipped to urban markets. In general, cities have high energy costs compared to rural areas. ■ *What are your major daily energy requirements and could you easily reduce them?* (Source: © Kim Newton/Woodfin Camp & Associates)

In Rome, as elsewhere in Europe, mini-cars are popular due to their fuel efficiency and ease of parking. ■ *Do research to discover the gas mileage of an average new car in the United States or Canada and compare it to that of a mini-car.* (Source: Barbara Miller and Bernard Wood)

everyone in the camp group, keeping only a small share for himself and his immediate family (Hawkes et al. 2001).

The distribution of personal goods such as clothing, beads, musical instruments, or smoking pipes is also equal. **Leveling mechanisms** are unwritten, culturally embedded rules that prevent an individual from becoming wealthier or more powerful than anyone else. They are maintained through social pressure and gossip. An important leveling mechanism among the Ju/'hoansi requires that any large game animal killed be shared with the group and its killer must be modest, insisting that the meat is meager and there is no fat at all (Lee 1969). Ju/'hoansi hunters gain no social status or power through their provision of meat. The same applies to other foragers. Leveling mechanisms are important in horticultural and pastoralist societies, too. For example, when someone's herd grows "too large," that person will be subject to social pressure to sponsor a large feast in which many of the herd animals are eaten.

Sharing is a key value among Native American groups such as the Cheyenne of the Great Plains region of the United States (Moore 1999:179–180). They have two distinct patterns of sharing: within one's extended family and with other families. Within the family, exchange

goes on continuously and includes not just food but also tools, jewelry, and even vehicles. A Cheyenne woman told anthropologist John Moore about her observations at a child-care center where Anglo people also took their kids: "'White people are funny,' she said, 'they spend half their time telling kids which toys are theirs, and the other half trying to get them to share'" (1999:179).

At the other end of the consumption continuum is consumerism, with the United States as the primary example, being the major consumerist country of the world. Since the 1970s, consumption levels in the United States have been the highest of any society in human history, and they show no sign of decline. The mass media send out seductive messages promoting consumerism as the way to happiness. Since China began to adopt some features of capitalism, it has quickly become a consumerist giant. In the world's poorest countries, too, rising numbers of middle- and upper-class people pursue consumerism. One estimate is that around 800 million people in "developing" and "transition" countries earn enough to be part of the consumerist economy (Myers 2000).

The growth of consumerism worldwide has some major costs:

■ *The environment and biological species diversity:* natural features such as rivers and lakes, forests, moun-

---

leveling mechanism: an unwritten, culturally embedded rule that prevents an individual from becoming wealthier or more powerful than anyone else.

consumption fund: a category of a personal or household budget used to provide for consumption demands.

---

tains, and beaches; nonhuman primates and hundreds of other species; and substances such as oil, gold, and diamonds

- *The world's cultural diversity:* people who live in environments being destroyed by consumerism (these people currently occupy the tropical rainforests, circumpolar regions, deserts, and mountain areas)
- *The poor, everywhere:* people whose real and relative incomes place them in poverty and who experience an ever-widening gap between themselves and the well-off and the super-rich

Minimalism was sustainable over hundreds of thousands of years, for most of humanity's time on earth. The amount of goods that the world's population consumed in the past fifty years equals what was consumed by all previous generations in human history.

In the United States, the attention given to the negative effects of consumerism tends to focus on the natural environment (especially "unspoiled" places for vacations) rather than to consumerism's endangerment of indigenous peoples and other nonindustrialized people, minimalists who "tread lightly on the land." The tragic irony is that more people in the United States probably know about an endangered bird species, the spotted owl, than about any single endangered human group—and there are many. Some countries have policies that seek to control consumerism and its negative effects. The government of Sweden has invested in public transportation and bicycle paths in cities in order to reduce the use of cars (Durning 1993). London recently placed a tax on cars entering the city. San Francisco is working on a plan to recycle dog waste and use it to create energy.

As consumerism spreads through globalization, a change in the social relations involved in consumption also occurs. In small-scale societies—such as those of foragers, horticulturalists, and pastoralists—consumption items are typically produced by the consumers themselves for their own use. If not, they are likely to be produced by people with whom the consumer has a personal, face-to-face relationship—in other words, *personalized consumption.* Everyone knows where products came from and who produced them. This pattern contrasts markedly with consumption in our contemporary globalized world, which is termed *depersonalized consumption.* Multinational corporations manage the production of most of the goods that people in industrialized countries consume. These products often are multisourced, with parts assembled in diverse parts of the world by hundreds of unknown workers. Depersonalized consumption, by distancing consumers from workers who actually produce goods, makes it more possible for workers to be exploited (see Critical Thinking box).

Even in the most industrialized contexts, depersonalized consumption has not completely replaced personalized consumption. The popularity of farmers' markets in urban centers is an example of personalized consumption in which the consumer buys apples from the person who grew them and with whom the consumer may have a friendly conversation, perhaps while sampling one of the apples. A reaction against depersonalized consumption supports regional markets in southern France where, even though many of the products come from far away, the marketers create a pretense of personalized production in order to satisfy their customers' preferences (de la Pradelle 2006).

Consumption Funds

Anthropologists define a **consumption fund** as a category within a person's or household's budget used to provide for his or her needs and demands. Cross-cultural analysis reveals five categories that appear to be relevant universally. The five funds are:

- *Basic needs fund:* for food, beverages, shelter, clothing, fuel, and the tools involved in producing or providing for them
- *Recurrent costs fund:* for maintenance and repair of tools, animals, machinery, and shelter
- *Entertainment fund:* for leisure activities
- *Ceremonial fund:* for social events such as rituals
- *Rent and tax fund:* for payments to landowners or governments for use of land, housing, or civic responsibilities

The categories apply universally, but the proportion of the budget allocated to each category varies widely and in relation to the mode of consumption. Remember: The "spending" involved may be in time, labor, or money, depending on the cultural context.

In the budget of free-ranging foragers, the largest share of expenditures goes into the basic needs fund. Foragers in temperate climates, however, spend far fewer hours per week collecting food than those in circumpolar climates. The next most important consumption fund among foragers is the recurrent costs fund, which supports repair and maintenance of tools and baskets, weapons, and shelter. Smaller shares are devoted to the entertainment fund and the ceremonial fund. Nothing goes into the rent and tax fund, because access to all land and other resources is free.

Consumption budgets in consumerist cultures differ in several ways from those in foraging, minimalist cultures. First, the absolute size of the budget is larger. People in agricultural and industrial/informatics societies work longer hours (unless they are unemployed), so they "spend" more of their time and labor providing for their consumption than foragers. Depending on their class position, they may have weekly cash budgets that are worth far more than their earnings due to stored wealth. Second, the relative size of the consumption funds varies

Critical Thinking

CAN THE INTERNET CREATE RESPONSIBLE CONSUMERS?

One important feature of increasingly globalized production is that the role of the producer is hidden from the consumer. Furthermore, many products are assembled with parts from all over the world, created by many invisible workers. Daniel Miller (no relation to the author) says that such labor invisibility and product depersonalization make it all too easy for consumers to be irresponsible and to support practices that are harmful to the distant, unseen laborers (2003). Most consumers are happy enough to blame the higher profits of multinational corporations for the poor treatment of producers. Miller points out, however, that the major responsibility lies with us, the consumers. It is our search for the cheapest possible goods that drives the commercial competition that results in further exploitation of workers. Consumers must be persuaded to pay more in order to facilitate better conditions for producers.

If consumers were educated about the actual dynamics of production and the role of the laborers, they would be more likely to make wiser and more responsible choices about which products to buy. For example, they would avoid products made by the more exploitative companies or by less ecologically responsible companies. And they might be willing to pay higher prices to discourage abuse of workers and of the environment.

Miller sees a lack of attention to consumer education in the school curriculum in his home country, the United Kingdom. It is extraordinary, he says, that we call people "educated" who know more about ancient Rome or physics than about the products they consume every day. Most students will never use the higher math or physics that they study in school, he says, but they will be consumers for the rest of their lives. So why not provide consumer education for students?

Miller devised an Internet education project for schoolchildren that would teach them about the role of workers in relation to the products the children consume in order to link the human faces of producers with the commodities. Having discovered the importance of "interactivity" from his earlier fieldwork on people's use of the Internet in Trinidad, he created a plan for an interactive narrative about a product. The Internet could enable students to talk in real time with actual producers going about their work. To avoid a power differential between workers and viewers, the producers should be able to question the students (the consumers) about their lives as well. This interaction would include, in the case of a relatively simple product like a banana, not just the plantation worker but also the wider process of

Child labor is prominent in many modes of production. In this photograph, a girl picks coffee beans in Guatemala. ■ *Should a child have the right to work, or should more international pressure be brought to bear against child labor?* (Source: © Sean Sprague/Stock Boston, LLC)

banana production and marketing: plantation managers, packers, and transporters. The students would choose a banana company, webcams would be supplied to the workers, and both students and workers would be connected on-line once a week. In order to push the reality of production all the way, Miller hopes that students would actually end up eating the same bananas that they saw being produced.

This is a big project, even for just a single commodity. Miller is well aware that people cannot, within reason, learn everything about the production of everything they consume. He suggests that three exemplary products be chosen for the education project, starting with the banana. The second product should be more complex to illustrate multiple sourcing. The third product might be locally produced by a small-scale firm.

Miller sought government funding for his project but was denied. Undaunted, he published an article in a journal in order to share his idea and inspire others to develop similar consumer education projects elsewhere. This Critical Thinking box asks you, as students of cultural anthropology, to consider his project.

CRITICAL THINKING QUESTIONS

- Is Miller's idea of enhancing the school curriculum in this way important?

- Is it feasible?

- What suggestions do you have for two products in addition to bananas?

in household budgets cross-culturally. Taking as an example an imagined middle-class person in the United States, his or her consumption funds might look like this, compared to a forager: The basic needs fund is a small portion of the total budget, given the increased overall size of the budget. This finding is in line with the economic principle that budgetary shares for food and housing (basic needs) decline as income rises. For example, someone who earns a total of $1,000 a month and spends $800 on food and housing spends 80 percent of his budget in that category. Someone who makes $10,000 a month and spends $2,000 a month on food and housing spends only 20 percent of her budget in this category, even though she spends more than twice as much as the first person, in an absolute sense. The largest share of the budget is the rent and tax fund. In some agricultural contexts, tenant farmers have to pay one-third to one-half of their crops to the landlord as rent. Income taxes claim well over 50 percent of personal income in countries such as Japan, Sweden, the Netherlands, and Italy. The entertainment fund receives a large share, larger than the ceremonial fund.

Theorizing Consumption Inequalities

Amartya Sen, an economist and a philosopher, proposed the theory of entitlements in order to explain why some groups suffer more than others during a famine (1981). An **entitlement** is a culturally defined right to provide for one's life needs. According to Sen, everyone has a set, or "bundle," of entitlements. For example, a person might own land, earn cash from a job, be on welfare, or live off an inheritance. Some entitlements are more secure and lucrative than others. *Direct entitlements* are the most secure form. In an agricultural society, for example, owning land that produces food is a direct entitlement. *Indirect entitlements* depend on exchanging something in order to obtain consumer needs: labor, animal hides, money, or food stamps. Because indirect entitlements involve dependency on other people or institutions, they are riskier bases of support than direct entitlements are. When a factory shuts down, animal hides drop in value, or a food stamp program ends, a person depending on those entitlements is in trouble. During times of economic decline, scarcity, or disaster, people with indirect entitlements are the most vulnerable to impoverishment, hunger, and forced displacement.

Entitlements Cross-Culturally

Entitlements vary depending on the type of economic system. In foraging societies, everyone has the same entitlement bundle. Entitlements are mainly direct, with the exception of infants and very old people who depend on sharing from group members for food and shelter. In industrial capitalist societies, entitlements are mainly indirect. People who grow all their own food are a small proportion of the total population. Even they depend on indirect entitlements for electricity and inputs required for maintaining their lifestyles. In highly monetized economies, the most powerful entitlements are those that provide a large and steady cash income, such as a good job. Other strong entitlements include home ownership, savings, stocks and bonds, and a retirement fund.

Internationally, entitlement theory exposes contrasts between countries that have secure and direct access to life-supporting resources and those that do not. Countries that produce food surpluses have a more secure entitlement to food than nations that are dependent on imports, for example. Replacing food crops with **cash crops,** or plants grown primarily for sale, such as coffee or tobacco, rather than for own-use, shifts a country from having mainly direct food entitlements to having mainly indirect entitlements. The same applies to access to energy sources that may be important for transportation to work or for heating homes. Direct access to energy resources is preferable to indirect access. This formula, however, leaves out the important factor of political power as exercised by the core countries of today's global economy. Many core countries lack direct access to critical resources, notably oil, yet they use political force to maintain access to such resources.

At the state (country) level, governments affect people's entitlements through policies related to employment, welfare programs, health care, and tax structures, among others. Political leaders and powerful policy-makers decide how many people will live in poverty and how many will be allowed to become rich, or even super-rich. They decide on whether or not to fund programs that transfer wealth from the rich to the poor or, the opposite, as is the case with regressive tax structures that tax lower-income people at higher rates than the rich.

THINKING OUTSIDE THE BOX

ESTIMATE YOUR MONTHLY EXPENDITURES in terms of the five funds. What proportion of your total expenditures goes to each fund? Do your expenditures fit well within the five categories or are different categories needed?

THINKING OUTSIDE THE BOX

WHAT IS IN YOUR personal entitlement bundle? Conduct a self-analysis of your daily consumption needs (food, shelter, entertainment, and other things) and how you provide for them. Then, imagine how you would provide for these needs if, starting today, your usual entitlements no longer had any value.

entitlement: a culturally defined right to life-sustaining resources.

cash crop: a plant grown primarily for sale rather than own-use.

The entitlement concept can also be applied to intra-household entitlements. Households do not always provide equal entitlements for all members. A household member who is employed and earns wages, for example, has a more secure position than someone who does not. Commonly, men have more secure entitlements than women. Inheritance practices may ensure that certain children, often sons, receive assets such as land or the family business, while others, often daughters, are excluded. Intra-household entitlements may also affect the distribution of food and health care.

During crises, entitlement structures often become glaringly clear. Famines are a good example. *Famine* is defined as massive levels of death resulting from food deprivation in a geographically widespread area. Most people think that famines are caused by overpopulation or by natural disasters such as droughts and floods. Comparative analyses of many famine situations prove, however, that neither overpopulation nor natural disasters are sufficient explanations for famine (Sen 1981). Calculations of world food supply in relation to population prove that there is enough food produced every year to feed the world's population. Furthermore, although natural factors are often catalysts of famine, they do not always cause famine.

Hurricane Andrew of 1992 devastated much of Florida but state and federal agencies rushed aid to the stricken area. In Louisiana and Mississippi, the hurricanes of 2005 caused many deaths, massive loss of private and commercial property, and displacement of thousands of people. But they did not cause a famine. Anthony Oliver-Smith, an anthropologist who specializes

Homeless children rest by a storefront grate in Ho Chi Minh City, Vietnam. ■ *Consider how the entitlement system affected children under pure socialism, compared to the current transition to a more capitalist system.* (Source: Edward Keller III)

in disasters, has said that there is no such thing as a purely natural disaster (2002). His point is that culture always shapes the patterns of suffering and loss. The social structure of suffering following the 2005 hurricanes in Louisiana and Mississippi had clear lines according to "race"/ethnicity and class, with low-income African Americans being the hardest hit in every respect.

Entitlement analysis can help improve the effectiveness of humanitarian aid during famines and other crises (Harragin 2004). During the famine in southern Sudan in 1988 (see Map 16.7, p. 443), relief workers failed to understand the local cultural pattern of sharing, which extends to the last cup of rice. As food supplies decreased, local people continued to share whatever food was available. The result was that many people were surviving, but barely. When the food supply declined even more, the social safety net was unable to stretch further, and suddenly hundreds of people were dying. If relief workers had known about the culture of sharing until death, they might have been able to forecast the breaking point before it happened and to bring in food aid sooner.

Three Consumption Microcultures

This section provides examples of three consumption microcultures: class, gender, and "race." Microcultures have distinct entitlement patterns, related levels of health and welfare, and identity associated with consumption. Depending on the cultural context, social inequality may play an important role and have major effects on human welfare.

Class and the Game of Distinction in Israeli Birthday Parties Class differences, defined in terms of levels of income, are reflected in distinctive consumption patterns. Although class differences in consumption may seem too obvious to be worth studying, they constitute an important and growing area in anthropology.

A landmark study about consumer preferences, or "tastes," was conducted by a team of French researchers led by French anthropologist/sociologist Pierre Bourdieu (1984). They sent questionnaires to several thousand people, based on a national sample, and received 1,000 responses. Statistical analysis of the responses revealed clear class patterns in, for example, choice of favorite painters or pieces of music. Preferences corresponded with educational level and father's occupation. An overall pattern of *distance from necessity* in tastes and preferences characterized members of the educated upper classes, who were more likely to prefer abstract art. Their goal was to keep "necessity" at a distance. In comparison, the working classes were closer to "necessity," and they preferred realist art. Bourdieu provides the concept of the game of distinction in which people of the upper classes continually adjust their preferences to distance themselves from the lower classes, whereas members of the lower classes tend to adopt aspects of upper-class preferences in order to gain status.

Cross-culturally, events such as weddings, funerals, and children's birthday parties are often occasions requiring large expenditures that send messages about the status (real or aspired) of the hosts. Children's birthday parties are a less-studied topic but one with much potential, especially since such parties are becoming increasingly popular in cultures around the world. In Israel, children's birthday parties have recently become expensive events among middle-class and upper-class urbanites (Goldstein-Gidoni 2003). Parents hire birthday party professionals to create special themes. "Around the World" themes are popular, especially those drawing on Japanese, Spanish, South American, and Middle Eastern motifs. A current craze for Japanese culture, such as gardens and food, means that the Japanese theme is one of the most popular. "Around the World" birthday party themes are ostensibly to help the children learn about other places and people. At the same time, they make a statement about how cosmopolitan, well-off, and stylish the hosts are.

Not everyone, everywhere, buys into the game of distinction. Many individuals and wider social movements actively resist the spread of upper-class consumption patterns and promote alternative cultural practices.

Gender and Deadly Food in Papua New Guinea

Consumption patterns are often marked by gender and related to discrimination and inequality. Specific foods may be considered "men's food" or "women's food." Beverage consumption is often related to gender, too. In cultures where alcoholic beverages are consumed, the general pattern is that men drink more than women, and certain types of alcoholic beverages are more likely to be consumed by men or women. Gender may play into what are considered appropriate quantities of food.

An example of lethal gender inequalities in food consumption comes from highland Papua New Guinea (see Map 4.1). The story begins with the eruption of a mysterious disease, with the local name of *kuru,* among the Fore (pronounced FOR-AY), a horticultural people (Lindenbaum 1979). Between 1957 and 1977, about 2,500 people died of kuru. A marked gender pattern in the deaths emerged: Most victims were women. The first signs of kuru are shivering tremors, followed by a progressive loss of motor ability along with pain in the head and limbs. People with kuru could walk unsteadily at first but would later be unable to get up. Death occurred about a year after the first symptoms appeared.

American medical researchers revealed that kuru was a neurological disease. Australian cultural anthropologist Shirley Lindenbaum pinpointed the cultural cause of kuru: cannibalism. Kuru victims had eaten the flesh of deceased people who had died of kuru. Most of the kuru victims were women. Lindenbaum sought to explain the

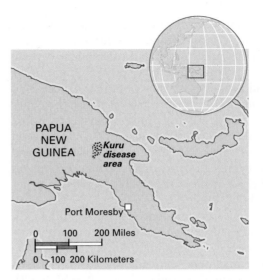

MAP 4.1 Location of the Kuru Epidemic in Papua New Guinea.

gender bias in the disease. She learned that among the Fore, it was considered acceptable to cook and eat the meat of a deceased person, although it was not a preferred food. The preferred source of animal protein is meat from pigs, and men receive preferential access to the best food. Fore women had begun to eat human flesh more often because of increased scarcity of pigs. Population density in the region had risen, more land was being cultivated, and forest areas had decreased. Pigs live in forest areas, so as their habitat became more restricted, their numbers declined. The Fore could not move to more pig-abundant areas because they were bounded on the east, west, and north sides by other groups. The south was a harsh and forbidding region. These factors, combined with the Fore's male-biased system of protein consumption, forced women to turn to the less-preferred protein source of human flesh. By eating the flesh, including brains, of kuru victims, they contracted the disease.

"Race" and Children's Shopping in New Haven

Throughout the world, in countries with "race"-based social categories, inequalities in consumption and quality of life exist, often in spite of anti-discrimination legislation. In the United States, racism and racial discrimination affect many areas of life from access to housing, neighborhood security and services, schooling, health, and whether or not a person is likely to have a taxi pass him or her by or be stopped by a police officer for speeding. Racial inequality between Black and White Americans has risen steadily since the 1970s in terms of income, wealth, and property ownership, especially house-ownership (Shapiro 2004:3–4). Those at the top of the income distribution have increased their share of the wealth most. The share of total income that goes to the top 1 percent of families is nearly the same size as the total income share of the bottom 40 percent.

How is this happening in a country supposedly dedicated to equality of opportunity? A large part of the answer lies in the simple fact that, in a capitalist system, inequality leads to more inequality through the transfer of wealth and property across generations. Those who have wealth and property are able to establish their children's wealth through college tuition payments, house down payments, and other financial gifts. The children of poor parents have to provide for their education and housing costs from their wages alone, a fact which makes it far less likely that they will be able to pursue higher education or buy a home.

Elizabeth Chin was a graduate student in anthropology at Yale University when she decided to do her dissertation research on consumption patterns among schoolchildren in a poor, African American neighborhood in New Haven, Connecticut (2001) (see Map 4.2). In terms of per capita income, Connecticut is the wealthiest state in the United States. It also harbors some of the most severe poverty and racial inequality in its major cities. Chin describes New Haven as a "patchwork of clearly delineated neighborhoods that can veer quite suddenly from the abjectly poor to the fabulously wealthy" (2001:vii). These zones are largely divided into White and Black groups who are fearful and suspicious of each other. During her research in "Newhallville," Chin found that the Black and White cultural worlds are clearly separate and deeply unequal. In the Black neighborhood, 50 percent of children age 5 and under were living in poverty.

Chin formed a relationship with one fifth-grade class of twenty-two students. She spent time in the classroom. She explored the neighborhood with some of the children, visited with them and their families in their homes, and accompanied them on shopping trips to the mall. The children are bombarded with media messages about consumption but they have little money to spend. Some receive an allowance for doing household chores, some receive small amounts of pocket money on an ad hoc basis, and some earn money from small-scale ventures such as a cucumber stand. They learn about the basics of household finances and the costs of daily life early on. Seeing their families strain every day to put meals on the table teaches them about the negative effects of overindulgence: "From divvying up the milk to figuring out where to sleep there is an emphasis on sharing and mutual obligation" (2001:5).

These practical lessons shape how the children spend their money when they go to the mall. Practicality and generosity guide their shopping choices. In order to learn about the children's decisions, Chin would give a child $20 and go with him or her to the mall. Most of the girls spent over half their money on gifts for family members, especially their mothers and grandmothers (2001:139). The girls knew their mothers' shoe sizes and clothing sizes. One boy, just before school was to start in the fall,

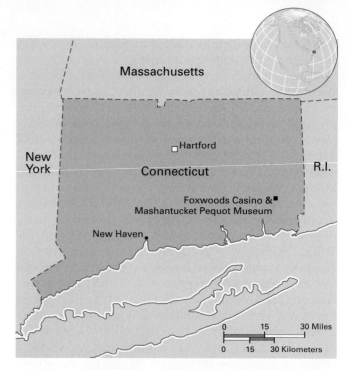

MAP 4.2   Connecticut, United States. In terms of per capita income, Connecticut is the wealthiest state in the United States. Its population of about 3.5 million includes a majority of Whites (76 percent), predominantly of Italian, Irish, and English descent. Blacks and Latinos constitute about 10 percent of the population each. Native Americans are 0.3 percent.

spent $10 on a T-shirt to wear on the first day of school, $6 on a pair of shorts, and the rest on school supplies: pencils, pens, notebook paper, and a binder (2001:135). In her two years of research, Chin never heard a Newhallville child nag a caretaker about buying him or her something or whine about personal consumption desires.

Birthday parties are rare events in Newhallville. The one birthday party Chin observed involved an $18 ice-cream cake. Birthday gifts are few. One girl received three gifts on her tenth birthday: a jumprope and a bingo game from her mother, wrapped in brown paper made from a grocery bag, and an inexpensive plastic toy from her grandmother (2001:72). There was no party, but her mother baked a chocolate cake for her.

Forbidden Consumption: Food Taboos

Cultural anthropologists have a long-standing interest in trying to explain culturally specific *food taboos,* or rules about prohibited foods. Cultural materialists and symbolic anthropologists disagree about why food taboos exist.

What Cultural Materialism Says

Cultural materialist Marvin Harris asks why there are Jewish and Muslim taboos on eating pig when pig meat is so enthusiastically consumed in many other parts of the world (1974). He says, "Why should gods so exalted as Jahweh and Allah have bothered to condemn a harmless and even laughable beast whose flesh is relished by the greater part of mankind?" (1974:36). Harris proposes that we consider the role of environmental factors during early Hebrew times and the function of this prohibition in terms of its fit to the local ecology:

> Within the overall pattern of this mixed farming and pastoral complex, the divine prohibition of pork constituted a sound ecological strategy. The pig is thermodynamically ill-adapted to the hot, dry climate of the Negev, the Jordan Valley, and the other lands of the Bible and the Koran. Compared to cattle, goats, and sheep, the pig has an inefficient system for regulating its body temperature. Despite the expression "To sweat like a pig," it has recently been proved that pigs can't sweat at all. (1974:41–42)

Raising pigs in this context would be a luxury. On the other hand, in "pig-loving" cultures of Southeast Asia and the Pacific, climatic factors, including temperature, humidity, and the presence of forest cover (good for pigs) promote raising pigs. There, pigs offer an important protein source that complements the major root crops: yams, sweet potatoes, and taro. Harris acknowledges that not all religiously sanctioned food practices can be explained ecologically and that food practices often serve to communicate and promote social identity. But analysis of food consumption should always consider ecological and material factors of production as basic.

Preparation for a feast in the highlands of Papua New Guinea where people place much value on consuming roasted pig meat. ■ *What are the high-status foods in your cultural world(s)? Propose a cultural materialist and a meaning-centered theory for a food item of your choice.* (Source: © David Austen/Stock Boston LLC)

THINKING OUTSIDE THE BOX

YOU HAVE INVITED Jesus, the Buddha, Mohammad, and Moses to dinner. What are you serving?

What Symbolic Anthropologists Say

Symbolic anthropologist Mary Douglas argues, in contrast to Harris, that what people eat has less to do with the material conditions of life (the environment or hunger) than with what food means and how food communicates meaning and identity (1966). For Douglas, people's emic categories about food provide a mental map of the world and people's place in it. *Anomalies,* or things that do not fit into culturally defined categories, become reminders to people of moral problems or things to avoid.

Douglas uses a symbolic approach in examining food categories and anomalies as laid out in the Old Testament book of Leviticus. One rule says that people may eat animals with cloven hoofs and that chew a cud. On the basis of this rule, animals that do not satisfy both criteria are anomalies, and such animals are considered unclean and are taboo as food. These anomalies include camels, pigs, and hares. A pig, for example, has cloven hoofs, but it does not chew a cud. In the interpretation of Douglas, the food rules in Leviticus are a symbolic system defining completeness and purity (the animals one can eat) in contrast to incompleteness and impurity (the animals one cannot eat). By extension, she argues, people who know these rules and follow them are constantly reminded of God's perfection, completeness, and purity. When people follow these rules, they communicate their identity as pure and godly to other people. Thus, according to Douglas, food choices are not about the nutritional content of the food; rather, they have to do with symbols and meaning. She downplays studying the "practical" aspects of food because, she says, that distracts analysts from studying the meaning of food.

Anthropologists, no matter which perspective they favor about food taboos, recognize that there is more to food than just eating. Douglas emphasizes the importance of food rules as codes, ways of communicating meaning, and this interpretation is clearly valid. Harris says that economic and political aspects of food choices must be considered for a full understanding.

Culture and Exchange

Exchange is the transfer of something that may be material or immaterial between at least two persons, groups, or institutions. Cultural anthropologists have done much

Everyday Anthropology

THE RULES OF HOSPITALITY

In much of the Middle East, where women spend most of their time in the domestic domain, social visits among women are eagerly anticipated and carefully planned events with complex rules about what foods and drinks should be served (Wikan 1982). In Oman, when women go outside the home, they wear head veils, face masks, and full-length gowns. Their main social activity consists of visits to other women in their homes. A typical visit involves sitting, chatting, and eating snacks.

Social etiquette dictates what should be served and how. Coffee and dates are the traditional entertainment foods offered to close neighbors. Biscuits (cookies), inexpensive caramels, and popcorn are increasingly favored snacks. The number of dishes offered is important. Between neighbors who interact on a daily basis a single dish is typical. All other visitors should be offered at least two plates, with different contents, or else the hostess will be considered stingy. In the case of many guests, the number of plates must be increased, with a minimum of four plates, and the variety of snacks must be greater. If a hostess wishes to honor one or two guests, she may offer them three or four plates of different snacks. Another rule of visitor etiquette requires that approximately half of the food served should be left for the hostess' household (1982:130–132).

Cooked food, such as meat and sweets, is served when one entertains guests at weddings, seasonal feasts, and burials. With cooked food, the hosts may never eat with their guests: "Even if the consequence is that the guest must eat all alone, in a separate room, it would be disrespectful to arrange it otherwise" (1982:133).

A Bedu (Bedouin) woman of Muscat, Oman, wearing traditional face covering. ■ (Source: © Charles O. Cecil)

FOOD FOR THOUGHT

- How do these Omani rules of hospitality resemble or contrast with rules of hospitality you know?

research on gifts and other forms of exchange, starting with Malinowski's work on the kula (review Culturama, Chapter 2, p. 39) and Boas's research on potlatching. In all economic systems, individuals and groups exchange goods and services with others, so exchange is a cultural universal. But variation exists in what is exchanged, how goods are exchanged, when exchange takes place, and the meaning of exchange.

What Is Exchanged?

The items that people exchange range from seashells to stocks and bonds and may be purely utilitarian (see Figure 4.2). Items of exchange may carry meanings and have a history, or "social life," of their own, as prized kula items do (Appadurai 1986).

In contemporary industrial societies, money is the major item of exchange, and such economies are referred to as *monetized*. In *nonmarket economies,* money plays a less important role, and time, labor, and goods are prominent exchange items. As nonmarket economies are connected, through globalization, they are confronted with the (to them) peculiar and mysterious meaning of Western money. Often, they localize the meanings of money, by treating particular bills as more special than others. In many cultures, money has completely replaced other valued items of exchange, such as shell wealth in Papua New Guinea.

Nonmonetary exchange exists in contemporary industrial societies, too. Hosting dinner parties, exchanging gifts at holiday times, and sharing a bag of potato chips with a friend are examples of common forms of nonmonetary exchange. Some scholars would even include caresses, kisses, loyalty, and glances (Blau 1964).

Omani biotech scientist, Ms. Wahida al-Amri, at work in her lab in the Omani Marine Science and Fisheries Center. ■ *Assume you are going to Oman for a semester abroad. What should you know about the culture before you go?* (Source: © Charles O. Cecil)

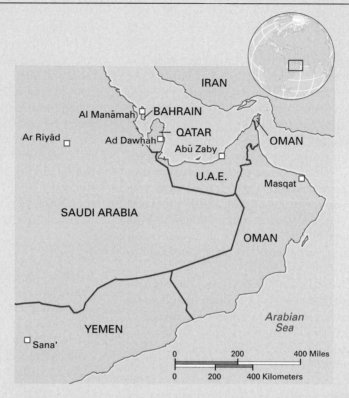

MAP 4.3 Oman. The Sultanate of Oman is mainly a vast desert plain with a hot and dry climate. The population of nearly 3 million includes over 500,000 non-nationals who are immigrant laborers. The economy is based mainly on crude oil. The major religion is Ibādī Islam, a more liberal version of Islam than Sunni or Shi'a Islam. Arabic is the official language, with English a widely spoken second language. Several local dialects are spoken including the Omani dialect of Arabic.

Material Goods

Cross-culturally, food is one of the most common exchange goods both in everyday life and on ritual occasions. Daily meals involve some form of exchange, as do most ceremonies and rituals. In many cultures, arranging a marriage involves many stages of food gifts and countergifts exchanged between the families of the couple. Wedding exchanges among the Nias of northern

Category	Selected Examples
Material Goods	Food to family and group members Gifts for special occasions such as weddings Money
Nonmaterial Goods	Myths, stories, rituals Time, labor
People	Offspring in marriage Slavery

FIGURE 4.2 Items of Exchange

Sumatra, Indonesia (see Map 8.3, p. 209), provide an illustration of a complex set of exchanges. From the betrothal to the actual marriage, a scheduled sequence of events occurs at which culturally stipulated food and other gifts are exchanged between the families of the bride and groom (Beatty 1992).

At the first meeting between the families, when the prospective groom expresses his interest in a betrothal, he and his party visit the bride's house and are fed. The guests receive the lower jaw of a pig (the portion of honor), and they take away with them raw and cooked portions of the pig for the father of the groom-to-be (1992:121). Within the next week or two, the prospective groom brings a gift of three to twelve pigs to confirm the engagement. He returns the container used for the pig meat given to him on the previous visit, filled with a certain kind of nut. The groom gives more pigs and gold as the major gift to seal the marriage. For many years following the wedding, the two families continue to exchange gifts.

On a more everyday level, exchanges of food and beverages are important in friendships. Among friends, food exchanges involve their own, largely unconscious rules of etiquette (see Everyday Anthropology box).

Exchanging alcoholic beverages is an important feature of many communal, ritual events in Latin America. In a highland village in Ecuador, the San Juan fiesta is the high point of the year (Barlett 1980). The fiesta consists of four or five days during which small groups of celebrants move from house to house, dancing and drinking. The anthropologist reports on the event:

> I joined the groups consisting of the president of the community and the elected alcaldes (councilmen and police), who were accompanied by their wives, a few friends, and some children. We met each morning for a hearty breakfast at one house, began drinking there, and then continued eating and drinking in other homes throughout the day and into the evening. . . . Some people drink for only one or two days, others prefer to make visits mainly at night, while some people drink day and night for four days. (1980:118–119)

Guests who drink at someone's house will later serve their former hosts alcohol in return. Functional theorists (review Chapter 1) would view this ritual exchange as contributing to social cohesion.

Symbolic Goods

Intangible valuables such as myths (sacred stories) and rituals (sacred practices) may be exchanged in ways similar to material goods. In the Balgo Hills region of Aus-

tralia (see Map 4.4), long-standing exchange networks transfer myths and rituals among regionally dispersed groups of women (Poirier 1992). The women may keep important narratives and rituals for a limited time and then must pass them on to other groups. One is the Tjarada, a love-magic ritual with an accompanying narrative. The Tjarada came to the women of Balgo Hills from the north. They kept it for about fifteen years and then passed it on to another group in a ceremony that lasted for three days. During the time that the Balgo Hills women were custodians of the Tjarada, they incorporated some new elements into it. These elements are retained even after its transfer to the next group. Thus, the Tjarada contains bits of local identity of each group that has had it. A sense of community and responsibility thereby develops and is sustained among the groups that have held the Tjarada.

Labor

In labor-sharing groups, people contribute labor to other people on a regular basis (for seasonal agricultural work such as harvesting) or on an irregular basis (in the event of a crisis such as the need to rebuild a barn damaged by fire). Labor-sharing groups are part of what has been called a "moral economy" because no one keeps formal records on how much any family puts in or takes out. Instead, accounting is socially regulated. The group has a sense of being a moral community based on years of trust and sharing. In Amish communities of North America (see Culturama, Chapter 5, p. 122), sharing labor is a central part of life. When a family needs a new barn that requires group labor, a barn-raising party is called. Many families show up to help. Adult men provide manual labor, and adult women provide food for the event.

Money

For most of humanity's existence, people did not purchase things. They collected or made things they needed themselves, shared, or exchanged items for other things. The invention of money is recent, only a few thousand years ago. **Money** refers to a medium of exchange that can be used for a variety of goods (Godelier 1971:53). Money exists cross-culturally in such diverse forms as shells, salt, cattle, furs, cocoa beans, and iron hoes.

Modern money, in the form of coins and paper bills, has the advantages of being portable, divisible, uniform, and recognizable (Shipton 2001). On the other hand, modern money is vulnerable to economic changes such as inflation, which reduce its value. The use of modern

---

money: a medium of exchange that can be used for a variety of goods.

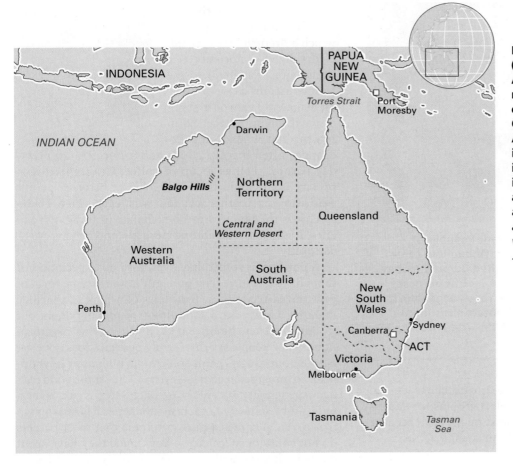

MAP 4.4 The Balgo Hills (Wirrimanu) Region in Western Australia. The Balgo Hills community is located on the northern edge of the Tanami and Great Sandy Deserts. One of Australia's most isolated indigenous desert settlements, it nevertheless has a flourishing art center. Balgo paintings and glass are highly sought after by collectors. ■ *To learn about Balgo art and artists, visit www.aboriginalartonline.com/regions/balgo.*

money is spreading throughout the world. Nonmonetary cultures, however, often adopt modern money in limited ways. They may prohibit its use in religious exchanges or in life-cycle rituals such as marriages. All forms of money, even modern money, are symbolic. They have meaning to the user, and they are associated with the user's identity and sense of self. The color and design of a credit card, for example, may signify status, such as "platinum" for the biggest spenders. As the European Union was forming, lengthy discussion was devoted to what the new currency would look like. As e-money becomes increasingly used, it will be interesting to see what kinds of meaning are attached to it.

People

Exchange in human beings relegates humans to objects. Throughout history, some people have been able to gain control of other people and treat them as items of exchange, as in slavery and human trafficking. The enslavement of people from many regions of Africa during European colonialism from the fifteenth to nineteenth centuries stands as one of the most heinous processes of treating humans as commodities in the full light of day, with no legal sanctions involved for slave traders or own-

ers. This process cruelly transformed thousands of people into property that could be bought and sold, used and abused, and even murdered.

A long-standing debate in anthropology concerns women as objects of exchange in marriage. Lévi-Strauss proposed many years ago that the exchange of women between men is one of the most basic forms of exchange among humans (1969 [1949]). He based his assertion on the universality of some sort of *incest taboo*, which he defined as a rule preventing a man from marrying or cohabiting with his mother or sister (Chapter 8 provides the current definition). Such a rule, he says, is the logic driving the exchange of women among men: "The fact that I can obtain a wife is, in the final analysis, the consequence of the fact that a brother or father has given her up" (1969:62). Thus, the avoidance of incest forces men to develop exchange networks with other men and, by extension, leads to the emergence of social solidarity more widely. For Lévi-Strauss, the incest taboo provides the foundation for human social organization.

Feminist anthropologists say that this theory overlooks much ethnographic evidence to the contrary. Men do not have rights over women in many foraging societies; instead, women make their own choices about partners (Rubin 1975). In many horticultural and agricultural

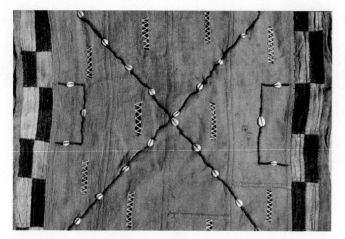

This raffia cloth, from the Democratic Republic of Congo, is woven from palm fibers. Throughout central Africa, raffia cloth functions as limited-purpose money, or money that can be used only for specific purposes, such as marriage or compensation for wrongdoing. It cannot be used for commercial transactions such as buying food, a house, or a car. ■ (Source: J. Marshall—Tribaleye Images/Alamy)

THINKING OUTSIDE THE BOX PROPOSE SOME EXAMPLES of what might qualify as a "pure gift."

societies of Southeast Asia, men do not exchange women (Peletz 1987). Instead, women select grooms for daughters. This pattern turns Lévi-Strauss on his head because it involves women organizing the exchange of men.

Modes of Exchange

Parallel to the two contrasting modes of consumption described earlier (minimalism and consumerism) two distinct modes of exchange can be delineated (see Figure 4.3). They are:

- **Balanced exchange:** a system of transfers in which the goal is either immediate or eventual balance in value.
- **Unbalanced exchange:** a system of transfers in which one party attempts to make a profit.

Balanced Exchange

The category of balanced exchange contains two subcategories based on the social relationship of the two parties involved in the exchange and the degree to which a "return" is expected. **Generalized reciprocity** is a transaction that involves the least conscious sense of interest in material gain or thought of what might be received in return, and when. Such exchanges often involve goods and services of an everyday nature, such as a cup of coffee. Generalized reciprocity is the main form of exchange between people who know each other well and trust each other. Therefore, it is the main form of exchange in foraging societies. It is also found among close kin and friends cross-culturally.

A **pure gift** is something given with no expectation or thought of a return. The pure gift is an extreme form of generalized reciprocity. Examples of a pure gift include donating money for a food drive, or making donations to famine relief, blood banks, and religious organizations. Some people say that a truly pure gift does not exist because one always gains something, no matter how difficult to measure, in giving—even if it is just the good feeling of generosity. Parental care of children is said to be a pure gift by some, but others do not agree. Those who say that parental care is a pure gift argue that most parents do not consciously calculate how much they have spent on their children with the intention of "getting it back" later on. Those who do not consider parental care a pure gift say that even if the "costs" are not consciously calculated, parents have unconscious expectations about what their children will "return" to them, whether the return is material (care in old age) or immaterial (making the parent feel proud).

Expected reciprocity is the exchange of approximately equally valued goods or services, usually between people of roughly equal social status. The exchange may occur simultaneously between both parties, or it may involve an understanding about the time period within which the exchange will be completed. This aspect of timing contrasts with generalized reciprocity, in which there is no fixed time limit for the return. In expected reciprocity, if the second party fails to complete the exchange, the rela-

---

balanced exchange: a system of transfers in which the goal is either immediate or eventual equality in value.
unbalanced exchange: a system of transfers in which one party seeks to make a profit.
generalized reciprocity: exchange involving the least conscious sense of interest in material gain or thought of what might be received in return.

pure gift: something given with no expectation or thought of a return.
expected reciprocity: an exchange of approximately equally valued goods or services, usually between people roughly equal in social status.
redistribution: a form of exchange that involves one person collecting goods or money from many members of a group who then, at a later time and at a public

event, "returns" the pooled goods to everyone who contributed.
market exchange: the buying and selling of commodities under competitive conditions in which the forces of supply and demand determine value.
trade: the formalized exchange of one thing for another according to set standards of value.

FIGURE 4.3 Keeping Track of Exchange

	Balanced Exchange			Unbalanced Exchange	
	Generalized Reciprocity	**Expected Reciprocity**	**Redistribution**	**Market Exchange**	**Theft, Exploitation**
Actors	Kin, friends	Trading partners	Leader and pooling group	Buyers/sellers	Nonkin, nonfriends, unknown
Return	Not calculated or expected	Expected at some time	Feast and give-away	Immediate payment	No return
Example	Buying coffee for a friend	Kula	Moka	Internet shopping	Shoplifting

tionship will break down. Balanced reciprocity is less personal than generalized reciprocity and, according to Western definitions, more "economic."

The kula is an example of a system of expected reciprocity (review Culturama, Chapter 2, p. 39). Men exchange necklaces and armlets, giving them to their exchange partners after keeping them for a while. Partners include neighbors as well as people on far-away islands who are visited via long canoe voyages on high seas. Trobriand men are distinguished by the particular armlets and necklaces that they exchange, and certain armlets and necklaces are more prestigious than others. One cannot keep one's trade items for long because the kula code dictates that "to possess is great, but to possess is to give." Generosity is the essence of goodness, and stinginess is the most despised vice. Kula exchanges should involve items of equivalent value. If a man trades a very valuable necklace with his partner, he expects to receive in return a very valuable armlet as a *yotile* (equivalent gift). At the time, if one's partner does not possess an equivalent item, he may have to give a *basi* (intermediary gift). The basi stands as a token of good faith until a proper return gift can be given. The *kudu* ("clinching gift") will come later and balance the original gift. The equality of exchange ensures a strong bond between the trading partners and is a statement of trust. When a man arrives in an area where it may be dangerous because of previous raids or warfare, he can count on having a friend to give him hospitality.

Redistribution is a form of expected reciprocity in which one person collects goods or money from many members of a group and provides a social return at a later time. At a public event, even several years later, the organizer "returns" the pooled goods to everyone who contributed by sponsoring a generous feast. Compared to the two-way pattern of exchange involved in reciprocity, redistribution involves some "centricity." It contains the possibility of inequality because what is returned may not always equal, in a material sense, what each individual

contributed. The pooling group may continue to exist, however, because it benefits from the leadership skills of the person who mobilizes contributions. If a neighboring group threatens a raid, people turn to their redistributive leader for political leadership (discussed further in Chapter 10).

Unbalanced Exchange

Market exchange, a prominent form of unbalanced exchange, is the buying and selling of commodities under competitive conditions in which the forces of supply and demand determine value and the seller seeks to make a profit (Dannhaeuser 1989:222). In market transactions, the seller and buyer may or may not have a personal relationship. They may or may not be social equals. Their exchange is not likely to generate social bonding. Many market transactions take place in a *marketplace*, a physical location in which buying and selling occur. The market system evolved from other, less formal contexts of **trade,** formalized exchange of one thing for another according to set standards of value.

The market system is associated with regional specialization in producing particular goods and trade between regions. Certain products are often identified with a town or region. In Oaxaca, Mexico (see Map 5.4, p. 128), some villages are known for their blankets, pottery, stone grinders, rope, and chili peppers (Plattner 1989). In Morocco, the city of Fez (see Map 5.3, p. 127) is famous for its blue-glazed pottery, whereas the Berber people of the Atlas Mountains are known for their fine wool blankets and rugs. Specialization develops with illegal commodities, too. For example, Jamaican marijuana is well known for its high quality, and many tourists travel to Jamaica, especially the Negril beach area, in order to buy this product.

Marketplaces range from informal, small stands that appear in the morning and disappear at night, to huge multistoried shopping centers. One variety found in

The weekly market in Pistoia, a small town near Firenze (Florence), Italy, is set up each Saturday next to the main church. According to government regulations, all food items are supposed to have labels that identify where they were grown. ■ (Source: Barbara Miller and Bernard Wood)

In China, many marketers are women. These two women display their wares in a permanent food market in a city about an hour's drive from Shanghai. ■
Assume you are at this market and would like to cook a chicken for dinner. What steps do you take to make that happen? (Source: Barbara Miller)

many parts of the world is a *periodic market,* a site for buying and selling that takes place on a regular basis (for example, monthly) in a particular location but without a permanent physical structure. Sellers appear with their goods and set up a table with perhaps an awning. In contrast, *permanent markets* are built structures situated in fixed locations. Marketplaces, however, are more than just places for buying and selling. They involve social interactions and even performances. Sellers solicit customers, shoppers meet and chat, government officials drop by, religious organizations may hold services, and traditional healers may treat toothaches. The particularities of how markets are structured, spatially and socially, and how culture shapes market transactions are rich topics for ethnographic research.

Ted Bestor conducted research over many years in Tsukiji (pronounced tsee-kee-jee, with all syllables equally stressed), the world's largest fish market, located in Tokyo (2004). Tsukiji connects large-scale corporations that supply most of the seafood with small-scale family-run firms that continue to dominate Tokyo's retail food trade. Bestor describes the layout of the huge market, with inner and outer sections as a basic division. The outer market attracts younger, more hip shoppers looking for unusual, trendy gourmet items and a more authentic-seeming shopping experience. It contains sushi bars, noodle stalls, knife shops, and chopstick dealers, as well as temples and graveyards. The inner market contains eleven fresh produce market subdivisions. The seafood section by far overshadows the "veggie" markets in size and transaction level. It is subdivided into several main buildings where auctions occur, activities such as deliveries and dispatches take place, and rows of retail stalls serve 14,000 customers each morning. Bestor gained insight into the verbally coded conversations between experienced buyers and sellers in the stalls that are more likely to yield a better price than what an inexperienced first-time buyer will get. Stalls do not typically post prices, so buyers and sellers have to negotiate them. The verbal codes involve phrases such as "morning mist on a white beach" which, depending on the number of syllables in the phrase, conveys a price offer.

American-style shopping malls may appear to be depersonalized marketplaces, but much social and cultural life goes on in malls, especially among young people who go there to meet their friends. Shopping on the Internet is the latest form of consumption, and one that poses a research challenge for anthropologists because it is "site-less."

Other Forms of Unbalanced Exchange

Several forms of unbalanced exchange other than market transactions exist. In extreme instances, no social relationship is involved; in others, sustained unequal relationships are maintained over time between people. These forms include taking something with no expectation of giving any return. They can occur in any mode of production but are most likely to be found in large-scale societies where more options (other than face-to-face) for balanced exchange exist.

Gambling *Gambling*, or gaming, is the attempt to make a profit by playing a game of chance in which a certain item of value is staked in hopes of acquiring the much larger return that one receives if one wins the game. If one loses, that which was staked is lost. Gambling is an ancient practice and is common cross-culturally. Ancient forms of gambling include dice throwing and card playing. Investing in the stock market can be considered a form of gambling, as can gambling of many sorts through the Internet. Although gambling may seem an odd category within unbalanced exchange, its goals of making a profit seem to justify its placement here. The fact that gambling within "high" capitalism is on the rise justifies anthropological attention to it. In fact, some scholars have referred to the present stage of Western capitalism as *casino capitalism*, given the propensity of investors to play risky games in the stock market (Klima 2002).

Native American gambling establishments in the United States have mushroomed in recent years. Throughout the United States, Native American casinos are so financially successful that they are perceived as an economic threat to many state lotteries. The Pequot Indians of Connecticut (see Map 4.2, p. 100), a small tribe of around 200 people, now operate the most lucrative gaming establishment in the world, Foxwoods Resort and Casino, established in 1992 (Eisler 2001). The story of this success hangs on the creativity of one man: Richard "Skip" Hayward who became the chief of his now-rich tribe. An unemployed shipbuilder in the 1970s, he granted his grandmother's wish that he revive the declining tribe. Hayward used the legal system governing Native Americans to his advantage and forged links with powerful people such as Malaysian industrialist Lim Goh Tong and President Bill Clinton (to whose campaign the Pequot donated half a million dollars).

Through gaming, many other Native American groups have become successful capitalists. An important question is what impact casinos will have on Native American people (see Lessons Applied box).

Theft *Theft* is taking something with no expectation or thought of returning anything to the original owner for it. It is the logical opposite of a pure gift. Anthropologists have neglected the study of theft, no doubt a reasonable response because theft is an illegal activity that is difficult to study and might involve danger.

Workers at Tsukiji, the world's largest fish market in Tokyo, transport frozen tuna on hand carts for the upcoming auction. ■ *For a research project, learn more about Ted Bestor's research on Tsukiji.* (Source: Bob Krist/CORBIS)

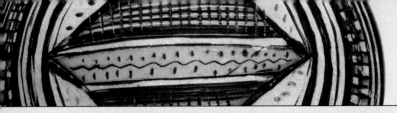

Lessons Applied

EVALUATING INDIAN GAMING IN CALIFORNIA

In 2006, the Center for California Native Nations (CCNN) at the University of California at Riverside released an evaluation of the effects of Indian gaming in California (Spilde Contreras 2006). Kate Spilde Contreras, applied cultural anthropologist, directed the multidisciplinary team that included anthropologists, political scientists, economists, and historians.

The research objective was to evaluate the social and economic effects of Indian gaming operations on tribal and local governments in California. The study relies mainly on public data, especially the 1990 and 2000 U.S. Censuses, to supply a "before" and "after" picture during the initial growth phase of Indian gaming in the state. To learn about more recent changes, the research team conducted surveys of tribal and local government officials and in-depth case studies of individual tribal governments.

Findings indicate two important factors that shape the effects of Indian gaming in California: gaming establishments are owned by tribal governments, and gaming establishments are located on existing tribal trust lands. Therefore, gaming revenues support community and government activities of the tribal communities, and employment generation is localized within the tribal communities.

Indian reservations in California are more economically heterogeneous than elsewhere in the United States.

Since the development of gaming, it similarly has a larger inequality across gaming and nongaming reservations than in the rest of the country. By 2000, the fastest average income growth on California reservations occurred on gaming reservations. A policy response to this situation is a tribal-state gaming contract, the Revenue Sharing Trust Fund (RSTF) that provides for sharing of gaming revenue with nongaming communities.

Spilde Contreras's team also considered the effects on gaming beyond the reservation. They found that areas within ten miles of gaming reservations experienced significant employment increases, greater income growth, and more educational expansion than those farther away. Given the fact that reservations in California are located in the poorest regions, this location effect is progressive.

Although the income and other effects of gaming in California are clearly substantial for Indians and their neighbors, Spilde Contreras points to the large gaps that still exist between conditions on Indian reservations and those for most Americans.

FOOD FOR THOUGHT

- Consider the development of Native American casinos from the theoretical perspective of structure versus agency. (Review the discussion of these perspectives in Chapter 1.)

One rare study of theft focused on food stealing by children in West Africa (Bledsoe 1983). During fieldwork among the Mende people of Sierra Leone (see Map 6.3, p. 160), Caroline Bledsoe learned that children in town stole fruits such as mangoes, guavas, and oranges from neighborhood trees. Bledsoe at first dismissed cases of food stealing as rare exceptions, but then she realized that she "rarely walked through town without hearing shouts of anger from an adult and cries of pain from a child being whipped for stealing food" (1983:2). Deciding to look into children's food stealing more closely, she asked several children to keep diaries. Their writings were dominated by themes of *tiefing*, the local term for stealing. Fostered children, who are temporarily placed in the care of friends or relatives, do more food tiefing than children living with their birth families do. Such food stealing can be seen as children's attempts to compensate for their less-than-adequate food shares in their foster homes.

Stealing as a conscious attempt to alter an unfair entitlement system underlies an analysis of the looting that occurred in Los Angeles in 1992 following the announcement of the Rodney King verdict (Fiske 1994). This looting was an outcome of the economic inequities faced by the African American community of South Central Los Angeles.

Between 1982 and 1989, 131 factories closed in LA with the loss of 124,000 jobs. . . . The jobs that were lost were ones that disproportionately employed African Americans . . . in the four years before 1982, South Central, the traditional industrial core of LA, lost 70,000 blue-collar jobs. In Black eyes, this pattern is produced not by a raceless free market, but by racism encoded into economics: To them the 50 percent Black male unemployment in South Central does not look like the result of neutral, let alone natural, economic laws. (1994:469–470)

How is this context related to exchange? One interpretation is that the looting expressed deep-seated resentment about economic discrimination. It was a form of political protest. The media's use of the word *looting* linked the uprising to the domain of crime, leaving prison as the only solution. Framing the uprising as a law-and-order issue diverted the public's attention from its roots in severe economic discrimination.

Much theft worldwide is motivated by greed. Cultural anthropologists, for obvious reasons, have not done research on high-level theft involving expensive commodities such as drugs, gems, and art, nor have they examined corporate financial malpractice as a form of theft. Given the ethical principle of informed consent, it is highly unlikely that any anthropologist would be given permission to study such criminal activity, even if the researcher was willing to risk his or her life by entering such dangerous domains.

Exploitation *Exploitation,* or getting something of greater value for less in return, is a form of extreme and persistent unbalanced exchange. Slavery is a form of exploitation in which people's labor power is appropriated without their consent and with no recompense for its value. Slavery is rare among foraging, horticultural, and pastoralist societies. Social relationships that involve sustained unequal exchange do exist between members of different social groups that, unlike pure slavery, involve no overt coercion and entail a certain degree of return by the dominant member to the subdominant member. Some degree of covert compulsion or dependence is likely to be present, however, in order for relationships of unequal exchange to endure.

Relationships between the Efe, who are "pygmy" foragers, and the Lese, who are farmers, in the Democratic Republic of Congo (formerly Zaire) exemplify sustained unequal exchange (Grinker 1994) (see Map 4.5). The Lese live in small villages. The Efe are seminomadic and live in temporary camps near Lese villages. Men of each group maintain long-term, hereditary exchange partnerships with each other. The Lese give cultivated foods and iron to the Efe, and the Efe give meat, honey, and other forest goods to the Lese.

Each Efe partner is considered a member of the "house" of his Lese partner, although he lives separately. Their main link is the exchange of food items, a system conceptualized by the Lese not as trade but as sharing of co-produced goods by partners living in a single unit. Evidence of inequality exists, however, in these relationships, with the Lese having the advantage. The Efe provide much-wanted meat to the Lese, but this role gives them no status. Rather, it is the giving of cultivated foods by the Lese to the Efe that conveys status. Another area of inequality is marital and sexual relationships. Lese men may marry Efe women, and their children are considered Lese. Efe men, however, cannot marry Lese women.

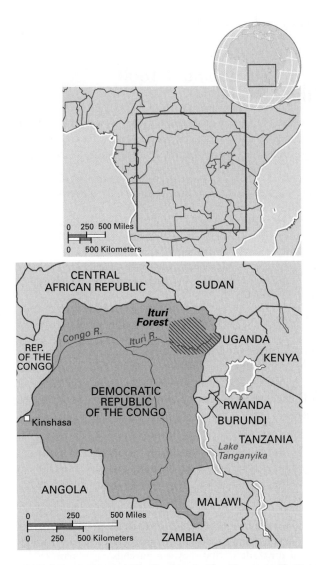

MAP 4.5 Lese and Efe Region in the Democratic Republic of Congo. The Lese and Efe live in the Ituri Forest, a dense tropical rainforest in the northern part of the Congo River Basin. Cultural Survival supports the Ituri Forest Peoples Fund which promotes the health and education of Efe foragers and Lese farmers. ■ *Go to the Internet to learn more about the projects of the Ituri Forest Peoples Fund.*

Changing Patterns of Consumption and Exchange

Powerful market forces controlled by the core countries are the main factors affecting changing patterns of consumption and exchange. Local cultures, though, variously adopt and adapt globalizing products and their meanings. Sometimes they resist them outright. This section presents examples of change in consumption in the Amazon and the former USSR and two trends in exchange in the United States. The last section returns to the potlatch.

Sugar, Salt, and Steel Tools in the Amazon

Katherine Milton, a biological anthropologist, has studied the nutritional effects of Western contact on the consumption patterns and health of indigenous foragers in the Brazilian Amazon. She comments:

> Despite the way their culture traditionally eschews possessions, forest-living people embrace manufactured goods with amazing enthusiasm. They seem to appreciate instantly the efficacy of a steel machete, ax, or cooking pot. It is love at first sight. . . . There are accounts of Indian groups or individuals who have turned their backs on manufactured goods, but such people are the exception. (1992:40)

The attraction to Western goods has its roots in the early decades of the twentieth century, when the Brazilian government sought to "pacify" Amazonian groups by placing cooking pots, machetes, axes, and steel knives along trails. This technique proved so successful that it is still used to "contact" remote groups. According to Milton,

> Once a group has been drawn into the pacification area, all its members are presented with various trade goods—standard gifts include metal cooking pots, salt, matches, machetes, knives, axes, cloth hammocks, T-shirts, and shorts. . . . Once the Indians have grown accustomed to these new items, the next step is to teach them that these gifts will not be repeated. The Indians are now told that they must work to earn money or must manufacture goods for trade so that they can purchase new items.

Unable to contemplate returning to life without steel axes, the Indians begin to produce extra arrows or blowguns or hunt additional game or weave baskets beyond what they normally need so that this new surplus can be traded. Time that might, in the past, have been used for other tasks—subsistence activities, ceremonial events, or whatever—is now devoted to production of barter goods. (1992:40)

Adoption of Western foods has negatively affected the nutrition and health of indigenous Amazonian peoples. They have begun to use table salt and refined sugar. Previously, they consumed small quantities of salt made by burning certain leaves and collecting the ash, and sugar came from wild fruits, in the form of fructose. Sucrose, in contrast, tastes exceptionally sweet, and the Indians get hooked on it. Tooth decay, obesity, and diabetes are new and growing health risks. Milton comments, "The moment manufactured foods begin to intrude on the indigenous diet, health takes a downward turn" (1992:41).

Social Inequality in Russia and Eastern Europe

As the countries of the former Soviet Union entered the global market economy, income inequality within those countries grew dramatically. The new rich own mansions and Mercedes-Benz cars. The influx of Western goods, including sugared soft drinks and junk food, has been nicknamed "pepsistroika" by an anthropologist who did fieldwork in Moscow around the time of the transition to capitalism (Lempert 1996). Advertising messages encourage people to adopt new diets that include unhealthy amounts of rich food.

Skiers and snowboarders line up to ride the lift to the top of the Middle East's first indoor ski resort, Ski Dubai, at the Mall of the Emirates in Dubai. Ski Dubai is housed in one of the world's largest malls and features a snow park with a twin track bobsled ride and a ski slope with five runs. ∎
Plan a fantasy two-week trip to Dubai: How will you get there, where will you stay, where will you eat, what will you do, and how much will the trip cost? (Source: Stephanie Kuykendal/CORBIS)

A member of the Kayapo tribe of Brazil eats a popsicle during a break in a meeting of indigenous peoples to protest a dam-building project. Tooth decay, diabetes, and obesity are rising among indigenous peoples worldwide as a result of changing consumption patterns. ■ (Source: © Wilson Melo/CORBIS)

An upscale car dealer in Moscow uses a cell phone to communicate with customers. His car lot stands on what was a sports ground during the Soviet era. ■ *Conduct research on the social distribution of wealth in several post-Soviet countries.* (Source: © Caroline Penn/CORBIS)

From 1961 to 1988, consumption of calories, proteins, and fats in what are now Russia and Eastern Europe were above the level recommended by the World Health Organization and exceeded those of most middle-income countries worldwide (Cornia 1994). These countries had full employment and little income inequality, so the high consumption levels were widely shared. This is not to say that diets were perfect. Especially in urban areas and among lower-income groups, people's diets contained less good-quality meat, fruits, vegetables, and vegetable oils. People tended to overconsume cholesterol-heavy products (eggs and animal fats), sugar, salt, bread, and alcohol.

Income levels and consumption quality have fallen among the newly created poor. Now, there are two categories of poor people: the *ultra-poor* (those whose incomes are below the subsistence minimum, or between 25 and 35 percent of the average wage) and the *poor* (those whose incomes are above the subsistence minimum but below the social minimum, or between 35 and 50 percent of the average wage). The largest increases in

the number of ultra-poor occurred in Bulgaria, Poland, Romania, and Russia, where between 20 and 30 percent of the population are ultra-poor and another 20 to 40 percent are poor. Overall calorie and protein intake fell significantly. People in the ultra-poor category substitute less expensive sources of nutrients. They now consume more animal fats and starch, and less milk, animal proteins, vegetable oils, minerals, and vitamins. Rates of low-birthweight babies have risen in Bulgaria and Romania, reflecting the deterioration in maternal diets, and the rate of childhood anemia has risen dramatically in Russia.

Global Networks and Ecstasy in the United States

In the late 1990s, a sharp increase in the use of ecstasy occurred in the United States (Agar and Reisinger 2003). Ecstasy, or MDMA (an abbreviation for its long chemical name), is an illicit drug that produces a high without, apparently, leading to clinical dependence. Fieldwork and interviews in Baltimore, Maryland, revealed that ecstasy use "took off" in the late 1990s as the "up and coming" drug of choice among youth. As one research participant commented: "A lot of people I know like rolling, taking a pill of ecstasy and going to like a club or going to a school dance. I mean, alcohol is up and coming among like teenagers, like it's always been, but I think ecstasy's making a pretty powerful fight" (2003:2).

Official statistics confirmed this rise: In 1998, 10 percent of Baltimore County high school seniors reported that they had tried ecstasy; in 2001, the number had increased to nearly 20 percent. Nationwide statistics on reported use, arrests of distributors, and numbers of MDMA-related seizures reveal a similar pattern of

Culturama

The Kwakwaka'wakw of Canada

Several Northern First Nations recently adopted the name Kwakwaka'wakw to refer to a cluster of twenty linguistically related groups of Canada's Pacific Northwest region (Macnair 1995). It means "the people who speak Kwak'wala." It replaces the earlier term Kwakiutl, which refers to only one of the several groups and is insulting to members of the other groups to be so named.

Their territory includes many islands as well as the waterways and deep inlets penetrating the Coast Mountains, a region of dense forests and sandy beaches. In earlier times, travel was mainly by canoe. Families moved seasonally with all their belongings packed in the canoe (Macnair 1995).

The Kwakwaka'wakw are famous for aspects of their material culture, including tall, carved wooden totem poles, canoes, masks, and serving bowls, as well as richly decorated capes, skirts, and blankets.

Cedar is vital to the Kwakwaka'wakw. They use its wood for the objects just mentioned and the inner bark for garments. Women pounded the bark strips with a whalebone beater until the fibers separated and became soft. They wove the strips on a loom or handwove them into mats used for sleeping on.

The first contact with Whites occurred in 1792, when explorer Captain George Vancouver arrived (Macnair 1995). At that time, the Kwakwaka'wakw population was perhaps 8,000. Franz Boas arrived in 1886 and carried out research with the help of George Hunt, born of an English father and a high-ranking Tlingit (Northwest Coast) mother.

In the late nineteenth century, colonial authorities and missionaries disapproved of matters such as marriage arrangements and the potlatch, and enacted legislation to promote change, including a ban on potlatching from 1884 to 1951. The people continued, however, to potlatch in secret.

The Royal British Columbia Provincial Museum (RCBM) in Victoria, British Columbia, Canada, worked closely with Kwakwaka'wakw communities to document their potlatches and promote cultural revitalization (Kramer, personal communication 2006). The first legal potlatch of recent times, hosted by Mungo Martin in 1953, was held outside the RCBM.

Readings

Boas, Franz. *Ethnology of the Kwakiutl.* Washington, DC: Government Printing Office, 1921.
Audrey Hawthorn, *Kwakiutl Art.* Seattle: University of Washington Press, 1979.
Bill Holm, *Smoky Top: The Art and Times of Willie Seaweed.* Seattle: University of Washington Press, 1983.

Videos

In the Land of the War Canoes: A Drama of Kwakiutl Life in the Northwest (1914; re-released by milestone Film & Video, 1992).
Raven Tales: How Raven Stole the Sun (Simon James, producer; NMAI, 2004).

Website

Museum of Anthropology, University of British Columbia, First Nations Collections; www.moa.ubc.ca/collections

Thanks to Jennifer Kramer, University of British Columbia, for reviewing this material.

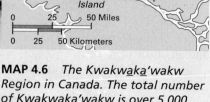

Canoes and their crews from other Kwakwaka'wakw villages gather at Alert Bay in 1999 to help celebrate the opening of the newly built Big House (left). ■ (Source: © Vickie Jensen) *Kwakwaka'wakw students practice the hamat'sa dance at a school in Alert Bay, under the tutelage of K'odi Nelson (right).* ■ (Source: © Vickie Jensen)

MAP 4.6 *The Kwakwaka'wakw Region in Canada. The total number of Kwakwaka'wakw is over 5,000 people.*

increased use during this period. What accounts for this change? Two anthropologists conducted research to assess their hypothesis that there was a major change in the systems that produced and delivered the drug, leading to increased availability.

The standard story of the supply chain goes like this: Ecstasy is produced in the Netherlands and Belgium, distributed to the United States by Israelis, with a fuzzy role for Russian organized crime along the way. Two anthropologists studied websites and media reports in 2000 and discovered a much more complicated story. They found a network of multiple and shifting production sites all over the world, including the largest illicit drug lab ever reported in Canadian history. Distribution channels are also highly diffuse. Although the simpler story may have been true in 1998, it was no longer true two years later. Perhaps as demand rose in the United States and elsewhere, this rise prompted the development of a wider network of production and distribution.

Credit Card Debt

Some markets, worldwide, have long allowed buyers to purchase goods on *credit*, which involves payment over time. Informal credit is usually based on personal trust and face-to-face interaction. Only recently did the invention of the credit card make credit purchasing a widespread and growing phenomenon. Credit card companies in the United States have created astounding new levels of debt across many social and economic levels: "New electronic technology in the 1970s and deregulation in the 1980s offered retail bankers exciting opportunities to experiment with credit as a commodity, and they did experiment, wildly, at 'penetrating the debt capacity' of varied groups of Americans" (B. Williams 1994:351).

In the United States, the primary users of credit cards are between 25 and 44 years old with flat or falling incomes. Many people use credit cards to pay for their college education, or set up a household, or buy a car or major household appliances. Charging the costs of leisure activities, such as a vacation trip, is another major use of credit cards. Maintaining a running debt to credit card companies has become an expected part of life for many people and a habit not easily changed. Attitudes about credit card debts vary. Some people express feelings of guilt similar to having a drug dependency. One woman in a study of credit card debt in the Washington, DC, area said, "Last year I had a charge-free Christmas. It was like coming away from drug abuse" (B. Williams 1994:354). Another expressed gratitude: "I wouldn't be able to go to college without my credit card" (1994:355).

Continuities and Resistance: The Enduring Potlatch

Potlatching among native peoples of the northwest coast of the United States and Canada was subjected to decades of opposition from Europeans and Euro-Americans (Cole 1991). The missionaries opposed potlatching as an un-Christian practice. The government thought it was wasteful and excessive, out of line with their goals for the "economic progress" of the Indians. In 1885, the Canadian government outlawed the potlatch. Of all the Northwest Coast tribes, the Kwakwaka'wakw (see Culturama) resisted this prohibition most strongly and for the longest time. In Canada, potlatches are no longer illegal. But it took a long battle to remove restrictions.

Reasons for giving a potlatch today are similar to those in the past: naming children, mourning the dead, transferring rights and privileges, celebrating marriages, and raising totem poles (Webster 1991). The length of time devoted to planning a potlatch, however, has changed. In the past, several years were involved compared to about a year now. Still, it takes much organization and work to accumulate enough goods to ensure that no guest goes away empty-handed, and the guest list may include between 500 and 1,000 people. Another change is in the kinds of goods exchanged. Typical potlatch goods now include crocheted items (such as cushion covers, blankets, and potholders), glassware, plastic goods, manufactured blankets, pillows, towels, articles of clothing, and sacks of flour and sugar. The potlatch endures but changes.

The Big Questions Revisited

WHAT is consumption in cross-cultural perspective?

Consumption includes a person's "intake" in terms of eating or other ways of using things and "output" in terms of spending or using resources to obtain those things. Anthropologists delineate two major modes of consumption. The first is minimalism, which is characterized by finite needs, the means of satisfying them, and sustainability. The second is consumerism, the mode of consumption with infinite needs, the inability to satisfy all needs, and lack of sustainability. Foraging societies typify the minimalist mode of consumption. Horticulture, pastoralism, and farming are associated with mixed patterns of consumption, with a rising trend toward consumerism. The consumerist mode of consumption is most clearly associated with industrialism/informatics.

In nonmarket economies, most consumers either produce the goods they use themselves or know who produced them. This is called personalized consumption. In market economies, consumption is largely depersonalized through globalized mass production. The increase in depersonalized consumption may put workers at greater risk of exploitation because consumers are alienated from producers.

Anthropologists define five consumption funds the proportions of which vary in different economic systems. Microcultures such as "race"/ethnicity, class, and gender are linked to specific consumption patterns. Such patterns may involve inequalities that affect human welfare.

A long-standing area of interest in cultural anthropology is cross-cultural patterns of food taboos and why such taboos exist. Cultural materialists provide interpretations that consider the ecological and environmental contexts of such food taboos and how taboos make sense to people's material lives. Symbolic/interpretive anthropologists interpret food taboos as systems of meaning that give people a sense of identity and communicate that identity to others.

WHAT is exchange in cross-cultural perspective?

Exchange refers to the transfer of goods, both material and intangible, or services between people, groups, or institutions. Cross-culturally, people and groups exchange a wide variety of goods and services. Nonmarket exchange long existed without the use of money. Modern money is now found throughout most of the world, though some groups restrict its use.

Anthropologists define two major modes of exchange. The first is balanced exchange in which items of roughly equal value are exchanged over time between people who have a social relationship. Balanced exchange reinforces social ties. In unbalanced exchange, the value of items transferred is unequal and there may or may not be a social relationship between the seller and buyer.

Market exchange, the main form of unbalanced exchange, is a transaction in which the seller's goal of making a profit overrides social relationships. Markets exist in many forms. Some are impermanent and irregular; some are impermanent and regular, as in a weekly farmer's market; and others are permanent. Recent technological developments have led to the creation of virtual marketplaces in which buyers and sellers never meet face to face

HOW are consumption and exchange changing?

Globalizing capitalism is leading to many changes in consumption and exchange around the world. Globalization appears to differentially benefit securely entitled people in core countries.

Many indigenous peoples are attracted by Western goods, such as steel axes and processed food. In order to obtain these goods, they have to have cash, so they are lured into the cash economy and subject to the fluctuations of the world labor market. The nutritional and health status of many such groups has declined with the adoption of Western-style foods, especially large amounts of sugar and salt in food.

The transition following the break-up of the USSR created vast disparities in income and human well-being. Throughout the post-Soviet world, average health and nutrition levels fell.

A prominent trend in consumption and exchange is credit card shopping. More people are buying on credit, accumulating large debts, and struggling to keep up with high interest payments.

KEY CONCEPTS

balanced exchange, p. 106
cash crop, p. 97
consumerism, p. 92
consumption fund, p. 95
entitlement, p. 97
expected reciprocity, p. 106

generalized reciprocity, p. 106
leveling mechanism, p. 94
market exchange, p. 107
minimalism, p. 92
mode of consumption, p. 92
mode of exchange, p. 92

money, p. 104
potlatch, p. 92
pure gift, p. 106
redistribution, p. 107
trade, p. 107
unbalanced exchange, p. 106

SUGGESTED READINGS

Theodore C. Bestor. *Tsukiji: The Fish Market at the Center of the World*. Berkeley: University of California Press, 2004. This ethnography of Tsukiji, the huge fish market in Tokyo, describes how it is a workplace for thousands of people, a central node in the Japanese fishing industry, and part of the global economy.

Denise Brennan. *What's Love Got to Do With It? Transnational Desires and Sex Tourism in the Dominican Republic*. Durham, NC: Duke University Press, 2004. This account of global sex tourism is located in the town of Sosúa, Dominican Republic, where Afro-Dominican and Afro-Haitian women sell sex to foreign, White tourists.

Michael F. Brown. *Who Owns Native Culture?* Cambridge, MA: Harvard University Press, 2003. This book documents the efforts of indigenous peoples to redefine heritage as a resource over which they claim proprietorship. It considers specific cases and proposes strategies for defending the rights of indigenous people within a market system.

Brenda Chalfin. *Shea Butter Republic: State Power, Global Markets, and the Making of an Indigenous Commodity*. New York: Routledge, 2004. This ethnography focuses on the changing role of shea butter production in northeastern Ghana in relation to the growing global market for shea butter in cocoa products and personal care products.

Elizabeth Chin. *Purchasing Power: Black Kids and American Consumer Culture*. Minneapolis: University of Minnesota Press, 2001. The author did research with a fifth-grade class in a low-income, African American neighborhood in New Haven, Connecticut. These 10-year-olds, motivated by a strong sense of family responsibility, spend their money mainly on practical items and gifts for family members rather than status symbols.

Maris Boyd Gillette. *Between Mecca and Beijing: Modernization and Consumption among Urban Chinese Muslims*. Stanford, CA: Stanford University Press, 2000. For centuries, the Han majority have labeled Chinese Muslims, or Hui, of northwest China as a "backward" minority. Although the government seeks to "modernize" the Hui, the Hui challenge government policy by maintaining Islamic values.

Karen Tranberg Hansen. *Salaula: The World of Secondhand Clothing in Zambia*. Chicago: University of Chicago Press, 2000. *Salaula* is the local term for used clothing in Zambia. It is the focus of this study of the widespread appeal of secondhand Western clothing in this West African country.

Betsy Hartmann and James Boyce. *Needless Hunger: Voices from a Bangladesh Village*. San Francisco: Institute for Food and Development Policy, 1982. Fieldwork in rural Bangladesh shows that poverty and hunger there are the result of severe class inequalities in economic entitlements. The book points to the role of foreign aid in perpetuating inequalities and offers positive suggestions for change.

Dwight B. Heath. *Drinking Occasions: Comparative Perspectives on Alcohol and Culture*. New York: Taylor & Francis, 2000. This book provides an ethnological review of alcohol consumption and looks at questions such as when people drink alcohol, where people drink, who drinks and who does not, what people drink, and why people drink.

Ann Kingsolver. *NAFTA Stories: Fears and Hopes in Mexico and the United States*. Boulder, CO: Lynne Reiner Publishers, 2001. The author collected and followed stories about NAFTA (North American Free Trade Agreement) during the early 1990s as told by everyday people in Mexico City and two cities in Morelos, Mexico. She worked collaboratively with a Mexican anthropologist for both ethical reasons and legal requirements and considers her research, and her book, an example of activist social documentation.

Bill Maurer. *Mutual Life, Limited: Islamic Banking, Alternative Currencies, Lateral Reason*. Princeton, NJ: Princeton University Press, 2005. This comparison of Islamic bankers who seek to avoid interest with local currency proponents who seek to provide an alternative to capitalist financial mechanisms shows how both resist and sometimes replicate Western capitalism.

Linda J. Seligmann, ed. *Women Traders in Cross-Cultural Perspective: Mediating Identities, Marketing Wares*. Stanford, CA: Stanford University Press, 2001. The chapters include attention to historic patterns of women's participation in Mexico's markets, and case studies of contemporary women marketeers in Java, South India, Ghana, the Philippines, Morocco, and Hungary.

5

Birth and Death

The Big Questions

- WHAT are the modes of reproduction cross-culturally?

- HOW does culture shape fertility in different contexts?

- HOW does culture shape mortality in different contexts?

Two sisters of the Tarahumara people of northern Mexico. The Tarahumara once occupied most of the present-day state of Chihuahua but retreated to the Copper Canyon area in the mountains after the arrival of the Spanish colonialists. (*Source: © William Coupon/CORBIS*)

- A common belief among Hindus in India is that men are weakened by sexual intercourse because semen is a source of strength and it takes a long time to replace even a drop. Yet India has a high rate of population growth.

- The Chinese government policy of urging couples to have only one child significantly decreased the population growth rate. It also increased the death rate of female infants to the extent that there is now a shortage of brides.

- The highest birth rates in the world are found among the Mennonites and Hutterites in the United States and Canada. In these Christian groups, women, on average, bear nine children.

Such population puzzles can be understood using anthropological theories and methods. Population dynamics, along with many other examples of human variation in births and deaths, are culturally shaped and change over time. This chapter looks at some aspects of *demography,* the study of population dynamics in cross-cultural perspective. Whereas demographers compile statistical reports, cultural anthropologists contribute understanding of what goes on behind the numbers and provide insights about the causes of demographic trends. For example, demographers may find that fertility rates are falling more rapidly in one nation than in another. They may be able to correlate falling fertility rates with certain factors such as changing literacy rates or economic growth. Cultural anthropologists studying the causes and processes involved in the declining birth rates would pay attention to many factors that are not included in official censuses or other statistical sources. For example, they would collect information about people's values about children, their aspirations for their children, and the source of changing values.

Demography includes three areas: **fertility** (births), or the rate of population increase from reproduction; **mortality** (deaths), or the rate of population decline in general or from particular causes; and **migration**, or the movement of people from one place to another. When cultural anthropologists study these processes, they tend to focus on small populations and examine the relationships between population dynamics and other aspects of culture such as gender roles, social inequality, sexual beliefs and behavior, marriage, household structure, child care, and health and illness.

This chapter first discusses three modes of reproduction. It then examines how and to what extent culture shapes the processes of birth and death.

Culture and Reproduction

Cultural anthropologists have enough data to support the construction of three **modes of reproduction,** or the predominant pattern of fertility in a culture. They correspond roughly to three of the major modes of production (see Figure 5.1):

- *Foraging mode of reproduction:* Level rates of population growth associated with moderate birthrates and moderate death rates. This mode of reproduction existed for most of human prehistory.

- *Agricultural mode of reproduction:* High rates of population growth associated with higher birth rates than death rates. It emerged with farming and sedentism (permanent settlements).

- *Industrialism/informatics mode of reproduction:* Low and declining rates of population growth associated with low birth rates and low deaths rates. It emerged beginning in the mid-nineteenth century and is associated with richer countries.

Horticulturalists and pastoralists, depending on the context, exhibit a mixture of the foraging mode of reproduction and the agricultural mode of reproduction. Anthropologists have done less research on reproduction among horticulturalists and pastoralists, so it is impossible to provide as much detail for them.

The Foraging Mode of Reproduction

Nancy Howell conducted a classic study in anthropological demography based on fieldwork conducted with the Ju/'hoansi in the 1970s (Howell 1979) (review Culturama in Chapter 1, p. 22). She found that *birth intervals* (the time between a birth and the next birth) among the Ju/'hoansi are often several years in duration. What accounts for these long birth intervals? Two factors are most important: breastfeeding and women's low level of body fat. Frequent and long periods of breastfeeding inhibit progesterone production and suppress ovulation. Also, a certain level of body fat is required for ovulation. Ju/'hoansi women's diets contain little fat, and their regular physical exercise as foragers keeps their body fat level low, further suppressing ovulation. Thus, diet and work are key factors underlying Ju/'hoansi population dynamics.

Ju/'hoansi women, during the time of the study, typically had between two and three live births of which two children survived into adulthood. This mode of repro-

---

fertility: the rate of births in a population, or the rate of population increase in general.

mortality: deaths in a population, or the rate of population decline in general or from particular causes.

migration: the movement of a person or people from one place to another.

mode of reproduction: the predominant pattern of fertility and mortality in a culture.

pronatalism: an ideology promoting many children.

FIGURE 5.1 Modes of Production and Reproduction

Foraging	Agriculture	Industrialism/Informatics
Population Growth Moderate birth rates Moderate death rates	**Population Growth** High birth rates Declining death rates	**Population Growth** Industrialized nations—negative population growth Developing nations—high
Value of Children Moderate	**Value of Children** High	**Value of Children** Mixed

Fertility Control
Indirect means
  Low-fat diet of women
  Women's work and exercise
  Prolonged breastfeeding
  Spontaneous abortion
Direct means
  Induced abortion
  Infanticide
	Fertility Control
	Increased reliance on direct means
	Pronatalist techniques
	  Herbs
	Direct means
	  Induced abortion
	  Infanticide
		Fertility Control
		Direct methods grounded in science
		  and medicine
		Chemical forms of contraception
		In vitro fertilization
		Abortion

Social Aspects
Homogeneous fertility
Few specialists
	Social Aspects
	Emerging class differences
	Increasing specialization
	  Midwifery
	  Herbalists
		Social Aspects
		Stratified fertility
		  Globally, nationally, and locally
		Highly developed specialization

duction is adaptive to the Ju/'hoansi environment and sustainable over time. Among the Ju/'hoansi who have become farmers or laborers, fertility levels have increased. Their diet contains more grains and dairy products, and they are less physically active.

The Agricultural Mode of Reproduction

Agriculture and sedentism are associated with the highest fertility rates of any mode of production. **Pronatalism,** an ideology promoting many children, emerges as a key value of farm families. It is prompted by the need for a large labor force to work the land, care for animals, process food, and do marketing. In this context, having many children is a rational reproductive strategy related to the mode of production. Thus, people who live in family farming systems cross-culturally have their own "family planning"—which is to have many children.

The groups with the highest fertility rates worldwide are the Mennonites and Hutterites, European-descent Christians of the United States and Canada. Women in these groups typically have between eight and ten children who survive into adulthood. A closely related religious cultural group, the Amish (see Culturama), also have high fertility rates.

Global variation in fertility in farming populations does exist, however, partly because of recent declines due to re-

duced demands for family labor. High rates of seven or more children per woman exist in several low-income, agricultural countries of Africa, such as Niger (8.0 births per woman), Guinea-Bissau (7.1 births per woman), Mali (7.1 births per woman), and Somalia (7.0 births per woman) (Population Reference Bureau 2005). Lower rates, of two or three children per woman, are found in many agricultural countries in South America, such as Venezuela, Chile, and Argentina.

Within countries, significant variation often exists in different regions, between urban and rural areas, and among different ethnic and class groups. In the Kilimanjaro region of northern Tanzania (see Map 5.2), East Africa, fertility is lower than in the country as a whole, perhaps because the region has an unusually active family planning program (Larsen and Hollos 2003). Within the Kilimanjaro region, fertility is lower among women who are economically better-off, have more years of education, choose their husbands, and have an equitable marital relationship. This study is just one of many that demonstrate the importance of women's status in shaping fertility.

In rural North India, sons are especially important in farming families. As young boys, they learn to do farm

THINKING OUTSIDE THE BOX

CHOOSE A COUNTRY and do Internet research to locate fertility data about internal patterns, such as state-by-state, regional, ethnic, class, urban/rural, education levels, or other variables.

Culturama

The Old Order Amish of the United States and Canada

The Amish are Christians who live in rural areas of the United States and Canada. In the early twenty-first century, their total population was about 200,000. Their ancestry traces to German-speaking, Swiss Anabaptists in the sixteenth century. To escape religious persecution, they migrated to North America, starting in the early eighteenth century and continuing into the mid-nineteenth century. There are no Amish in Europe today.

The term *Old Order Amish* refers to the main body of the Amish people. A small minority, known as *New Order Amish,* broke off from the Old Order in the late 1960s. Both groups use horse-drawn transportation, but the New Order Amish accept more technology.

The Amish speak a German-derived dialect. They wear modest and conforming clothing. They avoid using electricity from power grids but solar-generated electricity and 12-volt batteries are allowed. Education beyond the eighth grade is seen as unnecessary. A basic theme in Amish life is the need to guard against "worldly" (non-Amish, mainstream U.S.) values, dependencies, and hurriedness, and to maintain the family as a unit that lives and works together. Working with one's own hands is valued, as are humility and modesty. Farm-ing is the traditional means of livelihood among the Amish.

The Amish have high fertility rates, on average six or seven live births per woman. Even though some children leave and join "the English" (non-Amish), their population is doubling every twenty years. In Lancaster County, Pennsylvania, the heartland of the Old Order Amish, a steep rise in population growth starting in the 1970s has exceeded the availability of farmland (Kraybill and Nolt 2004). Now, several hundred Amish businesses exist, many small scale and operated from the home but many others are large scale and earn millions of dollars per year. Amish who enter business try to retain Amish values of family solidarity by working at home and selling products from their home. Many, though, work in businesses away from home, with the English.

Amish youth have the opportunity of deciding whether to be baptized into the faith when they are 16 years old. At this time, called *rumspringa* in Pennsylvania Dutch, or "running around," the young people are allowed to explore the customs of the English world including television. Most stay at home during rumspringa, spending time with Amish friends on the weekends. In rare cases, some experiment with alcohol, drugs, and sex (Shachtman 2006). After rum-springa, around 90 percent of Amish teenagers decide to accept Amish ways and be baptized, choosing a lifestyle that emphasizes humility and community solidarity rather than the "worldly" lifestyle of individualism and competition.

Readings

Donald B. Kraybill, *The Riddle of Amish Culture.* Baltimore: Johns Hopkins University Press, 2001.

Donald B. Kraybill and Steven M. Nolt. *Amish Enterprise: From Plows to Profits,* 2nd ed. Baltimore: The Johns Hopkins University Press, 2004.

Kathleen McLary. *Amish Style: Clothing, Home Furnishings, Toys, Dolls, and Quilts.* Bloomington: Indiana University Press, 1993.

Tom Shachtman. *Rumspringa: To Be or Not to Be Amish.* New York: North Point Press, 2006.

Video

The Amish: A People of Preservation (Heritage Productions, 1996).

Website

Amish Teens Tempted in Devil's Playground. www.npr.org/programs/morning/features/2002/may/amish

Thanks to Donald B. Kraybill, Elizabethtown College, for reviewing this material.

Members of an Amish household sit around their kitchen table (left). ■ (Source: © David & Peter Turnley/CORBIS) *A farmer mows alfalfa with a team of mules and a gasoline engine to power the mower (right). This mechanism enhances his farm work but does not break the Old Order Amish rule against using tractors in the field.* ■ (Source: Barbara Miller and Bernard Wood)

MAP 5.1 *Old Order Amish Population of North America. The states of Ohio (55,000), Pennsylvania (37,000), and Indiana (37,000) have the largest number of Old Order Amish.*

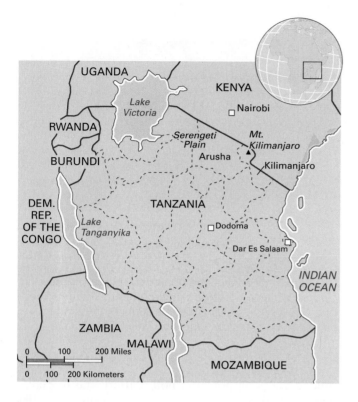

MAP 5.2 Tanzania. The United Republic of Tanzania is named after its mainland region, Tanganyika, and Zanzibar off its east coast. Its population is nearly 37 million. The capital city moved from Dar es Salaam to Dodoma in 1996, but many government offices remain in "Dar." Agriculture is the basis of the economy, and over 80 percent of the population is rural. Tanzania has substantial natural resources, especially gold. More than 120 different ethnic groups live in Tanzania. The national language is Swahili, a Bantu language, with English as a second official language. Many local languages are also spoken.

India in the late 1950s to promote the idea of small families, the farmers expressed dismay (Mamdani 1972). To them, a large family, especially many sons, is a sign of wealth and success, not poverty and failure. Having many children in a family farming system makes sense.

The Industrial/Informatics Mode of Reproduction

In industrial societies, either capitalist or socialist, reproduction declines to the point of **replacement-level fertility,** in which the number of births equals the number of deaths, leading to maintenance of current population size, or **below-replacement-level fertility,** in which the number of births is less than the number of deaths, leading to population decline (see Figure 5.2). Children in

work with their father. As adults, they are responsible for the plowing and for protecting the family land from encroachment by neighboring farmers and animals. When Western family planning experts visited villages in North

FIGURE 5.2   Some Countries with Below-Replacement-Level Fertility (Fertility Rates Below Two Births per Woman), Late 1990s

Country	Fertility Rate	Country	Fertility Rate	Country	Fertility Rate
Armenia	1.4	Dominica	1.9	Norway	1.8
Australia	1.7	Finland	1.7	Poland	1.4
Austria	1.3	France	1.8	Portugal	1.5
Azerbaijan	1.9	Germany	1.3	Romania	1.3
Barbados	1.8	Greece	1.3	Russia	1.2
Belarus	1.3	Hungary	1.3	Singapore	1.5
Belgium	1.6	Italy	1.2	Slovakia	1.4
Bosnia-Herzegovina	1.6	Ireland	1.9	Slovenia	1.2
Bulgaria	1.1	Japan	1.3	Spain	1.2
Canada	1.5	Kazakhstan	1.7	Sweden	1.5
China	1.8	Korea, South	1.5	Switzerland	1.5
Croatia	1.5	Lithuania	1.3	Taiwan	1.5
Cuba	1.6	Luxembourg	1.7	Thailand	1.9
Cyprus	1.9	Macedonia	1.9	Trinidad & Tobago	1.7
Czech Republic	1.1	Martinique	1.8	Ukraine	1.3
Denmark	1.7	Netherlands	1.6	United Kingdom	1.7

Source: From *2000 World Population Data Sheet.* Washington, DC: Population Reference Bureau. Copyright © 2000. Reprinted by permission of Population Reference Bureau.

replacement-level fertility: a situation when births equal deaths, leading to maintenance of current population size.

below-replacement-level fertility: a situation in which births are fewer than deaths, leading to population decline.

these contexts are less useful in production because of the reduced labor demands of industrialism. Furthermore, children in most industrialized countries must attend school and therefore cannot work for their families much during the school year. Parents respond by having fewer children and by investing more resources in them.

Population changes during the industrial mode of reproduction correspond to what demographers call the **demographic transition,** a process during which the agricultural pattern of high fertility and high mortality becomes the industrial pattern of low fertility and low mortality. There are two phases in the demographic transition model (see Figure 5.3). In the first phase, mortality declines because of improved nutrition and health, so population growth rates increase. The second phase occurs when fertility also declines. At this point, low rates of population growth occur.

Cultural anthropologists think the demographic transition model is too narrow because it attributes only one cause to declining population growth: industrialism (Ginsberg and Rapp 1991). They point to examples of other causes. China, for example, began to reduce its population growth rate well before widespread industrialism (Xizhe 1991). Strong government policies and a massive family planning program caused China's demographic transition.

The industrial/informatics mode of reproduction has three distinguishing features. First, social inequality is reflected in population patterns, referred to as *stratified reproduction.* Typically, middle-class and upper-class people tend to have few children, with high survival rates.

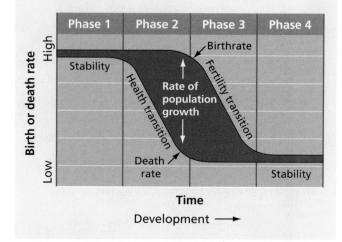

FIGURE 5.3   Model of the Demographic Transition
(Source: Nebel and Wright, Environmental Science: The Way the World Works, *7th ed. © 2000. Adapted by permission of Pearson Education, Inc. Upper Saddle River, NJ.)*

Among the poor, however, both fertility and mortality rates are high. Brazil, a newly industrializing state, has the world's most extreme income inequality. Parallel to its economic inequality is extremely stratified reproduction (discussed later in this chapter's section on mortality). Increasing international migration to core countries adds to variation in population dynamics within them. In France, the government promotes pronatalism to address its population deficit, but pronatal messages and pro-

Firefighters survey the scene after a fire in a six-story apartment building in Paris, France, in 2005, that was home to low-income African immigrants. The fire killed seventeen people, of whom half were children, and injured thirty more. ■ *What is your opinion on the role of government in ensuring that everyone lives in safe housing?* (Source: © Victor Tonelli/ReutersCORBIS)

demographic transition: the change from the agricultural pattern of high fertility and high mortality to the industrial pattern of low fertility and low mortality.

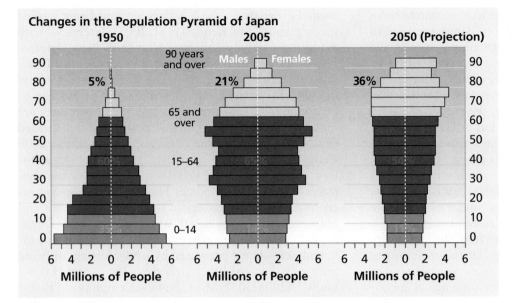

Changes in the Population Pyramid of Japan

1950	2005	2050 (Projection)

90 years and over · 65 and over · 15–64 · 0–14

Males · Females

5% · 21% · 36%

Millions of People · Millions of People · Millions of People

FIGURE 5.4 Changes in the Population Pyramid of Japan *(Source: Adapted from* Statistical Handbook of Japan, *Statistics Bureau, MIC, Japan.)*

grams are aimed at the "authentic" French population. In contrast, low-income immigrants from Mali, West Africa, living in Paris, receive antinatalist messages in clinics (Sargent 2005). Immigrant fertility, rather than being desired by the French government, is a matter of concern, as it strains public resources such as schools and hospitals. The fact that the immigrants are poor, Black, and Muslim, with a culture that values many children, places them in stark contrast to the "authentic" French people who are relatively well-off, White, and have few children.

A second characteristic of industrial/informatics contexts is population aging. In Japan, the total fertility rate declined to replacement level in the 1950s and later reached the below-replacement level (Hodge and Ogawa 1991). Japan is currently experiencing a decline in population growth of about 15 percent per generation and, simultaneously, rapid aging of the population. As many people enter the senior category, they create a population bulge that is not balanced by the number of younger people (see Figure 5.4). A population projection for the year 2050 suggests that the bulge will increase.

A third distinguishing feature of industrial/informatics demographies is the high level of involvement of scientific (especially medical) technology in all aspects of pregnancy: prevention, termination, and becoming pregnant in the first place (Browner and Press 1995, 1996). This trend is accompanied by increasing levels of specialization in providing the new services.

Culture and Fertility

Culture shapes human fertility from its very start, if that can be taken as sexual intercourse or some other form of fertilization of an ovum. Cultural practices and beliefs about pregnancy and birth affect the viability of the fetus during its gestation as well as the infant's survival and health.

Sexual Intercourse

Sexual intercourse usually involves private, sometimes secret, beliefs and behaviors. Anthropological research on sexual practices is thus particularly challenging. The ethics of participant observation prohibit intimate observation or participation, so data can be obtained only indirectly. Biases in people's verbal reports about sexual beliefs and behavior are likely for several reasons. People may be too shy or otherwise unwilling to discuss sex or, conversely, boastful and inflating the truth. Many people may simply be unable to answers questions such as "How many times did you have sexual intercourse last year?" If people do provide detailed information, it might be inappropriate for an anthropologist to publish it because of the need to protect confidentiality.

Bronislaw Malinowski wrote the first anthropological study of sexuality (1929), based on his fieldwork in the Trobriand Islands (review Culturama in Chapter 2, p. 39). In his book, he discusses the sexual lives of children, sexual techniques, love magic, erotic dreams, husband–wife jealousy, and other topics. Since the late 1980s, cultural anthropologists have paid increasing attention to the study of sexuality, especially "risky" practices related to sexually transmitted diseases (STDs), including HIV/AIDS.

When to Begin Having Intercourse?

Biologically speaking, sexual intercourse between a fertile female and a fertile male is normally required for human reproduction, although artificial insemination is becoming a widely used option in some contexts. Biology, interacting with environment and culture, defines the time span within which a female is fertile: from **menarche** (pronounced MEN-ARE-KEE), the onset of menstruation, to **menopause,** the cessation of menstruation. Globally, the beginning of menarche varies from between 12 to 14 years of age (Thomas et al. 2001). Generally, girls in richer countries reach menarche a few years earlier than girls in poorer countries do. For example, the estimated age at menarche in Japan is 12.5 years, but in Haiti it is 15.5 years. Worldwide, a trend is for the age at menarche to become earlier. The reasons for this change are not completely clear. Diet and activity patterns are likely factors involved. The underlying assumption is that today's diets and lifestyles are a sign of "progress" and thus earlier age at menarche is an indicator of social well-being.

Average age at menopause varies from the late forties to the early fifties, with later ages in richer countries (Thomas et al. 2001). According to a review of studies worldwide, in France, the latest average age at menopause is 52 years. Diet and activity level, again, are accepted as causes for regional differences. A woman's lifetime fertility also appears to be involved: Women who have more children reach menopause earlier than women who have few or no children.

Cultures, however, socialize children about the appropriate age to begin sexual intercourse, and cultural rules are more variable than the biological marker of menarche. Cultural guidelines vary by gender, class, race, and ethnicity. In many cultures, sexual activity should begin only with marriage. This rule often applies more strictly to females than to males. In Zawiya, a Muslim town of northern Morocco (see Map 5.3), a bride's virginity is highly valued, whereas that of the groom is ignored (Davis and Davis 1987). Most brides conform to the ideal. Some unmarried young women do engage in premarital sex, however. If they choose to have a traditional wedding, they must somehow meet the requirement of producing blood-stained wedding sheets after the first night. If the bride and the groom have been having premarital sexual relations, the groom may assist in the deception by nicking a finger with a knife and bloodying the sheets himself. Another option is to buy fake blood sold in drugstores.

In many cultures, young women are married immediately after menarche, and they expect, and hope, to become pregnant right away. Thus, so-called teenage pregnancy is often a desired condition instead of a social problem, as perceived by many Western health experts (Ginsberg and Rapp 1991). In contrast to Western norms, many people worldwide would find the concept of a 30-year-old, first-time mother as physically dangerous for the woman and quite bizarre.

A distinction can be made between *intended pregnancy,* which is hoped for and planned for, and *unin-*

tended pregnancy, which occurs without being wished for or planned for (Kendall et al. 2005). Interviews with many inner-city, low-income women in New Orleans, Louisiana, revealed women's ambivalence (mixed feelings) about early pregnancy. The women, who are predominantly African American, state a preference to postpone their first pregnancy, yet teen birth rates are high among the New Orleans poor, who constituted nearly 30 percent of the city's population in the 2000 Census. The average age in the study population for first sexual intercourse was 16 years, and few use contraception at this early age. Those who do use contraception reported a variety of problems: headaches and cramping with pills and heavy bleeding with Depo-Provera. The teenage girls expressed several reasons for having sex—being pressured by a boy, feelings of being grown up, because other girls are doing it, and "I don't know." (2005:303). Most, however, emphasized that it is better to postpone pregnancy until after finishing high school or college. One 17-year-old said, "You should concentrate on school . . . put yourself first . . . you can't do that if you are caring for a baby" (2005: 303).

A structurist view critiquing official U.S. public disapproval of urban African American teen mothers emphasizes the role of class differences (Geronimus 2003). Delayed childbearing may be adaptive for middle-class and upper-class Americans, but early childbearing makes sense when viewed within the structural constraints of inner-city poverty, violence, insecurity, and shorter life expectancies. The dominant message in the United States that teenage childbearing is wrong is, in this view, a form of moral and racist condemnation that should be revised to take into account the realities of people's lives in contexts radically different from the middle-class American dream.

Intercourse Frequency and Fertility

Cross-culturally, the frequency of sexual intercourse varies widely. The relationship between frequency of sexual intercourse and fertility, though, is not simple. A common assumption is that people in cultures with high fertility rates have sexual intercourse frequently. Without modern birth control, such as condoms, the birth control pill, and the intrauterine device (IUD), intercourse frequency would seem, logically, to produce high rates of fertility.

A classic study of reported intercourse frequency among Euro-Americans in the United States and Hindus in India throws this assumption into question (Nag 1972). The Indians had intercourse far less frequently (less than twice a week) than the Euro-Americans did

---

menarche: the onset of menstruation.   **menopause:** the cessation of menstruation.

A bride wearing traditional wedding clothing in the city of Meknès, Morocco. ■ *In your microculture, does a bride's wedding dress convey any messages about her virginity?* (Source: © Stephanie Dinkins/Photo Researchers, Inc.)

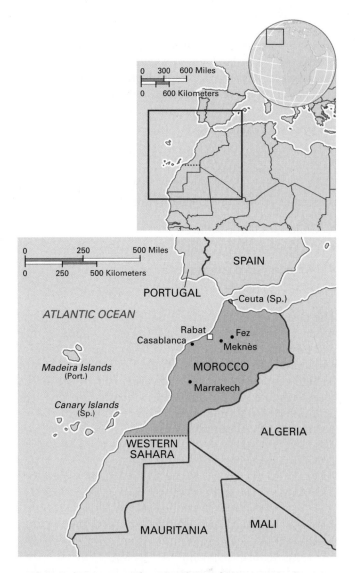

MAP 5.3   Morocco. The Kingdom of Morocco is the westernmost country of the Arab world. A border dispute continues with the Western Sahara, which Morocco has administered since 1975. Morocco's population is 30 million people. The terrain ranges from coastal lowlands to rugged interior mountains. Morocco's economy is based on mining phosphates, remittances, and tourism. It is one of the world's largest producers and exporters of cannabis and the world's largest per capita consumer of sugar. Most Moroccans are Sunni Muslims of Arab, Berber, or mixed Arab-Berber descent. The official language is classical Arabic but a dialect, Moroccan Arabic, is widely spoken. Over 40 percent of the people speak a variety of Berber.

(two to three times a week) in all age groups. Several features of Indian culture limit the frequency of sexual intercourse. The Hindu religion teaches the value of sexual abstinence, thus providing ideological support for limiting sexual intercourse. Hinduism also suggests that one should abstain from intercourse on many sacred days: the first night of the new moon, the first night of the full moon, and the eighth day of each half of the month (the light half and the dark half), and sometimes on Fridays. As many as 100 days each year could be observed as non-sex days. Another factor is Hindu men's belief in what anthropologists term the *lost semen complex*. An anthropologist learned about this complex during his fieldwork in North India:

> Everyone knew that semen was not easily formed; it takes forty days and forty drops of blood to make one drop of semen. . . . Semen of good quality is rich and viscous, like the cream of unadulterated milk. . . . Celibacy was the first requirement of true fitness, because every sexual orgasm meant the loss of a quantity of semen, laboriously formed. (Carstairs 1967:83–86, quoted in Nag 1972:235)

The fact remains, however, that fertility is higher in India than in many other parts of the world where such religiously based restrictions on sexual intercourse do not exist. Obviously, sheer frequency of intercourse is not the explanation because it takes only one act of sexual intercourse at the right time of the month to create a pregnancy. The point of this discussion is to show that "reverse reasoning" (assuming that high fertility means people have nothing better to do than have sex) is wrong. The cultural dynamics of sexuality in India function to restrain sexual activities and thus keep fertility lower than it otherwise would be.

Fertility Decision Making

This section explores decision making about fertility at the family, national, and global levels. Within the context of the family unit, decision makers weigh factors influencing why and when to have a child. At the national level, governments plan their overall population goals on the basis of goals that are sometimes *pronatalist* (favoring many births) and sometimes *antinatalist* (opposed to many births). At the global level, powerful economic and political interests influence the reproductive policies of countries and, in turn, of families and individuals.

At the Family Level

Within the family, parents and other family members consider, consciously or unconsciously, the value and costs of children (Nag 1983). Four factors are most important in affecting the desire for children:

- Children's labor value
- Children's value as old-age support for parents
- Infant and child mortality rates
- Economic costs of children

The first three factors have a positive effect on fertility: When children's value is high in terms of labor or old-age support, fertility is likely to be higher; when infant and child mortality rates are high, fertility rates tend to be high in order to "replace" offspring who do die. In the case of child costs—including direct costs (for food, education, clothing) and indirect costs (employment opportunities that the mother gives up)—the relationship is negative. Higher costs reduce the desire for children. Industrialism raises child costs and lowers their value dramatically because it tends to avoid using child labor. Mandatory school attendance also pulls children out of the workforce and may involve direct costs for fees, uniforms, and supplies. States that provide old-age security and pension plans further reduce the need for children.

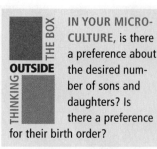

THINKING OUTSIDE THE BOX

IN YOUR MICRO-CULTURE, is there a preference about the desired number of sons and daughters? Is there a preference for their birth order?

Husbands and wives may not always have the same preferences about the number of desired children. In a highland village in the Oaxaca region of southern Mexico (see Map 5.4), men want more children than women do (Browner 1986). Of women with only one child, 80 percent were content with their present family size. Most men (60 percent) who were satisfied with their present family size had four or more children. One woman said, "My husband sleeps peacefully through the night, but I have to get up when the children need something. I'm the one the baby urinates on; sometimes I have to get out of bed in the cold and change both our clothes." (1986:714).

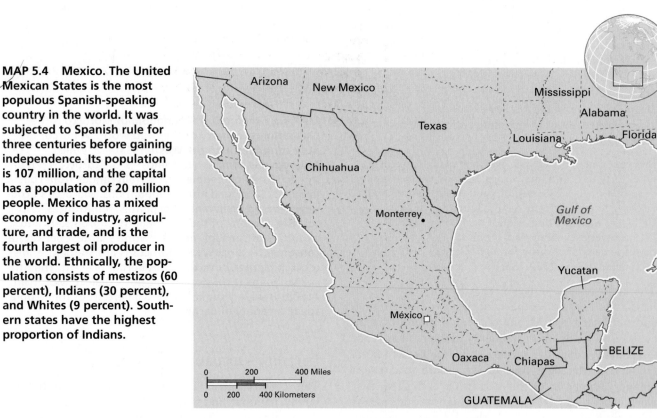

MAP 5.4 Mexico. The United Mexican States is the most populous Spanish-speaking country in the world. It was subjected to Spanish rule for three centuries before gaining independence. Its population is 107 million, and the capital has a population of 20 million people. Mexico has a mixed economy of industry, agriculture, and trade, and is the fourth largest oil producer in the world. Ethnically, the population consists of mestizos (60 percent), Indians (30 percent), and Whites (9 percent). Southern states have the highest proportion of Indians.

---

sex-selective infanticide: the killing of an infant or child because of its sex.

Depending on the gender division of labor and other social features, families may prefer sons, daughters, or a balance of each. Son preference is widespread, especially in Asia and the Middle East, but it is not universal (Williamson 1976). Throughout much of Southeast Asia, people prefer a balanced number of sons and daughters. Daughter preference is found in some parts of Africa south of the Sahara and some Caribbean populations.

In Tokugawa, Japan, during the eighteenth and nineteenth centuries, husbands and wives had differing preferences about the gender of their first child (Skinner 1993). Tokugawa wives, as is still common in Japan, preferred to have "first a girl, then a boy." This saying is related to the benefit of having a daughter to help the mother in her work and to care for the next child, especially a hoped-for son. Husbands, in contrast, favored a son-first strategy because a son helps them in their farm work. Husbands and wives tried to achieve their goals with the one method available: **sex-selective infanticide,** or the killing an infant or child because of its sex. Depending on their relative power, either the husband or the wife would prevail in the decision making about whether an infant would be kept alive. Three categories of marital power are defined, based on age differences between the spouses at the time of marriage:

- *Low husband power:* The wife is older than the husband (5 percent of marriages).

- *Intermediate husband power:* The ages of husband and wife are about equal (60 percent).

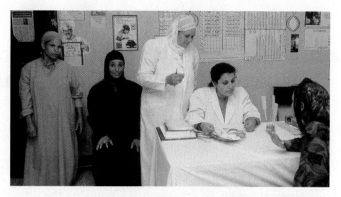

A family planning clinic in Egypt. Throughout much of the world, Western-style family planning advice is controversial because it may conflict with local beliefs and values. ■ *In your cultural experience, what is the prevailing attitude about family planning?* (Source: © Barry Iverson/Woodfin Camp & Associates)

- *High husband power:* The husband is older than the wife (35 percent).

In households with high husband power, 84 percent of first-born children kept alive were boys, compared to 34 percent in households with low husband power (see Figure 5.5). Households with more balanced marital power had a roughly equal number of first-born boys and girls (53 percent).

At the State Level

State governments formulate policies that affect rates of population growth within their boundaries. These policies vary from being antinatalist to pronatalist, and they vary in terms of the methods of fertility management promoted. Factors that affect government policies include economic factors such as projected jobs and employment levels, public services, maintaining the tax base, filling the ranks of the military, maintaining ethnic and regional proportions, and dealing with population aging.

The former Soviet Union faced significant planning challenges created by the contrasts between the below-replacement fertility of the "European" areas and high fertility rates in the Central Asian and Muslim regions of Tajikistan and Kyrghizstan (see Map 11.4, p. 297). Many countries, such as Japan and France, are concerned about declining population growth rates. Israel is openly pronatalist, a position related to its political interests in boosting its population level.

In many countries, abortion at any stage of fetal development is illegal. Illegality

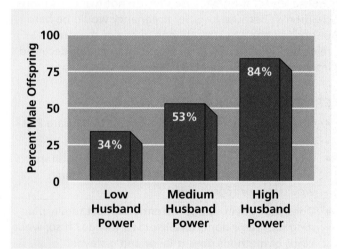

FIGURE 5.5 Gender of First-Born Child According to Spouse Power in the Household, Tokugawa, Japan
(*Note:* Under normal conditions, one would expect roughly equal percentages of male and female births.)
(*Source:* From "Conjugal Power in Tokugawa Japanese Families: A Matter of Life or Death" by William G. Skinner, in *Sex and Gender Hierarchies,* ed. by Barbara D. Miller. Copyright © 1993. Reprinted by permission of Cambridge University Press.)

THINKING OUTSIDE THE BOX

PROFESSOR KIMBER HADDIX MCKAY, who teaches at the University of Montana, invited representatives from Sexual Abstinence and Family Education (SAFE) to address her class. Read her report at http://zmagsite.zmag.org/Images/bader0105.html.

ARE FAMILY PLANNING PROGRAMS IN BANGLADESH COERCIVE?

Beginning in the 1980s, leaders in the United States began to cast a critical eye on Western family planning programs. Conservative politicians and some religious groups opposed U.S. support of abortion services and other forms of population control, both domestically and internationally. At the same time, critics on the left claimed that the Western-supported family planning programs in the so-called developing countries fail to support women's reproductive rights in various ways: providing inadequate services, using coercive tactics such as financial incentives, and pushing sterilization in favor of other methods that allow women more choice. This Critical Thinking box compares the perspectives of two anthropologists on family planning programs in Bangladesh in terms of women's reproductive rights.

Betsy Hartmann's fieldwork in a village and its surrounding region gave her a negative view of the family planning programs there (1987). The programs were vigorously promoting various methods, including birth control pills, the injectible Depo-Provera, and intrauterine devices (IUDs). But they did not provide adequate medical screening, supervision, and follow-up. Many women experienced problems and became disillusioned with family planning. Instead of improving the existing programs, the government's response was to intensify the promotion of female sterilization.

Hartmann argues that the programs denied women control over their reproduction. She does not dispute the value of family planning programs if they are well designed and well run. Her criticism is based on the lack of good services and safe options for women. She also pointed out the social inequity of population control programs, since they target the poorest women for sterilization and use what Hartmann views as coercive incentives. The financial incentive for sterilization was Taka 175, equivalent to several weeks' wages. In addition, women received an item of clothing worth about Taka 100, and men received an item of clothing worth about Taka 50. In some cases, food was also given. For impoverished people, these incentives mean that a family will be able to have food in a context of great need. A finding

that supports her position is that the number of sterilizations increased during the autumn months when food was scarcest. Thus, people are not freely choosing to be sterilized. Instead, poverty drives them to it, with the lure of the incentives that may seem minor to us but are significant to people struggling each day to provide food for their family.

Barbara Pillsbury, in contrast, defends the family planning program in Bangladesh (1990). She was hired by a U.S. agency to survey the situation there and write a report in response to criticisms from Hartmann and others. Her assessment is based on a review of studies conducted on female sterilization in Bangladesh, rather than on firsthand fieldwork (she has much experience in the field elsewhere, mainly in Africa). Her review indicates that the government of Bangladesh, international aid agencies, and nongovernmental organizations invested substantial efforts in program monitoring and program evaluations to ensure that women's rights and choice are protected.

In Pillsbury's view, the critics are wrong about coerciveness. She argues that the compensation payment is not an important influence on the decision of whether to be sterilized. Pillsbury says that free choice, not incentives, prompt Bangladeshis to seek sterilization. They choose sterilization because they do not want any more children or because another pregnancy would be hard on the woman's health. No one in any of the studies reviewed said that he or she was compelled or deceived into getting sterilized (1990:183).

CRITICAL THINKING QUESTIONS

- How would Betsy Hartmann respond to Barbara Pillsbury?

- If you were hired as an anthropological consultant to follow up on this debate, what further research would you propose to do?

- Does your government currently support family planning programs domestically or worldwide? If so, what kinds of methods does it favor and disfavor?

does not mean that women do not seek abortions, however; rather, the services are underground and unmonitored in terms of safety. The use of condoms is a controversial issue in the United States, with official government policy favoring "abstinence only" for unmarried people and disfavoring the promotion of condom use even though

condoms help prevent sexually transmitted diseases (STDs). In many African countries where various forms of Pentecostal Christianity are increasingly popular, a similar situation exists (Pfeiffer 2004). The Church emphasizes abstinence outside marriage and disapproves of condom use.

At the Global Level

The most far-reaching layer that affects fertility decision making occurs at the international level, where global power structures such as pharmaceutical companies and religious leaders influence country-level and individual-level decision making. In the 1950s, there was a wave of enthusiasm among Western nations for promoting family planning programs of many types in so-called developing countries. In the 1990s, the United States adopted a more restricted policy toward family planning, withdrew support for certain features such as abortion, and began to promote abstinence as the foundation of population control (see Critical Thinking box).

Fertility Control

People in all cultures since prehistory have had ways of influencing fertility, including ways to increase it, reduce it, and regulate its spacing. Some ways are direct, such as using herbs or medicines that induce abortion. Others are indirect, such as long periods of breastfeeding, which reduce the chances of conception. Hundreds of direct indigenous fertility control methods are available cross-culturally (Newman 1972, 1985).

Women waiting their turn at the clinic in Bazarak, eastern Afghanistan. Patriarchal norms prevent Afghan women from going to clinics, and the geographical terrain and distance make it difficult to get to a clinic in cases of emergency. Rates of maternal mortality in remote areas of Afghanistan are probably the highest in the world. ■ *What is the maternal mortality rate in your home country and how does it vary by region, class, or ethnicity?* (Source: © Reza; Webistan/CORBIS)

Research in Afghanistan during the 1980s found over 500 fertility-regulating techniques in just one region (Hunte 1985). In Afghanistan, as in most nonindustrial cultures, it is women who possess this information. Specialists, such as midwives or herbalists, provide further expertise. Of the total number of methods in the Afghanistan study, 72 percent were for increasing fertility, 22 percent were contraceptives, and 6 percent were used to induce abortion. Most methods involve plant and animal substances. Herbs are made into tea and taken orally. Some substances are formed into pills, some steamed and inhaled as vapors, some vaginally inserted, and others rubbed on the woman's stomach.

The next section considers two methods of family planning: induced abortion, which is a long-standing form of family planning, and, the most recent, the *new reproductive technologies (NRTs)*.

Induced Abortion

A review of 400 societies found that induced abortion was practiced in virtually all of them (Devereaux 1976). Cross-culturally, attitudes toward induced abortion range from absolute acceptability to conditional approval (abortion is acceptable but only under specified conditions), tolerance (abortion is regarded with neither approval nor disapproval), and opposition and punishment for offenders. Methods of inducing abortion include hitting the abdomen, starving oneself, taking drugs, jumping from high places, jumping up and down, lifting heavy objects, and doing hard work. Some methods clearly are dangerous to the pregnant woman. In Afghanistan, a midwife inserts into the pregnant woman an object such as a wooden spoon or stick treated with copper sulphate to cause vaginal bleeding and eventual abortion of the fetus (Hunte 1985).

The reasons women seek to induce abortion are usually related to economic and social factors (Devereaux 1976). Pastoralist women, for example, frequently carry heavy loads, sometimes for long distances. This lifestyle does not allow women to care for many small children at one time. Poverty is another frequent motivation. A woman who is faced with a pregnancy in the context of limited resources may find abortion preferable to bearing a child that cannot be fed. Culturally defined "legitimacy" of a pregnancy and social penalties for bearing an illegitimate child provide long-standing motivations for abortion, especially in Western societies.

Some governments intervene in family decisions to regulate access to abortion, either promoting it or forbidding it. Since the late 1980s, China has pursued a rigorous campaign to limit population growth (Greenhalgh 2003). Its One-Child-per-Couple Policy, announced in 1978, allowed most families to have only one child. It involved strict surveillance of pregnancies, strong group disapproval directed toward women pregnant for the

In Japan, people regularly visit and decorate *mizuko,* small statues in memory of their "returned" fetuses. ■ *In your cultural world, what is the definition and status of a fetus? Does a fetus have rights?* (Source: © Bettmann/CORBIS)

second time or more, and forced abortions and sterilizations. Inadvertently, this policy simultaneously led to an increase in female infanticide, as parents, prompted by son preference, killed or abandoned infant daughters.

Religion and abortion are often related, but there is no simple relationship between what a particular religion teaches about abortion and what people actually do. Catholicism forbids abortion, but thousands of Catholic women have sought abortions throughout the world. Predominantly Catholic countries have laws making induced abortion illegal. This is the case in Brazil where, in spite of the law and Catholic beliefs, many women, especially poor women, resort to abortion. In one impoverished shantytown in the city of Recife (see Map 10.1, p. 264), one-third of the women said that they had aborted at least once (Gregg 2003:71–72). Illegal abortions are more likely to have negative effects on women's health than safe, legal abortion services. Although solid statistics are difficult to obtain, one estimate for Bahia is that at least one-fourth of all maternal deaths were due to complications of abortion (McCallum 2005:222).

Islamic teachings forbid abortion. Abortion of female fetuses is nonetheless practiced covertly in Pakistan and by Muslims in India. Hinduism teaches *ahimsa,* or nonviolence toward other living beings, including a fetus whose movements have been felt by the mother. Thousands of Hindus, however, seek abortions every year. In contrast, Buddhism provides no overt rulings against abortion. Japanese Buddhism teaches that all life is fluid and that an aborted fetus is simply "returned" to a watery world of unshaped life and may later come back (LaFleur 1992). This belief is compatible with people's frequent use of induced abortion as a form of birth control in Japan.

The New Reproductive Technologies

Women's reproductive rights are an important contemporary issue worldwide. These rights range from the choice of seeking abortion to the right to bear a second child (in China). They include the issue of the right to decide to abort a fetus on the basis of its gender, physical disabilities, or other characteristics. Since the early 1980s, new forms of reproductive technology have been developed and have been made available in many places around the world.

One recent development is the ability to gain genetic information about the fetus, which can be used by parents in deciding whether to continue or stop the pregnancy. In the United States and some European countries, amniocentesis is a legal test used to reveal certain genetic problems in the fetus, such as Down syndrome and spina bifida. Some anthropologists question the social justice involved in this testing.

Rayna Rapp conducted local fieldwork on genetic testing among poor women in New York City (1993). In the United States, amniocentesis is now so common that it is can be considered a "ritual of pregnancy," especially among the educated, urbanized, White middle and upper classes. But the situation in the Prenatal Diagnosis Laboratory (PDL), where Rapp did participant observation, is quite different. The PDL of the City of New York was established in 1978 to offer amniocentesis to low-income women who are mainly African American or Latina. When a counselor at the PDL recommends an amniocentesis procedure, many people refuse, rather than welcoming it as a so-called ritual of pregnancy.

Rapp witnessed many counseling sessions. She interviewed several "refusers" in their homes about their attitudes toward the testing and why they rejected the counselor's advice. One Haitian father firmly rejected prenatal testing: "The counselor says the baby could be born retarded. They always say Haitian children are retarded. What is this retarded? Many Haitian children are said to be retarded in the public schools. If we send them to the Haitian Academy (a community-based private school) they learn just fine" (1993:392).

Although medical innovations such as amniocentesis are promoted as "advances for women," Rapp finds that poor women who are advised to seek genetic testing during their pregnancy are not fully aware of all that is involved. She argues that the new technology and the increased "choice" it offers does not empower them. Instead, it overpowers them.

In vitro fertilization (IVF) procedures are an increasingly important part of the new reproductive technologies. This procedure, designed to bypass infertility, is highly sought after by many couples in Western countries, especially middle- and upper-class couples, among whom infertility is inexplicably high. It is also becoming more available in cities worldwide (Inhorn 2003). As IVF spreads globally, people interpret it within their own cultural frameworks. In much of the United States and the United Kingdom, where IVF first became available, people consider its use to be an indication of "reproduction gone awry," of natural inadequacy, and failure (Jenkins and Inhorn 2003). In Athens, Greece, middle-class urban women who seek IVF see it as natural because it helps them realize a key aspect of their feminine nature through pregnancy and birth (Paxson 2003). Their husbands are less positive about IVF, as they feel that it

bypasses their role in conception. A study of male infertility in two Middle Eastern cities, Cairo in Egypt and Beirut in Lebanon, reveals how closely linked masculine identity is with male fertility (Inhorn 2004). In these cities, infertile men face serious social stigma and feelings of deep inadequacy. In addition, third-party donation of sperm is not acceptable according to Islam.

Medical institutional culture also varies worldwide in terms of its attitudes toward in vitro fertilization. In Japan, a doctor who performed an IVF procedure was expelled by the leading obstetric society in 1998 (Jordan 1998). Japanese societal values in relation to reproduction are complicated: They oppose surgery because it cuts the body, but they allow abortion. Birth control pills are illegal. The growing public demand in Japan for new reproductive techniques is opposed by the medical profession.

Culture and Death

Cultural anthropologists have studied mortality less than fertility (Bledsoe and Hirschman 1989). Mortality is difficult to research in a typical fieldwork period. In a year, several births might occur in a village of 1,000 people, but fewer infant deaths will occur and perhaps no murders or suicides. Another reason for the difference in research emphasis between fertility and mortality is the greater availability of funding for fertility studies, given the worldwide concern with population growth and family planning.

In the aftermath of Hurricane Katrina in 2005, a corpse lies covered as evacuees line the streets outside the convention center in New Orleans, Louisiana. After acknowledging that the initial federal effort to aid victims had failed, President George W. Bush deployed additional U.S. troops to the area. ■ *Using the Internet, learn what roles cultural anthropologists played in the posthurricane situation in the Gulf Coast area.* (Source: Shannon Stapleton/CORBIS)

Cultural factors often put certain people at more risk than others of dying from a certain cause and at a particular age. Consider patterns of death from car accidents. The rate of severe car accidents is higher among men and is associated with high-risk driving behavior, such as driving at high speeds and under the influence of alcohol (Hakamies-Blomqvist 1994). Among older drivers in Finland, an increase in fatal accidents occurs among female drivers. The explanation is related to the fact that, throughout their lives, women have had substantially less driving experience in terms of mileage and conditions because more men have jobs to which they commute. Women's relative lack of driving experience places them at a disadvantage when it comes to coping with the effects of aging on driving.

Analysts place the causes of death in three categories:

- *Proximate:* a factor, or factors, closest to the actual death

- *Intermediate:* a factor, or factors, that led to the proximate cause of death

- *Ultimate:* a factor, or factors, underlying both intermediate and proximate causes of death

Consider the death of an infant born into in a low-income group, in a poor country, who dies within a few days. Dehydration was recorded as the cause of death on the infant's death certificate, and that is the proximate cause of death. But why was the baby dehydrated? A closer look into the situation might show that the baby was malnourished. Malnutrition leads to diarrhea and subsequent dehydration. Malnutrition could be considered the intermediate cause of death. But why was the baby malnourished? Maybe the family was so poor that the mother was weak and malnourished and could not breastfeed the baby. Perhaps the baby died during a period of extreme food scarcity in the area. Perhaps the baby was an unwanted third daughter and no one tried to keep her alive. The question of ultimate causation entails an analysis of underlying factors that increase the risk of death. The next section provides some examples of how culture shapes death.

Infanticide

Infanticide, or the deliberate killing of offspring, is widely practiced cross-culturally, although it is rarely a frequent or common practice (Dickemann 1975, 1979; Divale and Harris 1976; Scrimshaw 1984). Infanticide takes two major forms: it can be direct infanticide or indirect infanticide (Harris 1977). *Direct infanticide* is the death of an infant or child resulting from actions such as beating, smothering, poisoning, or drowning.

Indirect infanticide, a more subtle process, may involve prolonged practices such as food deprivation, failure to take a sick infant to a clinic, or failure to provide warm clothing in winter.

The most frequent motive for direct infanticide reported cross-culturally is that the infant was "deformed" or very ill (Scrimshaw 1984:490–491). Other motives for infanticide include sex of the infant, an adulterous conception, an unwed mother, the birth of twins, and too many children in the family. A study of 148 cases of infanticide in contemporary Canada found that the mothers convicted of killing their offspring were relatively young and lacked financial and family resources to help them (Daly and Wilson 1984).

Family Resource Constraints and Child "Fitness"

In all cultures, parents have expectations for their children. If an infant appears to be unable to meet these expectations, parental disappointment and detachment might occur and may result in lethal neglect or direct infanticide.

Culturally accepted infanticide has long existed among the Tarahumara (pronounced tara-oo-MAR-a), indigenous people who live in Chihuahua state, northern Mexico (see Map 5.4, p. 128) (Mull and Mull 1987). The approximately 70,000 rural Tarahumara live in a harsh area. Houses are made of logs with dirt floors and no running water or electricity. The Tarahumara grow corn and beans and raise sheep and goats, mainly for their own use. Human strength is valued in children as well as in adults. Children begin helping with herding and child care early in their lives. Dennis Mull first learned about a case of infanticide when he was working as a volunteer physician in a hospital. A 12-month-old girl who had been admitted several months earlier developed a complication requiring the amputation of half her foot. During her recovery period, her mother's visits became less frequent. In conversations with the medical staff, the mother expressed restrained but deep anger about her daughter's disability. Some time after the child was dismissed from the hospital, she died. It was generally understood in the community that the child was a victim of indirect infanticide. One person explained, "Well, after all, with only half a foot she'd never be able to walk right or work hard. She might never find a husband" (1987:116–117).

Among the poor of northeastern Brazil, indirect infanticide is also related to harsh conditions and poverty

THINK OF a context where it would be feasible for an anthropologist to study mortality.

THINKING OUTSIDE THE BOX

infanticide: the killing of an infant or child.

These Tarahumara women of Chihuahua state, Mexico, are making tesgüino. Tesgüino is an alcoholic beverage made from fermented maize (corn). It is of central importance in the secular and religious lives of the Tarahumara. The Tarahumara region often experiences extended drought and food shortages and poverty is prevalent. ■ (Source: © Lindsay Hebberd/CORBIS)

(Scheper-Hughes 1992). In a shantytown called Bom Jesus, in the state of Pernambuco, Brazil, life expectancy is low. Available data on infant and child mortality in Bom Jesus since the 1960s led anthropologist Nancy Scheper-Hughes to coin the painfully ironic phrase, *the modernization of mortality*. The modernization of mortality in Brazil is class based, mirroring a deep division in entitlements between the rich and the poor. Economic growth in Brazil has brought rising standards of living for many. The *infant mortality rate* (deaths of children under the age of 1 year per 1,000 births) declined dramatically in recent decades. This decline, however, is unevenly distributed. High infant death rates are concentrated among the poorest classes of society. Poverty forces mothers to selectively (and unconsciously) neglect babies that seem sickly or weak, sending them to heaven as "angel babies" rather than struggling to keep them alive. People's religious beliefs, a form of Catholicism, provide psychological support for indirect infanticide by allowing mothers to believe that their dead babies are safe in heaven (this ethnographic case is discussed further in Chapter 6).

When the infant's gender is the basis for infanticide, females tend to be the target (Miller 1997 [1981]:42–44). Among foraging groups, female infanticide is found among some circumpolar groups of North America. This practice is likely related to the importance of raising males who will provide food through large-game hunting. Among horticultural societies, a correlation exists between the level of intergroup warfare and the practice of female infanticide (Divale and Harris 1976). Warfare places high value on raising males and diverts resources and support from females.

Son preference, discussed earlier in this chapter, is linked to indirect female infanticide in contemporary China, the Republic of Korea, Hong Kong, India, Pakistan, and parts of the Middle East (see Everyday Anthropology box). In these countries, son preference is related to a complex set of cultural factors, including the gender division of labor, kinship patterns, and marriage costs.

Suicide

Suicide occurs in all societies, but whether it is viewed as a positive or negative act varies. In some contexts, suicide is considered a crime. Religions take various positions on suicide. Catholicism defines suicide as a sin, and suicide rates tend to be lower in Catholic countries than in Protestant countries (Durkheim 1951 [1897]:152). Buddhism does not consider suicide a punishable crime, and Buddhists have sometimes used suicide as a form of political protest.

Suicide terrorism is a term that has become prominent since the September 11, 2001, attacks on the United States. Those attacks, as well as many others carried out in the Middle East and elsewhere by people of several different religious and political persuasions, involve the suicide of one or more people with the intention of killing other people as well (Andriolo 2002). Islam condemns suicide and teaches that hell awaits those who commit it. But certain reinterpretations, among Philippine Muslims, for example, see purposeful suicide killings as being outside Islamic teachings but nonetheless justifiable on other grounds. A few pages in the manual that the September 11 hijackers had with them related their actions to raids that the prophet Muhammad conducted to consolidate

A PREFERENCE FOR SONS

Prospective parents in all cultures may ask themselves questions such as: Will my baby be healthy? Will I have a girl or a boy? Throughout much of Asia, the baby's gender is often as important as the health of the baby. The preference for sons is especially strong in northern India.

The population of India has 55 million fewer females than males. Much of this gap is caused by indirect female infanticide and sex-selective abortion (Miller 1997 [1981]). These practices cause the **sex ratio,** or the number of males per 100 females in a population, to become unbalanced. The scarcity of girls is most extreme in northern India. In this region, it is common for mothers to breastfeed infant daughters less often and for a shorter period of time than they do their sons. Hospitals admit twice as many boys as girls, not because more boys are sick than girls but because family decision makers are more willing to allocate time and money to the health of boys than of girls.

The regional pattern corresponds with two features of the economy: production and marriage exchanges. The northern plains are dominated by *dry-field wheat cultivation,* which requires intensive labor inputs for plowing and field preparation and then moderate amounts of field labor for sowing, weeding, and harvesting, with women assisting in the latter tasks as unpaid family labor. Production in southern and eastern India relies more on *wet rice cultivation,* in which women form the bulk of the paid agricultural labor force. In much of southern India, women sometimes participate equally with men in agricultural planning and decision making.

Paralleling this regional difference in the gender division of labor is a contrast in costs related to marriage. In the North, marriage typically requires, especially among the propertied groups, a **dowry,** or **groomprice**—the transfer of money and goods from the bride's family to the groom's family. Marriage costs in the South among both propertied and unpropertied groups may involve **brideprice** or **bridewealth**—the transfer of money and goods from the groom's side to the bride's father, along with a tradition of passing gold jewelry through the female line from mother to daughter. In recent years, however, dowry has been spreading throughout India.

From a parent's perspective, the birth of several daughters in the northern system is a financial drain. In

A low-income, itinerant vendor in a small town in India's Himalayan region proudly displays her son. Son preference is spreading from the North Indian plains region throughout India. ■ (Source: Barbara Miller)

the North, the more sons per daughter in the household the better: More dowries coming in will finance a "better" marriage of a daughter. In the South, a daughter is considered a valuable laborer and source of wealth. Importantly, much of northern dowry and southern brideprice circulates. In the North, an incoming dowry can be used to finance the marriage of the groom's sister. In the South, cash received at the marriage of a daughter can be used for the marriage of her brother.

sex ratio: the number of males per 100 females in a population.
dowry: the transfer of cash and goods from the bride's family to the newly married couple and to the groom's family.
groomprice: the transfer of cash and goods, often large amounts, from the bride's family to the groom's family.
brideprice or **bridewealth:** the transfer of cash and goods from the groom's family to the bride's family and to the bride.

The economic costs and benefits to a household of having sons versus daughters in India also vary by class. Middle-class and upper-class families, especially in the North, tend to keep girls and women out of the paid labor force. Thus, daughters are a greater economic liability among them. Among the poor, where girls, as well as boys, may earn money in the informal sector (such as doing piece-work at home), daughters are less of a burden. This class difference is mirrored in marriage costs. Among the poor, marriage costs are lower than among the middle and upper classes. They often involve balanced transfers between the bride's and groom's families.

Thus, poverty is not the major cause of son preference and daughter disfavor in India. Instead, the cause is the desire to maximize family status and wealth. If parents have two sons and one daughter in the North Indian marriage system, then two dowries come in with the brides of the sons and only one dowry will be paid out. The incoming dowries can be used to finance an impressive outgoing dowry of one's daughter that will attract a high-status husband. If northern parents have two daughters and one son, the ratio of incoming to outgoing wealth changes dramatically. This situation will impoverish a family.

FOOD FOR THOUGHT

- Have you, or anyone you know, experienced a feeling of being less valued as a child than other children in the family? If you are an "only child," you will need to ponder experiences of your friends.

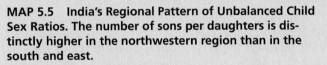

■ Juvenile sex ratios of 106 boys per girls and above
■ Juvenile sex ratios below 106 boys per girls

0   400   800 Miles

0   400   800 Kilometers

MAP 5.5   India's Regional Pattern of Unbalanced Child Sex Ratios. The number of sons per daughters is distinctly higher in the northwestern region than in the south and east.

Sania Mirza of India lunges for a return from Marion Bartoli of France during the U.S. Open tennis tournament in Flushing Meadows, New York, in 2005. A Muslim and world-class tennis player, Mirza is the "poster girl" for India's public education campaign to promote awareness of the value of daughters. Slogans urge parents to have daughters and to care for them because their daughter may be the next Sania Mirza. At the same time, some conservative Islamic groups criticize Mirza for wearing immodest clothing. ■ (Source: © Brian Snyder/ Reuters/CORBIS)

his position, thus portraying their actions as acceptable and even heroic. Many Islamic scholars, however, reject this reasoning.

Some religions place a positive value on *martyrdom*, or a person facing and accepting death for a sacred cause. Linking personal martyrdom with killing is also found in secular political movements. The young Tamil woman who blew herself up, along with India's former prime minister, Rajiv Gandhi (Indira Gandhi's eldest son), is an example of a secular, political martyr-assassin. Her motivation was support for Tamil ethnic separatism in northern Sri Lanka.

Throughout much of Asia and the South Pacific, suicide is considered a noble and honorable act. When Cheyenne Brando, daughter of actor Marlon Brando and Tahitian actress Tarita, committed suicide in Tahiti, the local mayor called her suicide "a beautiful gesture" (Gliotto 1995:70). Honorable suicide is also found in Japan, where it is related to a strong commitment to group goals and a feeling of failure to live up to those goals (Lebra 1976). Suicide in these societies is a way of "saving face."

Sati (pronounced SUT-TEE), or the suicide of a wife after the death of her husband, has been practiced by Hindus in India for several hundred years and occasionally into the present. According to Hindu scriptures, a woman whose husband dies performs an act of great honor if she voluntarily joins his corpse on the funeral pyre and burns to death. No one knows how common sati was in the past, but its ideal is still upheld by conservative Hindus. The most recent reported sati took place in the northern state of Rajasthan, in 1987, by a young widow named Roop Kanwar. Historians and social scientists have debated the degree of agency, or free will, involved in such suicides, as there is evidence of direct coercion in some cases—for example, when a widow is drugged or physically forced onto the pyre. Indirect coercion is also culturally embedded in the belief that a woman whose husband dies is to blame for his death: Perhaps she did not serve him with enough devotion, pray or fast for him enough, or give him enough food. The life of surviving widows is difficult, involving loss of status, shame, and material deprivation.

Since the mid-1950s, suicide rates have increased by 60 percent worldwide (Buvinic and Morrison 2000). Around one million people take their own lives each year, and that number continues to rise. Suicide has long been most prevalent in the industrialized, urbanized societies of Europe. In the late twentieth century, however, suicide rates rose steeply in several developing nations, such as Sri Lanka and Samoa (Kearney and Miller 1985). This rise appears to be driven by a widening gap between

A temple in Rajasthan, northern India, dedicated to women who have committed sati. ■ *Consider various examples of suicide in different cultures and be prepared to debate whether explanations of structure or agency seem more relevant.* (Source: © Lindsey Hebberd/CORBIS)

aspirations, especially of youth, and limited ways of achieving these aspirations due to economic constraints. Even more recently, suicide among youth in many Amazonian tribal groups has risen steeply (Jeter 2004). Forcibly displaced from their traditional territories, these people live on reservations that are squeezed more and more each year by encroaching development. They are impoverished, grieving for their lost heritage and lifestyle, and despairing. The only available work in sugar cane refineries and alcohol processing plants is extremely arduous and pays little. Faced with a bleak future, many young people end their lives, usually by hanging. One man commented, "It is a curse to have to cut your chil-

---

femicide: the murder of a person based on the fact of her being female.

genocide: the destruction of a culture and its people through physical extermination.

ethnocide: the destruction of a culture without physically killing its people.

dren down . . . we are living in a time of a great plague" (2004:A22)

In the United States and Canada, the highest suicide rates occur among Indian or First Peoples' populations, especially among youth (EcoHawk 1997). In the recently created Nunavut Territory of Canada's eastern Arctic (see Map 1.2, p. 12), suicide among the native Inuit people is the most serious problem facing the new government (Tester and McNicoll 2004). Suicide rates in Nunavut are six times higher than in the southern provinces, and males aged 15 to 29 are most likely to commit suicide. A compelling interpretation of this situation is that four aspects of *colonial stress* are related to the high suicide rates: stress of identity and self-definition, stress of isolation, and stress of changing intergenerational relations. In this region, colonialism refers to domination by the Canadian state, with the 1960s and 1970s being a particularly intense period. During this time, the government attempted to repress Inuit identity through various assimilation strategies, including imposition of the English language. One result was loss of Inuit self-esteem, or *inuusittiaqarniq*, a process that affected young men the most, given intergenerational expectations for them and their inability to fulfill these expectations.

Epidemics

Epidemics are diseases that spread rapidly and widely throughout populations. Throughout humanity's evolution, major epidemics such as the European plague dramatically affected population numbers and challenged people's social and psychological coping mechanisms. The major epidemic of modern times, HIV/AIDS, has been identified only since the 1980s. It has had a substantial mortality effect over the past two decades.

Currently, sub-Saharan countries are the most affected by the HIV epidemic, with most deaths occurring among adults of parent age (Nyambedha, Wandibba, and Aagaard-Hansen 2003). These deaths are tragic in themselves, but they also create huge numbers of orphaned children. Global estimates are that 10 million children under the age of 15 have lost their mother or both parents to AIDS. In Kenya alone, it is estimated that there are 1.5 million orphaned children. Community-based interventions to help these disadvantaged children would benefit from attention to local cultural factors (see Lessons Applied box).

Violence

Violent death can be the result of private, interpersonal conflict, or it can occur in a public arena, either through informal conflict between individuals or groups, such as gang fights, or formal conflict, such as war. Violent death can be direct, as when someone kills someone else with a weapon, or indirect, as when a government fails to provide food for people during a disaster. Often, culture shapes the victim pattern of violent death.

Private Violence: Wife Killing

Throughout the world, private violence resulting in death is all too common. One example, infanticide, was discussed earlier. Lethal spousal violence is known to exist throughout most of the world in varying degrees, although dependable statistics are unavailable. In the case of spouses, far more women are killed by husbands or male partners than vice versa.

In India, beginning in the 1980s, many cases of *dowry death* were reported. This term refers to the murder of a wife, characteristically committed by a husband but often in collusion with his mother. The means involve throwing a flammable substance over the woman and then lighting her on fire. Especially prevalent in the major cities of northern India, these murders are motivated by obsessive material greed and the attempt to extract wealth from the wife's family through a stream of demanded gifts. If the bride's family cannot comply, the bride's life is endangered. This form of **femicide** or murder of a person based on being female, is related to the low value of women in India, especially in the North and among many of the status-seeking middle and upper classes.

Public Violence

Two common forms of lethal public violence that anthropologists study are warfare and genocide (discussed further in Chapter 11). This section focuses on their effects on mortality. The few anthropological studies that have addressed mortality from warfare cross-culturally reveal that among horticultural societies, warfare is the leading cause of male deaths (Divale and Harris 1976). Horticulture's requirement for large territories puts many groups in conflict with one another. In recent decades, conflicts with outsiders have increased; for example, the Yanomami of the Brazilian and Venezuelan Amazon region (see Map 3.4, p. 73) are squeezed by outsiders such as cattle ranch developers and miners (Ferguson 1990). This external pressure impels them to engage in intergroup raids that often result in the deaths of male fighters and also sometimes of women, who may be captured and killed. In some especially vulnerable groups of Yanomami, up to one-third of all adult males die as a result of intergroup raids and warfare. In contrast, in industrialized societies, the death rates of men actively involved in warfare are a much smaller proportion of the total death rate, being replaced by such causes as automobile accidents and heart disease.

Some scholars distinguish **genocide**, the destruction of a culture and its people through physical extermination, from **ethnocide**, the destruction of a culture without

Lessons Applied

TAKING CULTURAL PATTERNS INTO ACCOUNT FOR IMPROVED ORPHAN CARE IN KENYA

The steep rise in the number of orphans in Africa, due to the HIV/AIDS epidemic, calls for new thinking about how to care for these children. Traditional kin-based support systems are breaking down under the strain. Child care in many African contexts involves parents, grandparents, and other family members. But now, this social safety net is not enough.

Many nongovernmental agencies are helping to design community-based services for AIDS orphans. Cultural anthropologists can assist in increasing the effectiveness of these services. Information about local cultural practices and beliefs can be used to tailor programs to fit particular communities. Anthropologists have long known that "one-size-fits-all" programs, designed by outsiders without attention to local culture, are less effective than they could be or, at worst, they may fail disastrously.

One anthropological study undertaken to provide such vital cultural information was conducted in western Kenya in an area bordering Lake Victoria (Nyambedha, Wandibba, and Aagaard-Hansen 2003) (see Map 6.2, p. 158). The Luo are the predominant ethnic group in the region. The area is poor, and most Luo practice small-scale farming and obtain some additional income from fishing, migrant labor, and informal gold mining. Recurrent droughts lead to frequent crop failures. Children are important in the local economy: They work on farms, planting, weeding, and harvesting and doing other important tasks such as collecting firewood, herding animals, fetching water, and fishing. Clean water is scarce. Health services provided by a Christian mission and the government are of poor quality and not affordable for most people.

The Luo define an orphan as someone under the age of 18 who has lost either one or both parents; thus, they refer to single and double orphans. (The Luo definition differs from the usual international definition: someone under the age of 15 who has lost both parents.) The Luo say that the neediest are double orphans.

The large and sudden increase in the number of orphans creates strains on the community as people come to realize that their traditional pattern of caring for orphans within the kinship structure is not adequate. The traditional generosity of kin seems to be declining. At the same time, a long-standing pattern of spending a lot of money on funerals means that resources that could go to orphans instead go to burial and after-burial rituals.

Community-based organizations such as churches and women's groups in this region are doing little to help the orphans, although in other areas they are more active. The study provides a baseline of the population of orphans, information about their specific needs and coping strategies, and insights about community views of the problem. It points to the particular needs of different types of orphans and the varying strengths of different family structures in caring for orphans.

The authors reject the idea of constructing an orphanage as a way of dealing with the problem. They offer no specific suggestions for community-based programs, but it is easy to see that the following would help: financial support to single-parent and grandparent caretakers, waiving or community funding of the school fees for orphans, and a social movement to divert some of the money used for funerals to orphan care.

FOOD FOR THOUGHT

- Has the issue of AIDS orphans in Africa come to your attention before? How was the issue presented? If it had not come to your attention, what might explain its relative invisibility?

---

physically killing its people. The Chinese occupation of Tibet, the Khmer Rouge's massacres in Cambodia, the Serbian-Bosnian conflict, the Hutu-Tutsi conflict in Rwanda, and the Indonesian government's actions in pre-independence East Timor are examples of politically motivated genocide.

Genocide of indigenous peoples has been occurring for centuries as imperialist powers and profit-seeking explorers and settlers have intentionally brought about the extinction of entire peoples (Maybury-Lewis 2002). During the nineteenth century, British settlers in Tasmania, an island off the southern coast of Australia (see Map 4.4, p. 105), carried out an overt campaign to exterminate the indigenous Tasmanians. In other cases, mass killings were used as a means of terrorizing survivors into performing forced labor, as, for example, in the rubber plantations

Thousands of refugees from Sudan's Darfur region have fled to neighboring Chad where they find shelter in camps such as this one. ■ *Assume you have a job as a refugees' advocate with Refugees International (www.refugeesinternational.org) and you are assigned to assess living conditions in this camp. What are the five most important questions you will pursue when you are in the field?* (Source: © Radu Sigheti/Reuters/CORBIS)

Public policies can be instruments of indirect violence, or *structural violence,* which lead to "excess" deaths. One such case is documented in Mongolia (Janes and Chuluundorj 2004). Beginning in 1990, Mongolia put into place several economic reforms as it transitioned from a socialist state to market capitalism: removal of restrictions on international trade, lifting of price controls, decollectivation of herds, privatization of state-run enterprises, and marked reduction in government services. The immediate consequences were food shortages to near-famine, widespread unemployment, rising urban crime, increase in alcoholism, emergent social inequality, and the collapse of the health-care system. During the early 1990s, the *maternal mortality rate* (measured as deaths of women related to pregnancy and birth per 100,000 live births) rose steeply. In 1990, the maternal mortality rate in Mongolia, as a whole, was 119. By 1994, it rose to its peak of 240. Since then, the maternal mortality rate began to decline. In 1999, it was around 180, still far higher than it was before the reforms. Mongolian women paid a heavy price for the postsocialist transition policies.

of Peru and the Democratic Republic of Congo. These examples of imperialist genocide were driven by greed and supported by a racist ideology that considered indigenous people less than human. Today, greed-driven and carelessly planned development projects such as large dams (discussed in Chapter 16) are often an indirect form of genocide when they completely disrupt where indigenous people live, force them to resettle, and subject them to new diseases and suicidal despair.

The legacy of mistreatment, forced relocation, and discriminatory policies experienced by Native Americans in the United States and First Peoples in Canada continues to play out in much higher rates of mortality in these populations compared to the general population (Brave Heart 2004). The situation among the Lakota and Dakota/Nakota peoples (see Map 5.6) living on reservations is grim. Mortality rates are three times higher than the U.S. average. Tuberculosis death rates are more than six times higher. Alcoholism mortality rates are 29 percent higher. Suicide rates for the northeastern part of South Dakota are the second highest in the Indian Health Service areas, exceeded only by those in Alaska. These rates should be viewed in the context of unemployment levels of over 70 percent, cumulative losses of resources and culture over generations, and the breakdown of spiritual and social supports. Native American and First People leaders are working hard to devise programs to help alleviate despair, substance abuse, and the intergenerational transfer of suffering.

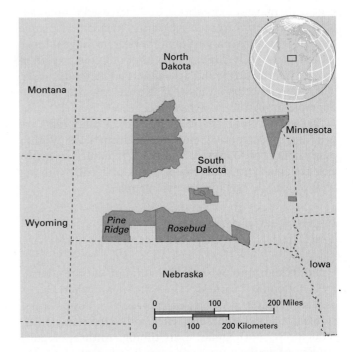

MAP 5.6 Indian Reservations in South Dakota. South Dakota has a total population of 755,000 of which 88 percent are White and 8 percent are Native American. The geography consists of prairie, low-lying hills, and the Black Hills. Before European colonialism, the region was inhabited by the Sioux and Northern Cheyenne. South Dakota is nicknamed "The Mount Rushmore State" because of the massive stone carving of four U.S. presidents in the Black Hills, the state's major tourist attraction. Indian tribes in the area object to the sculpture since it is carved into one of their most sacred sites.

The Big Questions Revisited

WHAT are the modes of reproduction cross-culturally?

Cultural anthropologists study how culture shapes fertility, or the number of births in a population. They classify the cross-cultural data on fertility into three modes of reproduction, or the dominant pattern of fertility in a culture. The three modes of reproduction are tied to three modes of production: foraging, agriculture, and industrialism/informatics. For thousands of years, foragers maintained a balanced level of population through direct and indirect means of fertility regulation.

With farming and sedentarization, a different mode of reproduction emerged. Farming provided different foods, especially more starchy foods, and increased food availability. The effect of sedentarization means that people are not constantly moving, and they can manage to raise more children. The highest rates of population growth in human history are found among settled agriculturalists. The contemporary Amish of North America are an example of high-fertility farmers.

In industrial/informatics economies, fertility rates are generally low or at a below-replacement level. Within many countries, both rich and poor, economic inequalities are linked to different patterns of fertility among well-off people and low-income people.

HOW does culture shape fertility in different contexts?

Cultural anthropologists find that, in all cultures, fertility is not purely "natural." No woman, anywhere, bears as many children as her biological capacity allows. Cross-culturally, many techniques exist for increasing fertility, reducing it, and regulating its timing. Anthropological studies of indigenous fertility-regulating mechanisms reveal hundreds of different methods, including the use of herbs and other natural sources for inhibiting or enhancing fertilization and for inducing abortion if an undesired pregnancy occurs. In nonindustrial societies, the knowledge and practice of fertility regulation were largely unspecialized and available to all women. Early specializations included midwives and herbalists.

In industrialism/informatics, substantial scientific and medical specialization exists. In these contexts, most women do not control reproductive knowledge and expertise. Technological innovations are emerging, especially to address increasing rates of infertility. Class-stratified access to fertility-regulating methods exists globally and within countries. Artificial insemination and in vitro fertilization are challenging religions to develop new policies.

HOW does culture shape mortality in different contexts?

Population growth and change are also affected through the cultural shaping of death. The practice of infanticide, or the deliberate killing of a child, is of ancient origin, and it still exists today. In some cases, people resort to infanticide because of limited family economic resources. In others, motivating factors appear to be perceptions about the "fitness" of the child or gender preferences. Infanticide can be direct or indirect. Both types of infanticide exist in parts of India, China, and elsewhere in Asia where people strongly prefer sons. This practice results in highly unbalanced sex ratios in these populations, and many activists and politicians are concerned about these situations. Deaths from suicide, from epidemics, and from public and private violence also follow cultural fault lines. Suicide rates are rising worldwide. No longer mainly a European practice, suicide is rising dramatically among young people in colonized contexts and many developing countries. Birth and death—far from being random, natural events—are cultural events to a large extent.

KEY CONCEPTS

below-replacement-level fertility, p. 123
brideprice or bridewealth, p. 136
demographic transition, p. 124
dowry or groomprice, p. 136
ethnocide, p. 129
femicide, p. 129

fertility, p. 120
genocide, p. 139
infanticide, p. 134
menarche, p. 126
menopause, p. 126
migration, p. 120

mode of reproduction, p. 120
mortality, p. 120
pronatalism, p. 121
replacement-level fertility, p. 123
sex ratio, p. 136
sex-selective infanticide, p. 129

SUGGESTED READINGS

Kamran Asdar Ali. *Planning the Family in Egypt: New Bodies, New Selves.* Austin: University of Texas Press, 2002. The author, a Pakistani doctor and anthropologist, provides a critique of family planning policies and programs in Egypt that pressure women to act in the country's interest by limiting their fertility. Most Egyptian women's families and religion, in contrast, are pronatalist.

Caroline Bledsoe and Barney Cohen, eds. *Social Dynamics of Adolescent Fertility in Sub-Saharan Africa.* Washington, DC: National Academy Press, 1993. An anthropologist and a demographer examine country-level survey data on cultural factors related to high fertility rates among adolescents in sub-Saharan Africa. They discuss patterns of adolescent sexuality; attitudes toward marriage; women's status, knowledge, and practice of contraception; and the role of education.

Nadia Taysir Dabbagh. *Suicide in Palestine: Narratives of Despair.* London: Hurst & Company, 2005. The author, who is the daughter of a Palestinian refugee, studied the rising rates of suicide in Ramallah, the West Bank. She examines recent trends in the context of Arab values, the family, and the political economy. In-depth examination of several cases of suicide by men and women reveal no simple pattern.

John D. Early and Thomas N. Headland. *Population Dynamics of a Philippine Rain Forest People: The San Ildefonso Agta.* Gainesville: University of Florida Press, 1998. This study describes longitudinal population dynamics of an Agta group of Luzon Island, the Philippines. It draws on a forty-four–year quantitative database on fertility, mortality, and migration, starting when the Agta were forest foragers and including their present situation as small-scale farmers.

Thomas E. Fricke. *Himalayan Households: Tamang Demography and Domestic Processes.* New York: Columbia University Press, 1994. This book presents findings from a local study of population patterns and change in one region of Nepal. It includes chapters on the subsistence economy, fertility and mortality, the life course, household dynamics, and recent changes.

Jessica L. Gregg. *Virtually Virgins: Sexual Strategies and Cervical Cancer in Recife, Brazil.* Stanford, CA: Stanford University Press, 2003. Research in a favela, or shantytown, in northeast Brazil, and in a maternity clinic, as well as interviews with many impoverished women of the favela, show how they attempt to deal with racism, sexism, poverty, and violence. The women establish relationships with men in order to be able to feed their children.

W. Penn Handwerker, ed. *Births and Power: Social Change and the Politics of Reproduction.* Boulder, CO: Westview Press, 1990. An overview chapter by the editor is followed by case studies about the Inuit of Canada, the Bariba of West Africa, the Mende of Sierra Leone, Hungary, Bangladesh, and the United States.

Jennifer Johnson-Hanks. *Uncertain Honor: Modern Motherhood in an African Crisis.* Chicago: University of Chicago Press, 2005. Educated women among the ethnic Beti people of southern Cameroon delay motherhood as a modern form of honor. This strategy is related to their formal education, their Catholicism, and the uncertain economic context in the region.

Nancy Howell. *Demography of the Dobe !Kung.* New York: Academic Press, 1979. This classic book describes the demography of a group of South African foragers before they were sedentarized. It considers how anthropological methods contribute to demographic analysis of small-scale societies, causes of illness and death, fertility and sterility, and population growth rates.

Marcia C. Inhorn. *Infertility and Patriarchy: The Cultural Politics of Gender and Family Life in Egypt.* Philadelphia: University of Pennsylvania Press, 1996. Based on fieldwork in Alexandria, this book uses narratives from several infertile Egyptian women to show how the women and their families deal with cultural pressures to bear children.

Leith Mullings and Alaka Wali. *Stress and Resilience: The Social Context of Reproduction in Central Harlem.* New York: Kluwer Academic, 2001. Documenting the daily efforts of African Americans to contend with oppressive conditions, this ethnography focuses on the experiences of women during pregnancy. It details their strategies for coping with the strains that their economic and social context places on them.

Nancy Scheper-Hughes. *Death without Weeping: The Violence of Everyday Life in Brazil.* Berkeley: University of California Press, 1993. This book is a landmark "ethnography of death," based on fieldwork in a shantytown in northeastern Brazil. The author argues that extreme social inequality in Brazil creates a stratified demography in which impoverished people, living within a context of everyday structural violence, have high rates of fertility and high rates of infant mortality.

Nancy Scheper-Hughes and Carolyn Sargent, eds. *Small Wars: The Cultural Politics of Childhood.* Berkeley: University of California Press, 1998. The chapters in this collection explore infant and child mortality and health in a wide array of contexts, including Japan, Ecuador, the United States, Israel, Mexico, Portugal, the Dominican Republic, Cuba, England, Croatia, and Brazil.

Andrea S. Wiley. *An Ecology of High-Altitude Infancy: A Biocultural Perspective.* New York: Cambridge University Press, 2004. Ladakh is a district in India's far north, high in the Himalayas. Wiley's several years of fieldwork there focused on the links between biology and culture in birth, infant health and survival, and women's reproductive health. A final section considers the relevance of the findings for policies to improve infant survival and women's health.

6

Personality and Identity over the Life Cycle

The Big Questions

- WHAT is the scope of psychological anthropology?

- HOW does culture shape personality and identity from birth through adolescence?

- HOW does culture shape personality and identity in adulthood through old age?

Young boys of the Shan people, Thailand, participating in the Poi Sang Long festival. This annual event culminates in the initiation of boys into the Buddhist monkhood for a minimum of two years. (*Source: Kevin R. Morris/CORBIS*)

Psychological anthropology addresses many of the topics of contemporary Western psychology: personality, identity, learning, memory, the emotions, sexuality and gender, and so-called mental-health problems. Anthropological evidence from cultures around the world suggests that Western psychological concepts are not universally valid, including the definition of what is "normal." As always, an anthropological approach reveals richly varying local ways of being a person.

This chapter focuses on individuals within their cultural context. A major area of interest is how cultures shape **personality,** an individual's patterned and characteristic way of behaving, thinking, and feeling. Another interest is how culture shapes a person's *identity:* a person's sense of self and relations with others. Much of the subject matter of this chapter is referred to as **ethnopsychology,** the study of how various cultures define and create personality, identity, and mental health. This chapter considers "normal" human development, and Chapter 7 provides material on problematic aspects of psychology.

Culture, Personality, and Identity

Cultural anthropologists think that personality is largely formed through *enculturation* (sometimes called socialization), learning of culture through both informal and formal processes. They study how various cultures enculturate their members into having different personalities and identities. Cultural anthropologists also investigate how personalities vary according to cultural context, and some ask why such variations exist. Others study how changing cultural contexts affect personality, identity, and well-being over the life cycle. The following discussion situates contemporary psychological anthropology in the context of its historical development in North America.

The Culture and Personality School

Psychological anthropology is rooted in the so-called Culture and Personality School, an intellectual movement that began in the United States in the 1930s and persisted through the 1970s. Anthropologists in this group were influenced by Freudian theories, especially:

- The importance of childhood experiences in shaping personality and identity
- The symbolic analysis of people's dreams, words, and stories

They differed from Freud, however, in rejecting universalism. Working within the Boasian tradition of historical particularism (Chapter 1), they believed that each culture has a unique history that provides a unique context for shaping personality types and behavior within that culture. Their studies focused on revealing cross-cultural differences in child-rearing practices, personality types, and key symbols.

Personality and Child Rearing

In the early 1930s, Margaret Mead went to the Sepik River area of northern Papua New Guinea (see Map 1.4, p. 19) and studied gender in three different groups. She found striking differences in male and female personalities and behavior in each group (1963 [1935]). Among the Arapesh, both men and women had nurturant and gentle personalities. Both valued parental roles and both participated equally in child care. All Arapesh males and females behaved according to what is stereotypically defined as "female" in Western cultures. Among the Mundugumor, in contrast, both males and females corresponded to the Western stereotype of "male" behavior. In general, adults were assertive, aggressive, loud, and even fierce. Both mothers and fathers treated children with indifference. The situation among the third group, the Tchambuli, was equally surprising to Mead and her readers: The men fussed about their looks, gossiped with each other most of the day, and did little productive work. The women were competent and responsible, providing most of the family food through fishing and gardening. Tchambuli women played a dominant role in the family and their personalities reflected their position.

Since all three groups Mead studied share similar biological traits, her findings indicate that gender is culturally defined and constructed rather than being inborn. Mead's research showed that differences in tenderness or neglect when holding, breastfeeding, and bathing infants led to different personalities. This view had an enormous impact on changing people's thinking about the best way to care for babies in North America during the mid-twentieth century and is still prominent in psychological anthropology today.

Cultural Patterns and National Character

Ruth Benedict, a student of Mead's and a leading figure of the Culture and Personality School, argued that particular personality types characterize whole cultures and even entire countries. She proposed that cultures are formed through the unconscious selection of a few cul-

---

personality: an individual's patterned and characteristic way of behaving, thinking, and feeling.
ethnopsychology: the study of how vari-

ous cultures define and create personality, identity, and mental health.
cultural configuration: Ruth Benedict's theory that cultures are formed through

the unconscious selection of a few cultural traits that interweave to form a cohesive pattern shared by all members of the culture.

Margaret Mead, during her later years of fieldwork, observes children's interactions in Sicily. ■ *Have you ever attempted to observe small children's behavior for research purposes? How would such research differ from doing research among teenagers or adults?* (Source: © Ken Heyman/Woodfin Camp & Associates)

tural traits from a "vast arc" of potential traits (1959 [1934]. The selected traits interweave to form a **cultural configuration,** a cohesive pattern of beliefs and behaviors shared by everyone in the culture. Benedict formulated this theory while doing research on Native American cultures. The Pueblo Indians of the American Southwest, in her view, had personalities that exemplified a "middle road," involving moderation in all things and avoiding excess and violence. She termed the Pueblo an "Apollonian" culture, after the Greek deity Apollo. In contrast, she labeled the Kwakwaka'wakw of the Pacific Northwest "Dionysian," after the Greek god of revelry and excess (and drinking wine). She chose this term because of their potlatches, high levels of expressive emotionality, and colorful art, architecture, and textiles (review Culturama, Chapter 4, p. 114).

Benedict, along with many other American anthropologists, worked for the U.S. government as an applied anthropologist during World War II (Price 2004). The U.S. Office of War Information commissioned her to analyze "the Japanese personality" and to provide findings that could be used to help the United States defeat the Japanese. Because she could not do fieldwork in

Japan during wartime, she did "anthropology at a distance." She consulted secondary sources (newspapers, magazines, movies) and she interviewed Japanese Americans. Her book, *The Chrysanthemum and the Sword* (1969 [1946]), lists what she saw as essential features of Japanese personality and character: the importance of *on* (obligation, the necessity to repay gifts and favors), the concept of virtue, the value of self-discipline, the importance of keeping one's name honorable, and the significance of maintaining rules of etiquette. Her interpretations influenced U.S. policy toward Japan during the postwar occupation.

THINKING OUTSIDE THE BOX

CHOOSE A CULTURAL CONTEXT with which you are familiar: your hometown, your college, or whatever culture with which you most closely identify. Assume that you are Ruth Benedict. What term(s) will you use to label your cultural group?

Following Benedict's work on Japan, psychological anthropologists undertook many studies that defined personality types and core values of entire countries. According to contemporary anthropological standards, however, such studies suffer from being:

■ *Ethnocentric:* They classify cultures according to Western psychological values and features.

■ *Reductionist:* They emphasize only one or two features.

■ *Totalizing:* They obscure internal and local variation in their construction of a monolithic national character such as "the French," "the English," or "the Japanese."

Nonetheless, psychological anthropologists still consider it valid to typify localized cultures in terms of valued personality traits so long as a more scientific research approach is employed. One such study is based on fieldwork in three areas of Wales (see Map 6.1). This project combined methods of interviewing people about what is true "Welshness" along with observations of behavior in everyday situations (Trosset and Caulkins 2001). Results show a high degree of consensus among the interviewees that was confirmed by the observations. Five characteristics are the most important: egalitarianism, martyrdom, emotionalism, performance, and nostalgia (see Figure 6.1). Welsh people in this study perceive many of these characteristics as providing a distinction between themselves and "the English."

Class and Personality

Pursuing a different line of thinking, two cultural anthropologists of the mid-twentieth century looked at how poverty shapes personality. George Foster's research among low-income family farmers in Mexico led him to propose a model called the **image of the limited good** (1965). In this worldview, people believe that the resources or wealth available within their group are finite, or limited. In such a finite system, if someone becomes wealthier, other people necessarily become poorer. The analogy of a pie illustrates how the image of the limited good works. If a group of eight people equally divides a pie, everyone gets the same size piece. But if one person takes two pieces, only six pieces remain for the other seven people, thus shrinking their share. The image of the limited good, according to Foster, coexists with personality traits such as jealousy and suspiciousness, as people guard against anyone taking a larger piece of the pie.

Oscar Lewis (1966) proposed a related concept, the **culture of poverty,** to explain the personality and behavior of the poor and why poverty persists. He typified low-income Mexican people as, among other things, lacking a future time orientation and planning. Therefore, poor people cannot change their situation and they are trapped in poverty.

Today, these theories appear to be ethnocentric products of their time. During the period of mid–twentieth-century capitalist growth in the United States, valued personality characteristics were self-assertion, aggressive competitiveness, and forward-thinking, along with belief in infinite resources and an ever-expanding pie of wealth. At the time that Foster and Lewis were doing research, anthropologists did not highlight either structurist factors or human agency in relation to people's wealth or poverty. In spite of the limits of these theories, Lewis and Foster are still remembered as major figures in North American anthropology. Lewis wrote valuable ethnographies about people living in poverty in Mexico, Puerto Rico, and the United States, and Foster played an important role in building the subfield of medical anthropology.

Recent ethnopsychology studies attempt to be less ethnocentric by emphasizing the terms and meanings important in other cultures. They also bring attention to structural factors that affect personality and identity as well as to the importance of human agency such as active resistance among poor and marginalized people to their situation. Along with studying poor and marginalized groups, psychological anthropologists now also study personality formation in middle-class and upper-class groups. Ethnographic research in Japan shows how corporate culture shapes the personality and identity of mid-

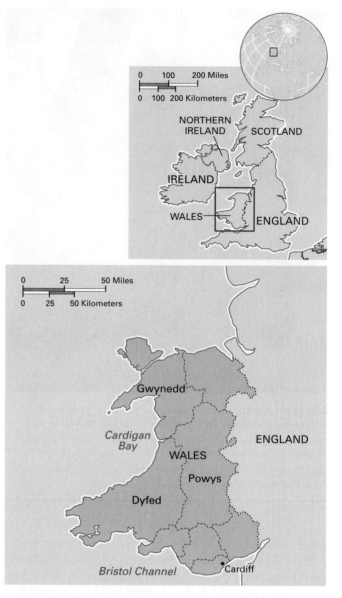

MAP 6.1 Wales. Wales, or Cymru (prounounced COME-ree) is one of the four countries of the United Kingdom. Its population of 3 million is 96 percent White British with Asian origin residents constituting another 2 percent. Mining has been an important part of the economy since the eighteenth century. Given the natural beauty of much of Wales, tourism is important and growing. Welsh and English are the official languages. The main religion is Christianity, with the Presbyterian Church of Wales the largest denomination.

image of the limited good: George Foster's theory that in nonindustrial cultures, people have a characteristic worldview of finite resources or wealth such that if someone in the group increases his or her wealth, other people will necessarily lose out.

culture of poverty: Oscar Lewis's theory that the personality characteristics of the poor trap them in poverty.

person-centered ethnography: anthropological research that focuses on the individual and how the individual's psychology and subjective experience both shape and are shaped by the wider culture.

FIGURE 6.1 Five
Characteristics of Welsh
Personhood

Value		Behavior
Egalitarianism	All people are equal and personal ties are more important than status.	Social introductions and interactions emphasize personal ties.
Martyrdom	The best acts are done on behalf of the group and may involve self-sacrifice.	Mothers labor for the family; protestors go to jail.
Emotionalism	Interactions with people should show emotion.	Anger is preferable to detachment; arguing is from the heart.
Performance	Differences exist between private and public self, with the public self more performative.	An aspiring community leader disclaims interest in the position.
Nostalgia	Sadness is shown for something lost.	Feels homesick; returns home to visit the graves of parents each year.

Source: Trosset and Caulkins (2001:66–68, 71–73).

dle- and upper-class men in urban Japan (see Everyday Anthropology box).

Person-Centered Ethnography

The newest direction in psychological anthropology is called **person-centered ethnography,** research that focuses on the individual or self, and how the individual's psychology and subjective experience both shape and are shaped by her or his culture (Hollan 2001). Gaining an emic view about individual people and their perceptions is the paramount goal. Thus, person-centered ethnographic research focuses on what people say about their perceptions and experiences. Like Western psychology and psychiatry, it is fundamentally discourse based rather than observation based. Yet most person-centered ethnographies situate details about individuals and what they say about their experience within the wider cultural context, because individuals and their cultures are interactive.

One such person-centered ethnography focuses on notions of the self in a mountainous village in eastern Nepal (see Map 7.5, p. 193) (Hardman 2000). In this region, family farming is the major occupation and an egalitarian principle of exchange prevails. In opposition to many broad statements from nonanthropologists about "Asian mentalities" and the lack of a concept of an autonomous self in "Asian societies," this study found clear evidence of a concept of individuality and interpersonal difference in *niwa*. As one villager commented, there are as many different niwa as there are faces. But people do not express their individual niwa in public.

With increasing social change, however, niwa is beginning to be exhibited in public more often. For example, some women are demonstrating their niwa as initiative and agency by selling beer and liquor. Young people are expressing opinions in public. So far, the prevailing view is that such expressions of individuality should not go so far as to upset accepted views of propriety, which include frugality, charitable giving, and feelings of conscience and shame. In this cultural context, the self and individualism can exist but within cultural bounds.

As many psychological anthropologists direct their attention to the details of individual perceptions and experience, others insist on the value of the comparative, ethnological method (Moore and Mathews 2001). They ask, for example, how does a Nepali villager's concept of niwa compare to people's notions of the self in other cultural contexts? Are there private/public notions of self elsewhere, and, if so, how does that distinction play out? The study of the individual provides a clear example of the fruitful tension between ethnography and ethnology.

Personality and Identity Formation from Infancy through Adolescence

In Euro-American culture, commonly accepted life stages include infancy, childhood, adolescence, middle age, and old age (psychologists and other experts con-

CORPORATE INTERESTS AND MALE PERSONALITY FORMATION

In all cultures, parents and other caretakers, consciously or consciously, raise children in ways that relate to their future roles as adults. Research in Tokyo, Japan (see Map 2.2, p. 41), on the personality of *salarymen* reveals links between men's personality with the demands of the business world (Allison 1994). Salarymen are men who work in the high-paced corporate world of urban Japan. They are nicknamed "7–11 men" because they leave home early in the morning and return late at night. Many Tokyo salarymen eat dinner with their family only a few times a year.

In the Japanese corporation, hierarchies are clear, total loyalty is required, work hours are long, and the pressure to perform is high. Regular socializing at the club solidifies bonds between salarymen and strengthens their loyalty to the corporation. After work, groups of about five to ten men go out together to expensive nightclubs. A few drinks and light snacks can result in a tab for hundreds of dollars. The corporation the salarymen work for picks up the bill. At the club, men relax and have fun. A trained hostess sits with the men, keeping the conversation moving along in a lightly playful tone. Her job is to flatter and flirt with them and make them feel good.

Anne Allison did participant observation while working as a nightclub hostess. She found that conversations are full of teasing and banter, with much of it directed at the hostess and most of it derogatory: The hostess's breasts are too small, her hair is not right, and so on. The hostess must take all of this with a smile, and even joke along with it: "Yes, I have no breasts at all." Allison calls this type of banter "breast talk." How should this focus on the female breast be interpreted? Salarymen's nightclub behavior is related to their childhood experiences. Given the near total absence of the father from the home scene, the mother is the main caretaker. Maternal attention is focused on sons and their school achieve-

Japanese salarymen singing karaoke. (Source: © Barry Lewis/Alamy)

ments. A mother's primary goal is that her son will do well in school, gain admission to a top university, and then get a job with a large corporation. The corporations pay well, guarantee lifelong employment, and provide substantial benefits after retirement.

Salarymen's behavior in nightclubs can be viewed as both a product of and a reaction to this strong maternal involvement. In nightclub culture, a man has guaranteed control over a desirable woman who flatters him and flirts with him. She will never control him because, after a few hours of fun, he leaves and there is no enduring relationship. Club culture, however, provides only temporary ego gratification for a salaryman and is addictive. He needs to return again and again for reinforcement. This fact keeps salarymen away from their homes, leaving their own sons in the isolated care of the mothers.

FOOD FOR THOUGHT

- How might this example be related to the increasing amount of time that men in the United States, and elsewhere, spend watching porn on the Internet?

---

cerned with human development construct even finer substages). These life-cycle stages are based on biological features such as the ability to walk, puberty, and capacity for parenthood (Bogin 1988). Although this model assumes that all its life-cycle markers have universal relevance, cultural anthropologists find striking variation in how different cultures construct life stages and how such stages are quite unrelated to biology

(Johnson-Hanks 2002). For example, one might think that the biological fact of having a baby places a female into the life stage of "mother," but such is not always the case. The cross-cultural construction of life stages sometimes uses markers that Western biology recognizes, and sometimes not. The following sections consider personality formation and identity according to general Western categories.

Birth and Infancy

This section first considers the cultural context of birth itself. It then discusses cultural variations in infant care and how they may shape personality and identity. Last, it deals with the topic of gender identity formation in infancy.

The Birth Context

The cultural context of birth affects an infant's psychological development. Brigitte Jordan (1983), a pioneer in the cross-cultural study of birth, conducted comparative research on birth practices in Mexico, Sweden, Holland, and the United States. She studied the birth setting, including its location and who is present, the types of attendants and their roles, the birth event, and the postpartum period. Among Maya women in Mexico, the midwife is called in during the early stages of labor. One of her tasks is to give a massage to the mother-to-be. She also provides psychological support by telling stories, often about other women's birthing experiences. The husband is expected to be present during the labor so that he can see "how a woman suffers." The woman's mother should be present, along with other female kin, such as her mother-in-law, godmother, sisters, and friends. Thus, a Maya mother is surrounded by a large group of supportive people.

In the United States, hospital births are the norm. The newborn infant is generally taken to the nursery, where it is wrapped in cloth and placed in a plastic crate under bright lights rather than being cared for by a family member. Some critics argue that the hospital-based system of highly regulated birth is extremely technocratic and too managed, alienating the mother—as well as other members of the family and the wider community—from the birthing process and the infant (Davis-Floyd 1992). This critique has led to consideration of how to improve the way birth is conducted.

The Western medical model of birth contrasts sharply with non-Western practices. Sometimes they come into direct conflict. In such situations, anthropological expertise can mediate such conflict by providing what medical specialists now refer to *cultural sensitivity,* or cultural awareness and respect (see Lessons Applied box).

Bonding

Many contemporary Western psychological theorists say that parent–infant contact and bonding at the time of birth is crucial for setting in motion parental attachment to the infant. Western specialists say that if this bonding is not established at the time of the infant's birth, it will not develop later. Explanations for juvenile delinquency or other unfavorable child development problems often include reference to lack of proper infant bonding at birth.

Nancy Scheper-Hughes (1992), whose research in a Brazilian shantytown appeared in Chapter 5, questions Western bonding theory. She argues that bonding does not necessarily have to occur at birth to be successful. Her observations in Brazil show that many low-income mothers do not exhibit bonding with their infants at birth. Bonding occurs later, if the child survives infancy, when it is several years old. She proposes that this pattern of later bonding is related to the high rate of infant mortality among poor people of northeast Brazil. If women were to develop strong bonds with their newborn infants, they would suffer untold amounts of grief. Western bonding is adaptive in low-mortality/low-fertility societies in which strong maternal attachment is reasonable because infants are likely to survive.

In Bom Jesus, a shantytown in northeastern Brazil, a doctor at the local clinic told this mother that her son was dying of anemia and that she needed to feed him red meat. The mother said, "Now, where am I going to find the money to feed my hopeless son rich food like that?" ■ *What is your perspective on Western bonding theory, and how did you come to have this view?* (Source: Nancy Scheper-Hughes)

MEDIATING CULTURAL CONFLICT ABOUT THE TREATMENT OF A NEWBORN BABY IN A U.S. HOSPITAL NURSERY

Birth practices aim to ensure that the baby will develop properly, and they vary dramatically cross-culturally. This example considers an instance of cultural conflict about treatment of a newborn. It takes place in a hospital that had recently been built in a suburban community in the central United States to provide services for its rapidly growing immigrant population (Deitrick 2002). Most of the nurses on staff were long-time residents of the community and had graduated from a local community college, where their training included no attention to cultural differences.

The conflict arose upon the birth of a baby to a Turkish immigrant family. The infant had not yet been brought to the mother's room, but family members had arrived to welcome the new baby. With them was a Muslim religious leader who came to administer the traditional honey blessing to the infant before his first feeding. This mandatory ritual ensures a sweet life for the baby.

The nurse in charge denied the family access to the baby, saying that he first must have a medical examination and that unpasteurized honey could not be given to him. The baby's father was upset and claimed that the blessing must be administered because whatever the baby first tastes determines the quality of its life.

Fortunately, a nurse who also had training in cultural anthropology, Lynn Deitrick, entered into the discussions and was able to act as a **cultural broker**, a person—often but not always an anthropologist—who is familiar with the practices and beliefs of two different cultures and can promote cross-cultural understanding to prevent or mediate conflicts. She listened to the views of the Turkish family and learned that only a tiny amount of honey would be placed on the baby's tongue for the blessing. She suggested a compromise to the medical staff whereby the baby would be taken for ten minutes to the mother's room and the Muslim cleric could administer the blessing. The attending physician agreed, saying that she was not "on record" as approving the blessing but that she understood its importance. Deitrick took the baby to the family and returned ten minutes later to find a smiling mother and father. The baby then underwent blood tests and other medically required procedures. He was discharged in good health—and assured of a sweet life—two days later.

FOOD FOR THOUGHT

- In your cultural world, what are some practices at birth that are considered essential for ensuring the baby's welfare?

Caregiver–Infant Proximity

Across cultures, wide differences exist in how much time an infant spends in close contact with caregivers. Euro-American cultures stand at one extreme, with infants spending much of their time not in physical contact with a caregiver (Keller et al. 2005). In a city in northern Germany, spot-check observations of families with infants from 2 to 3 months old found that the babies were on their own, with no caregiver in view, 40 percent of the time. In contrast, in research sites in rural Northern India and Cameroon, West Africa, infants spend less than 10 percent of their time away from physical contact with caregivers. In these cultural settings, caregivers spend much time rocking babies, holding and feeding them, massaging them, and bouncing them. Typical German personalities are, in fact, more autonomous than in cultures that focus on group connectedness.

Where the Baby Sleeps

Where and with whom the infant sleeps may also be related to the development of connected or autonomous personalities. The underlying hypothesis motivating research on sleeping patterns is the following: Little or no infant–parent co-sleeping promotes "strong ego formation" (in other words, an autonomous self with a high degree of independence), whereas long periods of parent–infant co-sleeping foster "weak ego formation" (a person with little sense of autonomous selfhood and a high degree of interpersonal connectedness).

This hypothesis finds confirmation in data from Japan where mothers and infants co-sleep for several years—longer, on average, than other world cultures (Caudill and Plath 1966). The long period of infant co-sleeping seems to match the high degree of social connectedness of Japanese people. The hypothesis, however, is not con-

cultural broker: a person who is familiar with the practices and beliefs of two cultures and can promote cross-cultural understanding to prevent or mediate conflicts.

A Euro-American infant exhibiting autonomy. ■ *If you were from a culture in which infants spend little time on their own, what would you think about the baby in this picture, its caretakers, and its culture?* (Source: Brand X Pictures/Alamy)

firmed in a study of personality formation among the Basque people of Spain (Crawford 1994) (see Map 2.5, p. 51). Most of the Basque women interviewed had slept in their parents' room for two to three years. The women who had been co-sleepers had both greater ego strength and a stronger sense of social connectedness than women who had not been co-sleepers. Thus, co-sleeping does not necessarily prevent the development of an autonomous ego and sense of self.

Gender in Infancy

Anthropologists distinguish between *sex* and *gender* (review definitions in Chapter 1). Sex is something that everyone is born with. In the view of Western science, it has three biological markers: genitals, hormones, and chromosomes. A male has a penis, more androgens than estrogens, and the XY chromosome. A female has a vagina, more estrogens than androgens, and the XX chromosome. Increasingly, scientists are finding that these two categories are not airtight. In all populations, some people are born with indeterminate genitals, similar proportions of androgens and estrogens, and chromosomes with more complex distributions than simply XX and XY. Thus, a continuum model of gender is more accurate than a strict binary model.

Gender, in contrast, is a cultural construction and is highly variable across cultures (B. Miller 1993). In the view of most cultural anthropologists, a high degree of human "plasticity" (or personality flexibility) allows for substantial human variation in personality and behavior. More biologically inclined anthropologists, however, continue to insist that many sex-linked personality characteristics are inborn.

Two major problems are involved in testing for innate (inborn) characteristics. First, one needs data on infants before they are subject to cultural treatment. Such data are, however, impossible to obtain because cultures start shaping the infant from the moment of birth through handling and treatment by others. Cultural effects may begin even in the womb, through exposure to sound and motion. Second, studying and interpreting the behavior of infants is fraught with potential bias on the part of the observers.

Studies of infants have focused on assessing the potential innateness of three major Euro-American personality stereotypes (Frieze et al. 1978:73–78):

- Whether infant males are more aggressive than infant females
- Whether infant females are more social than infant males
- Whether infant males are more independent than infant females

What is the evidence? Boy babies cry more than girl babies, and some people believe this is evidence of higher levels of inborn aggression in males. An alternative interpretation is that baby boys, on average, tend to weigh more than girls at birth. They therefore are more likely to have a difficult delivery from which it takes time to recover, so they cry more, but not because of aggressiveness. In terms of sociality, baby girls smile more often than boys, and some researchers claim this difference confirms innate personality characteristics. But caretakers smile more at baby girls than they smile at baby boys. Thus, the more frequent smiling of girls is likely to be a learned, culturally shaped behavior. In terms of independence or dependence, studies thus far reveal no clear differences in how upset baby boys and girls are when separated from their caretakers. Taken as a whole, studies seeking to document innate gender differences through the behavior of infants are not convincing.

Cultural anthropologists who take a constructionist view make two further points. They note that, if gender differences are innate, it is odd that cultures go to so much trouble (and they do) to enculturate offspring into a particular gender. Also, if gender differences are innate, then they should be the same throughout history and across all cultures, which they clearly are not. This chapter explores cross-cultural examples of the construction of gender at various stages of the life cycle starting with childhood.

Socialization during Childhood

The concept of "the child" as a special age category may have emerged first in Europe in recent centuries (Ariès 1962). In art, portraits of children became commonplace only in the seventeenth century. Other changes occurred at the same time: new interest in children's behavior, more elaborate terminology about children and childhood, and special clothing for children instead of small-sized versions of adult clothing. The special focus on "the child" is associated with the emergence of industrial capitalism's need for an ever-expanding market. "The child" became a new niche for sales and prompted the production of clothes, books, and toys specifically for children. In many nonindustrialized cultures, especially among the poor, "the child" is not the subject of such specialized consumption. In such situations, children take on adult tasks at an early age.

Mode of Production and Child Personality

The Six Cultures Study (mentioned in Chapter 3) is a classic cross-cultural research project designed to provide comparative data on how children's activities and tasks shape their personalities (Whiting and Whiting 1975). Researchers used parallel methods at six sites (see Figure 6.2), observing children between the ages of 3 and 11 years. They recorded behavior, such as caring for and being supportive of other children; hitting other children; and performing tasks such as child care, cooking, and errands. The data collected were analyzed in terms of two major personality types: nurturant-responsible and dependent-dominant. A *nurturant-responsible personality* is characterized by caring and sharing acts toward other children. The *dependent-dominant personality* involves fewer acts of caregiving, more acts that assert dominance over other children, and more need for care by adults.

FIGURE 6.2   Groups in the Six Cultures Study

Horticultural Groups
Gusii people of Kenya
Maya people of Oaxaca, Mexico
Tarong people, Philippines

Intensive Agriculture or Industrial Groups
Taira village, Okinawa, Japan
Rajput people, village in North India
Middle-class Euro-Americans in Orchard Town, New England, United States

Source: Whiting and Whiting (1975).

Of all six cultures, the Gusii children of southwestern Kenya (see Map 6.2, p.158) had the highest frequency of a nurturant-responsible personality type. Gusii children were responsible for the widest range of tasks and at earlier ages than children in any other culture in the study, often performing tasks that an Orchard Town, United States, mother does. Although some children in all six cultures took care of other children, Gusii children (both boys and girls) spent the most time doing so. They began taking on this responsibility at a very young age, between 5 and 8 years old.

In contrast, Orchard Town children had the highest frequency of the dependent-dominant personality type. The differences correlate with the mode of production. The people in Kenya, Mexico, and the Philippines all had more nurturant-responsible children and their economies are reliant on horticulture. The study sites in Japan, India, and the United States were based on either intensive agriculture or industry. How do these different modes of production influence child personality? The key underlying factor is women's work roles. In the horticultural societies, women are an important part of the labor force and spend much time working outside the home. Their children take on many family-supportive tasks and thereby develop personalities that are nurturant-responsible. When women are mainly occupied in the home, as in the second group of cultures, children have fewer tasks and less responsibility. They develop personalities that are more dependent-dominant.

This study has many implications for Western child development experts. For one thing, what happens when the dependent-dominant personality develops to an extreme level—into a *narcissistic personality*? A narcissist is someone who constantly seeks self-attention and self-affirmation, with no concern for other people's needs. Consumerism supports the development of narcissism via its emphasis on identity formation through ownership of self-defining goods (clothing, electronics, cars) and access to self-defining services (vacations, therapists, fitness salons). The Six Cultures Study suggests that involving children more in household responsibilities might result in less self-focused personality formation and more nurturant-responsible people.

Informal Learning

Games and toys shape personality universally, though in different ways and with different effects. Among the Yanomami, young boys learn to be future hunters by shooting small arrows from small bows at small targets

THINKING OUTSIDE THE BOX

TRY TO RECALL your daily activities when you were 5 years old, 10 years old, and 15 years old. What tasks did you do? In terms of the Six Cultures Study categories, which type of personality do you have?

A Yanomami boy acquiring skills necessary for hunting and warfare through play *(left)*. ■ (Source: © Napoleon A. Chagnon/AnthroPhoto) **An American boy playing a video game** *(right)*. ■ *Consider examples of children's games that may provide learning and skills related to adult roles in your culture.* (Source: © Bill Varie/CORBIS)

such as beetles. They learn to kill animals without sentimentality. In contrast, caring for animals as pets is a prominent part of child socialization in the West, where many animals are taboo as food. Some games, such as chess, teach strategic thinking that appears to be correlated with sociopolitical patterns of hierarchy and obedience.

The media play an extremely important role in child personality formation. One study examined children's cartoon shows aired on U.S. television in the 1980s and how they support stereotypical Euro-American gender roles (Williams 1991). Content analysis reveals two types of shows, one featuring interpersonal relationships and one featuring battles:

One was aimed at little girls and included groups of characters joined by relational values. "Rainbow Brite" had a set of multicolored friends; both friends and kin surrounded "My Little Pony." . . . "Strawberry Shortcake" presided over a group, mostly little girls. . . . At the other extreme are programs that toy companies intended for boys. . . . All presented heroes on teams. . . . Teammates had no common ties or work other than those involving

fighting. Each good team faced an evil team that chased, attacked, captured, and deceived them. (1991:114–115)

Boy-focused cartoon shows emphasized the importance of group identity in the face of "the enemy." Enemy teams look different from the heroes: the Thundercats (heroes) battle the Mutants (enemies), and He-Man (hero) takes on Skeletor (enemy).

Formal Schooling

Schools have important effects on personality and identity formation. Worldwide, schools vary in terms of their accessibility and quality. For example, not all countries provide for universal primary education. Even in those that do provide universal schooling, there may be wide gaps in quality for children of different microcultures. Within countries, poorer children are more likely to face problems enrolling and remaining in school. Beside the fact of an inadequate number of schools, poor families may need their children to work and contribute to the household income. Malnourished and exhausted children have difficulty concentrating in class, and their level of achievement is likely to be lower than that of better-off children. Teachers, however, may interpret their performance as a sign of bad attitude or laziness rather than the result of poverty.

School systems that offer inadequate learning experiences, home situations that are unsupportive, and political elements in the wider society often combine to constrain girls' achievement in school. Furthermore, "tracking" female students into domestic roles characterizes formal education throughout much of the world. In Israel, all-girl Zionist-Orthodox boarding schools aim to strengthen the religiosity of girls and prepare them for married life. But they also emphasize academic excellence, and the girls are highly motivated to achieve. The curriculum includes lectures, lessons, religious activities, and volunteer community work. Religious study excludes the canonic texts, promoting instead everyday religious practice and emphasis on morality, wifehood, childrear-

Two schoolgirls of Oman. The female literacy rate in Oman is about 50 percent, whereas the male literacy rate is 75 percent. Gender inequality in literacy is not, however, universal in Arab countries. ■ *Do research to learn about variations in gender and literacy in Arab countries.* (Source: © Charles O. Cecil)

Schoolchildren in Japan exhibiting eagerness to participate in class. ■ *What else can you read from this photograph about these Japanese schoolchildren? How does that compare to your school experience at this age?* (Source: © Nichol Katz/Woodfin Camp & Associates)

ing, and purity. A study of girls in such schools takes into account the interplay of religion and gender (Rapoport, Garb, and Penso 1995). Close supervision of the girls is maintained by teachers, peers, and older girls who serve as "big sisters." Even during free time, the girls are supposed to discuss religion. According to the school teachings, a woman's modesty is part of her essence. The ideal is invisibility and muteness in the public world. Girls learn that their sexuality is a secret, hidden treasure to be guarded with self-restraint, a key virtue that contrasts with how secular girls behave. One student commented, "For example, I walk by some [secular] girl with exposed legs, so she has no value, she simply presents herself as

puberty: a time in the human life cycle that occurs universally and involves a set of biological markers and sexual maturation.

adolescence: a culturally defined period of maturation from the time of puberty until adulthood.

an object, she doesn't say, first look for my character . . . and I feel very proud that I am modest" (1995:54). Some girls, however, described the dilemma created by the Zionist-Orthodox emphasis on women's family roles, the pressure for academic achievement, and personal aspirations for a career. Their only options are relinquishing aspirations for academic excellence or finding a career that accommodates family responsibilities and modesty rules.

Oppressed minority groups often find that formal schooling in the mainstream society is another context for discrimination and marginalization. Standard curricula reflect mainstream values and exclude or denigrate those of minority groups. Native Americans and First Nations people of Canada are developing community-based schools with curricula that combine standard subjects such as mathematics with learning that is necessary for true personhood in their local community (Manuelito 2005). Students learn their native language, kinship system, history, and skills such as telling stories, cooking, hunting, and weaving. Some are adapting the teaching of such subjects as mathematics in culturally meaningful ways (Lipka et al. 2005). Combining mainstream and local concepts and ways of learning was effective in an experimental math program among the Yup'ik, indigenous people of Alaska. Such a program has substantial implications for students' learning and for strengthening their sense of identity and self-esteem.

Schools and social inequality are intimately related. Schools may be places where social barriers are reduced and opportunities for marginalized students enhanced. Or they may reinforce existing social gaps. No simple story exists for any cultural context but, clearly, schools possess the potential for social progress as well as for social control and maintenance of conformity.

Adolescence and Identity

The transition from "childhood" to "adulthood" involves certain biological events as well as cultural events. This section provides ethnographic insights about the cultural construction of the transition to adulthood.

Is Adolescence a Universal Life-Cycle Stage?

Puberty is a time in the human life cycle that occurs universally and involves a set of biological markers. In males, the voice deepens and facial and body hair appear; in females, menarche and breast development occur; in both males and females, pubic and underarm hair appear and sexual maturation is achieved. **Adolescence,** in contrast, is a culturally defined period of maturation from around the time of puberty until the attainment of adulthood, usually marked by becoming a parent, getting married, or becoming economically self-sufficient.

Some scholars say that all cultures define a period of adolescence. A comparative study using data on 186 societies argues for the universal existence of a culturally defined phase of adolescence (Schlegel 1995; Schlegel and Barry 1991). The researchers point to supportive evidence in the fact that people in cultures as diverse as the Navajo and the Trobriand Islanders have special terms comparable to the U.S. term *adolescent* to refer to a person between puberty and marriage. Following a biological determinist, Darwinian model, they interpret the supposedly universal phases of adolescence as being adaptive in an evolutionary sense (Schlegel 1995:16). The logic is that adolescence provides training for parenthood and thus contributes to enhanced reproductive success and survival of parents' genes.

Other anthropologists view adolescence as culturally constructed and as highly variable, and thus impossible to explain on only biological grounds. These researchers point out that people in many cultures recognize no period of adolescence. In some others, identification of an adolescent phase is recent. Moroccan anthropologist Fatima Mernissi (1987), for example, states that adolescence became a recognized life-cycle phase for females in Morocco only in the late twentieth century. "The idea of an adolescent unmarried woman is a completely new idea in the Muslim world, where previously you had only a female child and a menstruating woman who had to be married off immediately so as to prevent dishonorable engagement in premarital sex" (1987:xxiv).

Another line of evidence supporting a constructionist view is that, in different cultures, the length and elaboration of adolescence varies for males and females. In many horticultural and pastoralist societies where men are valued as warriors, as among the Maasai, a long period between childhood and adulthood is devoted to training in warfare and developing solidarity among males (see Culturama). This adolescent period has nothing to do with training for parenthood. Maasai females, on the other hand, move directly from being a girl to being a wife and have no culturally marked adolescent period. They learn adult roles when they are children.

Long periods of male initiation among some highland groups in Papua New Guinea that involve institutionalized homosexual relationships also do not fit within the sociobiological interpretation. Gilbert Herdt conducted research with the Sambia, highland horticulturalists, and learned about their secret male initiation practices (1987). The Sambia believe that, in order for a young boy to mature into a healthy adult, he must join a secret, all-male initiation group. A boy becomes a partner of a senior male who regularly transfers his semen to the youth orally. The Sambia believe that the youth is nourished by ingesting semen. After a period of time in the initiation group, the "grown" youth rejoins society as a man. At that time he will marry a woman and raise children.

Culturama

The Maasai of Kenya and Tanzania

The Maasai (sometimes spelled Masai), before recent changes, made their living mainly as cattle herders. Their ancestral lands cover a large area crossing from Kenya into Tanzania, but far less than what they had before European colonialism. During the colonial era, they lost 75 percent (over 15 million acres) of their ancestral land (Oloi-Dapash 2002). Since then, the governments of Kenya and Tanzania continued to claim Maasai land. In the last two decades of the twentieth century, the Maasai lost over one million acres of land to White farmers, development projects, national parks, and game reserves. The Maasai now come into frequent conflict with outsiders who are fencing the land, preventing the free movement of wildlife, and disturbing what was a more stable lifestyle. Several indigenous and international nongovernmental organizations are advocating for the return of land to the Maasai.

The Maasai population is roughly 500,000. Most live in the traditional Maasai region, but many have migrated to cities in Kenya and Tanzania for work. Many have obtained prominent positions, as head of Kenya Airways, for example. Some have traveled to Europe and North America to attend college.

For many Maasai men, the traditional rite of passage is now augmented by the need to go to the city and earn money, or to go abroad and gain a Ph.D. in order to prove one's manhood.

Maasai life revolves around cattle, although the people also keep sheep and goats. Property rights invest cattle ownership in men only though in the past, before the concept of "ownership" existed, men and women had overlapping rights in livestock. Elder men occupy leadership positions. A married woman manages her husband's cattle and has rights to its products, notably milk and hides, for household consumption. Ownership of the cattle passes from father to sons. Women build and maintain the houses, which were formerly low, dome-shaped, earthen constructions but are now taller and with thatched roofs. They have a say in who enters the house, thus giving them some domestic status (Hodgson 2004). Modern houses are made from commercial materials obtained with cash. Women's domestic status related to control of the house has declined. Maasai women are increasingly involved in beadwork for sale to tourists.

The Maasai share much with each other, including food and sexual part-ners. Young Maasai men and women are free to have sexual liaisons with multiple partners. Young married women, whose husbands are much older than they, frequently have lovers. The increase in urban migration has brought HIV/AIDS to the Maasai (May 2003). Their relatively free sexual relations mean that the disease could spread rapidly. Nongovernmental organizations are working hard to raise awareness of the risk of HIV/AIDS among the Maasai and to urge young Maasai in the cities to abstain from sex or to use condoms.

Readings

Elizabeth Gilbert. *Broken Spears: A Maasai Journey.* New York: Atlantic Monthly Press, 2003.

Dorothy L. Hodgson. *Once Intrepid Warriors: Gender, Ethnicity, and the Cultural Politics of Maasai Development.* Bloomington: Indiana University Press, 2001.

Videos

The Masai Today: Changing Traditions (Films Media Group, 2003).

Masai Women (Disappearing World, 1994).

Thanks to Dorothy L. Hodgson, Rutgers University, for reviewing this material.

A Maasai warrior's mother shaves his head during part of his initiation ceremony into adulthood (left). This ritual validates her status as a mother as well as her son's adulthood. ■ (Source: © Robert Caputo/National Geographic Image Collection) *Maasai women own no land and no animals (right). Their hand-made jewelry is theirs, however, to have, to give, and to sell.* ■ (Source: © Barry D. Kass)

MAP 6.2 *Maasai Region of Kenya and Tanzania. An estimated 350,000 Maasai live in Kenya and 150,000 in Tanzania. Sixteen major sections of Maasai exist throughout the region. The climate is semi-arid and arid.*

In some cultures, females have long adolescent phases during which they live separated from the wider group and gain special knowledge and skills (J. Brown 1978). After this period of seclusion, they re-emerge as full-fledged women and marry.

A cultural explanation exists for why gender affects whether a young person has an adolescent phase of life. Cultural materialism (Chapter 1) offers an explanatory framework that accounts for variation. In this perspective, a prolonged and marked period of adolescence is likely to be preparation for any of several culturally valued adult roles: worker, warrior, or parent. Confirmation comes from the finding that extended adolescence for females in many nonindustrial societies occurs in cultures where adult females are important as food producers (J. Brown 1978).

Globalization is spreading Western patterns of adolescence to the middle and upper classes around the world. Globally, the age at marriage has risen steadily in the past few decades as young people attend college or university and then find employment before starting a family. At the same time, class differences in the adolescent phase of the life cycle are widening. Those who are poor have short periods of adolescence, or none at all. They spend little, if any, time in formal education, and they are likely to become parents when young.

Coming of Age and Gender Identity

Margaret Mead made famous the phrase "coming of age" in her book *Coming of Age in Samoa* (1961 [1928]). It can refer generally to the period of adolescence or specifically to a ceremony or set of ceremonies that marks the boundaries of adolescence. What are the psychological aspects of such special events for the children who go through them? Some of the ceremonies have a sacrificial element, with symbolic death and rebirth (Ingham 1996:183–184). Most coming of age ceremonies are gender specific, highlighting the importance of adult roles of men and women. These ceremonies often involve marking the body of the initiate in some way. Such marking may include scarification, tattooing, and genital surgery. In many societies, adolescent males undergo genital surgery that involves removal of part of the skin around the tip of the penis. Without this operation, the boy would not become a full-fledged male. In others, girls undergo genital cutting of various types which, similarly, is the only way to become a real woman.

A young Maasai male, in a first-person account of his initiation into manhood, describes the "intolerable pain" he experienced following the circumcision, as well as his feeling of accomplishment two weeks later when his head was shaved and he became a warrior: "As long as I live, I will never forget the day my head was shaved and I emerged a man, a Maasai warrior. I felt a sense of control over my destiny so great that no words can accurately describe it" (Saitoti 1986:71).

Less common worldwide is **female genital cutting (FGC)**, a Western term referring to several forms of genital surgery practiced on females (Gruenbaum 2001). These practices may involve the excision of part or all of the clitoris, part or all of the labia, and (the least common practice) *infibulation*, the stitching together of the vaginal entry, leaving a small aperture for drainage of menstrual blood. These procedures are performed when the girl is between 7 and 15 years of age. Many people practice some form of female genital cutting in the Sahelian countries extending from Africa's west to east coast (see Map 16.6, p. 442). It is also found in Egypt, in some groups of the Middle East (particularly among Bedu tribes), and among some Muslim groups in South and Southeast Asia. In terms of religion, FGC is often, but not always, associated with people who are Muslim. In Ethiopia, some Christian groups practice it. Genital cutting occurs in many groups in which female labor participation is high, but in others where it is not.

Scholars have yet to provide an explanation for the regional and social distribution of female genital cutting. Anthropologists who study this practice ask the people involved for their views. Many young girls say they look forward to the ceremony so that they will be free from childhood tasks and can take on the more respected role of an adult woman. In other cases, anthropologists have reported hearing statements of resistance (Fratkin 1998:60). Fewer issues force the questioning of cultural relativism more clearly than female genital cutting (see Critical Thinking box).

Initiation rites often involve themes of death and rebirth as the initiate loses his or her former identity and emerges with a new one. Abigail Adams conducted research during the early 1990s on initiation rituals at what was then a men's military school, the Virginia Military Institute (2002). Freshmen students, called "Rats," are each assigned to an upperclassman, called a "Dyke." The freshman year involves continuous humiliation and other forms of abuse for the Rats. Dykes treat their Rats like infants, telling them how to eat, bathe, and talk and yelling at them in baby talk. Another tradition is called the Rape of the First Sentinel. When the first Rat does

THINKING OUTSIDE THE BOX

IN YOUR CULTURAL WORLD, what economic roles are associated with long periods of seclusion and learning (for example, a college education)? Which are not? Are there gender variations?

---

female genital cutting: a term used for a range of genital cutting procedures, including the excision of part or all of the clitoris, excision of part or all of the labia, and sometimes infibulation, the stitching together of the vaginal entry.

Critical Thinking

CULTURAL RELATIVISM AND FEMALE GENITAL CUTTING

In cultures that practice female genital cutting (FGC), it is a necessary step toward full womanhood. The procedure is required for a woman to be considered marriageable. Fathers say that an uncircumcised daughter is unmarriageable and will bring no brideprice. Others say that removing the labia makes a woman beautiful by removing "male" parts. The prevailing Western view, increasingly shared by many people who have long practiced female genital cutting, is that FGC is both a sign of low female status and an unnecessary cause of women's suffering.

Female genital cutting is linked with several health risks, including those related to the surgery itself (shock, infection) and future genito-urinary complications (Gruenbaum 2001). Infibulation scars the vaginal canal and may lead to problems during childbirth, sometimes causing the death of the infant and mother. Having a new bride's husband "open" her, using a stick or knife to loosen the aperture, is both painful and an opportunity for infection. After giving birth, a woman is usually reinfibulated, and the process begins again. Health experts say that repeated trauma to the woman's vaginal area increases the risk of contracting HIV/AIDS.

The Western view argues that the effects of both clitoridectomy and infibulation on a woman's sexual enjoyment are highly negative—for one thing, clitoral orgasm is no longer possible. Some experts also say that FGC is related to the high level of infertility in many African countries, although a comparative study of fertility data from the Central African Republic, Côte d'Ivoire, and Tanzania found no clear relationship between FGC and infertility (Larsen and Yan 2000).

Outsiders often view these practices in oversimplified terms and in the most extreme forms. What are the views of insiders? Is there any evidence for agency? Or is it all structure and should anthropologists support FGC liberation movements? One voice that transcends insider/outsider divisions is that of Fuambai Ahmadu, who was born and raised in Washington, DC. She is descended from a prominent Kono lineage in Sierra Leone and has done research for her doctorate in anthropology on female genital cutting in the Gambia (2000).

In 1991, Ahmadu traveled to Sierra Leone with her mother and other family members for what she refers to as her "circumcision." Upon her return, she wrote about her intiation experience and what it meant to her. Although the physical pain was excruciating (in spite of the use of anesthetics), "the positive aspects have been much more profound" (2000:306). Through the initiation she became part of a powerful female

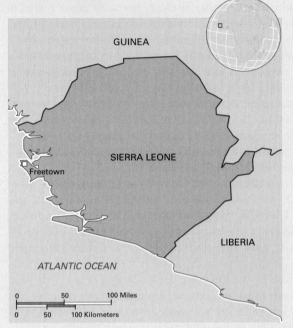

MAP 6.3 Sierra Leone. The Republic of Sierra Leone was an important center of the Transatlantic Slave Trade. Its capital, Freetown, was established in 1972 as a home for African slaves who fought with the British during the American Revolution. Sierra Leone's coast is covered with mangrove swamps while the interior is plateau, forests, and mountains. The population is 6 million people. Sierra Leone suffered a terrible civil war from 1991 to 2002, causing thousands of deaths and the displacement of 2 million people. It has the lowest per capita income in the world. English is the official language, but most people speak tribal languages.

world. Her analysis addresses the effects of genital cutting on health and sexuality. Ahmadu argues that Westerners exaggerate these issues by focusing on infibulation (which she says is rarely practiced) rather than on the less extreme forms. She adds, however, that if global pressures against the practice continue, she will go along with that movement and support "ritual without cutting" (2000:308).

CRITICAL THINKING QUESTIONS

- Why do you think FGC is a prominent issue in human rights debates in the West, whereas male circumcision and other forms of initiation (such as fraternity and sorority hazing) are condoned?

- Where do you stand on FGC and why?

- What kinds of cultural remodeling of the female body are practiced in your culture?

guard detail, the seniors attack him, rip off some of his clothes, spray him with shaving cream, and throw rotten food and used chewing tobacco at him. A "good Rat" takes it "like a man." The Rats who make it through the first year have strong bonds with the Dykes who are their mentors. In turn, the Rats serve them by making their beds and shining their shoes.

The culminating initiation ritual for the Rats takes place during March. The town's firetruck sprays the outskirts of the campus to create a large area of mud. The Rats have to crawl through the mud while sophomores and juniors attack them, shout at them, push them down, sit on them, and fill their eyes, ears, faces, and clothes with mud. The Rats can barely see as they grope their way along, and many lose their pants. The ordeal continues over two banks of earth and a ditch, with continuous harassment from the sophomores and juniors. When the Rats finally reach the top of the second bank, the Dykes rush to greet them, tenderly wash the mud off them, and wrap them in blankets. The moment when the mud is washed away is the transition of the Rat into a cadet.

Adams interprets this ritual as a birthing event with the newborn emerging blinded by and covered with fluids, then cleaned and blanketed. One senior said that being a Dyke "is like having my own child" (2002:39). Many aspects of this ritual, however, are ambiguous, not least of which is the term "Dyke" for male "mothers" (or "fathers"?). The Breaking Out initiation ritual is no longer practiced at VMI. For many years, this all-male school insisted that it could not admit women because the presence of women would destroy the very essence of the school. In the mid-1990s, VMI, as the recipient of public funds, was under pressure to admit women in order

to be compliant with the law. After a drawn-out legal battle that ended up in the Supreme Court, VMI admitted its first women students in 1997. Break Out has been replaced with a long weekend series of events involving physical and field challenges. As of 2005, over 100 women applied for admission.

Consider what happens, in different cultural contexts, to the biological universal of menarche, or first menstruation. In some cultures, menarche is a time of elaborate celebration and community feasting. In other, more male-dominated cultures, there is no public mention of it. For example, in rural Turkey, parents do not discuss menstruation with young girls, and the girls are shocked at menarche (Delaney 1988:79). Menstruation for Turkish girls is a matter of shame and embarrassment. Islamic teachings say that menstruation is the result of Eve's disobedience against Allah. Eve allowed herself to be persuaded by Satan to eat a forbidden fruit, so she was punished by being made to bleed monthly. In contrast, Hindus in southern India celebrate a daughter's menarche with a family gathering, special food, and songs (Miller 1997 [1981]). In the absence of studies on the psychological impact of these differences, one can only speculate that being honored at a celebration would have positive effects on a girl's sense of self-esteem, whereas linking menstruation with shamefulness would have the opposite effect.

Sexual Identity and Gender Pluralism

Scholars have long debated whether sexual preferences and gender identity are biologically determined (ruled by genetic or hormonal factors) or culturally constructed and learned. Biological anthropologist Melvin Konner

Breaking Out, a rite of passage at a military academy in Virginia when it was an all-men's school. ■ *What rite of passage have you been through and how would you analyze it anthropologically?* (Source: Abigail Adams)

(1989) takes a middle position, saying that both factors play a part, but simultaneously warning that no one has a simple answer to the question of who is gay. Science has yet to produce a clear answer.

The cultural constructionist position emphasizes socialization and childhood experiences as more powerful than biology in shaping sexual orientation. These anthropologists find support for their position in the cross-cultural record and its cases in which people change their sexual orientation once, or sometimes more than once, during their lifetimes. The Sambia of Papua New Guinea are one example. In the Gulf state of Oman, the *xanith* is another example (Wikan 1977) (see Map 4.3., p. 103). A xanith is a man who, for a time, becomes more like a woman, wears female clothing, and has sex with other men. Later, the xanith returns to a standard male role, marries a woman, and has children. Thus, given the same biological material, some people assume different sexual identities over their lives.

No matter what one's theoretical perspective is, it is clear that homosexuals are discriminated against in many contexts where heterosexuality is the norm. In the United States, homosexuals are disproportionately victims of hate crimes, housing discrimination, and problems in the workplace, including wage and benefits discrimination. They often suffer from being stigmatized by their parents, peers, and the wider society. The psychological damage to their self-esteem by social stigma and discrimination is related to the fact that homosexual youth in the United States have substantially higher suicide rates than heterosexual youth.

Some cultures allow for a "third gender, which is neither purely "male" nor purely "female," according to a particular culture's definition of those terms. As with the xanith of Oman, these gender categories offer ways for "males" to cross gender lines and assume more "female" behaviors, personality characteristics, and dress. In some Native American groups, a **berdache** is a male (in terms of genitals) who opts to wear female clothing, may engage in intercourse with a man or a woman, and does female tasks such as basket weaving and pottery making (Williams 1992). A person may become a berdache in a variety of ways. Some people say that parents, especially if they have several sons, choose one to become a berdache. Others say that a boy who shows interest in typically female activities or who likes to wear female clothing is allowed to become a berdache. Such a child is a focus of pride for the family, never a source of disappointment or stigma.

A Zuni berdache, We'wha, wearing the ceremonial costume of Zuni women and holding a pottery bowl with sacred corn meal. ■ *Generate a hypothesis about why most cultural examples of cross-gender roles involve males assuming female roles and dress, rather than the other way around.* (Source: © The National Anthropological Archive/Smithsonian Institution)

During decades of contact with Euro-American colonizers, including Christian missionaries, the outsiders viewed the berdache role with disapproval and ridicule (Roscoe 1991). Native American cultures began to suppress their berdache tradition. Starting in the 1980s, as Native American cultural pride began to grow, the open presence of the berdache and the **amazon** (a woman who takes on male roles and behaviors) has returned. Contemporary Native American cultures, compared to mainstream White culture, are more accepting of gender role fluidity and the contemporary concept of being gay: "Younger gay Indians, upon coming out to their families,

---

berdache: a blurred gender category, usually referring to a person who is biologically male but who assumes a female gender role.

amazon: a person who is biologically female but takes on a male gender role.

hijra: term used in India to refer to a blurred gender role in which a person, usually biologically male, takes on female dress and behavior.

gender pluralism: the existence within a culture of multiple categories of femininity, masculinity, and androgyny that are tolerated and legitimate.

will sometimes have an elderly relative who takes them aside and tells them about the berdache tradition. A part-Choctaw gay man recalls that his full-blooded Choctaw grandmother realized he was gay and it was totally acceptable. . . . This respectful attitude eliminates the stress felt by families that harbor homophobia" (1991: 225).

In India, the counterpart of the Native American berdache is a **hijra.** Hijras dress and act like women but are neither truly male nor truly female (Nanda 1990). Many hijras were born with male genitals or with genitals that were not clearly male or female. Hijras have the traditional right to visit the home of a newborn, inspect

The South Korean transgender group "Lady" includes four transsexuals. ■ (Source: © Kim Kyung-Hoon/ Reuters/CORBIS)

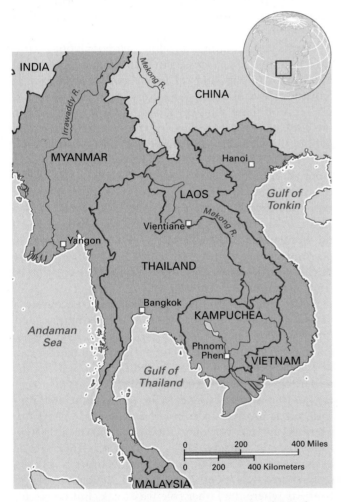

MAP 6.4   Mainland Southeast Asia. Mainland Southeast Asia comprises Myanmar, Thailand, Laos, Vietnam, Kampuchea, and Malaysia. Although each country has a distinct history, the region shares a tropical monsoon climate, emphasis on wet-rice agriculture, and ethnic contrasts between highlanders and lowlanders. Many national and ethnic languages exist. Languages in the Mon-Khmer language family have the most speakers. Theravada Buddhism, Islam, and Christianity are major religions. Growth in industry and informatics has created an economic upsurge in many parts of the region.

its genitals, and claim it for their group if the genitals are neither clearly male nor clearly female. Hijras born with male genitals may opt to go through an initiation ceremony that involves cutting off their penis and testicles. Hijras roam large cities of India, earning a living by begging from store to store (and threatening to lift their skirts if not given money). Because women do not sing or dance in public, hijras play an important role as performers in public events, especially as dancers or musicians. Mainstream people do not admire or respect hijras, and no family would be delighted to hear that their son has decided to become a hijra. Hijras are a stigmatized group, separated from mainstream society.

In mainland and island Southeast Asia, the situation is even more complex, with a wide range of gender options, or **gender pluralism.** Gender pluralism is the existence in a culture of multiple categories of femininity, masculinity, and androgyny which are tolerated and legitimate (Peletz 2006:310). In Thailand, three gender categories have long existed: *phuuchai* (male), *phuuyung* (female), and *kathoey* (transvestite/transsexual/hermaphrodite) (Morris 1994). Like the berdache and hijra, a kathoey is "originally" a male who crosses into the body, personality, and dress defined as female. Sexual orientation of kathoeys is flexible, including either male or female partners. In contemporary Thailand, explicit discussion and recognition of homosexuality exists, usually couched in English terms, conveying a sense of its foreignness. The words for lesbian are *thom* (from the word "tomboy") and *thut* (an ironic usage from the U.S. movie *Tootsie* about a heterosexual male transvestite). As in many parts of the world, reflecting the widespread presence of patriarchal norms, lesbianism in Thailand is a more suppressed form of homosexuality than male homosexuality.

Personality and Identity in Adulthood

Adulthood for most people means entering into some form of marriage, or long-term domestic relationship, and having children. This section considers the psychological aspects of parenthood and the "senior years."

Becoming a Parent

In Euro-American culture, a woman becomes a mother when she gives birth. **Matrescence** is the cultural process of becoming a mother (Raphael 1975). Like adolescence, matrescence varies cross-culturally in terms of duration and meaning. In some cultures, a woman is transformed into a mother as soon as she thinks she is pregnant. In others, she becomes a mother and is granted full maternal status only when she delivers an infant of the "right" sex, as in much of northern India, where son preference is strong.

Among the Beti people of southern Cameroon, West Africa, motherhood is not simply defined by having a child (Johnson-Hanks 2002). The Beti are both an ethnic group and a social status group of educated professionals. "School girl" is one category of young Beti women. If a school girl becomes pregnant, it is a matter of great shame. The girl is not considered to have entered a phase of motherhood even though she has borne a child. In this case, a biological marker does not bring about transition into a new life stage but instead creates ambiguity.

In many nonindustrial cultures, matrescence occurs in the context of supportive family members. Some cultures promote prenatal practices, abiding by particular food taboos, which can be regarded as part of matrescence. Such rules make the pregnant woman feel that she has a role in ensuring that the pregnancy turns out well. In the West, medical experts increasingly define the prenatal period as an important phase of matrescence, and they have issued many scientific and medical rules for potential parents, especially mothers (Browner and Press 1995, 1996). Pregnant women are urged to seek prenatal examinations, be under the regular supervision of a doctor who monitors the growth and development of the fetus, follow particular dietary and exercise guidelines, and undergo a range of tests such as ultrasound scanning. Some anthropologists think that such medical control of pregnancy leads to the greater likelihood of postpartum depression among mothers as a result of their lack of control in matrescence.

Fear is the predominant feeling that poor, young Afro-Brazilian mothers expressed in their narratives of birth-giving in a public hospital in the northeastern city of Salvador (McCallum and dos Reis 2005) (see Map 3.4, p. 73). For these women, giving birth in a run-down hospital where the medical staff are middle class and White, the lack of social support is one cause of their fear. The mother-to-be enters the hospital alone to confront an unfamiliar environment. The labor ward is full of women shrieking with pain. Any friendly interaction with the hospital staff is a source of uplift. Most women said that they missed their mothers and felt lonely. All the women's narratives, however, contained the theme of personal growth by learning to become stronger. Giving birth, in difficult circumstances, was a kind of ritual of transformation.

Patrescence, or the cultural process of becoming a father, is less marked cross-culturally than matrescence. One exception to this generalization is **couvade**, beliefs and customs applying to a father during his wife's pregnancy and delivery (Broude 1988:902). In some cases, the father takes to his bed before, during, or after the delivery, and he may experience pain and exhaustion. Couvade often involves rules for the expectant father. For example, he may not hunt a certain animal, eat certain foods, or cut objects. Early theories of why couvade exists relied on Freudian interpretations that men were seeking cross-sex identification (with the female role) in contexts where the father role was weak. But cross-cultural data on the existence of couvade indicates the opposite: Couvade occurs in societies where fathers have prominent roles in child care. In this view, couvade is one phase of patrescence: Their proper behavior helps ensure

---

matrescence: motherhood, or the cultural process of becoming a mother.
patrescence: fatherhood, or the cultural process of becoming a father.

couvade: customs applying to the behavior of fathers during and shortly after the birth of their children.

An Aka father and his son. Aka fathers are affectionate caretakers of infants and small children. Compared to mothers, they are more likely to kiss and hug children.
■ *How does this compare to a microculture with which you are familiar?* (Source: Barry Hewlett)

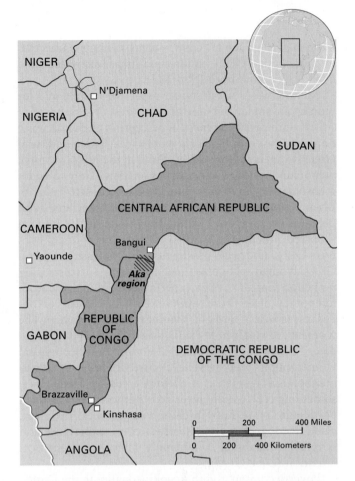

MAP 6.5   Aka Region of the Central African Republic and the Democratic Republic of Congo. The 30,000 Aka are tropical forest foragers who know hundreds of forest plants and animals. They eat roots, leaves, nuts, fruits, mushrooms, honey, grubs, caterpillars, and meat from monkeys, rats, mongooses, and porcupines. They trade meat to farmers for manioc and other cultivated foods. They are socially egalitarian, and their religious beliefs are indigenous. Diaka, their main language, is tonal. The Aka territory is seriously endangered by commercial loggers.

a good delivery and a healthy baby. Yet another interpretation of couvade is that it offers support for the mother. In Estonia, some people believe that a woman's birth pains will be less if her husband bears some of them (Oinas 1993).

The widespread pattern of women being the major caretakers of infants and children has led many people to think there is something biologically innate about females that makes them especially suited to caretaking roles. Most cultural anthropologists agree that child care is predominantly the responsibility of females worldwide— but not universally. They seek to provide a cultural construction explanation rather than a genetic or hormonal one. As evidence, they point to the cross-cultural variation in child-care roles. For example, throughout the South Pacific, child care is shared across families, and women breastfeed other women's babies. Paternal involvement varies cross-culturally as well. Among Aka foragers of the Central African Republic (see Map 6.5), paternal child care is prominent (Hewlett 1991). Aka fathers are intimate, affectionate, and helpful, spending half their time each day holding or within close reach of their infants. While holding their infant, fathers are more likely to hug and kiss them than mothers are. The definition of good fatherhood among the Aka means being affectionate toward children and assisting the mother when her workload is heavy. Among the Aka, gender equality prevails, and violence against women is unknown. The high level of paternal involvement in child care helps explain this pattern.

Middle Age

In industrial and postindustrial countries, the lower and upper boundaries of "middle age" are typically defined as being 30 and 70 years of age (Shweder 1998). A major turning point is now the fortieth birthday. Stanley Brandes explores the meanings of turning age 40 to U.S. middle-class men in a book entitled *Forty: The Age and the Symbol* (1985). The "forty syndrome" comprises feelings of restlessness, rebelliousness, and unhappiness that often lead to family break-ups. One possible reason behind this emphasis on age 40 as a turning point for males is that it is the current midpoint of a "typical" life span for a middle-class U.S. man. In cultures with shorter life spans, a so-called midlife crisis would necessarily occur at some point other than the age of 40 years, if it were to happen at all. Such a "crisis" seems strongly embedded in contemporary U.S. culture and its pervasive fear and denial of death (Shore 1998:103).

Menopause is a significant aspect of middle age for women in some, but not all, cultures. A comparative study examined differences in perception and experience of menopause among Maya women of Mexico and rural Greek women (Beyene 1989). Among the Maya women, menopause is not a time of stress or crisis. They consider menstruation an illness and look forward to its end. Menopause among these women is not associated with physical or emotional symptoms. None of the women reported hot flashes or cold sweats. No role changes were associated with menopause. In contrast, the rural Greek women recognized menopause as a natural phenomenon that all women experience and one that causes temporary discomfort, *exapi,* which is a phase of hot flashes, especially at night, that may last about a year. The women did not think exapi was serious and did not regard it as worthy of medical attention. Postmenopausal women emphasized the relief and freedom they felt. Postmenopausal women can go into cafes by themselves, something they would never do otherwise, and they can participate more fully in church ceremonies. In Japan, also, menopause is a minimally stressful experience and is rarely considered something that warrants medical attention (Lock 1993).

Poverty combines with racial inequality in the United States to create psychological insecurity and anxiety among many middle-aged African Americans. In a low-income neighborhood of Harlem, New York City, mid-dle-aged people have a strong work ethic in the face of declining employment opportunities (Newman 1998). Long-standing residents of Harlem have witnessed the rise in violent crime in their neighborhoods and the deaths of many young people. For these people, their old age security lies in the help they can count on from children and grandchildren. But children and grandchildren often get into trouble, and that spells disaster for their elders. As elders are asking themselves why there is so much trouble, they increasingly seek support in community organizations and churches.

THINKING OUTSIDE THE BOX

DO ANIMALS other than humans experience menopause?

The Senior Years

The "senior" life-cycle stage may be a development of contemporary human society because, like most other mammals, our early ancestors rarely lived beyond their reproductive years (Brooks and Draper 1998 [1991]). Cross-culturally, the category of the aged is variably recognized, defined, and valued. In many cultures, elders are highly revered and their life experiences are valued as the greatest wisdom. In others, aged people become burdens to their families and to society.

In general, the status and well-being of the elderly is higher when they continue to live with their families (Lee and Kezis 1979). This pattern is more likely to be found in nonindustrial societies than in industrialized ones,

Throughout Asia, it is the responsibility of children to care for their parents in thier old age. But the numbers of the elderly are growing, while reduced fertility means fewer family caretakers. ■ (Source: Barbara Miller)

Compared with the elderly of East Asia, many aged people in the United States have no family support and end up living on the street or in shelters. ■ (Source: © Douglas Kirkland/CORBIS)

where the elderly are increasingly experiencing a shift to "retirement homes." In such age-segregated settings, people have to create new social roles and ties and find new ways of gaining self-esteem and personal satisfaction. Research conducted in a retirement home in a small town in central New York state shows that having a pet promotes people's sense of well-being (Savishinsky 1991).

The Final Passage: Death and Dying

It may be that no one in any culture welcomes death, unless he or she is in very poor health and suffering greatly. The contemporary United States, with its dependence on medical technology, appears to play a leading role in resistance to death, often at high financial and psychological costs. In many other cultures, a greater degree of acceptance prevails.

A study of attitudes toward death and dying among Alaskan Inuits revealed a pervasive feeling that people are active participants in their death rather than passive victims (Trelease 1975). The person near death calls friends and neighbors together, is given a Christian sacrament, and then, within a few hours, dies. The author comments, "I do not suggest that everyone waited for the priest to come and then died right away. But the majority who did not die suddenly did some degree of planning, had some kind of formal service or celebration of prayers and hymns and farewells" (1975:35).

Terminally ill people, especially in industrial/informatic societies with a high level of medical technology, are likely to be faced with choices about how and where they should die: at home or in a hospital? Prolong life with "unusual means" or opt for "physician-assisted suicide"? Depending on the cultural context, the options are affected not only by the degree of medical technology and health-care services available but also by matters of kinship and gender role ideals (Long 2005). In urban Japan, terminally ill people have clear ideas of what is a "good death" and multiple "scripts" exist for a "good death." A modern script of dying in a hospital is widely accepted, because it reduces burdens on family members. But a value on dying surrounded by one's family members still prevails; this practice reassures the dying person that he or she will be remembered.

Proper treatment of the corpse is another important cultural aspect of death. Archaeological evidence suggests that the practice of burying corpses is only a few hundred thousand years old and likely originated in the Middle East. Since then, rituals associated with death have been elaborated around the world.

In many cultures, the inability to perform a proper burial and funeral for the deceased person is a cause of serious social suffering. Among refugees from Mozambique living in neighboring Malawi, the greatest cause of stress was being forced to leave behind deceased family members without providing a proper burial for them (Englund 1998). Such improperly treated deaths mean that the unhappy spirit of the deceased will haunt the living. This belief is related to the high rates of mental-health problems among the refugees. A culturally informed recommendation for reducing anxiety among the refugees is to provide them with money to travel home and to perform a proper funeral for their deceased relatives. In that way, the living may carry on in greater peace.

Anthropologists know little about people's grief at the death of a loved one or close community member. It might seem that sadness and grief, and a period of mourning, are only natural. But the outward expression of grief varies from extended, dramatic, public grieving that is overtly emotional to no visible sign of grief at all. The latter pattern is the norm in Bali, Indonesia (see Map 1.3, p. 15), where people's faces remain impassive at funerals and no vocal lamenting occurs (Rosenblatt, Walsh, and Jackson 1976). Do impassive faces and silence mean that the Balinese feel no sadness? Such different modes of expression of loss may be related to the healing process for the survivors by providing socially accepted rules of behavior—in other words, a script for loss. Either highly expressive public mourning or repressed grief may be equally effective, depending on the context.

Memorial to the 1995 terrorist bombing in Oklahoma City. Children's toys and stuffed animals mark the death of children in the child-care center of the building at the time of the explosion. ■ *If you were in charge of deciding what kind of memorial should mark the site of the 9/11 attack in New York City, what would your plans emphasize?* (Source: © Charles O. Cecil)

The Big Questions Revisited

WHAT is the scope of psychological anthropology?

Psychological anthropology is the study of individuals and their personalities and identities, within particular cultural contexts. In North American anthropology, psychological anthropology has its roots in the Culture and Personality School that emerged in the early part of the twentieth century. These anthropologists studied child-rearing patterns and their effect on personality, national patterns of personality, and the relationship between poverty and personality. More recently, psychological anthropologists have begun studying personality formation in Western and industrial/informatic cultures. The latest turn in psychological anthropology is an emphasis on person-centered ethnography and close attention to individual perceptions and experiences.

Compared to the Western discipline of psychology, psychological anthropology takes a much wider view of concepts such as personality and the self—a perspective gained through ethnographic research.

HOW does culture shape personality and identity from birth through adolescence?

Human psychological development begins from the moment of birth, if not before. Margaret Mead was a pioneer in showing how child-care practices such as breastfeeding, how the baby is held, and how much contact the infant has with others can affect personality formation, including gender identity. Her study of the Arapesh, Mundugumor, and Tchambuli peoples of Papua New Guinea showed that gender is a "plastic" (or malleable) aspect of human personality. Cross-cultural studies indicate that children's work roles and family roles correspond to personality patterns. Informal and formal learning, depending on cultural context, shape young people's sense of identity in various ways.

Adolescence, a phase of the life cycle around puberty and before adulthood, varies cross-culturally from being nonexistent to being long in duration and involving detailed training and elaborate ceremonies. "Coming of age" ceremonies may involve bodily cutting, which denotes membership of the initiate in a particular gender. In contrast to the clear distinction between "male" and "female" defined by Western science, many cultures have long-standing traditions of third-gender identities, especially for males or people of indeterminate biological sex markers, and gender pluralism.

HOW does culture shape personality and identity in adulthood through old age?

Reflecting the fact that women tend to be more involved than males in child care, cultures generally provide more in the way of enculturation of females for this role. In nonindustrial societies, learning about motherhood is embedded in other aspects of life, and knowledge about birthing and child care is shared among women. In industrialized cultures, science and medicine play a large part in defining the maternal role. This change reduces women's autonomy and fosters their dependence on external, nonfamily-based structures.

In general, the senior years are shorter in nonindustrialized societies than in industrial/informatics societies, in which life spans tend to be longer. Elder men and women in nonindustrial cultures are treated with respect, are considered to be highly knowledgeable, and retain a strong sense of their place in the culture. Increasingly in industrial/informatics societies, elderly people either remove themselves or are removed from their families and spend many years in age-segregated institutions. This transition tends to have negative implications for their psychological well-being.

Anthropologists know relatively little about how people in different cultures experience and express grief at the loss of a loved one. In some cultures, grief is openly expressed, whereas in others, it is repressed.

KEY CONCEPTS

adolescence, p. 157
amazon, p. 162
berdache, p. 162
couvade, p. 164
cultural broker, p. 152
cultural configuration, p. 147

culture of poverty, p. 148
ethnopsychology, p. 146
female genital cutting (FGC), p. 159
gender pluralism, p. 163
hijra, p. 163
image of the limited good, p. 148

matrescence, p. 164
patrescence, p. 164
person-centered ethnography, p. 149
personality, p. 146
puberty, p. 157

SUGGESTED READINGS

Evalyn Blackwood, ed. *The Many Faces of Homosexuality: Anthropological Approaches to Homosexual Behavior.* New York: Harrington Park Press, 1986. This text contains case studies of ritualized male homosexuality in Irian Jaya, the berdache in North America, hijras of India, lesbian relationships in Lesotho, and Mexican male homosexual interaction patterns in public.

Robbie E. Davis-Floyd. *Birth as an American Rite of Passage,* 2nd ed. with a new Preface. Berkeley: University of California Press, 2003. This book provides a cultural critique of the dominant U.S. model of birth as "technocratic" and patriarchal. The last two chapters consider the future of birthing in the United States and the increasing role of computers in obstetrics.

Ellen Gruenbaum. *The Female Circumcision Controversy: An Anthropological Perspective.* Philadelphia: University of Pennsylvania Press, 2001. The author draws on her more than five years of fieldwork in Sudan and discusses how change is occurring through economic development, the role of Islamic activists, health educators, and educated African women.

Charlotte E. Hardman. *Other Worlds: Notions of Self and Emotion among the Lohorung Rai.* New York: Berg, 2000. The author conducted fieldwork in a mountainous region of eastern Nepal to learn about one community's perception of what it means to be a person.

Susan Orpett Long. *Final Days: Japanese Culture and Choice at the End of Life.* Honolulu: University of Hawai'i Press, 2005. An increasing array of choices about how to die a "good death" now exists in Japan, mainly due to technological innovations. This study, conducted in an urban area, shows how people make end-of-life choices within the context of universal health care, kinship, and gender roles.

Susan McKinnon. *Neo-Liberal Genetics: The Myths and Moral Tales of Evolutionary Psychology.* Chicago: University of Chicago Press, 2005. Culturally based analysis of U.S.-based evolutionary psychology, as defined by such prominent scholars as Steven Pinker and David Buss, reveals that it is ethnocentric, myth creating, and linked to contemporary U.S. capitalist values. Evolutionary psychology's understandings of sex, gender, kinship, and social relations are at the center of the critique.

Judith Schachter Modell. *Ruth Benedict: Patterns of a Life.* Philadelphia: University of Pennsylvania Press, 1983. This biography provides insights into Benedict's development as an anthropologist, her research and writings, and her role in the Culture and Personality School.

Michael Moffatt. *Coming of Age in New Jersey: College and American Culture.* New Brunswick: Rutgers University Press, 1991. Based on a year's participant observation in a college dormitory in a university in the eastern United States, this study discusses sexuality, race relations, and individualism.

Mimi Nichter. *Fat Talk: What Girls and What Their Parents Say About Dieting.* Cambridge, MA: Harvard University Press, 2000. The author collected and analyzed interview data with adolescent girls in the United States, focusing on perceptions of weight, attachment to dieting, and the influence of their mothers' views and comments on weight.

Richard Parker. *Bodies, Pleasures and Passions: Sexual Culture in Contemporary Brazil.* Boston: Beacon Press, 1991. This ethnographic study of contemporary sexual culture in Brazil addresses such topics as sexual socialization, bisexuality, sadomasochism, AIDS, prostitution, samba, the symbolism of breasts, courting, and carnival.

Richard K. Reed. *Birthing Fathers: The Transformation of Men in American Rites of Birth.* New Brunswick, NJ: Rutgers University Press, 2005. The author interviewed fifty U.S. fathers, collected their narratives about birthing, and attended birthing classes. This book relates its findings to both classic and new themes in cultural anthropology such as the couvade, rites of passage, and ideas about the human body.

Jennifer Robertson, ed. *Same-Sex Cultures and Sexualities: An Anthropological Reader.* Malden, MA: Blackwell Publishing, 2004. The chapters in this book explore theory, biology and sexuality, language and sexuality, transsexuality, modernity and desire, and the globalization of gay sexual identity. Cultural contexts include North America, Japan, West Sumatra, South Africa, Bolivia, and more.

Joel S. Savishinsky. *Breaking the Watch: The Meanings of Retirement in America.* Ithaca, NY: Cornell University Press, 2000. Fieldwork in a nursing home in a small town in central New York state sheds light on the retirees themselves through vivid portraits of several, along with their own words on friendship in the home, finding purpose in life, and dealing with finances.

Joseph J. Tobin, David Y. H. Wu, and Dana H. Davidson. *Preschool in Three Cultures: Japan, China, and the United States.* New Haven, CT: Yale University Press, 1989. This book offers comparative insights about parents' reasons for sending children to preschool, including a concern that children learn cooperation in all three contexts and a contrast between the emphasis on academic learning in the United States and social learning in Japan.

John W. Traphagan. *Taming Oblivion: Aging Bodies and the Fear of Senility in Japan.* Albany: State University of New York Press, 2000. The author conducted fieldwork in a small town north of Tokyo to investigate people's attitudes and practices related to old age, especially as aging people attempt to prevent the onset of the *boke* condition, or what Westerners call senility.

7

Disease, Illness, and Healing

The Big Questions

- WHAT is ethnomedicine?

- WHAT are three major theoretical approaches in medical anthropology?

- HOW are disease, illness, and healing changing during globalization?

Steven Benally Jr., an apprentice medicine man, practices for a ceremony in his hogan on the Navajo Reservation near Window Rock, Arizona. An apprentice often studies for a decade or more. *(Source: © Kevin Fleming/CORBIS)*

Primatologist Jane Goodall once witnessed the consequences of a polio epidemic among the chimpanzees she was studying in Tanzania (Foster and Anderson 1978: 33–34). A group of healthy animals watched a stricken member try to reach the feeding area but did not help him. Another badly paralyzed chimpanzee was simply left behind when the group moved on. Humans also sometimes resort to isolation and abandonment of those who are ill and dying. But compared to our nonhuman primate relatives, humans have created more complex ways of interpreting health problems and highly creative methods of preventing and curing them.

Medical anthropology is one of the most rapidly growing areas of research in anthropology. This chapter presents a selection of findings from this subfield. It first describes how people in different cultures think and behave regarding health, illness, and healing. The second section considers three theoretical approaches in medical anthropology. The chapter concludes by discussing how globalization is affecting health.

Ethnomedicine

Since the early days of anthropology, the topic of **ethnomedicine,** or the study of cross-cultural health systems, has been a focus of study. A *health system* encompasses many areas: perceptions and classifications of health problems, prevention measures, diagnosis, healing (magical, religious, scientific, healing substances), and healers. Ethnomedicine has expanded its focus to include topics such as perceptions of the body, culture and disability, and change in indigenous or "traditional" healing systems, especially as resulting from globalization.

In the 1960s, when the term *ethnomedicine* first came into use, it referred only to non-Western health systems and was synonymous with folk medicine, popular medicine, or the now-abandoned term, primitive medicine. The early use of the term was ethnocentric. Contemporary **Western biomedicine (WBM)**, a healing approach based on modern Western science that emphasizes technology in diagnosing and treating health problems related to the human body, is an ethnomedical system, too. Medical anthropologists also study WBM as a cultural system intimately bound to Western values. Thus, the current meaning of the term *ethnomedicine* encompasses health systems everywhere.

South African healer Magdaline Ramaota speaks to clients in Durban. In South Africa, few people have enough money to pay for AIDS drugs. The role of traditional healers in providing psychological and social support for victims is extremely important. ■ *Do Internet research to learn about the current and projected rates of HIV/AIDS in African countries.* (Source: © AFP/CORBIS)

Perceptions of the Body

In Japan, the concept of *gotai* refers to the ideal of maintaining bodily intactness in life and death, to the extent of not piercing one's ears (Ohnuki-Tierney 1994:235). When Crown Prince Naruhitao was considering who to marry, one criterion for the bride was that she not have pierced ears. Underlying the value on intactness is the belief that an intact body ensures rebirth. Historically, a warrior's practice of beheading a victim was the ultimate form of killing because it violated the integrity of the body and prevented the enemy's rebirth. Gotai is an

---

ethnomedicine: the study of cross-cultural health systems.
Western biomedicine: a healing approach based on modern Western science that emphasizes technology for diagnosing

and treating health problems related to the human body.
disease: in the disease/illness dichotomy, a biological health problem that is objective and universal.

illness: in the disease/illness dichotomy, culturally specific perceptions and experiences of a health problem.

important reason for the low rates of surgery in Japan—compared to the United States—and the widespread popular resistance to organ transplantation.

Ideals about the female body are implicated in the high rate of caesarian births in Brazil (McCallum 2005). Ethnographic research in the city of Salvador, northeastern Brazil, reveals that vaginal childbirth is considered more "primitive," painful, and destructive of a woman's sexuality than caesarian delivery. One doctor said that "more and more, the vulva and the vagina are becoming the organs of sexuality and not parturition. . . . No worse thing can happen to a woman than that her husband take a mistress because (her vagina) is slack" (2005:226). When a pregnant woman asks how to avoid such problems, the doctor recommends a caesarian delivery as safe, practical, and having no "aesthetic damage."

Euro-American popular and scientific thinking emphasizes a separation of the mind from the body. Thus, Western medicine has a special category called "mental illness," which treats certain health problems as though they were located only in the mind. In contrast, in the many cultures in which a mind–body distinction does not exist, there is no category of "mental illness" and treatment is more holistic.

Another area of study related to the body is whether people consider the body to be a bounded physical unit, with healing focused on the body alone, or connected to a wider social context, in which case healing addresses the body within the wider social sphere (Fabrega and Silver 1973). Although Western biomedicine typically addresses a bounded, individual physical body, many other cultures situate an individual's physical body firmly within society. Variations in the definition of a living body versus a dead body are also prominent worldwide. Different organs may be seen as critical. In the United States, a person may be declared dead while the heart is still beating, so long as the brain is judged to be "dead." In many other cultures, people do not accept a brain-based definition of life and death (Ohnuki-Tierney 1994).

Defining and Classifying Health Problems

Emic diversity in labeling health problems presents a challenge for medical anthropologists and health-care specialists. Western labels, which biomedically trained experts accept as true, accurate, and universal, often do not correspond to the labels in other cultures. One set of concepts that medical anthropologists use to sort out the many cross-cultural labels and perceptions is the *disease/illness dichotomy*. In this model, **disease** refers to a biological health problem that is objective and universal, such as a bacterial or viral infection or a broken arm. **Illness** refers to culturally specific perceptions and experiences of a health problem. Medical anthropologists study both disease and illness, and they show how both

must be understood within their cultural contexts. Arthur Kleinman, medical anthropologist and physician, says that Western biomedicine focuses too narrowly on disease and neglects illness (1995). He advocates that biomedicine should pay more attention to the findings of

THINKING OUTSIDE THE BOX

IN YOUR MICROCULTURE, what are the prevailing perceptions about the body and how are they related to medical treatment?

medical anthropologists and broaden the understanding of health problems and their cultural construction.

A first step in ethnomedical research is to learn how people label, categorize, and classify health problems. Depending on the culture, the following may be bases for labeling and classifying health problems: cause, *vector* (the means of transmission, such as mosquitoes), affected body part, symptoms, or combinations of these. Often, knowledgeable elders are the repositories of this knowledge, and they pass it down through oral traditions. Among Native Americans of the Washington–Oregon region, many popular stories refer to health (Thompson and Sloat 2004). The stories convey messages about how to prevent health problems, avoid bodily harm, relieve afflictions, and deal with old age. For example, here is the story of Boil, a story for young children:

> Boil was getting bigger.
> Her husband told her to bathe.
> She got into the water.
> She disappeared. (2004:5).

Other, longer stories about Boil add complexities about the location of the boil and how to deal with particular boils, revealing indigenous patterns of classification.

This young man is carrying his teenage sister, Geralda, to a clinic in rural Haiti. She has tuberculosis. Tuberculosis worldwide now often exists in strains that are resistant to treatment with the usual drugs. ■ (Source: © Gilles Peress)

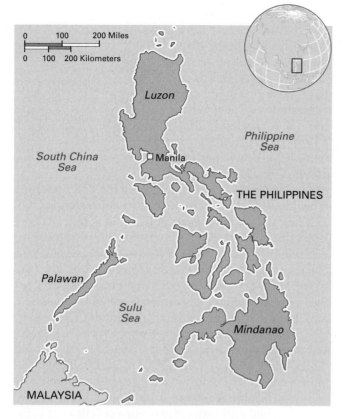

MAP 7.1   The Philippines. The Republic of the Philippines comprises over 7,000 islands of which around 700 are occupied. The population is over 85 million with two-thirds living on Luzon. The economy is based on agriculture, light industry, and a growing business processing outsourcing (BPO) industry. Over 8 million Filipinos work overseas and remit more than $12 billion a year, a large part of the GDP. Although Filipino and English are the official languages, more than 170 languages are spoken. The Philippines has the world's third largest Christian population with Roman Catholicism predominant.

FIGURE 7.1   Subanun Categories of *Nuka*, Skin-Related Health Problems

- Rash
- Eruption
- Inflammation
  - Eruption
  - Inflamed/Quasi-bite
  - Ulcerated
- Sore
  - Distal Ulcer
    Shallow
    Deep
  - Proximal Ulcer
    Shallow
    Deep
  - Simple Sore
  - Spreading Sore
- Ringworm
  - Exposed
  - Hidden
  - Spreading Itch
- Wound

Source: Adapted from Frake 1961:118, Figure 1.

A classic study among the Subanun people focused on their categories of health problems (Frake 1961). The Subanun, in the 1950s, were horticulturalists living in the highlands of Mindanao, in the Philippines (see Map 7.1). An egalitarian people, all Subanun, even young children, had substantial knowledge about health problems. Of their 186 labels for health problems, some are a single term, such as "itch," which can be expanded on using two words such as "splotchy itch." Skin diseases have several degrees of specificity (see Figure 7.1).

In Western biomedicine, panels of medical experts have to agree about how to label and classify health problems according to scientific criteria. Classifications and descriptions of thousands of afflictions are published in thick manuals that physicians consult before they give a diagnosis. In countries where medical care is privatized, the code selected may determine whether the patient's costs are covered by insurance or not. The *International Classification of Diseases (ICD),* now in its tenth edition (1993), is a major source for coding health problems according to Western biomedical standards. Even though it contains abundant details on many health problems and is carefully arranged according to a complex coding system, its categories often prove to be inadequate. For example, following the attacks on the United States of September 11, 2001, medical personnel who had to classify the cause of death of those who perished at the four sites and the health problems of survivors found the *ICD-10* codes of little help.

Another weakness of the *ICD-10* is that it is biased toward diseases that Western biomedicine recognizes and ignores health problems of many other cultures. Anthropologists have discovered the existence of many health problems around the world, often referred to as culture-specific syndromes. A **culture-specific syndrome** is a

---

culture-specific syndrome: a collection of signs and symptoms that is restricted to a particular culture or a limited number of cultures; also called "folk illness."

somatization: the process through which the body absorbs social stress and manifests symptoms of suffering.

FIGURE 7.2 Selected Culture-Specific Syndromes

Name of Syndrome	Distribution	Attributed Causes	Description and Symptoms
Anorexia nervosa	Middle- and upper-class Euro-American girls; globalizing	Unknown	Body wasting due to food avoidance; feeling of being too fat; in extreme cases, death
Hikikomori	Japan, males from adolescence through adulthood	Social pressure to succeed in school and pursue a position as a salaryman	Acute social withdrawal; refusal to attend school, or leave their room for months, sometimes years
Hwa-byung	Korea and Korean immigrants, especially elderly women	Stress, emotional disturbance, oppressive social relationships	Heavy feeling in the chest, perceived mass in the abdomen, problems sleeping, hot and cold flashes, anxiety, destructive impulsiveness
Koro	China and Southeast Asia, men	Unknown	Belief that the penis has retracted into the body
Peito aberto (open chest)	Northeastern Brazil, especially women, perhaps elsewhere among Latino populations	Excessive worry about others	Enlarges the heart and "bursts" through it causing "openings in the heart"
Retired Husband Syndrome (RHS)	Japan, older women whose husbands are retired	Stress	Ulcers, slurred speech, rashes around the eyes, throat polyps
Soufriendo del agua (suffering from water)	Valley of Mexico, low-income people, especially women	Lack of access to secure and clean water	Anxiety
Susto	Spain, Portugal, Central and South America, Latino immigrants in the U.S. and Canada	Shock or fright	Lethargy, poor appetite, problems sleeping, anxiety

Sources: Chowdhury 1996; Ennis-McMillan 2001; Faiola 2005; Gremillion 1992; Kawanishi 2004; Pang 1994; Rehbun 1994; Rubel, O'Nell, and Collado-Ardón 1984.

health problem with a set of symptoms associated with a particular culture (see Figure 7.2). Social factors such as stress, fear, or shock often are the underlying causes of culture-specific syndromes. Biophysical symptoms may be involved, and culture-specific syndromes can be fatal. **Somatization** refers to the process through which the body absorbs social stress and manifests symptoms of suffering.

For example, *susto,* or "fright/shock disease," is found in Spain and Portugal and among Latino people wherever they live. People afflicted with susto attribute it to events such as losing a loved one or having a terrible accident (Rubel, O'Nell, and Collado-Ardón 1984). In Oaxaca,

southern Mexico (see Map 5.4, p. 128) a woman reported that her susto was brought on by an accident in which pottery she had made was broken on its way to market. A man said that his susto came on after he saw a dangerous snake. Susto symptoms include appetite loss, lack of motivation, breathing problems, generalized pain, and nightmares. The researchers analyzed many cases of susto in three villages. They found that the people most likely to be afflicted were those who were socially marginal or experiencing a sense of role failure. For example, the woman with the broken pots had also suffered two spontaneous abortions and was worried that she would never have children. In Oaxaca, people with susto have higher mortality rates than other people. Thus, social marginality, or a deep sense of social failure, can place a person at a higher risk of dying. It is important to look at the deeper causes of susto and susto deaths.

Medical anthropologists first studied culture-specific syndromes in non-Western cultures. This focus created a bias in thinking that they exist only in "other" cultures. Now, anthropologists recognize that Western cultures also have culture-specific syndromes. Anorexia nervosa and a related condition, bulimia, are culture-bound syndromes found mainly among White middle-class adolescent girls of the United States, although some cases have been documented among African American girls in the United States and among young males (Fabrega and Miller 1995). Perhaps as a result of Western globalization, since the 1990s, cases have been documented in cities in Japan, Hong Kong, and India. Anorexia nervosa's cluster of symptoms includes self-perceptions of fatness, aversion to food, hyperactivity, and, as the condition progresses, continued wasting of the body and often death. No one has found a clear biological cause for anorexia nervosa, although some researchers claim that it has a genetic basis. Cultural anthropologists say that much evidence suggests a strong role of cultural construction. One logical result of the role of culture is that medical and psychiatric treatments are highly unsuccessful in curing anorexia nervosa (Gremillion 1992). Extreme food deprivation can become addictive and entrapping, and the affliction becomes *embodied*, intertwined with the body's biological functions. Extended fasting makes the body unable to deal with ingested food. Thus, medical treatment may involve intravenous feeding to override the biological block. Sometimes nothing works, and the affliction is fatal.

Pinpointing the cultural causes of anorexia nervosa, however, is not easy. Some experts cite societal pressures on girls that lead to excessive concern with looks, especially body weight. Others feel that anorexia is related to girls' unconscious resistance to overcontrolling parents. For such girls, food intake may be one thing over which they have power.

Ethno-etiologies

People in all cultures, everywhere, attempt to make sense of health problems and try to understand their cause, or etiology. Following anthropological practice, the term **ethno-etiologies** refers to cross-cultural variations in causal explanations for health problems and suffering.

Among the urban poor of northeastern Brazil, people consider several causal possibilities when they are sick

(Ngokwey 1988). In Feira de Santana, the second largest city in the state of Bahia (see Map 3.4, p. 73), ethno-etiologies can be natural, socioeconomic, psychological, or supernatural. Natural causes include exposure to the environment—for example: "Too much cold can provoke gripe; humidity and rain cause rheumatism; excessive heat can result in dehydration. . . . Some types of winds are known to provoke *ar do vento* or *ar do tempo,* a condition characterized by migraines. . ." (1988:795). Other natural explanations for illness take into account the effects of aging, heredity, personal nature (*natureza*), and gender. Contagion is another natural explanation, as are the effects of certain foods and eating habits. People also recognize the lack of economic resources, proper sanitation, and health services as structural causes of health problems. In the words of one person: "There are many illnesses because there are many poor" (1988:796). In the psychosocial domain, emotions such as anger and hostility cause certain health problems. In the supernatural domain, spirits and magic can cause health problems. The African-Brazilian religious systems of the Bahia region encompass many spirits who can inflict illness. They include spirits of the unhappy dead and devil-like spirits. Some spirits cause specific illnesses; others bring general misfortune. In addition, envious people with the evil eye (*ohlo grosso*) cast spells on people and cause much illness.

The people of Feira de Santana recognize several levels of causality. In the case of stomachache, they might blame a quarrel (*underlying cause*), which prompted the aggrieved party to seek the intervention of a sorcerer (*intermediate cause*), who cast a spell (*immediate cause*), which led to the resulting illness. The multilayered causal understanding opens the way for many possible avenues of treatment (see Figure 7.3).

The multiple understandings of etiology in Bahia contrast with the more narrowly scientific understandings of causality in Western biomedicine. The most striking difference is the tendency for biomedical etiologies to exclude as causal the many kinds of problems related to structural issues and social inequality. In contrast to the more narrow biomedical approach to causality, medical anthropologists use the term **structural suffering,** or social suffering, which refers to health problems that powerful forces such as poverty, war, famine, and forced migration cause (review the definition of the closely related concept, structurism, in Chapter 1). Structural

WHAT IS an example of a culture-specific syndrome in your microculture?

OUTSIDE THE BOX

THINKING

---

ethno-etiologies: culturally specific causal explanations for health problems and suffering.

structural suffering: human health problems caused by such economic and political situations as war, famine, terrorism, forced migration, and poverty. Also called structural affliction.

FIGURE 7.3 Three Levels of Causation for Morbidity and Mortality

Ultimate	Poverty
Intermediate	Lack of food, malnutrition
Immediate	Dehydration, diarrhea

conditions affect health in many ways, with effects ranging from anxiety and depression to death. An example of a culture-specific syndrome that clearly implicates structural factors as causal is *sufriendo del agua,* or "suffering from water" (Ennis-McMillan 2001).

Research in a poor community in the Valley of Mexico, located in the central part of the country (see Map 5.4, p. 128), reveals that "suffering from water" is a common health problem, especially among women. The cause is the lack of water for drinking, cooking, and washing. Women, who are responsible for cooking and doing the washing, cannot count on water coming from their taps on a regular basis. This insecurity makes the women feel anxious and constantly in a state of nervous tension. The lack of access to water also means that the people are at higher risk of cholera, skin and eye infections, and other biophysical problems. The development of piped water systems in the Valley of Mexico bypassed low-income communities in favor of servicing wealthier urban neighborhoods and supplying water for irrigation projects and the industrial sector. In Mexico, as a whole, nearly one-third of the population has inadequate access to water, in terms of quantity or quality.

Prevention

Many practices, based in either religious or secular beliefs, exist cross-culturally for preventing misfortune, suffering, and illness. Among the Maya of Guatemala (see Map 7.2), *awas* is a common childhood illness (Wilson 1995). Children born with awas have lumps under the skin, marks on the skin, or albinism. People say that awas is caused by events that happen to the mother during her pregnancy: She may have been denied food she desired or have been pressured to eat food she did not want, or she may have encountered a rude, drunk, or angry person (usually a man). To prevent awas in babies, the Maya are extremely considerate of pregnant women. A pregnant woman, like land before planting, is sacred. People make sure to give her the food she wants, and they behave with respect in her presence. The ideal is that a pregnant woman should be content. Proper social behavior is necessary for the health of the mother and baby.

Examples of ritual health protection worldwide include charms, spells, and sacred strings tied around parts of the body. An anthropologist working in rural

MAP 7.2 Central America. The countries of Central America share a similar geography as part of a long isthmus with a mountainous spine, active volcanoes, and rich soil. A federation that linked much of the region into the United Provinces of Central America existed from 1824 to 1838. The population of the region, around 40 million people, includes indigenous peoples and people of mixed indigenous and European ancestry. European colonialism has left a strong mark on the region, which is now heavily influenced by the United States and its interests in hemispheric hegemony.

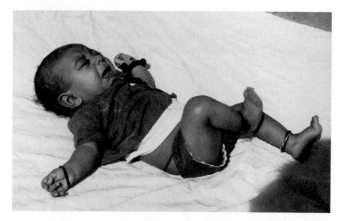

Throughout northern India, people believe that tying on strings provides protection from malevolent spirits and forces. This baby has five protective strings. ■ *What parallel forms of protection for infants would Western biomedicine require?* (Source: Barbara Miller)

One of the carved phalluses displayed in a northern Thai village to protect men from ghost attacks. ■ (Source: Mary Beth Mills)

northern Thailand (see Map 6.4, p. 163) learned about a health protection practice that involved the display of carved wooden phalluses throughout a village (Mills 1995). In 1990, fear of an attack by a widow spread throughout the area. It was based on several radio reports of unexplained deaths of Thai migrant men working in Singapore. People interpreted the sudden deaths of men as caused by widow ghosts. People believe that widow ghosts roam about, searching for men whom they take as their "husbands" and with whom they have sexual intercourse. Mary Beth Mills was conducting research in Baan Naa Sakae village at the time of the fear:

> I returned to Baan Naa Sakae village after a few days' absence to find the entire community of two hundred households festooned with wooden phalluses in all shapes and sizes. Ranging from the crudest wooden shafts to carefully carved images complete with coconut shell testicles and fishnet pubic hair, they adorned virtually every house and residential compound. The phalluses, I was told, were to protect residents, especially boys and men, from the "nightmare deaths" (*lai tai*) at the hands of malevolent "widow ghosts" (*phii mae maai*). (1995:249)

In the study area, spirits (*phii*) are a recognized source of illness, death, and other misfortunes. One variety of phii, a widow ghost is the sexually voracious spirit of a woman who has met an untimely and perhaps violent death. When a seemingly healthy man dies in his sleep, a widow ghost is blamed. The wooden phalluses hung on the houses were protection against a possible attack:

> Informants described these giant penises as decoys that would attract the interest of any phii mae maai which might come looking for a husband. The greedy ghosts would take their pleasure with the wooden penises and be satisfied, leaving the men of that household asleep, safe in their beds. (1995:251)

As the radio reports ceased, villagers' concerns about the widow ghosts died down, and the phalluses were removed.

Healing Ways

This section considers two approaches to healing, one in southern Africa and the other in Malaysia, Southeast Asia. It also discusses healers and healing substances.

Community Healing Systems

A general distinction can be drawn between private healing and **community healing**. The former addresses bodily ailments in social isolation, whereas the latter encompasses the social context as crucial to healing. Compared to Western biomedicine, many non-Western systems use community healing. An example of community healing comes from the Ju/'hoansi foragers of the Kalahari desert in southern Africa (review Culturama, Chapter 1, p. 22). Ju/'hoansi healing emphasizes the mobilization of community "energy" as a key element in the cure:

> The central event in this tradition is the all-night healing dance. Four times a month on the average, night signals

---

community healing: healing that emphasizes the social context as a key component and is likely to be carried out within the public domain.

humoral healing system: healing that emphasizes balance among natural elements within the body.

---

the start of a healing dance. The women sit around the fire, singing and rhythmically clapping. The men, sometimes joined by the women, dance around the singers. As the dance intensifies, *num* or spiritual energy is activated by the healers, both men and women, but mostly among the dancing men. As num is activated in them, they begin to *kia* or experience an enhancement of their consciousness. While experiencing kia, they heal all those at the dance. (Katz 1982:34)

The dance is a community event in which the entire camp participates. The people's belief in the healing power of num brings meaning and efficacy to the dance. Does community healing "work"? In both ethnic and Western terms, the answer is yes. It "works" on several levels. People's solidarity and group sessions may support mental and physical health, acting as a health protection system. When people fall ill, the drama and energy of the all-night dances may act to strengthen the afflicted in ways that Western science would have difficulty measuring. Clearly, in a small group of people, when one

A Ju/'hoansi healer in a trance, in the Kalahari desert, southern Africa. Most Ju/'hoansi healers are men, but some are women. ■ *In your microculture, what are the patterns of gender, ethnicity, and class among various kinds of healers?* (Source: © Irven DeVore/AnthroPhoto)

member falls ill and dies, the dances serve to support those who are grieving.

An important aspect of the Ju/'hoansi healing system is its openness. Everyone has access to it. The role of healer is also open. There is no special class of healers with special privileges. More than half of all adult men and about 10 percent of adult women are healers.

Humoral Healing Systems

Humoral healing systems are approaches to healing based on a philosophy of balance among certain elements within the body and within the person's environment (McElroy and Townsend 1996). In this system, food and drugs have different effects on the body and are classified as either "heating" or "cooling" (the quotation marks indicate that these properties are not the same as thermal measurements). Diseases are the result of bodily imbalances—too much heat or coolness—which must be counteracted through dietary changes or medicines that will restore balance.

Humoral healing systems have been practiced for thousands of years in the Middle East, the Mediterranean, and much of Asia. In the New World, indigenous humoral systems exist and sometime blend with those that Spanish colonialists brought with them. Humoralism has shown substantial resilience in the face of Western biomedicine, often incorporating into it the Western framework—for example, in the classification of biomedical treatments as either heating or cooling.

In Malaysia (see Map 1.3, p. 15), several different humoral traditions coexist, reflecting the region's history of contact with outside cultures. Malaysia has been influenced by trade and contact between its indigenous culture and that of India, China, and the Arab-Islamic world for around 2,000 years. Indian, Chinese, and Arabic health systems all define health as the balance of opposing elements within the body, although each has its own variations (Laderman 1988:272). Indigenous belief systems may have been compatible with these imported models because they also were based on concepts of heat and coolness.

Insights about these indigenous systems before outsiders arrived comes from accounts about the Orang Asli, indigenous peoples of the interior who are relatively less affected by contact. A conceptual system of hot–cold opposition dominates Orang Asli cosmological, medical, and social theories. The properties and meanings of heat and coolness differ from those of Islamic, Indian, or Chinese humoralism in several ways. In the Islamic, Indian, and Chinese systems, for example, death is the result of too much coolness. Among the Orang Asli, excessive heat is the primary cause of mortality. In their view, heat emanates from the sun and is associated with excrement, blood, misfortune, disease, and death. Humanity's hot blood makes people mortal, and their consumption of

Umbanda is a popular religion in Brazil and increasingly worldwide. Its ceremonies are often devoted to healing through spiritual means. In this session, tourists at the back of the room watch as Umbanda followers perform a dance related to a particular deity. ■ *What is your opinion on the role of spirituality in health and healing, and on what do you base this view?* (Source: © Ricardo Azoury/ CORBIS)

meat speeds the process. Heat causes menstruation, violent emotions, aggression, and drunkenness.

Coolness, in contrast, is vital for health. Health is protected by staying in the forest to avoid the harmful effects of the sun. This belief justifies the rejection of agriculture by some groups because it exposes people to the sun. Treatment of illness is designed to reduce or remove heat. If someone were to fall ill in a clearing, the entire group would relocate to the coolness of the forest. The forest is also a source of cooling leaves and herbs. Healers are cool and retain their coolness by bathing in cold water and sleeping far from the fire.

Extreme cold, however, can be harmful. Dangerous levels of coolness are associated with the time right after birth, because the mother is believed to have lost substantial heat. The new mother should not drink cold water or bathe in cold water. She increases her body heat by tying around her waist sashes that contain warmed leaves or ashes, and she lies near a fire.

Healers

In an informal sense, everyone is a "healer" because self-treatment is always the first consideration in dealing with a perceived health problem. Yet, in all cultures, some people become recognized as having special abilities to diagnose and treat health problems. Cross-cultural evidence indicates some common criteria of healers (see Figure 7.4).

Notable specialists include midwife, bonesetter (someone who resets broken bones), **shaman** (a healer who mediates between humans and the spirit world), herbalist, general practitioner, psychiatrist, nurse, acupuncturist, chiropractor, dentist, and hospice care provider. Some healing roles may have higher status, more power, and receive higher pay than others.

Several nonbiomedical healing specializations have declined due to pressures from and competition with Western biomedicine. Midwifery is an important example of a healing role that is endangered in many parts of the world as birth has become increasingly medicalized and brought into the institutional world of the hospital rather than the home. In Costa Rica (see Map 7.2), a recent government campaign to promote hospital births with a biomedical doctor in attendance has achieved a rate of 98 percent of all births taking place in hospitals (Jenkins 2003). This achievement means that midwives, especially in rural areas, can no longer support themselves, and they are abandoning their profession. The promotion of hospital births has destroyed the positive elements of community-based midwifery and its provision of social support and techniques such as massage for the mother-to-be.

Healing Substances

Around the world, thousands of different natural or manufactured substances are used as medicines for preventing or curing health problems. Anthropologists have spent more time studying the use of medicines in non-

---

shaman/shamanka: male or female part-time religious specialist who gains his or her status through direct relationship with the supernaturals, often by being "called."

phytotherapy: healing through the use of plants.

FIGURE 7.4 Criteria for Becoming a Healer

- *Selection:* Certain individuals may show more ability for entry into healing roles. In Western medical schools, selection for entry rests on apparently objective standards, such as pre-entry exams and college grades. Among the indigenous Ainu of northern Japan, healers were men who had a special ability to go into a sort of seizure called *imu* (Ohnuki-Tierney 1980).

- *Training:* The period of training may involve years of observation and practice and may be arduous and even dangerous. In some non-Western traditions, a shaman must make dangerous journeys, through trance or use of drugs, to the spirit world. In Western biomedicine, medical school involves immense amounts of memorization, separation from family and normal social life, and sleep deprivation.

- *Certification:* Healers earn some form of ritual or legal certification, such as a shaman going through a formal initiation ritual that attests to his or her competence.

- *Professional image:* The healer role is demarcated from that of ordinary people through behavior, dress, and other markers, such as the white coat in the West and the Siberian shaman's tambourine for calling the spirits.

- *Expectation of payment:* Compensation in some form, whether in kind or in cash, is expected for formal healers. Payment level may vary, depending on the status of the healer and other factors. In northern India, strong preference for sons is reflected in payments to the midwife that are twice as high for the birth of a son as for a daughter. In the United States, medical professionals in different specializations receive markedly different salaries.

Western cultures than that in the West, although a more fully cross-cultural approach is emerging that examines the use of Western pharmaceuticals (van der Geest, Whyte, and Hardon 1996).

Phytotherapy is healing through the use of plants. Cross-culturally, people know about and use many different plants for a wide range of health problems, including gastrointestinal disorders, skin problems, wounds and sores, pain relief, infertility, fatigue, altitude sickness, and more. Increasing awareness of the range of potentially useful plants worldwide provides a strong incentive for protecting the world's cultural diversity, because it is people who know about botanical resources (Posey 1990).

Leaves of the coca plant, for example, have for centuries been a key part of the health system of the Andean

These boys are selling hyssop, a medicinal herb, in Syria. In Unani (Islamic) traditional medicine, hyssop is used to alleviate problems such as asthma. ■ *Do research to learn more about hyssop and its medicinal uses.* (Source: © Ed Kashi/CORBIS)

Ingredients for traditional medicines available in a shop in Singapore include deer and antelope horns, monkey gall bladders, amber, freshwater pearls, and ginseng. ■ *Have you ever gone to a pharmacy in a non–Euro-American context? If so, what did you notice in terms of similarities and differences?* (Source: © William & Deni McIntyre/Photo Researchers, Inc.)

as arthritis and rheumatism. Thousands of people every year go to the Dead Sea, which lies beneath sea level between Israel and Jordan, for treating skin diseases (Lew 1994). The mud from the shore and the nearby sulfur springs relieves skin ailments such as psoriasis. German studies conclude that it is more cost-effective to pay for a trip to the Dead Sea than to hospitalize a psoriasis patient. In Japan, bathing in mineral waters is popular as a health-promotion practice.

Thousands of people in the United States and Canada visit "radon spas" every year, seeking the therapeutic effects of low doses of radon gas to alleviate the symptoms of chronic afflictions such as arthritis (Erickson 1999). In the United States, many radon spas are located in mines in the mountains of Montana. At one such spa, the Free Enterprise Mine, the recommended treatment is to go into the mine for one-hour sessions, two or three times daily, for up to a total of about thirty sessions. The mine contains benches and chairs, and clients read, play cards, chat, or take a nap. Some "regulars" come back every year and plan to meet up with friends from previous visits. Perhaps even less intuitively apparent in terms of potential therapeutic value is the practice of eating dirt (see Critical Thinking box).

Western patent medicines are increasingly popular worldwide. Although these medicines have many benefits, some negative effects include frequent use without prescription and overprescription. Sale of patent medicines is often unregulated, and self-treating individuals can buy them in a local pharmacy. The popularity and overuse of capsules and injections has led to a growing health crisis related to the emergence of drug-resistant disease strains.

region of South America (Allen 2002). Coca is important in rituals, in masking hunger pains, and in combatting the cold (Carter, Morales, and Mamani 1981). In terms of health, Andean people use coca to treat gastrointestinal problems, sprains, swellings, and colds. A survey of coca use in Bolivia showed a high prevalence rate. About 85 percent of 3,500 people reported that they use coca medicinally. The leaf may be chewed or combined with herbs or roots and water to make a *maté*, a medicinal beverage. Trained herbalists have specialized knowledge about preparing some matés. One maté, for example, is for treating asthma. Made of a certain root and coca leaves, it is taken three to four times a day until the patient is cured.

Minerals are also widely used for prevention and healing. For example, many people worldwide believe that bathing in water that contains high levels of sulphur or other minerals promotes health and cures ailments such

Three Theoretical Approaches in Medical Anthropology

The first major theoretical approach to understanding health systems emphasizes the importance of the environment in shaping health problems and how they spread. The second highlights symbols and meaning in people's expression of suffering and healing practices. The third points to the need to look at structural factors (political, economic, media) as the underlying causes of health problems.

The Ecological/Epidemiological Approach

The **ecological/epidemiological approach** examines how aspects of the natural environment interact with culture

ecological/epidemiological approach: an approach within medical anthropology that considers how aspects of the natural environment and social environment interact to cause illness.

WHY DO PEOPLE EAT DIRT?

Geophagia, the eating of earth, is a special form of *pica*, or habitual consumption of items that are not normally considered to be food (Reid 1992). It presents a fascinating puzzle that has been studied by medical anthropologists, cultural geographers, historians, and medical experts. Geophagia has been documented in the United States among some Native American groups and in the South among pregnant Euro-Americans and African Americans, among some indigenous peoples of South America, in the Mediterranean region, in rural India among women and children, and in some African cultures. It typically involves a preference for certain kinds of earth or clay, which is often baked before consumption, or formed into tablets, or mixed with other substances such as honey.

Some medical experts offer explanations for geophagia based on pathology—that is, people have something wrong with them which leads them to be geophagic in response. These conditions include anemia, colon perforation, fecal impaction, and severe tooth abrasion. In this view, anemic persons, for example, consume earth as an unconscious way of increasing iron levels. Therefore, increasing the level of iron in a person's diet would reduce the practice of geophagia. Other medical experts argue that the arrow of causation points in the opposite direction: Clay consumption reduces the body's ability to absorb iron, so it causes anemia. The anemia arguments are complex, and the data are often inconclusive

because of small samples or lack of good control groups. Thus, although an association between geophagia and anemia seems often (but not always) to exist, the direction of causation is undetermined.

Some medical anthropologists propose that geophagia may have a positive adaptive value on health. In this view, eating clay functions as a supplement to dietary minerals. Clay from markets in Ghana, for example, contains phosphorus, potassium, calcium, magnesium, copper, zinc, manganese, and iron. Another adaptive example is to prevent diarrhea. Many clays of Africa have compositions similar to that of Kaopectate, a Western commercial anti-diarrheal medicine. A third example of the possible adaptive effects of geophagia says that consuming clay may act as a detoxicant when people eat certain plant materials that may contain toxins. The clay prevents nausea or indigestion that would otherwise result. During famines, geophagia increases and may help people digest leaves, bark, and other unaccustomed and hard-to-digest foods. Laboratory rats react to exposure to chemical toxins or new foods by eating clay.

CRITICAL THINKING QUESTIONS

- Is it likely that only one of the above explanations for geophagia is correct in all cases? Why or why not?
- Could all of the above explanations be correct?
- Could none be correct? Why?

---

to cause health problems and to influence their spread throughout the population. According to this approach, research should focus on gathering information about the environmental context and social patterns that affect health, such as food distribution within the family, sexual practices, hygiene, and population contact. Research methods and data tend to be quantitative and etic, although a growing tendency is to include qualitative and emic data in order to provide context for understanding the quantitative data (review Chapter 2).

The ecological/epidemiological approach seeks to yield findings relevant to public health programs. It can provide information about groups that are at risk of specific problems. For example, although hookworm is common throughout rural China, epidemiological researchers learned that rice cultivators have the highest rates. The reason is that hookworm can spread through the night

soil (human excrement used as fertilizer) applied to the fields in which the cultivators work.

Another significant environmental factor that has important effects on health is urbanization. As archaeologists have documented about the past, settled populations living in dense clusters are more likely than mobile populations to experience a range of health problems, including infectious diseases and malnutrition (Cohen 1989). Such problems are apparent among many recently settled pastoralist groups in East and West Africa. One study compared the health status of two groups of Turkana men in northwest Kenya (see Map 6.2, p. 158): those who were still mobile pastoralists and those who lived in a town (Barkey, Campbell, and Leslie 2001). The two groups differ strikingly in diet, physical activities, and health. Pastoralist Turkana eat mainly animal foods (milk, meat, and blood), spend much time in rigorous

Guests are undergoing radon treatment at the Kyongsong Sand Spa in Haonpho-ri, North Korea. The spa, and its hot spring, has a 500-year history as a healing center. The treatment shown here is a "sand bath" used for chronic diseases such as arthritis, postoperative problems, and some female problems. ■ (Source: CORBIS)

physical activity, and live in large family groups. Settled Turkana men eat mainly maize and beans. Their sedentary (settled) life means less physical activity and exercise. In terms of health, the settled men had more eye infections, chest infections, backache, and cough/colds. Pastoralist Turkana men were not, however, free of health problems. One-fourth of the pastoralist men had eye infections, but among the settled men, one-half had eye infections. In terms of nutrition, the settled Turkana were shorter and had greater body mass than the taller and slimmer pastoralists.

Cities present many stressors to human health as well as opportunities for improved health through greater access to health care. Often, cities are comprised of diverse social categories, varying by class and ethnicity. These groups have different experiences of health stressors and opportunities. In the United States, the incidence of tuberculosis (TB) has increased in recent years, and this increase has occurred mainly in urban areas (DeFirdinando 1999). Tuberculosis is spread by infected humans, and its rate of spread is increased by crowding, poverty, poor housing, and lack of access to health care. In the United States, rates of tuberculosis are generally higher in southern than in northern states, with the exceptions of New York and Illinois, given their large urban populations. Beginning in the 1990s, outbreaks of multidrug-resistant mycobacterium tuberculosis

(MDRTB), a new strain of TB that is resistant to conventional drugs, led to its being recognized by public health authorities as a major "new" infectious disease.

Tuberculosis, and its several new strains, is also a frequent complication of HIV/AIDS. In New York City, far more people have TB and HIV/AIDS than can be accommodated in public hospitals. Homeless shelters are inadequate to care for the number of applicants who are not only homeless but also seriously ill with infectious diseases such as HIV/AIDS.

Colonialism and Disease

Anthropologists have applied the ecological/epidemiological approach to the study of the impaired health and survival of indigenous peoples resulting from colonial contact. Findings about the effects of colonial contact are negative, ranging from the quick and outright extermination of indigenous peoples to resilient adjustment, among other groups, to drastically changed conditions.

In the Western hemisphere, European colonialism brought a dramatic decline in the indigenous populations, although disagreement exists about the numbers involved (Joralemon 1982). Research indicates that the precontact New World was largely free of the major European infectious diseases such as smallpox, measles, and typhus, and perhaps also of syphilis, leprosy, and

historical trauma: the intergenerational transfer of the negative effects of colonialism from parents to children.

placebo effect or **meaning effect:** in Western science, a positive result from a healing method due to a symbolic or otherwise nonmaterial factor.

Women working in padi fields near Jinghong, southern China. Agricultural work done in standing water increases the risk of hookworm infection. ■ *Is hookworm a threat where you live? What is the major infectious disease in your home region?* (Source: © Peter Menzel/Stock Boston, LLC)

malaria. Therefore, the exposure of indigenous peoples to these infectious diseases likely had a massive impact, given the indigenous people's complete lack of resistance. One analyst compared colonial contact to a "biological war":

> Smallpox was the captain of the men of death in that war, typhus fever the first lieutenant, and measles the second lieutenant. More terrible than the conquistadores on horseback, more deadly than sword and gunpowder, they made the conquest by the whites a walkover as compared to what it would have been without their aid. They were the forerunners of civilization, the companions of Christianity, the friends of the invader. (Ashburn 1947:98, quoted in Joralemon 1982:112)

This quotation emphasizes the importance of the three major diseases in New World colonial history: smallpox, measles, and malaria. A later arrival, cholera, also had severe effects because its transmission through contaminated water and food thrives in areas of poor sanitation. Besides infectious diseases, indigenous populations were decimated by outright killing, enslavement and harsh labor practices, and the psychological ravages of losing one's livelihood, social ties and support, and access to ancestral burial grounds (see Maps 7.3 and 7.4).

Enduring effects of European colonialism among indigenous peoples worldwide include high rates of depression and suicide, low self-esteem, high rates of child and adolescent drug use, and high rates of alcoholism, obesity, and hypertension. **Historical trauma** refers to the intergenerational transfer of the emotional and psychological effects of colonialism from parents to children (Brave Heart 2004). It is closely associated with

substance abuse as a vehicle for attempting to cover the continued pain of historical trauma. Troubled parents create a difficult family situation for children who tend to replicate their parents' negative coping mechanisms. The concept of historical trauma helps to expand the scope of traditional epidemiological studies by drawing on factors from the past to explain the social and spatial distribution of contemporary health problems. Such an approach may prove more effective in devising culturally appropriate ways to alleviate health problems.

The Interpretivist Approach

Some medical anthropologists examine health systems as systems of meaning. They study how people in different cultures label, describe, and experience illness and how healing systems offer meaningful responses to individual and communal distress. These interpretivist anthropologists have examined aspects of healing, such as ritual trance, as symbolic performances. Claude Lévi-Strauss established this approach in a classic essay called "The Effectiveness of Symbols" (1967). He examined how a song sung during childbirth among the Kuna Indians of Panama (see Map 9.4, p. 243) helps women through a difficult delivery. The main point is that healing systems provide meaning to people who are experiencing seemingly meaningless forms of suffering. The provision of meaning offers psychological support to the afflicted and may enhance healing through what Western science calls the **placebo effect,** or **meaning effect,** a positive result from a healing method due to a symbolic or otherwise nonmaterial factor (Moerman 2002). In the United States,

MAP 7.3 Precolonial Distribution of Indian Tribes in the United States. Before the arrival of European colonialists, Indians were the sole occupants of the area. The first English settlers were impressed by the Indians' tallness and robust physical health.

depending on the health problem, between 10 and 90 percent of the efficacy of medical prescriptions lies in the placebo effect. Several explanatory factors may be involved in the meaning effect: the confidence and power of the person prescribing a treatment, the act of prescription itself, and concrete details about the medicine, such as its color, name, and place of origin (van der Geest, Whyte, and Hardon 1996). (See Everyday Anthropology box.)

Critical Medical Anthropology

Critical medical anthropology focuses on the analysis of how structural causes—such as the political economy, media, and inequality—affect the prevailing health sys-

tem, including types of afflictions, people's health status, and their access to health care. Critical medical anthropologists highlight how structural power, linked with the health system, perpetuate social inequality. Critical medical anthropologists have exposed the power of **medicalization,** or labeling a particular issue or problem as medical and requiring medical treatment when, in fact, its cause is structural.

Social Inequality and Poverty

Broad distinctions exist between the most common health problems of rich, industrial countries and those of poor, less industrial countries (United Nations Development Programme 1995). In the former, major causes of

critical medical anthropology: an approach within the cross-cultural study of health and illness involving the analysis of how economic and political struc-

tures shape people's health status, their access to health care, and the prevailing medical systems that exist in relation to them.

medicalization: labeling a particular issue or problem as medical and requiring medical treatment when, in fact, that issue or problem is economic or political.

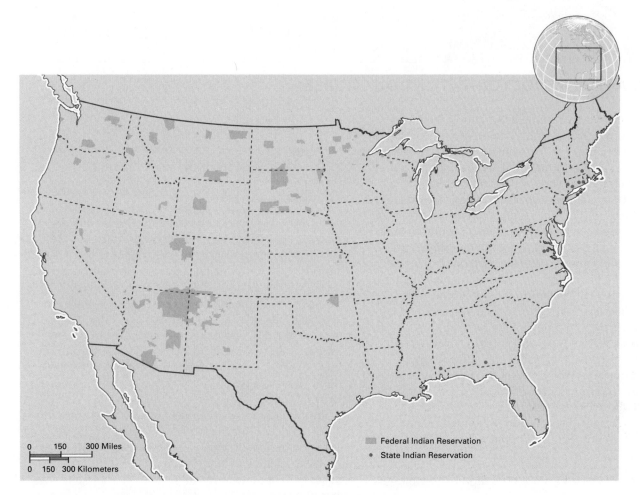

MAP 7.4   Designated Indian Reservations of the United States. Indian reservations today comprise a small percentage of the U.S. land mass. Reservations are allocated to "recognized tribes." Several states recognize no tribes. Many members of recognized tribes live off the reservations, often as poorly employed or unemployed urban residents. As discussed in Chapter 4, gaming revenues are helping to improve the income and living standards of some Indian tribes.

death are circulatory diseases, malignant cancers, HIV/AIDS, alcohol consumption, and tobacco consumption. In poor countries, tuberculosis, malaria, and HIV/AIDS are the three leading causes of death. Substantial evidence indicates that poverty is the primary cause of morbidity (sickness) and mortality (death) in both industrialized and developing countries (Farmer 2005). It may be manifested in different ways—for example, though child malnutrition in Chad or Nepal and through street violence among the urban poor of wealthy countries.

Throughout the developing world, rates of childhood malnutrition are inversely related to income. In other words, as income increases so does calorie intake as a percent of recommended daily allowances (Zaidi 1988:122). Thus, increasing the income levels of the poor is the most direct way to improve child nutrition and health. Yet, in contrast to this seemingly logical ap-

proach, many health and nutrition programs around the world focus on treating the outcomes of poverty rather than its causes.

Critical medical anthropologists describe the widespread practice of treating health problems caused by poverty with pills or other medical options. An example is Nancy Scheper-Hughes's research in Bom Jesus, northeastern Brazil, mentioned in Chapters 5 and 6 (1992) (see Map 3.4, p. 73). The people of Bom Jesus who experienced symptoms of weakness, insomnia, and anxiety received pills from the local doctor. But the people were, in fact, hungry and needed food. This medicalization of poverty serves the interests of pharmaceutical companies and helps to keep inequitable social systems in place.

Similar critical analyses show how Western psychiatry often treats symptoms and serves to keep people in their places rather than addressing root causes such as powerlessness, unemployment, and thwarted social aspira-

THE MEANING IN DOCTOR–PATIENT DISCOURSE

Probably most people at some point during their lives have had a conversation with a healer. Western biomedicine emphasizes the practical elements of such conversations: They transfer information from the patient to the doctor that leads to a diagnosis and treatment. Margaret Trawick, an interpretive anthropologist, emphasizes the "healing is in the meaning" approach in her study of Ayurvedic healers in Tamil Nadu, southern India (1988) (see Map 8.5, p. 215). Ayurvedic medicine is a widely used Indian health system based on texts composed from the beginning of the Common (or Christian) Era to about 1000 CE. Following humoral principles, Ayurvedic diagnosis takes into account whether bodily channels controlling the flow of life (vital air) are blocked or open.

A counseling session between an Ayurvedic physician and an elderly, poor woman in southern India reveals the themes of channels, processes of flow, points of connection (the heart is believed to be the center of all channels), and everyday activities that regulate the flow of life. Here are some clips from the doctor–patient conversation:

> D: Let's see your eyes. Let's see your pulse. Is your age over sixty?
> P: Probably.
> D: . . . Is there chest pain?
> P: A little.
> D: Does your heart flutter?

> P: It flutters . . .
> D: Is there pain in the joints?
> P: Yes. . . .
> D: Have you taken any treatment for this?
> P: I have taken no treatment at all. . . .
> (1988:138–139)

After the interview, the doctor offers dietary prescriptions to "quicken" the patient's body—such as avoidance of tamarind, because that causes "dullness," and eating light food so that it will not get crowded inside her. He also gives her a detailed daily regimen to follow: "Drink two coffees, in the morning a coffee and in the evening a coffee. Add palm sugar to the coffee, filter it and remove the dirt, add cow's milk and drink it. . . . Eat wheat grain made soft. At three o'clock drink only one cup of coffee. Eat more food than coffee" (1988:138–139). Finally, he gently tells her that, basically, she is growing old.

In this interaction, the meanings conveyed through the interview offer the woman a sense that the physician is taking her health complaints seriously. The detailed daily regimen gives her a feeling of self-efficacy. She takes with her a plan for things she can do to alleviate her distress.

FOOD FOR THOUGHT

- Provide an interpretivist view of an interaction that you have had with a doctor/healer.

---

tions. One example of psychiatric medicalization is the high rates of depression among women in North America and their treatment with psychotropic drugs.

Cultural Critique of Western Biomedical Training

Since the 1980s, critical medical anthropologists have studied Western biomedicine as a cultural system. They advocate for greater recognition of social factors in diagnosis and treatment, reduction of the spread of biomedical technology, and diversification of medical specialists to include alternative healing, such as massage, acupuncture, and chiropracty (Scheper-Hughes 1992).

Some of their work critiques Western medical school training and its emphasis on technology. Robbie Davis-Floyd examined the culture of obstetric training in the United States (1987). She interviewed twelve obstetri-

cians, ten male and two female. As students, they absorbed the technological model of birth as a core value of Western obstetrics. This model treats the body as a machine (recall the discussion of the technological model of birth in Chapter 5). The physician uses the assembly-line approach to birth in order to promote efficient production and quality control. One of the residents in the study explained, "We shave 'em, we prep 'em, we hook 'em up to the IV and administer sedation. We deliver the baby, it goes to the nursery and the mother goes to her room. There's no room for niceties around here. We just move 'em right on through. It's not hard to see it like an assembly line" (1987:292). The goal is the "production" of a healthy baby. The doctor is a technical expert in charge of achieving this goal, and the mother takes second place. One obstetrician said, "It is what we all were trained to always go after—the perfect baby. That's what we were trained to produce. The quality of the mother's

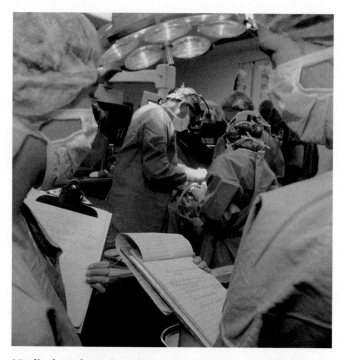

Medical students in training in a Western biomedical setting. These students are observing brain surgery. ■ *What does this scene convey about values and beliefs of Western medicine?* (Source: © Lara Jo Regan/Getty Images)

edge of medicine assumes supreme importance. As one informant put it,

> Medical school is not difficult in terms of what you have to learn—there's just so much of it. You go through, in a six-week course, a thousand-page book. The sheer bulk of information is phenomenal. You have pop quizzes in two or three courses every day the first year. We'd get up around 6, attend classes till 5, go home and eat, then head back to school and be in anatomy lab working with a cadaver, or something, until 1 or 2 in the morning, and then go home and get a couple of hours of sleep and then go out again. And you did that virtually day in and day out for four years, except for vacations. (1987:298–299)

Third, in a process termed *dehumanization*, medical school training works to erase humanitarian ideals through an emphasis on technology and objectification of the patient. One obstetrical student explained, "Most of us went into medical school with pretty humanitarian ideals. I know I did. But the whole process of medical education makes you inhuman . . . by the time you get to residency, you end up not caring about anything beyond the latest techniques you can master and how sophisticated the tests are that you can perform" (1987:299). The last two years of medical school and the four years of residency are devoted primarily to hands-on experience. The obstetrical specialization involves intensive repetition and learning of technical skills, including surgery. One obstetrician summed up the entire process of transformation: "It doesn't seem to matter—male or female, young or old, wealthy or poor—it is only the most unusual individual who comes through a residency program as anything less than a technological clone" (1987:307).

Davis-Floyd's study emphasizes how obstetricians learn to become dependent on technology as the basis of their expertise. Studies of other biomedical specializations, such as surgery, make the same point (Cassell 1991). The power and status of physicians are correlated with the complexity of the technology they use. Other studies reveal the human costs of the heavy reliance on technology rather than cultural understanding and interaction (Fadiman 1997).

experience—we rarely thought about that. Everything we did was to get that perfect baby" (1987:292).

This goal involves the use of sophisticated monitoring machines. One obstetrician said, "I'm totally dependent on fetal monitors, 'cause they're great! They free you to do a lot of other things. . . . I couldn't sit over there with a woman in labor with my hand on her belly, and be in here seeing 20 to 30 patients a day" (1987:291). Use of technology also conveys status to the physician: "Anybody in obstetrics who shows a human interest in patients is not respected. What is respected is interest in machines" (1987:291).

How do medical students learn to accept the technological model? Davis-Floyd's research points to three key processes. One way is through physical *hazing*, a harsh rite of passage involving, in this case, stress caused by sleep deprivation. The hazing extends throughout medical school and the residency period.

Second, medical school training in the United States involves a process of *cognitive retrogression* in which students relinquish critical thinking and thoughtful ways of learning. During the first two years of medical school, most courses are basic sciences, and students must memorize vast quantities of material. The sheer bulk of memorization forces students to adopt an uncritical approach. This mental overload socializes students into a uniform pattern, giving them tunnel vision in which the knowl-

Globalization and Change

With globalization, health problems move around the world and into remote locations and cultures more rapidly than ever before. The HIV/AIDS epidemic is one tragic example. Other new epidemics include SARS and avian (bird) flu. At the same time, Western culture, including biomedicine, is on the move. Perhaps no other aspect of Western culture, except for the capitalist market system and the English language, has so permeated the rest of the world as Western biomedicine. But the

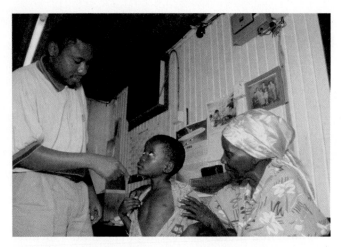

A woman takes her 8-year-old grandson, who has HIV/AIDS, to a clinic in Dar es Salaam, Tanzania. Throughout the world, increasing numbers of children are infected and, at the same time, are orphans because their parents have died of the disease. ■ *In your culture, what is the prevalence of HIV/AIDS among children?* (Source: © Sean Sprague/Stock Boston, LLC)

Social stigma often adds to the suffering of HIV/AIDS victims. The billboards, near Soweto in South Africa, promote condom use and seek to reduce social rejection and stigma. ■ (Source: Barbara Miller and Bernard Wood)

cultural flow is not one-way. Many people in North America and Europe are turning to forms of non-Western and nonbiomedical healing, such as acupuncture and massage therapy. This section considers new and emerging health challenges, changes in healing, and examples of how applied medical anthropology has increasing relevance.

New Infectious Diseases

The 1950s brought hope that infectious diseases were being controlled through Western scientific advances such as antibiotic drugs, vaccines against childhood diseases, and improved technology for sanitation. In North America, death from infections common in the late nineteenth and early twentieth centuries was no longer a major threat in the 1970s. In tropical countries, pesticides lowered rates of malaria by controlling the mosquito populations. The 1980s, however, were the beginning of an era of shaken confidence with the onset and rapid spread of the HIV/AIDS epidemic. New contexts for exposure and contagion are being created through increased international travel and migration, expansion of populations into previously uninhabited forest areas, changing sexual behavior, and overcrowding in cities. Several new and re-emerging diseases are related to unsafe technological developments. For example, soft

contact lenses can cause eye infections from a virus. Development projects such as dam construction and clearing forests often have negative health effects.

Diseases of Development

Diseases of development are health problems (both diseases and illnesses) caused or increased by economic development activities (Hughes and Hunter 1970). Examples of diseases in this category are schistosomiasis, river blindness, malaria, and tuberculosis. The construction of dams and irrigation systems throughout the tropical world has brought dramatically increased rates of schistosomiasis (a disease caused by the presence of a parasitic worm in the blood system). Over 200 million people suffer from this debilitating disease, with prevalence rates the highest in sub-Saharan countries in Africa (Michaud, Gordon, and Reich 2004). The larvae hatch from eggs and mature in slow-moving water such as lakes and rivers (see Figure 7.5). When mature, they can penetrate human (or other animal) skin with which they come into contact. Once inside the human body, the adult schistosomes breed in the veins around the human bladder and bowel. They send fertilized eggs through urine and feces into the environment. These eggs then contaminate water in which they hatch into larvae.

Anthropologists' research has documented steep increases in the rates of schistosomiasis at high dam sites in developing countries (Scudder 1973). This increased

disease of development: a health problem caused or increased by economic development activities that affect the environment and people's relationship with it.

medical pluralism: the existence of more than one health system in a culture, or a government policy to promote the integration of local healing systems into biomedical practice.

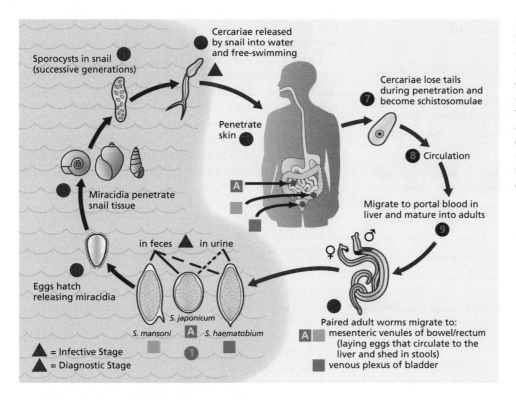

FIGURE 7.5 The Schistomomiasis Cycle. Cultural anthropologists are less interested in the technical details of the cycle of infection and re-infection as they are in the environmental, structural, and social context of the disease, and its social effects. (Source: Centers for Disease Control, www.dpd.cdc.gov/dpdx)

risk is caused by the dams slowing the rate of water flow. Stagnant water systems offer an ideal environment for development of the larvae. Opponents of the construction of large dams have used this information in support of their position.

New diseases of development continue to appear. One of these is Kyasanur forest disease, or KFD (Nichter 1992). This viral disease was first identified in 1957 in southern India:

> Resembling influenza, at onset KFD is marked by sudden chills, fever, frontal headaches, stiffness of the neck, and body pain. Diarrhea and vomiting often follow on the third day. High fever is continuous for five to fifteen days, during which time a variety of additional symptoms may manifest themselves, including gastrointestinal bleeding, persistent cough with blood-tinged sputum, and bleeding gums. In more serious cases, the infection progresses to bronchial pneumonia, meningitis, paralysis, encephalitis, and hemorrhage. (1992:224)

In the early 1980s, an epidemic of KFD swept through over thirty villages near the Kyasanur forest in Karnataka state, southern India (see Map 8.5, p. 215). Mortality rates in hospitals ranged between 12 and 18 percent of those admitted. Investigation revealed that KFD especially affected agricultural workers and cattle tenders who were most exposed to newly cleared areas near the forest. In the cleared areas, international companies established plantations and initiated cattle raising. Ticks were the vector transmitting the disease from the cattle to the people. Ticks had long existed in the local ecosystem, but thei,r numbers greatly increased in the cleared area, finding many inviting hosts in the cattle and in the workers. Thus, human modification of the ecosystem through deforestation and introduction of large-scale cattle raising caused the epidemic and shaped its social distribution.

Medical Pluralism

Contact between cultures may lead to a situation in which aspects of both cultures coexist: two (or more) different languages, religions, systems of law, or health systems, for example. The term **medical pluralism** refers to the presence of multiple health systems within a society. Medical pluralism provides both options and complications. First, something may be classified as a health problem in some cultures and not in others. For example, spirit possession is welcomed in some cultures but might be labeled schizophrenia by Western psychiatry. Second, the same issue may be classified as having a different cause (such as supernatural versus germ theories) and therefore require different treatments. Third, certain treatments may be rejected as violating cultural rules.

All of these issues affect how a particular culture will react to exogenous (outside) medical practices. In some cases, the coexistence of many forms of healing provides clients a range of choices and enhances the quality of health. In other cases, people are confronted by conflicting models of illness and healing, a situation that can result in misunderstandings between healers and clients and in unhappy outcomes.

Selective Pluralism: The Case of the Sherpa

The Sherpa of Nepal offer an unusual example of a capitalizing context in which preference for traditional healing systems remains strong along with the selective use of Western biomedicine (Adams 1988). Healing therapies available in the Upper Khumbu region in northeastern Nepal fit into three categories:

- Orthodox Buddhist practitioners, which include *lamas*, who Khumbu people consult for prevention and cure through their blessings, and *amchis*, who practice Tibetan medicine, a humoral healing system.
- Unorthodox religious or shamanic practitioners who perform divination ceremonies for diagnosis.
- Biomedical practitioners who work in a clinic that was first established to serve tourists. The clinic was established as a permanent medical facility in 1967 and many Sherpa selectively use it.

Thus, three varieties of health care now exist in the region, including Western biomedicine. Traditional healers are still thriving, unthreatened by changes brought by the tourist trade, the influx of new wealth, and notions of modernity. Sherpa choose among more options than before for treating their health problems.

The question of why Western biomedicine has not completely taken over other healing practices requires a complicated answer. One part of the answer is that high-mountain tourism does not deeply affect local production and social relations. Although it brings in new wealth, it does not require large-scale capital investment from outside as, for example, mega-hotel tourist developments have elsewhere. The Sherpa maintain control of their productive resources. Their family structures remain largely the same, and Sherpa kinship ties are important in the organization of tourist business.

Conflicting Explanatory Models

Compared to the positive aspects of the multiple health-care options in Upper Khumbu, in many other contexts, anthropologists have documented serious disjunctures between Western biomedicine and local health systems. Miscommunication often occurs between biomedical doctors and patients in matters as seemingly simple as a prescription that should be taken with every meal. The Western biomedically trained doctor assumes that this means three times a day. But some people do not eat three meals a day and thus they unwittingly fail to follow the doctor's instructions.

One anthropological study of a case in which death resulted from cross-cultural differences shows how complex the issue of communication across medical cultures is. The "F family" are immigrants from American Samoa (see Map 1.6, p. 26) living in Honolulu, Hawai'i (Krant-zler 1987). Neither parent speaks English. Their children are "moderately literate" in English but speak a mixture of English and Samoan at home. Mr. F was trained as a traditional Samoan healer. Mary, a daughter, was first stricken with diabetes at age 16. She was taken to the hospital by ambulance after collapsing, half-conscious, on the sidewalk near her home in a Honolulu housing project. After several months of irregular contact with medical staff, she was again brought to the hospital in an ambulance, unconscious, and she died there. Her father was charged with causing Mary's death through medical neglect.

Nora Krantzler analyzes this case from the perspectives of the Western medical providers and Samoan culture. Here is the biomedical view, beginning with Mary's first admission to the hospital:

> At that point, her illness was "discovered" and diagnosed as juvenile onset diabetes mellitus. She was initially placed in the Pediatric Intensive Care Unit for 24 hours, then transferred to a pediatric ward for about a week until her diabetes was "under good control." She, her parents, and her older sister were taught how to give insulin injections, and Mary was shown how to test her urine for glucose and acetone. She was given a 1-month supply of insulin. . . . She was further "counseled" about her diet. . . . She was then to be followed up with visits to the outpatient clinic. Following the clinic's (unofficial) policy of linking patients with physicians from their own ethnic group, she was assigned to see the sole Samoan pediatric resident. (1987:326–327)

Over the next few months, Mary was seen once in the clinic by a different resident (a physician at the stage of training following internship). She missed her next three appointments, came in once without an appointment, and was readmitted to the hospital on the basis of test results from that visit. At that time, she, her parents, and her older sister were once again advised about the importance of compliance with the medical advice they were receiving. Four months later, she returned to the clinic with blindness in one eye and diminished vision in the other. She was diagnosed with cataracts, and Dr. A, the Samoan physician, again advised Mary about the seriousness of her illness and the need for compliance. He wanted her to be admitted to the hospital to have the cataracts removed. Her father initially refused but then was persuaded. Dr. A wrote in Mary's chart:

> Her diabetes seemed to be very much out of control at the time but I was having a very difficult time with the patient and her father. . . . I consented to the father's wishes to have him supplement the insulin with some potion of his that he had prepared especially to control her sugar. . . . He did not believe that there was such an illness which would require daily injection for the rest of one's life and thanked me for my efforts but claimed that he would like to have total control of his daughter's illness at this time. (1987:328–329)

Culturama

The Sherpa of Nepal

The name Sherpa means "person." About 35,000 Sherpa live in Nepal, mainly in the northeastern region. Another 10,000 reside in Bhutan and Sikkim (Fisher 1990), and another 5,000 live in cities of Europe and North America.

In Nepal, the Sherpa are most closely associated with the Khumbu region. Khumbu is a valley set high in the Himalayas, completely encircled by mountains and with a clear view of Mount Everest (Karan and Mather 1985). The Sherpa have a mixed economy involving animal herding, trade between Tibet and India, small businesses, and farming, with the main crop being potatoes. Since the 1920s and the coming of Western mountaineers, Sherpa men became increasingly employed as guides and porters for trekkers and climbers. Many Sherpa men and women now run guest houses or work in guest houses as cooks, food servers, and cleaners.

The Sherpa are organized into eighteen separate lineages, or *ru* ("bones"), with marriage taking place outside one's birth lineage. Recently, they have begun marrying into other ethnic groups, thus expanding the definition and meaning of what it is to be Sherpa. Because of increased intermarriage, the number of people who can be considered Sherpa to some degree is 130,000. Status distinctions include "big people," "middle people," and "small people," with the middle group being the largest by far (Ortner 1999:65). The main privilege of those in the top level is not to carry loads. Those in the poorest level are landless and work for others.

The Sherpa practice a localized version of Tibetan Buddhism which contains non-Buddhist elements having to do with nature spiritualism that connects all beings. The place name Khumbu, for example, refers to the guardian deity of the region.

Tourism has been and still is a major change factor for the Sherpa. In Khumbu, the number of international tourists per year exceeds the Sherpa population.

Global warming is also having significant effects. Glaciers are melting, lakes are rising, and massive flooding is frequent. Some of the swollen lakes are in danger of breaking their banks (United Nations Environment Programme 2002). Many community development projects are aimed at reforestation, planting fruit orchards, and protecting and expanding local knowledge of medicinal herbs.

Readings

Vincanne Adams. *Tigers of the Snow and Other Virtual Sherpas: An Ethnography of Himalayan Encounters.* Princeton, NJ: Princeton University Press, 1996.

James Fisher. *Sherpas: Reflections on Change in Himalayan Nepal.* Berkeley: University of California Press, 1990.

Sherry Ortner. *Life and Death on Mt. Everest: Sherpas and Himalayan Mountaineering.* Princeton, NJ: Princeton University Press, 1999.

Video

Trekking on Tradition (Documentary Educational Resources, 1992).

Thanks to Vincanne Adams, University of California at San Francisco, for reviewing this material.

A Sherpa porter carries a load up a steep mountain path in the Himalayas. Porters earn relatively good wages, especially when they work for international tourists (left). ■ (Source: Royalty Free/CORBIS) *Among the many forms of medical treatment available to the Sherpa, shamanic healing remains a popular choice (right).* ■ (Source: Vincanne Adams)

MAP 7.5 *Nepal. The Kingdom of Nepal has a population of almost 30 million inhabitants. Most of its territory is in the Himalayas, and Nepal has eight of the world's ten highest mountains.*

The medical experts increasingly judged that "cultural differences" were the basic problem and that in spite of all their attempts to communicate with the F family, they were basically incapable of caring for Mary. Legal sanctions were used to force her family to bring her to the hospital for surgery.

The family's perspective, in contrast, was grounded in *fa'a Samoa*, the Samoan way. Their first experience in a large hospital occurred after Mary's collapse:

> When Mr. F first arrived at the hospital, he spoke with different hospital staff (using a daughter as a translator) and was concerned that there was no single physician caring for Mary. (Since it was a teaching hospital, she was seen by residents as well as by attending physicians.) He felt that the hospital staff members gave him different interpretations of Mary's illness, including discrepant results, leading him to perceive her care as experimental and inconsistent. The family also observed a child die while Mary was in the Intensive Care Unit, further reinforcing this perception and instilling fear over Mary's chance of surviving in this hospital. Partly due to language difficulties, they felt they did not get an adequate explanation of her problem over the course of her treatment. When they asked what was wrong with her, their perception was that "everyone said 'sugar.'" What this meant was not clear to the family; they were confused about whether she was getting too much sugar or too little. Mary's mother interpreted the explanations to mean she was not getting enough sugar, so she tried to give her more when she was returned home. Over time, confusion gave way to anger, and a basic lack of trust of the hospital and the physicians there developed. The family began to draw on their own resources for explaining and caring for Mary's illness, relying heavily on the father's skills as a healer. (1987:330)

From the Samoan perspective, the F family behaved logically and appropriately. The father, as household head and healer in his own right, felt he had authority. Dr. A, although Samoan, had been resocialized by the Western medical system and alienated from his Samoan background. He did not offer the personal touch that the F family expected. Samoans believe that children above the age of 12 are no longer children and can be expected to behave responsibly. Assigning Mary's 12-year-old sister to assist her with her insulin injections and recording results made sense to them. Also, the hospital in American Samoa does not require appointments. Cultural misunderstanding was the ultimate cause of Mary's death.

Applied Medical Anthropology

Applied medical anthropology, or **clinical medical anthropology,** is the application of anthropological knowledge to further the goals of health-care providers. It may involve improving doctor–patient communication in multicultural settings, making recommendations about culturally appropriate health intervention programs, or providing insights about factors related to disease that medical practitioners do not usually take into account. Applied medical anthropologists draw on ethnomedical knowledge and on any of the three theoretical approaches or a combination of them.

An example of the positive impact of applied medical anthropology is in the work of Robert Trotter on lead poisoning among Mexican American children (1987). The three most common sources of lead poisoning of children in the United States are:

- Eating lead-based paint chips
- Living near a smelter where the dust has high lead content
- Eating or drinking from pottery made with an improperly treated lead glaze

The discovery of an unusual case of lead poisoning by health professionals in Los Angeles in the 1980s prompted investigations that produced understanding of a fourth cause: a traditional healing remedy, *azarcon,* which contained lead, by many Mexican Americans. They use azarcon to treat a culture-specific syndrome called *empacho,* which is a combination of indigestion and constipation, believed to be caused by food sticking to the abdominal wall.

The U.S. Public Health Service asked Trotter to investigate the availability and use of azarcon. He went to Mexico and surveyed the contents of herbal shops. He talked with *curanderos* (local healers). His findings convinced the U.S. government to place restrictions on azarcon, and a related remedy called *greta.* Trotter also made recommendations about the need to provide a substitute remedy for the treatment of empacho that would not have harmful side effects. He offered ideas about how to advertise the substitute in a culturally effective way. Throughout his involvement, Trotter played several roles—researcher, consultant, and program developer— all of which brought anthropological knowledge to the solution of a public health problem.

Much work in applied medical anthropology involves health communication (Nichter 1996:327–328). Anthropologists can help health educators in the development of more meaningful messages through

- Addressing local health beliefs and health concerns
- Taking seriously all local illness terms and conventions
- Adopting local styles of communication

---

applied or **clinical medical anthropology:** the application of anthropological | knowledge to furthering the goals of health care providers.

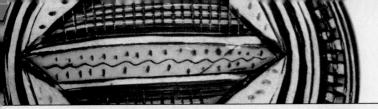

Lessons Applied

PROMOTING VACCINATION PROGRAMS IN DEVELOPING COUNTRIES

Vaccination programs in developing countries, especially as promoted by UNICEF, are introduced with much fanfare. But they are sometimes met with little enthusiasm by the target population. In India, many people are suspicious that vaccination programs are clandestine family planning programs (Nichter 1996). In other instances, fear of foreign vaccines prompts people to reject inoculations. Overall, acceptance rates of vaccination are lower than Western public health planners expected. To understand why, medical anthropologists conducted surveys in several countries. The results revealed that many parents have a partial or inaccurate understanding of what the vaccines protect against. Some people did not understand the importance of multiple vaccinations.

Public health promoters incorporated findings from the survey in two ways:

- Educational campaigns for the public that addressed their concerns
- Education for the public health specialists about the importance of understanding and paying attention to local cultural practices and beliefs

FOOD FOR THOUGHT

- What might be the three most important lessons for the public health specialists?

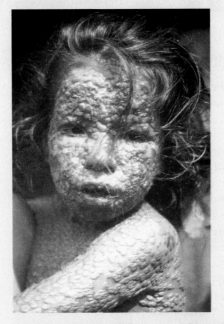

This photograph of a young girl in Bangladesh, taken in 1975, shows the raised bumps of smallpox infection which she contracted in 1973. In 1977, the World Health Organization announced that smallpox had been eradicated in Bangladesh. ■ *Research the status of smallpox in the world today.* (Source: © CDC/PHIL/CORBIS)

- Identifying subgroups within the population that may be responsive to different types of messages and incentives
- Monitoring the response of communities to health messages over time and facilitating corrections in communication when needed
- Exposing and removing possible victim blaming in health messages

These principles helped health-care officials understand local response to public vaccination programs in several countries of Asia and Africa (see Lessons Applied box).

Working Together: Western Biomedicine and Nonbiomedical Systems

Since 1978, the World Health Organization has endorsed the incorporation of local healing practices in na-tional health systems. This policy emerged in response to several factors. First is the increasing appreciation of the value of many non-Western healing traditions. Another is the shortage of trained biomedical personnel. Third is the growing awareness of the deficiencies of Western biomedicine in addressing a person's psychosocial context.

Debates continue about the efficacy of many traditional medical practices as compared to biomedicine. For instance, opponents of the promotion of traditional medicine claim that it has no effect on such infectious diseases as cholera, malaria, tuberculosis, schistosomiasis, leprosy, and others. They insist that it makes no sense to allow for or encourage ritual practices against cholera, for example, when a child has not been inoculated against it. Supporters of traditional medicine as one component of a pluralistic health system point out that biomedicine neglects a person's mind, soul, and social setting. Traditional healing practices fill that gap.

The Big Questions Revisited

WHAT is ethnomedicine?

Ethnomedicine is the study of health systems of specific cultures. Health systems include categories and perceptions of illness and approaches to prevention and healing. Research in ethnomedicine shows how perceptions of the body differ cross-culturally and reveals both differences and similarities across health systems in perceptions of illness and symptoms. Culture-specific syndromes are found in all cultures, not just non-Western societies, and many are now globalizing.

Ethnomedical studies of healing, healing substances, and healers reveal a wide range of approaches. Community healing systems are more characteristic of small-scale nonindustrial societies. They emphasize group interaction and treating the individual within the social context. Humoral healing systems seek to maintain balance in bodily fluids and substances through diet, activity, and behavior. In industrial/informatics societies, biomedicine emphasizes the body as a discrete unit, and treatment addresses the individual body or mind and frames out the wider social context. Biomedicine is increasingly reliant on technology and is increasingly specialized.

WHAT are three major theoretical approaches in medical anthropology?

Ecological/epidemiological medical anthropology emphasizes links between the environment and health. It reveals how certain categories of people are at risk of contracting particular diseases within various contexts in historical times and the present. The interpretivist approach focuses on studying illness and healing as a set of symbols and meanings. Cross-culturally, definitions of health problems and healing systems for these problems are embedded in meanings. Critical medical anthropologists focus on health problems and healing within a structurist framework. They ask what power relations are involved and who benefits from particular forms of healing. They analyze the role of inequality and poverty in health problems. Some critical medical anthropologists have critiqued Western biomedicine as a system of social control.

HOW are disease, illness, and healing changing during globalization?

Health systems everywhere are facing accelerated change in the face of globalization, which includes the spread of Western capitalism as well as new diseases and new medical technologies. The "new infectious diseases" are a challenge to health-care systems in terms of prevention and treatment. Diseases of development are health problems caused by development projects (such as dams) that change the physical and social environments.

The spread of Western biomedicine to many non-Western contexts is a major direction of change. As a consequence, medical pluralism exists in all countries. The availability of Western patent medicines has had substantial positive effects, but widespread overuse and self-medication can result in negative health consequences for individuals and more widely due to the emergence of drug-resistant disease strains.

Applied or clinical medical anthropologists play several roles in improving health systems. They may inform medical care providers of more appropriate forms of treatment, guide local people about their increasingly complex medical choices, help prevent health problems through changing detrimental practices, or improve public health communication by making it more culturally informed and effective.

KEY CONCEPTS

applied or clinical medical
  anthropology, p. 194
community healing, p. 178
critical medical anthropology, p. 186
culture-specific syndrome, p. 174
disease, p. 173
disease of development, p. 190
ecological/epidemiological approach,
  p. 182

ethno-etiology, p. 176
ethnomedicine, p. 172
historical trauma, p. 185
humoral healing system, p. 179
illness, p. 173
medicalization, p. 186
medical pluralism, p. 191
phytotherapy, p. 181
placebo effect, or meaning effect, p. 185

shaman, p. 180
somatization, p. 175
structural suffering, p. 176
Western biomedicine p. 172

SUGGESTED READINGS

Eric J. Bailey. *Medical Anthropology and African American Health.*
New York: Greenwood Publishing Group, 2000. This book
explores the relationship between cultural anthropology and
African American health-care issues. One chapter discusses how
to do applied research in medical anthropology.

Nancy N. Chen. *Breathing Spaces: Qigong, Psychiatry, and Healing in
China.* New York: Columbia University Press, 2003. This ethnography
explores *qigong* (pronounced CHEE-GUNG), a charismatic
form of healing popular in China that involves meditative breathing
exercises. The author links the growing practice of qigong in
China with the rise of capitalism and urban development.

Paul Farmer. *Pathologies of Power: Health, Human Rights, and the
New War on the Poor.* Berkeley: University of California Press,
2005. Farmer blends interpretive medical anthropology with critical
medical anthropology in his study of how poverty kills
through diseases such as tuberculosis and HIV/AIDS. He takes an
advocacy position.

Bonnie Glass-Coffin. *The Gift of Life: Female Spirituality and Healing
in Northern Peru.* Albuquerque: University of New Mexico
Press, 1998. The author examines women traditional healers in
northern Peru. She provides a descriptive account of their practices
and an experiential account about her experiences with two
healers who worked to cure her of a spiritual illness.

Stephanie Kane. *AIDS Alibis: Sex, Drugs and Crime in the Americas.*
Philadelphia: Temple University Press, 1998. Kane examines the
combined forces of sex, drugs, and crimes in Chicago and Belize.
An activist anthropologist, she critiques the U.S. war on drugs,
the war on crime, and public health programs.

Richard Katz, Megan Biesele, and Verna St. Davis. *Healing Makes
Our Hearts Happy: Spirituality and Cultural Transformation
among the Kalahari Ju/'hoansi.* Rochester, VT: Inner Traditions,
1997. This book presents the story of how traditional healing
dances help the Ju/'hoansi cope with recent and contemporary
social upheaval. Their healing dances help them maintain a sense
of community and are important for their cultural survival.

Arthur Kleinman and James L. Watson, eds. *SARS in China: Prelude
to Pandemic?* Stanford, CA: Stanford University Press, 2006. An
introduction and ten chapters consider such topics as SARS in
historical context, the epidemiology of SARS, public health
responses, economic and political consequences, social and psychological
consequences, and links with globalization.

Luisa Margolies. *My Mother's Hip: Lessons from the World of
Eldercare.* Philadelphia: Temple University Press, 2004. After the
author's mother broke her hip and entered a long-term care institution
in Florida, Margolies began her study of chronic illness
and eldercare. She chronicles her mother's case and interweaves a
cultural critique of elder health care in the United States, Medicaid,
and end-of-life questions such as resuscitation.

Carol Shepherd McClain, ed. *Women as Healers: A Cross-Cultural
Perspective.* New Brunswick, NJ: Rutgers University Press, 1989.
Case studies discuss women healers in Ecuador, Sri Lanka, Mexico,
Jamaica, the United States, Serbia, Korea, Southern Africa,
and Benin.

David McKnight. *From Hunting to Drinking: The Devastating
Effects of Alcohol on an Australian Aboriginal Community.*
New York: Routledge, 2002. Alcohol has had devastating effects
over a period of thirty years on Mornington Island, Australia.
McKnight discusses the history of drinking in Australia, causes of
excessive alcohol consumption, and vested interests of authorities
in the sale of alcohol on the island.

Daniel Moerman. *Meaning, Medicine and the "Placebo Effect."* New
York: Cambridge University Press, 2002. This book considers
medical practices in terms of how their meaning has an influence
on their effect. The author reviews many studies, mainly conducted
in the United States.

Ethan Nebelkopf and Mary Phillips, eds. *Healing and Mental Health
for Native Americans: Speaking in Red.* New York. AltaMira
Press, 2004. Chapters consider mental health and substance abuse
among Native North Americans and provide cases of healing that
involve Native American culture. Many of the authors are Native
Americans who are anthropologists, social workers, or social
psychologists.

Kathryn S. Oths and Servando Z. Hinajosa, eds. *Healing by Hand:
Manual Medicine and Bonesetting in Global Perspective.* New
York: AltaMira Press, 2004. Chapters explore varieties of "manual
medicine" such as massage therapy, bonesetting, chiropractics,
and osteopathy. Cases include the United States, Denmark,
Guatemala, Kenya, and Wales.

Merrill Singer. *Something Dangerous: Emergent and Changing Illicit
Drug Use and Community Health.* Long Grove, IL: Waveland
Press, 2005. This ethnography combines theory with research and
applied anthropology about drug use and public health responses
in the United States.

Paul Stoller. *Stranger in the Village of the Sick: A Memoir of Cancer,
Sorcery, and Healing.* Boston: Beacon Press, 2004. After being
diagnosed with lymphoma, the author enters the "village of the
sick" as he goes through diagnostic testing, chemotherapy, and
eventual remission. He offers observations about being a cancer
patient in the United States and describes how he found strength
through his earlier association with a West African healer.

Johan Wedel. *Santería Healing.* Gainesville: University of Florida
Press, 2004. This book discusses Santería healing in Cuba. The
author conducted interviews with priests and others knowledgeable
about Santería and observed many Santería consultations.

PART III
Social Organization

FREDY PECCERELLI, A FORENSIC ANTHROPOLOGIST,
risks his personal security working for victims of political violence in his homeland. Peccerelli is founder and executive director of the Guatemalan Forensic Anthropology Foundation (FAFG), a group that focuses on the recovery and identification of some of the 200,000 people, mostly indigenous Maya of the mountainous regions, that Guatemalan military forces killed or "disappeared" during the brutal civil war that occurred between the mid-1960s and the mid-1990s.

Peccerelli was born in Guatemala. His family immigrated to the United States when his father, a lawyer, was threatened by death squads. He grew up in New York and attended Brooklyn College in the 1990s. But he felt a need to reconnect with his heritage and began to study anthropology as a vehicle that would allow him to serve his country.

The FAFG scientists excavate clandestine mass graves, exhume the bodies, and identify them through several means, such as matching dental and/or medical records. In studying skeletons, they try to determine the person's age, gender, stature, ancestry, and lifestyle. DNA studies are few because of the expense. The scientists also collect information from relatives of the victims and from eyewitnesses of the massacres. Since 1992, the FAFG team has discovered and exhumed approximately 200 mass grave sites in villages, fields, and churches.

Anthropology in the Real World

Peccerelli sees the foundation's purpose as applying scientific principles to basic human concerns. Bodies of identified victims are returned to their families to allow them some sense of closure about what happened to their loved ones. Families can honor their dead with appropriate burial ceremonies.

The scientists also give the Guatemalan government clear evidence on the basis of which to prosecute the perpetrators of these atrocities. However, Guatemala was long structured in terms of a ruling military and a largely disenfranchised indigenous population. Many members of the former millitia are still in positions of power within the government.

Peccerelli, his family, and his colleagues have been harassed and threatened. Eleven of the FAFG scientists have received written death threats. Bullets have been fired into Peccerelli's home, and it has been burglarized. The United Nations and other human rights organizations have made it clear to the government that they support FARG's investigations, and exhumations continue with heightened security measures.

The American Association for the Advancement of Science, an organization committed to "advance science and serve society," honored Peccerelli and his colleagues in 2004 for their work in promoting human rights at great personal risk. In 1999, *Time* magazine and CNN chose Peccerelli as one of the fifty "Latin American Leaders for the New Millennium." During the same year, the Guatemalan Youth Commission named him an "icon" for the youth of the country.

Currently, Peccerelli is on sabbatical to work on a master's degree in forensic and biological anthropology at the University of Bournemouth, UK. He intends to return to Guatemala: "There is enough work for another twenty-five years."

8

Kinship and Domestic Life

The Big Questions

- HOW do cultures create kinship ties through descent, sharing, and marriage?

- WHAT is a household and what do anthropologists study about household life?

- HOW are kinship and households changing?

A Minangkabau bride in Sumatra, Indonesia, wears an elaborate gold headdress. Women play a central role among the Minangkabau. *(Source: © CORBIS)*

Learning how another kinship system works is as challenging as learning another language. Robin Fox became aware of this challenge during his research among the Tory Islanders of Ireland (see Map 8.1) (1995 [1978]). Some Tory Island kinship terms are similar to American English usage; for example, the word *muintir* means "people" in its widest sense, as in English. It can also refer to people of a particular social category, as in "my people," and to close relatives. Another similarity is in *gaolta,* the word for "relatives" or "those of my blood." Its adjectival form refers to kindness, like the English word *kin,* which is related to "kindness." Tory Islanders have a phrase meaning "children and grandchildren," also like the English term *descendants.* One major difference is that the Tory Island word for "friend" is the same as the word for "kin." This usage reflects the cultural context of Tory Island with its small population, all related through kinship. So, logically, a friend is also kin.

All cultures have ways of defining *kinship,* or a sense of being related to another person or persons. Rules about who are kinship can be either informal or formalized in law. From infancy, people begin learning about their particular culture's **kinship system,** the combination of rules about who are kin and the expected behavior of kin. Like one's language, one's kinship system is so ingrained that it is taken for granted as something natural rather than cultural.

This chapter first considers cross-cultural variations in kinship systems. It then focuses on a key unit of domestic life: the household. The last section provides examples of contemporary change in kinship patterns and household organization.

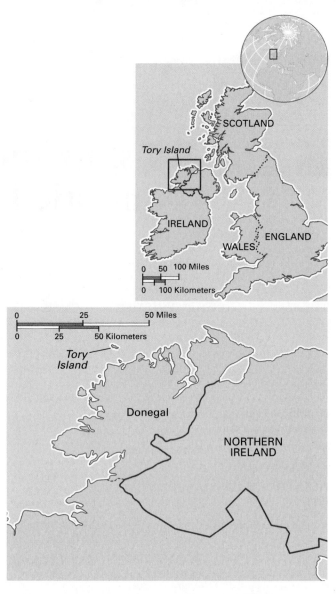

MAP 8.1   Ireland. Ireland's population is about 4 million. The geography is low central plains surrounded by a ring of mountains. Membership in the EU and the rising standard of living earned Ireland the nickname of the Celtic Tiger. Its economic opportunities are attracting immigrants from places as diverse as Romania, China, and Nigeria. Most people are Roman Catholics, followed by the Anglican Church of Ireland.

The Study of Kinship Systems

In all cultures, kinship systems are linked with modes of production and reproduction and prevailing symbols and beliefs (see Figure 8.1). Depending on the cultural context, various kinds of kinship systems shape children's personality development, influence marriage options, and affect the care of the aged. Nineteenth-century anthropologists found that kinship was the most important organizing principle in nonindustrial, nonstate cultures. The kinship group performs the functions of ensuring the continuity of the group by arranging marriages; maintaining social order by setting moral rules and punishing offenders; and providing for the basic needs of members by regulating production, consumption, and distribution. In large-scale industrial/informatics societies, kinship ties exist, but many other kinds of social ties draw people together.

Nineteenth-century anthropologists also discovered that definitions of who counts as kin differed widely from those of Europe and the United States. Western cul-

---

kinship system: the predominant form of kin relationships in a culture and the kinds of behavior involved.

kinship diagram: a schematic way of presenting data on kinship relationships of an individual (called "ego") depicting all of ego's relatives, as remembered by ego and reported to the anthropologist.

FIGURE 8.1 Modes of Production, Kinship, and Household Structure

Foraging	Horticulture	Pastoralism	Agriculture	Industrialism/Informatics
Descent and Inheritance Bilineal		Unilineal (matrilineal or patrilineal)		**Descent and Inheritance** Bilineal
Marital Residence Neolocal or bilocal		Matrilocal or patrilocal		**Marital Residence** Neolocal
Household Type Nuclear		Extended		**Household Type** Nuclear or single-parent or single-person

tures emphasize "blood" relations as primary, or relations through birth from a biological mother and biological father (Sault 1994). "Blood" is not a universal basis for kinship, however. Even in some cultures that do have a "blood"-based understanding of kinship, variations exist in defining who is a "blood" relative and who is not. For example, in some cultures, male offspring are considered of one "blood," whereas female offspring are not.

Behavior is a common nonblood basis for determining kinship. Among the Inuit of northern Alaska, people who act like kin are kin (Bodenhorn 2000). If a person ceases to act like kin, he or she stops being a kinsperson. So, someone might say that a certain person "used to be" his or her cousin. In this system, the kin of anyone considered kin are also one's kin.

Formal Kinship Analysis

Early anthropologists focused on finding out who is related to whom and in what way. Typically, the anthro-

pologist would conduct an interview with a few people, asking questions such as: What do you call your brother's daughter? Can you (as a man) marry your father's brother's daughter? What is the term you use to refer to your mother's sister? The anthropologist would ask an individual to name all his or her relatives, explain how they are related to the interviewee, and provide the terms by which they refer to him or her.

From this information, the anthropologist would construct a **kinship diagram,** a schematic way of presenting the kinship relationships of a particular individual, called *ego* (see Figure 8.2). This diagram depicts ego's relatives, as remembered by ego. In cultures where kinship plays a major role in social relations, ego may be able to provide information on dozens of relatives. When I (the author) took a research methods course as an undergraduate, I interviewed my Hindi language teaching assistant for a class assignment to construct a kinship diagram. He was from an urban, middle-class business family in India. He recalled over sixty relatives on both his father's and mother's sides, providing information for a much more

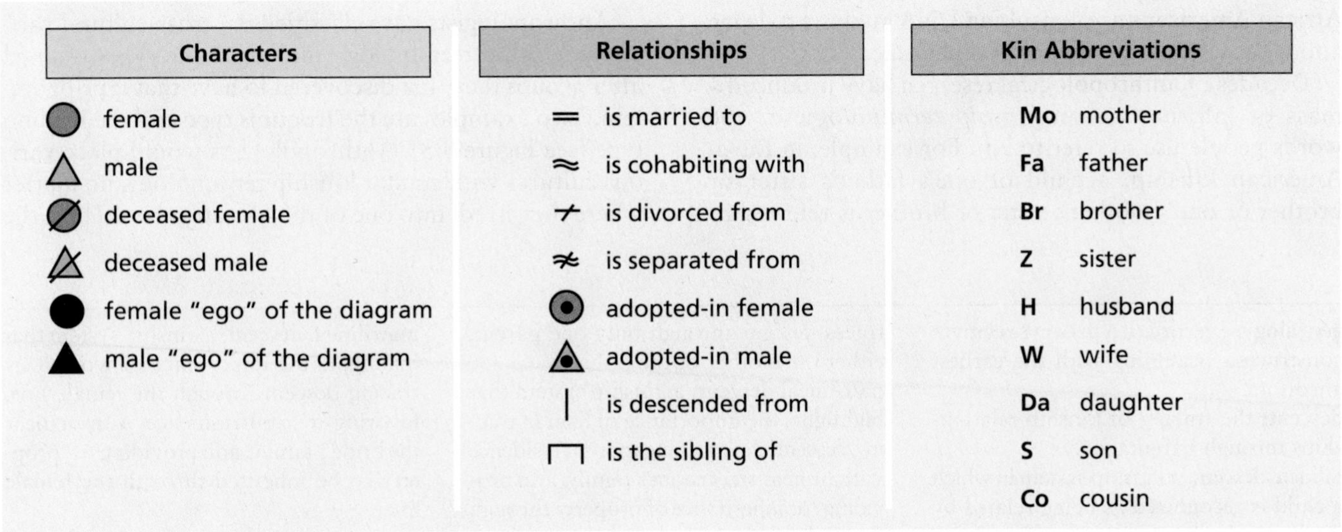

Characters		**Relationships**		**Kin Abbreviations**	
○	female	=	is married to	**Mo**	mother
△	male	≈	is cohabiting with	**Fa**	father
⊘	deceased female	⚊	is divorced from	**Br**	brother
△	deceased male	≉	is separated from	**Z**	sister
●	female "ego" of the diagram	⊙	adopted-in female	**H**	husband
▲	male "ego" of the diagram	◬	adopted-in male	**W**	wife
		|	is descended from	**Da**	daughter
		⊓	is the sibling of	**S**	son
				Co	cousin

FIGURE 8.2 Symbols Used in Kinship Diagrams

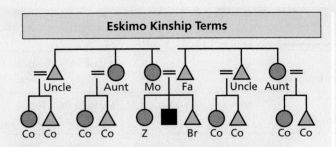

Eskimo Kinship Terms	Iroquois Kinship Terms

Eskimo kinship terminology, like that of most Euro-Americans, has unique terms for kin within the nuclear family that are not used for any other relatives: mother, father, sister, brother. This fact is related to the importance of the nuclear family. Another feature is that the same terms are used for relatives on both the mother's side and the father's side, a property that is related to bilineal descent.

Iroquois kinship terminology operates in unilineal systems. One result is that there are different terms for relatives on the mother's and father's sides and distinctions between cross and parallel cousins. Another feature is the "merging" of one's mother with one's mother's sister (both are referred to as "mother") and of one's father with one's father's brother (both are referred to as "father").

FIGURE 8.3 Two Kinship Naming Systems

extensive kinship diagram than I would have been able to provide for my middle-class, Euro-American relatives.

In contrast to a kinship diagram, a **genealogy** is a schematic way of presenting a family tree, constructed by beginning with the earliest ancestors that can be traced, then working down to the present. A genealogy, thus, does not begin with ego. When Robin Fox attempted to construct kinship diagrams beginning with ego, the Tory Islanders were uncomfortable with the approach. They preferred to proceed genealogically, so he followed their preference. Tracing a family's complete genealogy may involve archival research in the attempt to construct as complete a history as possible. In Europe and the United States, Christians have long followed a practice of recording their genealogy in the front of the family Bible. Many African Americans are consulting DNA analysts to learn about their ancestry and cultural heritage.

Decades of anthropological research have produced a mass of information on *kinship terminology,* or the words people use to refer to kin. For example, in Euro-American kinship, a child of one's father's sister or brother or one's mother's sister or brother is referred to by the kinship term "cousin." Likewise, one's father's sister and one's mother's sister are both referred to as "aunt," and one's father's brother and one's mother's brother are both referred to as "uncle." "Grandmother" and "grandfather" refer to the ascending generation on either one's father's or one's mother's side. This merging pattern is not universal. In some cultures, different terms apply to kin on one's mother's and father's sides, so a mother's sister has a different kinship term than a father's sister. In yet another type of kinship system, solidarity along lines of siblings of the same gender is emphasized. One's mother and one's mother's sisters all have the same term, which translates as "mother," a system found among the Navajo of the American southwest, for example.

Anthropologists have classified the cross-cultural variety in kinship terminology into six basic types, named after groups they first discovered to have that type of system. Two examples are the Iroquois type and the Eskimo type (see Figure 8.3). Anthropologists would place various cultures with similar kinship terminology, no matter where they lived, into one of the six categories. Thus, the

---

genealogy: a record of a person's relatives constructed beginning with the earliest ancestors.

descent: the tracing of kinship relationships through parentage.

bilineal descent: a kinship system in which a child is recognized as being related by descent to both parents.

unilineal descent: a kinship system that traces descent through only one parent, either the mother or the father.

patrilineal descent: a kinship system that highlights the importance of men in tracing descent, determining marital residence with or near the groom's family, and providing for inheritance of property through the male line.

matrilineal descent: a kinship system that highlights the importance of women by tracing descent through the female line, favoring marital residence with or near the bride's family, and providing for property to be inherited through the female line.

Yanomami are classified as having an Iroquois naming system. Contemporary anthropologists who study kinship have moved beyond these categories, since the six kinship types do not promote understanding of actual kinship dynamics. This text, therefore, merely presents two examples and avoids going into detail on the six classic types.

Kinship in Action

The formalism of early kinship studies led many students of anthropology, and some of their professors, to view kinship as a boring subject. Fortunately, a renewed interest in kinship shows how it is related to other topics, such as globalization, ethnic identity, reproductive decision making, and health (Carsten 2000).

Anthropologists who study kinship as a lived and changing aspect of life use varied methods of data gathering, rather than simply interviewing participants. Participant observation provides insights about who interacts with whom and what are the expected rights and responsibilities of kin. The life history method (see Chapter 2) reveals that kinship changes over an individual's lifetime and in relation to events such as migration, a natural disaster, or political change. *Focused life histories* are useful in targeting key events related to kinship, such as marriage or cohabitation, divorce, and widowhood/widowerhood. Anthropologists interested in population dynamics, for example, use focused life histories to learn at what age a woman began having sexual relations, how many pregnancies she had, if and when she had an abortion or bore a child, whether the child lived or died, and when she stopped having children.

Descent

Descent is the tracing of kinship relationships through parentage. It is based on the fact that everybody is born from someone else. Descent creates a line of people from whom someone is descended, stretching through history. But not all cultures reckon descent in the same way. Some cultures have a **bilineal descent** system, in which a child is recognized as being related by descent to both parents. Others have a **unilineal descent** system, which recognizes descent through only one parent, either the father or the mother. The distribution of bilineal and unilineal systems is roughly correlated with different modes of production (see Figure 8.1, p. 203). This correspondence makes sense because economies—production, consumption, and exchange—are closely tied to the way people are socially organized.

Unilineal Descent

Unilineal descent is the basis of kinship in about 60 percent of the world's cultures, making it the most common form of descent. This system tends to be found in societies with a fixed resource base, such as farmland or herds. Thus, unilineal descent is most common among pastoralists, horticulturalists, and farmers. Inheritance rules that regulate the transmission of property through only one line help maintain cohesiveness of the resource base.

Unilineal descent has two major forms. One is **patrilineal descent,** in which kinship is traced through the male line. The other is **matrilineal descent,** in which kinship is traced through the female line. In a patrilineal system, only male children are considered members of the kinship lineage. Female children "marry out" and become members of the husband's lineage. In matrilineal descent systems, only daughters are considered to carry on the family line, and sons "marry out."

Jack Goody (1976), a leading kinship theorist of the late twentieth century, proposed a broad comparison between the descent systems of rural sub-Saharan Africa and Eurasia. In sub-Saharan Africa, in horticultural groups, women are prominent as producers, reproducers, marketers, and decision makers. They have matrilineal descent, which reflects and maintains the importance of women. In rural Eurasia, in plow agriculture, men play the primary farming role while women do animal care, food processing, weeding, and harvesting. Patrilineal descent in agricultural Eurasia reflects and maintains male dominance.

Patrilineal descent is found among about 45 percent of all cultures. It occurs throughout much of India, East Asia, the Middle East, Papua New Guinea, northern Africa, and among some horticultural groups of sub-Saharan Africa. Margery Wolf's book, *The House of Lim* (1968), is a classic ethnography of patrilineal descent. Wolf lived for two years with the Lims, a Taiwanese farming household (see Figure 8.4, p. 207). In her book, she describes first the village setting and then the Lims' house, giving attention to the importance of the ancestral hall with its family altar, where the male household head meets guests. She next provides a chapter on Lim Han-ci, the father and household head, and then a chapter on Lim Hue-lieng, the eldest son. Wolf next introduces the females of the family: wives, sisters, and an adopted daughter. The ordering of the chapters reflects the importance of the *patriarch* (senior, most powerful male) and his eldest son, who will, if all goes according to plan, be next in line for the leadership position. Daughters marry out into other families. In-marrying females (wives, daughters-in-law) are always considered outsiders and are never fully merged into the patrilineage. The Lim's kinship system exemplifies strong patrilineality in that it heavily weights position, power, and property with males. In such systems, girls are raised "for other families" and are thus not fully members of their birth family. Likewise, they are never full members of their marriage family. The world's most strongly patrilineal

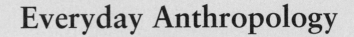
WHAT'S IN A NAME?

Naming children is always significant. Parents may follow cultural rules that a first-born son receives the name of his father's father or a first-born daughter receives the name of her mothers mother. Some parents believe that a newborn should not be formally named for a year or two and is instead referred to by a nickname. Others think that a name must convey some special hoped-for attribute of the child, or that a name should be unique.

The village of Ha Tsuen is located in the northwest corner of a rural area of Hong Kong (Watson 1986). About 2,500 people live in the village. All the males belong to the same patrilineage and all have the same surname of Teng. They are descended from a common male ancestor who settled in the region in the twelfth century. Daughters of Ha Tsuen marry into families outside the village, and marital residence is patrilocal.

Women do not own property, and they have no direct control of the means of production. Few married women are employed in wage labor. They depend on their husbands for financial support. Local politics is a male domain, as is all public decision making. A woman's status as a new bride is low, and the transition from daughter to bride can be difficult psychologically. Women's primary role is in reproduction, especially of sons. As a woman bears children, especially sons, her status in the household rises.

The local naming system reflects the power, importance, and autonomy of males. All children are first given a name referred to as their *ming* when they are a few days old. If the baby is a boy, the 30-day ceremony is as elaborate as the family can afford. It may include a banquet for many neighbors and the village elders and the presentation of red eggs to everyone in the community. For a girl, the 30-day ceremony may involve only a special meal for close family members. Paralleling this public expenditure bias toward sons is the thinking that

MAP 8.2 Hong Kong. The formal title of Hong Kong is the Hong Kong Special Administrative Region of the People's Republic of China. A world center of finance and trade, it lacks natural resources and agricultural land, so it imports most of its food and raw materials. With 7 million residents, Hong Kong's population density is high. Most of the population is ethnic Chinese, and many practice ancestor worship. Ten percent of the population is Christian. Religious freedom is protected through its constitution.

goes into selecting the ming. A boy's ming is distinctive and flattering. It may have a classical literary connection. A girl's ming often has negative connotations, such as "Last Child," "Too Many," or "Little Mistake." One com-

---

systems are found in East Asia, South Asia, and the Middle East (see Everyday Anthropology box.)

Matrilineal descent exists in about 15 percent of all cultures. It traces kinship through the female line exclusively, and the lineage consists of mothers and daughters and their daughters. It is found among many Native North American groups; across a large band of central Africa; among many groups of Southeast Asia and the Pacific, and Australia; in parts of eastern and southern India; in a small pocket of northern Bangladesh; and in parts of the Mediterranean coast of Spain and Portugal. Matrilineal societies vary greatly, from foragers to intensive agricultural societies (Lepowsky 1993:296). Most, however, are horticulturalist economies in which women dominate the production and distribution of food and other goods.

THINKING OUTSIDE THE BOX

IF YOU were going to write an ethnography of your family, like Wolf's book about the Lims, what chapter titles would you choose and what would be their sequence?

mon ming for a daughter is "Joined to a Brother," which implies the hope that she will be a lucky charm, bringing the birth of a son next. Sometimes, though, people give an uncomplimentary name to a boy such as "Little Slave Girl." The reason is protection, to trick the spirits into thinking the baby is only a worthless girl so that the spirits will do no harm.

Marriage is the next formal naming occasion. When a male marries, he is given or chooses for himself a *tzu,* or marriage name. Gaining a tzu is a key marker of male adulthood. The tzu is not used in everyday address, but appears mainly on formal documents. A man also has a *wai hao,* "outside name," which is his public nickname. As he enters middle age, he may take a *hao,* or courtesy name, which he chooses and which reflects his aspirations and self-perceptions.

In the case of a woman, her ming ceases to exist when she marries. She no longer has a name. Instead, her husband refers to her as *nei jen,* "inner person," since now her life is restricted to the domestic world of household,

husband's family, and neighborhood. People may also refer to her by *teknonyms,* or names for someone based on their relationship to someone else, such as "Wife of So and So" or "Mother of So and So." In old age, she becomes *ah po,* "Old Woman," like every other aged female in the village.

Throughout their lives, men accumulate more and better names than women. They choose many of the names themselves. Over the course of their lives, women have fewer names than men. Women's names are standardized, not personalized, and women never get to choose any of their names.

FOOD FOR THOUGHT

- Go to www.slate.com/id/2116505/ (*Trading Up: Where Do Baby Names Come From?* by Steven D. Levitt and Stephen J. Dubner) and read about the status game of child naming in the United States. How does your first name fit into this picture?

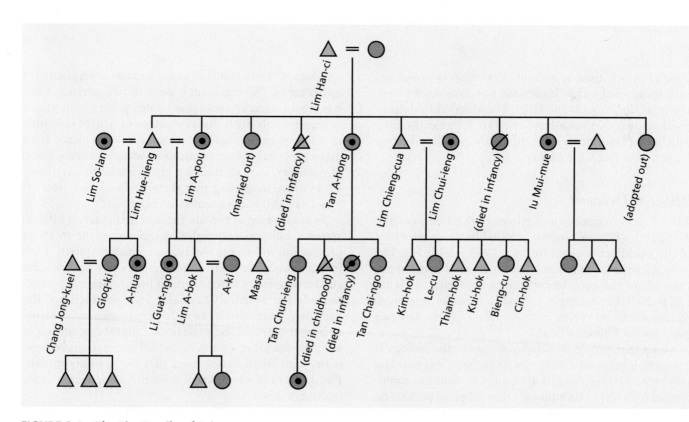

FIGURE 8.4 The Lim Family of Taiwan

Critical Thinking

HOW BILINEAL IS AMERICAN KINSHIP?

American kinship is a general model based on the bilineal descent system of Euro-Americans of the 1960s (Schneider 1968). According to this model, children are considered to be descended from both mother and father, and general inheritance rules suggest that property is divided equally between sons and daughters. Given the rich cultural diversity of the United States and Canada, most would now consider the label "American kinship" and its characterization as bilineal to be overgeneralized.

Even within the so-called American kinship of the 1960s, bilineality was not strictly followed. Indications of patrilineality include the practice of a wife dropping her surname at marriage and taking her husband's surname, and using the husband's surname for offspring. Although inheritance is supposedly equal among all offspring regardless of gender, often it is not. In many business families, the business is passed from father to sons, while daughters are given a different form of inheritance such as a trust fund. Increasing trends toward matrifocality are caused by high rates of divorce and the trend of more young children living with the mother than with the father.

In order to explore descent patterns, each student in the class should draw his or her own kinship diagram. Students should note their microculture or ethnicity at the top of the chart, choosing the label that they prefer. Then each student should draw a dotted line around the relatives with whom they live on a regular basis and a continuous line around the relatives with whom they feel "closest." As a group, students in the class should then consider the following questions about the kinship diagrams.

CRITICAL THINKING QUESTIONS

- How many students drew equal circles for residence and "closeness" around relatives on both parents' sides? How many emphasized the mother's side? How many emphasized the father's side?

- Do microcultural or ethnic patterns emerge in terms of the circled kin?

- From this exercise, what can be said about "American kinship"?

Often, but not always, matrilineal kinship is associated with recognized public leadership positions for women, as among the Iroquois and Hopi. The Minangkabau (pronounced mee-NAN-ka-bow, the last syllable rhyming with "now") of Indonesia are the largest matrilineal group in the world (see Culturama).

Bilineal Descent

Bilineal descent traces kinship from both parents equally to the child. Bilineal descent is found in about one-third of the world's cultures (Murdock 1965 [1949]:57). The highest frequency of bilineal descent is found at the opposite ends of the production continuum (refer to Figure 8.1, p. 203). For example, Ju/'hoansi foragers have bilineal descent as do urban professionals in North America (see Critical Thinking box).

Given that people worldwide recognize the biological connection between a baby and its parents, it is puzzling why most kinship systems are unilineal. Cultural evolutionists of the late 1800s thought that people in prehistoric societies did not understand the biological role of the father. Bilineal kinship, in their view, emerged with "higher

civilization" and unilineal kinship systems are remnants of earlier times. This argument is weak on two grounds. First, it is ethnocentric to claim that contemporary bilineal cultures, especially Euro-American cultures, are the only ones that recognize the father's biological role. Evidence from many unilineal cultures indicates widespread recognition of paternity. Second, foraging peoples tend to have bilineal kinship, suggesting that the world's earliest humans may have also had bilineal kinship.

In attempting to explain the low frequency of bilineal systems, cultural materialists suggest that the mode of production influences the type of kinship system. Both foraging and industrialism/informatics rely on a flexible gender division of labor in which both males and females contribute, relatively equally, to production and exchange. Logically, bilineal descent recognizes the roles of both the female and male lines. Bilineal descent is also adaptive for foraging and industrial populations because it fits with small family units that are spatially mobile. Flexibility in residence keeps open more opportunities for making a living.

Marital residence rules tend to follow the prevailing direction of descent rules (see Figure 8.1, p. 203).

The Minangkabau of Indonesia

The Minangkabau are the world's largest matrilineal culture, numbering between four and five million people (Sanday 2002). Most live in West Sumatra, Indonesia, and about 500,000 live in Malaysia. The Minangkabau are primarily farmers, producing substantial amounts of surplus rice. Many Minangkabau, both women and men, take up employment in Indonesian cities for a time and then return home.

In this strongly matrilineal kinship system, Minangkabau women hold power through their control of lineage land, its products, and agricultural employment on their land (Sanday 2002). Many have prominent positions in business, especially having to do with rice. Men are more likely to become scholars, merchants, and politicians. Inheritance of property, including farmland and the family house, passes from mothers to daughters.

Members of each submatrilineage, constituting several generations, live together in a lineage house or several nearby houses. Often, men and older boys live in a separate structure, such as the village mosque. In the household, the senior woman controls the power, and she makes decisions in all economic and ceremonial matters. The senior male of the sublineage has the role of representing its interests to other groups, but he is only a representative, not a powerful person in his own right.

Water buffaloes are important in both the Minangkabau rice economy and symbolically. The roofline of a traditional house has upward curves that echo the shape of water buffalo horns. Minangkabau women's festive headdress has the same shape. The Minangkabau are mostly Muslims, but they mix their Muslim faith with elements of earlier traditions and Hinduism. They have long-standing traditions of music, martial arts, weaving, wood carving, and making fine filigree jewelry of silver and gold.

Many of the traditional wooden houses and palaces in Western Sumatra are falling into a state of disrepair (Vellinga 2004). The matrilineal pattern of only women living in the house is changing and men and women are more likely to live together in nuclear households.

Readings

Evelyn Blackwood. *Webs of Power: Women, Kin, and Community in a Sumatran Village.* Lanham, MD: Rowman and Littlefield, 2000.

Kirstin Pauka. *Folk Theater, Dance, and Martial Arts of West Sumatra.* Ann Arbor: University of Michigan Press, 2002 (with CD-ROM).

Peggy Reeves Sanday. *Women at the Center: Life in a Modern Matriarchy.* Ithaca, NY: Cornell University Press, 2002.

Anne Summerfield and John Summerfield. *Walk in Splendor: Ceremonial Dress and the Minangkabau.* Los Angeles: UCLA Fowler Museum of Cultural History. Textile Series No. 4, 1999.

Thanks to Michael G. Peletz, Emory University, for reviewing this material.

A traditional wooden Minangkabau longhouse with its distinctive upward-pointing roof (left). The house interiors are divided into separate "bays" for submatrilineal groups. Many are no longer places of residence but are used as meeting halls or are falling into ruin. ■ (Source: © Wolfgang Kachler/CORBIS) *The symbolic importance of water buffaloes, apparent in the shape of traditional rooftops, is reiterated in the shape of girls' and women's ceremonial headdress (right). The headdress represents women's responsibilities for the growth and strength of Minangkabau culture.* ■ (Source: © Lindsay Hebberd/CORBIS)

MAP 8.3 *Minangkabau Region in Indonesia. The shaded area shows the traditional heartland of Minangkabau culture in western Sumatra. Many Minangkabau people live elsewhere in Sumatra and in neighboring Malaysia.*

Some members of a Bedu household in Yemen. Yemen is the most densely populated country of the Arabian peninsula. The Bedu are a small proportion of the Yameni population which is mainly sedentary. ■ (Source: © Norbert Schiller/The Image Works)

Patrilocality, or marital residence with or near the husband's family, occurs in patrilineal societies, whereas **matrilocality,** or marital residence with or near the wife's family, occurs in matrilineal societies. **Neolocality,** or marital residence in a place different from either the bride's or groom's family, is common in Western industrialized society. Residence patterns have political, economic, and social implications. The combination of matrilineal descent and matrilocal residence, for example, is often found among groups that engage in *long-distance warfare* (Divale 1974). Strong female household bonds maintain the domestic scene while the men are absent on military campaigns, as among the precolonial Iroquois of upstate New York (see Map 12.4, p. 326). Patrilineal descent and patrilocal residence promote the development of cohesive male-focused lineages that are associated with frequent *local warfare,* which requires the presence of a force of fighting men on the home front.

Sharing

Many cultures emphasize kinship ties based on acts of sharing and support. These relationships may be either informal or formally certified. Godparenthood and blood brotherhood are examples of sharing-based kinship that is ritually formalized.

Food Sharing   Sharing-based kinship is common in Southeast Asia, Papua New Guinea, and Australia

(Carsten 1995). Among inhabitants of one of Malaysia's many small islands, sharing-based kinship starts in the womb when the mother's blood feeds the fetus. After birth, the mother's breast milk nourishes the infant. This tie is crucial. A child who is not breastfed will not "recognize" its mother. Breastfeeding is also the basis of the incest rule. People who have been fed from the same breast are kin and may not marry. After the baby is weaned, its most important food is cooked rice. Sharing cooked rice, like breast milk, becomes another way that kinship ties are created and maintained, especially between women and children. Men are often away on fishing trips, in coffee shops, or at the mosque and so are not likely to have rice-sharing kinship bonds with children.

Adoption and Fostering   Another form of sharing-based kinship is the transfer of a child or children from the birth parent(s) to the care of someone else. *Adoption* is a formal and permanent form of child transfer. Common motivations for adoption include infertility and the desire to obtain a particular kind of child (often a son). Motivations for the birth parent to transfer a child to someone else include a premarital pregnancy in a disapproving context, having "too many" children, and having "too many" of a particular gender. Among the Maasai, a woman who has several children might give one to a friend, neighbor, or aged person who has no chil-

---

patrilocality: a kinship rule that defines preferred marital residence with or near the groom's kin.
matrilocality: a kinship rule that defines

preferred marital residence with or near the bride's kin.
neolocality: a kinship rule that defines preferred marital residence in a new lo-

cation not linked to either the bride's or the groom's parents' residence.

dren to care for her or him (review Culturama, Chapter 6, p. 158).

Since the mid-1800s, adoption has been a legalized form of child transfer in the United States. Judith Modell, cultural anthropologist and adoptive parent, studied people's experiences of adoptees, birth parents, and adoptive parents in the United States (1994). She found that the legal process of adoption reconstructs the adoptive relationship to be as much like a biological one as possible. In *closed adoption,* the adopted child receives a new birth certificate, and the birth parent ceases to have any relationship to the child. A recent trend is toward *open adoption,* in which adoptees and birth parents have information about each other's identity and are free to interact with one another. Of the twenty-eight adoptees Modell interviewed, most were interested in searching for their birth parents. The search for birth parents involves an attempt to discover "who I really am." For others, such a search is backward-looking and not a path toward formulating one's identity. Thus, in the United States, adoption legalizes sharing-based kinship but does not always replace a sense of descent-based kinship for everyone involved.

Fostering a child is sometimes similar to a formal adoption in terms of permanence and a sense of kinship. Or it may be temporary placement of a child with someone else for a specific purpose, with little or no sense of kinship. Child fostering is common throughout sub-Saharan Africa. Parents foster out children to enhance the child's chances for formal education or so that the child will learn a skill such as marketing. Most fostered children go from rural to urban areas and from poorer to better-off households. Fieldwork conducted in a neighborhood in Accra, Ghana (see Map 8.4), sheds light on

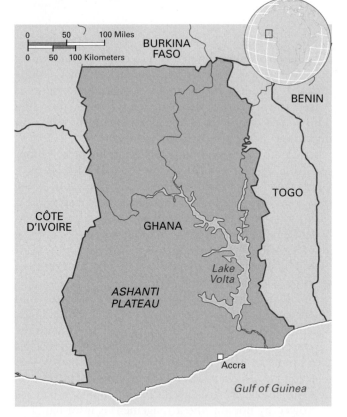

MAP 8.4   Ghana. The Republic of Ghana has over 20 million people. Ghana has rich natural resources and exports gold, timber, and cocoa. Agriculture is the basis of the domestic economy. Several ethnic groups exist, with the Akan people constituting over 40 percent of the population. English is the official language, but another eighty or so languages are also spoken. Over 60 percent of the people are Christian, 20 percent follow traditional religions, and 16 percent are Muslim.

An orphanage in Shanghai, China. Human rights activists in the 1990s claimed that abuse, especially of children with physical handicaps, was widespread in Chinese orphanages. Following this allegation, foreign media were invited to visit the Shanghai Children's Welfare Institute. ∎ *Have you ever visited an orphanage? If so, what were your impressions? Who is responsible for ensuring the quality of care of orphans in your microculture?* (Source: © Reuters/Will Burgess)

the lives of fostered children (Sanjek 1990). Child fostering in the neighborhood is common: About one-fourth of the children were foster children. Twice as many of the fostered children were girls as boys. School attendance is biased toward boys. All of the boys were attending school, but only four of the thirty-one girls were. An important factor affecting the treatment of the child is whether the fostered child is related to his or her sponsor. Although 80 percent of the fostered children as a whole were kin of their sponsors, only 50 percent of the girls were kin. People who sponsor nonkin girls make a cash payment to the girl's parents. These girls cook, do housecleaning, and assist in market work by carrying goods or watching the trading area. Fostered boys, most of whom are kin of their sponsors, do not perform such tasks because they attend school.

In villages of eastern Java, Indonesia, informal child fostering, or "borrowing," is common (Beattie 2002). The initiative for a child transfer, though, is not with the parents, but with the borrower. The borrower approaches the parents and tells them of a dream he or she had—of rescuing a child from a flood, for example. The parents have no choice but to lend their child. When a child is borrowed by nonkin, the arrangement is informal. The child takes turns spending time with both families, having a meal or nap here and there. When a kinsperson borrows a child, the arrangement is likely to be ritually

sealed. The new parents are renamed "mother" and "father," and the child calls the natural mother "elder sister." Whether or not a child is borrowed, all Javanese children have flexible living arrangements. They spend time in different houses, eating and sleeping wherever they feel at home.

Ritually Established Sharing Bonds   Ritually defined ties between adults and children born to other people are common among Christians, especially Catholics, worldwide. Relationships between godparents and godchildren often involve strong emotional ties and financial flows from the former to the latter. In Arembepe, a village in Bahia state in northeastern Brazil, children request a blessing from their godparents the first time they see them each day (Kottak 1992:61). Godparents give their godchildren cookies, candy, and money, and larger presents on special occasions.

Among the Maya of Oaxaca, Mexico (see Map 5.4, p. 128), godparenthood is both a sign of the sponsor's status and the means to increased status for the sponsor (Sault 1985). A parent's request that someone sponsor their child is a public acknowledgment of the sponsor's standing. The godparent gains influence over the godchild and can call on the godchild for labor. Being a godparent of many children means that the godparent can amass a large labor force when needed and gain further

marriage: a union between two people (usually), who are likely to be, but are not necessarily, co-resident, sexually involved with each other, and procreative.

incest taboo: a strongly held prohibition against marrying or having sex with particular kin.

status. Most godparents in Oaxaca are husband–wife couples, but many are women alone, a pattern that reflects the high status of Maya women.

Marriage

The third major basis for forming close interpersonal relationships is through marriage or other forms of "marriage-like" relationships, such as long-term cohabitation. This section focuses on marriage.

Toward a Definition   Anthropologists recognize that marriage exists in all cultures, though it may take different forms and serve different functions. What constitutes a cross-culturally valid definition of marriage is, however, open to debate. A standard definition from 1951 is now discredited: "Marriage is a union between a man and a woman such that children born to the woman are the recognized legitimate offspring of both parents" (Barnard and Good 1984:89). This definition says that the partners must be of different genders, and it implies that a child born outside a marriage is not socially recognized as legitimate. Exceptions exist to both these features cross-culturally. Same-gender marriages are legal in Denmark, Norway, and Holland. The legal status of same-gender marriage is still a matter of debate and disagreement throughout the United States and Canada.

In many cultures no distinction is made between legitimate and illegitimate children on the basis of whether they were born within a marriage. Women in the Caribbean region, for example, typically do not marry until later in life. Before that, a woman has sequential male partners with whom she bears children. None of her children is considered more or less "legitimate" than any other.

Jillian Armenante *(left)*, **actress on** *Judging Amy,* **and her bride, Alice Dodd, call friends and family after their marriage ceremony in City Hall, San Francisco, in 2004. The legality of same-sex marriage is a contentious issue in the United States.** ■ (Source: Deanne Fitzmaurice/ San Francisco Chronicle/CORBIS)

Other definitions of marriage focus on rights over the spouse's sexuality. But not all forms of marriage involve sexual relations; for example, the practice of *woman–woman marriage* exists among the Nuer of southern Sudan (see Map 16.7, p. 443) and some

THINKING OUTSIDE THE BOX   DO SOME RESEARCH on www.match.com to learn what cultural preferences people mention in their profiles.

other African groups (Evans-Pritchard 1951:108–109). In this type of marriage, a woman with economic means gives gifts to obtain a "wife," goes through the marriage rituals with her, and brings her into the residential compound just as a man would who married a woman. This wife contributes her productive labor to the household. The two women do not have a sexual relationship. Instead, the in-married woman will have sexual relations with a man. Her children, though, will belong to the compound into which she married.

The many practices that come under the heading of marriage make it impossible to find a definition that will fit all cases. One might accept the following as a working definition of **marriage**: a more or less stable union, usually between two people, who may be, but are not necessarily, co-residential, sexually involved with each other, and procreative with each other.

Selecting a Spouse   All cultures have preferences about whom one should and should not marry or with whom one should and should not have sexual intercourse. Sometimes these preferences are informal and implicit, and other times they are formal and explicit.

Rules of Exclusion

Some sort of **incest taboo**, or a rule prohibiting marriage or sexual intercourse between certain kinship relations, is one of the most basic and universal rules of exclusion. In his writings of the 1940s, Claude Lévi-Strauss dealt with the question of why all cultures have kinship systems. In his classic ethnological study, *The Elementary Structures of Kinship* (1969 [1949]), he argues that incest avoidance motivated men to exchange women between families (review the section on "Rights in People" in Chapter 4). This exchange, Lévi-Strauss says, is the foundation for social networks and social solidarity beyond the immediate group. Such networks promote trade between areas with different resources and peace through ties established by bride exchange. Genetic research suggests an alternative theory for universal incest taboos: Larger breeding pools help reduce the frequency of genetically transmitted conditions. Like the theory of Lévi-Strauss, the genetic theory is also functional. Each theory attributes the universal existence of incest taboos to their adaptive contribution, although in two different ways.

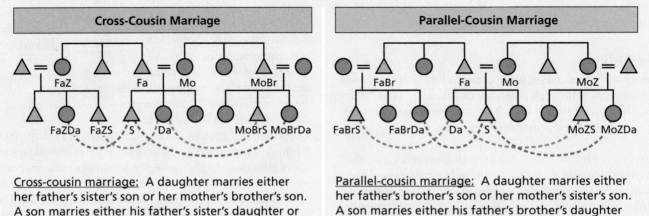

FIGURE 8.5 Two Major Types of Cousin Marriage

The most basic and universal form of incest taboo is against marriage or sexual intercourse between fathers and their children, and mothers and their children. In most cultures, brother–sister marriage has also been forbidden, but there are exceptions. The most well-known example of brother–sister marriage comes from Egypt at the time of the Roman Empire (Barnard and Good 1984:92). Brother–sister marriage was the norm among royalty. But the practice was common even among the general population, with between 15 and 20 percent of marriages between full brothers and sisters. Incest taboos do not universally rule out marriage with cousins. In fact, some kinship systems promote cousin marriage, as discussed next. Cousin marriage, like brother–sister marriage, builds tightly localized kin networks. In contrast, among the pastoralist Nuer of southern Sudan, the incest taboo includes all members of the patrilineage, which may be hundreds of people. This kind of incest taboo creates widely dispersed kinship networks.

Preference Rules

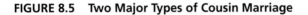

Many preference rules exist cross-culturally concerning whom one should marry. Rules of **endogamy**, or marriage within a particular group, stipulate that the spouse must be from a defined social category. In kin endogamy, cer-

tain relatives are preferred, often cousins. Two major forms of cousin marriage exist. One is marriage between **parallel cousins**, children of either one's father's brother or one's mother's sister—the term *parallel* indicates that the linking siblings are of the same gender (see Figure 8.5). The second is marriage between **cross-cousins**, children of either one's father's sister or one's mother's brother—the term *cross* indicates the different genders of the linking siblings. Parallel-cousin marriage is favored by many Muslim groups in the Middle East and northern Africa, especially the subform called *patrilateral parallel-cousin marriage,* which is cousin marriage into the father's line.

In contrast, Hindus of southern India favor *matrilateral cross-cousin marriage,* which is cousin marriage into the mother's line. Although cousin marriage is preferred, it nonetheless is a minority of all marriages in the region. A survey of several thousand couples in the city of Chennai (formerly called Madras) (see Map 8.5) in southern India showed that three-fourths of all marriages involved unrelated people, whereas one-fourth were between first cross-cousins or between uncle and niece, which is considered the same relationship as that of cross-cousins (Ramesh, Srikumari, and Sukumar 1989).

Readers who are unfamiliar with cousin marriage systems may find them objectionable on the basis of the

---

endogamy: marriage within a particular group or locality.
parallel cousin: offspring of either one's father's brother or one's mother's sister.
cross-cousin: offspring of either one's

father's sister or one's mother's brother.
exogamy: marriage outside a particular group or locality.
hypergyny: a marriage in which the groom is of higher status than the bride.

hypogyny: a marriage in which the bride is of higher status than the groom.
isogamy: marriage between status equals.

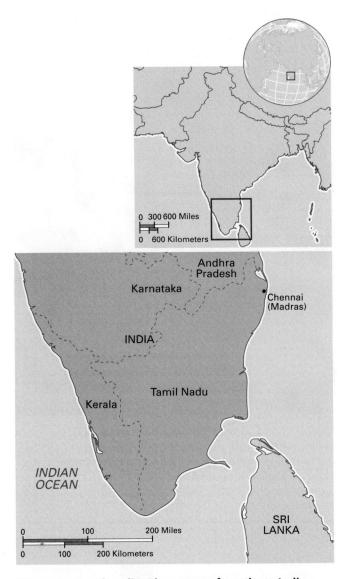

MAP 8.5 South India. The states of southern India, compared to the northern states, have lower population density, lower fertility rates, higher literacy rates, and less severe gender inequality. Agriculture is the mainstay of the region's economy and the population is predominantly rural. Industry, information technology, and business process outsourcing (BPO) are of increasing importance in cities such as Chennai and Bangalore.

potential genetic disabilities from close inbreeding. A study of thousands of such marriages in southern India, however, revealed only a small difference in rates of congenital problems compared to cultures in which cousin marriage is not practiced (Sundar Rao 1983). Marriage networks in South India are diffuse, extending over a wide area and offering many options for "cousins." This situation contrasts to the much more closed situation of a single village or town.

Endogamy may also be based on location. Village endogamy is preferred in the eastern Mediterranean among both Christians and Muslims. It is also the preferred pattern among Muslims throughout India and among Hindus of southern India. Hindus of northern India, in contrast, forbid village endogamy and consider it a form of incest. Instead, they practice village **exogamy**, or marriage outside a defined social group. For them, a spouse should live in a far-off village or town. In India, marriage distance is greater in the north than in the south, and northern brides are thus far less likely to be able to maintain regular contact with their birth family. Many songs and stories of northern Indian women convey sadness about being separated from their birth families.

Status considerations often shape spouse selection (see Figure 8.6). (The following discussion pertains to heterosexual marriage.) **Hypergyny**, or "marrying up," refers to a marriage in which the bride has lower status than the groom. Hypergyny is widely practiced in northern India, especially among upper-status groups. It is also prominent among many middle- and upper-class people in the United States. Women in top professions such as medicine and law have a difficult time finding an appropriate partner because there are few, if any, options for higher-status marriage partners. Women medical students in North America are experiencing an increased marriage squeeze because of status hypergyny. The opposite pattern is **hypogyny**, or "marrying down," a marriage in which the bride has higher status than the groom. Hypogyny is rare cross-culturally. **Isogamy**, marriage between partners who are status equals, occurs in cultures where male and female roles and status are equal.

Subtypes of status-based hypergyny and hypogyny occur on the basis of factors such as age and even height.

FIGURE 8.6 Status Considerations in Partner Selection (Heterosexual Pairing)

Hypergyny	The bride marries a groom of higher status.	The groom may be wealthier, more educated, older, taller.
Hypogyny	The bride marries a groom of lower status.	The bride may be wealthier, more educated, older, taller.
Isogamy	The bride and groom are status equals.	The bride and groom have similar wealth, education, age, height.

Men and women in Southeast Asia are similar in height and weight, as is the case with this couple from Bali, Indonesia. ■ *What are your cultural perceptions of the height of an ideal partner for you?* (Source: © Rick Smolan/Stock Boston, LLC)

The Taj Mahal, located in Agra, northern India, is a seventeenth-century monument to love. It was built by the Mughal emperor Shah Jahan as a tomb for his wife, Mumtaz Mahal, who died in childbirth in 1631. ■ *Name some other architectural monuments to love or marriage.* (Source: Jack Heaton)

Age hypergyny refers to a marriage in which the bride is younger than the groom, a common practice worldwide. In contrast, age hypogyny is a marriage in which the bride is older than the groom. Age hypogyny is rare cross-culturally but has been increasing in the United States due to the marriage squeeze on women who would otherwise prefer a husband of equal age or somewhat older.

Physical features, such as ability, looks, and appearance, are factors that may be explicitly or implicitly involved in spouse selection. Facial beauty, skin color, hair texture and length, height, and weight are variously defined as important. Height hypergyny (in which the groom is taller than the bride) is more common in male-dominated contexts. Height-isogamous marriages are common in cultures where gender roles are relatively equal and where *sexual dimorphism* (differences in shape and size of the female body compared to the male body) is not marked, as in much of Southeast Asia.

People with physical disabilities, particularly women, face constraints in marrying nondisabled partners (Sentumbwe 1995). Nayinda Sentumbwe, a blind researcher, conducted fieldwork with participants in education and rehabilitation programs for blind people in Uganda, central Africa. He realized that all of the married blind women in his study had blind spouses. Many of the married blind men had wives who were not blind. In exploring the reason for this pattern, Sentumbwe considered Ugandan gender roles, especially that of the housewife. People said that blindness decreases women's competence as wives and mothers and therefore reduces their desirability as spouses. Ugandan housewives have many roles: mother, hostess, housekeeper, keeper of the homestead, provider of meals, and provider of home-grown food, among others. Because a man wants a "competent" wife, blind women as partners are avoided. Ugandan men, however, often choose blind women as lovers. The relationship between lovers is private and does not involve social competence in the woman.

OUTSIDE THINKING THE BOX — WHAT IS your opinion about the relative merits of love marriages versus arranged marriages, and on what do you base your opinion?

The role of romantic love in spouse selection is debated by biological determinists and cultural constructionists. Biological determinists argue that feelings of romantic love are universal among all humans because they play an adaptive role in uniting males and females in care of offspring. Cultural constructionists, in contrast, argue that romantic love is an unusual factor influencing spouse selection (Barnard and Good 1984:94). The cultural constructionists point to variations in male and female economic roles to explain cross-cultural differences in the emphasis on romantic love. Romantic love is more likely to be an important factor in relationships in cultures where men contribute more to subsistence and where women are therefore economically dependent on men. Whatever the cause of romantic love, biological or cultural or both, it is an increasingly common basis for marriage in many cultures (Levine et al. 1995).

Within the United States, microcultural variations exist in the degree to which women value romantic love as a basis for marriage (Holland and Eisenhart 1990). One study interviewed young American women entering college from 1979 to 1981 and again in 1987 after they had graduated and begun their adult lives. The research sites were two southern colleges in the United States, one attended mainly by White Euro-Americans and the other by African Americans. A contrast between the groups of women emerged. The White women were much more influenced by notions of romantic love than the Black women. The White women were also less likely to have strong career goals and more likely to expect to be economically dependent on their spouse. The Black women expressed independence and strong career goals. The theme of romantic love supplies young White women with a model of the heroic male provider as the ideal, with her role being one of attracting him and providing the domestic context for their married life. The Black women were brought up to be more economically independent. This pattern is related to African traditions in which women earn and manage their own earnings and the racially discriminatory job market in the United States that places African American men at a severe disadvantage.

Arranged marriages are formed on the basis of parents' considerations of what constitutes a "good match" between the families of the bride and groom. Arranged marriages are common in many Middle Eastern, African, and Asian countries. Some theorists claim that arranged marriages are "traditional" and love marriages are "modern." They believe arranged marriages will disappear with modernity. Japan presents a case of an industrial/informatics economy with a highly educated population in which arranged unions still constitute a substantial proportion of all marriages, about 25 to 30 percent (Applbaum 1995). In earlier times, marriage partners would be found through personal networks, perhaps with the help of an intermediary who knew both families. Now, in large cities such as Tokyo and Osaka, professional matchmakers play an important role in finding marriage partners. The most important criteria for a spouse are the family's reputation and social standing, the absence of undesirable traits such as a case of divorce or mental illness in the family, education, occupation, and income.

The new billionaires of China (multimillionaires in terms of dollars) are men with wealth and interest in marrying a virgin woman (French 2006). They have turned to advertising to seek applications from prospective brides. In Shanghai, an enterprising lawyer began a business by managing the advertising and applicant screening for over fifty billionaires. On average, the process takes three months.

Marriage Gifts Most marriages are accompanied by exchanges of goods or services between the partners, members of their families, and friends (see Figure 8.7). The two major forms of marital exchanges cross-culturally are dowry and brideprice (defined in Chapter 5).

THINKING OUTSIDE THE BOX

IN YOUR MICROCULTURE, what are the prevailing ideas about wedding expenses and who should pay for them?

FIGURE 8.7 Major Types of Marriage Gifts and Exchanges

Dowry	Goods and money given by the bride's family to the married couple	European and Asian cultures; agriculturalists and industrialists
Groomprice	Goods and money given by the bride's family to the married couple and to the parents of the groom	South Asia, especially northern India
Brideprice	Goods and money given by the groom's family to the parents of the bride	Asian, African, and Central and South American cultures; horticulturalists and pastoralists
Brideservice	Labor given by the groom to the parents of the bride	Southeast Asian, Pacific, and Amazonian cultures; horticulturalists

Dowry is the transfer of goods, and sometimes money, from the bride's side to the new married couple for their use. The dowry includes household goods such as furniture, cooking utensils, and sometimes rights to a house. Dowry is the main form of marriage transfer in farming societies throughout Eurasia, from Western Europe through the northern Mediterranean and into China and India (Goody 1976). In northern India, dowry is more accurately termed *groomprice* because the goods and money pass not to the new couple but rather to the groom's family (Billig 1992). In China during the Mao era, the government considered dowry a sign of women's oppression and made it illegal. The practice of giving dowry in China has returned with increased personal wealth and consumerism, especially among the newly rich urban populations (Whyte 1993).

Brideprice, or bridewealth, is the transfer of goods or money from the groom's side to the bride's parents. It is more common in horticultural and pastoralist cultures. **Bride-service**, a subtype of brideprice, is a transfer of labor from the groom to his parents-in-law for a designated time period. It is still practiced in some horticultural societies, especially in the Amazon.

Many marriages involve gifts from both the bride's and the groom's side. For example, a typical pattern in the United States is that the groom's side is responsible for paying for the rehearsal dinner the night before the wedding, whereas the bride's side bears the costs of everything else.

Forms of Marriage

Cultural anthropologists distinguish two forms of marriage on the basis of the number of partners involved. **Monogamy** is marriage between two people—a male or female if the pair is heterosexual, or two people of the same gender in the case of a homosexual pair. Heterosexual monogamy is the most common form of marriage cross-culturally, and in many countries it is the only legal form of marriage.

Polygamy is marriage involving multiple spouses, a pattern allowed in many cultures (Murdock 1965 [1949]:24). Two forms of polygamous marriage exist. The more common of the two is **polygyny**, marriage of

Hausa dowry goods in Accra, Ghana. The most valuable part of a Hausa bride's dowry is the *kayan dak'i* ("things of the room"). It consists of bowls, pots, ornamental glass, and cookware which are conspicuously displayed in the bride's marital house so that the local women can get a sense of her worth. The bride's parents pay for these goods as well as other more utilitarian dowry goods such as everyday cooking utensils. ■ (Source: Deborah Pellow)

one man with more than one woman. **Polyandry,** or marriage between one woman and more than one man, is extremely rare. The only place where polyandry is prevalent is in the Himalayan region that includes parts of

---

bride-service: a form of marriage exchange in which the groom works for his father-in-law for a certain period of time before returning home with the bride.

monogamy: marriage between two people.

polygamy: marriage involving multiple spouses.

polygyny: marriage of one husband with more than one wife.

polyandry: marriage of one wife with more than one husband.

family: a group of people who consider themselves related through a form of kinship, such as descent, marriage, or sharing.

household: a group of people, who may or may not be related by kinship, who share living space.

nuclear household: a domestic unit con-taining one adult couple (married or partners), with or without children.

extended household: a co-residential group that comprises more than one parent-child unit.

stem household: a coresidential group that comprises only two married couples related through males, commonly found in East Asian cultures.

The woman on the lower right is part of a polyandrous marriage, which is still practiced among some Tibetan peoples. She is married to several brothers, two of whom stand behind her. The older man with the sash in the front row is her father-in-law. ■ *For people who have grown up in monogamous cultures, the daily dynamics of polyandry are difficult to imagine. Why do you think this is so?* (Source: © Thomas L. Kelly/Woodfin Camp & Associates)

Tibet, India, and Nepal. Nonpolyandrous people in the area look down on the people who practice polyandrous marriage as backward (Haddix McCay 2001).

Households and Domestic Life

In casual conversation, North Americans might use the words *family* and *household* interchangeably to refer to people who live together. Social scientists, however, propose a distinction between the two terms. A **family** is a group of people who consider themselves related through kinship. In North American English, the term includes both close or immediate relatives and more distant relatives. All members of a family do not necessarily live together or have strong bonds with one another.

A related term is the **household,** a person or persons who occupy a shared living space and who may or may not be related by kinship. Most households consist of members who are related through kinship, but an increasing number do not. An example of a nonkin household is a group of friends who live in the same apartment. A single person living alone also constitutes a household. This section of the chapter looks at household forms and organization cross-culturally and relationships between and among household members.

The Household: Variations on a Theme

This section considers three forms of households and the concept of household headship. The topic of female-headed households receives detailed attention because this pattern of headship is widely misunderstood.

Household Forms

Household organization is divided into types according to how many married adults are involved. The **nuclear household** (which many people call the nuclear family) is a domestic group that contains one adult couple (married or "partners"), with or without children. An **extended household** is a domestic group that contains more than one adult married couple. The couples may be related through the father–son line (making a *patrilineal extended household*) such as the Lims of Taiwan (see Figure 8.4 p. 207), through the mother–daughter line (a *matrilineal extended household*), or through sisters or brothers (a *collateral extended household*). Polygynous (multiple wives) and polyandrous (multiple husbands) households are *complex households*, domestic units in which one spouse lives with or near multiple partners and their children.

The precise cross-cultural distribution of these various types is not known, but some broad generalizations can be offered. First, nuclear households are found in all cultures but are the exclusive household type in about one-fourth of the world's cultures (Murdock 1965 [1949]:2). Extended households are the most important form in about one-half of all cultures. The distribution of these two household forms corresponds roughly with the modes of production (see Figure 8.3, p. 204). The nuclear form is most characteristic of economies at the two extremes of the continuum: in foraging groups and in industrialized/informatic societies. This pattern reflects the need for spatial mobility and flexibility in both modes of production. Extended households constitute a substantial proportion of households in horticultural, pastoralist, and farming economies.

In Japan, a subtype of the extended household structure has endured within the context of an industrial/postindustrial and urban economy. The *ie,* or **stem household,** is a variation of an extended household that contains two (and only two) married couples related through the male line. In it, only one son remains in the household, bringing in his wife, who is expected to perform the important role of caretaker for the husband's parents as they age. The ie is still widely preferred throughout much of East Asia, although it is increasingly difficult to achieve due to changing economic aspirations of children and lowered fertility rates. Aging parents find that none of their children is willing to live with them and take responsibility for their care. Some parents exert considerable pressure on an adult child to come and live with them (Traphagan 2000). A compromise is for an adult child

In China, the stem household system is changing because many people have one daughter and no son as a result of lowered fertility and the One-Child-Per-Family-Policy. ■ *Speculate about what the next generation of this household might contain.* (Source: © Keren Su/Stock Boston, LLC)

and his or her spouse to live near the parents but not with them.

Household Headship

The question of who heads a household is often difficult to answer. This section reviews some approaches to this question and provides insights into how cross-cultural perceptions about household headship differ.

The *head* is the primary person, or persons, responsible for supporting the household financially and making major decisions. This concept of household head is based on a Euro-American view that emphasizes the income contribution of the head who was traditionally a man. European colonialism spread the concept of the male, income-earning head of household around the world, along with laws that vested household authority in male headship.

The model of a male household head influences the way official statistics are gathered worldwide. If a household has a co-resident man and woman, there is a tendency to report the household as male headed. In Brazil, for example, the official definition of household head considers only a husband to be head of the household, regardless of whether he contributes to the household budget. Single, separated, or widowed women who are responsible for household support are deprived of the title of household head. If they happen to have a man visiting them on the day the census official arrives, he is considered to be the household head (de Athayde Figueiredo

and Prado 1989:41). Similarly, according to official reports, 90 percent of households in the Philippines are headed by males (Illo 1985). Philippino women, however, play a prominent role in income generation and budgetary control, and both partners share decision making. Thus co-headship would be a more appropriate label for many households in the Philippines and elsewhere.

Matrifocality refers to a household pattern in which a woman (or women) is the central, stable domestic figure around whom other members cluster (González 1970). In a matrifocal household, the mother is likely to be the primary or only income provider. The concept of matrifocality does not exclude the possibility that men may be part of the household, but they are not the central income providers or decision makers.

The number of woman-headed households is increasing worldwide, and these households are more likely to be poorer than other households. Most popular theories do not take into account ethnographic insights about the several possible causes of this form of household headship. A woman-headed household can come about if a partner never existed, if a partner existed at one time, but for some reason—such as separation, divorce, or death—is no longer part of the household, or if a partner exists but is not a co-resident because of migration, imprisonment, or some other form of separation. (Most thinking about woman-headed households assumes a heterosexual relationship and thus does not account for woman-headed households formed by a single woman with children either adopted or conceived through artificial

Members of a matrifocal household in rural Jamaica: two sisters and their children. ■ *What kind of household formation pattern is prevalent in your microcultural experience?* (Source: Barbara Miller)

---

matrifocality: a household system in which a female (or females) is the central, stable figure around whom other members cluster.

---

insemination, with or without a visiting woman partner.) Three prominent theories to account for the absence of a male spouse or partner (see Figure 8.8) are all "compensatory theories." They suggest that a woman-headed household emerges as a default system when "something is wrong" and men are unavailable as spouses. This view is based on the assumption that the heterosexual nuclear household is the normal and best pattern. Cultural anthropology suggests, instead, that a variety of household forms are to be expected, depending on such factors as men's and women's economic roles, especially access to work, wages, and the distribution of productive resources such as property. It is not simply the gender of the household head that is of importance in the healthy functioning of households. It has more to do with the resources that the head (or co-heads) has, both material and social, such as property ownership, a decent job, and living in a safe neighborhood.

Intrahousehold Dynamics

How do household members interact with each other? What are their emotional attachments, rights, and responsibilities? What are the power relationships between and among members of various categories, such as spouses, siblings, and those of different generations? Kinship systems define what the content of these relationships should be. In everyday life, people may conform more or less to the ideal. Cultural anthropologists have neglected the study of how household members enact or diverge from ideal roles and relationships on an everyday basis.

Spouse/Partner Relationships

This section discusses three areas of spousal relationships: marital satisfaction, sexual activity over the life course, and satisfaction within marriage and the "too good" wife in Japan.

A landmark sociological study of marriages in Tokyo in 1959 compared marital satisfaction of husbands and wives in love marriages and arranged marriages (Blood 1967). In all marriages, marital satisfaction declined over time, but differences between the two types emerged. The decline was greatest for wives in arranged marriages and least for husbands in arranged marriages. In love-match marriages, both partners' satisfaction dropped dramatically (a bit earlier for wives and a bit later for husbands), but both husbands and wives reported nearly equal levels of satisfaction after they had been married nine years or more.

Sexual activity of couples can be both an indication of marital satisfaction and a cause of marital satisfaction. Cultural anthropologists have not focused on gathering data about sexual intercourse frequency, but other social scientists have collected survey data. Analysis of reports of marital sex from a 1988 survey in the United States shows that frequency per month steadily declines with the duration of marriage, from an average of twelve times per month for people age 19 to 24, to less than once a month for people 75 years of age and older (Call, Sprecher, and Schwartz 1995). Older married people have sex less frequently. Less happy people have sex less frequently. Within each age category, sex is more frequent among three categories of people:

- Those who are cohabiting but not married
- Those who cohabited before marriage
- Those who are in their second or later marriage

In seeking to learn whether such decline is more widespread, an anthropologist and a statistician joined forces to analyze data from a survey conducted with over 90,000 women in 19 developing countries (Brewis and Meyer 2004). One of the survey questions was: When was the last time you had sexual intercourse (presumably with one's spouse)? The results were aggregated at the country level, which precludes the kind of localized information that cultural anthropologists prefer. Even at the country level, interesting findings emerged. Significant reductions in frequency over time occur in all countries except for Burkina Faso, West Africa. The honeymoon effect, of having more frequent sex in the first year of marriage, is significant in only five countries: Benin, Brazil, Ethiopia, Kazakhstan, and Mali. Burkina Faso couples have a significantly lower frequency of reported marital sex during the first year of marriage. These intriguing results need to be followed up by research on local cultural beliefs and practices related to marital sex.

Cultures everywhere define the proper role of a wife or husband. In Japan, a "good wife" should care for her husband's needs and make sure that any problems in the household do not erupt into the public domain (Borovoy 2005). Many Japanese salarymen consume substantial amounts of alcohol after work (review Chapter 6, p. 150). They return home late and drunk. It is the duty of the "good wife" to get the husband to eat something and go to bed, so that he can make it to work the next day. These wives face a profound cultural dilemma: If they continue to perform well the role of the "good wife," they are "codependent" in the husband's alcohol abuse, and are contributing to the problem. Many middle-class Japanese wives are joining support groups to help them deal with this dilemma and to build new roles for themselves beyond that of the "good wife."

Sibling Relationships

Sibling relationships are an understudied aspect of intrahousehold dynamics. Suad Joseph (1994) provides an example on this topic from her research in a working-class neighborhood of Beirut, Lebanon. She became friendly with several families and was especially close to

FIGURE 8.8   Households Headed by Women: Three Theories and Cultural Critique

1. The *slavery theory* says that the high frequency of woman-headed households among African Americans in the Western hemisphere is the heritage of slavery, which intentionally broke up marital ties. Problems with this theory are:

- The slave system denied legal standing to adult pairings because owners did not want their slaves committed to lifetime relationships, and wives and husbands were separated. These impositions were not accepted by the slaves and their descendants. Once freed, Black Americans sought to create durable unions they had been denied during slavery (Hacker 1992:69). Two-parent families were the norm among Black Americans following the Civil War through the mid-twentieth century.

- If slavery were the cause of woman-headed households, all slave-descendant groups would have this household form. But this is not the case. In Jamaica, which is populated mainly by descendants of African slaves, percentages of woman-headed households vary between rural and urban areas (Miller and Stone 1983). Likewise, in the United States, no generic "Black household" exists, just as there is no generic "White household."

- In the United States, percentages of woman-headed households during the twentieth century increased in roughly the same proportion among Blacks and Whites. Thus, similar factors may underlie the changes for both populations.

- The distribution of woman-headed households throughout the world is more widespread than the distribution of New World Colonial slavery.

2. According to the *poverty theory*, woman-headed households are adaptations to poverty. Problems with this theory are:

- Not all low-income populations worldwide have high rates of woman-headed households. Within the United States, significant ethnic differences exist: Low-income Chinese, Japanese, and other Asian peoples have low frequencies of woman-headed households. Many low-income Latino communities have dual-parent families (Pelto, Roman, and Liriano 1982:40). Poverty should be considered along with male and female income-earning options within the wider political economy.

- In the Caribbean region and throughout Latin America, the association between poverty and woman-headed households is strong. But underlying this association are some positive findings. In the Caribbean region, about one-third of all households have been woman-headed over the past few decades (Massiah 1983; Marcoux 2000). The

women have "visiting unions," involving a steady sexual relationship but separate residences. Many women commented that they sometimes expect and hope for financial support from their male partner or "baby father" (Massiah 1983). Many others emphasized the value they place on freedom from a husband or permanent partner. One woman said, "Being single fits in with my independent thinking" (1983:41). Another commented on her visiting union: "I like freedom, so I'm keeping it like it is."

3. According to the *unbalanced sex ratio theory*, woman-headed households occur in contexts of high male emigration or other situations causing a shortage of males. The sheer unavailability of partners limits marriage. This theory is the strongest of the three. The following case from Galicia, northwest Spain, is one example.

In Galicia, the local economy, inheritance rules, and household formation are related (Kelley 1991). This coastal region has long had a high percentage of households headed by unmarried women. In the village of Ezaro, about one-fourth of all baptisms in the latter half of the nineteenth century were born to unmarried women.

This proportion declined in the twentieth century, but the region is still distinctive. In Ezaro, households headed by unmarried mothers constitute over 10 percent of the total. Little or no stigma is attached to unwed motherhood in Galicia, in contrast to the generally high value that Mediterranean people place on marriage and male honor through control of the sexuality of female family members. In Ezaro, woman household heads often hold honored positions.

This unusual system is related to Galicia's high rates of male emigration. The scarcity of men promotes flexible attitudes toward women's roles. In Ezaro, women are in charge of agricultural work. They inherit land and gain prestige and power from owning and managing agricultural land: "Women's work is considered so critical to the prestige of the household in Ezaro that success at work is the single most important factor in the community's evaluation of a woman's character (and in her own self-evaluation). The good woman in Ezaro is the hardworking woman" (1983:572). Thus, a woman's work is more important than her marital status.

Inheritance practices in Galicia reflect the importance of women's agricultural work. The goal is to ensure continuity of the *casa*, the house, which includes both the physical structure and its members. Parents usually give one of their children a larger share of the inheritance, making that child the principal heir. Mothers often choose daughters, and thus a single woman can be head of an estate.

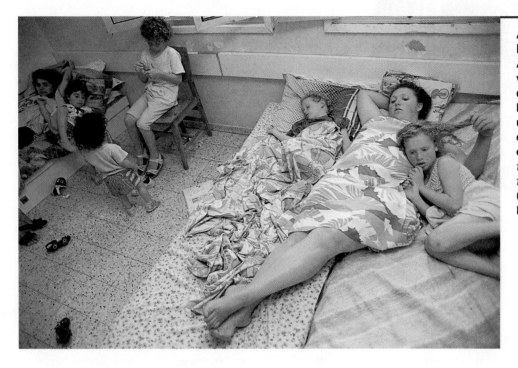

A shared bedroom in a battered woman's shelter, Tel Aviv, Israel. Many people wonder why abused women do not leave their abusers. Part of the answer lies in the unavailability and low quality of shelters throughout much of the world. ■ *What other factors might prevent women from leaving their abusers?* (Source: © David Wells/The Image Works)

Hanna, the oldest son in one of them. Hanna was an attractive young man, considered a good marriage choice, with friends across religious and ethnic groups. He seemed peace loving and conscientious. Therefore, the author reports, "I was shocked . . . one sunny afternoon to hear Hanna shouting at his sister Flaur and slapping her across the face" (1994:50). Aged 12, Flaur was the oldest daughter. "She seemed to have an opinion on most things, was never shy to speak her mind, and welcomed guests with boisterous laughter. . . . With a lively sense of humor and good-natured mischief about her, neighbors thought of her as a live wire" (1994:50). Further observation of the relationship between Hanna and Flaur suggested that Hanna was playing a fatherly role to Flaur. He was especially irritated with her if she lingered on the street near their apartment building, gossiping with other girls: "He would forcibly escort her upstairs to their apartment, slap her, and demand that she behave with dignity" (1994:51). Adults in the household thought nothing was wrong. They said that Flaur enjoyed her brother's aggressive attention. Flaur herself commented, "It doesn't even hurt when Hanna hits me." She said that she hoped to have a husband like Hanna.

An interpretation of this brother–sister relationship, common in Arab culture, is that it is part of a socialization process that maintains and perpetuates male domination in the household: "Hanna was teaching Flaur to accept male power in the name of love . . . loving his sister meant taking charge of her and that he could discipline her if his action was understood to be in her interest. Flaur was reinforced in learning that the love of a man could include that male's violent control and that to receive his love involved submission to control" (1994:52). This close and unequal sibling relationship persists throughout life. Even after marriage, a brother maintains a position of responsibility toward his sister and her children, as does a married sister toward her brother and his children. This loyalty can lead to conflict between husband and wife as they vie for support and resources from their spouse in competition with their siblings.

Domestic Violence

Domestic violence can occur between domestic partners, parents and children, and siblings. This section concerns the first of these. Violence between domestic partners, with males dominating as perpetrators and women as victims, seems to be found in nearly all cultures, although in varying forms and frequencies (J. Brown 1999). A cross-cultural review reveals that wife beating is more common and more severe in contexts where men control the wealth. It is less common and less severe where women's work groups exist (Levinson 1989). The presence of women's work groups is related to a greater importance of women in production and matrifocal residence. These factors provide women with the means to leave an abusive relationship. For example, among the Garifuna, an African-Indian people of Belize, Central America (see Map 7.2, p. 177), incidents of spouse abuse occur, but they are infrequent and not extended (Kerns 1999). Women's solidarity in this matrifocal society limits male violence against women.

Increased domestic violence worldwide throws into question the notion of the house as a refuge or place of

ETHNOGRAPHY FOR PREVENTING WIFE ABUSE IN RURAL KENTUCKY

Domestic violence in the United States is reportedly highest in the state of Kentucky. An ethnographic study of domestic violence in Kentucky revealed several cultural factors that are related to the high rate of wife abuse (Websdale 1995). The study included interviews with fifty abused wives in eastern Kentucky as well as with battered women in shelters, police officers, shelter employees, and social workers.

Three categories of isolation exist in rural Kentucky and make domestic violence particularly difficult to prevent:

- *Physical isolation:* The women reported a feeling of physical isolation in their lives. Abusers' tactics were more effective because of geographical isolation:

    The batterer's strategies, according to the women, included removing the phone from the receiver (for example, when leaving for work) . . .; locking the thermostat, especially in winter, as a form of torture; disabling motor vehicles to reduce or eliminate the possibility of her leaving the residence; destroying motor vehicles; closely monitoring the odometer reading on motor vehicles (a simple yet effective form of control due to the lack of alternative means of transportation); driving recklessly to intimidate his partner; discharging firearms in public (for example, at a battered woman's pet). (1995:106–107)

It is difficult to leave an abusive home located many miles from the nearest paved road, especially if the woman has children. No public transportation serves even the paved road. Nearly one-third of households had no phones. Getting to a phone to report abuse results in delay and gives police the impression that the call is less serious.

    Physical remoteness delays response time to calls for help and increases a woman's sense of hopelessness. Sheriffs have acquired a very poor reputation among battered women in the region for not attending domestic calls at all.

- *Social isolation:* Aspects of rural family life and gender roles lead to a system of "passive policing." In rural Kentucky, men are seen as providers and women are strongly tied to domestic work and child rearing. When women do work, their wages are about 50 per-

cent of men's wages. Residence is often in the vicinity of the husband's family, which creates isolation of a woman from the potential support of her natal family and restricts help seeking in the immediate vicinity because the husband's family is likely to be nonsupportive. Police officers, especially local ones, view the family as a private unit, a man's world. They are less inclined to intervene and arrest husbands whom they feel should be dominant in the family. In some instances, the police take the batterer's side, share the batterer's understandings of the situation, and have similar beliefs in a man's right to control his wife.

- *Institutional isolation:* Battered women in rural areas face special problems in using the limited services of the state. The fact that abused women often know the people who run the services ironically inhibits the women from approaching them, given values of family privacy. In addition, social services for battered women in Kentucky are scarce. Other institutional constraints include less schooling for rural women than urban women; lack of child-care centers to allow mothers the option to work outside the home; inadequate health services, with doctors appearing unfamiliar with domestic violence; and religious teaching of fundamentalist Christianity that supports patriarchal values, including the idea that it is women's duty to stay in a marriage, to "weather the storm."

The ethnographic findings suggest some recommendations. Most important is that women need more and better employment opportunities to reduce their economic dependency on abusive partners. To help address this need, rural outreach programs should be strengthened. Expanded telephone subscriptions would help decrease rural women's institutional isolation. Because of the complexity of the social situation in Kentucky, and the complicity of some law-enforcement personnel, no single solution will suffice.

FOOD FOR THOUGHT

- Think of some ways in which the structural conditions in Kentucky differ from or resemble those in another context where wife beating occurs.

security. In the United States, there is evidence of high and increasing rates of intrahousehold abuse of children (including sexual abuse), violence between spouses or partners, and abuse of aged family members. Anthropological research will help policy-makers and social workers better understand the factors affecting the safety of individuals within households and to be able to design more effective programs to promote personal safety (see Lessons Applied box).

Household Transformations

The composition and sheer existence of a particular household can change as a consequence of several factors, including divorce, death, and possible remarriage. This section reviews anthropological findings on these topics.

Divorce and Kinship Patterns   Divorce and separation, like marriage and other forms of long-term union, are cultural universals, even though they may be frowned on or forbidden. Marriages may break up for several reasons: The most common are voluntary separation and death of one of the partners. Globally, variations exist in the legality and propriety of divorce. Some religions, such as Roman Catholicism, prohibit divorce. In Muslim societies, divorce by law is easier for a husband to obtain than for a wife. Important research questions about marital dissolution include the causes for it, the reasons why divorce rates appear to be rising worldwide, and the implications for the welfare of children of divorced parents and other dependents.

One hypothesis for why divorce rates vary cross-culturally says that divorce rates will be lower in cultures with unilineal descent. In such cultures, a large descent group has control over and interests in offspring and control over in-marrying spouses due to their dependence (Barnard and Good 1984:119). Royal lineages, with their strong interests in maintaining the family line, are examples of groups especially unlikely to favor divorce, because divorce generally means losing control of offspring. In bilineal foraging societies, there is more flexibility in both marriage and divorce. The hypothesis, in general, appears to have some merit.

Another question is the effect of multiple spouses on divorce. A study in Nigeria, West Africa, found that two-wife arrangements are the most stable, whereas marriages involving three or more wives have the highest rates of disruption (Gage-Brandon 1992). Similar results come from an analysis of household break-up in a polyandrous group of Tibetan people living in northwestern Nepal (see Map 7.5, p. 193) (Haddix McCay 2001). Wealth of the household is an important factor affecting household stability, but the number of brothers is another strong factor. Polyandrous households comprising two brothers are far less likely to break up than those with four or more brothers. An additional factor, although more difficult to quantify, are the social support and networks that a brother has beyond the polyandrous household. Only with such social support will he be able to build a house and establish a separate household on his own.

Widow(er)hood   The position of a widow or widower carries altered responsibilities and rights. Women's position as widows is often marked symbolically. In Mediterranean cultures, a widow must wear modest, simple, and black-colored clothing, sometimes for the rest of her life. Her sexuality is supposed to be virtually dead. At the same time, her new "asexual" status allows her greater spatial freedom than before. She can go to public coffeehouses and taverns, something not done by women whose husbands are living.

Extreme restrictions on widows are recorded for parts of South Asia where social pressures on a widow enforce self-denial and self-deprivation, especially among the propertied class. A widow should wear a plain white sari, shave her head, eat little food, and live an asexual life. Many widows in India are abandoned, especially if they have no son to support them. They are considered polluting and inauspicious. Widows elsewhere experience symbolic and life-quality changes much more than do widowers. For example, in South Africa, a widower's body is not marked in any significant way except to have his head shaved. He is required to wear a black button or armband for about six months. A widow's body is marked by shaving her head, smearing a mixture of herbs and ground charcoal on her body, wearing black clothes made from an inexpensive material, and covering her face with a black veil and her shoulders with a black shawl. She may wear her clothes inside out, wear one shoe, eat with her left hand, or eat from a lid instead of a plate (Ramphele 1996:100).

Changing Kinship and Household Dynamics

This section provides examples of how marriage and household patterns are changing. Many of these changes have roots in colonialism whereas others are the result of recent changes effected by globalization.

Change in Descent

Matrilineal descent is declining worldwide as a result of both European colonialism and contemporary Western globalization. European colonial rule in Africa and Asia contributed to the decline in matrilineal kinship by registering land and other property in the names of assumed male heads of household, even where females were the heads (Boserup 1970). This process eroded women's previous rights and powers. Western missionaries contributed to transforming matrilineal cultures into patrilineal systems (Etienne and Leacock 1980). European colonial influences led to the decline of matrilineal kinship among Native North Americans. Before European colonialism, North America had one of the largest distributions of matrilineal descent worldwide, although not all Native North American groups were matrilineal. A comparative study of kinship among three reservation-based Navajo groups in Arizona shows that matrilineality is stronger where conditions most resemble the pre-reservation era (Levy, Henderson, and Andrews 1989). Among the Minangkabau of Indonesia (review Culturama, this chapter), three factors are related to the decline of matrilineal kinship (Blackwood 1995):

- Dutch colonialism promoted the image of male-headed nuclear families as an ideal.

- Islamic teachings idealize women as wives and men as household heads.

- The modernizing Indonesian state has a policy of naming males as household heads.

Change in Marriage

Although the institution of marriage in general remains prominent, many of its details are changing. New forms of communication are affecting ways of finding a potential partner and courtship. In a village in western Nepal (see Map 7.5, p. 193) people's stories of their marriages reveal that arranged marriages have decreased and elopement has increased since the 1990s. Through interviews with dozens of married women, Laura Ahern learned of the growing importance in the 1990s of love letters in establishing marital relationships (2001). Dating is not allowed, so sending love letters is how young people court. One woman offered to share a love letter from her husband and gave permission for it to be copied. Eventually, many other villagers did the same. Of the 200 letters Ahern collected, 170 were written by men and 30 by women. Typically, the man starts the correspondence. For example, one man's love letter contains the following lines: "I'm helpless and I have to make friends of a notebook and pen in order to place this helplessness before you. . . . I'll let you know by a 'short cut' what I want to say: Love is the union of two souls. The 'main' meaning of love is 'life success.' I'm offering you an invitation to love" (2001:3). Love letters became possible only in the 1990s because of increased literacy rates in the village. Literacy facilitated self-selected marriages and thus supported an increasing sense of personal agency among the younger people of the village.

Nearly everywhere, the age at first marriage is rising. The later age at marriage is related to increased emphasis on completing a certain number of years of education before marriage and to higher material aspirations such as being able to own a house. Marriages between people of different nations and ethnicities are increasing, partly because of growing rates of international migration. Migrants take with them many of their marriage and family practices. They also adapt to rules and practices in their area of destination. Pluralistic practices evolve, such as conducting two marriage ceremonies—one conforming to the "original" culture and the other the culture in the place of destination.

THINKING OUTSIDE THE BOX

WHAT FORMS of communication do young people use to "court" someone in your cultural world? How was it different in your parents' time?

Marriage crises are situations in which people who want to marry cannot do so for one reason or another. They appear to be more frequent now than in the past, at least as perceived and reported by young people in the so-called marriage market. Two examples illustrate variations in how a marriage crisis comes about and how it plays out for those caught up in it. In a town of about 38,000 in rural Niger, West Africa, the marriage crisis involves young men's inability to raise the necessary funds for the brideprice, and additional gifts to the bride's family (Masquelier 2005). Among these Muslim, Hausa-speaking people, called Mawri, marriage is the crucial ritual that changes a boy into a man. Typically, a prospective groom receives financial assistance from his kin and friends. In Niger, the economy has been declining for some time, and typical farm or other wages are worth less than they were in earlier times. Marriage costs for the groom have not declined, however—quite the opposite. Wealthy young men can afford to give a car to the bride's parents as a wedding gift. But most young Mawri men cannot afford such gifts and are caught in the marriage crisis. They remain sitting at home in their parents' house, something that only females do. The many young, marriage-age women who remain single gain a reputation of being immoral, as they occupy a new and suspect social space between girl and wife.

On the opposite side of the world, a case study of a marriage crisis for African American women in Syracuse, New York, reveals the role of state policies promoted by the government of President George W. Bush (Lane et al. 2004). The Bush government has earmarked millions of dollars to promote two-parent, heterosexual families. During the George W. Bush era an increasing number of African American men were imprisoned. Besides high rates of imprisonment, African American men die violent deaths at much higher rates than other ethnic populations. In Syracuse, a city of around 150,000 in postindustrial decline in central New York State, there are four African American women for every one African American man, compared to an equal ratio among Whites.

A newly married husband and wife and their relatives in front of a church in Seoul, Republic of Korea. ■ *How does this wedding group resemble or differ from a wedding you have attended?* (Source: © Noboro Komine/Photo Researchers, Inc.)

Given the strong preference for ethnic endogamous marriages, it is statistically impossible for many African American women to get married.

Weddings are important, culture-revealing events in themselves. Style changes in weddings worldwide abound. Factors of changes to consider are the ceremony, costs, appropriate clothing, and the possibility of a honeymoon. The globalization of Western-style "white weddings" promotes the adoption of many features familiar in the West: a white wedding gown for the bride, a multilayered wedding cake, and certain kinds of floral arrangements. What the bride and groom wear is an expression of their personal identity as well as the cultural identity of their families and larger social group. Clothing choice may reflect adherence to "traditional" values or may reject those in favor of more "modern" values. Euro-American trends are prominent worldwide. Throughout much of East and Southeast Asia, advertisements and upscale stores display the Western-style white wedding gown (but less so in India, where white clothing for women signifies widowhood and is inauspicious). On the other hand, resurgence of local styles is occurring in some contexts, such as in Morocco, where there is a trend for "modern" brides to wear a Berber costume (long robes and silver jewelry characteristic of the rural, mountain pastoralists) at one stage of the wedding ceremony.

Changing Households

Globalization is creating rapid change in household structure and intrahousehold dynamics. One assumption is that the frequency of extended households will decline with industrialization and urbanization and the frequency of nuclear households will rise. Given what this chapter mentioned earlier about the relationship between nuclear households and industrialism/informatics, it is highly possible that with the spread of this mode of production, nuclear households will increase, too.

This projection finds strong confirmation in the changes that have occurred in household structure among the Kelabit people of highland Borneo since the early 1990s (Amster 2000) (see Map 8.6). One Kelabit settlement was founded in 1963 near the Indonesian border. At the time, everyone lived in one longhouse with over twenty family units. It was a "modern" longhouse, thanks to roofing provided by the British army and the innovation of private sleeping areas. Like more traditional longhouses, though, it was an essentially egalitar-

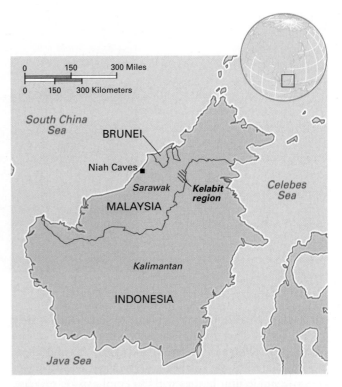

MAP 8.6   Kelabit Region in Malaysia. The Kelabit people's homeland is the Kelabit Highlands in Sarawak, a plateau ringed by mountain peaks that are forest-covered. One of Malaysia's smallest indigenous tribes, they number around 6,000 people, or 0.4 percent of Sarawak's population of 1.5 million, and .03 percent of Malaysia's total population of 22 million. Less than one-third of the Kelabit people live in the highlands.

A modern-style Kelabit longhouse built in the 1990s *(top)*. It is the home of six families who formerly lived in a twenty-family longhouse, seen in the background, which is being dismantled. Since the 1990s, houses built for a nuclear unit have proliferated in the highlands *(bottom)*. These houses stand on the site of a former multi-unit longhouse. ■ (Source: Matthew Amster)

ian living space within which individuals could freely move. Today, that longhouse is no more. Most of the young people have migrated to coastal towns and work in jobs related to the offshore oil industry. Most houses are now single-unit homes with an emphasis on privacy. The elders complain of a "bad silence" in the village. No one looks after visitors with the old style of hospitality. There is no longer one common longhouse for communal feasts and rituals.

International migration is another major cause of change in household formation and internal relationships (discussed further in Chapter 15). Dramatic reductions in fertility can occur in one generation when members of a farming household in, for example, Taiwan or Egypt, migrate to England, France, Canada, or the United States. Having many children makes economic sense in their homeland, but not in the new destination. Many such migrants decide to have only one or two children. They tend to live in small, isolated nuclear households. International migration creates new challenges for relationships between parents and children. The children often become strongly identified with the new culture and have little connection with their ancestral culture. This rupture creates anxiety for the parents and conflict between children and parents over issues such as dating, dress, and career goals.

In 1997, the people of Norway were confronted with a case of kidnapping of an 18-year-old Norwegian citizen named "Nadia" (Wikan 2000). Her parents took her to Morocco and held her captive there. The full story is complicated, but the core issues revolve around conflict between Moroccan and Norwegian family values. Nadia's parents felt that she should be under their control and that they had the right to arrange her marriage in Morocco. Nadia had a Norwegian concept of personal autonomy. In the end, Nadia and her parents returned to Norway, where the courts ruled that, for the sake of the family, the parents would not be jailed for kidnapping their daughter. The case brought stigma to Nadia among the Muslim community of Norway, who viewed her as a traitor to her culture. She now lives at a secret address and avoids publicity. An anthropologist close to this case who served as an expert cultural witness during the trial of her parents reports that, in spite of her seclusion, Nadia has offered help to other young women.

Change in everyday life in households is an understudied topic. Basic outlines of the near future in industrial/informatic societies point to the reduced economic dependence of women on men as wage earners and the possible decline of heterosexual marriage (Cherlin 1996: 478–480). These changes, in turn, will lead to increased movement away from nuclear household living and to increased diversity in household forms. During the second half of the twentieth century, household size in the United States shrank from an average of 3.2 in 1970 to 2.6 persons in 2000 (Fields and Casper 2000). The current situation contains several seemingly contradictory patterns first noted in the early 1980s by two sociologists (Cherlin and Furstenberg 1992 [1983]):

- The number of unmarried couples living together has more than tripled since 1970.
- One out of four children does not live with both parents.
- At current rates, half of all marriages in the United States made during the 1980s will end in divorce.

At the beginning of the twenty-first century, three kinds of households are most common in the United States: households composed of couples living in their first marriage, single-parent households, and households formed through remarriage. A new fourth category is the *multigenerational household,* in which an "adult child" (or "boomerang kid") lives with his or her parents. About one in three unmarried adults between the ages of 25 and 55 share a home with their mother or father or both (*Psychology Today* 1995 [28]:16). In the United States, adult offspring spend over 2 hours a day doing household chores, with adult daughters contributing about 17 hours a week and adult sons 14.4 hours. Daughters spend most of their time doing laundry, cooking, cleaning, and washing dishes. Sons are more involved in yard work and car care. Parents in multigenerational households still do three-quarters of the housework.

Kinship and household formation are certainly not dull or static. Just trying to keep up with changing patterns in North America is a daunting task, to say nothing of the challenge of keeping up with changes worldwide.

The Big Questions Revisited

HOW do cultures create kinship ties through descent, sharing, and marriage?

Key differences exist between unilineal and bilineal descent systems. Within unilineal systems, further important variations exist between patrilineal and matrilineal systems in terms of property inheritance, residence rules for married couples, and the relative status of males and females. Worldwide, unilineal systems are more common than bilineal systems. Within unilineal kinship systems, patrilineal kinship is more common than matrilineal kinship.

A second important basis for kinship is sharing. Sharing one's child with someone else through either informal or formal processes is probably a cultural universal. Sharing-based kinship is created through food transfers, including breastfeeding (in some cultures, children breastfed by the same woman are considered kin and cannot marry). Ritualized sharing creates kinship, as in the case of godparenthood.

The third basis for kinship is marriage, another universal factor, even though definitions of marriage may differ substantially. All cultures have rules of exclusion and preference rules for spouses.

WHAT is a household and what do anthropologists study about household life?

A household may consist of a single person living alone or may be a group comprising more than one person who may or may not be related by kinship; these individuals share a living space and, often, financial responsibilities for the household.

Nuclear households consist of a mother and father and their children, but they also can be just a husband and wife without children. Nuclear households are found in all cultures but are most common in foraging and indus-

trial societies. Extended households include more than one nuclear household. They are most commonly found in cultures with a unilineal kinship system. Stem households, which are most common in East Asia, are a variant of an extended household in which only one child, usually the first born, retains residence with the parents.

Household headship can be shared between two partners or can be borne by a single person, as in a woman-headed household. Study of intrahousehold dynamics between parents and children and among siblings reveals complex power relationships as well as security, sharing, and sometimes violence. Household break-up comes about through divorce, separation of cohabiting partners, or death of a spouse or partner.

HOW are kinship and households changing?

The increasingly connected world in which we live is having marked effects on kinship formation and household patterns and dynamics. Matrilineal systems have been declining in distribution since European colonialist expansion beginning in the 1500s.

Many aspects of marriage are changing, including a trend toward later age at marriage in many developing countries. Although marriage continues to be an important basis for the formation of nuclear and extended households, other options (such as cohabitation) are increasing in importance in many contexts, including urban areas in developed countries.

Contemporary changes in kinship and in household formation raise several serious questions for the future, perhaps most importantly about the care of dependent members such as children, the aged, and disabled people. As fertility rates decline and average household size shrinks, kinship-based entitlements to basic needs and emotional support disappear.

KEY CONCEPTS

SUGGESTED READINGS

Irwin Altman and Joseph Ginat, eds. *Polygynous Families in Contemporary Society.* Cambridge: Cambridge University Press, 1996. This book provides a detailed account of polygyny as practiced in two fundamentalist Mormon communities of Utah, one rural and the other urban.

Dorothy Ayers Counts, Judith K. Brown, and Jacquelyn C. Campbell, eds. *To Have and to Hit: Cultural Perspectives on Wife Beating.* Champaign/Urbana: University of Illinois Press, 1999. Chapters include an introductory overview, and cases from Australia, southern Africa, Papua New Guinea, India, Central America, the Middle East, and the Pacific.

Jamila Bargach. *Orphans of Islam: Family, Abandonment, and Secret Adoption in Morocco.* Lanham, MD: Rowman and Littlefield, 2002. According to Islam, adoption is not legal. Many Muslim childless couples, however, secretly adopt children and cover up their identity. Most adoptees are second-class members of their new families and cannot inherit property.

Amy Borovoy. *The Too-Good Wife: Alcohol, Codependency, and the Politics of Nurturance in Postwar Japan.* Berkeley: University of California Press, 2005. This book explores the experiences of middle-class women in Tokyo who participated in a weekly support meeting for families of substance abusers. The women attempt to cope with their husbands' alcoholism while facing the dilemma that being a good wife may be part of the problem.

Deborah R. Connolly. *Homeless Mothers: Face to Face with Women and Poverty.* Minneapolis: University of Minnesota Press, 2000. Poor, White women on the margin of mainstream society in Portland, Oregon, describe how they attempt to be good mothers with no money, no home, and no help.

Helen Bradley Foster and Donald Clay Johnson, eds. *Wedding Dress across Cultures.* New York: Berg, 2003. Chapters examine the evolution and ritual functions of wedding attire in cultures such as urban Japan, First Peoples of Alaska, Swaziland, Morocco, Greece, and the Andes.

Sara L. Friedman. *Intimate Politics: Marriage, the Market, and State Power in Southeastern China.* Cambridge, MA: Harvard University Press, 2006. Village culture along China's southeastern coast is distinct from mainstream Han culture. Women have much autonomy, are important in production, and have strong networks with other women. This woman-centered culture conflicts with official state reforms.

Jennifer Hirsch. *A Courtship after Marriage: Sexuality and Love in Mexican Transnational Marriages.* Berkeley: University of California Press, 2003. This study uses an innovative method of pairing thirteen migrant women living in Atlanta, Georgia, with thirteen nonmigrant counterparts in two rural towns in Mexico to learn about marriage and life within marriage.

Suad Joseph, ed. *Intimate Selving in Arab Families: Gender, Self, and Identity.* Syracuse, NY: Syracuse University Press, 1999. Chapters discuss family life and relationships in Arab culture with attention to connectivity, gender inequality, and the self. Case studies are from Lebanon and Egypt.

Laurel Kendall. *Getting Married in Korea: Of Gender, Morality and Modernity.* Berkeley: University of California, 1996. This book examines preferences about desirable spouses, matchmaking, marriage ceremonies and their financing, and the effect of women's changing work roles on their marital aspirations.

Judith S. Modell. *A Sealed and Secret Kinship: The Culture of Policies and Practices in American Adoption.* New York: Bergahn Books, 2002. This book presents examples of parents, children, kin, and nonkin of adoptive families in the United States. The author addresses adoption reform, adoptee experiences of searching for their birth parents, and changes in welfare policy.

Ellen Oxfeld. *Blood, Sweat, and Mahjong: Family and Enterprise in an Overseas Chinese Community.* Ithaca, NY: Cornell University Press, 1993. Situated in Calcutta, this ethnography provides insights about a Chinese family business and how it is organized.

Richard Parkin and Linda Stone, eds. *Kinship and Family: An Anthropological Reader.* Oxford, England: Blackwell Publishing, 2004. This collection traces the history of the anthropological study of kinship from the early 1900s to the present. It includes classical and contemporary works and situates them all in the context of major theoretical debates.

Sulamith Heins Potter. *Family Life in a Northern Thai Village: A Structural Study in the Significance of Women.* Berkeley: University of California Press, 1977. This ethnography of matrifocal family life in rural Thailand focuses on work roles, rituals, and intrafamily relationships.

Margaret Trawick. *Notes on Love in a Tamil Family.* Berkeley: University of California Press, 1992. This reflexive ethnography takes a close look at the daily dynamics of kinship in one Tamil (South Indian) family. Attention is given to sibling relationships, the role of older people, children's lives, and love and affection.

Toby Alice Volkman, ed. *Cultures of Transnational Adoption.* Durham, NC: Duke University Press, 2005. Chapters discuss Korean adoptees as a global family, transational adoption in North America, shared parenthood among low-income people in Brazil, and representations of "waiting children."

9

Social Groups and Social Stratification

The Big Questions

- WHAT is the range of cross-cultural variation of social groups?

- WHAT is social stratification, and what are its effects on people?

- WHAT is civil society?

A young woman of the Kabylie people, a Berber group of Algeria, wears a headband that signifies mourning during a public march to protest the government's denial of human rights to the Kabylie people. *(Source: © Tiz/CORBIS SYGMA)*

In the early 1800s, when French political philosopher Alexis de Tocqueville visited the United States and characterized it as a "nation of joiners," he implied that people in some cultures are more likely to join groups than others. The questions of what motivates people to join groups, what holds people together in groups, and how groups deal with leadership and participation have intrigued scholars in many fields for centuries.

This chapter focuses on nonkin groups and microculture formation. Chapter 1 defined several factors related to microcultures: class, "race," ethnicity, gender, age, region, and institutions such as prisons and retirement homes. So far, chapters in this book have discussed how microcultures affect fieldwork and how they vary in different economies and reproductive and kinship systems. This chapter looks at how they relate to group identity and structure and the relationships among different groups in terms of hierarchy and power. It first examines a variety of social groups ranging from small scale to large scale and then considers inequalities among social groups.

Social Groups

A **social group** is a cluster of people beyond the domestic unit who are usually related on grounds other than kinship, although kinship relationships may exist between people in the group. Two basic categories exist: the **primary group**, consisting of people who interact with each other and know each other personally, and the **secondary group**, consisting of people who identify with each other on some common ground but who may never meet with one another or interact with each other personally.

Members of all social groups have a sense of rights and responsibilities in relation to the group which, if not maintained, could mean loss of membership. Because of its face-to-face nature, membership in a primary group involves more direct accountability about rights and responsibilities than secondary group membership. When discussing different kinds of groups, social scientists also draw a distinction between *informal groups* and *formal groups* (March and Taqqu 1986:5):

- Informal groups are smaller and less visible.

- Members of informal groups have close, face-to-face relationships with one another; members of formal groups may or may not know each other.

- Organizational structure is less hierarchical in informal groups.

- Informal groups do not have legal recognition.

Modes of economies affect the formation of social groups, the greatest variety being found in agricultural and industrial/informatics societies (see Figure 9.1). One theory suggests that mobile populations, such as foragers and pastoralists, are less likely to develop enduring social groups beyond kin relationships. Although foragers and pastoralists have less variety of social groups, they do not completely lack social groupings. A prominent form of social group among foragers and pastoralists is an age set, a group of people close in age who go through certain rituals, such as circumcision, at the same time.

A related hypothesis is that settled and densely populated areas will have more social groups as a way to organize society. Again, this may be generally true, but important variations exist. Both informal and formal groups appear to be varied and active in Africa, Latin America, and Southeast Asia, but less so in South Asia (Uphoff and Esman 1984). In Bangladesh (see Map 9.1), a densely populated and agrarian country of South Asia, indigenous social groups are rare. The most prominent ties beyond the immediate household are kinship based (Miller and Khan 1986). In spite of the lack of indigenous social groups, however, Bangladesh has gained world renown for its success in forming local credit groups through an organization called the Grameen Bank, which gives loans to poor people to help them start small businesses.

In northern Thailand's Chiangmai region (see Map 6.4, p. 163), in contrast, many longstanding social groups exist (Potter 1976). The village, as a group, supports the Buddhist temple, the temple library, the monastery and school, irrigation canals, the cremation grounds, and the village roads. Within this overall structure, several more formal and focused groups exist: the temple committee that arranges festivals; the school committee; the Young People's Club (youth from about the age of 15 until their marriage who assist at village ceremonial functions); the village dancers (about a dozen young, unmarried women who host intervillage affairs); the funeral society (which provides financial aid for funeral services); neighborhood groups that take turns sending food to the temple for the monks; and irrigation work groups. The reasons why some cultures have strong and enduring social groups and others do not await further exploration.

The following sections describe a wide variety of social groups starting with the most face-to-face, primary

---

social group: a cluster of people beyond the domestic unit who are usually related on grounds other than kinship.

primary group: a social group in which members meet on a face-to-face basis.

secondary group: people who identify with each other on some basis but may never meet with one another personally.

FIGURE 9.1 Modes of Social Organization

Foraging	Horticulture	Pastoralism	Agriculture	Industrialism/Informatics
Characteristics Informal and primary Egalitarian structure Ties based on balanced exchange		Ritual ties	**Formal and secondary** Recognized leadership Dues and fees	**Characteristics**
Functions Companionship			Special purposes Work, war, lobbying government	**Functions**

Types of Social Groups
Friendship
	Friendship
	Age-based work groups
	Gender-based work groups
			Friendship
			Status Groups:
			  Class, race, ethnicity, caste, age, gender
			Institutional Groups:
			  Prisons, retirement homes
			Quasi-Political Groups:
			  Human rights, environmental groups
				Types of Social Groups
				Friendship
				Urban youth gangs
				Clubs, associations

groups of two or three people based on friendship. The discussion moves to larger and more formal groups with explicit goals, such as countercultural groups and activist groups.

MAP 9.1 Bangladesh. The People's Republic of Bangladesh is located on a deltaic floodplain with rich soil but also serious risk of flooding. One of the world's most densely populated countries, its nearly 150 million people live in an area about the size of the state of Wisconsin. Bangladesh is the third-largest Muslim majority country.

Friendship

Friendship refers to close social ties between at least two people that are informal, are voluntary, and involve personal, face-to-face interaction. Generally, friendship involves people who are nonkin, but in some cases kin are also friends (recall the Tory Islanders discussed in Chapter 8). Friendship fits in the category of a primary social group. One question that cultural anthropologists ask is whether friendship is a cultural universal. Two factors make it difficult to answer this question. First, insufficient cross-cultural research exists to answer the question definitively. Second, defining friendship cross-culturally is problematic. It is likely, however, that something like "friendship" is a cultural universal but shaped in different degrees from culture to culture (see Everyday Anthropology box).

Social Characteristics of Friendship

People choose their friends and friends remain so on a voluntary basis. Even so, the criteria for who qualifies as a friend may be culturally structured. For instance, gender segregation may prevent cross-gender friendships and promote same-gender friendships, and racial segregation limits cross–"race" friendships. Another characteristic of friendship is that friends are supportive of each other, psychologically and sometimes materially. Support is mutual, shared back and forth in an expectable way (as

THINKING OUTSIDE THE BOX

WHAT CATEGORIES of friends do you have? Are some kinds of friends "closer" or "truer" than others, and if so, why?

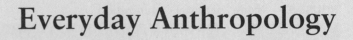

MAKING FRIENDS

People's activities often provide a shared interest that supports the development of friendship ties. In Andalucia, southern Spain (see Map 2.5, p. 51), the gender division of labor means that men and women pursue separate kinds of work and thus have differing friendship patterns (Uhl 1991). Men's work takes place outside the house and neighborhood either in the fields or in manufacturing jobs. Women devote most of their time to unpaid household work within the domestic domain. This dichotomy is somewhat fluid, however, as women's domestic roles sometimes take them to the market or the town hall.

For men, an important category of friend is an *amigo*, a friend with whom one casually interacts. This kind of friendship is acted out and maintained in the context of bars, drinking together night after night. Bars are a

man's world. Amigos share common experiences of school, sports and hobbies, and working together. In contrast, women refer to their friends either with kin terms or as *vecina*, "neighbor," reflecting women's primary orientation to family and neighborhood.

Differences between men and women also emerge in the category of *amigos(as) del verdad*, or "true friends." True friends are those with whom one shares secrets without fear of betrayal. Most men have many more true friends than the women do, a pattern that reflects their wider social networks.

FOOD FOR THOUGHT

- What different categories of friends do you have? Are some kinds of friends "closer" or "truer" than others?

in balanced exchange, see Chapter 4). Friendship generally occurs between social equals, although there are exceptions, such as friendships between older and younger people, a supervisor and a staff worker, or a teacher and a student.

Sharing stories is often a basis of friendship groups. In a study of male peer groups focused on interactions in rumshops in Guyana, South America (see Map 9.2), Indo-Guyanese men who have known each other since childhood reaffirm their solidarity through spending time, every day, at the rumshop eating, drinking, and regaling each other with stories (Sidnell 2000). Through shared storytelling about village history and other aspects of local knowledge, men display their equality with each other. The pattern of storytelling, referred to as "turn-at-talk," in which efforts are made to include everyone as a storyteller in turn, also serves to maintain equality and solidarity. These friendship groups are tightly knit, and the members can call on one another for economic, social, political, and ritual help.

Cell phone use among low-income people in Jamaica has wide use for "linking up," or creating extensive networks that include close friends, possible future sexual partners, and members of one's church (Horst and Miller 2005). Phone numbers of kin are also prominent on people's cell phone number lists. Participant observation and interviews with a sample of both rural and urban Jamaicans reveals that cell phone use is frequent, and Jamaicans are keenly aware of their call lists and how often they have kept in touch with the many individuals

on their lists. By linking up periodically with people on their lists, low-income Jamaicans maintain friendship and other ties with people who they can call on when they need support. Cell phones allow a more extensive network of friends and other contacts than was previously possible.

Friendships in Prison

Prisons, like colleges and universities, are social institutions with limited populations among whom friendship relationships may develop. In the case of colleges and universities, people are there voluntarily and have a good idea about how long they will be there. It makes sense to form enduring bonds with friends and classmates. In the context of prisons, people are not there voluntarily, and the formation of social ties is limited.

One factor that affects the formation of friendship in prisons is the duration of the sentence. A study that explored this issue first had to deal with the difficulty of doing participant observation. A research team of two people included an "insider" and an "outsider" (Schmid and Jones 1993). The "insider" was an inmate serving a short-term sentence who did participant observation, conducted interviews, and kept a journal. The "outsider," a sociologist, met with this inmate weekly to discuss findings (he also did the analysis). The inmate researcher was a male, so this study deals only with male prisoners. Furthermore, because his was a short-term sentence, the study's findings concern the effects of short-term sen-

MAP 9.2 Caribbean Countries of South America. The ethnically and linguistically diverse countries of the Caribbean region of South America include Guyana, Suriname, and French Guiana. Guyana (pronounced GAI-a-na), or the Co-operative Republic of Guyana, is the only South American country whose official language is English. Other languages are Hindi, Wai Wai, and Arawak. Its population is around 800,000. The Republiek Suriname, or Surinam, was formerly a colony of the Netherlands and is the smallest independent state in South America. Its population is 440,000. Dutch is the official language but most Surinamese also speak Sranang Tongo, or Surinaams, a mixture of Dutch, English Portuguese, French, and local languages. French Guiana is an overseas department of France and is thus part of the European Union. The smallest political unit in South America, its population is 200,000. Its official language is French but several other languages are spoken, including indigenous Arawak and Carib.

tencing (of one or two years) on social relationships among inmates.

Three stages of short-term inmate adaptation are typical. First, inmates experience uncertainty and fear based on their images of what life is like in prison. They avoid contact with other prisoners and guards as much as possible. The next stage involves the creation of a survival niche. The prisoner has selective interactions with other inmates and may develop a "partnership" with another inmate. Partners hang around together and watch out for each other. In the third phase, the prisoner anticipates his eventual release, transfers to a minimum security area, increases contact with outside visitors, and begins the transition to the outside. In this stage, partners begin to detach from each other as one of the pair moves toward the outside world.

Friendship among the Urban Poor

Carol Stack's study of how friendship networks promote economic survival among low-income, urban African Americans is a landmark contribution (1974). She conducted fieldwork in the late 1960s in "The Flats," the poorest section of a Black community in a large, midwestern city. She found extensive networks of friends "supporting, reinforcing each other—devising schemes for self help, strategies for survival in a community of severe economic deprivation" (1974:28). Close friends, are referred to by kin terms.

People in the Flats, especially women, maintain a set of friends through exchange: "swapping" goods (food, clothing) needed by someone at a particular time, sharing "child keeping," and giving or lending food stamps

and money. Such exchanges are part of a clearly understood pattern—gifts and favors go back and forth over time. Friends thus bound together are obligated to each another and can call on each other in time of need. In opposition to theories that suggest the breakdown of social relationships among the very poor, this research documents how poor people strategize and cope through social ties.

In a low-income neighborhood in Rio de Janeiro, Brazil, men play dominoes and drink beer while others observe. ■ *Discuss a comparable scene of female leisure activities in your microcultural experience.* (Source: © Stephanie Maze/Woodfin Camp & Associates)

Clubs and Fraternities

Clubs and *fraternities* are social groups that define membership in terms of a sense of shared identity and objectives. They may comprise people of the same ethnic heritage (such as the Daughters of the American Revolution in the United States), occupation or business, religion, or gender. Although many clubs appear to exist primarily to serve functions of sociability and psychological support, deeper analysis often shows that these groups have economic and political roles as well.

Women's clubs in a lower-class neighborhood in Paramaribo, Suriname (see Map 9.2), have multiple functions (Brana-Shute 1976). Here, as is common elsewhere in Latin America, clubs raise funds to sponsor special events and support individual celebrations, meet personal financial needs, and send cards and flowers for funerals. Members attend each other's birthday parties and death rites as a group. The clubs thus offer the women psychological support, entertainment, and financial help. A political aspect exists, too. Club members often belong to the same political party and attend political rallies and events together. These women constitute political interest groups that can influence political outcomes. Politicians and party workers confirmed that real pressure is exerted on them by women individually and in groups.

College fraternities and sororities are highly selective groups that serve a variety of explicit functions, such as entertainment and social service. They also form bonds between members that may help in securing jobs after graduation. Few anthropologists have studied the "Greek system" on U.S. campuses. One exception is Peggy Sanday, who was inspired to study college fraternities after the gang rape of a woman student by several fraternity brothers at the campus where she teaches. In her book, *Fraternity Gang Rape: Sex, Brotherhood, and Privilege on Campus* (1990), she explores initiation rituals; the role of pornography, ritual dances, and heavy drinking at parties; and how they are related to a pattern of male bonding solidified by victimization and ridicule of women. Gang rape, or a "train," is a prevalent practice in some, not all, fraternities. Fraternity party invitations may hint at the possibility of a "train." Typically, the brothers seek out a "party girl"—a somewhat vulnerable young woman who may be especially needy of acceptance or especially high on alcohol or other substances (her drinks may even have been "spiked"). They take her to one of the brother's rooms, where she may or may not agree to have sex with one man—often she passes out. Then a "train" of men have sex with her. Rarely prosecuted, the male participants reinforce their sense of privilege, power, and unity with one another through this group ritual involving abuse of a female outsider.

Members of a fraternity at the University of Texas at Austin engage in public service by planting trees at an elementary school. ■ *What knowledge do you have of the positive and negative social aspects of college fraternities and sororities? How could anthropological research provide a clearer picture?* (Source: © Bob Daemmrich/Stock Boston, LLC)

Cross-culturally, men's clubs in which strong male–male bonds are created and reinforced by the objectification and mistreatment of women are common, but not universal. They are especially associated with cultures where male–male competitiveness is an important feature of society (Bird 1996) and in which warfare and group conflict are frequent. In many indigenous Amazonian groups, the men's house is fiercely guarded from being entered by women. If a woman trespasses on male territory, she is punished by gang rape. One interpretation is that men have a high degree of anxiety about their identity as fierce warriors and as sexually potent males (Gregor 1982). Maintaining their identity as fierce and forbidding toward outsiders involves taking an aggressive position in relation to women of their own group.

As far as is known, women do not tend to form androphobic ("man-hating" or otherwise anti-male) clubs, the logical parallels of gynophobic ("woman-hating" or otherwise anti-female) men's clubs. College sororities are not mirror images of college fraternities. They may involve sometimes psychologically brutal hazing of new members, but they do not involve abusive behavior toward men. Women's groups and organizations, even if vocally anti-male, do not involve physical abuse of males.

Countercultural Groups

Several kinds of groups comprise people who, for one reason or another, are outside the "mainstream" of society and resist conforming to the dominant cultural pat-

---

youth gang: a group of young people, found mainly in urban areas, who are often considered a social problem by adults and law enforcement officials.

A participant in the annual gathering of U.S. bikers in Washington, DC, July 2005. Bikers share a sense of identity based on a particular lifestyle and mode of transportation, but many subgroups exist with distinct values and symbols ■ (Source: Mark L. Weiss)

tern, as in the so-called hippie movement of the 1960s. This section considers examples of countercultural groups. One similarity among these groups, as with clubs and fraternities, is the importance of bonding through shared initiation and other rituals.

Youth Gangs

The term *gang* can refer to a variety of groups, such as one's friends, as in "I think I'll invite the gang over for pizza" (Short 1996:325). The more specific term **youth gang** refers to a group of young people, found mainly in urban areas, who are often considered a social problem by adults and law enforcement officials (Sanders 1994: 5–15).

Youth gangs vary in terms of how formally they are organized. Gangs—like clubs and fraternities—often have a recognized leader, formalized rituals of initiation for new members, and symbolic markers of identity such as tattoos or special clothing. An example of an informal youth gang with no formal leadership hierarchy or initiation rituals is that of the "Masta Liu" in Honiara, the capital city of the Solomon Islands in the South Pacific (Jourdan 1995) (see Map 9.3). The primary unifying feature of the male youth who become Masta Liu is the fact that they are unemployed. Most have migrated to the city from the countryside to escape what they consider an undesirable lifestyle there: working in the fields under control of their elders. Some liu live with extended kin in the city; others organize liu-only households. They spend their time wandering around town (*wakabaot*) in groups of up to ten: "They stop at every shop on their way, eager to look at the merchandise but afraid to be kicked out by the secu-

rity guards; they check out all the cinemas only to dream in front of the preview posters ... not even having the $2 bill that will allow them to get in; they gaze for hours on end, and without moving, at the electronic equipment displayed in the Chinese shops, without saying a word: one can read in their gaze the silent dreams they create" (1995:210).

Street gangs are a more formal variety of youth gang. They generally have leaders and a hierarchy of membership roles and responsibilities. They are named, and their members mark their identity with tattoos or "colors." Much popular thinking associates street gangs with violence, but not all are involved in violence. An anthropologist who did research among nearly forty street gangs in New York, Los Angeles, and Boston learned much about why individuals join gangs, providing insights that also contradict popular thinking (Jankowski 1991). One common perception is that young boys join gangs because they are from homes with no male authority figure with whom they could identify. In the gangs studied, about half of the gang members were from intact nuclear households. Another common perception is that the gang replaces a missing feeling of family. This study showed that the same number of gang members reported having close family ties as those who did not.

What, then, might be the reasons why someone joins an urban gang? The research revealed that many gang members had a particular personality type called a

> **THINKING OUTSIDE THE BOX**
>
> THINK OF some examples in which socially excluded groups have contributed to changing styles of music, dress, and other forms of expressive culture of so-called mainstream groups.

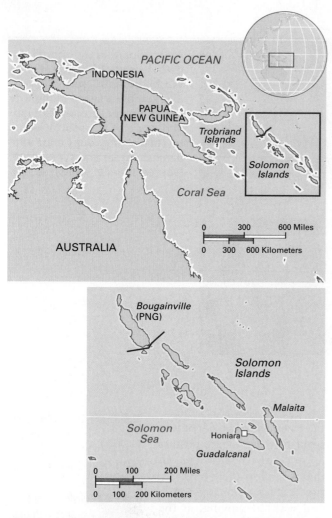

MAP 9.3 The Solomon Islands. This country consists of nearly 1,000 islands. Its capital, Honiara, is located on the island of Guadalcanal. The Solomons were the site of some of the bitterest fighting during World War II. Most of the people earn a living through small-scale farming and fishing. Commercial exploitation of local timber has led to severe deforestation. The population is 540,000. Over seventy languages are spoken, and four have recently gone extinct. The majority of the people are Christian, mainly Anglican.

Members of the gang "18" in San Salvador, El Salvador, passing time on the street. The group's leader prohibits the use of alcohol and drugs except on Saturdays and Sundays. ■ *Consider how the social life of gangs worldwide is affected by contemporary globalization.* (Source: © Jerome Sessini/In Visu/CORBIS)

defiant individualist. The defiant individualist type has five traits: intense competitiveness, mistrust or wariness, self-reliance, social isolation, and a strong survival instinct. A structurist view suggests that poverty, especially urban poverty, leads to the development of this kind of personality structure. Within the context of urban poverty, such a personality structure becomes a reasonable response to the prevailing economic obstacles and uncertainty.

In terms of explaining the global spread of urban youth gangs, structurists point to global economic changes in urban employment opportunities. In many countries, the declining urban industrial base has created persistent poverty in inner-city communities (Short

1996:326). At the same time, aspirations for a better life have been promoted through schooling and the popular media. Urban gang members, in this view, are the victims of large structural forces beyond their control. Research with gang members shows that they are not passive victims of structural forces, however: Many of these youth want to be economically successful, but social conditions channel their interests and skills into illegal pursuits rather than into legal pathways to achievement.

Body Modification Groups

One of the many countercultural movements in the United States includes people who have a sense of community strengthened through forms of body alteration. James Myers (1992) did research in California among people who feel they are a special group because of their interest in permanent body modification, especially genital piercing, branding, and cutting. Fieldwork involved participant observation and interviews. Myers was involved in six workshops organized especially for the San Francisco SM (sadomasochist) community; he attended the Fifth Annual Living in Leather Convention held in Portland, Oregon, in 1990; and he spent time in tattoo and piercing studios, as well as talking with students and others in his hometown who were involved in these forms of body modification. The study population included males and females, heterosexuals, gays, lesbians, bisexuals, and SMers. The single largest group was SM homosexuals and bisexuals. The study population was mainly White, and most had either attended or graduated from college.

Myers witnessed many modification sessions at workshops: Those seeking modification go up on stage and

A Tahitian chief wears tattoos that indicate his high status *(left)*. ■ (Source © Charles & Josette Lenars/CORBIS)
A woman with tattooed arms and pierced nose in the United States *(right)*. ■ *In your microcultural experience, what do tattoos mean to you when you see someone with them?* (Source: © Royalty-Free/CORBIS)

have their chosen procedure done by a well-known expert. Whatever the procedure, the volunteers exhibit little pain (usually a sharp intake of breath at the moment the needle passes through or the brand touches skin). After that critical moment, the audience breathes an audible sigh of relief. The volunteer stands up and adjusts clothing, and members of the audience applaud. This public event is a kind of initiation ritual that binds the expert, the volunteer, and the group together. Pain has long been recognized as an important part of rites of passage, providing an edge to the ritual drama. The audience in this case witnesses and validates the experience and also becomes joined to the initiate through witnessing.

A prominent motivation for seeking permanent body modification was a desire to identify with a specific group of people. As one informant said,

It's not that we're sheep, getting pierced or cut just because everyone else is. I like to think it's because we're a very special group and we like doing something that sets us off from others. . . . Happiness is standing in line

at a cafeteria and detecting that the straight-looking babe in front of you has her nipples pierced. I don't really care what her sexual orientation is, I can relate to her. (1992: 292)

Work Groups

Work groups are organized to perform specific tasks, although they also may have other functions, including sociality and friendship among members. They are found in all modes of production, but they are more prominent in nonindustrialized horticultural and agricultural communities where land preparation, harvesting, or repair of irrigation canals require large inputs of labor that exceed the capability of a single household unit. In her classic study of the Bemessi people of Cameroon, West Africa, Phyllis Kaberry (1952) describes a labor group system called a *tzo*, which is translated as "working bee." Among the Bemessi, women were responsible for horticulture. Related to this role, women were also responsible for organizing collective work. For preparing corn beds, ten to twelve women worked on each others' plots. For weeding, smaller groups of three to four women formed. At the end of the work day, the women have a meal of fish provided for them by their husbands.

Youth work groups are common in African regions south of the Sahara, particularly in settled, crop-growing areas. The major responsibility of the youth groups is providing field labor. The group members work one or more days in the village chief's fields for no reward or pay. They also maintain public paths and the public meeting area, construct and maintain roads between villages, build and repair canals, combat brush fires, maintain the village mosque, and prevent animals from grazing where they aren't allowed (Leynaud 1961). Girls' groups exist, but in patrilocal contexts they are less durable because marriage and relocation break girls' ties with childhood companions (Hammond 1966:133). As adults, however, women in African cultures have many types of associations, such as mothers' groups, savings groups, and work groups.

Irrigation organizations are formal groups devoted to maintaining irrigation canals and distributing the water. These organizations are responsible for a highly valued good, and they tend to develop formal leadership and membership rules and roles. Because watershed systems cross large regions, irrigation organizations often provide links among many local groups.

The important role these organizations play is illustrated in the Chiangmai region of northern Thailand (see Map 6.4, p. 163). At the village level, care of the irrigation canals is a constant concern (Potter 1976). Each year the main dam across the Ping River is washed away by floods and must be rebuilt. This task requires two weeks of concentrated labor by all the farmers who use the system. The main canal has to be cleared at least once a year and the smaller ones more often. These tasks require much organization. In the Chiangmai region, the administration has three tiers. At the highest level is the overall leader of the irrigation group, who is chosen by three local political leaders. The head is a wealthy man of high social status. At the next lower tier are the heads of each major canal in the system. At the local level is the village irrigation leader, chosen by the village farmers. Irrigation leaders have many duties, including keeping detailed records and arbitrating disputes. They receive some benefits, such as exemption from either furnishing irrigation labor or paying a proportion of their land tax, or they can keep part of the revenues from fines levied against those who are delinquent in providing labor.

Allocating water from the canals requires careful administration. As is often the case, water is allocated proportionally according to land holdings (Coward 1976, 1979). Farmers who are downstream are more likely to be deprived of their fair share than farmers who are upstream and can divert more water to their fields. In order to deal with conflicts that arise from this built-in inequity in one area of the Philippines, subgroups of farmers formed to meet and discuss distribution problems.

Another administrative issue is corruption, such as water theft, in which a farmer taps off water out of turn (Price 1995). Water theft in Egypt, as elsewhere, is more common as distance from the main canal increases. Farmers further from the source feel they are justified in their actions because they get less water through the normal distribution system than farmers closer to the source.

Cooperatives

Cooperatives are a form of economic group with two key features: Surpluses are shared among the members, and decision making follows the democratic principle of one person, one vote (Estrin 1996). Agricultural and credit cooperatives are the most common forms of cooperatives worldwide, followed by consumer cooperatives. We will look at two examples of cooperatives to see how human agency, within different structures, can bring about positive results. In the first case, the cooperative gives its members economic strength and checks the power of the richest farmers in one region of India. In the second case, women craft producers in Panama achieve economic position within the world market and also build social ties and political leadership skills.

Farmers' Cooperatives in Western India

In India's western state of Maharashtra, the sugar industry is largely owned and operated through farmer cooperatives (Attwood 1992). Most shareholders are small farmers, producing just one or two acres of sugar cane. Yet the sugar industry, owned and managed cooperatively, is huge, almost as large as the state's iron and steel industry. In contrast, in the northern states where sugar cane is grown, cooperatives are not prominent.

How and why are sugar cooperatives so successful in this region? The answer lies in the different pattern of social stratification. The rural social stratification system in Maharashtra is simpler than in northern India. In most villages, the Marathas are the dominant caste, but here they constitute even more of a majority and control even more village land than is typical of dominant castes. They also have stronger local ties with each other because their marital arrangements are locally centralized. Thus, they have a better basis for cooperating with each other in spite of class differences among themselves. Large farmers dominate the elected board of directors of the cooperatives. These "sugar barons" use their position to gain power in state politics. However, within the cooperatives their power is held in check. They do not form cliques that exploit the cooperatives to the detriment of the less wealthy. In fact, large farmers cannot afford to alienate the small and midsize farmers, for that would mean economic ruin for the cooperative and the loss of their own profits.

The technology of sugar cane processing requires wide participation of the farmers. Mechanization involves investing in expensive heavy equipment. The machinery cannot be run at a profit unless it is used at full capacity during the crushing season. If small and midsize farmers were displeased with their treatment, they might decide to pull out of the cooperative and put their cane into other uses. Then capacity would be underused and profits would fall.

Craft Cooperatives in Panama

In Panama's east coastal region, indigenous Kuna women have long sewn beautiful *molas,* or cloth with appliquéd designs (see Map 9.4). This cloth is made for their own use as clothing (Tice 1995). Since the 1960s, molas have been important items for sale both on the world market and to tourists who come to Panama. Revenue from selling molas is an important part of the household income of the Kuna. Some women continue to operate independently, buying their own cloth and thread and selling their molas either to an intermediary who exports them or in the local tourist market. But many other women have joined cooperatives that offer them greater economic security. The cooperative buys cloth and thread in

Kuna Indian woman selling molas, San Blas Islands, Panama. ■ *Learn more about molas from the Web.* (Source: © Wolfgang Kaehler)

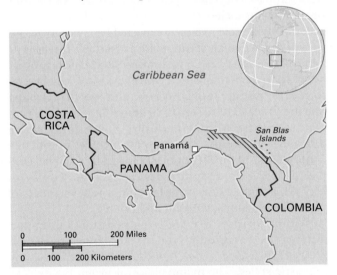

MAP 9.4 Kuna Region in Panama. The Kuna are an indigenous people who live mainly in the eastern coastal region of Panama, including its offshore islands. Some live in cities and a few live in villages in neighboring Colombia. Each community has its own political organization, and the Kuna as a whole are organized into the Kuna General Congress. The Kuna population is around 150,000. Most speak Kuna, or Dulegaya ("People's Language") and Spanish. They follow traditional religious practices, often with a mixture of Christian elements. Farming, fishing, and tourism are important parts of the economy.

bulk and distributes it to the women. The women are paid almost the entire sale price for each mola, with only a small amount of the eventual sale prices being taken out for cooperative dues and administrative costs. Their earnings are steadier than what the fluctuating tourist season offers.

Beyond the initial economic reasons for joining the cooperative, other benefits include the use of the cooperative as a consumer's cooperative (buying rice and sugar in bulk for members), as a source of mutual strength and support, and as a place for women to develop greater leadership skills and to take advantage of opportunities for political participation in the wider society.

Self-Help Groups

Recent years have seen a worldwide proliferation of *self-help groups,* or groups formed to achieve specific personal goals, such as coping with illness or bereavement, or lifestyle change, such as trying to exercise more or lose weight. Self-help groups also increasingly use the Internet to form virtual support communities. Anthropologists who study these groups focus on why members join, on rituals of solidarity, and on leadership and organization patterns.

An ethnography of Alcoholic Anonymous groups in Mexico City, or simply Mexico (see Map 5.4, p. 128) reports that most members are low-income, working-class males (Brandes 2002). Most of these men migrated to Mexico City from rural areas several decades earlier to find work and improve their standard of living. Their drinking problems are related both to their poverty and to the close links between alcohol consumption and male gender identity in Mexico (a "real man" consumes a lot of alcohol). Through a dynamic of shared stories and regular meetings, AA members in Mexico City achieve a high rate of sobriety.

The success of AA in Mexico is leading to a rapid proliferation of groups. Membership is growing at about 10 percent a year, a remarkably high rate of growth for a self-help organization. At the end of the twentieth century, Latin America accounted for almost one-third of the world AA membership. Thus, a model of a middle-class self-help organization that originated in the United States has been culturally localized by low-income men throughout Latin America.

Social Stratification

Social stratification consists of hierarchical relationships between different groups—as though they were arranged in layers or "strata." Stratified groups may be unequal on a variety of measures, including material resources, power, human welfare, education, and symbolic attributes. People in groups in higher positions have privileges not experienced by those in lower-echelon groups, and they are likely to be interested in maintaining their privileged position. Social stratification appeared late in human history, most clearly with the emergence of agriculture. Now some form of social stratification is nearly universal.

Analysis of the categories—such as class, "race," gender, and age—that form stratification systems reveals a crucial difference among them: the degree to which membership in a given category is an **ascribed position,** based on qualities of a person gained through birth, or an **achieved position,** based on qualities of a person gained through action. Ascribed positions may be based, for example, on one's "race," ethnicity, gender, age, and physical ability. These factors are generally out of the control

of the individual, although some flexibility exists for gender (through surgery and hormonal treatments) and for certain kinds of physical conditions. Also, one can sometimes "pass" as a member of another "race" or ethnic group. Age is an interesting ascribed

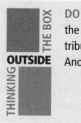

DO RESEARCH on the current global distribution of Alcoholics Anonymous.

category because an individual goes through several different status levels associated with age. Achievement as a basis for group membership means that a person belongs on the premise of some valued attainment. Ascribed systems are thus more "closed" and achievement-based systems more "open" in terms of mobility within the system (either upward or downward). Some scholars of social status believe that increasing social complexity and modernization led to an increase in achievement-based positions and a decline in ascription-based positions. In the next section, we look at the way key social categories define group membership and relations of inequality among groups.

The Concept of Status Groups

Societies place people into categories—student, husband, child, retired person, political leader, or member of Phi Beta Kappa—referred to as a person's **status,** or position or standing in society (C. Wolf 1996). Each status has an accompanying role, which is expected behavior for someone of a particular status, and a "script" for how to behave, look, and talk. Some statuses have more prestige attached to them than others (the word *status* can be used to mean prestige, relative value, and worth). Groups, like individuals, have status, or standing in society. German sociologist Max Weber called lower-status groups *disprivileged* groups. These groups include, in different contexts and in different times, physically disabled people, people with certain illnesses, such as leprosy or HIV/AIDS, indigenous peoples, minorities, members of particular religions, women, and others.

Within societies that have marked status positions, different status groups are marked by a particular lifestyle, including goods owned, leisure activities, and linguistic styles. The maintenance of group position by higher-status categories is sometimes accomplished by exclusionary practices in relation to lower-status groups through a tendency toward group in-marriage and socializing only within the group.

---

social stratification: hierarchical relationships between different groups as though they were arranged in layers or "strata."
ascribed position: a person's standing in society based on qualities that the person has gained through birth.

achieved position: a person's standing in society based on qualities that the person has gained through action.
status: a person's position, or standing, in society.

mechanical solidarity: social bonding among groups that are similar.
organic solidarity: social bonding among groups with different abilities and resources.

Class: Achieved Status

Social class (defined in Chapter 1) refers to a person's or group's position in society defined primarily in economic terms. In many cultures, class is a key factor in determining a person's status, whereas in others, it is less important than, for example, birth into a certain family. However, class and status do not always match. A rich person may have become wealthy in disreputable ways and never gain high status. Both status and class groups are secondary groups, because a person is unlikely to know every other member of the group, especially in large-scale societies. In most instances, they are also informal groups; there are no recognized leaders or elected officials of the "urban elite" or the "working class." Subsegments of these large categories do organize themselves into formal groups, such as labor unions or exclusive clubs for the rich and famous. Class can be both ascribed and achieved because a person who is born rich has a greater than average chance of living an upper-class lifestyle.

In capitalist societies, the prevailing ideology is that the system allows for upward mobility and that every individual has the option of moving up. Some anthropologists refer to this ideology as *meritocratic individualism*, the belief that rewards go to those who deserve them (Durrenberger 2001). This ideology would seem to be most valid for people with decent jobs rather than menial workers or the unemployed, but in fact the ideology is widely held outside the middle class. In the United States, the pervasive popular belief in rewards for equal opportunity and merit is upheld and promoted in schools and universities, even in the face of substantial evidence to the contrary.

Conservative governments have long sought to weaken labor unions, and they continue to promote the fantasy of a classless society based on meritocratic individualism to support their anti-union policies. Anthropologists who take a structurist perspective point to the power of economic class position in shaping a person's lifestyle and his or her ability to choose a different one. Obviously, a person who was born rich can, through individual agency, become poor, and a poor person can become rich. But in spite of exceptions to the rule, a person born rich is more likely to lead a lifestyle typical of that class, just as a person born poor is more likely lead a lifestyle typical of that class.

The concept of class was central to the theories of Karl Marx. Situated within the context of Europe's Industrial Revolution and the growth of capitalism, Marx wrote that class differences, exploitation of the working class by the owners of capital, class consciousness among workers, and class conflict are forces of change that would eventually spell the downfall of capitalism. In contrast to Marx's approach, French sociologist Emile Durkheim viewed social differences (including class) as the basis for social solidarity (1966 [1895]). He distinguished two major forms of societal cohesion: **mechanical solidarity**, social cohesion among similar groups, and **organic solidarity**, social cohesion among groups with different abilities and resources. Mechanical solidarity creates less enduring relationships because it involves little mutual need. Organic solidarity builds on need and provides complementary resources to different groups, thus creating stronger bonds than mechanical solidarity does. Durkheim placed these two concepts in an evolutionary framework, saying that in nonindustrial times, the division of labor was only minimally specialized: Everyone did what everyone else did. With increasing social complexity and economic specialization, organic solidarity emerged as increasingly important.

"Race," Ethnicity, and Caste: Ascribed Status

Three major ascribed systems of social stratification are based on divisions of people into unequally ranked groups on the basis of "race," ethnicity (defined in Chapter 1), and caste, a ranked group, determined by birth, often linked to a particular occupation and to South Asian cultures. Like status and class groups, these three categories are secondary social groups, because no one can have a personal relationship with all other members of the entire group. Each system takes on local specificities depending on the context. For example, "race" and ethnicity are interrelated and overlap with conceptions of culture in much of Latin America, although differences in what they mean in terms of identity and status occur in different countries in the region (de la Cadena 2001). For some, the concept of *mestizaje*, or racial mixture, refers to people who are disenfranchised and cut off from their Indian roots, but for others, it can refer to literate and successful people who retain indigenous cultural practices. One has to know the local system of categories and meanings attached to them to understand the dynamics of inequality that go with them.

Systems based in difference defined in terms of "race," ethnicity, and caste share with each other, and with class-based systems, some important features. First, they relegate large numbers of people to particular levels of entitlement to livelihood, power, security, esteem, and freedom (Berreman 1979 [1975]:213). This simple fact should not be overlooked. Second, those with greater entitlements dominate those with lesser entitlements. Third, members of the dominant groups tend—consciously or unconsciously—to seek to maintain their position. They do this through institutions that control ideology among the dominated and through institutions that physically suppress potential rebellion or subversion by the dominated (Harris 1971, quoted in Mencher 1974:469). Fourth, in spite of efforts to maintain systems

Critical Thinking

WHAT'S MISSING FROM THIS PICTURE?

Read the following summary from a news item entitled "Baseball Team Members Who Used KKK Symbol Will Receive Multi-Cultural Training" (Jet 1996). Then consider how anthropological research could provide a fuller understanding of racism in its social context.

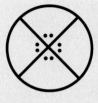

A county school board in Virginia opted not to punish members of the state champion high school baseball team who used a Ku Klux Klan symbol. The team members drew the symbol in the dirt before games for good luck. Investigators believe that the symbol represents four hooded Klansmen looking down a hole, the last thing a Black victim would see after being dropped down a well by Klansmen. The school superintendent decided to reprimand the coaches, and the school board voted to send the students for "multicultural training."

This brief news item tells us some things about the case but provides little information that would lead to deeper understanding of the cultural context. If a cultural anthropologist decided to do in-depth fieldwork in the community, what kinds of research questions would be most important? Here are some examples:

- The racial composition of the team
- The racial composition of the school leadership (superintendent), coaches, and other local leaders
- The pattern of racial and class stratification in the community in which the school is located
- Other possible forms of racist thinking and behavior in the community
- Any generational differences that might exist in racist thinking and behavior in this community
- The reactions of different community members to the behavior of members of the high school baseball team; the reactions of the coaches; and the reactions to the school superintendent's decision about how to treat the baseball players
- Social programs in the schools and wider community that might reduce racism

CRITICAL THINKING QUESTIONS

- How does cultural anthropology differ from journalism in terms of research goals? In terms of research methods? In terms of research results and how they are presented?

- What are the comparative strengths and weaknesses of each approach?

---

of dominance, instances of subversion and rebellion do occur, indicating the potential for agency among the oppressed.

"Race"

Racial stratification is a relatively recent form of social inequality. It results from the unequal meeting of two formerly separate groups through colonization, slavery, and other large-group movements (Sanjek 1994). Europe's "age of discovery," beginning in the 1500s, ushered in a new era of global contact. In contrast, in relatively homogeneous cultures, ethnicity is a more important distinction than "race." In contemporary Nigeria, for example, the population is relatively homogeneous, and ethnicity is the more salient term (Jinadu 1994). A similar situation prevails in Rwanda and other African states.

A key feature of racial thinking is its insistence that behavioral differences among peoples are "natural," inborn, or biologically caused (in this, it resembles sexism, ageism, and casteism). Throughout the history of racial

Boys in a small town of Brazil exhibit the skin-color diversity in the Brazilian population. ■ *If you were a census taker and had to categorize the "race" of these boys on the basis of physical features, what categories would you use?* (Source: © David G. Houser/CORBIS)

In 2003, the Treatment Action Campaign (TAC) began a program of civil disobedience to prompt the government of South Africa to sign and implement a National Prevention and Treatment Plan for HIV/AIDS. The TAC uses images of Hector Peterson, the first youth killed in the Soweto uprising against apartheid, and slogans such as "The Struggle Continues: Support HIV/AIDS Treatment Now." ■ *Take a position, and be prepared to defend it, on whether the government should take responsibility for preventing and treating HIV/AIDS in any country, rich or poor.* (Source © Gideon Mendel/CORBIS)

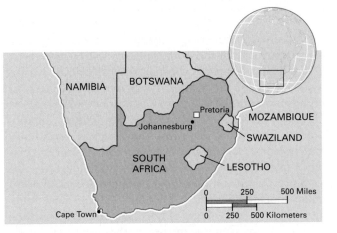

MAP 9.5   South Africa. The Republic of South Africa (which has eleven official names in different languages), had the highest level of colonial immigration of any country of Africa. Its rich mineral wealth attracted interest from global powers through the Cold War era. Of its population of over 46 million people, 80 percent are Black South Africans. The rest are of mixed ethnic backgrounds (referred to as "Coloureds"), Indian (from India), or White descendants of colonial immigrants. South Africa has eleven offical languages, and it recognizes eight nonofficial languages. Afrikaans and English are the major languages of the administration. Nonofficial languages include those of the San and other indigenous peoples.

categorizations in the West, such features as head size, head shape, and brain size have been accepted as the reasons for behavioral differences. Writing early in the twentieth century, Franz Boas contributed to de-linking supposed in-born, racial attributes from behavior (review Chapter 1). He showed that people with the same head size but from different cultures behaved differently and that people with various head sizes within the same cultures behaved similarly. For Boas and his followers, culture, not biology, is the key explanation for behavior. Thus "race" is not a biological reality; there is no way to divide the human population into "races" based on certain biological features. Yet, *social race* and racism exist. In other words, the concept of "race" in many contexts has a social reality in terms of people's entitlements, status, and treatment. In spite of some progress in reducing racism in the United States in the twentieth century, racial discrimination persists (see Critical Thinking box). One way of understanding this persistence is to see racial discrimination as linked to class formation, rather than separate from it (Brodkin 2000). In this view, racial stereotyping and discrimination function to keep people in less desirable jobs, or unemployed, as necessary aspects of advanced industrial capitalism, which depends on there being a certain number of low-paid workers and even a certain amount of unemployment.

Racial classifications in the Caribbean and in Latin America involve complicated systems of status classification. This complexity results from the variety of contact over the centuries between peoples from Europe, Africa, Asia, and indigenous populations. Skin tone is one basis of racial classification, but it is mixed with other physical features and economic status as well. In Haiti, for example, racial categories take into account physical factors such as skin texture, depth of skin tone, hair color and appearance, and facial features (Trouillot 1994). Racial categories also include a person's income, social origin, level of formal education, personality or behavior, and kinship ties. Depending on how these variables are combined, a person occupies one category or another—and may even move between categories. Thus, a person with certain physical features who is poor will be considered to be a different "color" than a person with the same physical features who is well-off.

An extreme example of racial stratification was the South African policy of apartheid, legally sanctioned segregation of dominant Whites from non-Whites. White dominance in South Africa (see Map 9.5) began in the early 1800s with White migration and settlement. In the 1830s, slavery was abolished. At the same time, increasingly racist thinking developed among Whites (Johnson 1994:25). Racist images, including visions of Africans as lazy, out of control, and sex driven, served as the rationale for colonialist domination in place of outright slavery. In spite of years of African resistance to White domination, the Whites succeeded in maintaining and increasing their control for nearly two centuries. In South Africa, Blacks constitute 90 percent of the population, a numerical majority dominated, through strict apartheid, by the White minority until only recently. Every aspect of life for the majority of Africans was far worse than for the Whites. Every measure of life quality—infant mortality, longevity, education—showed great disparity between the Whites and the Africans. In addition to physical deprivation, the Africans experienced psychological suffering through constant insecurity about raids from the police and other forms of violence.

Since the end of apartheid in South Africa in 1994, many social changes have taken place. One study describes the early stages of the dismantling of apartheid in the city of Umtata, in the southeastern part of the country (Johnson 1994). Before the end of apartheid, Umtata "was like other South African towns: all apartheid laws were in full force; public and private facilities were completely segregated; only whites could vote or serve in the town government; whites owned all the major economic assets" (1994:viii). When the change came, Umtata's dominant Whites bitterly resisted at first. They did not want to lose their privileges, and they feared reprisals by the Africans. These things did not happen, however. The initial stages of transition brought "neoapartheid," in which White privilege was not seriously threatened. Then members of the dominant group began to welcome the less tense, "nonracial" atmosphere.

In contrast to the explicitly racist discrimination of South African apartheid, racism exists within contexts where no public discourse about "race" or racism is found—where instead there is silence about it (Sheriff 2000). In such a context, the silence works to allow racial discrimination to continue in ways that are as effective as a clearly stated policy such as apartheid, or perhaps even more so because it is more difficult to critique and dismantle an institution whose existence is denied.

Ethnicity

Ethnicity is a sense of group membership based on a shared sense of identity (Comaroff 1987). Identity may be based on the perception of shared history, territory, language, or religion, or a combination of these. Ethnicity can be a basis for claiming entitlements to resources (such as land, buildings, or artifacts) and for defending or regaining those resources.

States are interested in managing ethnicity to the extent that it does not threaten security. China has one of the most formalized systems for monitoring its many ethnic groups, and it has an official policy on ethnic minorities, meaning the non-Han groups (Wu 1990). The government lists a total of fifty-four groups other than the Han majority, which constitutes about 94 percent of the total. The other 6 percent of the population is made up of these fifty-four groups, about 67 million people. The non-Han minorities occupy about 60 percent of China's land mass and are located in border or "frontier" areas such as Tibet, Yunnan, Xinjiang, and Inner Mongolia. Basic criteria for defining an ethnic group include language, territory, economy, and "psychological disposition." The Chinese government establishes strict definitions of group membership and group characteristics; it even sets standards for ethnic costumes and dances. The Chinese treatment of the Tibetan people is especially severe and can be considered an attempt at ethnocide (annihilation of the culture of an ethnic group by a dominant group). The Chinese government's treatment of Tibetan traditional medicine over the past several decades illustrates how the Han majority uses certain aspects of minority cultures.

In 1951, China forcibly incorporated Tibet, and the Chinese government undertook measures to bring about the social and economic transformation of what was formerly a decentralized, Buddhist feudal regime. This transformation has caused increasing ethnic conflict between Tibetans and Han Chinese, including demonstrations by Tibetans and crackdowns from the Chinese. Traditional Tibetan medicine has become part of the Chinese–Tibetan conflicts because of its cultural significance and importance to religion in Tibetan society (Janes 1995:7). Previously based on a model of apprenticeship training, it is now westernized and involves several years of classroom-based, lecture-oriented learning followed by an internship. At Tibet University, only half of all formal lecture-based instruction is concerned with traditional Tibetan medicine. Curriculum changes have reduced the integrity of Tibetan medicine: It has been separated from its Buddhist content, and parts of it have been merged with a biomedical approach. Some might say that overall, traditional Tibetan medicine has been "revived" in China, but stronger evidence supports the argument that the state has co-opted it and transformed it for its own purposes.

People of one ethnic group who move from one niche to another are at risk of exclusionary treatment by the local residents. Roma (formerly called gypsies by outsiders but considered a derogatory term by the Roma), are a **diaspora population**, a dispersed group living out-

THINKING OUTSIDE THE BOX

WITH WHICH ethnic or other kind of social group do you identify? What are the bases of this identification? Is your social group relatively high or low in terms of social status?

---

diaspora population: dispersed group of people living outside their original homeland.

caste system: a social stratification system linked with Hinduism and based on a person's birth into a particular group.

dalit: the preferred name for the socially defined lowest groups in the Indian caste system, meaning "oppressed" or "ground down."

side their original homeland, and are scattered throughout Europe and the United States (see Culturama).

A less difficult but still not easy adjustment is being experienced by Indo-Canadians (immigrants from India to Canada). In research among a sample of nearly 300 Indo-Canadians in Vancouver, British Columbia, about half of all the respondents reported experiencing some form of discrimination in the recent past (Nodwell and Guppy 1992). The percentage was higher among men (54 percent) than among women (45 percent). The higher level for men was consistent across the four categories: verbal abuse, property damage, workplace discrimination, and physical harm. Verbal abuse was the most frequent form of discrimination, reported by 40 percent of both men and women. Indo-Canadians of the Sikh faith who were born in India say that they experience the highest levels of discrimination in Canada. Apparently, however, their actual experience of discrimination is not greater than for other Indo-Canadians. The difference is that Sikhs who were born in India are more sensitive to discrimination than others. Sikhism, as taught and practiced in India, supports a strong sense of honor, which should be protected and, if wronged, avenged. This study helps explain differences in perception of discrimination among ethnic migrants. It does not, however, explain why such high levels of discriminatory treatment exist in a nation committed to ethnic tolerance.

Caste

The **caste system** is a social stratification system linked with Hinduism and based on a person's birth into a particular group. It exists in its clearest form in India, among its Hindu population, and in other areas of Hindu culture such as Nepal, Sri Lanka, and Fiji. The caste system is particularly associated with Hindu peoples because ancient Hindu scriptures are taken as the foundational sources for defining the major social categories called *varnas* (a Sanskrit word meaning "color") (see Figure 9.2). The four varnas are the *brahmans*, who were priests; the *kshatriya*, or warriors; the *vaishya*, or merchants; and the *shudras*, or laborers. Of these, men of the first three varnas go through a ritual ceremony of initiation and "rebirth" after which they may wear a sacred thread across their chest, indicating their purity and high status as "twice-born." Beneath the four varna groups are people considered so low that they are outside the caste system itself, hence the English term "outcast." Another English term for them is "untouchables," since people of the upper varnas avoided any kind of contact with them in order to maintain their purity. Mahatma Gandhi, himself a member of an upper caste, renamed them *harijans* (or "children of god") in his attempt to raise their status into that of the shudras. Currently, members of this category have adopted the term **dalit**, which means "oppressed" or "ground down."

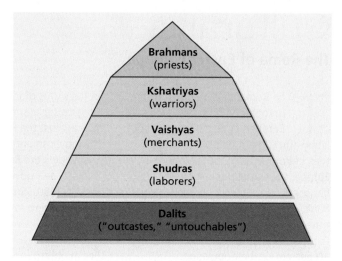

FIGURE 9.2 **Model of the Varna System in India** Within each of the major categories presented here, numerous castes and subcastes exist. The shape of the model is intended to suggest that the higher-ranking categories include fewer numbers of people than lower-ranking categories. The name for the priestly varna is variously transliterated into English as brahman or brahmin.

The four traditional varnas and the dalit category contain many hundreds of locally named groups called castes, or, more appropriately, *jatis* (birth group). The term *caste* is a Portuguese word meaning "breed" or "type." Portuguese colonialists first used it in the fifteenth century to refer to the closed social groups they encountered (Cohn 1971:125). Jati, a more emic term, conveys the meaning that a Hindu is born into his or her group. Jatis are ascribed status groups. Just as the four varnas are ranked relative to each other, so are all the jatis within them. For example, the jati of brahmans is divided into priestly and nonpriestly subgroups, the priestly brahmans are separated into household-priests, temple-priests, and funeral-priests; the household-priests are broken down into two or more categories; and each of those are divided into subgroups based on lineage ties (Parry 1966:77). Within all these categories exist well-defined status hierarchies.

Status levels also exist among dalits. In western Nepal, which, like India, has a caste system, dalit artisans such as basket-weavers and ironsmiths are the highest tier (Cameron 1995). They do not touch any of the people beneath them. The second tier includes leatherworkers and tailors. The bottom tier comprises people who are "untouchable" to all groups, including other dalits, because their work is extremely polluting according to Hindu rules. This category includes musicians (because some of their instruments are made of leather and they perform in public) and sex workers.

Indian anthropologist M. N. Srinivas (1959) contributed the concept of the *dominant caste* to refer to the

Culturama

The Roma of Eastern Europe

The Roma, better known by the derogatory term "Gypsies," are Europe's largest minority population. They live in nearly all the countries of Europe and Central Asia. In Europe, their total population is between 7 and 9 million people (World Bank 2003). They are most concentrated in the countries of Eastern Europe, where they constitute around 10 percent of the population.

Roma history is one of mobility and marginality ever since several waves of migrants left their original homeland in northern India between the ninth and fourteenth centuries CE (Crowe 1996). For many Roma in Europe, their lifestyle continues to involve movement. Temporary camps of their wagons often appear overnight on the outskirts of a town. Settled Roma typically live in marginalized areas that lack decent housing, clean water, and good schools. Most members of mainstream society look down on, and even despise, the Roma.

In Budapest, Hungary, the Roma minority is the most disadvantaged ethnic group (Ladányi 1993). Not all Roma in Budapest, however, are poor. About 1 percent have gained wealth. The other 99 percent live in substandard housing in the slums of inner Pest. Since the fall of state socialism in Hungary, discrimination against the Roma has increased. The government of Hungary has a policy that allows the Roma a degree of local minority self-government (Schaft and Brown 2000). Some Roma communities are mobilizing to improve their living conditions.

In Slovakia, one-third of the Roma live in ghetto-like enclaves called *osada* (Scheffel 2004). The heaviest concentration of osadas is in the eastern province. These settlements lack clean water, sewage treatment, reliable electricity, access to decent housing, good schools, and passable roads. These settlements exist in close proximity to affluent neighborhoods of ethnic Slovaks, or "Whites." In one village, Svinia (pronounced SVIH-neeyah), roughly 700 Roma are crowded together on a hectare of swampy land while their 670 ethnic Slovak neighbors own over 1,400 hectares of land (2004:8).

As more Eastern European countries seek to enter the European Union, they are initiating programs to improve Roma living conditions and enacting laws to prevent discrimination. Field research in Slovakia suggests that the government, in fact, is doing little to improve the lives of the Roma. The situation for the Roma in Hungary, in contrast, is more hopeful. After Hungary's accession to the European Union in 2004, it elected two Roma to the EU Parliament. In Bulgaria, the Roma won a court case in 2005 declaring that segregated schools were unconstitutional.

Readings

David Z. Scheffel. "Slovak Roma on the Threshold of Europe." *Anthropology Today*, 20 (1): 6–12, 2004.
———. *Svinia in Black and White: Slovak Roma and Their Neighbors.* Peterborough, Ontario: Broadview Press, 2005.
Carol Silverman. "Persecution and Politicization: The Roma of Eastern Europe." *Cultural Survival Quarterly*, 19 (2): 43–49, 1995.

Video

Suspino: A Cry for Roma. (Bullfrog Films, 2003).

Websites

www.svinia.net
www.nationalgeographic.com/ngm0104/feature4/media2.html [online interactive feature]

Thanks to David Z. Scheffel, Thompson Rivers University, for reviewing this material.

The Roma settlement of Svinia in 1993 (left). The standard of living has not improved since then, but the population has increased by nearly 50 percent, resulting in serious overcrowding and high levels of stress. Roma children's access to school facilities is severely restricted (right). A few Romani schoolchildren participate in the school lunch program but in a separate room next to the cafeteria. ■ (Source: David Z. Scheffel)

MAP 9.6 *Roma Population in Eastern Europe. Romania has the highest number of Roma of any country in the world, between one and two million. Macedonia has the highest percentage of Roma.*

tendency for one caste in any particular village to control most of the land and, often, to be numerically preponderant as well. Brahmans are at the top of the social hierarchy in terms of ritual purity, and they are often, but not always, the dominant caste. Throughout northern India, it is common for jatis of the kshatriya varna to be the dominant village group. This is the case in Pahansu village, where a group called the Gujars is dominant (Raheja 1988). The Gujars constitute the numerical majority, and they control most of the land (see Figure 9.3). Moreover, they dominate in the *jajmani system*, a patron-provider system in which landholding patrons (jajmans) are linked, through exchanges of food for services, with brahman priests, artisans (blacksmiths, potters), agricultural laborers, and other workers such as sweepers. In Pahansu, Gujars have power and status as the major patrons, supporting many different service providers who are beholden to them.

Some anthropologists have described the jajmani service system as one of mutual interdependence (organic solidarity, to use Durkheim's term) that provides security for the less well-off. Others argue that the system benefits those at the top to the detriment of those at the bottom. This perspective, from "the bottom up," views the patron-service system and the entire caste system as one of exploitation by those at the top (Mencher 1974). The benign interpretation is based on research conducted among the upper castes who present this view. From low-caste people's perspective, it is the patrons who have the power. Dissatisfied patrons can dismiss service providers, refuse them loans, or not pay them. Service providers who are dissatisfied with the treatment they receive from their patrons have little recourse. In addition, male

Only a special category of brahman priests can officiate at the Chidambaram temple in southern India. Here, members of an age-mixed group sit for a moment's relaxation. ■ *Name some other groups in which membership cuts across age differences.* (Source: Barbara Miller)

patrons often demand sexual access to females of service-providing households.

Throughout South Asia, the growth of industrial manufacturing has reduced the need for some service

FIGURE 9.3   Caste Ranking in Pahansu Village, North India

Caste Name	Traditional Occupation	Number of Households	Occupation in Pahansu
Gujar	agriculturalist	210	owner cultivator
Brahman	priest	8	priest, postman
Baniya	merchant	3	shopkeeper
Sunar	goldsmith	2	silversmith, sugar cane press operator
Dhiman (Barhai)	carpenter	1	carpenter
Kumhar	potter	3	potter, tailor
Nai	barber	3	barber, postman
Dhobi	washerman	2	washerman
Gadariya	shepherd	4	agricultural laborer, weaver
Jhivar	water-carrier	20	agricultural laborer, basket-weaver
Luhar	ironsmith	2	blacksmith
Teli	oil-presser	2	beggar, cotton-carder, agricultural laborer
Maniharan	bangle-seller	1	bangle-seller
Camar	leatherworker	100	agricultural laborer
Bhangi	sweeper	17	sweeper, midwife

Source: Adapted from Raheja 1988:19.

A village carpenter in front of his house in a north Indian village. The status of carpenters is midlevel, between the landholding elites or brahman priests and those who deal with polluting materials such as animal hides or refuse. ■ *In your culture, what social status do carpenters, toolmakers, or other skilled manual laborers have?* (Source: Barbara Miller)

dominance. The rich upper-caste leaders sponsor important annual festivals, thereby regularly restating their claim to public prominence (Mines 1994).

Social mobility within the caste system has traditionally been limited, but instances have been documented of group "up-casting." Several strategies exist, including gaining wealth, affiliation or merger with a somewhat higher jati, education, migration, and political activism (Kolenda 1978). A group that attempts to gain higher jati status takes on the behavior and dress of twice-born jatis. These include men wearing the sacred thread, vegetarianism, nonremarriage of widows, seclusion of women from the public domain, and the giving of larger dowries for the marriage of a daughter. Some dalits have opted out of the caste system by converting to Christianity or Buddhism. Others are becoming politically organized through the Dalit Panthers, a social movement seeking greater power and improved economic status for dalits.

The Indian constitution of 1949 declared that discrimination on the basis of caste is illegal. Constitutional decree, however, did not bring an end to these deeply structured inequalities. In the late twentieth century, the government of India instituted policies to promote the social and economic advancement of dalits, such as reserving for them places in medical schools, seats in the government, and public-sector jobs. This "affirmative action" plan has infuriated many of the upper castes, especially brahmans, who feel most threatened. Is the caste system on the decline? Surely aspects of it are changing. Especially in large cities, people of different jatis can "pass" and participate on a more nearly equal basis in public life—if they have the economic means to do so.

providers, especially tailors, potters, and weavers. Many of these people have left their villages to work in urban areas. The tie that remains the strongest is between patrons and their brahman priests, whose ritual services cannot be replaced by machines.

The caste system involves several mechanisms that maintain it: marriage rules, spatial segregation, and ritual. Marriage rules strictly enforce jati endogamy. Marriage outside one's jati, especially in rural areas and particularly between a higher-caste female and lower-caste male, is cause for serious, even lethal, punishment by caste elders and other local power-holders. Among urban educated elites, a trend toward inter-jati marriages is emerging.

Spatial segregation functions to maintain the privileged preserve of the upper castes and to remind the lower castes continually of their marginal status. In many rural contexts, the dalits live in a completely separate cluster; in other cases, they have their own neighborhood sections into which no upper-caste person will venture. Ritual rules and practices also serve to maintain

Civil Society

Civil society consists of the social domain of diverse interest groups that function outside the government to organize economic, political, and other aspects of life. It has a long history in Western philosophy, and many different definitions have been proposed by thinkers such as John Locke, Thomas Paine, Adam Smith, and Karl Marx (K. Kumar 1996:89). According to the German philosopher Hegel, civil society encompasses the social groups and institutions between the individual and the state. Italian social theorist Gramsci wrote that there are two basic types of civic institutions: those that support the state, such as the church and schools, and those that oppose state power, such as trade unions, social protest groups, and citizens' rights groups.

civil society: the collection of interest groups that function outside the government to organize economic and other aspects of life.

Civil Society for the State: The Chinese Women's Movement

In many instances, governments seek to build civil society to further their goals. The women's movement in China is an example of such a state-created organization. Canadian anthropologist Ellen Judd (2002) conducted a study of the women's movement in China, within the constraints that the government imposes on anthropological fieldwork by foreigners. Under the Mao leadership, foreign anthropologists were not allowed to do research of any sort in China. The situation began to change in the 1980s when some field research, within strict limitations, became possible.

Judd has developed a long-term relationship with China over several decades, having lived there as a student from 1974 to 1977, undertaking long-term fieldwork there in 1986, and returning almost every year since for research or some other activity, such as being involved in a development project for women or attending the Beijing Fourth World Conference on Women. According to Judd, "These various ways of being in China all allowed me some interaction with Chinese women and some knowledge of their lives" (2002:14). In her latest project to study the Chinese women's movement, she wanted to conduct research as a cultural anthropologist would normally do, through intensive participant observation over a long period of time.

Even now, the Chinese government prohibits such research, keeping foreigners at a distance from everyday life. Judd was not allowed to join the local women's organization or to speak privately with any of the women. Officials accompanied her on all household visits and interviews. She was allowed to attend meetings, however, and she had access to all the public information about the goals of the women's movement, which is called the Women's Federations. A policy goal of the Chinese government is to improve the quality of women's lives, and the Women's Federations were formed to address that goal. The government oversees the operation at all levels, from the national level to the township and village. The primary objective is to mobilize women, especially rural women, to participate in literacy training and market activities.

Judd's fieldwork, constrained as it was by government regulations and oversight, nevertheless yielded some insights. She learned, through interviews with women members, about some women who have benefited from the programs, and she discovered how important education for women is in terms of their ability to enter into market activities. The book she wrote is largely descriptive, focusing on the "public face" of the Women's Federations in one locale. Such a descriptive account is the most that can emerge from research in China at this time. Given that the women's organizations are formed by and for the government, this example stretches the concept of civil society to—and perhaps beyond—its limits.

Activist Groups

Activist groups are groups formed with the goal of changing certain conditions, such as political repression, violence, and human rights violations. In studying activist groups, cultural anthropologists are interested in learning what motivates the formation of such groups, what their goals and strategies are, and what leadership patterns they exhibit. Sometimes anthropologists join the efforts of activist groups and use their knowledge to support these groups' goals (see Lessons Applied box).

Many, but certainly not all, activist groups are initiated and organized by women. CO-MADRES of El Salvador (see Map 15.4, p. 411) is an important, women-led social movement in Latin America (Stephen 1995). CO-MADRES is a Spanish abbreviation for an organization called, in English, the Committee of Mothers and Relatives of Political Prisoners, Disappeared and Assassinated of El Salvador. It was founded in 1977 by a group of mothers protesting the atrocities committed by the Salvadoran government and military. During the civil war that lasted from 1979 until 1992, a total of 80,000 people died and 7,000 more disappeared—1 in every 100 El Salvadorans.

The initial group comprised nine mothers. A year later, it had grown to nearly thirty members, including some men. In 1979, the group made its first international trip to secure wider recognition. This developed into a full-fledged and successful campaign for international solidarity in the 1980s, with support in other Latin American countries, Europe, Australia, the United States, and Canada. The group's increased visibility earned it repression from the government. Its office was bombed in 1980 and then four more times after that. Forty-eight members of CO-MADRES have been detained since 1977; five have been assassinated. Harassment and disappearances continued even after the signing of the Peace Accords in January 1992: "In February 1993, the son and the nephew of one of the founders of CO-MADRES were assassinated in Usulutan. This woman had already lived through the experience of her own detention, the detention and gang rape of her daughter, and the disappearance and assassination of other family members" (1995:814).

In the 1990s, CO-MADRES focused on holding the state accountable for human rights violations during the civil war, as well as some new areas, such as providing better protection for political prisoners, seeking assurances of human rights protection in the future, working against domestic violence, educating women about political participation, and initiating economic projects for women. The work of CO-MADRES, throughout its history, has incorporated elements of both the "personal" and the "political," concerns of mothers and other family members for lost kin and for exposing and halting abuses of the state and military. The lesson

Lessons Applied

ANTHROPOLOGY AND COMMUNITY ACTIVISM IN PAPUA NEW GUINEA

A controversial issue in applied anthropology is whether or not an anthropologist should take on the role of community activist or act as an advocate on behalf of the people among whom they have conducted research (Kirsch 2002). Some say that anthropologists should maintain a neutral position in a conflict situation and simply offer information on issues—information that may be used by either side. Others say that it is appropriate and right for anthropologists to take sides and help support less powerful groups against more powerful groups. Those who endorse anthropologists taking an activist or advocacy role argue that neutrality is never truly neutral: By seemingly taking no position, one indirectly supports the status quo, and information provided to both sides will generally serve the interests of the more powerful side in any case.

Stuart Kirsch took an activist role after conducting field research for over fifteen years in a region of Papua New Guinea that has been negatively affected by a large copper and gold mine called the Ok Tedi mine (see Map 1.4, p. 19). The mine releases 80,000 tons of mining wastes into the local river system daily, causing extensive environmental damage that in turn affects people's food and water sources. Kirsch has joined with the local community in its extended legal and political campaign to limit further pollution and to gain compensation for damages suffered. He explains his involvement with the community as a form of reciprocal exchange. The community members have provided him with information about their culture for over fifteen years. He believes that his knowledge is part of the people's cultural property and that they have a rightful claim to its use.

Kirsch's support of the community's goals took several forms. First, his scholarly research provided documentation of the problems of the people living downstream from the mine. Community activists incorporated his findings in their speeches when traveling in Australia, Europe, and the Americas to spread awareness of their case and gather international support. During the 1992 Earth Summit, one leader presented the media with excerpts from an article by Kirsch during a press conference held aboard the Greenpeace ship, *Rainbow Warrior II*, in the Rio de Janeiro harbor. Second, he worked closely with local leaders, helping them decide how best to convey their views to the public and in the court. Third, Kirsch served as a cultural broker in discussions among community members, politicians, mining executives, lawyers, and representatives of nongovernmental organizations (NGOs) in order to promote solutions for the problems faced by people living downstream from

Yonggom people gather at a meeting in Atkamba village on the Ok Tedi River to discuss legal proceedings in 1996. At the end of the meeting, leaders signed an agreement to an out-of-court settlement, which was presented to the Victorian Supreme Court in Melbourne, Australia. The current lawsuit concerns the Yonggom people's claim that the 1996 settlement agreement has been breached. ■ (Source: Courtesy of Stuart Kirsch)

the mine. Fourth, he convened an international meeting of environmental NGOs in Washington, DC, in 1999 and secured funding to bring a representative from the community to the meeting.

In spite of official reports recommending that the mine be closed in 2001, its future remains uncertain. No assessment of past damages to the community has been prepared. As the case goes on, Kirsch will continue to support the community's efforts by sharing with them the results of his research, just as they have for so long shared their culture with him. Indigenous people worldwide are increasingly invoking their rights to anthropological knowledge about themselves. According to Kirsch, these claims require anthropologists to rethink their roles and relationships with the people they study. It can no longer be a relationship in which the community provides knowledge and the anthropologist keeps and controls that knowledge for his or her intellectual development alone. Although the details are still being worked out, the overall goal must be one of collaboration and cooperation.

FOOD FOR THOUGHT

* Consider the pros and cons of anthropological advocacy, and decide what position you would take on the Ok Tedi case. Be prepared to defend your position.

learned from the case of CO-MADRES is that activist groups formed by women can be based on issues related to the domestic domain (murdered sons and other kin), but their activities can extend to the top of the public political hierarchy.

Another example of activist group formation under difficult conditions comes from urban Egypt (Hopkins and Mehanna 2000). The Egyptian government frowns on overt political action outside the realm of the government. Although Egyptian citizens are deeply concerned about environmental issues such as waste disposal, clean air and water, and noise, group formation for environmental causes is not easily accomplished. People interviewed in Cairo reported that they rarely discuss environmental issues with one another. One example of environmental concern, however, did result in the closing of a highly polluting lead smelter. In this case, the people in the affected neighborhood banded together around this particular issue and called attention to the situation in the public media, prompting high-level officials to take up their case. They were successful partly because their target was localized—one relatively small industry—and also because the industry was so clearly guilty of polluting the environment. This effort, however, did not lead to the formation of an enduring group.

In many post-USSR states, concern about the environment has prompted the emergence of many nongovernmental groups. In Poland, youth activism related to the environment grew in strength beginning in the late 1980s (Glínski 1994:145). This was the first generation to come after Stalin that had not experienced martial law, so the youth had less fear of organizing than their parents. Furthermore, the government's policy of limited liberalization involves concessions to social groups and the interests they expressed, and the mass media have greater freedom of expression. In opposition to dominant values of the 1960s and 1970s, members of the early phase of the Polish green movement promoted nonviolence, distance from the political system, and an ironic and gentle way of communicating their interests. The government promoted distance between it and the youth environmental groups in several ways: It ignored environmental issues, many political elites actively sought to marginalize the youth movement, and police units were dispatched against public protests of the youth groups (for example, demonstrations in the late 1980s and early 1990s against construction of a nuclear power plant and a dam).

The 1990s brought a second phase in youth involvement when preliminary dialogue between some organizations and the Ministry of Environmental Protection took place. The ministry established a special office and organized monthly meetings with representatives of the youth groups. The groups themselves are becoming

A march of the "Mothers of the Disappeared" in Argentina. This organization of women combines activism motivated by personal causes (the loss of one's child or children to political torture and death) and wider political concerns (state repressiveness in general). ■ *How many activist groups in your culture can you name, and what are their goals?* (Source: © Peter Menzel/Stock Boston, LLC)

more formally organized as nongovernmental organizations, and their activities receive support from national and international foundations and ecological groups. This example of the change in the role and organization of a social movement unfolded in the postsocialist context of Poland, but it shares general features with youth movements in other places, such as increased political involvement, organizational sophistication, and global linkages.

New Social Movements and Cyberpower

Social scientists have begun to use the term *new social movements* to refer to the many social activist groups that emerged in the late twentieth century around the world. (Chapter 16 presents some examples in the context of international development.) These groups are often formed by oppressed minorities such as indigenous peoples, ethnic groups, women, and the poor. Increasingly, they involve networks wider than the immediate social group. Most recently, they are taking advantage of cybertechnology to broaden their membership, exchange ideas, and raise funds (Escobar 2002).

Cyber-enhanced social movements are important new political actors and the source of promising ways to resist, transform, and present alternatives to current political structures. The importance of cybernetworking has not gone unnoticed by formal political leaders, who are paying increased attention to enhancing their personal websites and those of their parties.

The Big Questions Revisited

WHAT is the range of cross-cultural variation of social groups?

Social groups can be classified in terms of whether all members have face-to-face interaction with one another, whether membership is based on ascription or achievement, and how formal the group's organization and leadership structure are. They extend from the most informal, face-to-face groups, such as those based on friendship, to groups that have formal membership requirements and whose members are widely dispersed and never meet each other. All groups have some criteria for membership, often based on a perceived notion of similarity in terms of gender or class identity, work roles, opposition to mainstream culture, economic goals, or self-improvement.

Many groups require a formal ritual of initiation of new members. In some cases, initiation into the group involves dangerous or frightening activities that serve to bond members to one another through a shared experience of helplessness.

WHAT is social stratification, and what are its effects on people?

Social stratification consists of hierarchical relationships between and among different groups, usually based on some culturally defined concept of status. Depending on the context, categories such as class, "race," ethnicity, gender, sexual preference, age, and ability may determine group and individual status.

The degree of social inequality among different status groups is highly marked in agricultural and industrial/informatics societies. Marked status inequalities are not characteristic of most foraging societies. Status inequalities are variable in pastoralist and horticultural societies, with leveling mechanisms typically at play to prevent the formation of severe inqualities.

India's caste-based system is an important example of a rigid structure of severe social inequality based on a person's birth group. According to ancient Hindu scriptures, the population is divided into mutually exclusive groups with different rights and privileges. Discrimination on the basis of caste is banned by the Indian constitution, yet it still exists, as does racism in other contexts even though formally illegal.

WHAT is civil society?

Civil society consists of groups and organizations that, although they are not part of the formal government, perform similar or complementary economic, political, or social functions. Civil society groups can be divided into those that support government policies and initiatives, and thus further the interests of government, and those that oppose government policies and actions, such as environmental protest groups.

Some anthropologists who study activist groups decide to take an advocacy role and apply their knowledge to further the goals of the community. This direction in applied anthropology is related to the view that anthropological knowledge is partly the cultural property of the people who have shared their lives and insights with the anthropologist.

New forms of information and communication technology are helping civil society groups gain visibility and stay in touch with their supporters.

KEY CONCEPTS

achieved position, p. 244
ascribed position, p. 244
caste system, p. 249
civil society, p. 252
dalit, p. 249

diaspora population, p. 248
mechanical solidarity, p. 245
organic solidarity, p. 245
primary group, p. 234
secondary group, p. 234

social group, p. 234
social stratification, p. 244
status, p. 244
youth gang, p. 239

SUGGESTED READINGS

Sandra Bell and Simon Coleman, eds. *The Anthropology of Friendship*. New York: Berg, 1999. The editors provide an introductory chapter on enduring themes and future issues in the anthropological study of friendship. The nine essays discuss friendship in contemporary Melanesia, historical friendship as portrayed in Icelandic sagas, friendship in the context of a game of dominoes in a London pub, how friendship creates support networks in northern Europe, and the globalization of friendship ties revealed through an East African case.

Gerald Berreman. *Caste and Other Inequities: Essays on Inequality*. Delhi, India: Folklore Institute, 1979. These essays on caste and social inequality in India were written over a period of twenty years. Topics include caste and economy, caste ranking, caste and social interaction, and a comparison of caste with "race" in the United States.

Stanley Brandes. *Staying Sober in Mexico City*. Austin: University of Texas Press, 2002. This ethnography of Alcoholics Anonymous groups in Mexico City focuses on how these groups help low-income men remain sober through social support. Although emphasizing the role of human agency in these men's attempts to remain sober, the author reminds us that the high rate of alcoholism among poor Mexican men must be viewed in the context of structural conditions that make life very difficult.

Liliana Goldin, ed. *Identities on the Move: Transnational Processes in North America and the Caribbean Basin*. Austin: University of Texas Press, 2000. This collection offers essays on identity formation and change in the process of voluntary migration or displacement and on how states label and exclude transnationals, often in racialized ways.

Thomas A. Gregor and Donald Tuzin, eds. *Gender in Amazonia and Melanesia: An Exploration of the Comparative Method, 2001.* Berkeley: University of California Press, 2001. Two anthropologists, one a specialist on indigenous peoples of Amazonia and the other on Papua New Guinea, are the editors of this volume, which includes a theoretical overview chapter and then several chapters addressing similarities and differences between cultures of the two regions in domains such as fertility cults, rituals of masculinity, gender politics, and age-based gender roles.

Steven Gregory and Roger Sanjek, eds. *Race*. New Brunswick: Rutgers University Press, 1994. Each editor provides an introductory chapter, and other contributions discuss aspects of racism in the United States and the Caribbean, how "race" articulates with other inequalities, and racism in higher education and anthropology.

Cris Shore and Stephen Nugent, eds. *Elite Cultures: Anthropological Perspectives*. New York: Routledge, 2002. This volume contains two introductory chapters and a concluding chapter framing twelve ethnographic cases from around the world. Issues addressed are how elites in different societies maintain their positions, how elites represent themselves to others, how anthropologists study elites, and the implications of research on elites for the discipline of anthropology.

Karin Tice. *Kuna Crafts, Gender and the Global Economy*. Austin: University of Texas Press, 1995. This ethnographic study looks at how the tourist market has affected women's production of molas in Panama and how women have organized into cooperatives to improve their situation.

Kevin A. Yelvington. *Producing Power: Ethnicity, Gender, and Class in a Caribbean Workplace*. Philadelphia, PA: Temple University Press, 1995. This ethnography examines class, "race," and gender inequalities as linked processes of social stratification within the context of a factory in Trinidad and in the wider social sites of households, neighborhoods, and global interconnections.

10

Politics and Leadership

The Big Questions

- WHAT does political anthropology cover?

- WHAT are the major cross-cultural forms of political organization and leadership?

- HOW are politics and political organization changing?

A political leader of the Ashanti people, Ghana. British colonialists referred to such leaders with the English term "chief" although the term "king" might have been more appropriate. *(Source: © Henning Cristoph/DAS FOTOARCHIV/Peter Arnold)*

Recent news headlines:

Violence Continues in Afghanistan

North Korea Admits Having Nuclear Weapons

States Dump on Gay Marriage

Setback for U.N. Draft Resolution on Lebanon

Evolution Fight Shifts Direction in Kansas Vote

U.S. Border Reopens to Canadian Cattle

In Nashville, Sounds of Political Uprising from the Left

Report Calls for Tighter Rules in Nursing Home Evacuations

Future of the Insurgency in Iraq

These events are cultural happenings related to public power and politics. Anthropologists in all four fields address political and legal topics. Archaeologists study the evolution of centralized forms of political organization and the physical manifestations of power in monumental architecture, housing, and material possessions. Primatologists do research on dominant relationships, coalitions, and aggression among nonhuman primates. Linguistic anthropologists analyze power differences in interpersonal speech, the media, political propaganda, and more.

Political anthropology, a subfield of cultural anthropology, addresses the area of human behavior and thought related to power: who has it and who does not, degrees of power, bases of power, abuses of power, political organization and government, and relationships between political and religious power

Politics and Culture

Cultural anthropologists take a broader view of *politics* than political scientists do because their cross-cultural data indicate that many kinds of behavior and thought (in addition to formal party politics, voting, and government) are political. Cultural anthropologists offer important examples of political systems that might not look like political systems at all to people who have grown up in large states. This section explores basic political concepts from an anthropological perspective and raises the question of whether political systems are universal to all cultures.

British anthropologists, especially Bronislaw Malinowski and A. R. Radcliffe-Brown, long dominated theory making in political anthropology. Their approach, referred to as functionalism (review the discussion of this concept in Chapter 1), emphasized how institutions such as political organization and law promote social cohesion. Later, the students of these two teachers developed divergent theories. For example, in the late 1960s, some scholars began to look at aspects of political organization that pull societies apart. The new focus on disputes and conflict prompted anthropologists to gather information on dispute cases and to analyze the actors involved in a particular conflict.

This approach was later countered by a swing toward a more macro view that examines politics, no matter how local, within a global context (Vincent 1996). The global perspective prompted studies of colonialism and neocolonialism. Ann Stoler's book, *Capitalism and Confrontation in Sumatra's Plantation Belt, 1870–1979* (1985), on the history and cultural impact of Dutch colonialism in Indonesia, is a pioneer study in the anthropology of colonialism. Since the 1980s, the experiences of "subaltern" peoples (those subordinated by colonialism) and "subaltern movements" in former colonized regions have attracted research attention, particularly from native anthropologists of decolonizing countries.

The history of political anthropology in the twentieth century illustrates the theoretical tensions between the individual-as-agent approach and the structurist perspective that sees people as constrained in their choices by larger forces.

Politics: The Use of Power, Authority, and Influence

This book uses the term *politics* to refer to the organized use of public power, as opposed to the more private micropolitics of family and domestic groups. **Power** is the ability to bring about results, often through the possession or use of forceful means. Closely related to power are authority and influence. **Authority** is the right to take certain forms of action. It is based on a person's achieved or ascribed status or moral reputation. Authority differs from power in that power is backed up by the potential use of force and power can be wielded by individuals without their having authority in the moral sense.

Influence is the ability to achieve a desired end by exerting social or moral pressure on someone or some

---

power: the capacity to take action in the face of resistance, through force if necessary.

authority: the ability to take action based on a person's achieved or ascribed status or moral reputation.

influence: the ability to achieve a desired end by exerting social or moral pressure on someone or some group.

political organization: the existence of groups for purposes of public decision making and leadership, maintaining so-

cial cohesion and order, protecting group rights, and ensuring safety from external threats.

band: the political organization of foraging groups, with minimal leadership and flexible membership.

---

group. Unlike authority, influence may be exerted from a low-status and marginal position. All three terms are relational. A person's power, authority, or influence exists in relation to other people. Power implies the greatest likelihood of a coercive and hierarchical relationship, and authority and influence offer the most scope for consensual, cooperative decision making. Power, authority, and influence are all related to politics, power being the strongest basis for action and decision making—and potentially the least moral.

Politics: Cultural Universal?

Is politics a human universal? Some anthropologists would say no. They point to instances of cultures with scarcely any institutions that can be called political, with no durable ranking systems, and with very little aggression. Foraging lifestyles, as a model for early human evolution, suggest that nonhierarchical social systems characterized human life for 90 percent of its existence. Only with the emergence of private property, surpluses, and other changes did ranking systems, government, formal law, and organized aggression emerge. Also, studies show how dominance seeking and aggression are learned behaviors, emphasized in some cultures and among some segments of the population, such as the military, and deemphasized among others, such as religious leaders, healers, and child-care providers. Being a good politician or a five-star general is a matter of socialization (see Everyday Anthropology box).

Other anthropologists argue that despite a wide range of variation, politics is a human universal. Every society is organized to some degree by kinship relationships, and many anthropologists would not draw a clear boundary between how kinship organizes power and how political organization organizes power.

Political Organization and Leadership

Political organization is the existence of groups for purposes such as public decision making and leadership, maintaining social cohesion and order, protecting group rights, and ensuring safety from external threats. Power relationships situated in the private domain—within the household, for example—may be considered "political" and may be related to wider political realities, but they are not forms of political organization. Political organizations have several features, some of which overlap with those of the groups and organizations discussed in Chapter 9:

- *Recruitment principles:* Criteria for determining admission to the unit.

- *Perpetuity:* Assumption that the group will continue to exist indefinitely.

- *Identity markers:* Particular characteristics that distinguish it from others, such as costume, membership card, or title.

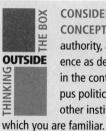

CONSIDER THE CONCEPTS of power, authority, and influence as defined here in the context of campus politics or in some other institution with which you are familiar.

- *Internal organization:* An orderly arrangement of members in relation to each other.

- *Procedures:* Prescribed rules and practices for behavior of group members.

- *Autonomy:* Ability to regulate its own affairs. (Tiffany 1979:71–72)

Cultural anthropologists cluster the many forms of political organization that occur cross-culturally into four major types (see Figure 10.1). The four types of political organization correspond, generally, to the major economic modes. Recall that the categories of economies represent a continuum, which suggests that there is overlap between different types rather than clear boundaries; this overlap exists between types of political organization as well.

Bands

A **band,** the form of political organization associated with foraging groups, involves flexible membership and the lack of formal leaders. Because foraging has been the predominant mode of production for almost all of human history, the band has been the most long-standing form of political organization. A band comprises between twenty people and a few hundred people at most, all related through kinship. These units come together at certain times of the year, depending on their foraging patterns and ritual schedule.

Band membership is flexible: If a person has a serious disagreement with another person or a spouse, one option is to leave that band and join another. Leadership is informal, with no one person named as a permanent leader. Depending on events, such as organizing the group to relocate or to send people out to hunt, a particular person may come to the fore as a leader for that time. This is usually someone whose advice and knowledge about the task are especially respected.

All members of the group are social equals, and a band leader has no special status. He has a certain degree of authority or influence, as perhaps a respected hunter or storyteller, but he does not have power, nor can he enforce his opinions on others. Social leveling mechanisms prevent anyone from accumulating much authority or influence. Political activity in bands involves mainly decision making about migration, food distribution, and

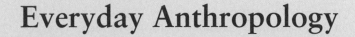

SOCIALIZATION AND WOMEN POLITICIANS

Parental attitudes and child-rearing practices affect children's involvement as adults in public political roles. Chunghee Sarah Soh's (1993) research in the Republic of Korea reveals how variation in paternal roles affects daughters' political leadership roles. Korean female members of the National Assembly can be divided into two categories: elected members (active seekers) and appointed members (passive recipients). Korea is a strongly patrilineal and male-dominated society, so female political leaders represent "a notable deviance from the usual gender-role expectations" (1993:54). This "deviance" is not stigmatized in Korean culture; rather, it is admired within the category of yŏgŏl. A yŏgŏl is a woman with "manly" accomplishments. Her personality traits include extraordinary bravery, strength, integrity, generosity, and charisma. Physically, a yŏgŏl is likely to be taller, larger, and stronger than most women and to have a stronger voice than other women. Why do some girls grow up to be a yŏgŏl?

Analysis of the life histories of elected and appointed female legislators offers clues about differences in their socialization. Elected female legislators were likely to have had atypical paternal experiences of two types: either an absent father or an atypically nurturant father. Both of these experiences facilitated a girl's socialization into yŏgŏl qualities, or, in the words of Soh, into developing an androgynous personality that combines both masculine and feminine traits. In contrast, the presence of a "typical" father results in a girl developing a more "traditional" female personality that is submissive and passive.

Representative Kim Ok-son greets some of her constituents who are members of a local Confucian club in Seoul, Republic of Korea. She is wearing a men's-style suit and has a masculine haircut. ■ (Source: Chunghee Sarah Soh)

An intriguing question follows from Soh's findings: What explains the socialization of different types of fathers—those who help daughters develop leadership qualities and those who socialize daughters for passivity?

FOOD FOR THOUGHT

- Given your microcultural experience, what socialization factors do you think might influence boys or girls to become politicians?

---

resolution of interpersonal conflicts. External conflict between groups is rare because territories of different bands are widely separated and the population density is low.

The band level of organization barely qualifies as a form of political organization because groups are flexible, leadership is ephemeral, and there are no signs or emblems of political affiliation. Some anthropologists argue that "real" politics did not exist in undisturbed band societies.

Tribes

A **tribe** is a more formal type of political organization than the band. Typically associated with horticulture and pastoralism, tribal organization developed about 10,000 to 12,000 years ago, with the emergence of these modes of production. A tribe is a political group that comprises several bands or lineage groups, each with similar language and lifestyle and each occupying a distinct territory. These groups may be connected through a clan

---

tribe: a political group that comprises several bands or lineage groups, each with similar language and lifestyle and occupying a distinct territory.

FIGURE 10.1 Modes of Political Organization

Foraging	Horticulture	Pastoralism	Agriculture	Industrialism/Informatics
Political Organization				**Political Organization**
Band	Tribe	Chiefdom	Confederacy	State
Leadership				**Leadership**
Band leader	Headman/Headwoman	Chief		King/queen/president
	Big-man	Paramount chief		prime minister/emperor
	Big-woman			
Social Conflict				**Social Conflict**
Face-to-face	Armed conflict	War		International war
Small-scale	Revenge killing			Technological weapons
Rarely lethal				Massively lethal
				Ethnic conflict
				Standing armies
Social Control				**Social Control**
Norms				Laws
Social pressure				Formal judiciary
Ostracism				Permanent police
				Imprisonment

Social Control

Increased population density and residential centralization ⟶

More surpluses of resources and wealth ⟶

More social inequality/ranking ⟶

Less reliance on kinship relations as the basis of political structures ⟶

Increased internal and external social conflict ⟶

Increased power and responsibility of leaders ⟶

Increased burdens on the population to support political organization ⟶

structure in which most people claim descent from a common ancestor, although they may be unable to trace the exact relationship. Kinship is the primary basis of membership. Tribal groupings contain from 100 to several thousand people. Tribes are found in the Middle East, South Asia, Southeast Asia, the Pacific, and Africa, as well as among Native Americans.

A tribal headman or headwoman (most are male) is a more formal leader than a band leader. Key qualifications for this position are being hardworking and generous and possessing good personal skills. A headman is a political leader on a part-time basis only, yet this role is more demanding than that of a band leader. Depending on the mode of production, a headman will be in charge of determining the times for moving herds, planting and harvesting, and setting the time for seasonal feasts and celebrations. Internal and external conflict resolution is also his responsibility. A headman relies mainly on authority and persuasion rather than on power. These strategies are effective because tribal members are all kin

and have loyalty to each other. Furthermore, exerting force on kinspersons is generally avoided.

Among many horticultural groups of the Amazonian rainforest, such as the Kayapo (see Map 10.1), tribal organization is the dominant political pattern. Each local tribal unit, which is itself a lineage, has a headman (or perhaps two or three). Each tribal group is autonomous, but recently many have united temporarily into larger groups, in reaction to threats to their environment and lifestyle from outside forces.

Pastoralist tribal formations are often linked into a *confederacy*, a loose umbrella organization linking several local tribal units or segments that maintain substantial autonomy. Normally, the local segments meet together rarely, perhaps only at an annual festival. In case of an external threat, however, the confederacy gathers together under one leader to deal with the problem. Once the threat is removed, local units resume their autonomy. This equality and autonomy of tribal units having the ability to unite and then disunite, is referred

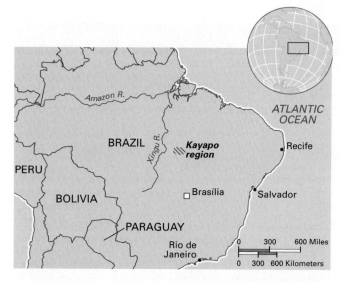

MAP 10.1 Kayapo Region in Brazil. The Kayapo live in several rainforest villages in the Matto Grosso plains region, south of the Amazon River. Their total population is around 7,000. The Kayapo use their traditional political organizing skills to help them deal with outsiders who seek to pursue commercial logging, mining, and hydroelectric development in the area.

Chief Paul Payakan, leader of the Kayapo, a group of indigenous horticulturalists living in the rainforest of the Brazilian Amazon. Payakan was instrumental in mobilizing widespread resistance in the region against the construction of a hydroelectric dam. ■ *Have you read in newspapers, or seen on television, news about the Kayapo or other Amazonian tribes recently? If so, what was the issue? If not, locate an update about the Kayapo on the Web.* (Source: © Hank Wittemore/CORBIS SYGMA)

to as a **segmentary model** of political organization. It exists among pastoralists worldwide (Eickelman 1981). For example, the Qashqa'i, pastoralists of Iran (see Map 3.5, p.74) have three levels of political organization: subtribe, tribe, and confederacy (Beck 1986). Leaders at each level deal with wider authorities and external forces on behalf of the tribespeople and communicate information to other levels. Leaders also help people in time of economic need.

Leadership among the Qashqa'i combines both ascribed and achieved features (review the definitions of these terms in Chapter 9). Subtribe headmen's positions are based mainly on achievement. Both *khans* (tribe leaders) and *ilkhanis* (confederacy leaders) are members of noble lineages. They gain their positions through patrilineal descent, with the eldest son favored. The role of the Qashqa'i ilkhani is similar in many ways to that of a chief (described in the next section).

The increased power of the state in recent decades has undermined the role of tribal leaders such as Borzu Qermezi, headman of one segment of the Qashqa'i tribe (Beck 1991). The state government formulated new policies regulating migratory schedules, pasture use, and prices of animal products. These new rules constrained the power of tribal leaders. Along with others, Borzu Qermezi lost significance to his followers, and they withdrew their support from him.

Big-Man and Big-Woman Leadership

In between tribal and chiefdom organizations is the **bigman system** or **big-woman system**, a form of political organization in which individuals build a political base and gain prestige, influence, and authority through a system of redistribution based on personal ties and grand feasts (as mentioned in Chapter 4). Anthropological research in Melanesia, a large region in the South Pacific including Papua New Guinea, established the existence

---

segmentary model: type of political organization in which smaller units unite in the face of external threats and then disunite when the external threat is absent.
big-man or big-woman system: a form of political organization midway between tribe and chiefdom involving reliance on the leadership of key individuals who develop a political following through personal ties and redistributive feasts.

moka: a strategy for developing political leadership in highland Papua New Guinea that involves exchanging gifts and favors with individuals and sponsoring large feasts where further gift giving occurs.

of the big-man type of politics, and most references to it are from this region (Sahlins 1963; Strathern 1971). Personalistic, favor-based political groupings are, however, also found elsewhere.

The political ties of a successful big-man or big-woman includes people in several villages. A big-man tends to have greater wealth than his followers, although people continue to expect him to be generous. The core supporters of a big-man tend to be kin, with extended networks including nonkin. A big-man has heavy responsibilities. He is responsible for regulating internal affairs, such as the timing of crop planting, and external affairs, such as intergroup feasts, trade, and war. In some instances, a big-man is assisted in carrying out his responsibilities by a group of other respected men. These councils include people from the big-man's different constituencies.

In several tribes in the Mount Hagen area of the Papua New Guinea highlands (see Map 1.4, p. 19), an aspiring big-man develops a leadership position through a process called **moka,** mentioned in Chapter 4 (Strathern 1971). Moka is a strategy for developing political leadership that involves exchanging favors and gifts, such as pigs, and sponsoring large feasts where further gift giving occurs. A crucial factor in big-manship in the Mount Hagen area is having at least one wife. An aspiring big-man urges his wives to work harder than ordinary women in order to grow more food to feed more pigs. The number of pigs a man has is an important measure of his status and worth. Given the importance of a wife or wives in maintaining a large collection of pigs, a man whose parents die when he is young is at an extreme disadvantage because he lacks financial support for the bridewealth required for marriage. Without parents, he has no bridewealth, no wife, no one to feed and care for pigs, no resource base for moka, and no chance of becoming a big-man.

A married man will use his wife's (or wives') production as a basis for developing and expanding exchange ties with contacts throughout the region. An aspiring big-man builds moka relationships first with kin and then beyond. By giving goods to people, he gains prestige over them. The recipient will later make a return gift of somewhat greater value. The exchanges go back and

Throughout much of the South Pacific, big-man and big-woman politics has long involved the demonstration of generosity on the part of the leaders, who are expected to be able to mobilize resources for impressive feasts such as this one on Tanna Island. ■ *How does this political system resemble or differ from a political system with which you are familiar?* (Source: © Kal Muller/ Woodfin Camp & Associates)

forth, over the years. The more he gives, and the more people in his exchange network, the greater prestige the big-man develops.

Although big-manship is an achieved position, analysis of the family patterns of big-manship in the Mt. Hagen area shows that most big-men are the sons of big-men (see Figure 10.2). This is particularly true of major big-men, of whom over three-quarters were sons of former big-men. It is unclear whether this pattern results from the greater wealth and prestige of big-man families, from socialization into big-manship through paternal example, or from a combination of these aspects.

With few exceptions, the early anthropological literature about tribal politics among indigenous peoples of Melanesia portrays men as dominating public exchange networks and the public political arenas. Women as wives are mentioned as important in providing the material basis for men's political careers. A study of Vanatinai (see Map 10.1, p. 264), however, a Pacific island that

	Father Was a Big-Man	Father Was Not a Big-Man	Totals
Major Big-Men	27	9	36
Minor Big-Men	31	30	61
Total	58	39	97

FIGURE 10.2 Family Background of Big-Men in Mt. Hagen, Papua New Guinea

Source: From The Rope of Moka: Big-Men and Ceremonial Exchange in Mount Hagen, New Guinea, p. 209, by Andrew Strathern. Copyright © 1971. Reprinted by permission of Cambridge University Press.

is gender-egalitarian, reveals the existence of big-women as well as big-men (Lepowsky 1990). In this culture, both men and women can gain power and prestige by sponsoring feasts at which valuables are distributed, especially mortuary feasts (feasts for the dead). Although more Vanatinai men than women are involved in political exchange and leadership building, some women are extremely active. These women lead sailing expeditions to neighboring islands to visit their exchange partners who are both male and female, and they sponsor lavish feasts attended by many people. On Vanatinai, big-women also include powerful sorcerers, famous healers, and successful gardeners.

Contact with European colonial culture gave men a political edge that they had not had before on Vanatinai. The Europeans traded with men for goods and approached women mainly for sexual relations. Formal government councils were established. Thus far, all councilors on Vanatinai have been male. In addition, some Vanatinai men have received training in the English language, the language of government, and thus have another advantage. In other cases, European domination led to more political equality between men and women with the imposition of "pacification," which ended local warfare and thereby eliminated one of the traditional paths to power for men.

Chiefdoms

A **chiefdom** is a form of political organization that includes permanently allied tribes and villages under one chief, a leader who possesses power. Compared to most tribes, chiefdoms have large populations, often numbering in the thousands. They are more centralized and socially complex. Hereditary systems of social ranking and economic stratification emerge in chiefdoms. Social divisions exist between the chiefly lineage(s) and nonchiefly groups. Chiefs and their descendants have higher status than commoners, and intermarriage between the two strata is forbidden. Chiefs are expected to be generous, but they may have a more luxurious lifestyle than the rest of the people.

The chiefship is an "office" that must be filled at all times. When a chief dies or retires, he or she must be replaced. In contrast, the death of a band leader or big-man or big-woman does not require that someone else be chosen as a replacement. A chief has more responsibilities than a band or tribal leader. He or she regulates production and redistribution, solves internal conflicts, and plans and leads raids and warring expeditions. Criteria for becoming a chief are clearly defined. Besides ascribed

Chief Joseph, or Hin-mah-too-yah-lat-kekt (Thunder Rolling Down the Mountain), of the Nez Perce, was born in northeastern Oregon in 1840. His father, Joseph the Elder, had been an active supporter of peace with the Whites and signed an agreement establishing the Nez Perce Reservation. In 1863, following the discovery of gold, the government took back almost six million acres of the land and attempted to force the Nez Perce onto the much reduced territory. After Joseph the Elder died, Joseph the Younger was elected Chief. He favored peace but continued White encroachments on Nez Perce land and government attempts to forcibly relocate his people prompted him to lead a war of resistance. ■ *Go the Internet and read his famous speech of surrender delivered in 1877.* (Source: Christie's Images/CORBIS)

criteria (birth in a chiefly lineage or being the first son or daughter of the chief), achievement is also important. Achievement is measured in terms of personal leadership skills, charisma, and accumulated wealth. Chiefdoms have existed throughout the world.

Anthropologists and archaeologists are interested in how and why chiefdom systems evolved as an intermediary unit between tribes and states and in what the political implications of this evolution are (Earle 1991). Several political strategies support the expansion of

chiefdom: a political unit of permanently allied tribes and villages under one recognized leader.

matriarchy: a society in which women are dominant in terms of economics, politics, and ideology.

power in chiefdoms: controlling more internal and external wealth and distributing feasting and gift exchanges that create debt ties; improving local production systems; applying force internally; forging stronger and wider external ties; and controlling ideological legitimacy. Depending on local conditions, different strategies were employed. Internal control of irrigation systems was the most important factor in the emergence of chiefdoms in prehistoric southeastern Spain, whereas control of external trade was more important in the prehistoric Aegean region (Gilman 1991).

Gender and Leadership in Chiefdoms

Much evidence about leadership patterns in chiefdoms comes from historical examples. Prominent chiefs—men and women—are documented in colonial archives and missionary records. Many historical examples of women chiefs and women rulers come from West Africa, including the Queen Mother of the Ashanti of Ghana and of the Edo of Nigeria (Awe 1977).

Oral histories and archival records show that Yoruba women had the institution of the *iyalode,* chief of the women. The iyalode was the women's political spokesperson in the "council of king makers," the highest level of government. She was a chief in her own right, with chiefly insignia, including the necklace of special beads, a wide-brimmed straw hat, a shawl, personal servants, special drummers, and bell ringers. She also had her own council of subordinate chiefs. The position of iyalode was based on achievement. The most important qualifications were her proven ability as a leader, economic resources to maintain her new status as chief, and popularity. Tasks included settling disputes via her court and meeting with women to formulate women's stand on such policy issues as the declaration of war and the opening of new markets. Although she represented all women in the group and had widespread support among women, she was outnumbered at the council of king makers because she was the only female and the only representative of all women.

The Iroquois of central New York provide a case of women's indirect political importance (J. K. Brown 1975) (see Map 3.3, p. 73). Men were chiefs, but women and men councilors were the appointing body. Most adult males were gone for extended periods, waging war as far away as Delaware and Virginia. Women controlled production and distribution of the staple crop, maize. If the women did not want warriors to leave for a particular campaign, they would refuse to provide them with maize, thereby vetoing the plan. Some have said that the Iroquois are an example of a **matriarchy,** or a society in which women are dominant in terms of economics, politics, and ideology. But most anthropologists think that the Iroquois are better characterized as an egalitarian society, because women did not control the society to the exclusion of men

nor did they oppress men as a group. Men and women participated equally on the councils.

Why do women play greater political roles in some chiefdoms than in others? The most satisfactory answers point to women's economic roles as the primary basis for political power, as among the Iroquois and many African horticultural societies. In contrast, the dominant economic role of men in Native American groups of the prairies, following the introduction of the horse by the Spanish and the increased importance of buffalo hunting by men, supported male-dominated political leadership in Indian groups such as the Cheyenne.

A marked change in leadership patterns in chiefdoms in the past few hundred years is the decline of women's political status due to European and North American colonial and missionary influences (Etienne and Leacock 1980). For example, British colonialists redefined the institution of iyalode in Nigeria. Now "she is no longer a member of any of the important councils of government. Even the market, and therefore the market women, have been removed from her jurisdiction, and have been placed under the control of the new local government councils in each town" (1980:146).

THINKING OUTSIDE THE BOX WHAT IMAGES do you have of Pocahontas and what is their source? Do some research to trace her story and perhaps compare it to the depiction of Pocahontas in the Walt Disney movie about her.

Pocahontas played an important role in Native American–British relations during the early colonial period. ■ (Source: North Wind Picture Archives)

Ethnohistorical research on chiefdoms in Hawai'i provides another example of powerful women chiefs in precolonial times (Linnekan 1990). Following Captain Cook's arrival in 1778, a Western-model monarchy was established. By the time the United States annexed the islands in 1898, indigenous Hawaiian leaders had been completely displaced by westerners.

Confederacies

Parallel to the situation discussed in the section on tribes, an expanded version of the chiefdom occurs when several chiefdoms are joined in a confederacy. Such a group is headed by a chief of chiefs, "big chief," or paramount chief. Many prominent confederacies existed, for example, in Hawai'i in the late 1700s, the Iroquois league of five nations that stretched across New York state, the Cherokee of Tennessee, and the Algonquins who dominated the Chesapeake region in present-day Virginia and Maryland. In the Algonquin confederacy, each village had a chief, and the regional council was composed of local chiefs and headed by the paramount chief. Powhatan, father of Pocahontas, was paramount chief of the Algonquins when the British arrived in the early 1600s.

In the New World, chiefdom confederacies were supported financially by contributions of grain from each local unit. Kept in a central storage area where the paramount chief lived, the grain was used to feed warriors during external warfare that maintained and expanded the confederacy's borders. A council building existed in the central location, where local chiefs came together to meet with the paramount chief to deliberate on questions of internal and external policy.

States

A **state** is a centralized political unit encompassing many communities, a bureaucratic structure, and leaders who possess coercive power. Earliest evidence of the state form of political organization comes from Mesopotamia, China, India, and Egypt, perhaps as early as 4000 BCE. States emerged with the development of intensive agriculture, increased food surpluses, increased population density, and the emergence of cities. The state is now the form of political organization in which all people live. Band organizations, tribes, and chiefdoms exist, but they are incorporated within state structures.

Many theories exist about why the state evolved (Trigger 1996). Demographic theory says that population density drove the need for central mechanisms for social control. Economic theory argues that the state emerged in response to the increased surpluses of food production in the Neolithic era, which produced sufficient wealth to support a permanent ruling class. Political theory says that the state arose as a necessary structure to manage increased competition for land and access to food surpluses. Marxist theory says that the state emerged to maintain the dominance of the ruling class. Rather than emphasizing a single causal factor, most scholars now include multiple causes in their theories of the origin of states. Cultural anthropologists, however, are now more interested in how states become and remain states than why they first emerged.

The Power of the State

Cultural anthropologists seek to learn how states operate and relate to their citizens. Their research shows that states have much more power compared to bands, tribes, and chiefdoms (see Figure 10.3). Religious beliefs and symbols are often closely tied to the power of state leadership: The ruler may be considered to be a deity or part deity, or may be a high priest of the state religion, or perhaps be closely linked with the high priest, who serves as advisor. Architecture and urban planning remind the populace of the greatness of the state. In pre-Columbian Mexico, the central plaza of city-states, such as Tenochtitlan (founded in 1345), was symbolically equivalent to the center of the cosmos and was thus the locale of greatest significance (Low 1995). The most important temples and the residence of the head of state were located around the plaza. Other houses and structures, in decreasing order of status, were located on avenues in decreasing proximity to the center. The grandness and individual character of the leader's residence indicate power, as do monuments—especially tombs to past leaders or heroes or heroines. Egypt's pyramids, China's Great Wall, and India's Taj Mahal are a few of the world's great architectural reminders of state power.

In democratic states where leaders are elected by popular vote and in socialist states where political rhetoric emphasizes social equality, expense and elegance are muted by the adoption of more egalitarian ways of dress (even though in private, these leaders may live relatively opulent lives in terms of housing, food, and entertainment). The earlier practice of all Chinese leaders wearing a "Mao jacket," regardless of their rank, was a symbolic statement of their anti-hierarchical philosophy. A quick glance at a crowd of people, including the Prime Minister of Canada or Britain or the President of the United States, would not reveal who was the leader because

---

state: a centralized political unit encompassing many communities and possessing coercive power.

in-kind taxation: a system of mandatory non-cash contributions to the state.

---

dress differences are avoided. Even members of British royalty wear "street clothes" on public occasions where regalia are not required.

Local Power and Politics in Democratic States

The degree to which states influence the lives of their citizens varies, as does the ability of citizens to influence the political policies and actions of their governments. Some anthropologists, as citizens, use their knowledge of culture at home or abroad to influence politics in their own countries (see the Lessons Applied box). So-called totalitarian states have the most direct control of local politics. In most other systems, local politics and local government are granted some degree of power. In highly centralized states, the central government controls public finance and legal institutions, leaving little power or autonomy in these matters to local governments. In decentralized systems, local governments are granted some forms of revenue generation (taxation) and the responsibility of providing certain services.

Local politics of varying types continue to exist within state systems, their strength and autonomy being dependent on how centralized the state apparatus is. This section describes village politics in Japan, factional politics in Belize that link different localities, and local electoral politics in France to illustrate varying patterns of local political dynamics.

In Japan, relatively egalitarian systems of local power structures exist in villages and hamlets. Families subtly vie for status and leadership roles through gift giving, as is common in local politics worldwide (Marshall 1985). Egalitarianism prevails as a community value, but people strive to be "more than equal" by making public donations to the buraku, or hamlet. The custom of giving a gift to the community is a way that hamlet families can improve their positions in the local ranking system. In one hamlet, all thirty-five households recently gave gifts to the community on specified occasions: the forty-second birthday of male family members, the sixty-first birthday of male family members, the seventy-seventh birthday of male family members, the marriage of male family members, the marriage of a female family member whose husband will be the household successor, the birth of the household head or successor couple's first child, and the construction of a new house. These occasions for public gift giving always include a meal to which members of all hamlet households are invited. Since the 1960s, it has also become common to give an item that is useful for the hamlet, such as a set of fluorescent light fixtures for the hamlet hall, folding tables, space heaters, and vacuum cleaners.

THINKING OUTSIDE THE BOX

WHAT ARE some key symbols of state power in your home country?

FIGURE 10.3   The Powers of States

- *States define citizenship and its rights and responsibilities.* In complex societies, since early times, not all residents were granted equal rights as citizens.

- *States monopolize the use of force and the maintenance of law and order.* Internally, the state controls the population through laws, courts, and the police. Externally, the state uses force defensively to maintain its borders and offensively to extend its territory.

- *States maintain standing armies and police* (as opposed to part-time forces).

- *States keep track of the number, age, gender, location, and wealth of their citizens through census systems that are regularly updated.* A census allows the state to maintain formal taxation systems, military recruitment, and policy planning, including population settlement, immigration quotas, and social benefits such as old-age pensions.

- *States have the power to extract resources from citizens through taxation.* All political organizations are supported by contributions of the members, but variations

occur in the rate of contributions expected, the form in which they are paid, and the return that members get in terms of services. In bands, people voluntarily give time or labor for "public projects" such as a group hunt or a planned move. Public finance in states is based on formal taxation that takes many forms. **In-kind taxation** is a system of mandatory, non-cash contributions to the state. For example, the Inca state used a labor tax, to finance public works such as roads and monuments and to provide agricultural labor on state lands. Another form of in-kind taxation in early states required that farmers pay a percentage of their crop yield. Cash taxes, such as the income tax that takes a percentage of wages, emerged only in the past few hundred years.

- *States manipulate information.* Control of information to protect the state and its leaders can be done directly (through censorship, restricting access to certain information by the public, and promotion of favorable images via propaganda) and indirectly (through pressure on journalists and television networks to present information in certain ways).

Afghanistan Prime Minister Hamed Karzai wears a carefully assembled collection of regional political symbols. The striped cape is associated with northern tribes. The Persian-lamb hat is an Uzbek style popular in the capital city, Kabul. He also wears a tunic and loose trousers, which are associated with villagers, and sometimes adds a Western-style jacket as well. His clothing implies a statement of unity and diversity about his country. ■ *Study clothing styles of other state leaders and see if you can "read" their symbolic messages.* (Source: © Reuters NewMedia Inc./CORBIS)

nomic differences between the two villages are important. In Mt. Hope, the government provided residents with land and established a marketing board to purchase villagers' crops. Farmers grow rice for the domestic market

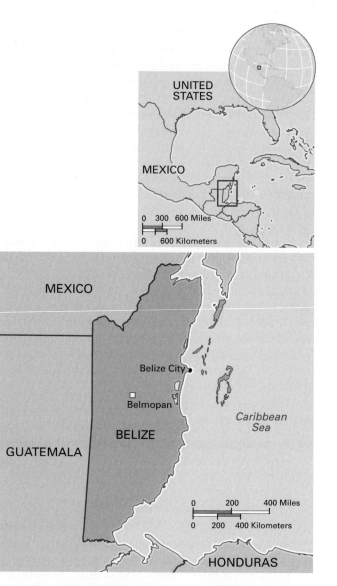

MAP 10.2   Belize. The only English-speaking country in Central America, Belize was a British colony known as British Honduras until 1973. Agriculture and international tourism are the most important parts of the economy. The population is 300,000 and growing rapidly, since Belize's fertility rate is among the highest in the world. The dominant religion is some form of Christianity, especially Roman Catholicism. English is the official language, but the most commonly used language is Belizean Kriol, spoken by 70 percent of the population as a first language. Mayan languages are spoken in the west and north.

Local politics within a democratic framework may involve another type of gift giving and exchange in the interest of maintaining or gaining power. People in elected positions of power give favors in expectation of political loyalty in return. In these cases, various factions vie with each other. A **faction** is a politically oriented group whose members are mobilized and maintained by a leader to whom the ties of loyalty are lateral—from leader to follower (Brumfiel 1994). Factions tend to lack formal rules and formal succession in their leadership.

Two villages in Belize show a contrast in the development and role of factional politics (Moberg 1991) (see Map 10.2). One village, Mt. Hope, is faction free; the other village, Charleston, has divisive factionalism. Eco-

faction: a politically oriented group with strong lateral ties to a leader.

Lessons Applied

CULTURAL KNOWLEDGE FOR ENGAGED CITIZENSHIP

Several times during the 1980s and 1990s, David Price conducted fieldwork on rural development and irrigation in Egypt. Following a trip to Egypt in October 2002, he, along with other Middle East scholars from his region in Washington State, held a series of meetings with their congressional representative (Price, personal communication, 2003). Their goal was to convince the congressman to change his upcoming vote from authorizing military action against Iraq to opposing it. In meetings with the congressman, Price emphasized his firsthand, street-level knowledge of Egyptian people's opinions about, and probable reactions to, such a war. He stressed how U.S. pressures on Egypt's president Mubarak could destabilize U.S. interests in Egypt and how U.S. military action would strengthen the position of Islamic fundamentalists throughout the Middle East. Price gave his congressman (and the congressman's wife, a former World Bank economist) copies of editorials and other papers he had written.

A few weeks after the vote, Price happened to meet up with the congressman and his wife. They both remarked how his information on everyday Egyptians' interpretations of U.S. actions had prompted them to rethink the congressman's position. On the basis of Price's insights, the congressman was also inspired to ask probing questions of CIA and State Department briefing personnel regarding the instability that U.S. military action in Iraq could bring to Egypt, as well as probing questions pertaining to U.S. threats to withhold aid to Egypt if it opposed military action.

FOOD FOR THOUGHT

- Choose a contemporary political issue, and compose a mock letter to the government representative of your home district supporting a position on that issue. Imagine that you are a cultural anthropologist with relevant knowledge to back up your position. What will you say in your letter?

---

and citrus crops for export. Citrus growers account for about half of Mt. Hope's households, receive more than three-fourths of its total income, and control about 87 percent of the land. In Charleston, most men work in small-scale fishing augmented by part-time farming. Lack of a road that would allow export of agricultural crops has inhibited the development of commercial agriculture. Start-up costs for citrus cultivation (fertilizer, insecticide, tractors) are prohibitive for most Charleston households. Charleston is "racked by intense intergroup conflict," and that includes factional conflict that divides kin groups: "One of the village's most acrimonious political conflicts exists between two brothers whose relationship deteriorated when the allies of one brother were excluded from a cooperative that the other had organized" (1991:221). Intense factionalism in Charleston is sustained by outside political party patronage and favor giving. Local faction leaders vie with one another to obtain grants and other benefits from the state. In return, national political parties look to Charleston as a base for developing political loyalties. The national parties have bypassed Mt. Hope because economic development created less dependence on state favors for projects such as a cooperative or a road. Charleston was ripe for political manipulation; Mt. Hope was not.

In rural France, family ties and family reputation influence who becomes an elected local leader (Abélès 1991).

The department of Yonne, located in the Burgundy region (see Map 10.3) southeast of Paris, is the "provincial heartland" of France. Fieldwork there was devoted to understanding how individuals gained access to local political office, and it involved interviewing local politicians, attending town council meetings, and following local elections. France is divided into 36,000 communes that are grouped in ninety-six departments. Communes and departments are the major arenas for local politics. At the commune level, elected officials are the mayor and town councilors. Several political parties contest the elections—the Socialist party, the Union for French Democracy, and others, including scattered support for the Communist party.

A successful candidate for either commune or department positions should have local roots and come from a distinguished family. Typically, the same family names recur again and again. In one town, the Truchots and the Rostains dominated public life for over a half century. Both families were grain and wine merchants. Another factor influencing electoral choice is a bias toward incumbents. The monopoly of political office by a certain family is perceived by local people to contribute to order and peace. Thus, local roots, reputation, and networks combine with a value placed on continuity as the ingredients for electoral success in rural France (see Critical Thinking box). This combination is summed up in the

Critical Thinking

HOW "OPEN" IS DEMOCRATIC ELECTORAL POLITICS?

In France, the only legal requirements for office are French citizenship and age. Other than that, elected positions are, in principle, open to anyone interested in contesting them. According to the perspective that emphasizes human agency in shaping behavior and events, one would hypothesize nearly complete openness in elections and low predictive value of "name" or "family" in determining electoral success. But such "openness" does not seem to be the case in rural Burgundy (Bourgogne) and may not exist elsewhere.

In comparison, consider the dynamics of the local political system(s) in which you have lived.

MAP 10.3   France. The French Republic comprises a wide variety of landscapes throughout its many departments, both on the mainland (Metropolitan France) and in its overseas departments and territories. France possesses the second largest Exclusive Economic Zone (EEZ) in the world, after the United States. The population of Metropolitan France is 61 million people. France is one of the most ethnically diverse countries of the world, with over half of its population claiming a foreign background. The official language is French, although several regional languages are spoken throughout Metropolitan France, along with immigrant communities' languages that include many African languages, several varieties of Chinese, Khmer, and Turkish.

CRITICAL THINKING QUESTIONS

- What are the criteria in your home country for eligibility to hold office?
- Do all eligible people appear to run for office on an equal basis?
- Do all eligible people appear equally successful in being elected?
- How do the electoral success patterns of candidates resemble or differ from that described for rural Burgundy?

concept of legitimacy. "To enjoy legitimacy is to belong to a world of eligible individuals, those to whom responsibilities can be entrusted. Legitimacy is an elusive quality at first glance: certain individuals canvassing the votes of their fellow-citizens are immediately recognized as legitimate, while others, despite repeated efforts, are doomed to failure. . . . It is as though a candidate's legitimacy is something people instinctively recognize" (1991:265).

Gender and Leadership in States

Most contemporary states are hierarchical and patriarchal, excluding members of lower classes and women from equal participation. Some states are less male dominated than others, but none is female dominated. One view of gender inequality in states suggests that increasing male dominance with the evolution of the state is

nation: a group of people who share a language, culture, territorial base, political organization, and history.

Secretary of State Condoleeza Rice arrived at the Weisbaden Army Airfield in February 2005 to introduce U.S. president George W. Bush and first lady Laura Bush to American troops based in Germany. ■ *What messages is she conveying in her dress?* (Source: © Michael Probst—AP)

differences range from an average of 40 percent female parliamentarians in the Nordic states to 8 percent in Arab states.

A few contemporary states have or have recently had women as prime ministers or presidents. Powerful women leaders of the twentieth century include Indira Gandhi in India, Golda Meir in Israel, Margaret Thatcher in the United Kingdom, and Benazir Bhutto in Pakistan. Often, female heads of state are related by kinship (as wife or daughter) to former heads of state. Indira Gandhi, for example, was the daughter of the popular first prime minister of independent India, Jawaharlal Nehru (she was not related to Mahatma Gandhi). It is unclear, however, whether these women's leadership positions are explained by their inheriting the role or through the political socialization they may have received, directly or indirectly, as a result of being born into political families. In the early years of the twenty-first century, several women gained positions as heads of state: Michelle Bachelet as President of Chile, Angela Merkel as Chancellor of Germany, Ellen Johnson-Sirleaf as President of Liberia, and Tarja Halonen as President of Finland.

Women's leadership roles can also be indirect, as mothers or wives of male rulers, such as Eva Peron in Argentina as wife of the president and Hillary Clinton in the United States when she was First Lady. Women may also wield indirect political power through their children, especially sons. In Turkey, most parents consider politics an undesirable career for their children but more women than men are favorable toward their sons' political ambitions (Güneş-Ayata 1995:238–239). Mothers of male political leaders use their maternal position to influence politics. Direct political roles are largely closed to them.

based on male control of the technology of production and warfare (Harris 1993). Women in most cultures have limited access to these areas of power. In states that are more peaceful, such as Finland, Norway, Sweden, and Denmark, women's political roles are more prominent.

Strongly patriarchal contemporary states preserve male dominance through ideologies that restrict women's political power. In much of the Muslim Middle East, Central Asia, Pakistan, and northern India, the practice of purdah, female seclusion and segregation from the public world, limits women's public roles. In China, scientific beliefs that categorize women as less strong and dependable than men have long been used to rationalize the exclusion of women from politics (Dikötter 1998). Socialist states typically attempt to increase women's political roles, and the proportion of female members of legislative bodies is higher in socialist states than in capitalist democracies. But it is still not equal to that of men. Although women account for roughly half of the world's population, they form only, on average, 16 percent of the world's parliamentary members (Lederer 2006). The proportion has risen from 11.3 percent in 1995. Regional

In the early days of political anthropology, researchers examined the varieties of political organization and leadership and created the categories of bands, tribes, chiefdoms, and states. Contemporary political anthropologists are more interested in political dynamics and change, especially in how the preeminent political form, the state, affects local people's lives. This section covers selected topics in the anthropological study of political change.

Emerging Nations and Transnational Nations

Many different definitions exist for a nation, and some of them overlap with definitions given for a state (Maybury-Lewis 1997b:125–132). One definition says that a **nation** is a group of people who share a language, culture, territorial base, political organization, and history (Clay

A political rally of indigenous people in Bolivia. ■ *Do some research to discover the political concerns of indigenous peoples in Bolivia.* (Source: Roshani Kothari)

President Evo Morales of Bolivia, elected in 2005, is the country's first indigenous head of state. He opposes what he refers to as "savage capitalism" and supports policies to improve the conditions for indigenous people in Bolivia. As the new president, his first international tour was to several Latin American countries, including Cuba, thus breaking with the tradition of the United States as the first international destination of a new president. ■ (Source: David Mercado/Reuters/CORBIS)

1990). In this sense, a nation is culturally homogeneous, and the United States would be considered not a nation but rather a political unit composed of many nations. According to this definition, groups that lack a territorial base cannot be termed nations. A related term is the nation-state, which some say refers to a state that comprises only one nation, whereas others think it refers to a state that comprises many nations. An example is the Iroquois nation (see Map 3.3, p. 73).

Depending on their resources and power, nations and other groups may constitute a political threat to state stability and control. Examples include the Kurds in the Middle East (see Culturama, this chapter), the Maya of Mexico and Central America (see Culturama, Chapter 11), Tamils in Sri Lanka, Tibetans in China, and Palestinians in the Middle East. In response to this (real or perceived) threat, states seek to create and maintain a sense of unified identity. Political scientist Benedict Anderson, in his book *Imagined Communities* (1991 [1983]) writes about the efforts that builders of states employ to create a sense of belonging—"imagined community"—among diverse peoples. Strategies include the imposition of one language as the national language; the construction of monuments and museums that emphasize unity; and the use of songs, poetry, and other media messages to promote an image of a unified country. Some states, such as

China, control religious expression in the interest of promoting loyalty to and identity with the state. Another strategy is to draw on symbols of minority or ancestral groups and bring them into the center, thus creating a sense of belonging through recognition. Such recognition may also be interpreted as a form of co-optation, depending on the context. When South Africa launched its new Coat of Arms in 2000, then President Mbeke pointed out that the inclusion of a rock art drawing and a slogan in an extinct San language were intended to evoke both South Africa's distant past and its emerging identity as a socially complex and peaceful country.

Inspired by Anderson's writings, many anthropologists study state laws, policies, and other practices that seek to create a sense of unity out of diversity. Their work shows that attempts by states to force homogenization of nations and ethnic groups will inevitably

Supporters of independence for East Timor celebrate on the streets of Dili as Indonesian soldiers leave the capital in September 1999. ■ *Do Internet research to learn about the current political situation in East Timor. Who is the leader? What kind of government has been put in place?* (Source: © Reuters/Jason Reed)

group movements for autonomy have been suppressed, sometimes brutally, or lead to long-term internal conflicts. In spite of ongoing pressure to build strong states, several states are labeled as "weak," while others have "failed." Political theorists and U.S. leaders fear that weak states are easy targets for outside intervention and provide havens for terrorists. Thus, much international aid and military support goes to programs that aim at strengthening weak states. *Failed states* share features of a breakdown in law and order, economic deterioration, the collapse of service delivery such as education and health, a sharp decline in living standards, and loss of people's loyalty to the government (Wainwright 2003). Examples of failed states in recent times include Liberia, the Democratic Republic of the Congo, Sudan, and Somalia (see Map 10.5, p. 277). Today, Somalia exists in two separate units: Somaliland, which is relatively stable, and Puntland, a situation of warlordism and factional fighting.

With so many examples of weak states and failed states, some anthropologists ask if perhaps the idea of the state should be reconsidered (Graeber 2004). Options include the development of more, smaller states that correspond more closely to national/ethnic identities, or, on the other hand, the abandoning of country borders and creation of a global state within which all people could move freely. If, one could argue, the point of a state is to prevent human suffering by providing a benevolent structure that provides for people's welfare and human rights, and many states are unable to accomplish this goal, then perhaps other avenues must be explored.

Globalization and increased international migration also prompt anthropologists to rethink the concept of the

prompt resistance of varying degrees from those groups that wish to retain or regain autonomy. Mexico, for example, is promoting a unified identity centered in *mestizaje* (mestizo, or people of mixed Spanish and Indian ancestry) culture and heritage (Alonso 2004). Monuments and museums in Mexico City place mestizaje symbols at the forefront and draw links to Aztec ancestors. They suppress connections with both highland Indians and the Spanish colonialists in an attempt to forge a new sense of political nationalism and consciousness that values hybridity and mixture. Emphasizing the Aztecs as the cultural roots of Mexican heritage frames out other indigenous groups and further marginalizes their position in the imagined nation-state of Mexico. On the other side of the world, in the Middle East, the Kurds provide an example of an ethnic group spanning several countries whose cultural rights are consistently denied (see Culturama).

For the past few centuries, leading global powers have promoted the notion of the strong state as the best option for promoting world peace. To that end, minority

The Coat of Arms of South Africa, adopted in 2000, is meant to highlight democratic change and multicultural unity. ■ *For a class project, study the coat of arms of several countries in terms of their symbols and slogans.* (Source: Republic of South Africa)

Culturama

The Kurds of the Middle East

The Kurds are an ethnic group of between 20 to 30 million people, most of whom speak some dialect of the Kurdish language, which is related to Persian (Major 1996). The majority are Sunni Muslims. Kurdish kinship is strongly patrilineal and Kurdish family and social relations are male dominated.

Their home region, called Kurdistan ("Place of the Kurds"), extends from Turkey into Iran, Iraq, and Syria. This area is grasslands, interspersed with mountains, with no coastline. Before World War I, many Kurds were full-time pastoralists, herding sheep and goats. Following the war and the creation of Iraq, Syria, and Kuwait, many Kurdish herders were unable to follow their traditional grazing because they crossed the new country borders. Herders no longer live in tents year-round, though some do for part of the year. Others are farmers. In towns and cities, Kurds own shops, are professionals, and are employed in many different occupations.

Reliable population data for the Kurds in the Middle East do not exist, and estimates vary widely. About half of all Kurds, numbering between 10 and 15 million, live in Turkey where they constitute 20 percent or perhaps more of the total population. Approximately 6 million live in Iran, 4 to 5 million in Iraq, and 1.5 million in Syria. Others live in Armenia, Germany, France, and the United States.

The Kurds have attempted to establish an independent state for decades, with no success and often facing harsh treatment from government forces. In Turkey, the state used to refer to them as "Mountain Turks," and in many ways still refuses to recognize them as a legitimate minority group. Use of the Kurdish language is restricted in Turkey. The Kurds have faced similar repression in Iraq, especially following their support of Iran in the 1980–1988 Iran–Iraq war. Sadam Hussein razed villages and used chemical weapons against the Kurds. After the Persian Gulf War, 2 million Kurds fled to Iran. Many others have emigrated to Europe and the United States. Iraqi Kurds gained political autonomy from Baghdad in 1991 following a successful uprising aided by Western forces.

Many Kurds feel united by the shared goal of statehood, but several strong internal political factions and a guerrilla movement in Turkey also exist among the Kurds. Kurds in Turkey seek the right to have Kurdish-language schooling and television and radio broadcasts, and they would like to have their folklore recognized as well. The Kurds are fond of music and dancing, and Kurdish villages are known for their distinct performance styles.

Readings

Diane E. King. Asylum Seekers/Patron Seekers: Interpreting Iraqi Kurdish Migration. *Human Organization* 64(4):316–326.

Lokman I. Meho and Kelly Maglaughlin. *Kurdish Culture and Society: An Annotated Bibliography.* Westport, CT: Greenwood Press, 2001.

Martin Van Bruinessen. *Agha, Shaikh, and the State: On the Social and Political Organization of Kurdistan.* Atlantic Highlands, NJ: Zed Press, 1992.

Videos

Jiyan (Jano Rosebiani, dir., 2002).
Long Live the Bride . . . and the Liberation of Kurdistan (Hiner Saleem, dir., 1997).
Turtles Can Fly (Bahman Ghobadi, dir., 2004).

Website

www.kurd.org/kurdlinks.html

Thanks to Diane E. King, Brown University and Washington State University, for reviewing this material.

Kurdish sheep herders (left). Goat and sheep herding is still a major part of the Kurdish economy throughout Kurdistan. ■ (Source: blickwinkel/Alamy) *In Dohuk, Iraq, the Mazi Supermarket and Dream City are a combination shopping and amusement park (right). The goods in the market come mainly from Dubai and Turkey.* ■ (Source: Ed Kashi/CORBIS)

MAP 10.4 *Kurdish Region in the Middle East. Kurdistan includes parts of Iran, Iraq, Syria, Turkey, and Armenia. About half of the Kurds live in Turkey.*

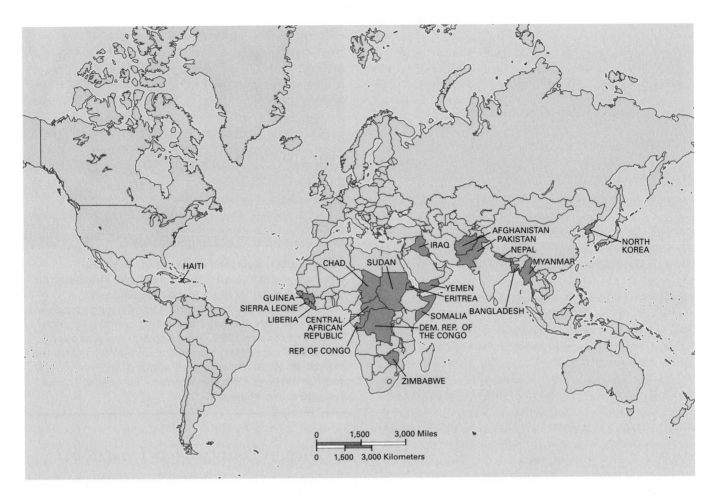

MAP 10.5 Failed States of the World, 2006. A failed state is defined as one in which the government does not have effective control over its territory, is not seen as legitimate by a significant proportion of its population, does not provide services and domestic security to its citizens, and lacks a monopoly on the use of force.

state (Trouillot 2001). The case of Puerto Rico (see Map 10.6) is particularly illuminating because of its continuing status as a quasi-colony of the United States (Duany 2000). Puerto Rico is neither fully a state of the United States nor an autonomous political unit with its own national identity. Furthermore, Puerto Rican people do not co-exist in a bounded spatial territory. By the late 1990s, nearly as many Puerto Ricans lived in the United States mainland as on the island of Puerto Rico. Migration to Puerto Rico also occurs, creating cultural diversity there. Migrants include returning Puerto Ricans and others from the United States, such as Dominicans and Cubans.

These migration streams—outgoing and incoming—complicate in two ways the sense of Puerto Rico as constituting a nation. First, half of the "nation" lives outside the home territory. Second, within the home territory, ethnic homogeneity does not exist because of the diversity of people who migrate there. The Puerto Ricans who are return migrants are different from the islanders because many have adopted English as their primary language. All of these processes foster the emer-

gence of a transnational identity, which differs from a national identity centered in either the United States or Puerto Rico. (Chapter 15 provides additional material on transnationalism.)

Democratization

Democratization is the process of transformation from an authoritarian regime to a democratic regime. This process includes several features: the end of torture, the liberation of political prisoners, the lifting of censorship, and the toleration of some opposition (Pasquino 1996:173). In some cases, what is achieved is more a relaxation of authoritarianism than a true transition to democracy, which would occur when the authoritarian regime is no longer in control. Political parties emerge, some presenting traditional interests and others oppositional.

THINKING OUTSIDE THE BOX

WHAT IS your position on states: Are they the best option for a peaceful world and for providing internal security and services for citizens? What are some examples of successful states?

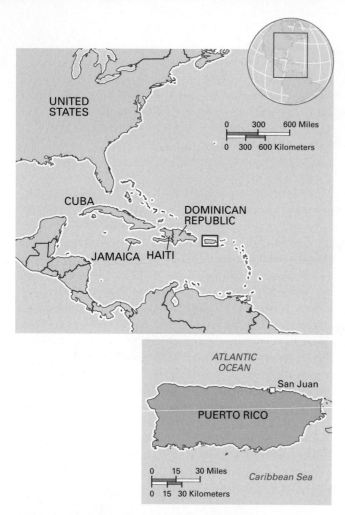

MAP 10.6 Puerto Rico. The Commonwealth of Puerto Rico is a U.S. territory with Commonwealth status. The indigenous population of the island, the Tainos, is extinct. Analysis of DNA of current inhabitants of Puerto Rico reveals a mixed ancestry, including the Taino, Spanish colonialists, and Africans who came to the island as slaves. The economy is based on agriculture, and sugar is the main crop. Tourism is also important, as are remittances. Official languages are Spanish and English. Roman Catholicism is the dominant religion, although Protestantism is increasing.

The wide variety of approaches to democratization is matched by varied outcomes (Paley 2002). Of the twenty-seven nations created from the former Soviet Union, nineteen are democracies, at least in name. All Western European states are democracies, as are the majority in the Western Hemisphere. The percentage is about half in Asia and the Pacific. Africa, with less than one-third, has the lowest percentage.

The transition to democracy appears to be most difficult when the change is from highly authoritarian socialist regimes. This pattern is partly explained by the fact that democratization implies a transition from a planned economy to one based on market capitalism (Lempert 1996).

Aung San Suu Kyi is the leader of the Burmese democracy and human rights movement. The daughter of Burma's national hero, Aung San, who was assassinated just before Burma gained its independence from the British, she has frequently been placed under house arrest since 1989. Aung San Suu Kyi was awarded the Nobel Peace Prize, the eighth woman to receive the award. ■ *What can you learn about Aung San Suu Kyi and her writings from the Internet?* (Source: © Daniel Simon/Gamma Images)

Women in Politics: New Directions?

Two questions arise in the area of changing patterns of women in contemporary politics: Is the overall participation of women at varying political levels increasing? Do women in politics bring more attention to women's issues such as the division of labor and wages, access to health care, and violence? The answer to the first question is yes, as noted earlier, although the increase is modest. In terms of the second question, none of these leaders except Bruntland of Norway had a record of supporting women's issues. One interpretation of this pattern is that women political leaders in male-dominated contexts become "like men" or have to avoid "feminist issues" in order to maintain their position.

Women still lack political status equal to that of men in all countries. In general, women are still marginalized from formal politics and must seek to achieve their goals either indirectly (as wives or mothers of male politicians) or through channels other than formal politics, such as grassroots movements.

In contrast, in some Native American groups, recovery of women's former political power is occurring (B. G. Miller 1994). In several communities, female participation in formal politics is increasing dramatically, and it is bringing more attention to issues that face women. This change is taking place within the context of colonialism's effects, which resulted in women's greatly decreased political roles compared to the pre-colonial era. One explanation for the recent improvement is that women are obtaining newly available managerial positions on reservations. These positions give women experience in dealing with the outside world and authority for assuming public office. In addition, they face less resistance from men than women in more patriarchal contexts do. Most Native Americans do not view women's roles as contradictory to public authority roles.

The resurgence in women's political roles among the Seneca of New York state and Pennsylvania echoes these themes (Bilharz 1995). From women's precolonial position of at least equal political power with men, Seneca women's political status had declined in many ways. Notably, when the constitution of the Seneca Nation was drawn up on a European model in 1848, only men were granted the right to vote. In 1964, Seneca women finally gained the right to vote. Even before enfranchisement, women were politically active and worked on committees formed to stop the building of Kinzua Dam in Pennsylvania. For Seneca women, job creation through the Seneca Nation of Indians (SNI) brought new employment opportunities. Although no woman has run for president of the Seneca Nation as yet and only a few women have been head of a reservation, many women hold elective offices of clerk and judge, and many women head important service departments of the SNI, such as in the areas of education and health. Women of the Seneca Nation still retain complete control over the "clearing" (the cropland), and "their primacy in the home has never been challenged" (1995:112). According to Bilharz, Seneca women have regained a position of equality.

Political Leadership in New Social Movements

The Rural Landless Workers' Movement (NSM) in Brazil is possibly the most dynamic social movement in Central and South America today (Veltmeyer and Petras 2002). This is a movement of small farmers united in a political struggle for social change especially through pro-poor programs of land redistribution and limitations on state power. Brazil's NSM is characterized by especially suc-

An Iraqi Shi'ite woman in the city of Najaf, south of Baghdad, casts her ballot in the 2005 parliamentary elections. **Promoting women's participation in democratic processes is challenging in contexts where women's role in the public domain is constrained.** ■ *What are the gender patterns in voter turn-out in your country?* (Source: © Faleh Kheiber/Reuters/Corbis)

California Congresswoman Lucille Roybal-Allard attending the Congressional Hispanic Caucus Party at the 2004 Democratic National Convention. ■ *Is the representation of various ethnic groups in the United States Senate and House of Representatives proportional to the country's major ethnic populations? If not, should it be?* (Source: © Zack Seckler/CORBIS)

cessful leaders who are able to mobilize and sustain popular support. Analysis of NSM leaders' characteristics finds the following features of successful leaders:

- Deep and continuing roots in the countryside
- Relatively more education and strong commitment to education
- Ability to solve problems and take practical action
- Shared vision of alternative social system
- Personality with style and mystique to sustain popular loyalty in difficult times
- High degree of optimism

The opposite of these characteristics define an unsuccessful political leader: origin in a distant social class from the constituency, from the same class but poorly educated, inspired by theory and ideology rather than being pragmatic, lacking in style and charisma, and with little sense of positive alternatives for the future.

Globalization and Politics

Since the seventeenth century, the world's nations have been increasingly linked in a hierarchical structure that is largely regulated through international trade. In the seventeenth century, Holland was the one core nation dominating world trade. It was then surpassed by England and France, which remained the two most powerful nations up to around 1900. In the early part of the twentieth century, challenges for world dominance were made by the United States and later Germany and Japan. The outcome of World War II placed the United States as leader of the "core" (see Chapter 3). Recently, Japan, the European Union, and China are playing larger roles.

Cultural anthropology's traditional strength has been the study of small, bounded local groups, so anthropologists have come late to the study of international affairs (Wilson 2000). Now, more anthropologists have enlarged their focus to the international level, studying both how global changes affect local politics and how local politics affect international affairs. Worldwide communication networks facilitate global politics. Ethnic politics, although locally initiated, increasingly has international repercussions. Migrant populations promote interconnected interests across state boundaries.

A pioneering study in "the anthropology of international affairs" is Stacia Zabusky's (1995) research on patterns of cooperation among international scientists at the European Space Agency (ESA). The ESA involves people from different European nations seeking to cooperate in joint ventures in space and, more indirectly, to promote peaceful relations in Europe. Zabusky attended meetings and interviewed people at the European Space Research and Technology Centre, ESA's primary production site, in the Netherlands. Focusing on people's work roles, their styles of reaching consensus at meetings, and the role of national differences in this cooperative effort, she found that language plays a key part in affecting cooperation. The official languages of the ESA are English and French, but most interactions take place in English. Some non-native English speakers felt that this gave the British an automatic advantage, especially in meetings where skill in speech can win an argument. A major divisive factor is the sheer geographic dispersal of the participants throughout Europe. This means that

A flight operation specialist of the European Space Agency (ESA) waits for the launch of Cryosat satellite in Darmstadt, near Frankfurt, Germany, in 2005. Cryosat will circuit on a polar orbit with the primary mission of testing the prediction that polar ice is thinning due to global warming. ■ (Source: © Alex Grimm/Reuters/CORBIS)

travel is a constant, as scientists and engineers convene for important meetings. Despite logistical problems, meetings are an important part of the "glue" that promotes cooperation above and beyond just "working together." Conversations and discussions at meetings allow people to air their differences and work toward agreement.

Zabusky concludes that the ESA represents an ongoing struggle for cooperation that is motivated by more than just the urge to do "big" science. "In working together, participants were dreaming about finding something other than space satellites, other than a unified Europe or even a functioning organization at the end of their travails. Cooperation indeed appeared to participants not only as an achievement but as an aspiration" (1995:197).

Culture exists at all levels of human interaction—local, national, international, and transnational and even in cyberspace—and power relations are embedded in culture at all these levels. Anthropologists are now contributing to debates about the definition and use of the term *culture* by international organizations such as UNESCO. Pleased as we are that such organizations are paying more attention to culture, our wish is that they would not use outdated concepts that portray cultures as nicely bounded entities with a simple list of traits, such as language, dress, and religion (Wright 1998; Eriksen 2001).

Anthropologists are also tackling the study of powerful international organizations such as NATO (Feldman 2003). Anthropologists must "study up," as Laura Nader urged us to do over three decades ago (1972), because people, power, and culture are "up" there. Anthropologists need to examine their own culture, which tends to be power-averse, to feel empathy with the powerless—with "the village people" and not the people who wield power at NATO. As one anthropologist urges, it is high time that anthropologists break their silence about institutions with lethal powers (Feldman 2003).

The Big Questions Revisited

WHAT does political anthropology cover?

Political anthropology is the study of power relationships in the public domain and how they vary and change cross-culturally. Political anthropology has moved from a mainly functional perspective about local political systems, characteristic of the first half of the twentieth century, to looking at more macro and global issues related to inequality and conflict and to the role of individual agency in contesting political structures.

Political anthropologists study the concept of power, as well as related concepts such as authority and influence. They have discovered differences between politics and political organization in small-scale societies and large-scale societies by examining issues such as leadership roles and responsibilities, the social distribution of power, and the emergence of the state. Although politics in some form or another is a cultural universal, cross-cultural studies show wide variation in the bases and extent of political leadership and the informality or formality of political organization.

WHAT are the major cross-cultural forms of political organization and leadership?

Patterns of political organization and leadership vary according to mode of production and global economic relationships. Foragers have a minimal form of leadership and political organization in the band. Band membership is flexible. If a band member has a serious disagreement with another person or a spouse, one option is to leave that band and join another. Leadership in bands is informal. A tribe is a more formal type of political organization than the band. A tribe comprises several bands or lineage groups, with a headman or headwoman as leader. Big-man and big-woman political systems are an expanded form of tribe, with leaders having influence over people in several different villages. Chiefdoms may include several thousand people. Rank is inherited, and social divisions exist between the chiefly lineage(s) and nonchiefly groups.

A state is a form of political organization with a bureaucracy and diversified governmental institutions designed to administer large and complex societies. State leaders possess coercive power and employ a variety of symbols to bolster their image. States arose in several locations with the emergence of intensive agriculture, increased surpluses, and increased population density. Most states are hierarchical and patriarchal. Strategies for building a sense of unity in culturally plural states may include imposition of one language as the national language, construction of monuments and museums, and promotion of songs, poetry, and other media-relayed messages about the homeland. Ethnic/national politics has emerged within and across states as groups compete for either increased rights within the state or autonomy from it. States are differentiated in terms of their strength and ability to carry out their responsibilities to their citizens. The concept of a failed state refers to a government that is unable to maintain order and provide services. In recent decades, several states, especially in Africa, are considered to be failed states. Globalization, increased transnational migration, and the development of international organizations such as the United Nations and the World Trade Organization are major contemporary forces that have certain powers that transcend states.

HOW are politics and political organization changing?

The anthropological study of change in leadership and political organization has documented several trends, most of which are related to the influences of European colonialism or contemporary capitalist globalization. Postcolonial nations struggle with internal ethnic divisions and pressures to democratize. Women as leaders of states are still a tiny minority. In some groups, however, women leaders are gaining ground, as among the Seneca. Globalized communication networks promote the growth of global politics. Cultural anthropologists have rarely addressed the topic of international political affairs and the role of international organizations such as the United Nations. They are, however, increasingly interested in demonstrating the usefulness of cultural anthropology in global peacekeeping and conflict resolution.

KEY CONCEPTS

authority, p. 260
band, p. 261
big-man or big-woman system, p. 264
chiefdom, p. 266
faction, p. 270

influence, p. 260
in-kind taxation, p. 269
matriarchy, p. 267
moka, p. 265
nation, p. 273

political organization, p. 261
power, p. 260
segmentary model, p. 264
state, p. 268
tribe, p. 262

SUGGESTED READINGS

Stanley R. Barrett. *Culture Meets Power.* Westport, CT: Praeger, 2002. The author examines why the concept of power has gained ascendancy in anthropology, seeming to eclipse the concept of culture. He argues that the concept of power is no less ambiguous than that of culture and that the two concepts both need to be considered in understanding contemporary affairs, including events such as the September 11, 2001, attacks on the United States.

Jane K. Cowan, Marie-Bénédicte Dembour, and Richard A. Wilson, eds. *Culture and Rights: Anthropological Perspectives.* New York: Cambridge University Press, 2001. This collection includes three overview/theoretical chapters, seven case studies that address issues such as child prostitution and ethnic and women's rights, and a chapter that critiques the UNESCO concept of culture.

Mona Etienne and Eleanor Leacock, eds. *Women and Colonization: Anthropological Perspectives.* New York: Praeger, 1980. This classic collection examines the impact of Western colonialism and missionary intervention on women of several indigenous groups of North America and South America, Africa, and the Pacific.

Magnus Fiskesjö. *The Thanksgiving Turkey Pardon, The Death of Teddy's Bear, and the Sovereign Exception of Guantáno.* Chicago: Prickly Paradigm Press, 2003. Cultural interpretation of the U.S. presidential ritual of "pardoning" a turkey every Thanksgiving sheds light on notions of the presidency and its power in the United States. The argument leads more broadly to questions of presidential clemency and pardons and the denial of rights to certain kinds of prisoners.

David Graeber. *Fragments of an Anarchist Anthropology.* Chicago: Prickly Paradigm Press, 2004. The author presents examples of nonstate societies as evidence that alternatives do exist and can function. He discusses the tendency of cultural anthropologists to favor small-scale, nonstate political organization as more peaceful and egalitarian than contemporary mega-states.

David H. Lempert. *Daily Life in a Crumbling Empire.* New York: Columbia University Press, 1996. This two-volume ethnography is based on fieldwork conducted in Moscow before perestroika. It is the first comprehensive ethnography of urban Russia and its economic, political, and legal systems and reforms.

Mark Moberg. *Citrus, Strategy, and Class: The Politics of Development in Southern Belize.* Iowa City: University of Iowa Press, 1992. The theoretical debate of structure versus agency frames this ethnography of household and village economies within the world economy and the transformation from factional politics to class formation. The author provides quantitative data as well as insights from five individual lives in a chapter entitled "Keep on Fighting It."

Dan Rabinowitz. *Overlooking Nazareth: The Politics of Exclusion in Galilee.* New York: Cambridge University Press, 1997. This ethnographic study of Palestinian citizens in an Israeli new town examines specific situations of conflict and cooperation and provides theoretical insights into nationalism and ethnicity. Biographical accounts of three Palestinians—a medical doctor, a basketball coach, and a local politician—are included.

Katherine Verdery. *The Political Lives of Dead Bodies: Reburial and Postsocialist Change.* New York: Columbia University Press, 1999. Post-USSR political changes in Eastern Europe involved a rethinking and revision of the past and forward thinking about the present. An understudied aspect of post-Communist political change in Eastern Europe involved the disposition of the bodies of dead political leaders, heroes, artists, and regular people. Many bodies were exhumed and relocated and have been given a new political "life."

Joan Vincent. *Anthropology and Politics: Visions, Traditions and Trends.* Tucson: The University of Arizona Press, 1990. This text presents a definitive history of the emergence of political anthropology, with a detailed presentation of theories and findings through the late 1980s.

Joan Vincent, ed. *The Anthropology of Politics: A Reader in Ethnography, Theory, and Critique.* Malden, MA: Blackwell Publishers, 2002. Over forty essays are arranged in four broad historical sections to demonstrate the dynamic interplay among theory, ethnography, and critique. First come classics of the Enlightenment (Adam Smith, Karl Marx, and others). There follows a section on early ethnographies (E. E. Evans-Pritchard and others), coupled with contemporary updates (such as Sharon Hutchinson). The third section is on colonialism and imperialism (Talal Asad, June Nash, and others), and the last focuses on cosmopolitanism (Aihwa Ong, James Ferguson, and others).

Jack M. Weatherford. *Tribes on the Hill.* New York: Rawson, Wade Publishers, 1981. This engagingly written analysis of politics within the United States Congress examines the effects of male privilege and seniority on ranking, lobbying tactics, and ritual aspects of the legislation process.

11
Social Order and Social Conflict

The Big Questions

- WHAT is the scope of legal anthropology?

- WHAT are cross-cultural systems for maintaining social order and social control?

- WHAT are cross-cultural patterns of social conflict and violence?

The antiglobalist movement has gained supporters worldwide. This is a scene from the Seattle demonstration during the Global Trade Meeting of 2000. *(Source: © Robert Sorbo/CORBIS)*

Many Maasai (review Culturama in Chapter 6, p. 158) now work in cities, interact with international tourists, and some attend universities. Most rural Maasai, however, have limited knowledge of global events. Some villages lack electricity, so there are no televisions. When Kimeli Naiyomeh returned to his village in a remote area of Kenya following his medical studies at Stanford University in California, he told the villagers stories that stunned them (Lacey 2002). They had not heard about the attacks on the United States on September 11, 2001. He described how massive fires destroyed buildings so high that they stretched into the clouds. The villagers could not believe that a building could be so tall that people jumping from it would die.

The stories about 9/11 saddened the villagers. They decided they should do something to help the victims. Cows are the most precious objects among the Maasai. As Kimeli Naiyomeh comments, "The cow is almost the center of life for us. . . . It's sacred. It's more than property. You give it a name. You talk to it. You perform rituals with it" (2002: A7). In June 2002, in a solemn ceremony, the villagers gave fourteen cows to the United States. After the cows were blessed, they were transferred to the deputy chief of the U.S. Embassy in Kenya. He expressed his country's gratitude and explained that transporting the cows to the United States would be difficult. The cows are being sold and the money will be used to support local Maasai schools.

This chapter discusses social order and peace, including informal arrangements and formal laws and systems of crime prevention and punishment. It begins with the cross-cultural study of social order then moves to a discussion of conflict and violence. Anthropologists in all four fields study social order and social conflict. Archaeologists examine artifacts such as weapons, remains of forts, and the waxing and waning of political centers in order to understand group conflict in the past. Primatologists study nonhuman primate patterns of cooperation, coalitions, and conflict. Linguistic anthropologists do research on social conflict related to state language policies and on how communication patterns in the courtroom and in international mediation influence outcomes.

Within cultural anthropology, this subject matter constitutes the subfield of legal anthropology. Over the course of the twentieth century, legal anthropology, like political anthropology (Chapter 10), moved from its original foundations in functionalism (the way a particular practice or belief contributes to social cohesion) toward the study of conflict. Launching the subfield through his classic book, *Crime and Custom in Savage Society* (1962 [1926]), functionalist Bronislaw Malinowski wrote that in the Trobriand Islands, social ties themselves promoted mutual social obligation and harmony. No separate legal institutions existed; instead, law was embedded in social life. The discovery that social relationships can perform the same functions as laws and courts was one of Malinowski's major contributions.

Several new directions have emerged in legal anthropology (Merry 1992):

- Law in postcolonial settings
- Legal discourse in courtrooms
- **Critical legal anthropology** (the study of how law and judicial institutions serve to maintain and expand dominant power interests rather than protecting marginal and less powerful people)
- Law, human rights, and globalization

Systems of Social Control

Social control is the process by which people maintain orderly life in groups (Garland 1996:781). Social control systems define agreed-upon rules and ways to ensure conformity to those rules. Because some people may violate the rules (what sociologists refer to as "deviant behavior"), social control systems include ways to deal with such breaches.

Social control systems include *internalized* social controls that exist through socialization for proper behavior, education, and peer pressure. They may also include formal systems of codified rules about proper behavior and punishments for deviation. In the United States and Canada, the Amish (review Culturama in Chapter 5, p. 122) and Mennonites rely on internalized social controls far more than most microcultural groups. These groups have no police force or legal system; the way social order is maintained is through religious teaching and group pressure. If a member veers from correct behavior, punishment such as ostracism ("shunning") may be applied.

Cultural anthropologists distinguish two major instruments of social control: norms and laws. A **norm** is an accepted standard for how people should behave that is usually unwritten and learned unconsciously through

---

critical legal anthropology: an approach within the cross-cultural study of law that examines how law and judicial systems serve to maintain and expand dominant power interests rather than protecting marginal and less powerful people.

social control: processes that maintain orderly social life, including informal and formal mechanisms.
norm: a generally agreed-upon standard for how people should behave, usually unwritten and learned unconsciously.

law: a binding rule created through enactment or custom that defines right and reasonable behavior and is enforceable by threat of punishment.

Amish men in a communal barn-raising in Pennsylvania.
■ *Think of an example of shared work from your microcultural experience.* (Source: © Paul Solomon/ Woodfin Camp & Associates)

socialization. All societies have norms. Norms include, for example, the expectation that children should follow their parents' advice, that people standing in line should be orderly, and that an individual should accept an offer of a handshake (in cultures where handshakes are the usual greeting) when meeting someone for the first time. In rural Bali, etiquette dictates certain greeting forms between people of different status: "Persons of higher status and power are shown very marked respect. . . . If [they are] seated, then others moving past them crouch" (Barth 1993:114). Enforcement of norms tends to be informal; for example, a violation may simply be considered rude and the violator would be avoided in the future. In others, direct action may be taken, such as asking someone who disrupts a meeting to leave.

A **law** is a binding rule created through custom or official enactment that defines correct behavior and the punishment for misbehavior. Systems of law are more common and more elaborate in state-level societies, but many nonstate societies have formalized laws. Religion often provides legitimacy for law. Australian Aborigines believe that law came to humans during the "dreamtime," a period in the mythological past when the ancestors created the world. Law and religion are synonymous in contemporary Islamic states. Secular Western states consider their laws to be religiously neutral. In fact, much Western law is based in Judeo-Christian beliefs.

This section considers forms of social control in small-scale societies as contrasted with large-scale societies. The former are characterized more by the use of norms. The latter, notably states, rely more on legal sanctions, although local-level groups, such as neighbors, practice social sanctions among themselves. The last part of the section presents findings from critical legal anthropology.

Social Control in Small-Scale Societies

THINKING OUTSIDE THE BOX

WHAT ARE some forms of conflict prevention and conflict resolution used among small-scale political groups in your cultural world. Which are more effective and why?

Among small-scale groups such as foragers, formal laws are rare. Because bands are small, close-knit groups, disputes are usually handled at the interpersonal level through discussion or one-on-one fights. An observer's notes on his conversation with some Kalahari foragers (see Map 1.5, p. 22) lend insight into social order in small groups (Ury 1990):

> They say that, if a man takes your bow and arrows, go to the man and tell him not to do it again. If your daughter wants to go off with a man you dislike, try to convince her not to go. If she does not agree, let her go. She will learn her lesson and eventually come back. In the most serious disputes, when a man runs off with another man's wife, the husband should go and get her and then move far away so the other man cannot come to get her. If his wife goes off with another man, the husband should go and fetch her again. If she refuses to come back, he should take the children and move far away, leaving her with the new man.

Group members may act together to punish an offender through shaming and ridicule. Emphasis is on maintaining social order and restoring social equilibrium, not hurtfully punishing an offender. Ostracizing an offending member (forcing the person to leave the group) is a common means of formal punishment. Capital punishment (execution) is rare. In some Australian Aboriginal societies, laws restrict access to religious rituals and paraphernalia to men who have gone through a ritual initiation. If an initiated man shared secrets with an uninitiated person, the elders would delegate one of their group to kill the offender. In such instances, the elders act like a court.

In nonstate societies, punishment is often legitimized through belief in supernatural forces and their ability to affect people. Among the highland horticulturalists of the Indonesian island of Sumba (see Map 1.3, p. 15), one of the greatest offenses is to fail to keep a promise (Kuipers 1990). Breaking a promise will bring on "supernatural assault" by the ancestors of those who have been offended by the person's misbehavior. The punishment may come in the form of damage to crops, illness or death of a relative, destruction of the offender's house, or having one's clothing catch on fire. When such a disaster occurs, the only recourse is to sponsor a ritual that will appease the ancestors.

Conflict resolution among horticulturalists relies on similar methods as among foragers, such as public shaming and ridicule. Discussing disputes in the Trobriand

Islands (see Map 2.1, p. 39) in the early twentieth century, Malinowski provides a functional interpretation:

> The rare quarrels which occur at times take the form of an exchange of public expostulation (*yakala*) in which the two parties assisted by friends and relatives meet, harangue one another, hurl and hurl back recriminations. Such litigation allows people to give vent to their feelings and shows the trend of public opinion, and thus it may be of assistance in settling disputes. (1926:60)

The overall goal in dealing with conflict in small-scale societies is to return the group to harmony. Village fission (breaking up) and ostracism are mechanisms for dealing with more serious, unresolvable conflict.

Social Control in States

In densely populated societies with more social stratification and more wealth, increased social stress occurs in relation to the distribution of surplus, inheritance, and rights to land. In addition, increased social scale means that not everyone knows everyone else. Face-to-face accountability exists only in localized groups. Three important factors of state systems of social control are:

- Increased specialization of roles involved in social control
- Formal trials and courts
- Power-enforced forms of punishment, such as prisons and the death penalty

Informal mechanisms of social control, however, exist alongside these formal systems at the local level. In the Lessons Applied box, an activist anthropologist provides a cultural critique of one example of informal social control in states.

Specialization

The specialization of tasks related to law and order—police, judges, lawyers—increases with the emergence of state organization. In nonstate societies, society at large determines right from wrong and punishes offenders, or the elders may have special authority and be called on for advice. In chiefdoms, special advisors, such as the "leopard-skin chief" of the Nuer of southern Sudan, played a key role in decision making about crime and punishment. The leopard-skin chief was distinguished by his knowledge and authority as well as the privilege of wearing a leopard-skin upper garment. Full-time professionals, such as judges and lawyers, emerged with the state. These professionals are often members of powerful social groups, a fact that perpetuates elite biases in the justice process itself. In the United States, the legal profession is committed to opposing discrimination on the basis of gender and ethnicity. Nonetheless, women and minorities are severely underrepresented in the legal profession. Minority women face a double bind and are especially underrepresented (Chanen 1995:105).

Policing is a form of social control that includes processes of surveillance and the threat of punishment related to maintaining social order (Reiner 1996). Police are the specific organization and personnel who discover, report, and investigate crimes. As a specialized group, police exist mainly in states. Japan's low crime rate has attracted the attention of Western law-and-order specialists, who think that it may be the result of the police system there. They are interested in learning whether solutions to U.S. crime problems can be found in such Japanese policing practices as neighborhood police boxes staffed by foot patrolmen and volunteer crime prevention groups organized on a neighborhood basis.

Fieldwork among police detectives in the city of Sapporo (see Map 2.2, p. 41) reveals aspects of Japanese culture and policing that promote low crime rates (Miyazawa 1992). In Japan, the police operate under high expectations that no false arrests will be made and that all arrests should lead to confession. In fact, the rate of confession is high. This pattern may be due to the fact that the police do an excellent job of targeting the guilty party, or it may result from the nearly complete control of interrogation by the police. They are allowed to keep suspects isolated for long periods of time, which can lead to wearing down resistance and potentially distorting the process of justice. The "enabling legal environment" in Japan gives more power to the police and less to the defendant than in U.S. law. For example, the suspect's statements are not recorded verbatim or taped. The detectives write them down and the suspect is asked to sign them.

Trials and Courts

In societies where spirits and ancestors define wrongdoing and punishment, a person's guilt is proved simply by the fact that misfortune has befallen him or her. If a person's crops were damaged by lightning, for instance, then that person must have done something wrong. In other cases, guilt may be determined through **trial by ordeal**, a way of judging guilt or innocence in which the accused person is put through a test that is often painful. An accused person may be required to place his or her hand in boiling oil, for example, or to have a part of his or her

---

policing: the exercise of social control through processes of surveillance and the threat of punishment related to maintaining social order.

trial by ordeal: a way of determining innocence or guilt in which the accused person is put to a test that may be painful, stressful, or fatal.

Lessons Applied

LEGAL ANTHROPOLOGIST ADVISES RESISTANCE TO "COERCIVE HARMONY"

This box shows how an anthropologist uses her cross-cultural insights to provide a critique of her own culture, with an eye to producing improved social relations (Nader 2001). Laura Nader has conducted extensive fieldwork in Latin America, as well as in the World Court in Europe. Her main interest lies in cross-cultural aspects of conflict and conflict resolution. In terms of her observations of her home country, the United States, she points out that leading politicians are currently emphasizing the need for unity, consensus, and harmony among the American people. But the United States, she points out, was founded by dissenters, and democracy depends on people speaking out. Democracy, in her view, supports the right to be indignant and the idea that "indignation can make Americans more engaged citizens" (2001:B13).

A professor of anthropology at the University of California at Berkeley, Nader fosters the expression of critique, opinion, and even indignation when she teaches. One of her students commented that "Dr. Nader is a pretty good professor, except she has opinions" (2001:B13). She took that as a compliment.

Nader feels that Europeans are generally less concerned about social harmony than are people in the United States. Americans consider it bad manners to be contentious, whereas in Europe, debate—even bitterly

contentious debate—is valued. She uses the term *coercive harmony* to refer to the informal but strong pressure in the United States to agree, to be nice, to avoid digging beneath the surface, to stifle indignation at the lack of universal health care or the low voter turnout in presidential elections. The unstated, informally enforced policy of coercive harmony labels cultural critique as bad behavior, as negative rather than positive. Nader finds it alarming that in a country that proclaims freedom as its primary feature, coercive harmony in fact suppresses contrary views and voices through the idiom of politeness, niceness, and friendliness.

How can this insight be used to improve the situation in the United States? Nader suggests one step: Make sure that critique, dissent, and indignation are supported in schools. Teachers should avoid contributing to the informal enforcement of social harmony and consensus and should instead proactively encourage critique.

FOOD FOR THOUGHT

- Watch several television interview shows with politicians on BBC, and compare their interview style to that seen on a U.S. station. (Try to see Jeremy Paxman, one of Britain's most infamous political interviewers.) How do the interview styles compare?

---

body touched by a red-hot knife. Being burned is a sign of guilt, whereas not being burned means the suspect is innocent.

The court system, with lawyers, judge, and jury, is used in many contemporary societies, although variation exists in how cases are presented and juries constituted. The goal of contemporary court trials is to ensure both justice and fairness. Analysis of actual courtroom dynamics and patterns of decision making in the United States and elsewhere, however, reveals serious problems in achieving these goals.

Prisons and the Death Penalty

Administering punishment involves doing something unpleasant to someone who has committed an offense. In small-scale societies, punishment is socially rather than judicially managed. As noted earlier, the most extreme form of punishment in small-scale societies is ostracism and only rarely death. Another common form of punishment in the case of theft or murder, especially in

Islamic cultures of the Middle East, is that the guilty party must pay compensation to members of the harmed family. The prison, as a place where people are forcibly detained as a form of punishment, has a long history, but probably emerged only with the state. The dungeons and "keeps" of old forts and castles are vivid evidence of the power of some people to detain and inflict suffering on others.

Long-term detention of prisoners did not become common until the seventeenth century in Europe (Foucault 1977). The first penitentiary in the United States was built in Philadelphia in the late 1700s (Sharff 1995). Percentages of imprisoned people vary widely around the world. The United States and Russia have high percentages compared to other contemporary Western countries: 550 and 470 prisoners per 100,000 population, respectively. The rate in the United Kingdom is about 100. The Scandinavian countries have among the lowest rates, under 60. In the United States, nearly two million people are in prison, and the "corrections industry" is a growing sector of society (Rhodes 2001).

Interior scene of the Cellular Jail in India's Andaman Islands, which was so named because all prisoners had single cells, arranged in rows, to prevent them from engaging in social interaction and possible collusion to escape or rebel. ■ *Find out about how prisons in your home country are designed.* (Source: Barbara Miller)

WHAT IS your position on the death penalty? How does your microculture shape your views?

THINKING OUTSIDE THE BOX

been documented in judicial systems around the world, including long-standing democracies. This section presents an example from Australia.

At the invitation of Aboriginal leaders in Australia, Fay Gale and her colleagues conducted research comparing the treatment of Aboriginal youth and White youth in the judicial system (1990). The question posed by the Aboriginal leaders was: Why are our kids always in trouble? Two directions can be pursued to find the answer. First, structural factors—such as Aboriginal displacement from their homeland, poverty, poor living conditions, and bleak future prospects—can be investigated. These factors might make it more likely for Aboriginal youth to commit crimes than the relatively advantaged White youth. Second, the criminal justice system can be examined to see whether it treats Aboriginal and White youth equally. The researchers decided to direct their attention to the judicial system because little work had been done on that area by social scientists. Australia, a former colony of England, adopted the British legal system, which claims to administer the law equitably. The research assessed this claim in one state, South Australia (see Map 4.4, p. 105).

Results show that Aboriginal youth are overrepresented at every level of the juvenile justice system, from apprehension (being caught by the police) through pretrial processes to the ultimate stage of adjudication (the

The death penalty (capital punishment) is rare in nonstate societies because condemning someone to death requires a great deal of power. A comparison of capital punishment in the contemporary United States with human sacrifice among the Aztecs of Mexico of the sixteenth century reveals striking similarities (Purdum and Paredes 1989). Both systems involve the death of mainly able-bodied males who are in one way or another socially marginal. In the United States, most people who are executed are non-White, have killed Whites, are poor, and have few social ties. Aztec sacrificial victims were mainly male war captives from neighboring states, but Aztec children were also sometimes sacrificed. The deaths in both contexts communicate a political message to the general populace about the state's power and strength, which is why they are highly ritualized and widely publicized events.

Social Inequality and the Law

Critical legal anthropologists examine the role of law in maintaining power relationships through discrimination against such social categories as indigenous people, women, and minorities. Systematic discrimination has

This man, in a military prison in Chechnya, is accused by the Russian government of participating with Chechen rebel forces. Human rights activists have been concerned about the mistreatment of prisoners in Chechnya for several years. ■ *What human rights do prisoners have in your country?* (Source: © EPA/CORBIS)

judge's decision) and disposition (the punishment): "A far greater proportion of Aboriginal than other young people follow the harshest route. . . . At each point in the system where discretion operates, young Aborigines are significantly more likely than other young persons to receive the most severe outcomes of those available to the decision-makers" (1990:3). At the time of apprehension (being caught by the police), the suspect can be either formally arrested or informally reported. A formal arrest is made to ensure that the offender will appear in court. Officers ask the suspects for a home address and whether they have a job. Aboriginal youth are more likely than White youth to live in a poor neighborhood in an extended family, and they are more likely to be unemployed. Thus, they tend to be placed in a category of "undependable," and they are formally arrested more than White youth for the same crime (see Figure 11.1). The next step determines whether the suspect will be tried in Children's Court or referred to Children's Aid Panels. The Children's Aid Panels in South Australia have gained acclaim worldwide for the opportunities they give to individuals to avoid becoming repeat offenders and take their proper place in society. But most Aboriginal youth offenders are denied access to them and instead have to appear in court, where the vast majority of youthful offenders end up pleading guilty. The clear and disturbing finding from this study is that the mode of arrest tends to determine each subsequent stage in the system.

Change in Legal Systems

Law-and-order systems, like other cultural domains, change over time. European colonialism since the seventeenth century has had major effects on indigenous systems. Legal systems of contemporary countries have to deal with social complexity that has its roots in colonialism and new patterns of migration.

European Colonialism and Indigenous Systems

Colonial governments, to varying degrees, attempted to learn about and rule their subject populations through what they termed *customary law* (Merry 1992). By seeking to codify customary law, colonial governments created fixed rules where flexibility and local variation had formerly existed. Often the colonialists totally ignored local customary law and imposed their own laws. Homicide, marriage, land rights, and indigenous religion were frequent areas of European imposition. Among the Nuer of southern Sudan, for example, British legal interventions resulted in confusion concerning blood feuds (Hutchinson 1996). In a case of homicide, Nuer practice requires either the taking of a life in repayment or the payment in cattle, depending on the relationship between the victim and the assailant, the type of weapon used, and the current rate of bridewealth as an index of value. In contrast, the British determined a fixed amount of indemnity, and they imprisoned people for committing murder. The Nuer interpreted being put in prison as a way of protecting the person from a reprisal attack.

When European administrators and missionaries encountered aspects of marriage systems different from their own, they often tried to impose their own ways. Europeans tried in most cases to stop polygamy as unChristian and uncivilized. In South Africa, however, British and Afrikaaner Whites tolerated the continuation of traditional marriage practices of South African peoples (Chambers 2000). So-called customary law, applying to the diverse practices of South African Black communities, permits a number of marriage forms that, despite their variety, share two basic features. First, marriage is considered a union between two families, not two individuals. Second, bridewealth is paid in nearly all groups, formerly in cattle and now in cash. These traditions made

	Aboriginal Youth (percent)	White Youth (percent)
Brought into system via arrest rather than police report	43.4	19.7
Referred to Children's Court rather than diverted to Children's Aid Panels	71.3	37.4
Proportion of court appearances resulting in detention	10.2	4.2

FIGURE 11.1 Comparison of Outcomes for Aboriginal and White Youth in the Australian Judicial System

Note: Most of these youths are male; data are from 1979 to 1984.
Source: From "Comparison of Outcomes for Aboriginal and White Youth in the Australian Judicial System," pg. 4, in *Aboriginal Youth and the Criminal Justice System: The Injustice of Justice?* by Faye Gale, Rebecca Bailey-Harris, and Joy Wundersitz. Copyright © 1990. Reprinted by permission of Cambridge University Press.

sense in a largely rural population in which men controlled the major form of movable wealth—cattle.

In the later part of the twentieth century, however, many Black South Africans no longer lived in rural areas within extended families, and most worked in the wage economy. In the view of South African Blacks in this context much of customary marriage law appeared inequitable to women. The 1994 Black-majority parliament that came to power adopted a new marriage law that eliminated a large part of the customary law. This change reflects a split between the views of "modernist" legislators, who favor gender equity in the law as provided for in the new constitution, and the views of rural elders, who feel that tradition has been forsaken.

Colonial imposition of European legal systems onto indigenous systems added another layer, and one that had preeminent power over others. **Legal pluralism** is a situation in which more than one way exists of defining acceptable and unacceptable behavior and ways to deal with the latter. It raises questions such as, should a case of murder in the Sudan be tried according to indigenous Sudanese principles or European ones? Several postcolonial countries are now in the process of attempting to reform their legal systems and develop more unified codes (Merry 1992:363). In some contexts, indigenous minority groups seek to have their customary law and practices gain greater recognition (see Culturama).

Law and Complexity

In situations where several cultural groups are subject to a single legal code, misunderstandings between the perspectives of both legal specialists and the affected people are likely and may result in conflict. For example, in the United States and Canada, female genital cutting (recall Chapter 6) is against the law. Members of some immigrant groups, however, wish to have their daughters go through this procedure. Cultural relativists (Ahmadu 2000, Shweder 2003) support people's freedom to pursue their traditional cultural practices.

The issue of whether Muslim girls can wear head scarves in school in non-Muslim countries is another example of cultural rights versus state laws (Ewing 2000). For many Muslims, the head scarf is a sign of proper Muslim society, a rejection of Western secularism, and an aspect of religious freedom. Westerners typically view the head scarf as a sign of women's oppression and as a symbol of resistance to the goals of schooling and values of modernity. In France, beginning in 1989, disputes have erupted over girls wearing head scarves in school. In 1994, the French education director stated that head scarves would not be permitted in school, yet

This scene occurred in Mantes-la-Jolie, France, in 1994. Female Muslim students who wish to wear a headscarf while attending public schools in France have been banned from doing so by the government. This ban has led to protests and court disputes for over a decade. ■ *What is the current position of the French government? What is the current position of your government on clothing allowed in public schools?* (Source: © Giry Daniel/CORBIS SYGMA)

Jewish boys, at that point, had been allowed to wear yarmulkes (head caps). Muslim leaders responded by taking the issue to court. As of 2007, the issue has not been settled.

Social Conflict and Violence

All systems of social control have to deal with the fact that conflict and violence may occur. This section considers the varieties of social conflict as studied by cultural anthropologists. Conflict can occur at any social level, from the private microlevel of the household to the public situation of international warfare.

Interpersonal Conflict

Interpersonal conflict encompasses a wide range of behavior, from arguments to murder. At the most microlevel, the household, interpersonal disputes are common (review Chapter 8's section on domestic violence). Some might say that it is easier to kill or be cruel to an anonymous enemy. But abusive and lethal conflict between people who are intimately related as lovers or family members is frequent cross-culturally. Dating violence

---

legal pluralism: a situation in which more than one way exists of defining acceptable and unacceptable behavior and ways to deal with the latter.

Culturama

The Māori of New Zealand

The term *Māori* refers to all indigenous people of New Zealand or Aotearoa. Their claim to specific territories is a matter of oral tradition, not law. About 530,000 Māori people live in New Zealand, representing 15 percent of the country's total population.

Traditionally, Māori livelihood was based on foraging, especially fishing, and horticulture. Now they are increasingly involved as wage workers in the industrial sector. Compared to the Paheka (European descent people), Māori have lower incomes and lower life expectancies, and higher rates of unemployment, infant mortality, and percentages of their population in prison (Olsen, Maxwell, and Morris 1995).

Māori consider themselves descended from the natural elements (Solomon and Watson 2001). Reciprocity with nature and care for nature are essential. Before cutting down a tree or taking fish from the sea, the Māori give a blessing. Of key importance is the protection of native places, plants, and animals, and the traditional knowledge about them that are related to their religion, medicine, art, and language.

Several tribes claim that their rights have been violated repeatedly since the Treaty of Waitungi was signed with the British in 1840 (Solomon and Watson 2001). The Treaty guarantees the Māori full and exclusive ownership of their lands, forests, fisheries, and other "treasured possessions." The tribes advocated for the establishment of a new organization, called the Waitungi Tribunal, to hear claims from any person of Māori descent about acts inconsistent with the Waitungi Treaty. Established in 1975, the Tribunal began meeting in the mid-1980s. Of it sixteen members, eight are Māori and eight are Paheka.

Tribunal hearings take place in the traditional community meeting area of the Māori (Solomon and Watson 2001). Witnesses are surrounded by extended family members with whom cultural knowledge is shared. The ancestors, represented in carvings around the meeting house, lend further support. The Māori language is used for testimony, with interpreters providing English translation.

In spite of the attempt to bring Māori culture to the fore in the Tribunal hearings, British legal procedure and government interests dominate. Māori input is often more of a token gesture. Government restrictions on funding for the Tribunal process result in long delays in scheduling a hearing, and over 1,000 cases are pending (Te Pareake Mead 2004). Furthermore, the current political environment is not sympathetic to Māori issues (Charters 2006).

Readings

Claire Charters, "An Imbalance of Powers: Māori Land Claims and an Unchecked Parliament." *Cultural Survival Quarterly, 30* (1), 32–35, 2006.

Aroha Te Pareake Mead. "He Paua, He Korowai, me Nga Waahi Tapu." *Cultural Survival Quarterly, 28* (1), 61–64, 2004.

Maui Solomon and Leo Watson. "The Waitungi Tribunal and the Māori Claim to the Cultural and Intellectual Heritage Rights Property." *Cultural Survival Quarterly, 24* (4), 46–50, 2000.

Video

Whale Rider (2003).

Website

Federation of Māori Authorities, www.foma.co.nz and www.kaitiakitanga.net.

Dr. Pita Sharples, or Ko Tākuta Pita Russell Sharples, leads a procession to Parliament in Wellington in 2004 (left). ■ *(Source: Ross Setford/Getty Images) Sharples, an academic and politician, is head of the Māori Party. Most Māori are Christian (right). Many denominations exist, and all are localized to some degree. This traditional Māori religious center is located on the east coast of North Island.* ■ (Source: © Robert Harding World Imagery/CORBIS)

MAP 11.1 *Māori Regions in New Zealand. The Māori name for New Zealand is Aotearoa. It is widely used but unofficial.*

among high school and college students is an increasing problem (Makepeace 1997, Sanday 1996).

Beyond the household, interpersonal conflict occurs between neighbors and residents of the same town or village, often over resources or territory. Since the 1970s, villagers of the Gwembe Valley in southern Zambia (see Map 11.2) have kept diaries documenting economic and demographic information and reports of disputes (Colson 1995). Over the years, the number of disputes has increased. There are two possible reasons for this change: Disputing may actually be on the rise because of the increased availability of beer and guns, or the people have become more willing to discuss negative features of their communities, or both. One thing is clear: Disputes still occur over the same issues: cattle damage to growing crops, land encroachment, inheritance, elopement and impregnation damages, marriage payments and marriage difficulties, slander, accusations of sorcery, theft,

physical violence, and the rights of senior people over the labor of younger men and women. One important new cause for disputes is debts.

A different pattern of interpersonal conflict emerges from interviews with 100 middle-class, U.S. suburbanites: "In the first five minutes of listening to suburbanites discuss neighbors, it became clear that dogs are the most worrisome population" (Perin 1988: 108). Problems include dogs roaming off the leash; barking; relieving themselves; chewing garbage bags; biting; and threatening children, joggers, and bicyclists.

How do U.S. suburbanites deal with conflicts about dogs? Some opt for a face-to-face solution; others resort to the dog warden after trying to talk to the neighbor several times. In taking the issue to court, every complaint has to be substantiated. A building inspector in Houston said, "The barking dog isn't as cut and dried a thing as it might seem. We watch it for a week. If we're going to court, we have to prove it's excessive. We have to keep numbers. People's first reaction to a barking complaint is that they're not in violation." (1988:113). Mutual hostility may continue for a long time. The seriousness of dog-related conflicts led to an expanded role of the courts. In Middlesex District Court in Massachusetts, one day each month is devoted to dog cases, and two days a month are needed in Portland, Oregon. In Santa Barbara, California, the city attorney's office provides professional mediation for dog-related disputes.

Banditry

Banditry is a form of aggressive conflict that involves socially patterned theft. It is usually practiced by a person or group of persons who are socially marginal and who gain a special social status from their illegal activity. Political scientists, sociologists, historians, and anthropologists have proposed various theories to explain why banditry appears at particular times and places more than others, why it is persistent in some contexts, and what sentiments inspire bandits. One theory is that bandits flourish in the context of weak states and decline as states grow stronger and increase their control of violence (Blok 1972). Another view is that banditry is a form of protest, expressing a yearning for a just world (Hobsbawm 1969). Neither theory can explain, however, the surge of banditry in late-nineteenth-century Egypt during the time of British colonialism (Brown 1990). British control was not weak, nor was this banditry an expression of anti-British sentiment (banditry existed in Egypt long before the British arrived). Instead, the answer appears to be that the British chose to high-

MAP 11.2 Zambia. The Republic of Zambia consists of high plateaus and mountains. Heavily mined by the British for its copper, Zambia has one of the highest poverty rates in the world. The prevalence of HIV/AIDS is also high. Zambia's population of about 11 million people consists of over seventy Bantu-speaking ethnic groups. Zambia has a very urbanized population with more than 2 million people living in the capital city of Lusaka. Small-scale farming is the basis of the rural economy. Christianity is the official religion, and several denominations exist as well as localized versions.

---

banditry: a form of aggressive conflict that involves socially patterned theft, usually practiced by a person or group of persons who are socially marginal and who may gain a mythic status.

feuding: long-term, retributive violence that may be lethal between families, groups of families, or tribes.

Anthropologist Michael Herzfeld (*far right*) observes and interacts with men at a coffeehouse while doing fieldwork on banditry and male identity in Crete. ■ *Do you think a woman anthropologist could conduct fieldwork on the same topics in Crete?* (Source: Cornelia Mayer Herzfeld)

light the presence of banditry as a social problem so that they could justify their presence and role in imposing law and order.

One anthropologist has, somewhat humorously, termed banditry "adventurist capital accumulation" (Sant Cassia 1993:793), but it is much more than that. For example, banditry, male identity and status, and the creation of social alliances are closely associated on the Greek island of Crete (Herzfeld 1985) (see Map 11.3). In this sheepherding economy, manhood and male identity depend on a local form of banditry: stealing sheep. "Coming out on the branch" is a metaphor for the attainment of manhood following a young man's first theft. This phrase implies that he is now a person with whom to be reckoned. To not participate in sheep raids is to be effeminate. Each theft, however, requires a countertheft in revenge, and so the cycle goes on. For protection of his flock from theft and to be able to avenge any theft that occurs, a shepherd relies heavily on male kin (both patrilineal kin and kin through marriage). Another important basis for social ties is sheep stealing itself. After a series of thefts and counterthefts and rising hostility between the two groups, a mediator is brought in to resolve the tension, the result being that the enemies swear to be loyal friends from then on. Male identity formation through sheep stealing in highland Crete is still strong, although it is declining as some shepherds take up farming. The government has sought, mainly unsuccessfully, to suppress the raiding and to define sheep stealing as a crime.

Analysis of many instances of banditry reveals that they often involve mythification of bandits (Sant Cassia 1993). In this process, the imagined character of the bandit becomes more significant than what the bandit actually did. The story of Phulan Devi, India's "Bandit Queen," contains many aspects of banditry mythifica-

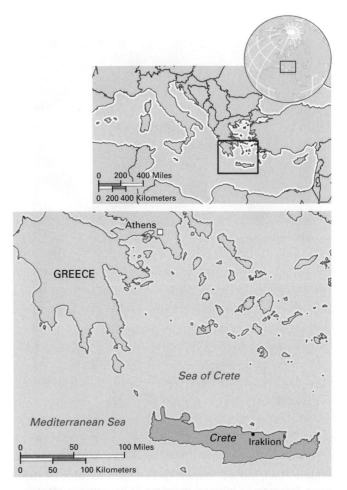

MAP 11.3 Crete. Crete is the largest of the Greek islands and, after Cyprus, the second largest in the eastern Mediterranean. Its terrain is mountainous interspersed with fertile plateaus. Farming is the traditional basis of the economy with tourism growing in importance.

tion: her low socioeconomic status, traditions of pastoralism, and raiding as honorable. Villagers have composed songs praising her, and a movie appeared in 1995 depicting her as a heroine who suffered, resisted, and ultimately triumphed.

Feuding

Feuding is a form of intergroup aggression that involves long-term, retributive violence that may be lethal between families, groups of families, or tribes. A concept of revenge motivates such back-and-forth violence between two groups. It is widely distributed cross-culturally.

Feuding long had an important role among the horticultural Ilongot people of the highlands of Luzon, in the Philippines (Rosaldo 1980) (see Map 7.1, p. 174). From 1883 to 1974, Ilongot feuds were structured around head-hunting as redress for an insult or offense. Manhood was defined by the taking of a first head, and fathers were responsible for transferring the elaborate knowledge of head-hunting to their sons. In 1972, the government banned head-hunting and attempted to stop

Phulan Devi, India's "Bandit Queen" and heroine of the poor, became an elected member of Parliament after eleven years in prison. Here, she participates in Parliament in New Delhi in 2000. She was assassinated in 2001. ■ *For a class project, read a biography of her, watch the video called "The Bandit Queen," read commentary on the Internet, and be prepared to comment on the "mythic" aspects of her life story.* (Source: AFP/CORBIS)

the Ilongot from practicing horticulture. The repercussions were devastating. The banning of head-hunting weakened father–son ties that had been solidified by the handing down of the elaborate techniques of head-hunting. The people said they were no longer Ilongots.

Sometimes contemporary change may lead to increased feuding, as in the case of Thull, a village in northern Pakistan of about 6,000 people (Keiser 1986). *Blood feuds,* which involve the death of someone in the enemy group, increased in frequency and intensity over a fifteen-year period in the 1960s and 1970s. Previously, there had been fights, usually expressing hostility between members of three patrilineal clans, but they rarely involved deadly weapons. According to the traditional honor code in this region, an act of avenging should not exceed the original

act: A blow should answer a blow, a death a death. For a murder, a man prefers to kill the actual murderer, but a father, adult brother, or adult son is a permissible substitute; killing women and children is unknown. Wrongs committed against a man through his wife, sister, or daughter are special, and whatever the transgression, the most appropriate response is to kill the offender. For example, staring at a man's wife or his daughter or sister (if she is of marriageable age) demands a deadly retaliation. Thus, according to some people in Thull, one man killed another man because he had apparently come to his house to catch a glimpse of his attractive young wife.

Why did blood feuds increase in Thull? The answer lies in the effects of economic change on the area. The government built a new road so that commercial logging could begin in the region. The logging involved local men in wage work and greatly increased the amount of cash available. The new road transformed local production from a blend of herding and farming to an emphasis on growing cash crops, especially potatoes. These changes led to increased tension among men, and they became more vigilant about defending their honor. Along with more cash came a dramatic rise in the number of guns. With more guns, feuding became more deadly.

Ethnic Conflict

Ethnic pluralism is a characteristic of most states in the world today. Ethnic conflict and grievances may result from an ethnic group's attempt to gain more autonomy or more equitable treatment (Esman 1996). It may also be caused by a dominant group's actions to subordinate,

The Hatfield clan in West Virginia in 1899. The long-standing feud between the Hatfields and the McCoys is part of American legend. ■ *What can you learn about the context of this conflict that would add complexity to its label as a blood feud?* (Source: © Bettmann/CORBIS)

revolution: a political crisis prompted by illegal and often violent actions of subordinate groups that seek to change the political institutions or social structure of a society.

oppress, or eliminate an ethnic group by genocide or ethnocide. In the past few decades, political violence has increasingly been enacted within states rather than between states, and intra-state violence constitutes the majority of the many "shooting wars" in the world today (Clay 1990). Political analysts and journalists often cite ethnicity, language, and religion as the causes of certain conflicts. It is true that ethnic identities give people an ideological commitment to a cause, but one must look beneath the labels to see whether deeper issues exist, such as claims to land, water, ports, and other material resources.

Consider Central Asia (see Map 11.4), a vast region populated by many ethnic groups, none of which has a pristine indigenous claim to the land. Yet, in Central Asia, every dispute appears on the surface to have an ethnic basis: "Russians and Ukrainians versus Kazakhs over land rights and jobs in Kazakhstan, Uzbeks versus Tajiks over the status of Samarkhand and Bukhara, conflict between Kirghiz and Uzbeks in Kyrgyzstan, and riots between Caucasian Turks and Uzbeks in the Fergana Valley of Uzbekistan" (Clay 1990:48).

Attributing the causes of all such problems to ethnic differences overlooks resource competition based on regional, not ethnic, differences. Uzbekistan has most of the cities and irrigated farmland, whereas Kyrgyzstan and Tajikistan control most of the water, and Turkmenistan has vast oil and gas riches. Competition among groups in these different regions appears to be "ethnic" while its roots are in the local and global political economy. So-called ethnic conflicts are waged in many different ways, from the cruelest and most gruesome killings and rapes to more subtle forms. Throughout the history of the state, and seemingly at increasing rates in recent decades, violence linked to ethnicity has led to the break-up of states and the forced displacement of millions of people (see Everyday Anthropology box).

Revolution

A **revolution** is a form of conflict involving illegal and usually violent actions by subordinate groups that seek to change the status quo (Goldstone 1996:740). Revolutions have occurred in a range of societies, including monarchies, postcolonial developing countries, and totalitarian states. Comparison of revolutions in modern times—England, 1640; France, 1789; Mexico, 1910; China, 1911; Russia, 1917; and Iran, 1979—reveal that their causes involve interrelated factors, such as a military crisis, a fiscal crisis, and a weak state. The process of revolution varies in terms of the degree of popular participation, the roles of radicals and moderates, and leadership.

MAP 11.4 Central Asian States. The five states of Central Asia are Kazakhstan, Turkmenistan, Uzbekistan, Kyrgyzstan, and Tajikistan. It is a large, landlocked region that is historically linked with pastoralism and the famous Silk Road, a trade route linking the Middle East with China. The region's terrain encompasses desert, plateaus, and mountains. Given its strategic location near several major world powers, it has often been a battleground of other states' interests. The predominant religion is Islam, and most Central Asians are Sunnis. Languages are of the Turkic language group. Central Asia has an indigenous form of rap-style music in which lyrical improvisers engage in battles, usually accompanied by a stringed instrument. These musical artists, or *akyns,* are now using their art to campaign for political candidates.

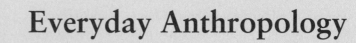

NARRATING TROUBLES

Refugee survivors of violence are especially at risk of various mental health problems, including what Western psychiatrists call post-traumatic stress disorder, or PTSD. It includes symptoms such as depression, anxiety, sleep disorders, and changes in personality. In treating refugee survivors in North America, several approaches have been used, including "narrative therapy," in which the sufferer tells about his or her experiences as a way of unloading the pent-up memories. Narrative therapy, also called the testimony method, is usually combined with other forms of therapy, such as support groups. The method involves asking the individual to tell in detail, in a safe and caring interpersonal setting, the story of what happened to him or her.

A study of twenty Bosnian refugees who now live in the United States sheds light on the positive effects of having survivors narrate their experiences of terror and suffering (Weine et al. 1995). Ten of the refugees in the study were male and ten were female. They belonged to six families and ranged in age from 13 to 62 years. All but one were Muslims, and all adults were married and had worked either inside or outside the home. Analysis of the testimony showed that all had experienced many traumatic events, the frequency increasing with a person's age. The number of traumatic events in the narratives did not differ by gender, but the qualitative aspects of the trauma did:

> Adult men were more likely to be separated from their families and to be held in concentration camps

where they suffered extreme deprivation and atrocities. Adult women (as well as adolescents of both genders) were often held briefly in detention camps and then they spent months fleeing from capture or being held in occupied territory where they were subjected to violence. (1995:537)

Almost all the refugees experienced the destruction of their homes, forced evacuation, food and water deprivation, disappearance of family members, exposure to acts of violence or death, detainment in a refugee camp, and forced emigration: "Nearly all the refugees emphasized the shock that came with the sudden occurrence of human betrayal by neighbors, associates, friends, and relatives" (1995:538).

The testimonies document the genocidal nature of the traumas directed at the entire Muslim Bosnian population. The traumas experienced were "extreme, multiple, repeated, prolonged, and communal" (1995:539). Some of the survivors carry with them constant images of death and atrocity. One man describes them as "films" that play in his head. In contrast, others have lost their memories of the events, and one woman was later unable to remember the trauma story she told three weeks earlier: "All kinds of things come together. Being expelled. Things we lost. Twenty years of work—then suddenly being without anything. . . . All the memories come at the same moment and it's too much" (1995:541).

The massiveness of their suffering, the psychiatrists report, extends beyond the bounds of the current diag-

---

Theorists argue about the different roles of rural and urban sectors in fostering revolution. Many revolutions occurred in agrarian countries and were propelled by rural participants, not by urban radicalism (Skocpol 1979; E. Wolf 1969). Such agrarian-based revolutions include the French, Russian, and Chinese revolutions. A rural-based movement also characterized many national liberation movements against colonial powers such as French Indo-China, Guinea-Bissau, Mozambique, and Angola (Gugler 1988). Algeria was a somewhat more urbanized country, but it was still about two-thirds rural in 1962 when the French finally made peace there. In these cases, the colonial power was challenged by a rural-based guerrilla movement that controlled crop production, processing, and transport and thus could strike at the heart of the colonial political economy.

In contrast, some revolutions have been essentially urban in character, as in Bolivia, Iran, and Nicaragua. The importance of cities in these revolutions is related to the fact that the countries were highly urbanized. Thus, revolutionary potential exists where resources are controlled and where the bulk of the population is located. Given the rapid urban growth in most developing countries, it is possible that the world is entering "the age of urban revolutions" (Gugler 1988).

The case of Cuba is mixed. Rural-based guerrillas played a prominent role in the revolution that placed

---

war: organized and purposeful group action directed against another group and involving lethal force.

MAP 11.5 Bosnia and Herzegovina. Formerly part of the Socialist Federal Republic, Bosnia and Herzegovina have a population of around 4 million people. Bosnia occupies the northern areas of the country, about four-fifths of the total area, whereas Herzegovina occupies the southern part. The country currently faces the challenges of postwar reconstruction following the Yugoslav War of 1992–1995. On a brighter note, it has one of the best income equality rankings in the world, placing eighth among 193 countries. Bosnia and Herzegovina are world champions in Paralympics volleyball, with a team consisting of players who lost their legs in the Yugoslav War.

nostic category of PTSD. Yet, in spite of their deep and extensive suffering, many Bosnian refugees in the United States are recovering and rebuilding their lives, perhaps in part due to the success of narrative therapy. Studies of this therapeutic approach among refugees of other cultures, however, reveal that some people are extremely reluctant to discuss their experiences, even in a supportive setting. Thus, narrative therapy may not be effective in all cultures.

FOOD FOR THOUGHT

- The Bosnian refugees described here have diverse stressful experiences, from violence in their homelands to going through Western therapeutic treatment in the United States. Have you ever had similar experiences? If so, what were your reactions and how did you cope with the stress?

Fidel Castro in power. The cities, however, provided crucial support for the guerrillas.

Warfare

Several definitions of **war** exist (Reyna 1994). One view is that war is an open and declared conflict between two political units. This definition would rule out many war-like conflicts, including the American–Vietnam War because it was undeclared. Or, is war simply organized aggression? This definition is too broad because not all organized violence can be considered warfare. Perhaps the best definition is that war is organized conflict involving group action directed against another group and involving lethal force (Ferguson 1994, quoted in Reyna 1994:30). Lethal force during war is legal if it is conducted according to the rules of battle.

Cultural variation exists in the frequency and seriousness of wars. Intergroup conflicts among free-ranging foragers that would fit the definition of war do not exist in the ethnographic record. The informal, nonhierarchical political organization among bands is not conducive to waging armed conflict. Bands do not have specialized military forces or leaders.

Archaeological evidence indicates that warfare may have emerged during the Neolithic era. Plant and animal domestication required extensive land use, and they were accompanied by increased population density. The resulting economic and demographic pressures put more and larger groups in more direct and intense competition

THINKING OUTSIDE THE BOX

HOW WOULD YOU define war? Given your definition, how many wars are currently ongoing and where are they?

YANOMAMI: THE "FIERCE PEOPLE"?

The Yanomami are a horticultural people living in dispersed villages of between 40 and 250 people in the Amazonian rainforest (Ross 1993). Since the 1960s, biological anthropologist Napoleon Chagnon has studied several Yanomami villages. He has written a widely read and frequently republished ethnography about the Yanomami, subtitled *The Fierce People* (1992 [1968]) and has helped produce several classic ethnographic films about them, including *The Feast* and *The Axe Fight*.

Chagnon's writings and films have promoted a view of the Yanomami as exceptionally violent and prone to lethal warfare. According to Chagnon, about one-third of adult Yanomami males die violently, about two-thirds of all adults had lost at least one close relative through violence, and over 50 percent had lost two or more close relatives (1992:205). He has reported that one village was raided twenty-five times during his first fifteen months of fieldwork. Although village alliances are sometimes formed, they are fragile and allies may turn against each other unpredictably.

The Yanomami world, as depicted by Chagnon, is one of danger, threats, and counterthreats. Enemies, human and supernatural, are everywhere. Support from one's allies is uncertain. All of this uncertainty leads to what Chagnon describes as the *waiteri complex,* a set of behaviors and attitudes that includes a fierce political and personal stance for men and forms of individual and group communication that stress aggression and independence. Fierceness is a dominant theme in socialization, as boys learn how to fight with clubs, participate in chest-pounding duels with other boys, and use a spear. Adult males are aggressive and hostile toward adult females, and young boys learn to be aggressive toward girls from an early age.

Chagnon provides a biological, Darwinian explanation for the fierceness shown by the Yanomami. He reports that the Yanomami explain that village raids and warfare are carried out so that men may obtain wives. Although the Yanomami prefer to marry within their village, a shortage of potential brides exists because of the Yanomami practice of female infanticide. Although the Yanomami prefer to marry endogamously, taking a wife from another group is preferable to remaining a bachelor. Men in other groups, however, are unwilling to give up their women—hence the necessity for raids. Suspicion of sorcery or theft of food are other valid reasons for raids. Chagnon argues that within this system, warfare contributes to reproductive success because successful warriors are able to gain a wife or more than one wife (polygyny is allowed). Thus, successful warriors will have higher reproductive rates than unsuccessful warriors. Successful warriors, Chagnon suggests, have a genetic advantage for fierceness, which they pass on to their sons, leading to a higher growth rate of groups with violent males through genetic selection for fierceness. Male fierceness, in this view, is biologically adaptive.

Marvin Harris, from the cultural materialist perspective, says that protein scarcity and population dynamics in the area are the underlying cause of warfare (1984). The Yanomami lack plentiful sources of meat, which is highly valued. Harris suggests that when game in an area becomes depleted, pressure rises to expand into the territory of neighboring groups, thus precipitating conflict. Such conflicts in turn result in high rates of adult male mortality. Combined with the effects of female infanticide, this meat-warfare complex keeps population growth rates down to a level that the environment can support.

A third view depends on historical data. Brian Ferguson (1990) argues that the high levels of violence among the Yanomami were caused by the intensified Western presence during the preceding 100 years. Furthermore,

---

with each other. Tribal leadership patterns facilitate mobilization of warrior groups for raids (recall the discussion of the segmentary model in Chapter 10). Tribal groups, though, do not have uniform levels of warfare. At one extreme, with reported high levels of warfare, are the Yanomami of the Amazon (see Map 3.4, p. 73 and Critical Thinking box).

Many chiefdoms have high rates of warfare and high casualty rates. They have increased capacity for war in terms of personnel and surplus foods to support long-range expeditions. The chief could call on his or her retainers as a specialized fighting force as well as the general members of society. Chiefs and paramount chiefs could be organized into effective command structures (Reyna 1994:44–45).

In states, standing (permanent) armies and complex military hierarchies are supported by increased material resources through taxation and other forms of revenue generation. Greater state power allows for more powerful and effective military structures, which in turn

Napoleon Chagnon (*center*) in the field with two Yanomami men, 1995. Chagnon has been accused of using distribution of goods to the Yanomami to gain their cooperation in his research, thereby markedly changing their culture. ■ (Source: © Antonio Mari)

diseases introduced from outside, especially measles and malaria, severely depopulated the Yanomami and greatly increased their fears of sorcery (their explanation for disease). The attraction to Western goods such as steel axes and guns would also increase intergroup rivalry. Thus, Ferguson suggests that the "fierce people" are a creation of historical forces, especially contact and pressure from outsiders.

Following on Ferguson's position but with a new angle, journalist Patrick Tierney points the finger of blame at Chagnon himself (2000). Tierney maintains that it was the presence of Chagnon, with his team of co-researchers and many boxes of trade goods, that triggered a series of lethal raids due to increased competition for those very goods. In addition, Tierney argues that Chagnon intentionally prompted the Yanomami to act fiercely for his films and to stage raids that created aggravated intergroup hostility beyond what had originally existed.

In 2001, the American Anthropological Association (AAA) established the El Dorado Task Force, charging it to examine five topics related to Tierney's allegations that Chagnon's and others' representations of the Yanomami may have had a negative impact on them and that the activities of anthropologists and others may have contributed to "disorganization" among the Yanomami. The report of the El Dorado Task Force appears on the AAA website (www.aaanet.org). Overall, the AAA position repudiates all charges against Chagnon and instead emphasizes the harmfulness of false accusations that may jeopardize future scientific research.

CRITICAL THINKING QUESTIONS

- Which perspective presented here on Yanomami men's behavior appears most persuasive to you and why?

- What relevance does this case have to the theory that violence is a universal human trait?

- Do you think it is possible that anthropological research could have such negative effects as increased violence among the study population?

increase the state's power. Thus, a mutually reinforcing relationship emerges between the military and the state. States are generally highly militarized, but not all are, nor are all states equally militarized. Costa Rica (see Map 14.2, p. 386) does not maintain an army, whereas Turkey has one of the world's largest.

Examining the causes of war between states has occupied scholars in many fields for centuries. Some experts have pointed to common, underlying causes, such as attempts to extend boundaries, secure more resources, ensure markets, support political and economic allies, and resist aggression from other states. Others point to humanitarian concerns that prompt participation in "just wars," to defend values such as freedom or to protect human rights that are defined as such by one country and are being violated in another.

Causes of war in Afghanistan have changed over time (Barfield 1994). Since the seventeenth century, warfare increasingly became a way in which kings justified their power in terms of the necessity to maintain independence

Members of the Turkish army special forces hang from a helicopter with their weapons and flags in 2002 as part of the celebration of the 79th anniversary of the foundation of the Turkish Republic. ■ *In your cultural world, what role do military forces play in celebrations of "statehood"?* (Source: © Reuters/CORBIS)

of Afghanistan would have required more extensive involvement and commitment, including introduction of a new economic and political system and ideology that would win over the population.

Current events show clearly that attacking and taking over a country are only the first stages in a process much more complicated than the term *regime change* implies. Afghanistan is still attempting to recover and rebuild after nearly three decades of war, although its problems of state integration and security have roots that go deeper than either the Soviet invasion or the U.S. occupation (Shahrani 2002). These roots include local codes of honor that value political autonomy and require vengeance for harm received, the moral system of Islam, the revitalized drug economy, and the effects of intervention from outside powers involving foreign governments and corporations, including Unocal of California, Delta Oil of Saudi Arabia, and Bridas of Argentina. The difficulty of constructing a strong state with loyal citizens in the face of these conflicting internal and external factors is great.

Cultural anthropologists, by and large, oppose war and have perhaps, therefore, avoided studying the institutions of war. Some cultural anthropologists are now doing research on topics such as the armed forces as social institutions, soldiers in the armed forces, and the effects of soldiers on the wider society. Much of this research could be termed **critical military anthropology**, the study of the military as a power structure. It takes a perspective of critique, viewing the armed forces as instruments of power and, often, repressive domination, and the process of *militarization* as problematic. Militarization refers to the intensification of labor and resources allocated to military purposes. Cultural anthropologists seek to provide insights that might lead to its control and reduction (Lutz 2002).

A study of the military in Bolivia (see Map 11.6) reveals that the young, male soldiers are recruited from the most powerless sections of society—minority farming groups, such as the Quechua and Aymara, and poor urban dwellers (Gill 1997). Serving as the foot soldiers, they risk death in combat more than the members of more powerful social groups, and they are more likely to suffer emotional abuse from their commanding officers. Military service is an obligation of all able-bodied Bolivian men, but many middle-class and upper-class men are able to avoid serving. It is also a prerequisite for many forms of urban employment. A more subtle, underlying motivation is that army service enables marginalized, powerless boys to express bravery, competence, and patriotism and thereby earn the respect and admiration of women as responsible adult males. The army instills a heightened sense of masculinity in its soldiers through basic training,

from outside forces such as the British and Czarist Russia. The last Afghan king was murdered in a coup in 1978. When the Soviet Union invaded in 1979, no centralized ruling group existed to meet it. The Soviet Union deposed the ruling faction, set up one of its own, and then killed over one million people, caused three million to flee the country, and millions of others to be displaced internally. In spite of the lack of a central command, ethnic and sectarian differences, and being outmatched in equipment by Soviet forces, the Afghanis waged a war of resistance that eventually wore down the Soviets, who withdrew in 1989.

This case suggests that war was a more effective tool of domination in the premodern period when it settled matters more definitively (Barfield 1994). In premodern times, fewer troops were needed to maintain dominance after a conquest, because continued internal revolts were less common and the main issue was defense against rivals from outside. Success in the Soviet Union's holding

---

critical military anthropology: the study of the military as a power structure in terms of its roles and internal social dynamics.

which lasts for three months and emphasizes the importance of male bonding and the link between masculinity and citizenship. A soldier who completes his service receives a *libreta militar,* or "military booklet," which documents his successful completion of duty and is used to help him obtain work in urban factories. The booklet is also useful in various transactions with the state and thus is a kind of ticket to citizenship. Better-off men simply pay a fee for the booklet. That is easy enough for them but impossible for poor men. Under President Evo Morales, it is now possible for indigenous people to attend officer training, something that was impossible previously (Gill 2006, personal communication).

In Israel, military service is a focal point of citizenship and nation building (Khanaaneh 2005). Service in the military, for all Jewish citizens, is also a pathway to full citizenship. Non-Jews in Israel, notably Palestinians who constitute one-fifth of Israel's population, are normally excluded from the military. Nonetheless, about 5,000 Palestinians living in Israel currently volunteer to serve in the Israeli military. Interviews with twenty-four Arab men and one Arab woman who served in various Israeli security branches—the army, border patrol, and police force—reveal the complexities and contradictions

MAP 11.6 **Bolivia. The Republic of Bolivia is situated in the Andes Mountains. It is the poorest country in South America although it is rich in natural resources, including the second largest oil field in South America after Venezuela. The population of 10 million includes a majority of indigenous people of nearly 40 different groups. The largest are the Aymara (2 million) and the Quechua-speaking groups (1.5 million). Thirty percent of the population is mestizo and 15 percent are of European descent. Two-thirds of the people are low-income farmers. The official religion is Roman Catholicism, but Protestantism is growing. Religious syncretism is prominent. Most people speak Spanish as their first language, although Aymara and Quechua are also common. Bolivia's popular fiesta known as *El carnaval de Oruro* is on UNESCO's list of Intangible Cultural Heritage.**

A child soldier named Alfred walks to a UN disarmament camp in the Liberian city of Tubmanburg in 2004. Many countries have programs in place to help child soldiers adjust to life after war. ■ *What might be the five most important challenges these children face in a postconflict situation?* (Source: © Emmanuel Tobey/Reuters/Corbis)

involved in their motivations and their identities as military personnel. These people are socially marginal in Israeli society because they are Arabs, and are even feared as security threats, but in their roles in the military they often gain positions of power and physical force. Joining the military is a way for non-Jews to achieve higher status through access to jobs, state land, educational subsidies, and low-interest loans. All of these entitlements are denied to non-serving Arabs. Being able to buy state land, however, raises a stark contradiction: The state policy of taking over Arab lands often involves confiscating land of Arabs who served in the military. In one instance in 2002, fifty homes of Arab Bedu who had served were confiscated. Thus, military service enables Arabs to buy back land that was originally theirs. Other contradictions arise when Arab members of the Israeli army have to carry out operations against other Arabs. Some of the soldiers justify their role by saying that their presence

Nonviolent Conflict

Mohandas K. Gandhi was one of the greatest designers of strategies for bringing about peaceful political change. Born in India, he studied law in London and then went to South Africa, where he worked as a lawyer serving the Indian community and evolved his primary method of civil disobedience through nonviolent resistance (Caplan 1987). In 1915, he returned to India, joined the nationalist struggle against British colonialism, and put into action his model of civil disobedience through nonviolent resistance, public fasting, and strikes.

Celibacy is a key feature of Gandhian philosophy because avoiding sex, in the Hindu view, helps maintain one's inner strength and purity (recall the lost semen complex mentioned in Chapter 5). Regardless of whether one agrees with Gandhi's support of sexual abstinence, the methods he developed of nonviolent civil disobedience have had a profound impact on the world. Martin Luther King Jr. and his followers adopted many of Gandhi's tactics during the U.S. civil rights movement, as did members of the peace movement of the 1960s and 1970s in the United States.

Most subordinate classes throughout history have not had the luxury of open, organized political activity because of its danger. Instead, people have had to resort to indirect ways of "working" the system. Political scientist and cultural anthropologist James Scott (1985) used the phrase "weapons of the weak" in the title of his book on rural people's resistance to domination by landlords and government through tactics other than outright rebellion or revolution. Weapons of the weak include "foot dragging," desertion, false compliance, feigned ignorance, and slander, as well as more aggressive acts such as theft, arson, and sabotage. One weapon of the weak that Scott overlooked is humor. Humor is an important part of Native American cultural resistance to domination by White society (Lincoln 1993). Instead of pitying themselves or lamenting the genocide that occurred as a result of European and Euro-American colonization, Native Americans have cultivated a sharp sense of humor. "Rez" (reservation) jokes travel like wildfire. Charlie Hill, for example, is notorious for his one-liners:

> The first English immigrants, he snaps, were illegal aliens—"Whitebacks, we call 'em." Hill imagines the Algonquians asking innocently, "You guys gonna stay long?" His Custer jokes are not printable ("Look at all those f—ing Indians!"—a barroom nude painting of Custer's last words). (1993:4–5)

Or, what did Native Americans say at Plymouth Rock? Answer: "There goes the neighborhood." Obviously, humor has not been the only source of strength for

Mahatma Gandhi (*left*), leader of the Indian movement for freedom from British colonial control, on his famous "Salt March" of 1930, in which he led a procession to the sea to collect salt in defiance of British law. He is accompanied by Sarojini Naidu, a noted freedom fighter.
■ *What are your images of Gandhi and how did you come by them?* (Source: © Bettmann/CORBIS)

Native Americans, but humor surely must be added to the list of weapons of the weak.

Maintaining World Order

Computer-operated war missiles, email, the Internet, satellite television, and jet flights mean that the world's states are more closely connected and better able to influence each other's fate than ever before. Modern weaponry means that such influences can be more lethal and more depersonalized. In the face of these realities, politicians, academics, and the public ponder the possibilities for world peace. Anthropological research on peaceful, local-level societies shows that humans are capable of living together in peace. The question is whether people living in larger groups that are globally connected can also live in peace. This section discusses two issues related to world order.

Women near Kabul, Afghanistan, look at replicas of land mines during a mining awareness program sponsored in 2003 by the International Committee of the Red Cross (ICRC). Afghanistan is still heavily mined, and rates of injury and mortality from mines are high. ■ *Do Internet research to learn about international organizations involved in de-mining.* (Source: © Reuters NewMedia Inc./CORBIS)

International Legal Disputes

Numerous attempts have been made, over time, to create institutions to promote world peace. The United Nations is the most established and respected of such institutions. One of the UN's significant accomplishments was its creation of the International Court of Justice, also known as the World Court, located in The Hague in the Netherlands (Nader 1995). In 1946, two-thirds of the Court's judges were American or Western European.

Representatives of ten NATO countries at the World Court in The Hague. This distinguished body of legal experts exhibits a clear pattern of age, gender, and ethnicity. ■ *What might be the implications of this pattern?* (Source: © Reuters/Fred Ernst)

Today, the Court has many judges from developing countries. Despite this more balanced representation, there has been a decline in use of the World Court and an increased use of international negotiating teams for resolving disputes between countries.

Laura Nader (1995) analyzed this decline and found that it follows a trend in the United States, beginning in the 1970s, to promote *alternate dispute resolution* (ADR). The goal was to move more cases out of the courts and to privatize dispute resolution. On the surface, ADR seems a more peaceful and more dignified option. Deeper analysis of actual cases and their resolution shows, however, that this bilateral process favors the stronger party. *Adjudication* (formal decree by a judge) would have resulted in a better deal for the weaker party than bilateral negotiation did. Thus, less powerful nations are negatively affected by the move away from the World Court.

The United Nations and International Peacekeeping

What role might cultural anthropology play in international peacekeeping? Robert Carneiro (1994) has a pessimistic response. Carneiro says that during the long history of human political evolution from bands to states, warfare has been the major means by which political units enlarged their power and domain. Foreseeing no logical end to this process, he predicts that war will follow war until superstates become ever larger and one mega-state is the final result. He considers the United Nations powerless in dealing with the principal obstacle to world peace, which is state sovereignty interests. Carneiro indicts the United Nations for its lack of coercive power and its poor record of having resolved disputes through military intervention in only a few cases. If war is inevitable, there is little room for hope that anthropological knowledge can be applied to peacemaking efforts.

Despite Carneiro's views, cultural anthropologists have shown that war is not a cultural universal and that different cultures have ways of solving disputes without resorting to killing. The cultural anthropological perspective of critical cultural relativism (review this concept in Chapter 1) can provide useful background on issues of conflict and prompt a deeper dialogue between parties.

One positive point emerges. The United Nations does provide an arena for airing disputes. This more optimistic view suggests that international peace organizations play a major role by providing analysis of the interrelationships among world problems and by helping others see the causes and consequences of violence (Vickers 1993:132). In addition, some people see hope for local and global peacemaking through nongovernmental organizations and local grassroots initiatives that seek to bridge group interests.

The Big Questions Revisited

WHAT is the scope of legal anthropology?

Legal anthropology encompasses the study of cultural variation in social order and social conflict. Early legal anthropologists approached the subject from a functionalist viewpoint that stresses how social institutions promote social cohesion and continuity. In contrast, the more recent approach of critical legal anthropology examines how law and judicial institutions serve to maintain and expand dominant power interests rather than protect marginal and less powerful people.

Legal anthropologists examine how legal systems change. Colonialism and contemporary globalization have affected indigenous systems of social control and law, often resulting in legal pluralism.

WHAT are cross-cultural systems for maintaining social order and social control?

Systems of social order and social control vary cross-culturally and over time. Social control is the process by which people maintain an orderly group life. They do so by designing rules for proper behavior and ensuring social conformity to these rules, including ways of dealing with people who do not adhere to the rules. Legal anthropologists distinguish between norms, which are a cultural universal, and laws, which are more associated with large-scale societies. A norm is a culturally accepted standard for how people should behave that is unwritten and learned unconsciously through socialization. Enforcement is usually informal and socially regulated. A law is a binding rule created through custom or official enactment with defined forms of punishment for violation, which may include death. Laws are associated with the development of professional specialization.

Social control in small-scale societies seeks to restore order more than to punish offenders. In small-scale societies, common forms of punishment are social shaming and shunning. States have power-related forms of punishment, including imprisonment and execution and a wide array of professional specializations involved in enacting punishment.

WHAT are cross-cultural patterns of social conflict and violence?

All cultures have to deal with the fact that disrepect for norms, interpersonal conflict, and violence on a wider scale may occur. Ethnographic evidence on levels and forms of conflict and violence indicate that high levels of violence, especially lethal violence, are not universal. They are more associated with the state than with other forms of political organization. Cross-culturally, social conflict ranges from face-to-face conflicts, as among neighbors or domestic partners, to larger group conflicts between ethnic groups and states. The immediate causes of interpersonal violence range from economic debt to problems with neighborhood dogs. Many forms of social conflict involve property in one way or another. Banditry is devoted to illegal transfer of property and also may involve one's cultural identity as a person of worth. Feuding is a form of intergroup violence that may go on for decades, with revenge for harm done in the past being the motivating factor and resource issues often underlying the interpersonal enmity.

So-called ethnic conflict appears to be on the rise in recent decades and is more common than interstate violence. Research suggests that much ethnic conflict is also about resources such as land, water, and oil. Beyond their causes, ethnic conflicts have generated massive suffering and the forced displacement of millions of people as either refugees or internally displaced people. Revolutions are intentionally planned forms of conflict, usually violent, by subordinate groups that seek to change the status quo. Many are rural based, others are urban based, and some are a mixture of the two. War is difficult to define. The best definition is that war is conflict involving organized group action directed against another group and involving lethal force. War is associated with the emergence of the state.

Many cultural anthropologists are turning their attention to global conflict and peacekeeping solutions. Key issues involve the role of cultural knowledge in global dispute resolution and how international or local organizations can help achieve or maintain peace.

KEY CONCEPTS

banditry, p. 294
critical legal anthropology, p. 286
critical military anthropology, p. 302
feuding, p. 295

law, p. 287
legal pluralism, p. 292
norm, p. 286
policing, p. 288

revolution, p. 297
social control, p. 286
trial by ordeal, p. 288
war, p. 299

SUGGESTED READINGS

Thomas Biolsi. *"Deadliest Enemies": Law and the Making of Race Relations on and off Rosebud Reservation.* Berkeley: University of California Press, 2001. This book examines the effects of contradictory U.S. laws about Indians within the context of the Sicangu Lakota, or Rosebud Sioux, and the non-Indians in south-central South Dakota.

Jack David Eller. *From Culture to Ethnicity to Conflict: An Anthropological Perspective on International Ethnic Conflict.* Ann Arbor: University of Michigan Press, 1999. Two introductory chapters discuss terminology and the relationships among culture, ethnicity, and conflict. Chapters provide case studies of Sri Lanka, the Kurds, Rwanda, Bosnia, and Québec.

Pamela Frese and Margaret Harrell, eds. *Anthropology and the United States Military: Coming of Age in the Twenty-First Century.* New York: Palgrave/Macmillan, 2003. This volume of collected essays contributes to knowledge in several core anthropological areas (such as kinship, the body, leadership, and meaning) by addressing army spouses, gender roles, weight control, anthrax vaccines, and the military advisor.

Leslie Gill. *The School of the Americas: Military Training and Political Violence in the Americas.* Durham, NC: Duke University Press, 2004. Located at Fort Benning, Colorado, the School of the Americas (SOA) is a U.S. Army center that trains soldiers and police, mostly from Latin America, in counterinsurgency techniques and combat skills. Gill attended classes, accompanied students and their families on shopping trips to the mall, and examined the effects of the SOA in Colombia and Bolivia.

Daniel M. Goldstein. *The Spectacular City: Violence and Performance in Urban Bolivia.* Durham, NC: Duke University Press, 2004. Situated within the context of the increasing crime that has accompanied the consolidation of Western capitalism in Bolivia, this ethnography explores how local political activism is expressed using traditional performance genres.

Thomas Gregor, ed. *A Natural History of Peace.* Nashville: University of Tennessee Press, 1996. This book contains essays on "what is peace?" reconciliation among nonhuman primates, the psychological bases of violent and nonviolent societies, case studies of Amazonia and American Indians, and international relations.

Hugh Gusterson. *Nuclear Rites: A Weapons Laboratory at the End of the Cold War.* Berkeley: University of California Press, 1996. This ethnographic study focuses on the nuclear research community of Livermore, California. It explores the scientists' motivations to develop nuclear weapons, the culture of secrecy, and the metaphors used in nuclear research.

Roger N. Lancaster. *Life Is Hard: Machismo, Danger, and the Intimacy of Power in Nicaragua.* Berkeley: University of California Press, 1992. This ethnography of everyday life in a barrio of Managua, Nicaragua, examines interpersonal violence as well as the wider issue of how living during a revolution affects people.

Mahmood Mamdani. *When Victims Become Killers: Colonialism, Nativism, and the Genocide in Rwanda.* Princeton, NJ: Princeton University Press, 2001. Mamdani examines the historical context of violence from the colonial era in order to understand root causes and how ethnic labels and identities change.

Beatiz Manz. *Paradise in Ashes: A Guatemalan Journey of Courage, Terror, and Hope.* Berkeley: University of California Press, 2004. This book traces the lives and deaths of some Guatemalan Maya villagers who left their impoverished homeland in the mountains to build a new life in the lowlands. In their new location, they became victims of state-sponsored violence. Many were murdered, and others were forced to flee into the jungle. The survivors have returned and are now attempting to rebuild their homes and lives.

Sally Engle Merry. *Human Rights and Gender Violence: Translating International Law into Local Justice.* Chicago: University of Chicago Press, 2005. This multisited study investigates the tensions between global laws that seek to protect women from violence and women's status in local contexts. Findings indicate that human rights law must be framed in local terms to be accepted.

Bruce Miller. *The Problem of Justice: Tradition and Law in the Coast Salish World.* Lincoln: University of Nebraska Press, 2001. The author compares several legal systems operating in the Northwest Coast region from Washington State to British Columbia. The effects of colonialism differ from group to group. Some are strong and independent, whereas others are disintegrating.

Carolyn Nordstrom. *Shadows of War: Violence, Power, and International Profiteering in the Twenty-First Century.* Berkeley: University of California Press, 2004. Nordstrom did fieldwork in Sri Lanka and Mozambique during times of war to reveal the shadow economy that surrounds and supports war. She focuses on informal trading networks that involve goods ranging from guns to food and the people who profit from this economy.

Jeffrey Rubin. *Decentering the Regime: Ethnicity, Radicalism and Democracy in Jchitán, Mexico.* Durham, NC: Duke University Press, 1997. Written by a political scientist who adopted the methods of cultural anthropology, this study analyzes how the Mexican state defines, represents, and relates to indigenous peoples and how indigenous peoples struggle against the state.

Jennifer Schirmer. *The Guatemalan Military Project: A Violence Called Democracy.* Philadelphia: University of Pennsylvania Press, 1998. This book is an ethnography of the Guatemalan military, documenting its role in human rights violations through extensive interviews with military officers and trained torturers.

June Starr and Mark Goodale, eds. *Practicing Ethnography in Law: New Dialogues, Enduring Methods.* New York: Palgrave Macmillan, 2002. Chapters address relationships between legal and feminist scholarship, between law and the media, and between law and globalization. Specific topics include human rights, witchcraft belief, immigration, and the value of ethnographic methods.

PART IV

Symbolic Systems

BRIAN CRAIK IS A FEDERAL RELATIONS AND ENVIRON-MENTAL IMPACT ASSESSMENT ANTHROPOLOGIST.
"Working together" is his basic principle for achieving First Nations' rights in Canada. In his current position, Craik is the director of federal relations for the Grand Council of the Crees. The Cree People, or Eeyouch or Eenouch, number over 14,000. They live in the area of eastern James Bay and southern Hudson Bay in northern Québec, Canada.

In working more than thirty years as an applied anthropologist, Craik has combined his anthropological training with political skills to assist the Cree in seeking social and environmental justice. Early in his career, he lived with the Waskaganish Cree for many years. He is the first anthropologist in the world to become fluent in the Cree language (Preston 2006). After studying for his doctorate in anthropology at McMaster University in the early 1970s and being the first student to pass his language exam in the Cree language, Craik began working as a consultant for various Cree communities on issues such as the proposed Nottaway-Broadback-Rupert Project.

In 1984, Craik joined Canada's Department of Indian Affairs and Northern Development. In that role, he helped to implement the James Bay and Northern Québec Agreement (JBNQA) that was signed in 1975. The JBNQA was a benchmark settlement related to land claims issues and compensation for damages. It awarded $225 million in compensation to the James Bay Cree and the Inuit of northern Québec to be paid by Canada and Québec. The agreement defined Native rights to the land and laid out various protections to ensure the maintenance of these rights in the face of the undesirable social and environmental effects of commercial development. As part of this effort, Craik worked on the passage of the Cree/Naskapi (of Québec) Act, Canada's first Aboriginal local government act, and helped assure the approval of related funding.

In 1987, Craik left the government to return to private consulting work. He worked with the Lubicon Crees of Alberta, the Inuit of Northern Quebec, the Micmac of Conn River, and the Mohawks of Kahnawake. In 1989, he advised the James Bay Cree on relations with the federal government and on the environmental and social issues related to the Great Whale Project. The Cree People appointed him to two of the environmental committees that reviewed the project. Craik played a central role in the 1989–1994 campaign that stopped the Great Whale River hydroelectric project. From 1997 to 1999, he negotiated an agreement between the Crees and Canada on Canada Manpower Services and has worked to implement the 2002 New Relationship Agreement between the Crees and the government of Québec and on the review of the Eastmain 1A–Rupert Diversion Project that it contains.

The Cree People have faced many threats to their lifeway, their culture, and their environment. The Grand Council of the Crees was formed in 1974 in response to the James Bay Hydroelectric Project (www.gcc.ca/gcc/fedrelations.php). Their political mobilization was inspired by the need to "stand in the way of development projects designed to serve others" (Craik n.d.). With Craik's long-term assistance in their struggle, they have sharpened their political and economic power and skills. They now choose when to block a destructive project or when to work to change the terms of a project in order to mitigate damage to their culture and land and to reap some of the benefits for their own group-defined development goals.

Anthropology *in the* Real World

12
Communication

The Big Questions

- HOW do humans communicate?

- WHAT are the links between communication, cultural diversity, and inequality?

- HOW does language change?

Tuareg men in Niger, West Africa, greeting each other. Tuareg men's greetings involve lengthy handshaking and close body contact. *(Source: © Charles O. Cecil)*

Most people are in almost constant communication—with other people, with supernaturals, or with pets. We communicate in face-to-face situations or indirectly through mail or email. **Communication** is the process of sending and receiving messages. Among humans, it involves some form of **language,** a systematic set of symbols and signs with learned and shared meanings. Language may be spoken, hand-signed, written, or conveyed through body movements, body markings and modifications, hairstyle, dress, and accessories.

This chapter is about human communication and language, drawing on work in both linguistic anthropology and cultural anthropology. It looks at communication with a wide-angle lens to include topics from word choice to language extinction. The chapter first discusses how humans communicate and what distinguishes human communication from that of other animals. Next, the chapter offers examples of language, microcultures, and inequality. The third section discusses language change from its origins in the distant past to contemporary concerns about language loss.

The Varieties of Human Communication

Humans can communicate with words, either spoken or signed, with gestures and other forms of body language such as clothing and hairstyle, and through methods such as telephone calls, "real" mail, and email.

Language and Verbal Communication

Specialists can get quite engaged in arguing about what a *language* is, how many languages there are in the world, and whether animals other than humans have language. Most agree that language and its subvarieties are systems of symbols and signs, and rules for their meaningful combination and use. The term **dialect** usually refers to a subvariety of language associated with a region, social class, or ethnic group. A speaker of the main language should be able to understand local dialects, though perhaps with difficulty.

Two Features of Human Language

Scholars of language, over many years, have proposed characteristics of human language that distinguish it from communication among other living beings. This section presents the two most robust of these.

First, human language has **productivity,** or the ability to create an infinite range of understandable expressions from a finite set of rules. This characteristic is a result of the rich variety of symbols and signs that humans use in their communication. In contrast, nonhuman primates have a more limited set of communicative resources. They rely on a **call system,** or a form of oral communication among nonhuman primates with a set repertoire of meaningful sounds generated in response to environmental factors. Nonhuman primates do not have the physiological capacity for speech that humans do. In captivity, however, some bonobos and chimpanzees have learned to communicate effectively with humans through sign language and by pointing to symbols on a chart. The world's most famous bonobo is Kanzi, who lives at the Great Ape Trust in Des Moines, Iowa (www .greatapetrust.org/bonobo/meet/Kanziiphp), can understand what humans are saying, and can respond by combining symbols on a printed board. He can also play simple video games, such as Ms. Pac-Man.

Second, human language emphasizes the feature of **displacement,** the ability to refer to events and issues beyond the immediate present. The past and the future, in this view, are considered to be *displaced domains.* They include reference to people and events that may never exist at all, as in fantasy and fiction. Some bonobos who have been raised by and live in a close relationship with humans do exhibit the ability for displacement (www.pbs.org/templates/story/story.php?storyID= 5541690). Thus, they have the capacity for displacement but, especially in the wild, are likely to use it far less than humans do.

In respect to productivity and displacement in human language, the case of language among the Pirahã of Brazil is challenging (Everett 2005) (see Map 12.1). Their language does not appear to emphasize either productivity or displacement, though both exist to some degree. The Pirahã are a group of 300 to 350 foragers living on a reservation in the Amazonian rainforest near the Maici River. Their language contains only three pronouns, few

---

communication: the conveying of meaningful messages from one person, animal, or insect to another.
language: a form of communication that is a systematic set of learned and shared symbols and signs shared among a group and passed on from generation to generation.

dialect: a way of speaking in a particular place or a variety of a language arising from local circumstances.
productivity: a feature of human language that offers the ability to communicate many messages efficiently.
call system: a form of oral communication among nonhuman primates with a set

repertoire of meaningful sounds generated in response to environmental factors.
displacement: a feature of human language that allows people to talk about events in the past and future.
phoneme: a sound that makes a difference for meaning in a language.

Primatologist Sue Savage-Rumbaugh, working with Kanzi, an adult male bonobo. Kanzi has been involved in a long-term project about ape language. He has learned to communicate with researchers using a variety of symbols. Some chimpanzees, bonobos, orangutans, and gorillas have learned to communicate using American Sign Language and symbols on computer keyboards. ■ (Source: © Frans Lanting/Minden Pictures)

words associated with time, no past-tense verbs, no color terms, and no numbers other than a word that translates into English roughly as "about one." Grammar is simple, with no subordinate clauses. Kinship terms are simple and few. The Pirahã have no myths or stories and no art other than necklaces and a few rudimentary stick figures. In spite of over 200 years of regular contact with Brazilians and neighboring Indians who speak a different language, the Pirahã remain monolingual.

MAP 12.1   Pirahã Reservation in Brazil. Linguistic anthropologist Daniel Everett helped to define the boundaries of the Pirahã reservation in the 1980s. With support from Cultural Survival and other sources, the demarcation was legally declared in 1994.

Since 1977, linguist Daniel Everett has lived with the Pirahã and learned their language, so it is unlikely that he has overlooked major aspects of their language. He insists that their language is in no way "primitive." It has extremely complex verbs and rich and varied uses of stress and intonation, referred to in linguistics as *prosody*. The Pirahã especially enjoy verbal joking and teasing, both among themselves and with researchers.

Formal Properties of Verbal Language

Human language can be analyzed in terms of its formal properties: sounds, vocabulary, and syntax (sometimes called grammar), which are the formal building blocks of all languages. But languages differ widely in which sounds are important, what words are important in the vocabulary, and how people put words together to form meaningful sentences.

Learning a new language usually involves learning different sets of sounds. The sounds that make a difference for meaning in a language are called **phonemes**. The study of phonemes is called *phonetics*. Sharon Hutchinson comments on her attraction to phonemes of the Nuer language of southern Sudan (see Map 16.7, p. 443):

As a native English speaker, I find the seeming airy lightness and rich melodic qualities of the Nuer language to be attractive. . . . The apparent "airiness" of the language stems from the fact that many Nuer vowels are heavily aspirated—that is, they are released with an audible bit of breath as in the English "hi" and "hea" in "behind" and "ahead." Indeed, one of the earliest obstacles I faced in trying to learn the language was to hear and to control the voice's "breathiness" or "nonbreathiness" in the pronunciation of various Nuer vowels. (1996:xv–xvi)

Compared to English, the Pirahã language appears to lack several features, such as the ability to count. According to Daniel Everett, who has spent many years learning about their culture and language, the Pirahã do not lead a culturally deprived life. They have happy and fulfilling leisure activities which include playing tag and other games. In spite of their wish to remain living as they are, their reservation is not secure from outside encroachment, and their lifestyle and culture are therefore endangered. ■ (Source: Daniel Everett)

A native English-speaker learning to speak Hindi, the major language of North India, must learn to produce and recognize several new sounds. Four different "d" sounds exist. None is the same as an English "d," which is usually pronounced with the tongue placed on the ridge behind the upper front teeth (try it). One "d" in Hindi, which linguists refer to as a "dental" sound, is pronounced with the tongue pressed firmly behind the upper front teeth (try it) (see Figure 12.1). Next is a dental "d" that is also aspirated (pronounced "with air"); making this sound involves the tongue being in the same position and a puff of air expelled during pronunciation (try it, and try the regular dental "d" again with no puff of air at all). Next is what is referred to as a "retroflex"

FIGURE 12.1 Dental and retroflex tongue positions. When making a dental sound, the speaker places the tongue against the upper front teeth (position A on the diagram). When making a retroflex sound, the speaker places the tongue up against the roof of the mouth (position B on the diagram).

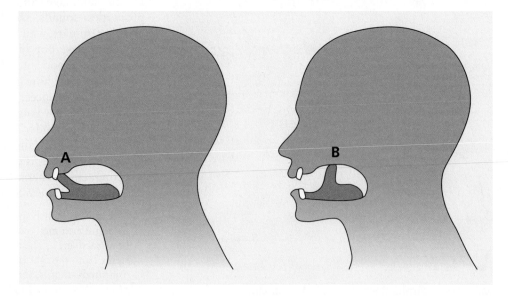

ethnosemantics: the study of the meaning of words, phrases, and sentences in particular cultural contexts.

sign language: a form of communication that uses mainly hand movements to convey messages.

FIGURE 12.2   Kinds of "Snow" the Saami Recognize Related to Reindeer Herding

- Firm, even snow that falls in mild weather
- Thickly packed snow caused by intermittent freezing/thawing and high winds
- Hard-packed snow formed by strong wind
- Dry, large-grained, water-holding snow at the deepest layers, closest to the ground, found in late winter and spring
- Snow that forms a hard layer after rain
- Ice sheet on pastures formed by rain on open ground that freezes
- A layer of frozen snow between other snow layers that acts as an ice sheet

Source: Jernsletten 1997.

sound, made by flipping the tongue back to the central dome of the roof of the mouth (try it, with no puff of air). Finally, there is the aspirated retroflex "d" with the tongue in the center of the roof of the mouth and a puff of air. Once you can do this, try the whole series again with a "t," because Hindi follows the same pattern with this letter as with the "d." Several other sounds in Hindi require careful use of aspiration and placement of the tongue for communicating the right word. A puff of air at the wrong time can produce a serious error, such as saying the word for "breast" when you want to say the word for "letter."

All languages have a *lexicon,* or vocabulary, which consists of all its meaningful words. Words are combined in phrases and sentences to create meaning. *Semantics* refers to the study of the meaning of words, phrases, and sentences. Anthropologists add the concept of **ethnosemantics,** the study of the meaning of words, phrases, and sentences in particular cultural contexts. They find that different languages classify the world in different ways, and categorize even such seemingly natural things as color and disease in different ways (recall the discussion of Subanun disease categories in Chapter 7). By doing ethnosemantic research, one can learn much about how people define the world and their place in it, how they organize their social lives, and what is of value to them. *Focal vocabularies* are clusters of words that refer to important features of a particular culture. For example, many circumpolar languages have rich focal vocabularies related to snow (see Figure 12.2).

Syntax, or grammar, consists of the patterns and rules by which words are organized to make sense in a string. All languages have rules for syntax, although they vary in form. Even within the languages of contemporary Europe syntactical variation exists. German, for exam-

ple, places verbs at the end of the sentence (try to compose an English sentence with its main verb at the end).

Nonverbal Language and Embodied Communication

This section reviews forms of language and communication that do not rely on verbal speech. Like verbal language, though, they are based on symbols and signs and have rules for their proper combination and meaning.

Sign Language

Sign language is a form of communication that uses mainly hand movements to convey messages. A sign language provides a fully competent communicative system for its users just as spoken language does (Baker 1999). Around the world, many varieties of sign language exist, including American Sign Language, British Sign Language, Japanese Sign Language, Russian Sign Language, and many varieties of indigenous Australian sign languages. Most sign languages are used by people who are hearing impaired as their main form of communication. Indigenous Australian sign languages, in contrast, are used by people who have the capacity for verbal communication. They switch to sign language in situations in which verbal speech is forbidden or undesirable (Kendon 1988). Verbal speech is forbidden in some sacred contexts and for widows during mourning. It is also undesirable when hunting.

Although sign languages are complete and complex languages in their own right, they are often treated as second-class versions of "real" languages. A breakthrough in recognition of the validity and communicative competence of sign languages came in 1983 when the government of Sweden recognized Swedish Sign Language as a native language. Such recognition is especially important in contexts where a person's sense of identity, and even citizenship itself, is based on the ability to speak an officially accepted language. Anthropologists collaborate with people who are deaf to help promote public understanding of the legitimacy of their language and to advocate for improved teaching of sign language (see Lessons Applied box).

Gestures are movements, usually of the hands, that convey meanings. Some gestures may be universally meaningful, but most are culturally specific and often completely arbitrary. Some cultures have more highly developed gesture systems than others. Black urban youths in the province of Gauteng, South Africa, in which the cities of Pretoria and Johannesburg are located, use a rich repertoire of gestures (Brookes 2004) (see Map 9.5, p. 247). Although some of the gestures are widely used and recognized, many vary by age, gender, and situation (see Figure 12.3). Men use more gestures than women do; the reason for this difference is not clear.

Lessons Applied

ANTHROPOLOGY AND PUBLIC UNDERSTANDING OF THE LANGUAGE AND CULTURE OF PEOPLE WHO ARE DEAF

Ethnographic studies of the communication practices and wider culture of people who are deaf have great importance and practical application (Senghas and Monaghan 2002). This research demonstrates the limitations

In Uganda, James Mwadha, a deaf attendee at a meeting for Action on Disability and Development (ADD), signs to others in the group. ADD seeks to promote the rights of disabled people. ■ (Source: © Penny Tweedie/CORBIS)

and inaccuracy of the "medical model" that construes deafness as a pathology or deficit and sees the goal as curing it. Instead, anthropologists propose the "cultural model," which views deafness simply as one possibility in the wide spectrum of cultural variation. (In this view a capital *D* is often used: Deaf culture.)

Deafness allows plenty of room for human agency. The strongest evidence of agency among people who are deaf is sign language itself, which exhibits adaptiveness, creativity, and change. This view helps to promote a nonvictim, nonpathological identity for people who are deaf and to reduce social stigma related to deafness.

Anthropologists working in the area of Deaf culture studies are examining how people who are deaf become bilingual—for example, fluent in both English and Japanese sign languages. Their findings are being incorporated in improved ways of teaching sign language.

FOOD FOR THOUGHT

- Choose five words and learn the signs for them in American Sign Language and in another culture's sign language. Are they the same or different, and how might one explain the similarity or difference?

Greetings, an important part of communication in every known culture, often involve gestures (Duranti 1997b). They are typically among the first communicative routines that children learn, as well as tourists and anyone trying to learn a foreign language. Greetings establish a social encounter. They typically involve both verbal and nonverbal language. Depending on the context and the social relationship, many variations exist for both the verbal and the nonverbal component. Contextual factors include the degree of formality or informality. Social factors include gender, ethnicity, class, and age.

Silence

Silence is another form of nonverbal communication. Its use is often related to social status, but in unpredictable ways. In rural Siberia, an in-marrying daughter-in-law has the lowest status in the household, and she rarely speaks (Humphrey 1978). In other contexts, silence is associated with power. In U.S. courts, lawyers speak the most, the judge speaks rarely but has more power than

a lawyer, while the silent jury holds the most power (Lakoff 1990).

Silence is an important component of communication among many Native American cultures. Anglo outsiders, including social workers, have sometimes misinterpreted this silence as a reflection of dignity or a lack of emotion or intelligence. How ethnocentric such judgments are is revealed by a study of silence among the Western Apache of Arizona (Basso 1972 [1970]) (see Map 12.2). The Western Apache use silence in four contexts:

THINKING OUTSIDE THE BOX

SPEND A WEEK observing how people greet each other, both verbally and nonverbally. What are your major findings?

- When meeting a stranger, especially at fairs, rodeos, or other public events. Speaking with a stranger immediately indicates interest in something such as money, work, or transportation, all possible reasons for exhibiting such bad manners.

child
Fingers of one hand are brought together at the tips pointing upwards.

father/male elder/boyfriend
Side of knuckle of forefinger, with thumb under chin, strokes chin downwards once or twice.

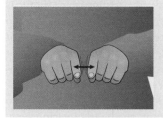

friendship
Sides of first fingers of each hand are tapped together several times.

girl/girlfriend
Thumb touches each breast starting with the breast opposite to the hand being used and then touches the first breast again.

secret lover
One hand placed under opposite armpit.

drunk (she/he is drunk)
Side of curved first finger is drawn across the forehead.

FIGURE 12.3   Some South African Gestures Used by a Man. *(Source: Adapted from Heather Brookes, "A Repertoire of South African Quotable Gestures," Journal of Linguistic Anthropology 14[2001]: 186–224.)*

- In the early stages of courting. Sitting in silence and holding hands for several hours is appropriate. Speaking "too soon" would indicate sexual willingness or interest. That would be immodest.

- When parents and children meet after the child has been away at boarding school. They should be silent for about fifteen minutes. It may be two or three days before sustained conversations are initiated.

- When "getting cussed out," especially at drinking parties.

An underlying similarity of all these contexts is the uncertainty, ambiguity, and unpredictability of the social relationships.

Body Language

Human communication, in one way or another, inevitably involves the body in sending and receiving messages. Beyond the mechanics of speaking, hearing, gesturing, and seeing, the body itself can function as a "text" that conveys messages. The full range of *body language* includes eye movements, posture, walking style, the way of standing and sitting, cultural *inscriptions* on the body such as tattoos and hairstyles, and accessories such as dress, shoes, and jewelry. Body language follows patterns and rules just as verbal language does. Like verbal language, the rules and meanings are learned, often unconsciously. Without learning the rules and meanings, one will commit communication errors, which are sometimes funny and sometimes serious.

Different cultures emphasize different body language channels more than others. Some are more touch oriented

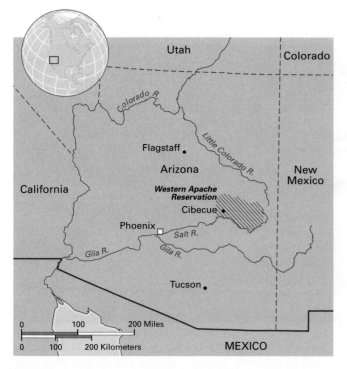

MAP 12.2   Western Apache Reservation in Arizona

Japanese business men meet each other, bow, and exchange business cards. Bowing is an important part of nonverbal communication in Japan. ■ *What is the role of bowing in your cultural world?* (Source: © Olympia/ PhotoEdit)

identity, class, gender, and more. In the United States, gender differentiation begins in the hospital nursery with the color coding of blue for boys and pink for girls. In some parts of the Middle East, public dress is black for women and white for men.

Covering or not covering various parts of the body with clothing is another culturally coded matter. Consider the different meaning of veiling/head covering in Egypt and Kuwait (MacLeod 1992). Kuwaiti women's head covering distinguishes them as relatively wealthy, leisured, and honorable, in contrast to the immigrant women workers from Asia who do not cover their heads. In contrast, the head covering in Egypt is done mainly by women from the lower and middle economic levels. For them, it is a way to accommodate conservative Islamic values while preserving their right to work outside the home. In Egypt, the head covering says, "I am a good Muslim and a good wife/daughter." In Kuwait, the headscarf says, "I am a wealthy Kuwaiti citizen."

In Japan, the kimono provides an elaborate coding system for gender and life-cycle stage (Dalby 2001). The higher one's status, the shorter the sleeve of one's kimono. Men's kimono sleeve comes in one length: short. Unmarried women's sleeve length is nearly to the ground, whereas a married woman's sleeve is nearly as short as that of a man's.

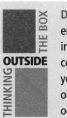

THINKING OUTSIDE THE BOX

DO YOU wear different-colored clothing in your everyday life compared to when you are "going out" or attending a special occasion such as a wedding or funeral? If yes, what are the differences and how do you explain them? If not, how do you explain that? Is there a "culture color code" at work?

than others, and some use facial expressions more. Eye contact is valued during Euro-American conversations, but in many Asian contexts, direct eye contact is considered rude or perhaps a sexual invitation.

Modification of and marks on the body, clothing, and hairstyles convey messages about age, gender, sexual interest or availability, profession, wealth, and emotions. Color of clothing can send messages about a person's

A horse race at Ascot, England, attended by members of the elite. ■ *If you were going to the races at Ascot and wanted to be dressed properly, what would you need to wear?* (Source: © 2004 Getty Images)

critical media anthropology: an approach within the cross-cultural study of law that examines how law and the judicial systems serve to maintain and expand dominant power interests rather than protecting marginal and less powerful people.

Lanita Jacobs-Huey's research on African American women's hair culture (review Chapter 2) reveals the links among women's hair, their talk about hair, and identity (2006). She also learned about the complex linguistic terminology that Black hairstylists use to refer to various hair styling procedures. Stylists use specialized language and language correction to affirm their identities as hair-care specialists. In hair-care seminars, cosmetology schools, client–stylist negotiations, and even Bible study meetings, Black cosmetologists distinguish themselves from "hairdressers" and unlicensed "kitchen beauticians" by asserting their status as "hair doctors" and divinely "gifted" stylists.

The *furisode* kimono is distinguished by its fine silk material, long sleeves, elaborate colors and designs. A girl's twentieth birthday gift is typically a furisode, marking her transition to young adulthood. Only unmarried women wear furisode, so wearing one is a statement of marital availability. Fluttering the long, wide sleeves at a man is a way to express love for him.
■ *Do sleeve styles and lengths in women's clothing convey special messages in your cultural world?* (Source: © Around the World in a Viewfinder/Alamy Images)

Two girls watch powwow dancing in eastern Pennsylvania. Hair styles may communicate gender, ethnic identity, and age, among other things. ■ (Source: Barbara Miller)

Communicating with Media and Information Technology

Media anthropology is the cross-cultural study of communication through electronic media such as radio, television, film, recorded music, the Internet, and print media, including newspapers, magazines, and popular literature (Spitulnik 1993). Media anthropology is an important emerging area that links linguistic and cultural anthropology (Allen 1994). Media anthropologists study the media process and content, the audience response, and the social effects of media presentations. **Critical media anthropology** asks to what degree access to its messages is liberating or controlling, and whose interests the media serve. It is especially active in examining journalism, television, advertising, and new information technology, as the following examples illustrate.

The Politics of Journalism

Mark Pedelty studied war correspondents in El Salvador to learn about journalists and journalistic practices during war (1995) (see Map 15.4, p. 411). He found that the lives and identities of war correspondents are highly charged with violence and terror: "War correspondents have a unique relationship to terror . . . that combines voyeurism and direct participation. . . . They need terror to . . . maintain their cultural identity as 'war correspondents'" (1995:2). The primary job of journalists, including war correspondents, is communication, of a specific sort. They gather information that is time sensitive and often brutal. Their job is to provide brief stories for the public. A critical media anthropology perspective reveals the important role of the news agency that pays their salary or, if they are freelancers or "stringers," that buys their story. War correspondents in El Salvador, Pedelty found, would write a story about the same event differently, depending on whether they were sending it to a U.S. newspaper or a European newspaper. How "accurate," then, is "the news"?

Gender and Japanese Television Programming

Most television programming in Japan presents women as housewives, performing traditional domestic roles (Painter 1996). Many Japanese women are now rejecting such shows. In response, producers are experimenting with new sorts of dramas in which women are shown as active workers and aggressive lovers. One such show is a ten-part serial that first aired in 1992 called *Selfish Women*. The story concerns three women: an aggressive single businesswoman who faces discrimination at work, a young mother who is raising her daughter alone while her photographer husband lives with another woman, and an ex-housewife who divorced her husband because she found home life empty and unrewarding. There are several male characters, but except for one, they are depicted as less interesting than the women.

The show's title is ironic. In Japan, men often label women who assert themselves as "selfish." The lead women in the drama use the term in a positive way to encourage each other: "Let's become even more selfish!" Although dramas like *Selfish Women* may not be revolutionary, they indicate that telerepresentations of gender in Japan are changing, largely through the agency of Japanese women.

Advertising for Latinos in the United States

Within the U.S. advertising market, one of the most sought-after segments is the Latino population, also called "the Hispanic market" in the advertising industry (Dávila 2002). Interviews with staff of sixteen Latino advertising agencies and content analysis of their adver-

tisements reveal their approach of treating Latinos as a unified, culturally specific market. The dominant theme, or *trope*, is that of "the family" as being the most important feature of Latino culture, in contrast to the stereotype of the Anglo population as more individualistic. Recent milk-promotion advertisements for the Anglo population show a celebrity with a milk moustache. The Latino version shows a grandmother cooking a traditional milk-based dessert with the caption, "Have you given your loved ones enough milk today?" (2002:270). In Spanish-language television and radio networks, a kind of "standard" Spanish is used, a generic form with no hint of regionalism or accent.

Latinos are, however, a highly heterogeneous population. By promoting a monolithic image of Latino culture, media messages may be contributing to identity change toward a more monolithic pattern. At the same time, they are certainly missing opportunities to tap into more specialized markets within the Latino population.

Crossing the Digital Divide in Rural Hungary

The term **digital divide** refers to social inequality in access to new and emerging information technology, especially access to up-to-date computers, the Internet, and training related to their use. Local attempts to overcome the digital divide between Hungary and countries in the European Union involve the development of the Hungarian Telecottage Association (HTA) (Wormald 2005) (see Map 12.3). The idea of the telecottage, which started in Sweden and Scotland, involves dedicating some space such as an unused workshop or part of a house, for public use in which a computer with Internet access is provided.

The HTA, centered in Bucharest, promotes village-based Internet access in order to improve the lives of rural people through enhanced communication. Most telecottages in Hungary are located in rural communities of fewer than 5,000 people. The HTA website provides announcements about funding opportunities and relevant news. While all this sounds highly populist and positive, some emerging interpersonal problems exist related to who gets access first to information for posting on the website and information hoarding by some managers.

Like the Hungarian villagers, many marginalized people around the world, including indigenous people, women, and youth, realize the importance of having access to the Internet and other information and communication technologies (ICT). These technologies can help people preserve and learn their ancestral languages, record traditional agricultural and medical knowledge,

---

digital divide: social inequality in access to new and emerging information technology, notably access to up-to-date computers, the Internet, and training related to their use.

MAP 12.3 Hungary. The Republic of Hungary has a population of around 10 million people. Its landscape is mainly plains with hills and low mountains to the north. One of the newest members of the European Union, Hungary has a growing economy. The main religion is Christianity, with Catholicism accounting for about half of the total; about 30 percent, however, are atheists. The Roma population, variously estimated at between 450,000, and 600,000, has increased rapidly in recent years. Magyar, the Hungarian language, is one of the few European languages that does not belong to the Indo-European language family but belongs instead to the Finno-Ugric family.

and otherwise protect their culture and improve their lives (Lutz 2005; Turner 2002).

Communication, Cultural Diversity, and Inequality

This section presents material about the links between language, microcultures, and social inequality. It begins with a brief discussion of research methods in the study of language. Two major models of the relationship between language and culture are presented next. Examples follow about class, gender and sexuality, "race" and ethnicity, and age.

Fieldwork Challenges

Research about human communication shares the basic methods of cultural anthropology: fieldwork and participant observation. Some topics require more specialized data gathering and analysis. The study of language relies heavily on tape recordings or video recordings of people and events (Kuipers 2004; Brookes 2004). The tapes are

then analyzed qualitatively or quantitatively. Video recordings, for example, may be subjected to a detailed *frame analysis* that can pinpoint when communication breaks down or misunderstandings occur.

Analysis of recorded linguistic data must be informed by knowledge of the cultural context. Bronislaw Malinowski, early in the twentieth century, pointed out that communication is always embedded in its cultural context. An example of a contextualized approach is a study in Western Samoa that tape recorded many hours of speech and also involved extensive participant observation in the community (Duranti 1994) (see Map 1.6, p. 26). Analysis of the transcriptions of the recorded talk revealed two major findings about how speech in village council meetings is related to social status: (1) turn-taking patterns and (2) particular words and grammatical forms to indirectly praise or blame others. Nonlinguistic data

A satellite dish now dominates the view of a village in Niger, West Africa. Throughout the world, the spread of electronic forms of communication have many and diverse social effects. ■ *Pretend you are a cultural anthropologist doing research on communication in this village. What do you want to study in order to assess the effects of satellite communication on the people and their culture?* (Source: © Charles O. Cecil)

A Samoan kava drinking ceremony begins. Kava is made from the roots of a plant in the black pepper family. The roots are dried, pounded, and mixed with water. A social beverage, kava is a relaxant also used for healing. ■ *Think of a parallel gathering in your cultural world in terms of expected forms of consumption, seating arrangements, and discourse patterns in terms of who speaks, taking turns, and the content of the discourse itself.* (Source: © Don Smetzer)

that helped inform these interpretations included observation of seating arrangements and the order of the distribution of *kava* (a ritually shared and mildly intoxicating beverage made from a local plant). Seating, kava drinking, and speech patterns all reflected and restated people's relative status.

Anthropologists who seek to study language in everyday use face the problem of the **observer's paradox,** the fact that the research process alters people's normal behavior (McMahon 1994:234). The mere presence of an anthropologist with a tape or video recorder affects how people speak and behave. Being studied often makes people speak and behave more "correctly" and more formally. The ways of dealing with the observer's paradox are:

- Observe and record speech outside an interview situation.

- Record speech in a group situation.

- Initiate role-plays in which participants act out a particular scene, such as arguing about something. The drama involved helps create a "natural" situation.

- Conduct structured interviews in which the participant is asked to perform speech tasks at varying levels of formality, starting with the most formal and moving to informal, open-ended conversation.

Study of communication, just like culture more generally, often involves translation from one language to another. In order to provide a reliable and meaningful translation, one has to understand more about a language than just vocabulary. Johannes Fabian once translated into English a song that occurred at the end of a play performed in a village in the southeastern region of the Democratic Republic of Congo (Fabian 1995) (see Map 4.5, p. 111). Many languages, perhaps over 200, are spoken within the borders of the DRC. French is used in government, education, and international commerce. Four African languages have official status. The play was in the Kiswahili language, one of the official languages. Fabian assumed that the final song was in Kiswahili, too, and thought the repeated use of the word *tutabawina* indicated that it was a fighting song. A Kiswahili speaker assisting him said it was a soccer song. The play was an improvisation created by the performers, so Fabian wrote to them for their insight. They told him that the text is a marching song in Kisela, a language spoken in the southeastern region of the country.

observer's paradox: the logical impossibility of doing research on natural communication events without affecting the naturalness sought.
Sapir-Whorf hypothesis: a theory in linguistic anthropology that says language determines thought.

sociolinguistics: a theory in linguistic anthropology that says that culture and society and a person's social position determine language.
critical discourse analysis (CDA): the study of the relations of power and inequality in language.

tag question: a question seeking affirmation, placed at the end of a sentence.

Language and Culture: Two Theories

During the twentieth century, two theoretical perspectives were influential in the study of the relationship between language and culture. They are presented here as two separate models but they actually overlap in real life and anthropologists tend to draw on both of them (Hill and Mannheim 1992).

The first was formulated by two early founding figures in linguistic anthropology, Edward Sapir and Benjamin Whorf. In the mid-twentieth century, they formulated an influential model called the **Sapir-Whorf hypothesis**, which says that people's language affects how they think. If a language has many words for different kinds of snow, for example, then someone who speaks that language can "think" about snow in more ways than someone can whose language has fewer "snow" terms. Among the Saami, whose traditional occupation was reindeer herding (see Culturama, p. 333), a rich set of terms exist for "snow" (review Figure 12.2, p. 315). If a language has no word for "snow," then someone who speaks that language cannot think of "snow." Thus, a language constitutes a *thought world* and people who speak different languages inhabit different thought worlds. This catchy phrase became the basis for *linguistic determinism,* a theory stating that language determines consciousness of the world and behavior. Extreme linguistic determinism implies that the frames and definitions of a person's primary language are so strong that it is impossible to learn another language fully or, therefore, to understand another culture fully. Most anthropologists see value in the Sapir-Whorf hypothesis, but not in its extreme form.

A second model for understanding the relationship between language and culture is proposed by scholars working in the area of **sociolinguistics,** the study of how cultural and social context shapes language. These theorists support a *cultural constructionist* argument that a person's context and social position shape the content, form, and meaning of their language. Most anthropologists see value in this model and agree that language and culture are interactive: Language shapes culture and culture shapes language.

Critical Discourse Analysis: Class, Gender and Sexuality, "Race" and Ethnicity, and Age

Critical discourse analysis (CDA) is an emerging area that focuses on the relations of power and inequality in language (Blommaert and Bulcaen 2000). This part of the chapter looks at distinctive communication styles, or *registers,* that include variation in vocabulary, grammar, and intonation. Critical discourse analysis reveals links between language and social inequality, power, and stigma as well as agency and resistance through language.

Class and Accent in New York City

William Labov launched the subfield of sociolinguistics with his classic study of accents among mainly Euro-American people of different socioeconomic classes in New York City (1966). For example, pronunciation of the consonant "r" in words such as *car, card, floor,* and *fourth* tends to be associated with upper-class people, whereas its absence ("caw," "cawd," "flaw," "fawth") is associated with lower-class people. In order to avoid the observer's paradox, Labov used informal observations of sales clerks' speech in three Manhattan department stores of different "class" levels: Saks (the highest), Macy's, and S. Klein (the lowest). Labov wanted to find out if the clerks in the different stores spoke with different class accents. He would approach a clerk and inquire about the location of an item that he knew was on the fourth floor. The clerk would respond, and then Labov would say, "Excuse me?" in order to prompt a more emphatic repeat of the word *fourth.* He found that the higher-status "r" was pronounced both the first and second times by 44 percent of the employees in Saks, by 16 percent of the employees in Macy's, and by 6 percent of the employees in S. Klein.

THINKING OUTSIDE THE BOX

THESE BROAD generalizations about Euro-American conversational styles do not apply to all situations. What are your microcultural rules about interruptions and taking turns?

Gender in Euro-American Conversations

Most languages contain gender differences in word choice, grammar, intonation, content, and style. Early studies of language and gender among white Euro-Americans revealed three general characteristics of female speech (Lakoff 1973):

- Politeness
- Rising intonation at the end of sentences
- Frequent use of **tag questions** (questions seeking affirmation placed at the end of sentences, such as, "It's a nice day, *isn't it?*")

Male speech, in general, is less polite, maintains a flat and assertive tone in a sentence, and does not use tag questions. Related to politeness is the fact that, during cross-gender conversations, men tend to interrupt women more than women interrupt men.

Deborah Tannen's popular book *You Just Don't Understand* (1990) shows how differences in conversational styles between white Euro-American men and women lead to miscommunication. She says that "women speak and hear a language of connection and intimacy, while men speak and hear a language of status and independence" (1990:42). Both men and women use *indirect response* (not really answering the question). Their differ-

MOTHERESE

Motherese, or "baby talk," is the special way mothers talk to their babies. Culturally widespread, it is a simplified register. Other simplified registers include "teacher talk," "foreigner talk," and talk to the elderly, lovers, and pets.

Linguistic anthropologist Elinor Ochs compared hundreds of hours of mother–infant "conversations" among Western Samoans and White middle-class (WMC) North Americans (1993). Among the WMC Americans, mothers used three basic verbal strategies: motherese, or other forms of simplification; guessing and negotiating meaning of messages that the child conveys; and praising the child's accomplishments. The WMC American mothers' baby talk included restricted vocabulary, baby talk words (the child's own version of words), shorter sentences, simplification of sounds (for example, avoiding consonant clusters in favor of consonant-vowel pairs), avoidance of complex sentences, topical focus on the here-and-now, exaggerated intonation, slower pace, repetition, and providing sentence frames for the child to complete. Baby talk is an important register in WMC American society because the culture is so child centered, yet it is primarily a register used by mothers and female caretakers.

Child centeredness also promotes the use of mothers' second strategy: verbal accommodation of the adult to the child. The WMC mothers, for example, often participated in conversation-like interactions with tiny infants, including greeting exchanges with a newborn. This pattern indicates the mother's willingness to take on the conversational work of both infant and mother. The WMC mothers responded to children's unintelligible speech by attempting to guess at the meaning: "Guessing involves attempting to formulate the child's intended message, which in turn may entail taking into consideration what the child is looking at, holding, what the child has just said and other clues" (1993:162).

In the third strategy, WMC mothers praised their children for activities beyond their competence—things they could not have done without the mother. For example, in joint activities, such as a mother and child building a block tower together, the mother praised the child as the sole builder, thus denying her participation and raising the position of the child.

Western Samoan mothers do not use a simplified register when talking with their infants and young children. Instead, Samoan has a simplified register used with foreigners, who historically were missionaries, government representatives, and other people in high social positions. Thus, accommodation of the speaker to the listener is appropriate, just as a host would accommodate to a guest. In the case of a child's unintelligible utterances, Western Samoan mothers ignore them or point out that they are unintelligible. In terms of praising, the first one to be praised should then praise the praiser. The praise usually contains the phrase "*Maaloo!*" ("Well done!"). After the first maaloo, a second maaloo should be returned to the producer of the first maaloo. Children in Western Samoa learn, through such bidirectional praising, to understand and articulate the contributions of others, including mothers.

Thus, Samoan women have a different position in their relationships with their children than the WMC mothers. Their children accommodate to them rather than the other way around, and their children praise and appreciate them.

FOOD FOR THOUGHT

- What is "motherese" like in your microculture?

---

ent motivations, however, create different meanings embedded in their speech:

Michele: What time is the concert?
Gary: You have to be ready by seven-thirty.
  (1990:289)

Gary sees his role as one of protector in using an indirect response to Michele's question. He feels that he is simply "watching out for her" by getting to the real point of her question. Michele feels that Gary is withholding information by not answering her directly and is maintaining a power position. A wife's indirect response to a question from her husband is prompted by her goal of being helpful in anticipating her husband's underlying interest:

Ned: Are you just about finished?
Valerie: Do you want to have supper now?
  (1990:289)

Women's speech cross-culturally is not universally accommodating, subservient, and polite. In cultural contexts in which women's roles are prominent and valued, their language reflects and reinforces their position. A comparison of how mothers talk to their infants in two cultures illustrates this point (see Everyday Anthropology box).

Gender and Politeness in Japanese, and Those Naughty Teenage Girls

Gender registers in spoken Japanese reflect gender differences (Shibamoto 1987). Certain words and sentence structures convey femininity, humbleness, and politeness. One important contrast between male and female speech is the attachment, by female speakers, of the honorific prefix "o-" to nouns (see Figure 12.4). This addition gives women's speech a more refined and polite tone.

A contrasting pattern of gendered language comes from the *Kogals*, young Japanese women roughly between 14 and 22 years of age, known for their "female-centered coolness" (Miller 2004). The term Kogal is a label created by the media. Kogals' self-reference term is *gyaru* ("girl"). The Kogals have distinctive language, clothing, hairstyles, make-up, attitude, and activities, all of which challenge prescriptive norms for young women. Their overall style is flashy and exuberant, combining global and local elements. Heavy users of cell phones, Kogals have created an extensive set of emoticons, or "face characters," far more complex than the American smiley face. Read vertically, they include icons for "wow," "ouch," "applause," and "I can't hear you." They have also invented a unique text message code for their cell phones that uses mixed scripts such as mathematical symbols and Cyrillic letters.

The spoken language of Kogals is a rich and quickly changing mixture of slang, some classic but much newly created. They create new words through compounds and by adding the Japanese suffix *-ru*, which turns a noun into a vowel, such as *maku-ru* ("go to McDonald's). They intentionally use strongly masculine language forms, openly talk about sex, and rework taboo sexual terms into new meanings. Reactions from mainstream society to Kogals are mixed, ranging from horror to fascination. No matter what, in the words of Laura Miller, they have cultural influence and are shaking up the gender order.

A Kogal in Tokyo's trendy Shibuyu district displays her cell phone that is covered with stickers. Her facial make-up and dress are characteristic of some, but not all, Kogals. Various Kogal make-up and dress styles, like their language, exist and keep changing. ■ (Source: Eriko Sugita/Reuters/CORBIS)

"Fat Talk" among Euro-American Adolescent Girls

In the United States, Euro-American adolescent girls' conversations exhibit a high level of concern with their body weight and image (Nichter 2000). A study of 253 girls in the eighth and ninth grades in two urban high schools of the Southwest reveals the contexts and meanings of *fat talk*. Fat talk usually starts with a girl commenting, "I'm so fat." The immediate response from her friends is, "No, you're not." Girls who use fat talk are typically not overweight and are not dieting. The weight of the girls in the study was within "normal" range, and none suffered from a serious eating disorder. Fat talk occurs frequently throughout a day. Sometimes it appears to function as a call for reinforcement from friends that the initiator is an accepted group member. In other cases, it occurs at the beginning of a meal. In this context, fat talk may function to absolve the girl from guilty feelings and to give her a sense of agency.

FIGURE 12.4   Male-Unmarked and Female-Marked Nouns in Japanese

	Male	Female
Box lunch	bentoo	obentoo
Money	kane	okane
Chopsticks	hasi	ohasi
Book	hon	ohon

(*Source:* From "The Womanly Woman: Manipulation of Stereotypical and Nonstereotypical Features in Japanese Female Speech," pg. 28, by Janet Shibamoto in *Language, Gender, and Sex in Comparative Perspective*, ed. by S.U. Philips, S. Steel, and C. Tanz. Copyright © 1987. Reprinted by permission of Cambridge University Press.)

Gay Language and Belonging in Indonesia

Many homosexual men in Indonesia speak *bahasa gay*, or "gay language," based on *bahasa Indonesia*, the national language (Boellstorff 2004). Indonesia is the world's fourth largest country in terms of population, with nearly 250 million citizens living in over 6,000 islands and speaking nearly 700 local languages. In spite of this diversity, bahasa gay is remarkably standardized. Bahasa gay has a distinctive vocabulary that plays humorously on mainstream language and provides a political commentary on mainstream life.

Some of the vocabulary changes involve sound-alikes; others add a suffix to a standard word. In terms of state power and the state's heterosexual image, Indonesian gays would seem to be a clearly excluded group. Nonetheless, bahasa gay is moving into mainstream culture where it conveys agency and freedom from official control.

Cuing among the Akwesasne Mohawks

Linguistic cues are words or phrases that preface a remark to indicate the speaker's attitude toward what is being said. Standard English cues include *maybe* and *in my opinion* (Woolfson et al. 1995). Three functions of cuing exist in Mohawk English, a version of English spoken by the Akwesasne people of the St. Lawrence River area (see Map 12.4). They are:

- The speaker's unwillingness or inability to verify the certainty of a statement
- Respect for the listener
- The inability to make statements that have to do with matters that are in the domain of religion

Frequent miscommunication occurs between the Akwesasne people and Anglo medical professionals. Analysis of doctor–patient conversations reveals the role that Akwesasne cuing plays, and how it is misinterpreted by the professionals. Here is a response to a question posed by an anthropologist about the kinds of diseases Akwesasne people had in the past, with the cues italicized:

> Hmm . . . That [tuberculosis] . . . was mostly, it well . . . they always said cirrhosis. . . . *It seems* like no matter what anybody died from . . . if they drank, it was cirrhosis. *I don't know* if anybody *really* knew a long time ago what anybody really died from. Even if the doctor requested an autopsy, the people would just say no . . . you know . . . it won't be done. So *I don't think* it was . . . you know . . . it was just what the doctor thought that would go down on the death certificate. (1995:506)

The Anglo medical practitioners misinterpret such clues as indications of indecisiveness or noncooperation. The Akwesasne speakers are following linguistic rules about truthfulness, humility, and the sacred.

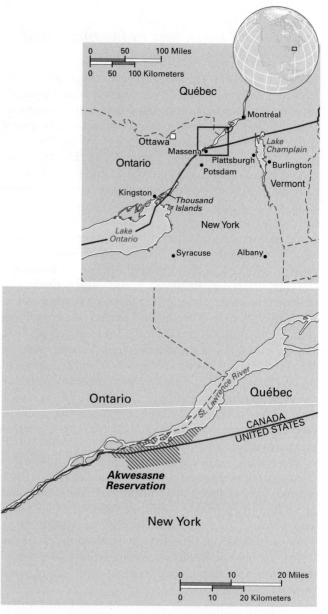

MAP 12.4 **Akwesasne Territory in New York State and Ontario, Canada. The Akwesasne Territory has an international border running through it with New York State on one side and two provinces of Canada on the other: Ontario and Québec. The Mohawk Council of Akwesasne comprises 12 District Chiefs and a Grand Chief. Since the 1960s, the Akwesasne Territory has been affected by environmental pollution of the water, soil, and food supply from industries along the St. Lawrence River. In 1987, the Akwesasne formed a Task Force to restore and protect the environment and the survival of their culture.**

African American English: Prejudice and Pride

The topic of African American English (AAE) or African American Vernacular English (AAVE), is complicated by racism, past and present (Jacobs-Huey 2006). Scholars debate whether AAE/AAVE is a language in its own right or a dialect of English. "Linguistic conservatives" who champion standard American Mainstream English (AME) view AAE as an ungrammatical form of English that needs to be "corrected." In the current linguistic hierarchy in the United States with AME at the top, speakers of AAE may be both proud of their language and feel stigmatized by those who judge AAE negatively and treat its speakers unfairly (Lanehart 1999).

African American English is a relatively new language, emerging out of slavery to develop a degree of standardization across the United States, along with many local variants. Some of its characteristic grammar results from its African roots. One of the most prominent is the use, or nonuse, of forms of the English verb "to be" (Lanehart 1999:217). In AAE, one says, "She married" which, in AME means, "she is married." Viewed incorrectly by outsiders as "bad" English, the sentence "She married" follows a grammatical rule in AAE. The fact that AME has its own grammar and usage rules is evident in the fact that when non-AME speakers attempt to speak it or imitate it, they often make mistakes (Jacobs-Huey 1997).

Ethnographic research among African American school-age children in a working-class neighborhood of southwest Philadelphia examined within-gender and cross-gender conversations, including *directives* (getting someone to do something), argument, he-said-she-said accusations, and storytelling (Goodman 1990). All of these speech activities involve complex verbal strategies that are culturally embedded. In arguments, the children may bring in imaginary events as a "put-on," preceded by the cue term "psych," or use words of a song to create and maintain playfulness within an argument. Much of their arguments involve highly ritualized insults that work quickly to return an insult to the original giver. When a group of girls were practicing some dance steps and singing, a boy said, "You sound terrible." A girl responded, "We sound just like you look" (1990:183). The study revealed the importance of verbal play and art among the children. It also showed that girls often excel at verbal competitions in mixed gender settings.

Children who grow up speaking a version of AAE at home and with peer groups face a challenge in schools where they are expected to perform in AME. Just like native Spanish speakers or any non–English-speaking new immigrants, African American children are implicitly expected to become bilingual in AAE and AME. More than vocabulary and grammar are involved. Teachers need to understand that African American children may have culturally distinct styles of expression that should be recognized and valued. For example, in narrative style, African American children tend to use a spiral pattern, skipping around to different topics before addressing the theme, instead of a linear style. Rather than being considered a deficiency, having AAE speakers in a classroom adds cultural diversity to those whose linguistic worlds are limited to AME.

Inspired by such findings, the Oakland School Board, in California, approved a resolution in 1996 to recognize *Ebonics*, or AAE, as the primary language, or vernacular, of African American students. The school developed a special teaching program, called the Bridge Program, in which AAE speakers were encouraged to learn Standard American English through a process of translation between AAE and SAE (Rickford 1997). After several months, students in the Bridge Program had progressed in their SAE reading ability much faster than African American students who were not in the program. Nevertheless, the program received so much negative publicity and raised such deeply sensitive questions about the best way to enhance minority student learning, that it was cancelled within the year. The underlying issues of the so-called *Ebonics controversy* are still unresolved. One of the thorniest questions debated is whether AAE/AAVE/Ebonics is so distinct (either as a separate language from SAE or a vernacular form) that schools should address it in their curriculum with special programs. If so, can it be dealt with in a positive way as a rich part of Black cultural heritage? Or should it be suppressed in public schools in favor of promoting SAE? No easy answers exist. According to John Rickford, a sociolinguist at Stanford University and an expert on AAE, the Bridge Program of using AAE to teach SAE was well intentioned and demonstrated persuasively that the approach works.

Language Change

Languages, like the cultures in which they are embedded, experience both continuity and change, and for similar reasons. Human creativity and contact lead to linguistic innovation and linguistic borrowing. War, imperialism, genocide, and other disasters may destroy languages. This section looks first at what is known about the origins of human language and provides a brief history of writing. Later sections discuss the role of European colonialism on languages, nationalism and language, world languages, and contemporary language loss and revitalization.

The Origins and History of Language

No one knows how verbal language began. Current evidence of other aspects of human cultural evolution suggest that verbal language started to develop between 100,000 and 50,000 years ago when early humans had both the physical and mental capacity for verbal communication and symbolic thinking. Before that, facial expressions, gestures, and body postures were likely important features of communication.

Early scholars of language were often misled by ethnocentric assumptions that the structure of European

An African bonobo male waves branches in a display of power *(top)*. (Source: © Gallo Images/CORBIS) **In the United States, women lacrosse players use sticks in a competitive sport invented by American Indians *(bottom)*. In the former, communication is clearly involved in the use of the branches.** ■ *Is there any communication going on with the use of sticks in lacrosse?* (Source: Ed Bock/CORBIS)

languages have. As discussed at the beginning of this chapter, the Pirahã language appears "simpler" in many ways when compared to English, as does the Pirahã culture, but both Pirahã and English have to be examined within their cultural contexts. Pirahã is a language that works for a rainforest foraging population. English works for a globalizing, technology-driven, consumerist culture. Languages of foraging cultures today can, with caution, provide insights about what foragers' language may have been like thousands of years ago. But they are not "frozen in time" examples of "stone age" language.

Historical Linguistics

Historical linguistics is the study of language change through history. It relies on many specialized methods that compare shifts over time and across space in aspects of language such as phonetics, syntax, and meaning. It originated in the eighteenth century with a discovery made by Sir William Jones, a British colonial administrator working in India. During his spare time, he studied Sanskrit, a classical language of India. He noticed strong similarities among Sanskrit, Greek, and Latin in vocabulary and syntax. For example, the Sanskrit word for "father" is *pitr,* in Greek it is *patér,* and in Latin it is *pater.* This was an astounding discovery for the time, given the prevailing European mentality that placed its cultural heritage firmly in the classical Graeco-Roman world and depicted the "Orient" as completely separate from "Europe" (Bernal 1987).

Following Jones's discovery, other scholars began comparing lists of words and grammatical forms in different languages: the French *père,* the German *Vater,* the Italian *padre,* the Old English *faeder,* the Old Norse *fadhir,* the Swedish *far.* These lists allowed scholars to determine degrees of closeness and distance in their relationships. Later scholars contributed the concept of **language families,** or languages descended from a parent language (see Figure 12.5). Descendant languages that are part of the same language are referred to as *sister languages,* such as French and Spanish.

Using comparative evidence from historical and contemporary Eurasian languages, historical linguists developed a hypothetical model of the original parent language, or *proto-language,* of most Eurasian languages. It is called *Proto-Indo-European (PIE).* Linguistic evidence suggests that PIE was located in Eurasia, either north or south of the Black Sea (see Map 12.5). From its area of origin, between 6,000 and 8,000 years ago, PIE spread into Europe, central and eastern Asia, and South Asia, where local variants developed over the centuries.

languages was normative and that languages with different structures were less developed and deficient. For example, they considered the Chinese language "primitive" because it lacks the kinds of verbs that European

historical linguistics: the study of language change using formal methods that compare shifts over time and across space in aspects of language such as phonetics, syntax, and semantics.

language family: languages descended from a parent language.

logograph: a symbol that conveys meaning through a form or picture resembling that to which it refers.

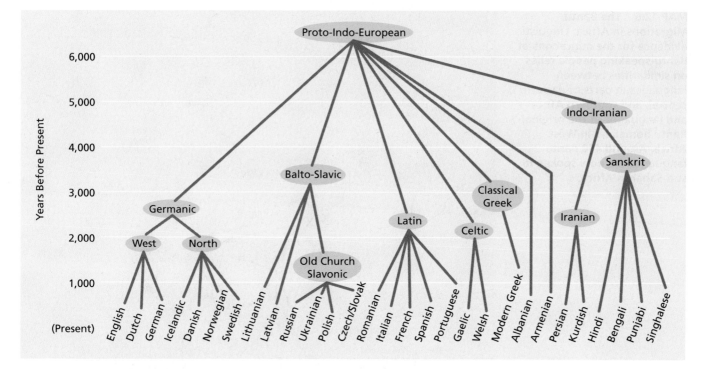

FIGURE 12.5 The Indo-European Language Family

MAP 12.5 Two Sites of Proto-Indo-European Origins. Two major theories about the location of PIE exist, with the site south of the Black Sea considered to be earlier.

Similar linguistic methods reveal the existence of the original parent form of the Bantu language family, *Proto-Bantu* (Afolayan 2000). Scholars can trace the so-called *Bantu expansion* in Africa starting around 5,000 years ago (see Map 12.6). Today, some form of Bantu language is spoken by over 100 million people in Africa, not to mention the number of people in the African diaspora worldwide. Over 600 African languages are derived from Proto-Bantu. According to linguistic analysis, the homeland of Proto-Bantu is the present-day countries of Cameroon and Nigeria, West Africa. It is likely that Proto-Bantu spread through population migration as the farming population expanded and moved, over hundreds of years, into areas occupied by indigenous foragers. Bantu cultural imperialism may have wiped out some local languages, although it is impossible to document possible extinctions. Substantial linguistic evidence, however, suggests some interactions between the farmers and the foragers through which standard Bantu absorbed elements from local languages.

Writing Systems

Evidence of the earliest written languages comes from Mesopotamia, Egypt, and China. The oldest writing system was in use in the fourth millennium BCE in Mesopotamia (Postgate, Wang, and Wilkinson 1995). All early writing systems used **logographs,** signs that indicate a word, syllable, or sound. Over time, some logographs retained their original meaning, others were kept but given more abstract meaning, and nonlogographic symbols were added (see Figure 12.6).

The emergence of writing is associated with the development of the state. Some scholars take writing as a

MAP 12.6   The Bantu Migrations in Africa. Linguistic evidence for the migrations of Bantu-speaking people relies on similarities between languages in parts of eastern, central, and southern Africa and languages of the original Bantu homeland in West Africa. Around 450 Bantu languages are now spoken in sub-Saharan Africa.

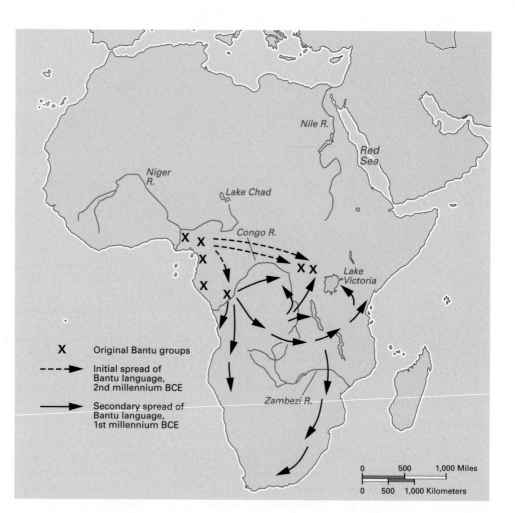

key diagnostic feature that distinguishes the state from nonstate political forms because recordkeeping was such an essential task of the state. The Inca empire, centered in the Peruvian Andes, is a notable exception to this generalization. It used **khipu,** or cords of knotted strings of different colors, for keeping accounts and recording events. Scholars are not quite sure how khipu worked in the past because their coding system is so complicated. Debates are ongoing as to whether khipu served as an actual language or more simply as an accounting system. Whatever is the answer, the world's largest empire in the fourteenth century relied on khipu.

Two interpretations of the function of early writing systems exist. The first is that early writing was mainly for ceremonial purposes because of its prevalence on tombs, bone inscriptions, or temple carvings. The second is that early writing was mainly for secular use in government recordkeeping and trade. The archaeological record is biased toward durable substances such as stone. Since ceremonial writing was intended to last, it was more likely to be inscribed on stone. Utilitarian writing,

in contrast, was more likely to have been done on perishable materials because people would be less concerned with permanence (consider the way you treat shopping lists). Compared to what has been preserved, more utilitarian writing, and other forms of nonceremonial writing must have existed.

The scripts of much of South and Southeast Asia originated in the Aramaic system of the Middle East (Kuipers and McDermott 1996). It spread eastward to India, where it took on new forms, and continued to move into much of Southeast Asia, including Indonesia and the Philippines but excluding Vietnam. The functions of the scripts vary from context to context. Writing for recordkeeping and taxation exists but is subordinate to, and carries less status than, writing for communication with the spirits, to record medical knowledge, and for love poetry. Writing love poetry is exalted and esteemed, and sometimes done in secret. Some love songs in the Philippine highlands have strict rules regulating such matters as how many syllables may be used per line. All adolescents seek to learn the rules of writing love poetry and to be able to write it well.

---

khipu: cords of knotted strings used during the Inca empire for keeping accounts and recording events.

pidgin: a contact language that blends elements of at least two languages and that

emerges when people with different languages need to communicate.

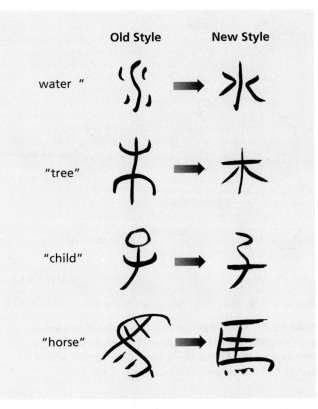

Old Style   New Style

water "

"tree"

"child"

"horse"

FIGURE 12.6 Logographic and Current Writing Styles in China *(Source: Courtesy of Molly Spitzer Frost.)*

Colonialism, Nationalism, and Globalization

European colonialism was a major force of language change. Not only did colonial powers declare their own language as the language of government, business, and education, but they often took direct steps to suppress indigenous languages and literatures. Widespread *bilingualism,* or competence in a language other than one's birth language, is one prominent effect of colonialism. Globalization is also having substantial and complex effects on language.

European Colonialism and Contact Languages

Beginning in the fifteenth century, European colonialism had dramatic effects on the people with whom it came into contact, as discussed elsewhere in this book. Language change is an important part of the story of colonialism and indigenous cultures. Depending on the type and duration of contact, it resulted in the development of new languages, the decline of others, and the extinction of many, along with the people who spoke them (Silverstein 1997). Two forms of new languages prompted by European colonialism are pidgins and creoles.

A **pidgin** is a language that blends elements of at least two parent languages and that emerges when two differ-

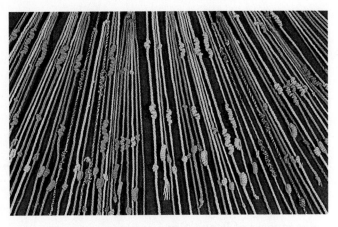

Khipu, or knotted strings, were the basis of state-level accounting in the Incan empire. The knots convey substantial information for those who could interpret their meaning. ■ *How do contemporary states keep track of official information?* (Source: © M. Vautier, Anthropological & Archaeological Museum, Lima, Peru/ Woodfin Camp & Associates)

ent cultures with different languages come in contact and need to communicate (Baptista 2005). All speakers have their own native language(s) but learn to speak pidgin as a second, rudimentary language. Pidgins are typically limited to specific functional domains, such as trade and basic social interactions. Many pidgins of the Western Hemisphere were the result of the Atlantic slave trade and plantation slavery. Owners needed to communicate with their slaves, and slaves from various parts of Africa needed to communicate with each other.

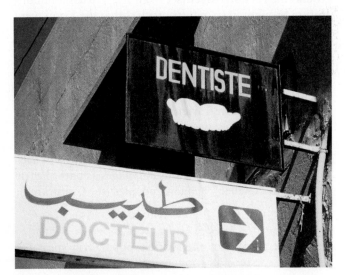

French colonialism added another cultural layer to Arabic influences in Morocco, resulting in many bilingual and trilingual shop signs. ■ *Where have you seen multilngualism in public use? What languages were used and why?* (Source: Barbara Miller)

A pidgin often evolves into a **creole,** which is a language descended from a pidgin with its own native speakers, richer vocabularies, and more developed grammar. Throughout the Western Hemisphere, many localized creoles have developed in areas such as Louisiana, Haiti, Ecuador, and Suriname. While a living reminder of the heritage of slavery, Creole languages and associated literature and music are also evidence of resilience and creativity in the African diaspora. Pidgins are common throughout the South Pacific. Tok Pisin, the pidgin language of Papua New Guinea, consists of a mixture of English, Samoan, Chinese, and Malayan. Tok Pisin is now a creole language and recognized as one of the official languages of Papua New Guinea.

Nationalism and Linguistic Assimilation

Nationalist policies of cultural assimilation of minorities have led to suppression and loss of local dialects and the extinction of many indigenous and minority languages throughout the world. Direct policies of linguistic assimilation include declaration of a *lingua franca,* or standard language and rules about the language of instruction in public schools. Indirect mechanisms include discrimination in hiring on the basis of language and social stigma.

The Soviet attempt to build a USSR-wide commitment to the state after the 1930s included mass migration of Russian speakers into remote areas, where they eventually outnumbered indigenous peoples (Belikov 1994). Russian officials burned books in local languages. Many children were forcibly sent away to boarding schools, where they were taught in Russian. The indigenous Komi traditionally formed the majority population in an area around the Pechora River (see Map 12.7). Russian immigration brought in so many outsiders that the Komi were outnumbered. The Russians initiated the use of the Russian language in schools, and the Komi people became bilingual. Eventually, the Komi language was so heavily influenced by Russian that it may be extinct.

This story can be repeated for many indigenous languages of the former Soviet Union. Enforced attendance at boarding schools was also a strategy of the United States, Canada, and Australia in their attempts to assimilate indigenous peoples. Often, Christian missionaries worked to suppress indigenous languages as part of their attempts to "civilize" "pagan" peoples (see Culturama).

Global Languages

Ninety-six percent of the world's population speaks 4 percent of the world's languages (Crystal 2000:14). The

MAP 12.7   Komi Region in Russia. The Komi were traditionally reindeer hunters. The Komi language belongs to the Finno-Ugric language family and is closer to Finnish and Estonian than to Russian.

eight most-spoken languages are Mandarin, Spanish, English, Bengali, Hindi, Portuguese, Russian, and Japanese. Languages that are gaining widespread currency are called **global languages,** or **world languages.** Global languages are spoken worldwide in diverse cultural contexts. As they spread to areas and cultures beyond their home area and culture, they take on new, localized identities. At the same time, the "mother language" picks up words and phrases from local languages (see Figure 12.7, p. 334).

English is the most globalized language in history (Bhatt 2001; Crystal 2003). British English was first transplanted through colonial expansion to the present-day United States, Canada, Australia, New Zealand, South Asia, Africa, Hong Kong, and the Caribbean. English was the dominant language in the colonies, used in government and commerce and taught in schools. Over time, regional and subregional varieties of English have developed, often leading to a "New English" that a native speaker from England cannot understand at all. So many varieties of English now exist that scholars are beginning to talk of the *English language family* that comprises varieties such as American English, Spanglish, Japlish, and Tex-Mex.

Global languages may act as both a form of linguistic and economic opportunity and a form of linguistic imperialism.

---

creole: a language directly descended from a pidgin but possessing its own native speakers and involving linguistic expansion and elaboration.

global language or **world language:** a language spoken widely throughout the world and in diverse cultural contexts often replacing indigenous languages.

The Saami of Lapland, or Sapmi

The Saami are indigenous, "fourth world" people who live in the northernmost stretches of Norway, Sweden, Finland, and western Russia (Gaski 1993). The area is called Lapland or Sapmi, the land of the Saami. The total Saami population is around 100,000 people, with the majority in Norway (Magga and Skutnabb-Kangas 2001).

At the time of the earliest written records of 1,000 years ago, all Saami hunted wild reindeer, among other land and sea species, and may have kept some tamed reindeer for transport (Paine 2004). Over time, herding domesticated reindeer developed and became the economic mainstay. In the past few hundred years, though, reindeer pastoralism declined to being a specialization of about 10 percent of the population. Settled Saami are farmers or work in trade, small-scale industry, handicrafts, services, and the professions.

Traditional Saami reindeer herding has been a family-based system. Men and women cared for the herd, and sons and daughters inherited equally the rights to the herd (Paine 2004). The value of social equality was strong, entailing both rights and privileges.

In their relationships with the modern state, the Saami have experienced discrimination, exclusion, loss of territorial rights, and cultural and linguistic repression. Specific risks to Saami cultural survival include being downwind of the prevailing winds after the 1986 Chernobyl disaster, being near the earlier Soviet atomic testing grounds in Siberia, having their ancestral territory and sacred spaces suffer environmental degradation from hydroelectric dam construction, and having grazing lands taken over for use as military training grounds (Anderson 2004).

State policies of cultural assimilation and forced Christianization in the twentieth century marginalized the Saami language and led to serious language loss (Magga and Skutnabb-Kangas 2001). Several Saami languages and dialects still exist, with spatially distant versions being mutually unintelligible (Gaski 1993:116). Language is of central cultural value to the Saami, and efforts to maintain it have been under way since the 1960s.

Besides the Saami language, a traditional song form, the *yoik,* is of particular importance (Anderson 2005). Yoik lyrics allow a subtle system of double meanings that can camouflage political content (Gaski 1997).

Readings

Myrdene Anderson. "Reflections on the Saami at Loose Ends." In Myrdene Anderson, ed., *Cultural Shaping of Violence: Victimization, Escalation, Response.* West Lafayette, IN: Purdue University Press, 2004, pp. 285–291.

Myrdene Anderson. "The Saami Yoik: Translating Hum, Chant, or/and Song." In Dinda Gorlée, ed., *Song and Significance: Virtues and Vices of Vocal Translation.* Amsterdam: Rodopi, 2005, pp. 213–233.

Harald Gaski (Ed.), *Sami Culture in a New Era: The Norwegian Sami Experience.* Seattle: University of Washington Press, 1997.

Ole Henrik Magga and Tove Skutnabb-Kangas. "The Saami Languages: The Present and the Future." *Cultural Survival Quarterly, 25* (2), 26–31, 2001.

Robert Paine. "Dam a River, Damn a People? Saami (Lapp) Livelihood and the Alta-Kautokeino Hydro-Electric Project and the Norwegian Parliament." *IWGIIA Document 45,* 1992.

Video

Even If a Hundred Ogres. (Introduced and narrated by Joanne Woodward. 1996. www.nativeVideos.com.)

Website

Saami Council, www.saamicouncil.net/.

Thanks to Myrdene Anderson, Purdue University, for reviewing this material.

The well-known Saami singer-songwriter Marie Boine performs at the Easter Festival in Kautokeino, Sapmi, north Norway (left). ■ (Source: © Anders Ryman/ Alamy) *A Saami herder, named Aslak, with his reindeer herd in Kautokeino (right).* ■ (Source: © Bryan and Cherry Alexander Photography/Alamy)

MAP 12.8 *Saami Region in Lapland, or Sapmi. Sapmi spreads across Norway, Sweden, Finland, and Russia's Kola Peninsula.*

FIGURE 12.7   Loan Words in North American English

Alcohol	Arabic, Middle East
Avocado	Nahuatl, Mexico/Central America
Banana	Mandingo, West Africa
Bogus	Hausa, West Africa
Candy	Arabic, Middle East
Caucus	Algonquin, Virginia/Delaware, North America
Chimpanzee	Bantu, West and Central Africa
Chocolate	Aztec Nahuatl, Mexico/Central America
Dungaree	Hindi, North India, South Asia
Gong	Malaysia, Southeast Asia
Hammock	Arawakan, South America
Hip/hep	Wolof, West Africa
Hurricane	Taino, Caribbean
Lime	Inca Quechua, South America
Moose	Algonquin, Virginia/Delaware, North America
Panda	Nepali, South Asia
Savannah	Taino, Caribbean
Shampoo	Hindi, North India, South Asia
Sugar	Sanskrit, South Asia
Tepee	Sioux, Dakotas, North America
Thug	Hindi, North India, South Asia
Tobacco	Arawak, South America
Tomato	Nahuatl, Mexico/Central America
Tundra	Saami, Lapland, Northern Europe
Tycoon	Japanese
Typhoon	Mandarin Chinese, East Asia
Zombie	Congo and Angola, Central and West Africa

Endangered Languages and Language Revitalization

The field of linguistic anthropology, as mentioned in Chapter 1, was prompted by the need to document disappearing indigenous languages in the United States. Today, anthropologists and other scholars, as well as descendant language communities themselves, are still concerned about the rapid loss of languages (Fishman 1991; Maffi 2005). The task of documenting declining languages is urgent. It is often accompanied by applied work to preserve and revive endangered and dying languages (see Critical Thinking box).

Scholars have proposed ways to assess degrees of language loss or decline (Walsh 2005). The general stages proceed from "shift" to extinction. **Language shift,** or language decay, is a category of language decline when speakers have limited vocabulary in their native language and more often use a new language in which they may be semifluent or fluent (Hill 2001). An intermediary stage, **language endangerment,** is judged to exist when a language has fewer than 10,000 speakers. Near-extinction is a situation in which only a few elderly speakers are still living. **Language extinction,** or language death, occurs when the language no longer has any competent users (Crystal 2000:11). Dialects follow a similar pattern of decline from decay to near-extinction to extinction. In 1777, Dolly Penreath, the last speaker of the Cornish dialect of British English died and Cornish became officially extinct (Lightfoot 2006:2).

Keeping track of endangered and dying languages is difficult because no one is sure how many languages have existed in the recent past and even now (Crystal 2000). Estimates of living languages today range between 5,000 to 7,000. Part of the explanation for the fuzzy numbers is the problem in separating languages from dialects. The largest number of languages of any world region is in New Guinea, an area comprising Papua New Guinea, Irian Jaya, and several neighboring, smaller islands but not including Australia (Foley 2000). In this area alone are some 1,000 languages, many from completely separate language families.

Language extinction is a serious problem worldwide. It is perhaps especially acute in the Australia/Pacific region, where 99.5 percent of the indigenous languages have fewer than 100,000 speakers (Nettle and Romaine 2000:40). The situation of indigenous languages in the Americas, Siberia, Africa, and South and Southeast Asia is increasingly serious. Over half of the world's languages have fewer than 10,000 speakers; a quarter have less than 1,000 speakers.

Linguistic diversity is closely tied to cultural survival and diversity. It is also closely tied to biological diversity. The greatest linguistic diversity is found in the same regions as the greatest biodiversity (Maffi 2005). These are areas where indigenous people live, the "keepers" of much of the world's cultural and biological heritage,

language shift or decay: condition of a language in which speakers adopt a new language for most situations, begin to use their native language only in certain contexts, and may be only semi-fluent and have limited vocabulary in their native language.

language endangerment: a stage in language decline when a language has fewer than 10,000 speakers.

language extinction: a situation, either gradual or sudden, in which language speakers abandon their native language in favor of a new language to the extent that the native language loses functions and no longer has competent users.

Critical Thinking

SHOULD DYING LANGUAGES BE REVIVED?

The Western media often carry articles about endangered biological species, such as certain frogs or birds, and the need to protect them from extinction. The reasons for concern about loss of biological species are many. One major factor is simply that biological diversity is a good thing to have on the earth. Opponents of taking special measures to protect endangered species find support for their position in a Darwinian view that progress involves competition and the survival of those species that can make it. Economic progress might mean building a new shopping center or airport with a massive parking lot. If that means the death and burial of a particular kind of trillium, so be it, in the name of "progress."

Some parallels exist between the survival of endangered languages and that of endangered biological species (Maffi 2005). Supporters of language preservation and revitalization can point to the sheer fact of diversity on earth as a good thing, a sign of a culturally healthy planet with room for everyone's language. They will argue that a people's language is an intrinsic part of their culture. Without language, the culture, too, will die.

Others take the Darwinian view that languages, like species, live in a world of competition. Language survival means that the strong and fit carry on while the weak and unfit die out. They may point out that preserving linguistic heritage is useless because dying languages are part of a past that no longer exists. They resist spending public funds on language preservation and regard revitalization programs as wasteful.

CRITICAL THINKING QUESTIONS

- Have you read or heard of an endangered biological species in the media recently? What was the species?
- Have you read or heard of an endangered language in the media lately? What was the language?
- Where do you stand on biological species preservation and on language preservation, and why?

including the knowledge of how to live a culturally and biologically sustainable life. Yet, they are also the people, languages, and biological species most in danger of extinction in the near future.

Efforts to revive or maintain local languages face many challenges (Fishman 2001). Political opposition

Indigenous language dictionaries and usage guides are available on the Web and may help indigenous peoples preserve their cultures. ■ *Check out The Internet Guide to Australian Languages.* (Source: © Robert Essel NYC/CORBIS)

may come from governments that fear local identity movements. Governments are often averse to devoting financial resources to supporting minority language programs. Deciding which version of an endangered language to preserve may have political consequences at the local level (Nevins 2004). Notable achievements have been made, however, with perhaps one of the most robust examples of language maintenance occurring in French-speaking Québec.

Approaches to language maintenance and revitalization must respond to local circumstances and factors such as how serious the degree of loss is, how many living speakers there are, what version of the language should be maintained or revived, and what resources for maintenance and revitalization programs are available. Major strategies include (Walsh 2005):

- Formal classroom instruction
- Master-apprentice system in which an elder teaches a nonspeaker in a one-on-one situation
- Web-based tools and services to support language learning

Each method has both promise and pitfalls. One thing is key: It takes living communities to activate and keep alive the knowledge of a language (Maffi 2003).

The Big Questions Revisited

HOW do humans communicate?

Human communication is the sending of meaningful messages through language. Language is a systematic set of symbols and signs with learned and shared meanings. It may be spoken, hand-signed, written, or conveyed through body movements, marking, or accessories. Languages include subvarieties such as dialects.

Human language has two characteristics that distinguish it from communicative systems of other living beings. It has productivity, or the ability to create an infinite number of novel and understandable messages, and displacement, the ability to communicate about the past, the future, and imaginary things.

Language consists of basic sounds, vocabulary, and syntax. Cross-culturally, however, languages vary substantially in the details of all three features.

Humans use many forms of nonverbal language to communicate with each other. Sign language is a form of communication that uses mainly hand movements to communicate. Silence is a form of nonverbal communication with its own cultural values and meaning. Body language includes body movements and placement in relation to other people, body modifications such as tattoos and piercing, dress, hairstyles, and odors.

Media anthropology sheds light on how culture shapes media messages and the social dynamics in media institutions. Critical media anthropology examines the power relations involved in the media.

WHAT are the links between communication, cultural diversity, and inequality?

In order to study language in society, anthropologists have to deal with the observer's paradox, or the difficulty of collecting data on language without affecting the object of study in the process. Translation is another challenge.

The Sapir-Whorf hypothesis places emphasis on how language shapes culture. Another model, called sociolinguistics, emphasizes how culture, and one's position in it, shape language. Many anthropologists draw on both models.

Critical discourse analysis studies the relations of power and inequality in language. Language can reveal social difference and reinforce exclusion. It can also empower oppressed people, depending on the context. In mainstream North America, women's speech is generally more polite and accommodating than that of men. In Japan, gender codes emphasize politeness in women's speech, but many young Japanese women, kogals, are creating a new linguistic style of resistance. Gay language in Indonesia is entering the mainstream as an expression of freedom from official control. Linguistic cuing among the Akwesasne Mohawks has been frequently misinterpreted by Anglo medical practitioners as a sign of indecisiveness or noncooperation. African American English (AAE) has evolved from the tragic heritage of slavery to become a standard language with many local variants.

HOW does language change?

The exact origins of human verbal language will never be known. The discovery of language families provides insights about human history and settlement patterns. The emergence of writing can be traced to around 6,000 years ago, with the emergence of the state in Mesopotamia. Scripts have spread widely throughout the world, with the Aramaic system the basis of scripts in South and Southeast Asia. The functions of writing vary from context to context. In some situations, official recordkeeping predominates, whereas in others, writing is important for courtship.

The recent history of language change has been influenced by the colonialism of past centuries and by Western globalization of the current era. Nationalist policies of cultural integration often involve the repression of minority languages and promotion of a *lingua franca*. Colonial contact created the context for the emergence of pidgin languages, many of which evolved into creoles. Western globalization supports the spread of English and the development of localized variants.

In the past 500 years, colonialism and globalization have resulted in the extinction of many indigenous and minority languages. Many others are in danger of dying. Applied anthropologists seek to preserve the world's linguistic diversity. They document languages and participate in designing programs for teaching dead and dying languages. Efforts to maintain or revive languages at risk face many challenges. One of the basic elements for success is to have living communities use the language.

KEY CONCEPTS

SUGGESTED READINGS

Keith H. Basso, *Wisdom Sits in Places: Landscape and Language among the Western Apache.* Albuquerque: University of New Mexico Press, 1996. Fieldwork on the Fort Apache Indian Reservation, Arizona, reveals the importance of natural places in people's everyday life, thought, and language.

David Crystal, *English as a Global Language,* 2nd ed. New York: Cambridge University Press, 2003. This book discusses the history, current status, and future of English as a world language. It covers the role of English in international relations, the media, international travel, education, and "New Englishes."

Joshua A. Fishman, ed. *Can Threatened Languages Be Saved?* Buffalo, NY: Multilingual Matters Ltd., 2001. Seventeen case studies examine language shift and language loss and the attempts to reverse such changes.

Marjorie H. Goodwin. *He-Said-She-Said: Talk as Social Organization among Black Children.* Bloomington: Indiana University Press, 1990. A study of everyday talk among children of an urban African American community in the United States, this book shows how children construct social relationships among themselves through verbal interactions, including disputes, pretend play, and stories.

Niloofar Haeri, *Sacred Language, Ordinary People: Dilemmas of Culture and Politics in Egypt.* New York: Palgrave Macmillan, 2003. Classical Arabic is the official language of all Arab states and the language of the Qur'an, but no Arabs speak it as their mother tongue. This book uses ethnographic research in Cairo to demonstrate the role that classical Arabic plays in how the state maintains its identity and in people's everyday lives.

Jennifer Hasty. *The Press and Political Culture in Ghana.* Bloomington: Indiana University Press, 2005. The author worked as a journalist in Accra, Ghana, while doing research on the practices of journalism at privately owned and state-operated daily newspapers. She discusses differences in ways of gathering the news, assigning beats, using sources, and writing articles. Underlying these contrasts is a generally unified sense of Ghanaian national identity as expressed in the printed news.

Joy Hendry. *Wrapping Culture: Politeness, Presentation and Power in Japan and Other Societies.* New York: Oxford University Press, 1993. This book explores the pervasive idiom and practice of "wrapping" in Japanese culture, including verbal language, gift giving, and dress. In verbal language, wrapping involves the use of various forms of respect, indicating social levels of the speakers, and the use of linguistic forms of beautification.

Lanita Jacobs-Huey. *From the Kitchen to the Parlor: Language and Becoming in African-American Women's Hair Care.* New York: Oxford University Press, 2006. Jacobs-Huey combines childhood experiences as the daughter of a cosmetologist with multisited fieldwork in the United States and England. She finds a rich and complex world centered on hair that relates to race, gender, religion, body esthetics, health, and verbal language.

William L. Leap. *Word's Out: Gay Men's English.* Minneapolis: University of Minnesota Press, 1996. Fieldwork among gay men in the Washington, DC, area produced this ethnography. It addresses gay men's speech as a cooperative mode of discourse, bathroom graffiti, and discourse about HIV/AIDS.

Julie Lindquist. *A Place to Stand: Politics and Persuasion in a Working-Class Bar.* New York: Oxford University Press, 2002. The author did participant observation while working as a bartender in a White, working-class bar in the U.S. Midwest. The book provides an ethnography of speaking within the bar as a context of cultural "performance" related to White, working-class identity.

Susan U. Philips, Susan Steele, and Christine Tanz, eds. *Language, Gender and Sex in Comparative Perspective.* New York: Cambridge University Press, 1987. Chapters explore women's and men's speech in Japan, Western Samoa, and Mexico; children's speech in U.S. preschools and in Papua New Guinea; and sex differences in how the brain is related to speech.

John R. Rickford and Russell J. Rickford. *Spoken Soul: The Story of Black English.* New York: John Wiley & Sons, 2000. The authors, a linguist and a journalist, describe the history and use of African American English in everyday conversation, religion, the performing arts, and literature. They explore the status of AAE in the United States and its relationship to issues of "race" and class.

Frank Salomon, *The Cord Keepers: Khipus and Cultural Life in a Peruvian Village.* Durham, NC: Duke University Press, 2004. The pre-Columbian Incas of the Andes used khipus, or knotted cords, to manage their empire. This ethnography describes the use of khipus in a contemporary Peruvian village where village leaders wear them on ceremonial occasions in order to signal their political identity and ancestry.

Lisa Philips Valentine. *Making It Their Own: Ojibwe Communicative Practices.* Toronto: University of Toronto Press, 1995. This ethnography examines speech events in a small Ojibwe community in northern Ontario, Canada. It considers speech variations among speakers, code switching, multilingualism, and church music.

Peter Wogan. *Magical Writing in Salasaca: Literacy and Power in Highland Ecuador.* Boulder, CO: Westview Press, 2004. This ethnography about highland people in Ecuador focuses on the importance and power of different forms of writing. The author describes writing in relation to ethnicity, the role of the state, social conflict, and religious beliefs and practices.

13
Religion

The Big Questions

- WHAT is religion and what are the basic features of religions?

- HOW do world religions illustrate globalization and localization?

- WHAT are some important aspects of religious change in contemporary times?

Uluru, Kata Tjuta National Park, Australia. Located roughly in the center of Australia in the Northern Territory and 280 miles south of Alice Springs, Uluru is an Aboriginal sacred site and a World Heritage Site. Tourists often want to make the arduous climb to the top, though the Anangu people who are the custodians urge people to consider other ways to enjoy the region. *(Source: © John Carnemolla/Australian Picture Library/CORBIS)*

When studying the religious life of people of rural northern Greece, anthropologist Loring Danforth observed rituals in which participants walk across several yards of burning coals (1989). They do not get burned, they say, because their faith and a saint protect them. Upon his return to the United States, Danforth met an American who regularly walks on fire as part of his New Age faith and organizes training workshops for people who want to learn how to firewalk. Danforth himself firewalked in a ceremony in rural Maine.

Not every anthropologist who studies religion undertakes such challenges during fieldwork, but they all share an interest in enduring questions about humanity's understanding of the supernatural realm and relationships with it: Why do some religions have many gods and others just one? Why do some religions practice sacrifice? Why do some religions have more participation by women? How do religions respond to changing conditions in the political economy?

Religion has been a cornerstone topic in cultural anthropology since the beginnings of the discipline. Over many decades, a rich collection of material has accumulated. The early focus was on religions of indigenous and tribal peoples. More recently, anthropologists are studying the major religions of state-level societies and the effects of globalization on religious change.

Christian firewalkers in northern Greece express their faith by walking on hot coals and reaffirm divine protection by not getting burned. ■ *Speculate on why some religious rituals involve physical and mental challenges. How do these challenges compare to physical and mental challenges in secular life, such as certain sports?* (Source: © Loring Danforth)

Religion in Comparative Perspective

This section sets the stage for the chapter by reviewing basic areas in the anthropology of religion, including how to define religion and a discussion of theories about the origin of religion. It also covers types of religious beliefs, rituals, and religious specialists.

What Is Religion?

Since the earliest days of anthropology, scholars have proposed various definitions of religion. In the late 1800s, British anthropologist Sir Edward Tylor defined religion as the belief in spirits. A more comprehensive, current definition says that **religion** is beliefs and actions related to supernatural beings and forces. This definition includes both beliefs and behavior, parallel to our definition of culture. This definition specifically avoids linking religion with belief in a supreme deity since no concept of a supreme deity exists in some religions, whereas others have multiple deities.

Religion is related to, but not the same as, a people's *worldview*, or way of understanding how the world came to be, its design, and their place in it (see Figure 13.1). Worldview is a broader concept and does not include the

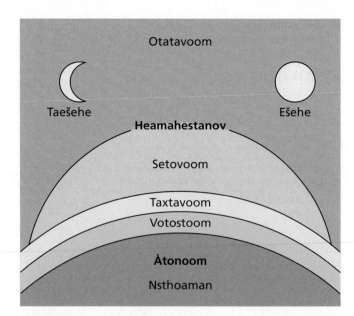

Otatavoom

Taešehe

Ešehe

Heamahestanov

Setovoom

Taxtavoom

Votostoom

Àtonoom

Nsthoaman

FIGURE 13.1 Cheyenne View of the Universe *(Source: John H. Moore,* The Cheyenne *[Malden, MA: Blackwell Publishers, 1996], p. 205.)*

---

religion: beliefs and actions related to supernatural beings and forces.

magic: the attempt to compel supernatural forces and beings to act in certain ways.

animism: the belief in souls or "doubles."

---

criterion of concern with a supernatural realm. An atheist has a worldview, but not a religious one.

Magic versus Religion

Sir Edward Tylor wrote that magic, religion, and science are alike in that they are different ways in which people have tried to explain the physical world and events in it. He considered science to be the superior, most rational of the three. Sir James Frazer, writing at about the same time as Tylor, defined **magic** as people's attempt to compel supernatural forces and beings to act in certain ways (1978 [1890]). He contrasted magic with religion, which he said is the attempt to please supernatural forces or beings. Frazer differentiated two general principles of magic:

- *The law of similarity,* which is the basis of *imitative magic.* It is founded on the assumption that if person or item X is like person or item Y, then actions done to person or item X will affect person or item Y. A familiar example is a voodoo doll. If someone sticks pins into a doll X that represents person Y, then person Y will experience pain or suffering.

- *The law of contagion,* which is the basis of *contagious magic.* It says that persons or things once in contact with a person can still have an effect on that person. Common items for working contagious magic include a person's hair trimmings, nail clippings, teeth, spit, blood, fecal matter, and the placenta of a baby. In cultures where contagious magic is practiced, people are careful about disposing of their personal wastes so that no one else can get hold of them.

Tylor, Frazer, and other early anthropologists supported an evolutionary model (review Chapter 1), with magic preceding religion. They evaluated magic as less spiritual and ethical than religion and therefore more "primitive." They assumed that, in time, magic would be completely replaced by the "higher" system of religion which, in turn, would be replaced by science as the most rational way of thinking. They would be surprised to see the widespread presence of magical religions in the modern world such as so-called Wicca, or Neo-Pagan, religion that centers on respect for the Earth, nature, and the seasonal cycle. An anthropologist who studied Wicca in the San Francisco Bay area learned about beliefs, rituals, and magical practices through participant observation (Magliocco 2004). One of the prominent Wicca symbols is the pentacle (see Figure 13.2).

Many people turn to magical behavior at certain times in their everyday lives, especially in situations of uncertainty. Magic, for example, is prominent in sports (Gmelch 1997 [1971]). Some baseball players in the United States repeat actions or use charms, including a special shirt or hat, to help them win. This practice is based on the assumption that if it worked before, it may work

FIGURE 13.2   A Pentacle. Sometimes called a pentagram, it is a five-pointed star surrounded by a circle. An important symbol in Neo-Pagan and Wikkan religions, the pentacle is also a magical tool used for summoning energies and commanding spirits.

again, following the law of contagion. In baseball, pitching and hitting involve more uncertainty than fielding, and pitchers and hitters are more likely to use magic. Magical practices are also common in farming, fishing, the military, and love.

THINKING OUTSIDE THE BOX

TAKE CAREFUL note of your daily thoughts and activities for a week in terms of how magic, religion, and science are involved. What did you learn?

Theories of the Origin of Religion

Many theorists adopt a functionalist approach in explaining why religion is such a pervasive aspect of human culture. According to this view, religion provides ways of explaining and coping with universal human problems such as life and death, illness, and misfortune.

Tylor's theory, proposed in his book *Primitive Culture* (1871), was based on his assumption that early human ancestors needed to explain the difference between the living and the dead. They therefore developed the concept of a soul that exists in all living things and departs from the body after death. Tylor named this way of thinking **animism,** the belief in souls or "doubles." Tylor speculated that the concept of the soul eventually became personified, and human-like deities were conceived. For Tylor, religion evolved from animism to *polytheism* (the belief in many deities) to *monotheism* (the belief in one supreme deity). Once again, this evolutionary model is proved wrong. Animistic beliefs exist in many religions, including, for example, Christian beliefs about visitations of the dead (Stringer 1999), and many contemporary religions are polytheistic.

French scholar Emile Durkheim presented a different functional theory in his book *The Elementary Forms of the Religious Life* (1965 [1915]). He speculated that early humans understood the benefits of social contact, so they developed symbols to represent the group and rituals to maintain continuity. Bronislaw Malinowski's functional theory says that rituals help reduce anxiety and uncertainty. Karl Marx took a class conflict approach to understanding how religion functions, emphasizing religion's role as an "opiate of the masses." Marx thought that religion provides a superficial form of comfort to the poor, masking the harsh realities of class inequality and thereby preventing uprisings against the rich.

Religion provides an important source of social cohesion and psychological support for many immigrant groups, whose places of worship attract both worshippers and cultural anthropologists interested in learning how religion fits into migrants' adaptation. This is a scene at a Lao Buddhist temple in Virginia. ■ *See what you can find out about Buddhism in North America from the Internet.* (Source: Ruth Krulfeld)

Another functional theory comes from symbolic analysis, as informed by Sigmund Freud's emphasis on the role of the unconscious. For Freud, religion is a "projective system" that expresses people's unconscious thoughts, wishes, and worries. Clifford Geertz provides a theoretical approach combining Durkheimian functionalism with symbolic analysis (1966). In his view, religions are primarily systems of meaning that provide for people a *model of life* (how to understand the world) and a *model for life* (how to behave in the world).

Varieties of Religious Beliefs

Religions comprise beliefs and behavior. Scholars of religion generally address belief systems first because they appear to inform patterns of religious behavior. Religious beliefs are shared by a group, sometimes by millions of people, and are passed on through the generations. Elders teach children through songs and narratives, artists paint the stories on rocks and walls, and sculptors create images in wood and stone that depict aspects of religious belief.

How Beliefs Are Expressed

Beliefs are expressed and transferred over the generations in two main forms:

- **Myth,** stories about supernatural forces or beings
- **Doctrine,** direct statements about religious beliefs

A myth is a narrative that has a plot with a beginning, middle, and end. The plot may involve recurrent motifs, the smallest units of narrative. Myths convey messages about the supernaturals indirectly, through the story itself, rather than by using logic or formal argument. Greek and Roman myths, such as the stories of Zeus, Athena, Orpheus, and Persephone, are world famous. Some people would say that the Bible is a collection of myths; others would object to that categorization as suggesting that the stories are not "real" or "sacred." Myths have long been part of people's oral tradition, and many are still unwritten.

Anthropologists ask why myths exist. Malinowski said that a myth is a *charter* for society in that it expresses core beliefs and teaches morality. Claude Lévi-Strauss, the most famous mythologist, saw myths as functional but in a philosophical and psychological way. In his view, myths help people deal with the deep conceptual contradictions between, for example, life and death and good and evil, by providing stories in which these dualities find a solution in a mediating third factor. These mythological solutions are buried within a variety of surface details in the myth. For example, many myths of the

---

myth: a narrative with a plot that involves the supernaturals.

doctrine: direct and formalized statements about religious beliefs.

San rock paintings in the Tsodillo Hills *(left)*, southwestern Botswana. Some of the paintings date back to 800 CE. The site is sacred to the San people. ■ (Source: © Galen Rowell/CORBIS) A stone sculpture at Mamallapuram, south India *(right)*, dating from the eighth or ninth century, depicts the triumph of the goddess Durga (riding the lion, left of center) over the bull-headed demon Mahishasura. ■ (Source: Simon Hiltebeitel)

Pueblo Indians of the U.S. Southwest juxtapose grass-eating animals (vegetarians) with predators (carnivores). The mediating third character is the raven, who is a carnivore but, unlike other creatures, does not have to kill to eat meat because it is a scavenger.

A cultural materialist perspective, also functionalist, says that myths store and transmit information related to making a living and managing economic crises (Sobel and Bettles 2000). Analysis of twenty-eight myths of the Klamath and Modoc Indians (see Map 13.1) reveals that subsistence risk is a consistent theme. The myths also describe ways to cope with hunger, such as skill in hunting and fishing, food storage, resource diversification, resource conservation, spatial mobility, reciprocity, and the role of supernatural forces. Thus, myths are repositories of knowledge related to economic survival, crisis management, and environmental management and conservation.

Doctrine, the other major form in which beliefs are expressed, explicitly defines the supernaturals, the world and how it came to be, and people's roles in relation to the supernaturals and to other humans. Doctrine is written and formal. It is close to law because it links incorrect beliefs and behaviors with punishments. Doctrine is associated with institutionalized, large-scale religions rather with than small-scale "folk" religions.

Doctrine can and does change (Bowen 1998:38–40). Over the centuries, various Popes have pronounced new doctrine for the Catholic Church. A papal declaration of 1854, made with the intent of reinvigorating European Catholicism, bestowed authenticity on the concept of the Immaculate Conception, an idea with substantial popular support.

Muslim doctrine is expressed in the Qu'ran, the basic holy text of the Islamic faith, which consists of revelations made to the prophet Muhammad in the seventh century, and in collections of Muhammad's statements and deeds (Bowen 1998:38). In Kuala Lumpur, Malaysia (see Map 8.3, p. 209), a small group of highly educated women called the Sisters in Islam regularly debate with members of the local *ulama*, religious authorities who are responsible for interpreting Islamic doctrine especially concerning families, education, and commercial affairs (Ong 1995). In recent years, the debates have concerned such issues as polygamy, divorce, women's work roles, and women's clothing.

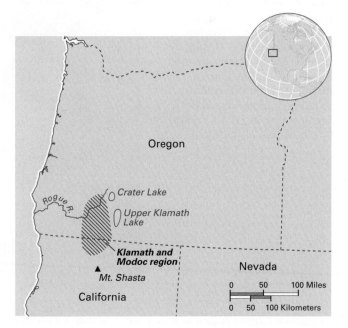

MAP 13.1 Klamath and Modoc Region in Oregon and Washington

Beliefs about Supernatural Forces and Beings

Supernaturals range from impersonal forces to those that look just like humans. Supernaturals can be supreme and all-powerful creators or smaller-scale, annoying spirits that take up residence in people through possession.

The term **animatism** refers to belief systems in which the supernatural is conceived of as an impersonal power. An important example is *mana*, a concept widespread throughout the South Pacific region, including Melanesia, Polynesia, and Micronesia. Mana is a force outside nature that works automatically; it is neither spirit nor deity. It manifests itself in objects and people and is associated with personal status and power, because some people accumulate more of it than others.

Some supernaturals are *zoomorphic*, deities in the shape, or partial shape, of animals. No satisfactory theory has appeared to explain why some religions develop zoomorphic deities, and for what purposes, and why others do not. Religions of classical Greece and Rome and ancient and contemporary Hinduism are especially rich in zoomorphic supernaturals. *Anthropomorphic* supernaturals, deities in the form of humans, are common but not universal. The human tendency to perceive of supernaturals in their own form was noted 2,500 years ago by the Greek philosopher Xenophanes, who lived sometime between 570 and 470 BCE. He said, "If cattle and horses, or lions, had hands, or were able to draw with their feet and produce the worlds which men do, horses would draw the forms of gods like horses, and cattle like cattle, and they would make the gods' bodies the same shape as their own" (Fragment 15). The question, though, of why some religions do and others do not have anthropomorphic deities is impossible to answer.

Anthropomorphic supernaturals, like humans, can be moved by praise, flattery, and gifts. They have emotions. They get annoyed if neglected, they can be loving and caring, or they can be distant and nonresponsive. Most anthropomorphic supernaturals are adults though some prominent anthropomorphic deities are children. Supernaturals tend to have similar marital and sexual relationships as the humans who worship them do. Divine marriages are heterosexual, and, in polygynous societies, male gods have multiple wives. Although many supernaturals have children, grandchildren are not prominent. In *pantheons* (collectivities of deities), a division of labor reflects specializations in human society. There may be deities of forests, rivers, the sky, wind and rain, agriculture, childbirth, disease, warfare, and marital happiness. The supernaturals have political roles and hierarchies. High gods, such as Jupiter and Juno of classical Roman religion, are all powerful with a range of less powerful deities and spirits below them.

Deceased ancestors can be supernaturals. Many African, Asian, and Native American religions have a cult of the ancestors in which the living must do certain things to please the dead ancestors and may also ask for their help in time of need. In contemporary Japan, ancestor veneration is the principal religious activity of many

Shizuko Maddox, a first-generation Japanese American, maintains a shrine for her husband in her house in Columbus, Ohio. Originally from Nagoya, Japan, she met her American husband, a member of the U.S. military, when he was stationed in Japan following World War II.
■ (Source: Rita Maddox)

animatism: a belief system in which the supernatural is conceived of as an impersonal power.

ritual: a patterned form of behavior that has to do with the supernatural realm.

families. Three national holidays recognize the importance of the ancestors: the annual summer visit of the dead to their home and the visits by the living to graves during the two equinoxes.

Beliefs about Sacred Space

Beliefs about sacred space probably exist in all religions, but such beliefs are more prominent in some religions than others. Sacred spaces, such as rock formations or rapids in a river, may or may not be permanently marked (Bradley 2000). Among the Saami (see Culturama in Chapter 12, p. 333), traditional religious beliefs were closely tied to sacred natural sites (Mulk 1994). The sites, often unmarked, included rock formations resembling humans, animals, or birds. The Saami sacrificed animals and fish at these sites until strong pressures from Christian missionaries forced them to repress their practices and beliefs. Many Saami today know where the sacred sites are, but they will not reveal them to outsiders.

Another important form of sacred space that has no permanent mark occurs in a domestic ritual conducted by Muslim women throughout the world called the *khatam quran,* the "sealing" or reading of the holy book, the Qu'ran (Werbner 1988). Among Pakistani migrants living in the city of Manchester, northern England (see Map 13.2), this ritual involves a gathering of women who read the Qu'ran and then share a ritual meal. The reason for gathering is to give thanks or seek divine blessing. During the ritual, the otherwise nonsacred space of the house becomes sacred. A "portable" ritual such as this one is especially helpful in migrant adaptation, because it can be conducted without a formally consecrated ritual space. All that is required is a supportive group of kin and friends and the Qu'ran.

Religions of the Aboriginal people of Australia are closely tied to sacred space. During a mythological past, called the Dream Time, the ancestors walked the earth and marked out the territory belonging to a particular group. People's knowledge of where the ancestors roamed is secret. In several cases that have recently been brought to the courts, Aboriginal peoples have claimed title to land that is being sought by commercial developers.

Anthropologists have sometimes become involved in these disputes, providing expert testimony documenting the validity of the Aboriginal claims to their sacred space. In one such case, secret Aboriginal knowledge about a sacred place and its associated beliefs was gender specific: It belonged to women and could not be told to men. The anthropologist who was hired to support the women's claims was a woman and could therefore be told about the sacred places, but she would not be able to convey that knowledge in court to the male judge. These cultural nuances demanded considerable ingenuity on the part of the anthropological consultant (see Lessons Applied box).

MAP 13.2 England. England is the largest of the constituent countries of the United Kingdom, and its population of 50 million accounts for 84 percent of the total. DNA analysis reveals that a majority of the English are of Germanic descent, as is their language. The terrain is mainly rolling hills, with some mountains in the north and east. London is by far the largest city, with Manchester and Birmingham competing for second place. English is the dominant language, with its diverse regional accents. Many different languages brought into the country by immigrant communities are spoken as first languages, including several South Asian languages, Polish, Greek, and Cantonese. An estimated 250,000 people speak British Sign Language. Although the Church of England is the state religion, everyone in England has the right to religious freedom.

In contrast to unmarked and secret sacred spaces, many religions make concerted efforts to mark and protect their sacred territory. Such claims to sacred space are frequently the basis of conflict between people of different faiths and between believers and commercial interests.

THINKING OUTSIDE THE BOX THINK OF some examples of sacred space, unmarked or marked, in your microculture. What patterns emerge?

Ritual Practices

A **ritual** is a patterned form of behavior that is focused on the supernatural realm. Many rituals are the enactment of beliefs expressed in myth and doctrine, such as the Christian ritual of communion. Rituals are distinct from *secular rituals,* such as a sorority or fraternity ini-

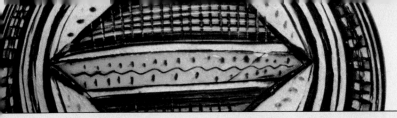

Lessons Applied

ABORIGINAL WOMEN'S CULTURE, SACRED SITE PROTECTION, AND THE ANTHROPOLOGIST AS EXPERT WITNESS

A group of Ngarrindjeri (prounounced NAR-en-jeery) women and their lawyer hired cultural anthropologist Diane Bell to serve as a consultant to them in supporting their claims to a sacred site in southern Australia (Bell 1998). The area on Hindmarsh Island was threatened by the proposed construction of a bridge that would cross sacred waters between Goolwa and the island. The women claimed protection for the area and sought prevention of the bridge building on the basis of their secret knowledge of its sacredness, knowledge passed down in trust from mother to daughter over generations. The High Commission formed by the government to investigate their claim considered it to be a hoax perpetrated to block a project important to the country.

Helping the women prove their case to a White, male-dominated court system was a challenging task for Diane Bell, a White Australian with extensive fieldwork experience among Aboriginal women. Bell conducted research over many months to marshal evidence for the validity of the women's claims. She examined newspaper archives, early recordings of ritual songs, and oral histories of Ngarrindjeri women. She prepared reports for the courtroom about women's sacred knowledge that were general enough to avoid violating the rule of women-only knowledge but detailed enough to convince the High Court judge that the women's sacred knowledge was authentic. In the end, the judge was convinced, and the bridge project was canceled in 1999.

FOOD FOR THOUGHT

- On the Internet, learn more about this case and other disputes in Australia about sacred sites.

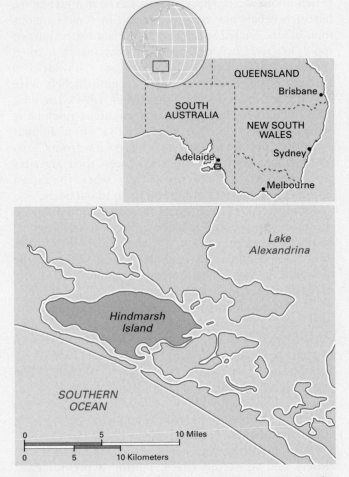

MAP 13.3 Hindmarsh Island in Southeast Australia. The Ngarrindjeri name for Hindmarsh Island is Kumarangk.

---

tiation or a common-law wedding, which are patterned forms of behavior with no connection to the supernatural realm. Some ritual events combine sacred and secular elements. The U.S. holiday of Thanksgiving originated as a Christian sacred meal with the primary purpose of giving thanks to God for the survival of the pilgrims (Siskind 1992). Its original Christian meaning is not maintained by everyone who celebrates the holiday today. Secular features of the holiday, such as watching football, are of greater importance than the ritual aspect of thanking God for plentiful food.

Anthropologists of religion categorize rituals in many ways. One division is based on how regularly the ritual is performed. Regularly performed rituals are called *periodic rituals*. Many periodic rituals are performed annually to mark a seasonal milestone such as planting or harvesting or to commemorate some important event. For example, an important periodic ritual in Buddhism,

---

life-cycle ritual: a ritual performed to mark a change in status from one life stage to another of an individual or group; also called *rite of passage*.

A gathering of modern-day Druids at Stonehenge, England. They are one of the several groups that have interests in the preservation of and access to this World Heritage Site. Debates concern possible changes in the location of nearby roads and planting or removing trees. The Druids claim that the site is important to their religion.
■ As a research project, learn about the various groups and preservation issues related to Stonehenge. (Source: © Adam Wolfitt/CORBIS)

Visakha Puja, or Buddha's Day, commemorates the birth, enlightenment, and death of the Buddha (all on one day). On this day, Buddhists gather at monasteries, hear sermons about the Buddha, and perform rituals such as pouring water over images of the Buddha. Calendrical events such as the shortest day of the year, the longest day, the new moon, and the full moon often shape ritual cycles. *Nonperiodic rituals,* in contrast, occur irregularly, at unpredictable times, in response to unscheduled events such as a drought or flood, or to mark events in a person's life such as illness, infertility, birth, marriage, or death.

Life-Cycle Rituals

Belgian anthropologist Arnold van Gennep (1960 [1908]) first proposed the category of life-cycle rituals in 1909. A **life-cycle ritual**, or rite of passage, marks a change in status from one life stage to another of an individual or group. Victor Turner's (1969) fieldwork among the Ndembu, horticulturalists of northwestern Zambia (see Map 11.2, p. 294) provides insights about the phases of life-cycle rituals. Turner found that, among the Ndembu, and cross-culturally, life-cycle rituals have three phases: separation, transition, and reintegration.

In the first phase, the initiate (the person undergoing the ritual) is separated physically, socially, or symbolically from normal life. Special dress may mark the separation. In many cultures of the Amazon and in East and West Africa, adolescents are secluded for several years in separate huts or areas away from the village. The transition phase, or liminal phase, is the time when the person is no longer in the previous status but is not yet a member of the next stage. *Liminality* often involves the learning of specialized skills that will equip the person for the new

status. Reintegration, the last stage, occurs when the initiate emerges and is welcomed by the community in the new status.

Differences in the cross-cultural distribution of puberty rituals for boys and girls reflect the economic value and status of males and females (review material in Chapter 6). Most societies have some form of puberty ceremony for boys, but puberty ceremonies for girls are less common. In societies where female labor is important and valued, girls have elaborate, and sometimes painful, puberty rites (J. Brown 1978). Where their labor is not important, menarche is unmarked and there is no puberty

An Apache girl's puberty ceremony. Cross-cultural research indicates that the celebration of girls' puberty is more likely to occur in cultures in which adult women have valued productive and reproductive roles. ■ *Can you generate a hypothesis about why this is the case? How does this theory apply to your microcultural experience?* (Source: © CORBIS)

Millions of Muslim pilgrims every year do the Hajj to Mecca, in Saudi Arabia. The Hajj is one of the Five Pillars of Sunni Islam and is also important in Shi'a Islam. A person who has done the Hajj is referred to as a *hajji*, a term of honor. ■ (Source: © Reuters/CORBIS)

ceremony. Puberty rites function to socialize future members of the labor force, among other things. For example, among the Bemba of northern Zambia, during her initiation, a girl learns to distinguish forty different kinds of mushrooms and which are edible and which are poisonous.

Pilgrimage

Pilgrimage is round-trip travel to a sacred place or places for purposes of religious devotion or ritual. Prominent pilgrimage places are Varanasi in India (formerly called Banaras) for Hindus; Mecca in Saudi Arabia for Muslims; Bodh Gaya in India for Buddhists; Jerusalem in Israel for Jews, Christians, and Muslims; and Lourdes in France for Christians. Pilgrimage often involves hardship, with the implication that the more suffering that is involved, the more merit the pilgrim accumulates. Compared to a weekly trip to church or synagogue, pilgrimage removes a person further from everyday life, is more demanding, and therefore is potentially more transformative.

Victor Turner applied his three sequences of life-cycle rituals to pilgrimage: The pilgrim first separates from everyday life, then enters the liminal stage during the actual pilgrimage, and then returns to be reintegrated into society in a transformed state. A person who has gone on a certain pilgrimage often gains enhanced public status.

Rituals of Inversion

In some rituals, normal social roles and relations are temporarily inverted. A functionalist perspective says that these rituals allow for social pressure to be released. They also provide a reminder about the propriety of normal, everyday roles and practices to which people must return once the ritual is over.

Carnival (or *carnaval* in Brazil) is a **ritual of inversion** with roots in the northern Mediterranean region. It is celebrated widely throughout southern Europe and the Western Hemisphere. Carnival is a period of riotous celebration before the Christian fast of Lent. It begins at different times in different places, but always ends on Mardi Gras (or Shrove Tuesday), the day before the fasting period of Lent begins. The word *carnival* is derived from Latin and means "flesh farewell," referring to Lent.

In Bosa, a town in Sardegna (Sardinia), Italy (see Map 13.4), carnival involves several aspects of social-role reversal and relaxing of usual social norms. The discotheques extend their hours, mothers allow their daughters to stay out late, and men and women flirt with each other and fondle each other in the discotheques and during masquerades in ways that are forbidden during the rest of the year (Counihan 1985). Carnival in Bosa has three major phases. The first is impromptu street theater and masquerades that take place over several weeks, usually on Sundays. The skits are social critiques of current events and local happenings. In the masquerades, men dress up as exaggerated women:

> Young boys thrust their padded breasts forward with their hands while brassily hiking up their skirts to reveal their thighs. . . . A youth stuffs his shirt front with melons and holds them proudly out. . . . The high school gym teacher dresses as a nun and lifts up his habit to reveal suggestive red underwear. Two men wearing nothing but bikinis, wigs, and high heels feign a stripper's dance on a table top. (1985:15)

The second phase occurs during the morning of Mardi Gras, when hundreds of Bosans, mostly men, dress in black, like widows, and flood the streets. They accost passersby, shaking in their faces dolls and other objects that are maimed in some way or bloodied. They shriek

---

ritual of inversion: a ritual in which normal social roles and order are temporarily reversed.

sacrifice: a ritual in which something is offered to the supernaturals.

at the top of their lungs as if mourning, and they say, "Give us milk, milk for our babies. . . . They are dying, they are neglected, their mothers have been gallivanting since St. Anthony's Day and have abandoned their poor children" (1985:16). The third phase, called Giolzi, takes place during the evening. Men and women dress in white, wearing sheets for cloaks and pillow cases for hoods. They blacken their faces. Rushing into the street, they hold hands and chant the word *Giolzi*. They storm at people, pretending to search their bodies for Giolzi and then say, "Got it!" It is not clear what Giolzi is, but whatever it is, it represents something that makes everyone happy.

Elements of class inequality and global capitalism emerge as important in the celebration of carnival in the historic city center of Puebla, Mexico (Churchill 2006). This area was declared a UNESCO World Heritage Site in 1987. Since then, entrepreneurs have made several

MAP 13.4   Italy. Officially the Italian Republic, the country includes the mainland and two large islands. In 2006, Italy had the seventh-highest GDP in the world and is home to the largest number of UNESCO World Heritage Sites. A mountain system forms the backbone of the peninsula, and the climate varies according to altitude. Its population of nearly 60 million people makes it one of the most densely populated countries in Europe. Roman Catholicism is the dominant religion. Recent waves of immigration, especially from northern Africa, have increased the number of Muslims to perhaps 1 million. The official language is standard Italian, descended from the Tuscan dialect centered in Firenze. Cherished dialects exist throughout the country, and people in some northern border provinces speak dialects of German and French.

proposals to improve the area, which is mainly inhabited by working-class people living in crowded, low-rent housing. One project would convert much housing into hotels, restaurants, and tourist shops. The plan would have gone forward on the basis that no "traditional culture" existed in the barrios, or neighborhoods. Anthropological research, however, revealed much "traditional culture," especially the working-class celebration of carnival. Armed with the concept of *intangible cultural heritage*, residents campaigned to protect their neighborhoods from demolition and "development." In Puebla, the principal figure of carnival is the *huehue*, a working-class man who masquerades as a rich landowner. He wears a mask to disguise his identity, and prances through the streets, head thrown back, and kicking up his heels. The men who take time off from work to perform in carnival are sometimes in danger of losing their jobs. City administrators have attempted to take over the celebration and replace the huehue with floats and "dignified" events that they believe will be more acceptable to tourists. This story, as so many others, is still in flux, as is carnival itself in Puebla and elsewhere.

Sacrifice

Many rituals involve **sacrifice,** or the offering of something for transfer to the supernaturals. Sacrifice has a long history throughout the world and is probably one of the oldest forms of ritual. It may involve killing and offering animals; or making human offerings (of whole people, parts of a person's body, or even bloodletting); or offering vegetables, fruits, grains, flowers, or other products. Flowers may be symbolic replacements for former animal sacrifices (Goody 1993).

Spanish documents from the sixteenth century describe the Aztec practice of public sacrifice of humans and other animals to please the gods. The details are gory and involve cutting the heart from living beings so that the blood spurts forth (see Critical Thinking box).

Religious Specialists

Not all rituals require the presence of a religious specialist, or someone with extensive, formal training, but all require some level of knowledge on the part of the performer(s) about how to do them correctly. Even the daily, household veneration of an ancestor requires some knowledge gained through informal learning. At the other extreme, many rituals cannot be done without a highly trained specialist.

Shamans and Priests

General features of the categories of shaman and priest illustrate key differences between these two types of specialists (many other specialists fit somewhere in between).

WHY DID THE AZTECS PRACTICE HUMAN SACRIFICE AND CANNIBALISM?

Evidence of state-sponsored human sacrifice among the Aztecs of Mexico comes from accounts written by the Spanish conquistadors (Harris 1977, 1989; Sanday 1986). The Aztec gods required human sacrifice. They "ate" human hearts and "drank" human blood. Most of the victims were prisoners of war, but many others were slaves, and sometimes young men and women, and even children. There is more to the ritual than sheer death of the sacrificial victims. The archives report that the dead were also eaten.

The victims were marched up the steep steps of the pyramid, held lying on their backs over a stone altar, and slit open in the chest by a priest, who wrenched out the heart, still beating, which was then burned in offering to the gods. The gods were satisfied.

The body was rolled down the other side of the temple, where it was retrieved by butchers and prepared for cooking. The skull was returned to the temple area to be displayed. No one knows for sure how many victims were sacrificed, but estimates are in the hundreds of thousands. At a single site, one chronicler reported that the display racks contained more than 100,000 skulls (Harris 1977:106). At one especially grand event, victims to be sacrificed were arranged in four lines, each two miles long. Priests worked for four days to complete the sacrifices.

Human sacrifice and cannibalism of any scale invite the question, "Why?" This box compares two theoretical perspectives: an etic view and an emic view. First, Michael Harner (1977) and Marvin Harris (1977, 1989) propose an etic, cultural materialist explanation based on factors in the regional ecology and the politics of Aztec expansionism. They say that the Aztec empire lacked sufficient amounts of animal sources of protein to satisfy its growing population. The ruling classes managed to maintain their supply of delicacies, such as dog, turkey, duck, deer, rabbit, and fish, but little was available for the poor.

Yet the rulers needed to support and retain the loyalty of their army in order to protect and expand the empire's boundaries, and they needed to keep the masses happy. Providing the gods with human hearts and blood was a powerful statement of the empire's strength. It had the additional benefit of yielding huge amounts of meat for soldiers and commoners. Such "cannibal redistribution" could be manipulated by the state to reward particular groups and to compensate for periodic shortages in the agricultural cycle.

Peggy Sanday (1986) rejects the cultural materialist perspective of Harris and Harner. She provides an emic, interpretive view based on texts describing the Aztec people's rationale and motives. Sacrifice and cannibalism, she says, followed religious logic and symbolism. They were practiced to satisfy the gods' hunger, not human hunger. According to Aztec religion, the gods require blood sacrifices in order for the universe to continue to operate. Human flesh was consumed not as an "ordinary meal" but as part of a religious identification with the gods, just as people would wear the skins of sacrificed victims in order to participate in their sacredness. Sanday says that the etic explanation, in focusing on the "business" aspects of Aztec sacrifice and cannibalism, has overlooked the tradition's religious meaning for the Aztecs.

CRITICAL THINKING QUESTIONS

- How do the two explanations differ in the data they use?
- Which do you find more convincing, and why?
- What other explanations might apply to Aztec human sacrifice and cannibalism?

A *shaman,* or *shamanka* (the female form with the "-ka" ending derives from the original Siberian usage), is a part-time religious specialist who gains status through a direct relationship with the supernaturals, often by being "called." A potential shaman may be recognized by special signs, such as the ability to go into a trance. Anyone who demonstrates shamanic abilities can become a shaman; in other words, this is an openly available role.

---

priest/priestess: male or female full-time religious specialist whose position is based mainly on abilities gained through formal training.
world religion: a term coined in the nineteenth century to refer to religions that had many followers, that crossed state borders, and that exhibited other features such as a concern with salvation.
religious pluralism: when one or more religions co-exist as either complementary to each other or as competitive systems.
syncretism: the blending of features of two or more cultures, especially used in discussion of religious change.

Shamans are more often associated with nonstate societies, yet faith healers and evangelists of the United States could fit in this category. One of the most important functions of shamanic religious specialists is healing (review Chapter 7).

In states, the more complex occupational specialization in religion means that there is a wider variety of types of specialists, especially what anthropologists refer to as *priests* (not the same as the specific modern role of the Catholic priest) and promotes the development of religious hierarchies and power structures. The terms **priest** and **priestess** refer to a category of full-time religious specialists whose position is based mainly on abilities gained through formal training. A priest may receive a divine call, but more often the role is hereditary, passed on through priestly lineages. In terms of ritual performance, shamans are more involved with nonperiodic rituals. Priests perform a wider range of rituals, including periodic state rituals. In contrast to shamans, who rarely have secular power, priests and priestly lineages often do.

Other Specialists

Many other specialized religious roles exist cross-culturally. *Diviners* are specialists who are able to discover the will and wishes of the supernaturals through techniques such as reading animal entrails. Palm readers and tarot card readers fit into the category of diviners. *Prophets* are specialists who convey divine revelations usually gained through visions or dreams. They often possess charisma, an especially attractive and powerful personality, and may be able to perform miracles. Prophets have founded new religions, some long-lasting and others short-lived. *Witches* use psychic powers and affect people through emotion and thought. Mainstream society often condemns witchcraft as negative. Some scholars of ancient and contemporary witchcraft differentiate between positive forms that involve healing and negative forms that seek to harm people.

World Religions and Local Variations

The term **world religions** was coined in the nineteenth century to refer to religions with many followers that crossed country borders and had a concern with salvation (the belief that human beings require deliverance from an imperfect world). At that time, the term referred only to Christianity, Islam, and Buddhism. It was later expanded to include Judaism, Hinduism, Confucianism, Taoism, and Shintoism. Because of the global importance of the African diaspora that began with the European colonial slave trade, a sixth category of world religions is included here that describes key elements shared among the diversity of traditional African belief systems.

For many centuries, the world religions have traveled outside their original borders through intentional attempts to expand and gain converts or through migration of believers to new locales. European colonialism was a major force that led to the expansion of Christianity through the missionary work of Protestant sects. Now, the increased rate of population migration (Chapter 15) and the expansion of television and the Internet give even greater impetus to religious movement and change. The designation of only five world religions is increasingly inappropriate, because many religions cross state boundaries and have "world" reach.

Cultural anthropologists emphasize that no world religion exists as a single, homogeneous entity. Each comprises many local variants, raising a "predicament" for centrally organized religions in terms of how to maintain a balance between standardization based on core beliefs and the local variations (Hefner 1998).

This section first discusses the five traditional world religions in terms of their history, distribution, and basic teachings (see Figure 13.3). It then provides examples of variations in local cultural contexts. When a world religion moves into a new cultural region, it encounters indigenous religious traditions. In many cases, the incoming religion and local religions coexist as separate traditions, either as complements or competitors, in what is called **religious pluralism. In religious syncretism,** elements of two or more religions blend together. It is most likely to occur when aspects of two religions form a close match with each other. For example, if a local myth involves a hero who has something to do with snakes, there may be a syncretistic link with the Catholic belief in St. Patrick, who is believed to have driven snakes out of Ireland.

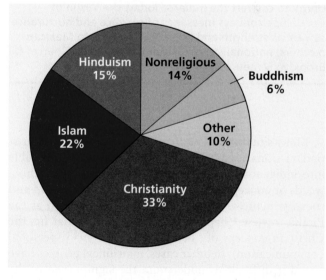

FIGURE 13.3 Population Distribution of Major World Religions

An early nineteenth-century painting of the Virgin of Guadalupe by Isidro Escamilla, a Mexican artist. The Virgin of Guadalupe, or Our Lady of Guadalupe, is Mexico's most popular image. Her depiction may involve syncretism with the indigenous Aztec goddess Tonantzin, part of a conscious strategy of Christian clergy to convert the Indians. Today, the Virgin of Guadalupe conveys messages of sacrifice and nurturance as well as strength and hope. She appeals to Mexican mothers, nationalists, and feminists alike. ■ (Source: © Brooklyn Museum of Art/CORBIS)

Many situations of nonfit can also be provided. Christian missionaries have had difficulty translating the Bible into indigenous languages because of lack of matching words or concepts, and because of differing kinship and social structures. Some Amazonian groups, such as the Pirahã (review Chapter 12), have no word that fits the Christian concept of "heaven" (Everett 1995, personal communication). In other cases, matrilineal peoples have found it difficult to understand the significance of the Christian construct of "god the father."

The two world religions that emphasize proselytizing, or seeking converts, are Christianity and Islam. Their encounters with indigenous religions have sometimes been violent, involving physical destruction of sacred places and objects (Corbey 2003). Common methods include burning, overturning, dismantling, or cutting up sacred objects, dumping them into rivers, and hiding them in caves. European Christian missionaries in the 1800s often confiscated sacred goods and shipped them to Europe for sale to private owners or museums. Both Christian and Islamic conversion efforts frequently involved the construction of their own places of worship on top of the original sacred site.

Hinduism

Around 900 million people in the world are Hindus. (*Note:* The population statistics for the world religions are rough averages derived from several Internet sources.) Most Hindus live in India, where Hinduism accounts for about 80 percent of the population. The other 20 percent live in the United States, Canada, the United Kingdom, Malaysia, Fiji, Trinidad, Guyana, and Hong Kong. A Hindu is born a Hindu, and Hinduism does not actively seek converts. The core texts of Hinduism are the four Vedas, which were composed in Sanskrit in northern India between 1200 and 900 BCE. Many other scholarly and popular texts and oral traditions exist to enrich the Hindu tradition, especially the *Mahabharata* (the story of a war between two lineages, the Pandavas and the Kauravas) and the *Ramayana* (the story of King Rama and his wife Sita). Throughout India, many local traditions exist, some of which contain elements from pre-Vedic times. Thus, Hinduism incorporates a diversity of ways to be a Hindu. It offers a rich polytheism and at the same time a philosophical tradition that reduces the multiplicity of deities into oneness.

Deities range from being a simple stone placed at the foot of a tree to elegantly carved and painted icons of gods such as Shiva, Vishnu, and the goddess Durga. Everyday worship of a deity involves lighting a lamp in front of the god, chanting hymns and mantras (sacred phrases), and taking *darshan* (sight of) the deity (Eck 1985). These acts bring blessings to the worshipper. Local variations of worship often involves deities and rituals unknown elsewhere. For example, firewalking is an important part of goddess worship in southern and eastern India (Freeman 1981; Hiltebeitel 1988) and among some Hindu groups living outside India, notably Fiji (C. Brown 1984).

Caste differences in beliefs and practices are also marked, even within the same village. Lower-caste deities prefer offerings of meat sacrifices and alcohol, whereas upper-caste deities prefer flowers, rice, and fruit. Yet, the "unity in diversity" of Hinduism has long been recognized as real, mainly because of the shared acceptance of at least some elements of Vedic thought.

A Nayar Fertility Ritual

The matrilineal Nayars of Kerala, South India (see Map 16.2, p. 420), perform a nonperiodic ritual as a remedy for the curse of the serpent deities who cause infertility in women (Neff 1994). This ritual illustrates the unity of Hinduism in several ritual elements: the use of a camphor flame and incense, the importance of serpent deities, and offering flowers to the deity. But locally specific elements arise from the matrilineal cultural context of Kerala.

The all-night ritual includes, first, women painting a sacred design of intertwined serpents on the floor. Several hours of worshipping the deity follow with the camphor flame, incense, and flowers. Music comes from drumming, cymbals, and singing. The presence of the deity is fully achieved when one of the women goes into a trance. Through her, matrilineal family members may speak to the deity and be blessed.

Among the Nayars, a woman's mother, mother's brothers, and brothers are responsible for ensuring that her desires for motherhood are fulfilled. They share her interest in continuing the matrilineage. What the women say during the trance is important. They typically draw attention to family disharmonies or neglect of the deities. This message diverts blame from the infertile woman for whom the ritual is being held. It reminds family and lineage members of their responsibilities for each other.

Hindu Women and Karma in Northern England

One of Hinduism's basic concepts is *karma*, translated as "destiny" or "fate." A person's karma is determined at birth on the basis of his or her previous life and how it was conducted. The karma concept has prompted many outsiders to judge Hindus as fatalistic, lacking a sense of agency. But anthropological research on how people actually think about karma in their everyday lives reveals much individual variation from fatalism to a strong sense of being in charge of one's destiny. One study looked at women's perceptions of karma among Hindus living in the city of Leeds, northern England (Knott 1996) (see Map 13.2, p. 345). Some of the women are fatalistic in their attitudes and behavior. One woman who had a strongly fatalistic view of karma said,

> When a baby's born . . . we have a ritual on the sixth day. That's when you name the baby, you know. And on that day, we believe the goddess comes and writes your future . . . we leave a blank white paper and a pen and we just leave it [overnight]. . . . So I believe that my future— whatever happens—is what she has written for me. That

Celebration of Holi, a spring festival popular among Hindus worldwide. In this scene in New Delhi, a young woman sprays colored water on a young man as part of the joyous event. The deeper meaning of Holi is tied to a myth about a demon. ■ *How is the arrival of spring marked in your microculture?* (Source: © AFP/CORBIS)

tells me [that] I have to do what I can do, and if I have a mishap in between I have to accept that. (1996:24)

Another woman said that her sufferings were caused by the irresponsibility of her father and the "bad husband" to whom she had been married. She challenged her karma and left her husband: "I could not accept the karma of being with Nirmal [her husband]. If I had done so, what would have become of my children?" (1996:25). Because Hindu women's karma dictates being married and having children, leaving one's husband is a major act of resistance.

Options for women seeking support when questioning or changing their karmic roles can be religious, such as praying more and fasting, or they can be secular, such as seeking the advice of a psychological counselor or social worker. Some Hindu women in England have become counselors, working in support of other women's independence and self-confidence. They illustrate how human agency can work against traditional religious rules.

Buddhism

Buddhism originated in a founding figure, Siddhartha Gautama (ca. 566–486 BCE), revered as the Buddha, or Awakened One (Eckel 1995:135). It began in northern India, where the Buddha grew up. From there, it spread throughout the subcontinent, into inner Asia and China, to Sri Lanka, and on to Southeast Asia. In the past 200 years, Buddhism has spread to Europe and North America. Buddhism's popularity subsequently faded in India, and Buddhists now constitute less than 1 percent of India's population. Its global spread is matched by a great diversity of doctrine and practice, to the extent that it is difficult to point to a single essential feature other than the importance of Gautama Buddha. No single text is accepted as authoritative for all forms of Buddhism. Many Buddhists worship the Buddha as a deity, but others do not. Instead, they honor his teachings and follow the pathway he suggested for reaching *nirvana,* or release from worldly life. The total number of Buddhists worldwide is around 400 million.

Buddhism arose as a protest against Hinduism, especially caste inequality, but it retained and revised several Hindu concepts, such as karma. In Buddhism, everyone has the potential for achieving nirvana (enlightenment and the overcoming of human suffering in this life), the ultimate goal of Buddhism. Good deeds are one way to achieve a better rebirth with each incarnation, until finally, release from *samsara* (the cycle of birth, reincarnation, death, and so on) is achieved. Compassion toward others, including animals, is a key virtue. Branches of Buddhism have different texts that they consider their canon. The major division is between the Theravada Buddhism practiced in Southeast Asia and the Mahayana Buddhism of Tibet, China, Taiwan, Korea, and Japan. Buddhism is associated with a strong tradition of monasticism through which monks and nuns renounce the everyday world and spend their lives meditating and doing good works. Buddhists have many and varied annual festivals and rituals. Some events bring pilgrims from around the world to Sarnath, near Varanasi, North

India, where the Buddha gave his first teaching, and to Gaya, where he gained enlightenment.

Local Spirits and Buddhism in Southeast Asia

Wherever Buddhism exists outside India, it is never the exclusive religion of the devotees because it arrived to find established local religions already in place (Spiro 1967). In Myanmar, Buddhism and indigenous traditions coexist without one being dominant (see Map 6.4, p. 163). Indigenous beliefs remained strong because they offer a way of dealing with everyday problems. According to Buddhism in Myanmar, a person's karma (as in Hinduism) is a result of previous births and determines his or her present condition. If something bad happens, the person can do little but suffer through it.

Indigenous supernaturalism, on the other hand, says that the bad thing happened because of the actions of capricious spirits called *nats.* Ritual actions can combat the influence of nats. In other words, nats can be dealt with, but karma cannot. The continuity of belief in nats can be seen as an example of human agency and creativity. People kept what was important to them from their traditional beliefs but also adopted aspects of the new religion.

Buddhism, however, became an important cultural force and the basis for social integration in Myanmar. One village, for example, had three Buddhist monasteries, with four resident Buddhist monks and several temporary monks. Every male child was ordained as a temporary member of the monastic order. Almost every villager observed Buddhist holy days. Although Buddhism is held to be the supreme truth, the spirits retain control when it comes to dealing with everyday problems such as a toothache or a monetary loss.

Other studies of religion in Southeast Asia provide examples in which there is more thorough blending of local religions with Buddhism (see Everyday Anthropology box).

Judaism

The first Judaic religious system was defined around 500 BCE, following the destruction of the Temple in Jerusalem by the Babylonians in 586 BCE (Neusner 1995). The early writings, called the Pentateuch, established the theme of exile and return as a paradigm for Judaism that endures today. The Pentateuch is also called the Five Books of Moses, or the Torah. Followers of Judaism share in the belief in the Torah as the revelation of God's truth through Israel, a term for the "holy people." The Torah explains the relationship between the supernatural and human realms and guides people in how to carry out the worldview through appropriate actions. A key feature of

Buddhism gained an established footing in Japan in the eighth century. The city of Nara was an important early center of Buddhism. Here, an emperor sponsored the casting of a huge bronze statue of the Buddha. ■ *Is there a Buddhist temple where you live? If so, have you visited it? If not, find out where the nearest one is, and visit it if possible.* (Source: Jack Heaton)

Everyday Anthropology

TATTOOS AND SACRED POWER

Fieldwork among Shan people in Thailand (see Map 6.4, p. 163) reveals the importance of tattooing, a tradition shared with much of Southeast Asia (Tannenbaum 1987). Shan tattooing blends aspects of Buddhism with local spirit beliefs and even elements of Hinduism as practiced by some groups in neighboring Myanmar.

The Shan have three general classes of tattoos:

- Tattoos that act on other people, causing them to like or fear the bearer, and that cause the spirits to be kind
- Tattoos that act on the bearer, increasing the bearer's skill
- Tattoos that create a barrier around the person that prevents animals from biting, knives from cutting, and bullets from entering the body

Tattoos are done in two colors—red and blue/black. The first two types tend to be done in red; the third type tends to be done in blue/black. Different designs are associated with each type. For example, the two-tailed lizard is a common tattoo in the first type.

The first type of tattoo is popular among many people, because it brings health to the bearer. It is the main type among women, used for illness prevention as well as for curing an illness. A person who falls ill may get a tattoo incorporating a letter of the Shan alphabet in the design, either on the calf, around a body joint, around the mouth, or on the top of the tongue. Some of the most powerful designs in this category are placed on the back or over the heart. The most powerful tattoo in this category, called the Five Buddha tattoo, is not allowed for women. Men who get this tattoo have to follow five Buddhist precepts at all times: refrain from killing, stealing, improper sexual behavior, lying, and intoxication. This tattoo is red, but it also includes exfoliated skin from a Buddhist monk. That makes this tattoo different from all others and makes its bearer like a monk. Whereas most tattoos in the first category cause other

people to look favorably on the bearer, the Five Buddha tattoo inspires fear and awe.

Tattoos in the second category, worn by men, are all related to words. Some increase people's memory and help them on exams. Others strengthen a person's speaking ability. The most powerful tattoos in this group give a person such great verbal skills that he or she can intimidate others. They increase courage as well. One tattoo in this category is the Saraswati tattoo, which depicts, among other things, the head of Saraswati, the Hindu goddess of knowledge, on the bearer's right shoulder. To call on Saraswati for help, the person brushes his or her lips on the tattoo.

The third category of tattoos, those that provide a protective barrier, has one subset that prevents bites from insects, snakes, dogs, cats, tigers, and so on. If the person has the tattoo and gets bitten nonetheless, the tattoo helps reduce the pain. A general anti-bite tattoo is a cat on the lower arm. More powerful tattoos in this third category protect people from weapons. They seal off the body. A person should be careful not to get too many of these tattoos, however, because they seal the body off completely and therefore prevent good fortune from entering it. Someone with many of these tattoos is likely to be poor or unlucky.

The Shan people do not question why or how their tattoos work. They simply believe that they do. They blend what anthropologists classify as magic with religious beliefs from Buddhism and Hinduism, in the case of the Saraswati tattoo. Sacred power is the key that links all these beliefs together into a coherent system for the Shan.

FOOD FOR THOUGHT

- What do people in your microculture do to get people to like them, to succeed on exams, and to protect the body from harmful intrusions?

all forms of Judaism is the identification of what is wrong with the present and how to escape, overcome, or survive that situation. Jewish life is symbolically interpreted as a tension between exile and return, given its foundational myth in the exile of the Jews from Israel and their period of slavery in Egypt.

Judaism is monotheistic, teaching that God is one, unique, and all powerful. Humans have a moral duty to follow Jewish law, to protect and preserve life and health, and to follow certain duties, such as observing the Sabbath. The high regard for human life is reflected in the general opposition to abortion within Jewish law and in

The Kotel, or Western Wall, in Jerusalem is a sacred place of pilgrimage, especially for Jews. Men pray at a section marked off on the left, women at the area on the right. Both men and women should cover their heads, and when leaving the wall area, women should take care to keep their faces toward it and avoid turning their backs to it. ■ *Think of some behavioral rules at another sacred place you know.* (Source: Barbara Miller)

on this hill. Later, King Solomon built the First Temple here in the middle of the tenth century BCE. It was destroyed by Nebuchadnessar in 587 BCE, when the Jews were led into captivity in Babylon. Around 500 BCE, King Herod built the Second Temple on the same site. The Kotel is a remnant of the Second Temple. Jews of all

opposition to the death penalty. Words, both spoken and written, are important in Judaism. There is an emphasis on truth telling in life and on the use of established literary formulas at precise times during worship. These formulas are encoded in a *sidur*, or prayer book. Dietary patterns distinguish Judaism from other religions; for example, rules of kosher eating forbid the mixing of milk or milk products with meat.

Contemporary varieties of Judaism range from conservative Hasidism to Reform Judaism, which emerged in the early 1800s. One difference between these two perspectives concerns the question of who is Jewish. Jewish law traditionally defined a Jewish person as someone born of a Jewish mother. In contrast, reform Judaism recognizes as Jewish the offspring of a Jewish father and a non-Jewish mother. Currently, the Jewish population numbers about 15 million worldwide, with about half living in North America, a quarter in Israel, and 20 percent in Europe and Russia. Smaller populations are scattered across the globe.

Who's Who at the Kotel

The most sacred place to all Jews is the Kotel, or Western Wall in Jerusalem (see Map 13.5). Since the 1967 war, which brought Jerusalem under Israeli rule, the Kotel has been the most important religious shrine and pilgrimage site of Israel. The Kotel is located at one edge of the Temple Mount (or Haram Sharif), an area sacred to Jews, Muslims, and Christians. According to Jewish scriptures, God asked Abraham to sacrifice his son Isaac

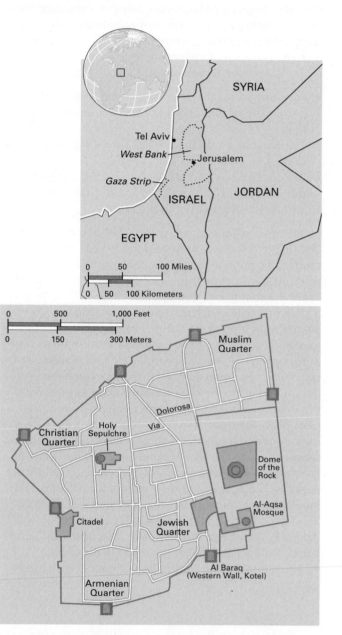

MAP 13.5 Sacred Sites in the Old City of Jerusalem, Israel. Jerusalem is the holiest city of Judaism, the third holiest city of Islam, and holy to some Christian denominations. The section called the Old City is surrounded by walls that have been built, razed, relocated, and rebuilt over several hundred years. The Old City contains four quarters: Armenian, Christian, Jewish, and Muslim, and many sacred sites such as the Kotel and the Via Dolorosa.

varieties and non-Jews come to the Kotel in vast numbers from around the world. The Kotel plaza is open to everyone, pilgrims and tourists. The wall is made of massive rectangular stones weighing between two and eight tons each. At its base is a synagogue area partitioned into men's and women's sections.

This single site brings together a variety of Jewish worshippers and secular visitors. The great diversity among the visitors is evident in the various styles of dress and gesture:

> The Hasid . . . with a fur shtreimel on his head may enter the synagogue area alongside a man in shorts who utilizes a cardboard skullcap available for "secular" visitors. American youngsters in jeans may ponder Israeli soldiers of their own age, dressed in uniform, and wonder what their lot might have been if they [had been] born in another country. Women from Yemen, wearing embroidered trousers under their dresses, edge close to the Wall as do women accoutred in contemporary styles whose religiosity may have been filtered through a modern education. . . . (Storper-Perez and Goldberg 1994:321)

In spite of plaques that state the prohibition against begging, beggars offer to "sell a blessing" to visitors. They may remind visitors that it was the poor who built the wall in the first place. Another category of people is young Jewish men who, in search of prospective "born again" Jews, "hang around" looking for a "hit" (in their words). Most of the hits are young Americans who are urged to take their Jewishness more seriously and, if male, to be sure to marry a Jewish woman. Other regulars are Hebrew-speaking men who are available to organize a prayer service. One of the most frequent forms of religious expression at the Kotel is the insertion of written prayers into the crevices of the wall.

The social heterogeneity of the Jewish people is thus transcended in a single space, creating some sense of what Victor Turner (1969) called *communitas,* a sense of collective unity out of individual diversity.

Passover in Kerala

The Jews of the Kochi area (formerly called Cochin) of Kerala, South India, have lived there for about 1,000 years (Katz and Goldberg 1989) (see Map 16.2, p. 420). The Maharaja of Kochi had respect for the Jewish people, who were mainly merchants. He relied on them for external trade and contacts. In recognition of this, he allowed a synagogue, which is still standing, to be built next to his palace. Syncretism is apparent in Kochi Jewish lifestyle, social structure, and rituals. Basic aspects of Judaism are retained, along with adoption of many aspects of Hindu practices.

Three aspects of syncretism with Hinduism are apparent in passover, one of the most important annual rituals of the Jewish faith. First, the Western/European passover celebration is typically joyous and a time of feasting. In contrast, the Kochi version has adopted a tone of austerity and is called "the fasting feast." Second, Kochi passover allows no role for children, whereas at a traditional seder (ritual meal) children usually ask four questions as a starting point of the narrative. The Kochi Jews chant the questions in unison. (In Hinduism, children do not have solo roles in rituals.) Third, a Kochi seder stresses purity even more than standard Jewish requirements. Standard rules about maintaining the purity of kosher wine usually mean that no gentile (non-Jew) should touch it. But Kochi Jews expand the rule to say that if the shelf or table on which the wine sits is touched by a gentile, the wine is impure. This extra level of "contagion" is influenced by Hindu concepts of pollution.

Christianity

Christianity has many ties with Judaism, from which it sprang, especially in terms of the Biblical teachings of a coming savior, or *messiah* (annointed one). It began in the eastern Mediterranean in the second quarter of the first century (Cunningham 1995:240–253). Most of the early believers were Jews who took up the belief in Jesus Christ as the messiah who came to earth in fulfillment of prophesies contained in the Hebrew scriptures. Today, Christianity is the largest of the world religions, with about 2 billion adherents, roughly one-third of the world's population. It is the majority religion of Australia, New Zealand, the Philippines, Papua New Guinea, most countries of Europe and of North and South America, and about a dozen southern African countries. Christianity is a minority religion throughout Asia, but Asian Christians constitute 16 percent of the world's total Christians and are thus a significant population.

Christians accept the Bible (Old and New Testaments) as containing the basic teachings of their faith, believe that a supreme God sent His son to earth as a sacrifice for the welfare of humanity, and look to Jesus as the model to follow for moral guidance. The three largest branches of Christianity are Roman Catholic, Protestant, and Eastern Orthodox. Within each of these branches, various denominations exist. Christianity has existed the longest in the Middle East and Mediterranean regions. In contemporary times, the greatest growth in Christianity is occurring in sub-Saharan Africa, parts of India, and Indonesia. It is currently experiencing a resurgence in Eastern Europe.

Protestantism among White Appalachians

Studies of protestantism in Appalachia describe local traditions that outsiders who are accustomed to standard, urban versions may view as "deviant." For example, some churches in rural West Virginia and North Carolina, called Old Regulars, practice three obligatory rit-

The Vatican in Rome *(left)*. The Vatican attracts more pilgrims/visitors each year than any religious site in the world. In the nearby neighborhood *(right)*, shops cater to pilgrims/visitors by offering a variety of religious and secular goods. ■ (Sources: Barbara Miller and Bernard Wood)

uals: footwashing, communion (a ritual commemorating the "Last Supper" that Jesus had with his disciples), and baptism (Dorgan 1989). The footwashing ceremony occurs once a year in conjunction with communion, usually as an extension of the Sunday service. An elder is called to the front of the church, and he preaches for ten to twenty minutes. A round of handshaking and embracing follows. Two deaconesses then come forward to "prepare the table" by uncovering the sacramental elements placed there earlier under a white tablecloth. The elements are unleavened bread, serving plates for the bread, cups for the wine, and a decanter or quart jar or two of wine. The deacons break the bread into pieces and the moderator pours the wine into the cups. Men and women form separate groups as the deacons serve the bread and wine. The deacons serve each other, and then it is time for the footwashing.

The moderator begins by quoting from the New Testament (John 13:4): "He riseth from supper, and laid aside his garments; and he took a towel and girded himself." The moderator takes a towel and basin from the communion table, puts water in it, and selects a senior elder and removes his shoes and socks. The moderator washes his feet slowly and attentively. Other members come forward and take towels and basins and take turns washing other's feet and having their feet washed. Soon "the church is filled with crying, shouting, and praising as these highly poignant exchanges unleash a flood of emotions" (1989:106). A functional interpretation of the ritual of footwashing is that it helps maintain social cohesion.

Another feature of worship in some small, Protestant churces in Appalachia, especially remote areas of rural West Virginia, involves the handling of poisonous snakes. This practice finds legitimation in the New Testament (Daugherty 1997 [1976]). According to a passage in Mark (16:15–18), "In my name shall they cast out devils; they shall speak with new tongues;

THINKING OUTSIDE THE BOX

VISIT THE Vatican website and explore the Vatican's position on the "DaVinci code" phenomenon.

they shall take up serpents; and if they drink any deadly thing, it shall not hurt them; they shall lay hands on the sick, and they shall recover." Members of "Holiness-type" churches believe that the handling of poisonous snakes is the supreme act of devotion to God. Biblical literalists, these people choose serpent handling as their way of celebrating life, death, and resurrection and of proving that only Jesus has the power to deliver them from death. Most serpent handlers have been bitten many times, but few have died.

One interpretation says that the risks of handling poisonous snakes mirror the risks of the environment. Rates of unemployment are high and many people are economically poor. The anthropological view about the importance of structure (Chapter 1) points to the fact that serpent handling increased when local people lost their land rights to big mining and forestry companies (Tidball and Toumey 2003:4). As their lives became more economically insecure, they turned to a way of increasing their sense of stability through a dramatic religious ritual. Outsiders might ask whether such dangerous ritual practices indicate that the people are psychologically disturbed. Psychological tests indicate that members of Holiness churches are more emotionally

A celebration of the Christian holy day of Palm Sunday in Port-au-Prince, Haiti. European colonialism brought African slaves to the "New World" and to Christianity through missionary efforts. Many forms of Christianity are now firmly established in the Caribbean region. ■ *Discover through a website or other source what the major Christian denominations in Haiti are.* (Source: Edward Keller III)

healthy, on average, than members of mainline Protestant churches.

Recent newspaper and television coverage of serpent handling sensationalizes these religious practices. In doing so, it adds a secular avenue to economic success for some of the most famous serpent handlers. One pastor, for example, got a better job offer from a coal mining company, which allowed him and his family to purchase a new house and car (Tidball and Toumey 2003:10).

The Last Supper in Fiji

Among Christians in Fiji (see Map 1.6, p. 26), the image of the "Last Supper" is a dominant motif (Toren 1988). This scene, depicted on tapestry hangings, adorns most churches and many houses. People say, "Christ is the head of this household, he eats with us and overhears us" (1988:697). The image's popularity is the result of its fit with Fijian notions of communal eating and kava drinking. Seating rules at such events place the people of highest status, such as the chief and others close to him, at the "above" side of the room, away from the entrance. Others sit at the "lower" end, facing the highly ranked people. Intermediate positions are located on either side of the person of honor, in ranked order.

Da Vinci's rendition of the Last Supper places Jesus Christ in the position of a chief, with the disciples in an ordered arrangement around him. "The image of an ordered and stratified society exemplified in people's positions relative to one another around the kava bowl

is encountered virtually every day in the village" (1988: 706). The disciples and the viewers "face" the chief and eat and drink together, as is appropriate in Fijian society.

Islam

Islam is based on the teachings of the prophet Muhammad (570–632) and is thus the youngest of the world religions (Martin 1995:498–513). The Arabic word *Islam* means "submission" to the will of the one god, Allah, through which peace will be achieved. Followers of Islam, known as Muslims, believe that Muhammad was God's final prophet. Islam has several denominations with essentially similar beliefs but also distinct theological and legal approaches. The two major schools of thought are Sunni and Shi'a. Sunnis are about 85 percent

The Hassan II Mosque was built for the sixtieth birthday of Morocco's previous king, Hassan II. It is the largest religious monument in the world, after Mecca, with space for 25,000 worshippers inside and another 80,000 outside. The minaret, 210 meters in height, is the tallest in the world. ■ (Source: Jack Heaton)

Culturama

Hui Muslims of Xi'an, China

The Hui, one of China's largest designated minorities, number around 10 million people. Most live in the northwestern part of the country. The state classifies the Hui as "backward" and "feudal" in comparison to China's majority Han population. Hui residents of Xi'an, however, reject the official characterization of them as less civilized and less modern than the Han majority (Gillette 2000).

About 60,000 Hui live in Xi'an, mainly in the so-called Old Muslim Area, which is dominated by small shops, restaurants, and mosques. The quality of housing and public services is inferior to that found elsewhere in the city. Parents worry that their children are not getting the best education and feel that the state is not providing adequate schooling in their neighborhood. Many Hui have taken steps to improve their houses themselves and to send their children to schools outside the district.

The Hui of Xi'an construct what they consider to be a modern and civilized lifestyle by choosing aspects of Muslim culture and Western culture. Their form of "progress" is visible in many aspects of their daily life, such as eating habits, dress styles, housing, religious practices, education, and family organization.

Being Muslim in China poses several challenges in relation to the dominant Han culture. Diet is one prominent example. The Qu'ran forbids four types of food to Muslims: animals that have not been consecrated to God and properly slaughtered, blood, pork, and alcohol (Gillette 2000:116). Three of the four rules apply to meat, and meat is the central part of a proper meal for Muslims. The Hui say that pork is especially impure. This belief differentiates the Hui clearly from other Chinese people for whom pork is a major food item. Given the Hui belief that the kinds of food one eats affect a person's essence and behavior, they view pork eaters with disdain.

Hui residents consider alcohol even more impure than pork (Gillette 2000:167). Hui of Xi'an do not drink alcohol. They avoid using utensils that have touched alcohol and people who are drinking it. Many Hui of Xi'an, however, make a living in the restaurant business, which caters to Chinese Han and foreign tourists. While selling alcohol boosts business, many Hui object to it. Several Hui formed the Anti-alcohol Committee to advocate for banning the sale of alcohol in restaurants in the Hui quarter and preventing customers from bringing their own alcohol. Some areas of the market section are alcohol-free zones. Committee members say that restricting alcohol has improved the quality of life by making the neighborhood more peaceful and orderly.

In 2003, an urban development project in the Old Muslim Quarter was launched with financial support from the Norwegian government (*People's Daily* 2003). The project will widen the main street, replace "shabby" housing and infrastructure, and restore crumbling buildings of historic interest. A commercial area will be dedicated to restaurants serving Hui food in recognition of the touristic appeal of traditional Hui specialties such as baked beef and mutton, buns with beef, mutton pancake, and mutton soup. It is unclear where alcohol consumption will fit into this plan.

Reading

Maris Boyd Gillette. *Between Mecca and Beijing: Modernization and Consumption among Urban Chinese Families.* Stanford, CA: Stanford University Press, 2000.

Thanks to Maris Boyd Gillette, Haverford College, for reviewing this material.

At a street stand in Xi'an (left), Hui men prepare and sell a noodle dish. Like Muslim men in many parts of the world, they wear a white cap. ■ (Source: Eddie Gerald/Alamy) *Hui women in Xi'an (right) participate in a ritual that commemorates Hui people who died in a massive conflict that spread across northwest China from 1862 to 1874.* ■ (Source: Maris Boyd Gillette)

MAP 13.6 *The City of Xi'an in China. Xi'an, the capital of Shaanxi province, is one of the most economically developed cities in the northwestern part of China.*

of the total Muslim population worldwide, with Shi'as about 15 percent. Sufism is a more mystical variant, with much smaller numbers of adherents. Many other sub-groups exist.

The Five Pillars of Islam are profession of faith in Allah, daily prayer, fasting, contributing alms for the poor, and pilgrimage to Mecca (the *Hajj*). They are central to Sunni Islam but less so to other branches of Islam such as the Shi'as and the Sufis.

The total number of Muslims worldwide is about 1.4 billion, making it the second largest religion. Muslim-majority nations are located in northern Africa; the Middle East, including Afghanistan, Pakistan, and Bangladesh in South Asia; and several nations in Central Asia and Southeast Asia. Most of the world's Muslims (60 percent) live in South Asia or Southeast Asia. Muslims live as minorities in many other countries, including China, where they seek to maintain their religious practices (see Culturama). Although Islam originally flourished among pastoralists, only 2 percent of its adherents now are in that category.

A common and inaccurate stereotype of Islam among many non-Muslims is that wherever it exists, it is the same. This erroneously monolithic model tends to be based on an image of conservative Wahhabist Islam as practiced in Saudi Arabia. It is only one of many "Islams." A comparison of Islam in highland Sumatra, Indonesia, and Morocco, North Africa, reveals differences that are the result of local cultural adaptations (Bowen 1992). Eid-ul-Adha, or the Feast of Sacrifice, is celebrated annually by Muslims around the world. It commemorates Ibrahim's willingness to sacrifice his son Ishmael (Isaac in Christian and Jewish traditions) to Allah. It occurs on

the tenth of the last month of the year, called Pilgrimage Month and marks the end of the Hajj. The ritual reminds Muslims of their global unity within the Islamic faith.

An important aspect of this ritual in Morocco (see Map 5.3, p. 127) involves the king publicly plunging a dagger into a ram's throat, a reenactment of Muhammad's performance of the sacrifice on the same day in the seventh century. Each male head of household follows the pattern and sacrifices a ram. Size and virility of the ram are a measure of the man's power and virility. Other men of the household stand to witness the sacrifice, while women and children are absent or in the background. After the ram is killed, the men come forward and dab its blood on their faces. In some villages, women play a more prominent role before the sacrifice by daubing the ram with henna (red dye), thus sanctifying it, and using its blood afterward in rituals to protect the household. These state and household rituals are symbolic of male power in the public and private domains—the power of the monarchy and the power of patriarchy.

In Isak, Sumatra (see Map 8.3, p. 209), the cultural context is less patriarchal and the political structure does not emphasize monarchy. Isak is a traditionalist Muslim village where people have been Muslims since the seventeenth century. They sacrifice many kinds of animals: chickens, ducks, sheep, goats, and water buffalo. The people believe that so long as the animal's throat is cut and the meat is eaten, the sacrifice satisfies God. Most sacrifices are family affairs and receive little public notice. They are done in the back of the house. Both women and men of the household refer to it as "their" sacrifice, and there are no signs of male dominance. Women may sponsor a sacrifice, as did one wealthy woman trader who sacrificed a buffalo (the cutting was done by a man).

The Moroccan ritual emphasizes fathers and sons, whereas the Isak ritual includes attention to a wider range of kin on both the husband's and wife's side, daughters as well as sons, and even dead relatives. In Isak, the ritual carries no centralized political meanings. The differences are not due to the fact that Moroccans know the scriptures better than Sumatrans do. The Isak area has many Islamic scholars who are familiar with the scriptures and regularly discuss them with each other. Rather, the two cultural contexts, including kinship and politics, shape the ritual to local realities.

African Religions

Many African religions are global. In earlier centuries, they spread outside Africa through the coerced movement of people as slaves. African diaspora religions are especially prominent in the United States, the Caribbean region, and Central and South America. This section summarizes some key features of African religions and

A sacred altar in a local African religion in Togo, West Africa. ■ *Can you distinguish some of the ritual elements displayed here? Are some incomprehensible to you? How would an anthropologist begin to learn about the beliefs involved in this religion?* (Source: © Gerd Ludwig/Woodfin Camp & Associates)

then offers two examples of African religions in the Western Hemisphere.

Features of African Religions

With its diverse geography, cultural variation, and history, Africa encompasses a wide range of religious affiliations, including many Muslims, Christians, Jews, Hindus, practitioners of indigenous religions, and people who follow some combination of these.

Indigenous African religions are difficult to typify, but some of their shared features are:

- Myths about a rupture that once occurred between the creator deity and humans
- A pantheon that includes a high god and many secondary supernaturals ranging from powerful gods to lesser spirits
- Elaborate initiation rituals
- Rituals involving animal sacrifices and other offerings, meals, and dances
- Altars within shrines as focal places where humans and deities meet
- Close links with healing

Although these features are fairly constant, African religions are rethought and reshaped locally and over time with complex and variable results (Gable 1995). In their home locations, they have been influenced by foreign religions, notably Islam and various types of Christianity. The out-migration of African peoples has brought African religions to new locations where they have been localized in their new contexts and also revitalized (Clarke 2004). Kamari Clarke's research on the Yorùbá revivalist religion in the United States took her from New York City to South Carolina and Nigeria. The focal point of her fieldwork was in Ọ̀yọ̀túnjí Village near Beaufort, South Carolina (see Map 14.3, p. 387). African American Yorùbá revivalists have created a place that reconstructs royal Yorùbá spiritual leadership and worship that helps some African Americans reconnect with their lost identity. In the words of Kamari Clarke, "Ritual initiations and rhythmic drumming echo in the endless hours of the night as residents remake their ancestral homeland outside the territory of Africa" (2004:51). The place, the rituals, and the music tie the people to Africa. Many Yorùbá-descent Americans, like other African Americans, go even further in their attempt to reconnect with their heritage. "Roots tourism" is a growing industry that provides culturally informed travel for African Americans to their places of ancestral origin in Africa.

Many religious syncretisms in North and South America combine African traditions with aspects of Christianity, indigenous Indian religions, and other traditions. Widely popular in Brazil are Afro-Brazilian religions such as *umbanda*, *santería*, and *condomblé* that appeal to people of all social classes, urban and rural, especially for providing social support and alleviation of stress (refer to photo on p. 180) (Burdick 2004).

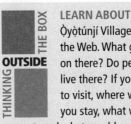

OUTSIDE THE BOX / THINKING

LEARN ABOUT Ọ̀yọ̀túnjí Village from the Web. What goes on there? Do people live there? If you went to visit, where would you stay, what would you eat, and what would you do?

Ras Tafari

Also called Rastafarianism, Ras Tafari is an Afro-Caribbean religion with its original roots in Jamaica. It is not known how many Rastafarians there are because they refuse to be counted (Smith 1995:23). Ras Tafari is an unorthodox, protest religion that shares only a few of the features of African religions just mentioned. It traces its history to several preachers of the early twentieth century who taught that Ras ("Prince") Tafari, then the Ethiopian emperor Haile Selassie, was the "Lion of Judah" who would lead Blacks to the African promised land.

Rastafarianism does not have an organized set of doctrines or written texts. Shared beliefs of the many diffuse groups in the Caribbean, the United States, and Europe include the belief that Ethiopia is heaven on earth, that Haile Selassie is a living god, and that all Blacks will be able to return to the homeland through his help. Since the death of Haile Selassie in 1975, more emphasis has been placed on pan-African unity and Black power, and less on Ethiopia.

Rastafarianism is particularly strong in Jamaica, where it is associated with reggae music, dreadlocks, and *ganja* (marijuana) smoking. Variations within the Rastafarian movement in Jamaica range from beliefs that one must fight oppression to the position that living a peaceful life brings victory against evil.

Directions of Religious Change

All religions have established mythologies and doctrines that provide for continuity in beliefs and practices. Yet

---

revitalization movement: a religious movement, usually organized by a prophetic leader, that seeks to construct a more satisfying situation by reviving all or parts of a religion that has been threatened by outside forces or by adopting new practices and beliefs.

cargo cult: a form of revitalization movement that emerged in Melanesia and New Zealand, in response to Western and Japanese influences.

nowhere are religions frozen and unchanging. Cultural anthropologists have traced the resurgence of religions that seemed to have been headed toward extinction through colonial forces, and they have documented the emergence of seemingly new religions. Likewise, they are observing the contemporary struggle of once-suppressed religions in socialist states to find a new position in the postsocialist world. Religious icons (carvings or other artistic renderings of Mary, for example), once a prominent feature in Russian Orthodox churches, had been removed and placed in museums. Now, the churches want them back.

Indigenous people's beliefs about the sacredness of their land are an important part of their attempts to protect their territory from encroachment and development by outside commercial interests. The world of religious change offers these examples, and far more, as windows into wider cultural change.

Revitalization Movements

Revitalization movements are social movements that seek to bring about positive change, either through reestablishing all or parts of a religion that have been threatened by outside forces or through adopting new practices and beliefs. Such movements often arise in the context of rapid cultural change and appear to represent a way for people to try to make sense of their changing world and their place in it. One such movement that emerged as a response of Native Americans to the invasion of their land by Europeans and Euro-Americans was the Ghost Dance movement (Kehoe 1989). In the early 1870s, a shaman named Wodziwob of the Paiute tribe in California declared that the world would soon be destroyed and then renewed: Native Americans, plants, and animals would come back to life. He instructed people to perform a circle dance, known as the Ghost Dance, at night.

The movement spread to other tribes in California, Oregon, and Idaho but ended when the prophet died and his prophecy was unfulfilled. A similar movement emerged in 1890, led by another Paiute prophet, Wovoka, who had a vision during a total eclipse. His message was the same: destruction, renewal, and the need to perform circle dances in anticipation of the impending event. The dance spread widely and had various effects. Among the Pawnee, it provided the basis for a cultural revival of old ceremonies that had fallen into disuse. The Sioux altered Wovoka's message and adopted a more overtly hostile stance toward the government and White people. Newspapers began to carry stories about the "messiah craze," referring to Wovoka. Ultimately, the government took action against the Sioux, killing Chief Sitting Bull and Chief Big Foot and about 300 Sioux at Wounded Knee. In the 1970s, the Ghost Dance was revived again by the American Indian Movement, an activist organization that seeks to advance Native American rights.

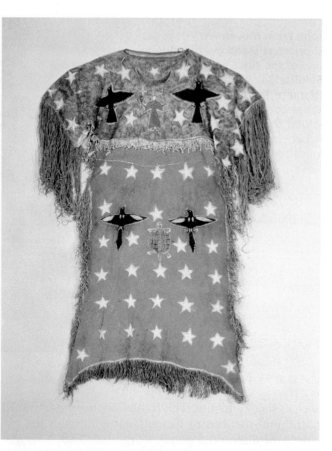

A Ghost Dance shirt of the Arapaho Indians of the Plains Region, with painted designs of birds, turtle, and stars. These specially decorated garments were believed to protect the wearer from the White man's bullets. ■ (Source: © Visual Arts Library [London]/Alamy)

Cargo cults are a type of revitalization movement that emerged in much of Melanesia (including Papua New Guinea and Fiji), and in New Zealand among the indigenous Māori people, in response to Western influences. Most prominent in the first half of the nineteenth century, cargo cults emphasize the acquisition of Western trade goods, or *cargo* in local terms. Typically, a prophetic leader emerges with a vision of how the cargo will arrive. In one instance, the leader predicted that a ship would come, bringing not only cargo but also the people's dead ancestors. Followers set up tables for the expected guests, complete with flower arrangements.

Later, after World War II and the islanders' experiences of aircraft arrivals bringing cargo, the mode of anticipated arrival changed to planes. Once again, people would wait expectantly for the arrival of the plane. The cargo cults emerged as a response to the disruptive effects of new goods being suddenly introduced into indigenous settings. The outsiders imposed a new form of exchange system that emphasized the importance of Western goods and suppressed the importance of indigenous valuables

John Frum Movement supporters stand guard around one of the cult's flag poles at Sulphur Bay village, on the island of Tanna, Vanuatu. ■ *What does this scene remind you of from your own cultural experience?* (Source: Lamont Lindstrom)

such as shells and pigs. This transformation undermined traditional patterns of gaining status through the exchange of indigenous goods. Cargo cult leaders sought help, in the only way they knew, in obtaining Western goods so that they could acquire social status in the new system.

Contested Sacred Sites

Religious conflict often becomes focused on sacred sites. One place of recurrent conflict is Jerusalem, where many religions and sects within religions compete for control of sacred terrain. Three major religions claim they have primary rights: Islam, Judaism, and Christianity. Among the Christians, several different sects vie for control of the Church of the Holy Sepulchre (see Map 13.5, p. 356). In India, frequent conflicts over sacred sites occur between Hindus and Muslims. Hindus claim that Muslim mosques have been built on sites sacred to Hindus. On some occasions, the Hindus have destroyed the mosques. Many conflicts that involve secular issues surrounding sacred sites also exist worldwide. In the United States, White racists have burned African American churches. In Israel, some Jewish leaders object to archaeological research because the ancient Jewish burial places should remain undisturbed.

The same situation exists for Native Americans in the Western Hemisphere, whose sacred sites and burial grounds have often been destroyed for the sake of urban growth, petroleum and mineral extraction, and even recreational sports. Resistance to such destruction is growing, with indigenous people finding creative ways to protect, restore, and manage their heritage.

Religious Freedom as a Human Right

According to a United Nations Declaration, freedom from religious persecution is a universal human right. Yet violations of this right by countries and by competing religions are common. Sometimes people who are persecuted on religious grounds can seek and obtain sanctuary in other places or nations. Thousands of Tibetan Buddhist refugees, including their leader the Dalai Lama, fled Tibet after it was taken over by the Chinese. Several Tibetan communities have been established in exile in India, the United States, and Canada, where the Tibetan people attempt to keep their religion, language, and heritage alive.

The post-9/11 policy enactments in the United States related to its campaign against terrorism are seen by many as dangerous steps against constitutional principles of personal liberty—specifically, as infringements on the religious rights of practicing Muslims. The prevalent mentality in the U.S. government, and in much of the general populace, links the whole of Islam with terrorism and thereby stigmatizes all Muslims as potential terrorists. Many anthropologists (for example, Mamdani 2002) have spoken out against the wrong-headedness and indecency of labeling an entire religion dangerous and putting all its members under the shadow of suspicion.

After the Chinese takeover of Tibet, many Tibetans became refugees, including the revered head of Tibetan Buddhism, the Dalai Lama. Buddhism, founded in India as a protest against Hinduism, is a minority religion in its homeland. It has millions of followers elsewhere, from Scotland to San Francisco. ■ *Do some research on Buddhism as a world religion to find out where it is now established.* (Source: AP/Wide World Photos)

Religions—like economies, reproduction, health systems, kinship and social organization, politics, and other areas of culture discussed in this book—are often the focal point of conflict and dissension and the source of conflict resolution. As an integral part of the heritage of humanity, they can be better understood from a cross-cultural and contextualized perspective, and such understanding can contribute to a more peaceful future.

The Big Questions Revisited

WHAT is religion and what are the basic features of religions?

Early cultural anthropologists defined religion in contrast to magic and suggested that religion was a more evolved form of thinking about the supernatural realm. They collected information on religions of non-Western cultures and constructed theories about the origin and functions of religion. Since then, ethnographers have described many religious systems and documented a rich variety of beliefs, forms of ritual behavior, and types of religious specialists. Beliefs are expressed in either myth or doctrine and often are concerned with defining the roles and characteristics of supernatural beings and how humans should relate to them.

Religious beliefs are enacted in rituals. They are periodic (regular) or nonperiodic (irregular). Some common rituals worldwide are life-cycle rites, pilgrimage, rituals of inversion, and sacrifice. Rituals are meant to be transformative for the participants. Many rituals require the involvement of a trained religious specialist such as a shaman/shamanka or priest/priestess. Compared to states, in nonstate societies, religious specialist roles are fewer, less formalized, and carry less secular power. In states, religious specialists are often organized into hierarchies, and many specialists gain substantial secular power.

HOW do world religions illustrate globalization and localization?

The five traditionally named world religions of longstanding are based on texts and generally agreed-on teachings. In order of historic age, they are Hinduism, Buddhism, Judaism, Christianity, and Islam. Christianity has the largest number of adherents, with Islam second and Hinduism third. As members of the world religions have moved around the world, religious beliefs and practices have become contextualized into localized variants. When a new religion moves into a culture, it may be blended with indigenous systems (syncretism), may coexist with indigenous religions in a pluralistic fashion, or may take over and obliterate the original beliefs.

Due to accelerated global population migration in the past few centuries, many formerly local religions now have a worldwide membership. African diaspora religions are particularly prominent in the Western Hemisphere, with a variety of syncretistic religions attracting many adherents.

WHAT are some important aspects of religious change in contemporary times?

Religious movements of the past two centuries have often been prompted by colonialism and other forms of social contact. In some instances, indigenous religious leaders and cults have arisen in the attempt to resist unwanted outside forces of change. In other cases, they evolve as ways of incorporating selected outside elements. Revitalization movements, such as the Ghost Dance movement in the United States plains region, look to the past and attempt to recover lost and suppressed religious beliefs and practices.

Issues of contemporary importance include the increasing amount of conflict surrounding sacred sites, hostilities related to the effects of secular power interests on religious institutions and spaces, and religious freedom as a human right.

KEY CONCEPTS

animatism, p. 344
animism, p. 341
cargo cult, p. 363
doctrine, p. 342
life-cycle ritual, p. 347
magic, p. 340

myth, p. 342
priest/priestess, p. 351
religion, p. 340
religious pluralism, p. 351
revitalization movement, p. 363
ritual, p. 345

ritual of inversion, p. 348
sacrifice, p. 349
syncretism, p. 351
world religion, p. 351

SUGGESTED READINGS

Paulo Apolito. *The Internet and the Madonna: Religious Visionary Experience on the Web*. Antony Shugaar, trans. Chicago: University of Chicago Press, 2003. This book traces the Christian cult of Mary as it has developed and grown through the medium of the World Wide Web. Apparitions, or sightings of Mary, are an important theme.

Diane Bell. *Ngarrindjeri Wurruwarrin: A World That Is, Was, and Will Be*. North Melbourne, Australia: Spinifex, 1998. This ethnography describes Ngarrindjeri women's struggles to protect their sacred land from encroachment by developers. It includes the women's voices, the perspective of the Australian government, the media, and disputes among anthropologists about what constitutes truth.

Janet Bennion. *Desert Patriarchy: Mormon and Mennonite Communities in the Chihuahua Valley*. Tucson: University of Arizona Press, 2004. The ethnographer, raised in a Mormon family in a desert region of the United States, reports on her fieldwork among Mormons in a desert region in Mexico. Three themes pervade Mormon life in both contexts: patriarchy, strong female networks, and religious fundamentalism.

Karen McCarthy Brown. *Mama Lola: A Vodou Priestess in Brooklyn*. Berkeley: University of California Press, 1991. This life story of Mama Lola, a Vodou practitioner, is set within an ethnographic study of a Haitian community in New York City.

Kamari Maxine Clarke. *Mapping Yorùbá Networks: Power and Agency in the Making of Transnational Communities*. Durham, NC: Duke University Press, 2004. The author studied Yorùbá (Nigerian) religious revivalism in Òyòtúnjí African Village, a reconstructed Yorùbá village in rural South Carolina, traveled with village members to other Yorùbá revivalist groups throughout the United States, and went on a pilgrimage with them to Nigeria.

Susan Greenwood. *Magic, Witchcraft and the Otherworld: An Anthropology*. New York: Berg, 2000. This book examines modern magic as practiced by Pagans in Britain, focusing on the Pagan view of the essence of magic as communication with an "otherworldly" reality. Chapters address witchcraft, healing, Goddess worship, and links between magic and morality.

Klara Bonsack Kelley and Harris Francis. *Navajo Sacred Places*. Bloomington: Indiana University Press, 1994. The authors report on the results of a research project undertaken to learn about Navajo cultural resources, especially sacred sites, and the stories associated with them in order to help protect these places.

Melvin Konner. *Unsettled: An Anthropology of the Jews*. New York: Penguin Compass, 2003. A biological anthropologist is the author of this cultural history of the Jewish people and their religion. It extends from the origins of Judaism among pastoralists in the Middle East during the Bronze Age through enslavement in the Roman Empire, to the Holocaust and the creation of Israel.

J. David Lewis-Williams and D. G. Pearce. *San Spirituality: Roots, Expression, and Social Consequences*. New York: AltaMira Press, 2004. This book examines the interplay of cosmology, myth, ritual, and art among the San people of southern Africa.

Anna S. Meigs. *Food, Sex, and Pollution: A New Guinea Religion*. New Brunswick, NJ: Rutgers University Press, 1983. Meigs provides an analysis of taboos surrounding food, sex, and vital bodily essences among the Hua people of Papua New Guinea.

Fatima Mernissi. *Beyond the Veil: Male–Female Dynamics in Modern Muslim Society*. Bloomington: Indiana University Press, revised edition, 1987. The author considers how Islam perceives female sexuality and regulates it on behalf of the social order.

Kathleen M. Nadeau. *Liberation Theology in the Philippines: Faith in a Revolution*. Westport, CT: Praeger Press, 2002. Based on fieldwork on the island of Cebu, this book examines grassroots Christian (Catholic) activism in service of the poor. The study is based in the context of how colonialism in the past created deep social inequalities and how globalization today creates rising consumption expectations. Catholic activist groups seek to redress injustices and work with the poor to create a better life for them.

Maureen Trudelle Schwarz. *Blood and Voice: Navajo Women Ceremonial Practitioners*. Tucson: University of Arizona Press, 2003. Contemporary Navajo women are increasingly taking on the ritual role of ceremonial Singer, formerly the domain of men. This book describes how women gain sacred knowledge, explains how they overcome the tradition that only men can be Singers.

Katharine L. Wiegele. *Investing in Miracles: El Shaddai and the Transformation of Popular Catholicism in the Philippines*. Honolulu: University of Hawai'i Press, 2005. This book examines the widespread popularity in the Philippines of a charismatic businessman who became a preacher, Brother Mike. Brother Mike appears at huge outdoor rallies and uses mass media to spread his message of economic prosperity within a Catholic framework.

14
Expressive Culture

The Big Questions

- HOW is culture expressed through art?

- WHAT do play and leisure activities reveal about culture?

- HOW is expressive culture changing in contemporary times?

Brazilian country music (*sertaneja*) singer Inaia performs at the opening ceremony of the Barretos Rodeo in Berretos in the Brazilian state of São Paolo. (*Source: © Douglas Engle/CORBIS*)

In 2006, the Louvre in Paris, one of the most famous art museums in the world, opened a new museum in the shadow of the Eiffel Tower to display so-called tribal art of Africa, Asia, the South Pacific, and the Americas. This project reflects the interest of France's president, Jacques Chirac, in non-Western art. It is also an example of the growing role of cultural anthropologists in helping museums provide contextual information for objects that are displayed, because Maurice Godelier, a specialist on Papua New Guinea, was closely involved in planning the exhibits (Corbey 2000). The new museum elevates "tribal" objects to the level of art, rather than placing them in a museum of natural history as is the practice in the United States. It does, however, segregate "tribal" art in a museum physically separate from the Louvre with all its "classic" treasures. This long-standing conceptual division, beginning in the European Enlightenment, links the West with "civilization" and non-Western peoples with that which is "uncivilized."

This chapter considers a vast area of human behavior and thought called **expressive culture,** or behavior and beliefs related to art, leisure, and play (definitions of these terms are provided later). It starts with a discussion of theoretical perspectives on cross-cultural art. The next section reviews findings from *museum studies,* in which scholars seek appropriate ways of representing culture in a museum context, and then looks cross-culturally at play and leisure activities. The last section provides examples of change in expressive culture.

Art and Culture

Compared to questions raised in art history classes you may have taken, cultural anthropologists have a rather different view of art and how to study it (see Critical Thinking box). Their findings, here as in other cultural domains, stretch and subvert the Western concepts and categories and prompt us to look at art within its context. Thus, anthropologists consider many products, practices, and processes to be art. They also study the artist and the artist's place in society. In addition, they ask questions about how art, and expressive culture more generally, is related to microcultural variation, inequality, and power.

What Is Art?

Are ancient rock carvings art? Is subway graffiti art? An embroidered robe? A painting of a can of Campbell's soup? Philosophers, art critics, anthropologists, and art lovers have all struggled with the question of *What is art?* The issue of how to define art involves more than mere word games. The way art is defined affects the manner in which a person values and treats artistic creations and those who create art.

Anthropologists propose broad definitions of art to take into account emic definitions cross-culturally. One definition says that **art** is the application of imagination, skill, and style to matter, movement, and sound that goes beyond the purely practical (Nanda 1994:383). Such culturally judged skill can be applied to any number of substances and activities and the product can be considered art—for example, a beautifully presented meal, a well-told story, or a perfectly formed basket. In this sense, art is a human universal, and no culture can be said to lack artistic activity completely, although the Pirahã appear to have very little art, no matter how broadly defined (review Chapter 12). The anthropological study of art considers the products of such human skill as well as the process of making art, variations in art and its preferred forms cross-culturally, and the way culture constructs and changes artistic traditions.

Within the general category of art, subcategories exist, sometimes denoting eras such as Paleolithic or modern art. Other subcategories are based on the medium of expression, such as graphic or plastic arts (painting, drawing, sculpture, weaving, basketry, and architecture); decorative arts (interior design, landscaping, gardens, costume design, and body adornment such as hairstyles, tattooing, and painting); performance arts (music, dance, and theater); and verbal arts (poetry, writing, rhetoric, and telling stories and jokes). All these are Western, English-language categories.

A long-standing distinction in the Western view exists between "fine art" and "folk art." This distinction is based on a Western-centric judgment that defines fine art as rare, expensive art produced by artists usually trained in the Western classical tradition. This is the kind of art that is included in college courses called Fine Arts. The implication is that all other art is less than fine and is more appropriately called folk art, ethnic art, primitive art, or crafts. Characteristics of Western fine art are as follows: The product is created by a formally schooled artist, it is made for sale on the market, it is clearly associated with a particular artist, its uniqueness is valued, and it is not primarily utilitarian but is rather "art for art's sake." In contrast, all the rest of the world's art that is non-Western and nonclassical is supposedly characterized by the opposite features:

- It is created by an artist who has not received formal training.

---

expressive culture: behavior and beliefs related to art, leisure, and play.
art: the application of imagination, skill, and style to matter, movement, and sound that goes beyond what is purely practical.

ethno-esthetics: cultural definitions of what art is.

Critical Thinking

PROBING THE CATEGORIES OF ART

Probably every reader of this book, at one time or another, has looked at an object on display in an art museum or in an art book or magazine and exclaimed, "But that's not art!" As a critical thinking research project on "what is art," visit two museums, either in person or on the Internet. One of these should be a museum of either fine art or modern art. The other should be a museum of natural history. In the former, examine at least five items on display. In the latter, examine several items on display that have to do with human cultures (that is, skip the bugs and rocks).

Take notes on all the items that you are examining. Then answer the following questions.

CRITICAL THINKING QUESTIONS

- What is it?
- What contextual explanation does the museum provide about the object?
- Was the object intended as a work of art or as something else?
- In your opinion, is it art or not, and why or why not?
- Compare your notes on the objects in the two types of museums. What do your notes tell you about categories of art?

- It is not produced for the market.
- The artist is anonymous and does not sign or individually claim the product.
- It is made primarily for everyday use, such as food procurement, processing, or storage; in ritual; or in war.

Closer examination of these two categories is in order. All cultures have art, and all cultures have a sense of what makes something art versus nonart. The term *esthetics* refers to agreed-on notions of quality (Thompson 1971:374). Before anthropologists proved otherwise, however, Western art experts considered that esthetics either did not exist or was poorly developed in non-Western cultures. We now know that esthetic principles, or established criteria for artistic quality, exist everywhere, whether or not they are written down and formalized. Franz Boas, from his wide review of many forms of art in nonstate societies, deduced principles that he claimed were universal for these cultures, especially symmetry, rhythmic repetition, and naturalism (Jonaitis 1995:37). These principles do apply in many cases, but they are not as universal as Boas thought.

Ethno-esthetics refers to local cultural definitions of what art is. The set of standards concerning wood carving in West Africa illustrates the importance of considering cross-cultural variation in the criteria for art (Thompson 1971). Among the Yorúbà of Nigeria, esthetic guidelines include the following:

- Figures should be depicted midway between complete abstraction and complete realism so that they resemble "somebody," but no one in particular (portraiture in the Western sense is considered dangerous).

- Humans should be depicted at their optimal physical peak, not in infancy or old age.
- Line and form should have clarity.

In South Africa, women paint colorful designs on the outside of houses. ■ *What kind of domestic art do you know how to do?* (Source: Roshani Kothari)

Yorùbá wood carving follows esthetic principles that require clarity of line and form, a polished surface that creates a play of light and shadows, symmetry, and the depiction of human figures that are neither completely abstract nor completely realistic. ■ *Have you ever seen African sculptures that follow these principles? Visit an African art museum on the Web for further exploration.* (Source: Courtesy of the Peabody Museum, Harvard University)

- ■ The sculpture should have the quality of luminosity achieved through a polished surface and the play of incisions and shadows.
- ■ The piece should exhibit symmetry.

Some anthropological studies have documented intracultural differences in esthetic standards as well as cross-cultural variation. For example, one anthropologist showed computer-generated graphics to the Shipibo Indians of the Peruvian Amazon and learned that the men liked the abstract designs, whereas the women thought they were ugly (Roe, in Anderson and Field 1993:257). If you are wondering why this difference would exist, consider the interpretation of the anthropologist: Shipibo men are the shamans and take hallucinogenic drugs that may give them familiarity with more "psychedelic" images.

Studying Art in Society

The anthropological study of art seeks to understand not only the products of art but also who makes it and why,

the role of art in society, and its wider social meanings. Franz Boas was the first anthropologist to emphasize the importance of studying the artist in society. Functionalism (review Chapter 1) was the most important theory informing anthropological research on art in the first half of the twentieth century. Anthropologists wrote about how paintings, dance, theater, and songs serve to socialize children into the culture, provide a sense of social identity and group boundaries, and promote healing. Art may legitimize political leaders and enhance efforts in war through body painting, adornment, and magical decorations on shields and weapons. Art may also serve as a form of social control, as in African masks worn by dancers who represent deities visiting humans to remind them of the moral order. Art, like language, can be a catalyst for political resistance or a rallying point for ethnic solidarity in the face of oppression.

The anthropology of art relies on a range of methods in data gathering and analysis. For some research projects, participant observation provides most of the necessary data. In others, participant observation is complemented by collecting and analyzing oral or written material such as video and tape recordings. Thus, strong ties often exist between cultural and linguistic anthropologists in the study of art.

Many anthropologists have become apprentices in an artistic tradition. For John Chernoff, learning to play African drums was an important part of building rapport during his fieldwork in Ghana and an essential aspect of his ability to gain an understanding of the importance of music in Ghanaian society (1979). His book, *African Rhythm and African Sensibility,* is one of the first reflexive ethnographies (recall Chapter 2), taking into account the position and role of the ethnographer and how they shape what the ethnographer learns. Reading the introduction to his book is the best way to become convinced that fieldwork in cultural anthropology is far more than simply gathering the data you think you need for the project you have in mind, especially if your project concerns processes of creativity and expression.

Chernoff makes the case that only by relinquishing a scientific approach can a researcher learn about creativity and how it is related to society. As one of his drumming teachers said, "The heart sees before the eyes." Chernoff had to do more than practice participant observation. His heart had to participate, too. During his early months in the field, Chernoff often found himself wondering why he was there. To write a book? To tell people back in the United States about Ghana? No doubt many of the Ghanaians he met wondered the same thing, especially given that his early efforts at drumming were pretty bad, although he did not realize it because he always drank copious amounts of gin before playing. Eventually, he became the student of a master drummer and went through a formal initiation ceremony. For the ceremony, he had to kill two chickens himself and eat

In Sumba, Indonesia, linguistic anthropologist Joel Kuipers interviews a ritual speaker who is adept at verbal arts performance. ■ *What is a form of verbal art in a microculture you know?* (Source: Joel Kuipers)

A woman in East Sumba weaves *ikat* cloth on a bamboo loom. Ikat is a style of weaving that uses a tie-dye process on either the warp or weft before the threads are woven that will create a design in the final product. Double ikat is when both warp and weft threads are tie-dyed before weaving. The motif on this piece of ikat is the Tree of Life flanked by roosters. ■ (Source: Lindsay Hebberd/CORBIS)

parts of them in a form that most North Americans will never see in a grocery store. Still, he was not playing well enough. He went through another ritual to make his wrist "smart" so that it would turn faster, like a cat chasing a mouse. For that ritual, he had to go into the bush, ten miles outside town, and collect ingredients. The ritual worked. Having a cat's hand was a good thing, but anthropologically it was more important to Chernoff that he had begun to gain an understanding of drumming in its social and ritual contexts.

Chernoff learned about Ghanaian family life and how it is connected to individual performers and to rituals that have to do with music. He also grew to see where his performance fell short and what he needed to do to improve. He gained great respect for the artists who taught him and admiration for their striving for respectability. Chernoff's personality was an important ingredient of the learning process. He comments, "I assumed that I did not know what to do in most situations. I accepted what people told me about myself and what I should be doing. . . . I waited to see what people would make of me. . . . By staying cool I learned the meaning of character" (1979:170).

Focus on the Artist

In the early twentieth century, Boas urged his students to go beyond the study of the products of art and study the artists. One role of the anthropologist, he said, is to add to the understanding of art by studying art from the artist's perspective. Ruth Bunzel's (1972 [1929]) research with Native American potters in the U.S. Southwest is a classic example of this tradition. While undergoing training as an apprentice potter, she paid attention to the vari-

ety of pot shapes and motifs and asked individual potters about their design choices. One Zuni potter commented, "I always know the whole design before I start to paint" (1972:49). A Laguna potter said, "I made up all my designs and never copy. I learned this design from my mother. I learned most of my designs from my mother" (1972:52). Brunzel discovered the importance of both past traditions and individual agency.

The social status of artists is another aspect of the focus on the artist. Artists may be revered and wealthy as individuals or as a group, or they may be stigmatized and economically marginal. In ancient Mexico, goldworkers were highly respected. In Native American groups of the Pacific Northwest coast, male carvers and painters had to be initiated into a secret society, and they had higher status than other men. Often a gender division exists. Among the Navajo of Arizona, women weave and men do silversmithing. In the Caribbean, women of African descent are noted for their carvings of calabashes (large gourds). In the contemporary United States, most famous and successful graphic artists are men, although the profession includes many women. The lives of artists and performers are often outside the boundaries of mainstream society or challenge the social boundaries.

In Morocco (see Map 5.3, p. 127), a *shikha* is a female performer who sings and dances at festivities, including life-cycle ceremonies such as birth, circumcision, and marriage (Kapchan 1994). These performers appear in a group of three or four with accompanying musicians. Their performance involves suggestive songs and body movements, including reaching a state of near-possession when they loosen their hair buns. With their long hair waving, they "lift the belt," a technique accomplished through an undulating movement that rolls the abdomen up to the waist. Their entertainment creates a lively atmosphere. "Through the provocative movements and loud singing of the shikhat, the audience is drawn up and into a collective state of celebration, their bodies literally pulled into the dance" (1994:93).

In their private lives, shikhat are on the social fringes, leading lives as single women who transgress limits applied to proper females. They own property, drink alcohol, smoke cigarettes, and may have several lovers. Most of the shikhat, therefore, have been rejected by their families and by the wider society. Middle- and upper-class women consider them vulgar and distance themselves from them.

Yet, shikhat who become successful, widening their performance spheres to large towns and cities, manage to save money and become landowners and gain economic status. Furthermore, the modern mass media are contributing to an increased status of shikhat as performers. Recordings of shikhat music are popular in Morocco. State-produced television broadcasts carry performances of regional shikhat groups as a way of presenting the diverse cultures of the country.

As with other occupations, the performing arts are more specialized in state-level societies. Generally, among free-ranging foragers, little specialization exists. Artistic activity is open to all, and artistic products are shared equally by all. Some people may be especially appreciated as singers, storytellers, or carvers. With increasing social complexity and a market for art, specialized training is required to produce certain kinds of art, and the products are sought after by those who can afford them. Class differences in artistic styles and preferences emerge along with the increasingly complex division of labor.

Microcultures, Art, and Power

Art forms and styles, like language, are often associated with microcultural groups' identity and sense of pride.

Kanye West performs on the main stage at the 2006 Coachella Valley Music and Arts Festival in Indio, California. ■ *Do your parents or grandparents know who Kanye West is?* (Source: © Lucas Jackson/Reuters/CORBIS)

For example, the Berbers of highland Morocco are associated with woolen carpets, Maya Indians with woven and embroidered blouses, and the Inuit of Alaska with small stone carvings of figurines. Cultural anthropologists provide many examples of linkages between various microcultural dimensions and power issues. In some instances, more powerful groups appropriate the art forms of less powerful groups. In others, forms of art are said to be expressive of resistance. One study reveals how political interests in Israel take ownership of ethnic artistic expression (see Everyday Anthropology box).

An example of how gender relations are played out in expressive culture comes from a study of male strip dancing in Florida (Margolis and Arnold 1993). Advertisements in the media tell women that seeing a male strip dancer is "their chance," "their night out." Going to a male strip is marketed as a time of reversal of traditional gender roles in which men are dominant and women submissive. Are gender roles actually reversed in a male stripper bar? The short answer is no. Women customers are treated like juveniles. As they stand in line waiting for the show to open, the manager instructs them on how to tip. They are symbolically dominated by the dancers, who take on various roles such as lion-tamers. The *dive-bomb* is further evidence of women's subordinate position. The dive-bomb is a form of tipping the dancer in which the woman customer gets on her hands and knees and tucks a bill held between her teeth into the dancer's g-string. The interpretation of all this behavior is that, rather than reversing the gender hierarchy, it reinforces it.

THE INVISIBLE HANDS THAT CRAFT SOUVENIRS

Tourists who buy arts and crafts souvenirs rarely learn much about the people who actually made the items. Yet they probably have some mental image of, for example, a village potter sitting at the wheel or a silversmith hammering at a piece of metal in a quaint workshop. Souvenir shops come in different varieties, from street stalls that sell a few items such as embroidered clothing or "ethnic" jewelry to national emporiums that offer a wide range of arts and crafts. An upscale store of the latter category in Israel, called Maskit, caters mainly to tourists (Shenhav-Keller 1993:183). Ethnographic study shows how the sellers "put Israeli society on display via its souvenirs." It also reveals how certain artists and craftspeople are selectively rendered invisible.

The tourist artifact, or souvenir, can be analyzed like a "text" that contains social messages. Looking at souvenirs this way reveals what both marketeers and tourists choose to preserve, value, and exchange (Clifford 1988:221). In the Maskit stores, three central themes in Israeli society are expressed in the choice and presentation of souvenirs: Israel's attitudes toward its ancient and recent past, its view of its religion and culture, and its approach to Arab Israelis and Palestinians. Shelly Shenhav-Keller (1993) conducted participant observation in the original Maskit store in Tel Aviv and interviewed Jewish Israeli, Arab Israeli, and Palestinian artists and artisans whose products were sold there.

Maskit, the Israel Center for Handicrafts, was founded by Ruth Dayan (then the wife of Moshe Dayan) as a Ministry of Labor project in 1954. Its purpose was "to encourage artisans to continue their native crafts in the new surrounding . . . to retain and safeguard the ancient crafts." (1988:183). Maskit was a success, and a chain of shops was eventually opened. As its status increased, Maskit came to be perceived as an "ambassador of Israel." Dignitaries who traveled from Israel abroad were loaded with gifts from the shop. Official visitors to Israel were given Maskit gifts.

The shop had two floors. The top floor, where the entrance was located, had five sections: fashion (women's clothing, wedding gowns, and dresses with three different styles of Arab embroidery); jewelry; ritual articles (candlesticks, goblets, incense burners); decorative items; and books. The larger lower floor had five thematic sections: the Bar-Mitzvah Corner with prayer books and other ritual items; the children's corner (clothing, games, toys, and T-shirts); the embroidery section (tablecloths, linens, pillow covers, wallets, eyeglass cases); the carpet section; and a large area for ceramics, glassware, and copperware.

Over the years, changes have occurred in who is producing the art sold in Maskit. Many of the original Jewish Israeli artists gained eminence and opened their own shops. Those who continue to supply Maskit specialize in ceramics, jewelry, carpet design, and ritual articles. These pieces are considered to have the status of art and may be displayed as an "individual collection" within the store. The amount of Jewish ethnic art has declined as the older artists have aged and their children have not taken up the craft. This change is most marked in Yemenite embroidery and silversmithing, the crafts that once dominated Maskit. Now, Arab embroidery is sought as a replacement.

After the 1967 Six-Day War, Arab Israeli and Palestinian craftsmanship became increasingly available with the incorporation of new areas within Israel, including the Occupied Territories. Most of the Arabs who were absorbed into the souvenir industry became hired laborers in factories and workshops owned by Maskit or by Israeli artisans who sold their works to Maskit. Maskit, however, provides no information about the creative role of Israeli Arabs or Palestinians. The carpets, for example, are presented simply as hand-woven Israeli carpets, even though Arab Israelis wove them.

FOOD FOR THOUGHT

- Do you know of another example in which something attributed to one ethnic group or culture is actually produced by people of a different group?

Not all forms of popular art and performance are mechanisms of social control and hierarchy maintenance. In the United States, for example, hip-hop and urban Black youths' verbal arts and rap music can be seen as a form of protest through performance (Smitherman 1997). Their lyrics report on their experience of economic oppression, the danger of drugs, and men's disrespect for women. The global spread of hip-hop and related music is another example of social resistance through song and performance.

Performance Arts

The performance arts include music, dance, theater, rhetoric (speech-making), and narrative (storytelling). One important area has developed its own name: **ethnomusicology,** the cross-cultural study of music. Ethnomusicologists study a range of topics, including the form of the music itself, the social position of musicians, how music interacts with other domains of culture such as religion or healing, and change in musical traditions. This section provides examples about music and gender in Malaysia, music and globalization in Brazil, and theater and society in India.

Music and Gender among the Temiar of Malaysia

An important topic for ethnomusicologists is gender differences in access to performance roles in music (for readers interested in doing research on this topic, see Figure 14.1). A cultural materialist perspective would predict that in cultures where gender roles are relatively egalitarian, access to and meanings in music will tend to be egalitarian. This is the case among the Temiar, a group of foragers of highland Malaysia (see Map 8.3, p. 208). Their musical traditions emphasize balance and complementarity between males and females (Roseman 1987).

Among the Temiar, kinship and marriage rules are flexible and open. Marriages are based on the mutual desires of the partners. Descent is bilineal (review Chapter 8), and marital residence follows no particular rule after a period of bride service. Marriages often end in separation, and serial monogamy is common. Men have a certain edge over women in political and ritual spheres. They are typically the village leaders, and they are the spirit mediums who sing the songs that energize the spirits. Historical records, however, indicate that women were spirit mediums in the past.

Although men singers are the nodes through which the songs of the spirits enter the community, women's performance role is significant and the male spirit-medium role is not of greater importance or status. The distinction between male leader and female chorus is blurred through overlap between phrases and repetition. The performance is one of general community participation with integrated male and female roles, just as in Temiar society in general.

Country Music and Globalization in Brazil

Linguistic anthropologist Alexander Dent studies the growing popularity of *música sertaneja,* Brazilian coun-

FIGURE 14.1 Five Ethnographic Questions about Gender and Music

If you were doing an ethnographic study of gender roles in musical performance, the following questions would be useful in starting the inquiry. But they would not exhaust the topic. Can you think of questions that should be added to the list?

1. Are men and women equally encouraged to use certain instruments and repertoires?

2. Is musical training available to all?

3. Do male and female repertoires overlap? If so, how, when and for what reasons?

4. Are the performances of men and women public, private, or both? Are women and men allowed to perform together? In what circumstances?

5. Do members of the culture give equal value to the performances of men and women? On what criteria are these evaluations based, and are they the same for men and women performers?

Source: From "Power and Gender in the Musical Experiences of Women," pp. 224–225, by Carol E. Robertson in *Women and Music in Cross-Cultural Perspective,* ed. by Ellen Koskoff. Copyright © 1987. Reprinted by permission of Greenwood Publishing Group, Inc., Westport, CT.

try music (2005). Although drawing on U.S. country music, *música sertaneja* is significantly localized within Brazilian social contexts. Brazilian performers creatively use North American country music songs, such as *Achy Breaky Heart* to convey messages that make sense in the Brazilian context about gender relationships, intimacy, the family, the past, and the importance of the countryside. In their performances and recordings, therefore, they may use an American genre to critique certain American-led processes such as rampant capitalism and globalization and to critique the Brazilian adoption of such Western ways.

A prominent feature of Brazilian country music is performance by a *dupla,* a duo of brothers. They emphasize their similarity in terms of physical looks by cutting their hair the same way and wearing similar clothes. Musically, they blend their voices without one voice dominating the other. When performing, they may sing part of a song with their arms over each other's shoulders and gazing at each other affectionately. In these ways, the *dupla* and their music emphasize kinship and caring as important aspects of Brazilian tradition that should be preserved.

---

ethnomusicology: the cross-cultural study of music.

theater: a form of enactment, related to other forms such as dance, music, parades, competitive games and sports, and verbal

art, that seeks to entertain through acting, movement, and sound.

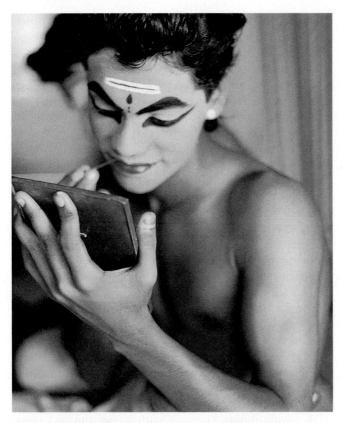

Many forms of theater combine the use of facial makeup, masks, and costumes to transform an actor into someone (or something) else. This Kathakali dancer is applying makeup before a performance in Kerala, South India. ■ *What forms of dance or theater in your microculture involve the use of facial makeup to depict a particular character?* (Source: Roshani Kothari)

A new use for classical dance-drama throughout India is for raising social awareness about problems such as excessive dowries and female infanticide. Street theater groups go into neighborhoods and act out skits, drawing members of the audience into dialogue with them. ■ (Source: Barbara Miller)

Theater and Myth in South India

Theater is a type of enactment that seeks to entertain through movement, and words related to dance, music, parades, competitive games and sports, and verbal art (Beeman 1993). Cross-culturally, strong connections exist among myth, ritual, and performance.

One theatrical tradition that offers an exuberant blend of mythology, acting, and music is the Kathakali ritual dance-drama of southern India (Zarrilli 1990). Stylized hand gestures, elaborate makeup, and costumes contribute to the attraction of these performances, which dramatize India's great Hindu epics, especially the *Mahabharata* (a story of warring lineages and divine intervention by the deity Krishna) and the *Ramayana* (the story of a good king, Rama, and his devoted wife, Sita). Costumes and makeup transform the actor into one of several well-known characters from Indian mythology. The audience easily recognizes the basic character types at their first entrance by the performers' costumes and makeup. Six makeup types exist to depict characters ranging from the most refined to the most

vulgar. Kings and heroes have green facial makeup, reflecting their refinement and moral uprightness. Vulgar characters are associated with black facial makeup and occasionally black beards. With their black faces dotted with red and white, they are the most frightening of the Kathakali characters.

Architecture and Decorative Arts

Like all art forms, architecture is interwoven with other aspects of culture. Architecture may reflect and protect social rank and class differences as well as gender, age, and ethnic differences (Guidoni 1987). Decorative arts— including interior decoration of homes and buildings, and external design features such as gardens—likewise reflect people's social position and "taste." Local cultures have long defined preferred standards in these areas of expression, but global influences from the West and elsewhere, such as Japan and other non-Western cultures, have been adopted and adapted by other traditions.

Architecture and Interior Design

Foragers, being highly mobile, build dwellings as needed and then abandon them (refer to the photo on p. 66 of Ju/'hoansi shelter). Having few personal possessions and no surplus goods, they need no permanent storage structures. The construction of dwellings does not require the efforts of groups larger than the family unit. Foragers' dwellings are an image of the family and not of the wider society. The dwellings' positioning in relation to each other reflects the relations among families.

More elaborate shelters and greater social cohesiveness in planning occur as foraging is combined with horticulture, as in the semipermanent settlements in the Amazon rainforest. People live in the settlement part of the year but break up into smaller groups that spread out into a larger area for foraging. Important decisions concern location of the site in terms of weather, availability of drinking water, and defensibility. The central plaza must be elevated for drainage, and drainage channels dug around the hearths. The overall plan is circular. In some groups, separate shelters are built for extended family groups; in others, they are joined into a continuous circle with connected roofs. In some cases, the headman has a separate and larger shelter.

Pastoralists have designed ingenious portable structures such as the teepee and the yert (refer to the photo on p. 89). The teepee is a conical tent made with a framework of four wooden poles tied at the top with thongs, to which are joined other poles to complete the cone; this frame is then covered with buffalo hide. A yert is also a circular, portable dwelling, but its roof is flatter. The covering is made of cloth. This lightweight structure is easy to set up, take down, and transport, and it is adaptable to all weather conditions. Encampments are often arranged the teepees or yerts in several concentric circles. Social status was the structuring principle, and the council of chiefs and the head chief were located in the center.

With the development of the state, urban areas grew and showed the effects of centralized planning and power, for example, in grid-style street planning rather than haphazard street placement. The symbolic demonstration of the power, grandeur, and identity of states was and is expressed architecturally through the construction of impressive urban monuments: temples, administrative buildings, memorials, and museums.

Interior decoration of domestic dwellings also became more elaborate. In settled agricultural communities and urban centers where permanent housing is the norm, decoration is more likely to be found in homes. Wall paintings, sculptures, and other features distinguish the homes of wealthier individuals. Research on interior decoration in contemporary Japan involved studying the contents of home decorating magazines and doing participant observation within homes (Rosenberger 1992). Findings reveal how people incorporate and localize selected aspects of Western decorating styles.

Home decorating magazines target middle- and upper-class Japanese housewives who seek to express their status through new consumption styles. A trend is the abandonment of three features of traditional Japanese design: *tatami*, *shoji*, and *fusuma*. Tatami are two-inch-thick mats, about three feet by six feet. A room's size is measured in terms of the number of tatami mats it holds. Shoji are the sliding screen doors of tatami rooms, one covered with glass and the other with translucent rice paper often printed with a design of leaves or waves. Fusuma are sliding wall panels made of thick paper; they are removable so that rooms can be enlarged for gatherings. The tatami room usually contains a low table in the center, with pillows for seating on the floor. A special alcove may contain a flower arrangement, ancestors' pictures, and a Buddhist altar. Futons are stored in closets around the edges and brought out at night for sleeping.

In distancing themselves from the old style, "modern" Japanese housewives make several changes. The kitchen has a central rather than marginal location and is merged with a space called the DK (dining-kitchen) or LDK (living-dining-kitchen), with wood, tile, or carpeting on the floor. Western products such as carpeting and curtains (instead of the fusuma, the tatami, and shoji) are used to cover surfaces and to separate rooms. The LDK has a couch, dining set, VCR, stereo, and an array of small items on display such as Western-style teapots, cuckoo clocks, and knick-knacks.

These design choices accompany deeper social changes that involve new aspirations about marriage and family relationships. Home decorating magazines promote the idea that the modern style brings with it happier children with better grades and closer husband–wife ties. Tensions exist, however, between these ideals and the realities of middle- and upper-class life in Japan. Women feel compelled to work either part time or full time to be able to contribute income for satisfying their new consumer needs. Yet, Japanese women are discouraged from pursuing careers and are urged to devote more time to domestic pursuits, including home decorating and child care, in order to provide the kind of life portrayed in the magazines. Children are in the conflicting position of being indulged as new consumer targets, while the traditional value of self-discipline still holds. Husbands are in the conflicting position of needing to be more attentive to wife and home, whereas the corporate world calls them for a "7–11" working day (review Chapter 6). Furthermore, the Western-style, happy nuclear family image contains no plan for the aged. The wealthiest Japanese families manage to satisfy both individualistic desires and filial duties because they can afford a large house in which they dedicate a separate floor for the husband's

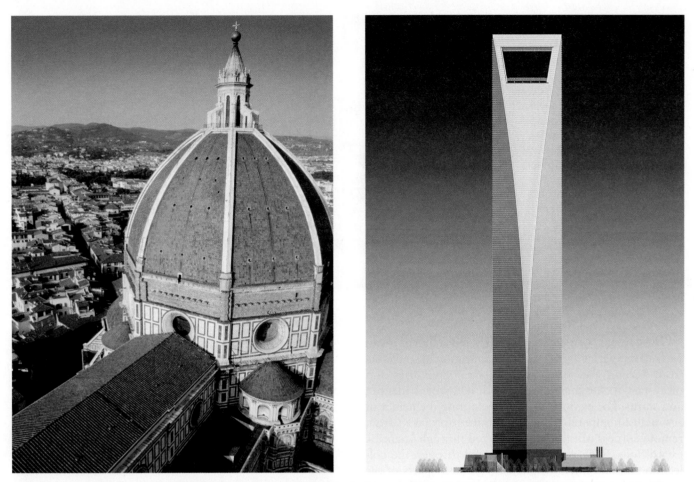

The Duomo in Florence, Italy (*left*). The Duomo, or Cathedral of Santa Maria del Fiore, was begun in 1296. Its massive dome, designed by architect and sculptor Filippo Brunelleschi, was not completed until 1436. The goal was to surpass in height and beauty all other edifices. It still physically dominates the city of Florence and also attracts vast numbers of tourists from around the world. ■ (Source: Andrew Ward/Life File) **A computer-enhanced photograph shows the newest design of the Shanghai World Financial Center in 2005 (*right*). According to its blueprint, the 101-story building will be taller than the current world's record holder, Malaysia's Petronas Twin Towers. The project is scheduled to be completed in 2008.** ■ (Source: Getty Images)

parents, complete with tatami mats. Less wealthy people have a more difficult time dealing with these conflicting values.

Gardens and Flowers

Gardens for use, especially for food production, are differentiated from gardens for decorative purposes. The concept of the decorative garden is not a cultural universal. Circumpolar peoples cannot construct gardens in the snow, and highly mobile pastoralists have no gardens because they are on the move. The decorative garden is a product of state-level societies, especially in the Middle East, Europe, and Asia (Goody 1993). Within these contexts, variation exists in what are considered to be the appropriate contents and design of a garden. A Japanese garden may contain no blooming flowers, focusing instead on the shape and placement of trees, shrubs, stones, and bodies of water.

Elite Muslim culture, with its core in the Middle East, has long been associated with formal decorative gardens. A garden, enclosed with four walls, is symbolically equivalent to the concept of "paradise." The Islamic garden pattern involves a square design with symmetrical layout, fountains, waterways, and straight pathways, all enclosed within walls. Islamic gardens often surrounded the tombs of prominent people. India's Taj Mahal (refer to the photo on p. 216), built by a Muslim emperor, follows this pattern, with one modification: The tomb is placed at one edge of the garden rather than in the center. The result is a dramatic stretch of fountains and flowers leading from the main gate up to the monument.

An early morning scene in the city of Den Haag (The Hague), in the Netherlands. Dutch people buy, on average, a dozen bouquets of cut flowers per year. Raising cut flowers is energy intensive, and people are encouraged to consider alternate gift ideas. ■ *How often do you buy cut flowers per year, and what are the occasions?* (Source: Barbara Miller and Bernard Wood)

The contents of a personal garden, like a dinner menu with all its special ingredients or a collection of souvenirs from around the world with all their memories and meanings, makes a statement about its owner's identity and status. For example, in Europe during the height of colonialism, imperial gardens contained specimens from remote corners of the globe, collected through scientific expeditions. Such gardens are created through the collection and placement of plants from many parts of the world. The practice of cultural displacement of diverse objects into a single collection with a new identity is called **heterotopia** (Foucault 1970). These gardens expressed the owner's worldliness and intellectual status.

Cut flowers are now important economic products; they provide income for gardeners throughout the world. They are also exchange items. In France, women receive flowers from men more than any other kind of gift (Goody 1993:316). In much of the world, special occasions require gifts of flowers: In the West, as well as in East Asia, funerals are times for displays of flowers. Ritual offerings to the deities in Hinduism are often flowers such as marigolds woven into a chain or necklace.

Flowers are prominent motifs in Western and Asian secular and sacred art, but less so in African art (Goody 1993). Some possible reasons for this variation include ecological and economic factors. Eurasia's more temperate environment possesses a greater variety of blooming plants than Africa's does. Sheer economic necessity in developing countries of Africa limits the amount of space that can be used for decorative purposes. In wealthy African kingdoms, prominent luxury goods include fab-rics, gold ornaments, and wooden carvings rather than flowers. This pattern of production is changing with globalization, however. Many African countries now grow flowers for export to the world market.

Museums and Culture

This section considers the concept of the museum and the debates about the role of museums in exhibiting and representing culture. Museum studies, in anthropology, include anthropologists who work in museums helping to prepare exhibits and anthropologists who study museums—what they choose to display and how they display it—as important sites of culture itself.

What Is a Museum?

A **museum** is an institution that collects, preserves, interprets, and displays objects on a regular basis (Kahn 1995:324). Its purpose may be esthetic or educational. The idea of gathering and displaying objects goes back at least to the Babylonian kings of the sixth century BCE who ruled in what is present-day Iraq (Maybury-Lewis 1997a). The term comes originally from a Greek word referring to a place where the *muses* (spirits who inspire thought and creativity) congregate, or a place to have philosophical discussions or see artistic performances. In Europe, the term *museum* came to denote a place where

---

heterotopia: the creation of an internally varied place by collecting things from diverse cultures and locations.

museum: an institution that collects, preserves, interprets, and displays objects on a regular basis.

repatriation: returning art or other objects from museums to the people with whom they originated.

A display of artifacts collected by British explorers and early anthropologists, shown with minimal labels and context, at the Powell-Cotton Museum in Kent, southeast England (*left*). This museum is moving toward exhibits that provide more context while also preserving some of its more "colonialist" exhibits as examples of museum displays of their time. ■ (Sources: Barbara Miller and Bernard Wood) In Port Blair, the Andaman Islands, the Anthropological Museum is a small building containing some artifacts but mainly photographs of the indigenous people (*right*). The most well-known and feared group (for their false reputation as cannibals) are the so-called Jarawa, shown here. Their photographs are the museum's main attraction. ■ (Source: Barbara Miller)

art objects were housed and displayed. Ethnographic and science museums came later, inspired by Europe's emerging interests in exploration in the 1500s and the accompanying scientific urge to gather specimens from around the world and classify them into an evolutionary history. The Western concept of the museum and its several forms has now diffused to most parts of the world.

The Politics of Exhibits

Within anthropology, the subfield of *museum anthropology* is concerned with studying how and why museums choose to collect and display particular objects (Ames 1992; A. Jones 1993). Museum anthropologists are at the forefront of debates about who gets to represent whom, the ownership of particular objects, and the public-service role of museums versus possible elitism. One major issue is whether objects from non-Western cultures should be exhibited, like Western art objects, with little or no ethnographic context (Clifford 1988; Watson 1997). Most anthropologists support the need for context, and not just for non-Western objects but for all objects on display. For example, a museum label of Andy Warhol's hyperrealistic painting of a can of Campbell's soup should include information on the social context in which such art was produced and some background on the artist. The anthropological view that all forms of expressive culture are context bound and are better understood and appreciated within their social context is, however, still rare among Western art historians and critics (Best 1986).

Another contentious issue concerns who should have control of objects in museums that were acquired through colonialism and neocolonialism. The issue of **repatriation,** or returning objects to their original peoples, is a matter of international and intranational concern. In the United States and Canada, many Native American groups have lobbied successfully for the return of ancestral bones, grave goods, and potlatch goods. In 1990, the United States passed the Native American Graves Protection and Repatriation Act (NAGRPA) after two decades of lobbying by Native American groups (Bray 1996; Rose, Green, and Green 1996). This act requires universities, museums, and federal agencies in the United States to inventory their archaeological holdings in preparation for repatriating skeletons to their Native American descendant communities. Estimates of the number of Native American skeletons in museums in the United States (not including Hawai'i) range from 14,000 to 600,000. Unknown numbers of other items are being inventoried for possible repatriation, a process that is stretching slender museum budgets (Watson 1997).

The break-up of the former Soviet Union prompted claims from several newly independent states seeking to retrieve artistic property that originated in their locale and had been taken to Soviet national museums in Moscow and St. Petersburg. Ukraine, for example (see

THINKING OUTSIDE THE BOX

DO SOME Internet research on the repatriation in Canada of potlatch goods.

Map 14.1) has asked for the return of about two million art objects (Akinsha 1992a).

Another dimension of dispute about art in Russia concerns the state and the church. The Soviet state put many icons and other religious objects in museums and turned churches into museums. The Russian Orthodox Church has been campaigning for the return of church property. Churches are demanding that all sacred objects of the church, church buildings, and masterpieces of church art confiscated by the state after 1917 be returned to the ownership of the Russian Orthodox Church (Akinsha 1992b:102). Art historians and museum officials worry that the churches lack the resources and the experience to care for these treasures. Another complication comes from occasional threats of theft and violence to museums by those who seek the return of icons to churches and monasteries. In response, some museums have removed certain pieces from display.

Play, Leisure, and Culture

This section turns to the area of expressive culture related to what people do for "fun." It is impossible to draw a clear line between the concepts of *play* or *leisure* and art or performance, however, because they often overlap. For example, a person could paint watercolors in her leisure time, yet simultaneously be creating a work of art. In most cases, though, play and leisure can be distinguished from other activities by the fact that they have no direct, utilitarian purpose for the participant. Dutch historian Johan Huizinga, in the 1930s, proposed some features of play (summarized in Hutter 1996):

- Play is unnecessary activity, and thus free action.
- Play is outside of ordinary life.
- Play is closed and limited in terms of time.
- Play has rules.
- Play contains chance and often tension.

Leisure activities often overlap with play, but many leisure activities, such as reading or lying on a beach, would not be considered play because they lack rules, chance, and tension. Within the broad category of play and leisure activities, several subcategories exist, including varieties of games, hobbies, and recreational travel. Although play and leisure, and their subcategories, may be pursued from a nonutilitarian perspective, they are often situated in a wider context of commercial and political interests. The Olympic Games are a good example of such complexities.

Cultural anthropologists study play and leisure within their cultural contexts as part of social systems. They ask, for example, why some leisure activities involve teams rather than individuals; what the social roles and

MAP 14.1   Ukraine. Ukraine became independent after the collapse of the Soviet Union in 1991. It is mostly fertile plains, or steppes, crossed by rivers. Since independence and privatization, the economy has been unstable with high inflation rates. Related to the economic crisis, sex trafficking of women became a serious problem, infant mortality rates rose, and the birth rate fell. The total population is around 50 million and declining. Ukrainian is the official language, though many people speak Russian, especially in the south and east. In reality, many people speak a mixture of both languages. Government policy is to promote Ukrainization, especially the increased use of the Ukrainian language. The dominant religion is Eastern Orthodox Christianity. The tradition of coloring Easter eggs began in Ukraine in pre-Christian times.

wa: Japanese word meaning discipline and self-sacrifice for the good of the whole.

Tony Stewart, driver of the No. 20 Home Depot Chevrolet, makes a pit stop during the NASCAR SEXTEL Cup Series Food City at Bristol Meyer Speedway in Tennessee. James Todd, a doctoral student at the University of California at Santa Cruz, is writing his dissertation on NASCAR racing and its culture. ■ *What kinds of things do you think he is learning?* (Source: © George Tiedemann/GT Images/CORBIS)

Clearing a stone platform over six and a half feet high, a young man from Nias, Indonesia, participates in the sport of *fahombe*. Formerly a method of training warriors to leap over walls of enemy villages during a raid and of demonstrating a man's readiness to marry, *fahombe* is now a popular sport in several islands off Sumatra. ■ (Source: © Lindsay Hebberd/CORBIS)

status of people involved in particular activities are; what the goals of the games are and how they are achieved; how much danger or violence is involved; how certain activities are related to group identity; and how such activities link or separate different groups within or between societies or countries.

Games and Sports as a Cultural Microcosm

Games and sports, like religious rituals and festivals, can be interpreted as reflections of social relationships and cultural ideals. In Clifford Geertz's terms, they are both *models of a culture,* depicting basic ideals, and *models for a culture,* socializing people into certain values and ideals. American football can be seen as a model for corporate culture in its clear hierarchy with leadership vested in one person (the quarterback) and its goal of territorial expansion by taking over areas from the competition.

A comparison of baseball as played in the United States and in Japan reveals core values about social relationships in each country (Whiting 1979). These differences emerge clearly when U.S. players are hired by Japanese teams. The U.S. players bring with them an intense sense of individualism, which promotes the value of "doing your own thing." This pattern conflicts with a primary value that influences the playing style in Japan: **wa,** meaning discipline and self-sacrifice for the good of the whole. In Japanese baseball, players must seek to achieve and maintain team harmony. Japanese baseball players have a negative view of extremely individualistic, egotistical plays and strategies.

Sports and Spirituality: Male Wrestling in India

In many contexts, sports are closely tied to religion and spirituality. Asian martial arts, for example, require forms of concentration much like meditation, leading to spiritual self-control. Male wrestling in India, a popular form of entertainment at rural fairs and other public events, involves a strong link with spiritual development and asceticism (Alter 1992).

Wrestlers in the village of Sonepur, India. These wrestlers follow a rigorous regimen of dietary restrictions and exercise in order to keep their bodies and minds under control. ■ *Think of another sport that emphasizes dietary restrictions.* (Source: © CORBIS. All Rights Reserved.)

In some ways these wrestlers are just like other members of Indian society. They go to work, and they marry and have families, but their dedication to wrestling involves important differences. A wrestler's daily routine is one of self-discipline. Every act—defecation, bathing, comportment, devotion—is integrated into a daily regimen of discipline. Wrestlers come to the *akhara* (equivalent to a gymnasium) early in the morning for practice under the supervision of a guru or other senior akhara member. They practice moves with different partners for two to three hours. In the early evening, they return for more exercise. In all, a strong young wrestler will do around 2,000 push-ups and 1,000 deep-knee bends a day in sets of 50 to 100.

The wrestler's diet is prescribed by the wrestling way of life. Wrestlers are mainly vegetarian and avoid alcohol and tobacco, although they do consume *bhang,* a beverage made of blended milk, spices, almonds, and concentrated marijuana. In addition to regular meals, wrestlers consume large quantities of milk, ghee (clarified butter), and almonds. These substances are sources of strength, because according to traditional dietary principles, they help to build up the body's semen.

Several aspects of the wrestler's life are similar to those of a Hindu *sannyasi,* or holy man, who renounces life in the normal world. The aspiring sannyasi studies under a guru and learns to follow a strict routine of discipline and meditation called yoga, and he adheres to a restricted diet to achieve control of the body and its life force. Both wrestler and sannyasi roles focus on discipline to achieve a controlled self. In India, wrestling does not involve the "dumb jock" stereotype that it sometimes does in North America. Rather, the image is of perfected physical and moral health.

Play, Pleasure, and Pain

Many leisure activities combine pleasure and pain. Serious injuries can result from mountain climbing, horseback riding, or playing touch football in the backyard. A more intentionally dangerous category of sports is **blood sports,** competition that explicitly seeks to bring about a flow of blood or even death. Blood sports may involve human contestants, humans contesting against animal competitors, or animal-animal contestants (Donlon 1990). In the United States and Europe, professional boxing is an example of a highly popular blood sport that has not yet been analyzed by anthropologists. Cultural anthropologists have looked at the use of animals in blood sports such as cockfights and bullfights. These sports have been variously interpreted as providing sadis-

tic pleasure, as offering vicarious self-validation (usually of males) through the triumph of their representative pit bulls or fighting cocks, and as the triumph of culture over nature in the symbolism of bullfighting.

Even the seemingly pleasurable leisure experience of a Turkish bath can involve discomfort and pain. One phase involves scrubbing the skin vigorously several times with a rough natural sponge, a pumice stone, or a piece of cork wood wrapped in cloth (Staats 1994). The scrubbing removes layers of dead skin and opens the pores so that the skin will be beautiful. In Turkey, an option for men is a massage that can be quite violent, involving deep probes of leg muscles, cracking of the back, and being walked on by the (often hefty) masseur. In Ukraine, being struck repeatedly on one's bare skin with birch branches is the final stage of the bath. Violent scrubbing, scraping, and beating of the skin, along with radical temperature changes in the water, are combined with valued social interaction at the bathhouse.

THINKING OUTSIDE THE BOX

IN YOUR cultural world, what are some examples of leisure activities that combine pleasure and pain? As a research project, conduct some informal interviews with participants to learn why they are attracted to such activities.

Leisure Travel

Anthropologists who study leisure travel, or tourism, have often commented that their work is taken less seriously than it should be because of the perspective that they are just "hanging out" at the beach or at five-star hotels. Research on tourism, however, can involve as much conflict and danger as anthropological study of any other topic. Violence is not unknown in tourist destinations, and such sites are sometimes the explicit focus of violence. Even when the research site is peaceful, anthropological investigation of tourism involves the same amount of effort as any other fieldwork.

Tourism is now one of the major economic forces in the world, and it has dramatic effects on people and places in tourist destination areas. A large percentage of worldwide tourism involves individuals from Europe, North America, and Japan traveling to the less industrialized countries. Ethnic tourism, cultural tourism, and ecotourism are attracting increasing numbers of travelers. They are often marketed as providing a view of "authentic" cultures. Images of indigenous people figure prominently in travel brochures and advertisements (Silver 1993; Bruner 2005).

---

blood sport: a form of competition that explicitly seeks to bring about a flow of blood, or even death, of human-human contestants, human-animal contestants, or animal-animal contestants.

Many international tourists increasingly prefer "cultural tourism" so that they can participate, for a while, in what is presented to them as a traditional cultural context. Safari tour groups in Africa, as in the case of this visit to Maasailand, combine exposure to wildlife and to the Maasai people. ■ *Go to the Web to learn about cultural tourism opportunities among the Maasai.* (Source: © Betty Press/Woodfin Camp & Associates)

Tourist promotional literature often presents a "myth" of other peoples and places and offers travel as a form of escape to a mythical land of wonder. In fact, research on Western travel literature shows that from the time of the earliest explorers to the present, it has been full of "primitivist" images about indigenous peoples. They are portrayed as having static or "stone age" traditions, remaining largely unchanged by the forces of Western colonialism, nationalism, economic development, and tourism itself (Bruner 2005). Tourists often seek to find the culture that the tourist industry defines rather than gaining a genuine, more complicated, and perhaps less photogenic view of it. For the tourist, obtaining these desired cultural images through mass tourism involves packaging the "primitive" with the "modern" because most tourists want comfort and convenience along with their "authentic" experience. Thus, advertisements minimize the foreignness of the host country, noting, for example, that English is spoken and that the destination is remote yet accessible, while simultaneously promoting primitivist and sometimes racist imagery.

The strains between accuracy in presenting a cultural experience, sensationalism, and social stigma emerge clearly in research on tourism in the coal-mining region of Appalachia in Virginia (LaLone 2003). Mary LaLone pinpoints some of the challenges in representing Appalachian culture with accuracy and dignity in relation to responding to marketing demands of tourists. For example, in portraying people's everyday lives, accuracy says that it is right to show people wearing shoes and using indoor plumbing, whereas tourists may expect and want to see displays of "hillbilly life" that emphasize poverty, shoelessness, outhouses, feuding, and "moonshining" (producing and consuming illicit alcohol). LaLone suggests that cultural anthropologists may help find a way toward heritage interpretation and presentation that provides a more complex view so that hosts retain their dignity, accuracy is maintained, and tourists learn more than they expected.

The anthropology of tourism has focused on the impact of global and local tourism on indigenous peoples and places. Such studies are important in exposing the degree to which tourism helps or harms local people and local ecosystems. For example, the formation of Amboseli National Park in Kenya (see Map 6.2, p. 158) negatively affected the access of the Maasai to strategic water resources for their herds (Honadle 1985, as summarized in Drake 1991). The project staff promised certain benefits to the Maasai if they stayed off the reserve, but many of those benefits (including shares of the revenues from the park) never materialized. In contrast, in Costa Rica local people were included in the early planning stages of the Guanacaste National Park (see Map 14.2) and play a greater role in the park management system.

Many studies show how local residents attempt to exercise agency and take an active role in transforming the effects of tourism to their advantage and designing

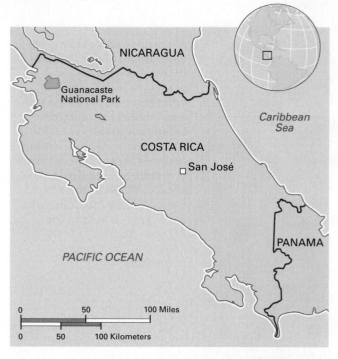

MAP 14.2   Costa Rica. The Republic of Costa Rica was the first country in the world to constitutionally abolish its army, and it has largely escaped the violence that its neighbors have endured. Agriculture is the basis of the economy with tourism, especially ecotourism, playing an increasing role. Most of the 4 million inhabitants of Costa Rica are descended from Spanish colonialists. Less than 3 percent are Afro-Costa Ricans, and less than 2 percent, or around 50,000, are indigenous people. Seventy-five percent of the people are Roman Catholic and 14 percent Protestant. The official language is Spanish.

and managing tourist projects (Stronza 2001; Natcher, Davis, and Hickey 2005; Miller 2005). The Gullah people of South Carolina are one such example (see Culturama); others are described in the last section of this chapter.

Change in Expressive Culture

Nowhere are forms and patterns of expressive culture frozen in time. Much change is influenced by Western culture through globalization, but influence does not occur in only one direction. African musical styles have transformed the U.S. musical scene since the days of slavery. Japan has exerted a strong influence on upper-class garden styles in the United States. Cultures in which tradition and conformity have been valued in pottery making, dress, or theater find themselves having to make choices about whether to innovate, and if so, how. Many contemporary artists (including musicians and playwrights) from Latin America to China are fusing ancient

and "traditional" motifs and styles with more contemporary themes and messages.

Changes occur through the use of new materials and technology and through the incorporation of new ideas, tastes, and meanings. These changes often accompany other aspects of social change, such as colonialism, global tourism, or political transitions.

Colonialism and Syncretism

Western colonialism had dramatic effects on the expressive culture of indigenous peoples. In some instances, colonial disapproval of particular art forms and activities resulted in their extinction. For example, when colonialists banned head-hunting in various cultures, this change also meant that body decoration, weapon decoration, and other related expressive activities were abandoned. This section provides an example of how colonial repression of indigenous forms succeeded, but only temporarily.

In the Trobriand Islands of Papua New Guinea (see Map 2.1, p. 39), British administrators and missionaries sought to eradicate the frequent tribal warfare as part of a pacification process. One strategy was to replace it with intertribal competitive sports (Leach 1975). In 1903, a British missionary introduced the British game of cricket in the Trobriands as a way of promoting a new morality, separate from the warring traditions. As played in England, cricket involves particular rules of play and a proper look of pure white uniforms. In the early stages of the adoption of cricket in the Trobriands, the game followed the British pattern closely. As time passed and the game spread into more parts of the islands, it developed localized versions.

Throughout the Trobriands, cricket was merged into indigenous political competition between big-men (Foster 2006). Big-men leaders would urge their followers to increase production in anticipation of a cricket match because matches were followed by a redistributive feast. The British missionaries had discouraged traditional magic in favor of Christianity, but the Trobriand Islanders brought war-related magic into cricket. For example, spells are used to help one's team win, and the bats are ritually treated in the way that war weapons were. Weather magic is also important. If things are not going well for one's team, a spell to bring rain and force cancellation of the game may be invoked.

Other changes occurred. The Trobrianders stopped wearing the crisp white uniforms and instead donned paint, feathers, and shells. They announced their entry into the host village with songs and dances, praising their team in contrast to the opposition. Many of the teams, and their songs and dances, draw on Western elements such as the famous entry song of the "P-K" team. (P-K is the name of a chewing gum. This team chose the name because the stickiness of gum is likened to the ability of their bat to hit the ball.) Other teams incorporated

The Gullah culture in South Carolina stretches along the coast, going inland about thirty miles (National Park Service 2005:10–11). The Gullah are descended from African slaves originating in West and Central Africa. In the early eighteenth century, Charleston, South Carolina, was the location of the largest trans-Atlantic slave market on the coast of British North America (National Park Service 2005:18).

The enslaved people brought with them many forms of knowledge and practice. Rice was a central part of their African heritage and identity. They knew how to plant it in swamps, harvest it, and prepare it. Gullah ancestors in colonial South Carolina were influential in developing *tidal irrigation methods* of rice growing, using irrigation and management of the tides to increase yields compared to yields from rainfall-dependent plantings.

Experts at net fishing, the Gullah made handwoven nets that are masterpieces of folk art. Their textile arts include a form of quilting, or sewing strips of cloth together into a larger piece. Gullah women combined their African quilting styles with those of Europeans to form new styles and patterns. Many quilts tell a story in their several panels.

Gullah cuisine combines African elements such as rice, yams, peas, okra, hot peppers, peanuts, watermelon, and sesame seeds with European ingredients, and Indian foods such as corn, squash, tomatoes, and berries (National Park Service 2005:62). Popular dishes are stews of seafood and vegetables served over rice. Rice is the cornerstone of the meal, and the family rice pot is a treasured possession passed down over the generations.

Gullah culture in South Carolina has become a major tourist attraction, including music, crafts, and cuisine. If there is a single item that tourists identify with the Gullah, it is sweetgrass baskets. Although basketmaking was once common among all Gullah people in South Carolina, it is thriving in the Charleston area largely due to a combination of tourist demand and the creativity of local artists. Both men and women "sew" the baskets. They sell them in shops in Charleston's historic center and along Highway 17.

As the success of the basketmakers has grown and the popularity of the baskets increased, so too has the need for sweetgrass. Sweetgrass baskets, thus, are a focal point of conflict between Gullah cultural producers and local economic developers who are destroying the land on which the sweetgrass grows. Since tourism in low country South Carolina is increasingly dependent on cultural tourism, some planners are trying to find ways to devote land to growing sweetgrass.

The story of the Gullah of South Carolina begins with their rich African cultural heritage through their suffering as slaves, to racism and social exclusion, and to their current situation in which their expressive culture is a key factor in the state economy.

Readings

Josephine Beoku-Betts. "We Got Our Way of Cooking Things." *Gender and Society, 9,* 535–555, 1995.

Virginia M. Geraty, *Gullah fuh Oonum: A Gullah English Dictionary.* Orangesburg, SC: Sandlapper Publishing, 1997.

National Park Service. *Low Country Gullah Culture: Special Resource Study and Final Environmental Impact Statement.* Atlanta: NPS Southeast Regional Office, 2005. www.nps.gov.

Dale Rosengarten. *Row upon Row: Sea Grass Baskets of the South Carolina Lowcountry.* Columbia: University of South Carolina Press, 1994.

Drummers at the Gullah Festival in Beaufort (pronounced BYOO-FORT) (left). The Festival celebrates the cultures and accomplishments of the Gullah people. (Source: © Bob Krist/CORBIS) The hands of Mary Jackson (right) are shown making a sweetgrass basket. (Source: © Karen Kasmauski/CORBIS)

MAP 14.3 *The Gullah Region of South Carolina. The heartland of Gullah culture is in the low country area of South Carolina, Georgia, and Florida, and on the Sea Islands.*

In the Trobriand Islands, British missionaries, in the late nineteenth century, tried to substitute their game of cricket for intertribal rivalries and warfare. It did not take long, however, for the Trobriand people to transform British rules and style to Trobriand ways. ■ *If you wanted to watch a cricket match, what would be the closest place for you to go?* (Source: © Wolfgang Kaehler/CORBIS)

sounds and motions of airplanes, objects that they first saw during World War II. The songs and dances are explicitly sexual and enjoyed by all, in spite of missionary attempts to suppress the "immoral" aspects of Trobriand culture. The Trobrianders have changed some of the rules of play as well. The home team should always win, but not by too many runs. In this way, guests show respect to the hosts. Winning is not the major goal. The feast after the match is the climax.

Tourism's Complex Effects

Global tourism has had varied effects on indigenous arts. Often, tourist demand for ethnic arts and souvenirs has led to mass production of sculpture or weaving or jewelry of a lesser quality than was created before the demand. Tourists' interests in seeing an abbreviated form of traditionally long dance or theater performances has led to the presentation of "cuts" rather than an entire piece. As a result, some scholars say that tourism leads to the decline in quality and authenticity of indigenous arts.

Tourist support for indigenous arts, however, is often the sole force maintaining them, because local people in a particular culture may themselves be more interested in foreign music, art, or sports. Vietnamese water puppetry is an ancient performance mode, dating back at least to the Ly Dynasty of 1121 (Contreras 1995). Traditionally, water puppet shows took place in the spring during a lull

in the farm work, or at special festival times. The stage for this performance art is either a small natural pond or an artificial water tank, with a backdrop that hides the puppeteers from the audience. They operate wooden puppets with bamboo poles, wires, and strings to make the puppets glide over the water as if on their own. Since the 1980s, water puppetry has grown in popularity among Vietnamese people and international tourists (Foley 2001). It has spread from its core area in the Red River Delta in the northern part of the country to being nationwide and from being a seasonal performance to being year-round.

One positive result of global tourism is the growing support for preservation of **material cultural heritage**, which includes sites, monuments and buildings, and movable objects considered of outstanding world value in terms of history, art, and science (Cernea 2001). UNESCO proposed the basic definition of material cultural heritage in 1972. Since then, many locations worldwide have been placed on its World Heritage List for preservation. In the Middle East and North Africa alone, sixty places are on UNESCO's list. Many invaluable sites and other aspects of material cultural heritage are lost to public knowledge through destructive engineering projects, war, looting, and private collecting.

Applied anthropologists are involved in promoting better stewardship of material cultural heritage. Some are motivated by a desire to preserve the record of human-

---

material cultural heritage: sites, monuments, buildings, and movable objects considered to have outstanding value to humanity. Also called cultural heritage.

intangible cultural heritage: UNESCO's view of culture as manifested in oral traditions, languages, performing arts, rituals and festive events, knowledge and

practices about nature and the universe, and craftmaking. Also called living heritage.

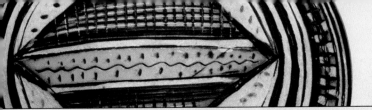

Lessons Applied

A STRATEGY FOR THE WORLD BANK ON CULTURAL HERITAGE

With headquarters in Washington, DC, and offices throughout the world, the World Bank is an international organization funded by member nations that works to promote and finance economic development in poor countries. Even though most of its permanent professional staff are economists, the Bank has begun to pay more attention to noneconomic factors that affect development projects. One of the major moves in that direction occurred in 1972 when the Bank hired its first anthropologist, Michael Cernea. For three decades, Cernea has drawn attention to the cultural dimensions of development, especially in terms of the importance of local participation in development projects and people-centered approaches to project-forced resettlement (when, for example, large dams are being planned). His most recent campaign is to convince top officials at the World Bank that the Bank should become involved in supporting cultural heritage projects as potential pathways to development.

The World Bank already has in place a "do no harm" rule when it approves and financially supports construction projects. Cernea agrees that a "do no harm" rule is basic to preventing outright destruction, but it is a passive rule and does nothing to provide resources to preserve sites. He wants the Bank to move beyond its "do no harm" rule and has written a strategy for it that is active, not passive. The strategy has two major objectives:

- The World Bank should support cultural heritage projects that promote poverty reduction and cultural heritage preservation by creating employment and generating capital from tourism.
- The projects should emphasize the educational value to local people and international visitors on the grounds that cultural understanding promotes value for goodwill and relations at all levels—local, state, and international.

Cernea also offers two suggestions for better management of cultural heritage projects: (1) selectivity in site selection on the basis of the impact in reducing poverty and (2) building partnerships for project planning and implementation among local, national, and international institutions.

FOOD FOR THOUGHT

- Find, on the Internet, the UNESCO World Heritage Site that is nearest to where you live. What does the site contain, and what can you learn about its possible or potential role in generating income for the local people?

---

ity for future generations, or for science. Others see that material cultural heritage, especially in poorer countries, can promote improvements in human welfare, and they endorse forging a link between material cultural heritage and sustainable development (see Lessons Applied box).

In 2003, UNESCO ratified a new policy aimed at protecting **intangible cultural heritage,** or living heritage manifested in oral traditions, languages, performing arts, rituals and festive events, knowledge and practices about nature and the universe, and craftmaking (http://portal.unesco.org/culture). Support for this policy is based on the understanding that intangible culture provides people with a sense of identity and continuity, promotes respect for cultural diversity and human creativity, is compatible with human rights promotion, and supports sustainable development. Through this initiative, member countries of the United Nations are to make lists of valuable forms of intangible culture and take steps to preserve them. This policy has stimulated discussion and debate among cultural anthropologists who see culture as more than a list

of traits, highly contextualized, always changing, and not amenable to being managed or preserved through policy mandates (Handler 2003).

Cultural anthropologists point to the fact that the preservation of expressive culture sometimes occurs as a form of resistance to outside development forces. One example of this phenomenon is the resurgence of the hula, a traditional Hawai'ian dance (Stillman 1996). Beginning in the early 1970s, the *Hawai'ian Renaissance* grew out of political protest, mainly against American colonialism. Hawai'ian youth began speaking out against encroaching development that was displacing indigenous people from their land and destroying their natural resources. They launched a concerted effort to revive the Hawai'ian language, the hula, and canoe paddling, among other things. Since then, hula schools have proliferated, and hula competitions among the islands are widely attended by local people and international tourists.

The 1990s saw the inauguration of the International Hula Festival in Honolulu, which attracts competitors

---

Classical dancers perform in Thailand. The intricate hand motions, with their impact augmented by metal finger extenders, have meanings that accompany the narrative being acted out. International tourism is a major support for such performance arts in Thailand. ■ *Learn about UNESCO's recent declaration about intangible cultural heritage and speculate on what it may mean for the preservation of particular cultural forms.* (Source: © Dallas and John Heaton/ CORBIS)

from around the world. Although the hula competitions have helped ensure the survival of this ancient art form, some Hawai'ians voice concerns. First, they feel that allowing non-Hawai'ians to compete is compromising the quality of the dancing. Second, the format of the competition violates traditional rules of style and presentation, which require more time than is allowed, so important dances have to be cut. Third, for Hawai'ians, hula has close ties to religious beliefs and stories about the deities (Silva 2004). Performing hula in a mainly secular format is offensive to the gods and violates the true Hawai'ian way.

Another approach to cultural heritage preservation that is not top-down is "people-first" cultural heritage projects (Miller 2005). These are projects designed by the people whose culture is to be preserved, designed for their benefit, and managed by them. A growing number of examples worldwide demonstrate the value of *people-first cultural heritage preservation* as having strong positive, measurable effects. One major area of impact is on the very survival of a culture through territorial entitlements, community security, poverty reduction, improved mental health, and educating youth in traditional knowledge. Other important domains where people-first cultural heritage preservation has demonstrable positive effects include minority rights, conflict prevention and resolution, and environmental conservation and sustainability.

An example of people-first heritage preservation with implications for territorial entitlements and cultural sur-

vival is the Waanyi Women's History Project, Northern Queensland, Australia (Smith, Morgan, and van der Veer 2003) (see Map 4.4, p. 105). This is a case of a community-driven project devoted to archiving cultural heritage and to establishing local community management. The "community" is a group of Waanyi women who value their family history as heritage. The traditional way of maintaining this heritage has been to pass it on verbally from mother to daughter. The women were interested in having a written record of their history and to record sites and places of significance to women. They hired an anthropologist consultant to collect and record their narratives. An interesting feature of this case, which contrasts with traditional academic research, is that the knowledge generated cannot be published. The role of the researcher is limited to supporting the aspirations of the Waanyi women.

The project had positive effects in providing a new source of income and thus reducing material deprivation and entitlement insecurity through the formal recognition of Waanyi custodial rights and the establishment of a National Park. It generated new sources of cash income for some Waanyi women through employment in the National Park as "cultural rangers" responsible for conservation of women's sites. This project is a clear case of a community-initiated and community-controlled heritage project. It involved concern for, and recognition of, community interests and goals. It produced benefits to the local people in terms of firmer entitlement to the land, new sources of income, skill acquisition, and pride.

The decorated façade of a domestic dwelling in Kano, northern Nigeria. ■ (Source: © Robert Frerck/Odyssey Productions, Inc.)

Post-Communist Transitions

Major changes have occurred in the arts in the states of the former USSR for two reasons: loss of state financial support and removal of state controls over subject matter and creativity. A new generation of talented young artists has appeared (Akinsha 1992c:109). They are looking for something new and different. Art for art's sake, independent from the socialist project, is now possible. Many of the new artists find inspiration in nostalgia for the popular culture of the 1950s and 1960s, such as a

pack of Yugoslav chewing gum, or the cover of a Western magazine. Commercial galleries are springing up, and a museum of modern art in Moscow opened in 1999.

Theater in China is passing through a transition period with the recent development of some features of capitalism. Since the beginning of the People's Republic in 1949, the arts have gone through different phases, from being suppressed as part of the old feudal tradition to being revived under state control. China's theater companies have experienced financial crises in recent times (Jiang 1994). Steep inflation means that actors can no longer live on their pay. Theater companies are urging their workers to find jobs elsewhere, such as making movies or videos, but this is not an option for provincial troupes. Local audience preferences have changed: "People are fed up with shows that 'educate,' have too strong a political flavor, or convey 'artistic values.' They no longer seem to enjoy love stories, old Chinese legends, or Euro-American theater. Most of the young people prefer nightclubs, discos, or karaokes. Others stay at home watching TV" (1994:73). The new materialism in China means that young people want to spend their leisure time having fun. For the theater, too, money now comes first. One trend is toward the production of Western plays.

For example, Harold Pinter's *The Lover* was an immediate success when it was performed in Shanghai in 1992 (Jiang 1994). In explaining its success, sex is a big part of the answer. The topic of sex was taboo in China for a long time and censored in theater and films. The producers of the play warned parents not to bring children with them, fueling speculation about a possible sex scene. Although *The Lover* contains only hints of sexuality, by Chinese standards it was bold. The actress's alluring dress had seldom, if ever, been seen by Chinese theatergoers in the early 1990s. There was also bold language: talk about female breasts, for example. Another feature was the play's focus on private life, interiority, and individual thoughts and feelings. This emphasis corresponds with a new focus on and cultivation of private lives in China. Change in the performing arts in China thus is being shaped both by changes in the local political economy and by globalization.

The Big Questions Revisited

HOW is culture expressed through art?

Cultural anthropologists choose a broad definition of art that takes into account cross-cultural variations. In the anthropological perspective, all cultures have some form of art and a concept of what is good art. Ethnographers document the ways in which art is related to many aspects of culture: economics, politics, human development and psychology, healing, social control, and entertainment. Art may serve to reinforce social patterns, and it may also be a vehicle of protest and resistance.

In state societies, especially in Europe, people began collecting art worldwide and placing it in museums a few hundred years ago. Later, ethnographic museums were established in Europe as the result of scientific and colonialist interest in learning about other cultures. Anthropologists study museum displays as a reflection of cultural values as well as sites where perceptions and values are formed. Many indigenous and formerly colonized people are reclaiming objects from museums as part of their cultural heritage.

WHAT do play and leisure activities reveal about culture?

Anthropological studies of play and leisure examine these activities within their cultural context. Cultural anthropologists view games as cultural microcosms, both reflecting and reinforcing dominant social values. Sports and leisure activities, although engaged in for nonutilitarian purposes, are often tied to economic and political interests. In some contexts, sports are related to religion and spirituality.

Tourism is a fast growing part of the world economy with vast implications for culture. Anthropologists who study tourism examine the impact of tourism on local cultures and questions of authenticity in the touristic experience. Tourism companies often market "other" cultures to appeal to the consumers, a phenomenon that perpetuates stereotypes and denigrates the "host" culture. Cultural anthropologists are working with the tourism industry to find better ways of representing culture that are more accurate, less stigmatizing to the host culture, and more informative for tourists.

HOW is expressive culture changing in contemporary times?

Major forces of change in expressive culture include Western colonialism, contemporary tourism, and globalization in general. As with other kinds of cultural change through contact, expressive culture may reject, adopt, and adapt new elements. Syncretism is a frequent occurrence, as exemplified in the Trobriand Islanders' co-optation and re-creation of cricket as a performative event leading up to a traditional feast.

In some cases, outside forces have led to the extinction of local forms of expressive culture. In others, outside forces have promoted continuity or the recovery of practices that had been lost. Resistance to colonialism and neocolonialism has inspired cultural revitalization, as in the Hawai'ian Renaissance. Post-communist states, in the past few decades, have reacted to freedom of expression and the privatization of art in various ways. Artists find new subject matter and audiences have more options.

KEY CONCEPTS

art, p. 370
blood sports, p. 384
ethno-esthetics, p. 371
ethnomusicology, p. 376

expressive culture, p. 370
heterotopia, p. 380
intangible cultural heritage, p. 389
material cultural heritage, p. 388

museum, p. 380
repatriation, p. 381
theater, p. 377
wa, p. 383

SUGGESTED READINGS

Eduardo Archetti. *Football, Polo and the Tango in Argentina*. New York: Berg, 1999. An Argentinian anthropologist examines expressive culture in Buenos Aires and how they are related to elite tastes, gender, and international competitiveness.

G. Whitney Azoy. *Buzkashi: Game and Power in Afghanistan*, 2nd ed. Long Grove, IL: Waveland, 2003. The first full-length ethnography of a sport, this study has been updated with a chapter on buzkashi as played through 2002. This game, which involves tribal groups of men on horseback competing for a goat or calf carcass, is probably ancestral to polo.

Tara Browner. *Heartbeat of the People: Music and Dance of the Northern Pow-Wow*. Urbana: University of Illinois Press, 2002. An ethnomusicologist of Choctaw heritage uses archival research on the pow-wow and participant observation to show how elements of the pow-wow in North America have changed.

Shirley F. Campbell. *The Art of Kula*. New York: Berg, 2002. The author focuses on designs painted on kula canoes and finds that kula art and its associated male ideology linked to the sea competes with female ideology and symbolism linked to the earth.

Rebecca Cassidy. *The Sport of Kings: Kinship, Class, and Thoroughbred Breeding in Newmarket*. New York: Cambridge University Press, 2002. This study of British thoroughbred racing is based on fieldwork conducted in Newmarket, England. How people discuss the horses, their breeding, and their capabilities relate to the British class system.

Michael M. Cernea. *Cultural Heritage and Development: A Framework for Action in the Middle East and North Africa*. Washington, DC: The World Bank, 2001. Following an overview of cultural heritage projects and possibilities in the Middle East and North Africa, Cernea presents a strategy to reduce poverty with high-impact cultural heritage projects.

John Miller Chernoff. *African Rhythm and African Sensibility: Aesthetics and African Musical Idioms*. Chicago: University of Chicago Press, 1979. This reflexive ethnography describes how Chernoff learned to play West African drums and to understand Ghanaian culture.

Michael Chibnik. *Carving Tradition: The Making and Marketing of Oaxcan Wood Carvings*. Austin: University of Texas Press, 2003. Chibnik examines the production of and international trade in Oaxacan wood carvings. Wood carving is not an indigenous art form in Oaxaca but was developed to appeal to tourists.

Timothy J. Cooley. *Making Music in the Polish Tatras: Tourists, Ethnographers, and Mountain Musicians*. CD included. Bloomington: Indiana University Press, 2005. This ethnographic study describes the musicians and music of the Tatra Mountains of southern Poland.

Robert Davis and Garry R. Marvin. *Venice: The Tourist Maze: A Cultural Critique of the World's Most Touristed City*. Berkeley: University of California Press, 2004. The authors include material on the beginnings of Venetian tourism in the late Middle Ages to its current form of mass entertainment through which Venetian residents are a minority in their hometown.

Patricia Fogelman Lange. *Pueblo Pottery Figurines: The Expression of Cultural Perceptions in Clay*. Tucson: University of Arizona Press, 2002. This book offers insights into Pueblo esthetics by focusing on the figurines made in the late nineteenth century. Their style departed from earlier ones as the artists responded to the presence of Anglo-Americans.

Alaina Lemon. *Between Two Fires: Gypsy Performance and Romani Memory from Pushkin to Post-Socialism*. Durham, NC: Duke University press, 2000. This book examines how theater in Moscow both liberates Roma in Russia and reinforces their status as stigmatized outsiders.

Beverly B. Mack. *Muslim Women Sing: Hausa Popular Song*. CD included. Bloomington: Indiana University Press, 2004. This ethnography provides an intimate portrait of the life and art of Hausa women singers in northern Nigeria. It shows how Hausa women exercise agency and creativity through music and dance.

Jay R. Mandle and Joan D. Mandle. *Caribbean Hoops: The Development of West Indian Basketball*. Amsterdam: Gordon and Breach Publishers, 1994. This book describes and analyzes the emergence of basketball (mainly men's basketball) as a popular sport in several Caribbean nations. It explores regional differences within the Caribbean.

Louise Meintjes. *Sound of Africa! Making Music Zulu in a South African Studio*. Durham, NC: Duke University Press, 2003. A South African anthropologist reveals the connections among music, culture, and state building. Focused on one studio in Johannesburg, this ethnography describes the roles of artists, sound engineers, emcees, and producers.

Laura Miller. *Beauty Up: Selling and Consuming Body Aesthetics in Japan*. Berkeley: University of California Press, 2006. The author, a linguistic anthropologist, examines the diversity of Japanese personal beauty practices for both males and females. She links eyelid surgery, body hair removal, and beauty products to a wider context of body esthetics.

Timothy Mitchell. *Blood Sport: A Social History of Spanish Bullfighting*. Philadelphia: University of Pennsylvania Press, 1991. Based on fieldwork and archival study, this book views bullfighting within the context of annual Spanish village and national fiestas, considers the role of the matador in society, and offers a psychosexual interpretation of the bullfight.

Stacy B. Schaefer. *To Think with a Good Heart: Wixárike Women, Weavers, and Shamans*. Salt Lake City: University of Utah Press, 2002. Weaving woolen textiles is a woman-centered activity among the Wixárike of western Mexico. Women generate income from weaving, and master weavers gain status.

R. Anderson Sutton. *Calling Back the Spirit: Music, Dance and Cultural Politics in Lowland South Sulawesi*. New York: Oxford University Press, 2002. The author describes many performance modes in South Sulawesi, Indonesia, from village ceremonies to studio-produced popular music. Accompanying the book is a CD.

PART V Contemporary Cultural Change

MAMPHELA RAMPHELE'S life story moves from her being subjected to racial apartheid and gender discrimination as a girl born in 1947 in rural Northern Transvaal, South Africa, to professional and personal achievement as a political activist, medical doctor, anthropologist, teacher, university administrator, mother, and (currently) one of the four managing directors of the World Bank.

As a child, Ramphele saw the injustices of apartheid inflicted on her family when the government retaliated against her relatives who worked for social equality. This experience spurred her on to political activism while she was still pursuing her education. Speaking of her school years, Ramphele says she felt confidence in her intelligence but had a difficult time overcoming the sense of inferiority that apartheid instilled in Black people.

In the early 1970s, Ramphele completed her medical studies at the University of Natal. She became a founder of South Africa's Black Consciousness movement to abolish segregation and injustice at a time when the nation's White government was engaged in some of the most brutally repressive activities in its history.

The consequence of her activism was federal censure under the Terrorism Act. Exiled for six years to Northern Transvaal, Ramphele worked with the rural poor, setting up community health programs. In the 1980s, she became a research fellow with the South African Development Research Unit at the University of Cape Town and earned a doctorate in anthropology. Her dissertation, *A Bed Called Home: Life in the Migrant Labour Hostels of Cape Town,* was later published as a book.

Ramphele also earned a BCom degree in administration and diplomas in tropical health and hygiene and public health. She served as senior research officer in the University of Cape Town's Department of Social Anthropology and, in 1996, became the first Black person and the first woman to be elected as vice-chancellor of the University of Cape Town.

Since 2000, Ramphele has been with the World Bank, the first South African to hold a position as managing director. In this position, she oversees the institution's human development activities in education; health, nutrition, and population; and social protection. She also monitors and guides the World Bank's relationships with client governments in strengthening socioeconomic support programs. In this capacity, she has worked to reduce child mortality, eradicate polio, and reduce the prevalence of HIV/AIDS, TB, and malaria.

Describing her work as "advocating with all my passion," Ramphele consults globally with several human rights initiatives. She was also an advisor to Nelson Mandela's government. She has received many awards and honors and has published books and articles on education, health, and social development.

In 2001, the South African Women for Women organization awarded Ramphele a Woman of Distinction Award that recognizes her "energetic leadership, her commitment to excellence, and her continuing dedication to transforming the lives of those around her."

Anthropology in the Real World

15

People on the Move

The Big Questions

- WHAT are the major categories of migration?

- WHAT are examples of the new immigrants in the United States and Canada?

- HOW do anthropologists contribute to migration policies and programs?

The so-called Marsh Arab people suffered under the rule of Saddam Hussein from government projects that drained their marshes and political repression. Many who fled the country as refugees are now returning and plans are under way for restoring some of the marshes. *(Source: © Nik Wheeler/CORBIS)*

The current generation of North American youth will move more times during their lives than previous generations. College graduates are likely to change jobs an average of eight times during their careers, and these changes are likely to require relocation.

Ecological, economic, familial, and political factors are causing population movements worldwide at seemingly all-time high levels. Research in anthropology shows, however, that frequent moves during a person's life and mass movements have occurred throughout human evolution. Foragers, horticulturalists, and pastoralists relocate frequently as a normal part of their lives.

Migration (defined in Chapter 5) is the movement of a person or people from one place to another. Its causes are linked to major aspects of life such as providing for one's food or for marriage. It often has profound effects on a person's economic and social status, for better or worse, as well as health, language, religious identity, and education. Thus, migration is of great interest to many academic subjects and professions. It is one of three core areas of demography, along with fertility and mortality (recall Chapter 5). Historians, economists, political scientists, sociologists, and scholars of religion, literature, art, and music have studied migration. The professions of law, medicine, education, business, architecture, urban planning, public administration, and social work have specialties that focus on the process of migration and the period of adaptation following a move. Experts working in these areas share with anthropologists an interest in such issues as the kinds of people who migrate, causes of migration, processes of migration, health and psychosocial adaptations to new locations, and implications for planning and policy.

Cultural anthropologists do research on many issues related to migration. They study how migration is related to economic and reproductive systems, health and human development over the life cycle, marriage and household formation, politics and social order, and religion and expressive culture. Because migration affects all areas of human life, this topic pulls together the material in preceding chapters of this book.

Given the breadth of migration studies, cultural anthropologists have used the full range of methods available, from individual life histories to large-scale surveys. Three differences distinguish research on migration studies from other areas of research in cultural anthropology:

- Anthropologists studying migration often have fieldwork experience in more than one location in order to understand the places of origin and estimation. Max-

Chinese Canadians mainly live in urban areas such as Vancouver and Toronto. In Vancouver, they constitute about 16 percent of the population. Vancouver's Chinatown is a vibrant tourist site as well as a place where Chinese Canadians reaffirm their cultural heritage, as in the celebration shown here of Chinese New Year. ■ *When does Chinese New Year take place, and how is the date determined?* (Source: © Annie Griffiths Belt/CORBIS)

ine Margolis (1994), for example, first did fieldwork in Brazil and then later studied Brazilian immigrants in New York City.

- Migration research is more likely to use both macro and micro perspectives. Studying migration challenges the traditional fieldwork focus on one village or neighborhood, creating the need to take into account national and global economic, political, and social forces (Basch, Glick Schiller, and Szanton Blanc 1994; Lamphere 1992).

- Anthropologists who do research about migrants tend to be involved in applied anthropology. Many oppor-

internal migration: population movement within state boundaries.

transnational migration: a form of population movement in which a person regularly moves between two or more countries and forms a new cultural identity transcending a single geopolitical unit.

push-pull theory: an explanation for rural-to-urban migration that emphasizes people's incentives to move based on a lack of opportunity in rural areas (the "push") compared to urban areas (the "pull").

tunities exist for anthropologists to contribute their knowledge and insights to improve government policies and programs related to migration. Anthropologists have been at the forefront of efforts to address the situation of people forced to move by war, environmental destruction, and massive building projects such as dams.

This chapter first presents information on the most important categories of migrants and the opportunities and challenges they face. The second section provides descriptions of several examples of immigrants to the United States and Canada. The last section considers urgent issues related to migration, such as human rights and risk assessment and prevention programs.

Categories of Migration

Migration encompasses many categories, depending on the distance involved; the migration's purpose, duration, and degree of voluntarism (was the move forced or more a matter of choice?); and the migrant's status in the new destination. Major differences exist in both causes and consequences between **internal migration,** movement within state boundaries, and *international migration,* moving to a different country. Moving to a new country, in general, involves more challenges in the process of relocation and in adjustment after arrival.

Categories Based on Spatial Boundaries

This section reviews the basic features of three categories of population movement defined in terms of the spatial boundaries crossed: internal migration, international migration, and transnational migration. **Transnational migration** is a form of population movement in which a person regularly moves back and forth between two or more countries and forms a new cultural identity transcending a single geopolitical unit (recall the discussion of transnationalism in Chapter 1).

Internal Migration

Rural-to-urban migration was the dominant form of internal population movements in most countries during the twentieth century. A major reason why people migrate to urban areas is the availability of work. According to the **push–pull theory** of labor migration, rural areas are increasingly unable to support population growth and rising expectations about the quality of life (*the push factor*). Cities (*the pull factor*) attract people, especially youth, for employment and lifestyle reasons. The push–pull model makes urban migration sound like

a simple function of rational decision making by people who have information on the costs and benefits of rural versus urban life, weigh that information, and then opt for going or staying. It is a theory closely related to the approach in anthropology emphasizing human agency, or choice (review Chapter 1). Many instances of urban migration, however, are shaped by structural forces that are beyond the control of the individual, such as economic need or political factors such as war (see Critical Thinking box).

The anonymity and rapid pace of city life and the likelihood of various degrees of stress caused by relocation pose special challenges for migrants from rural areas. Urban life, for example, increases the risk of hypertension (elevated blood pressure through stress or tension), which is related to coronary heart disease. In the Philippines (see Map 7.1, p. 174), hypertension is more common among urban migrants, both men and women, than among people living in their rural places of origin (Hackenberg et al. 1983). The relationship between elevated health risks resulting from psychosocial adjustment problems in rural-to-urban migration exists among international immigrants as well—for example, among Samoans who migrate to cities in California (Janes 1990).

International Migration

International migration has grown in volume and significance since 1945 and especially since the mid-1980s (Castles and Miller 1993). It is estimated that nearly 2 percent of the world's population lives outside of their home countries, or around 100 million people, including legal and undocumented immigrants. Migrants who move for work-related reasons constitute most of the people in this category. Over 35 million people from developing countries have migrated to industrialized countries in the past three decades. The driving forces behind this trend are economic and political changes that affect labor demands and human welfare.

The major destination countries of early international immigration are the United States, Canada, Australia, New Zealand, and Argentina. The immigration policies that these countries applied in the early twentieth century are labeled "White immigration" because they explicitly limited non-White immigration (Ongley 1995). In the 1960s in Canada, changes made immigration policies less racially discriminatory and more focused on skills and experience. The "White Australia" policy formally ended in 1973. In both the Canadian and Australian cases, a combination of changing labor needs and interest in improving their international image prompted the reforms. During the 1980s and the 1990s, the United States, Canada, and Australia experienced large-scale immigration from new sources, especially from Asia, and—to the United States—from Latin America and the Caribbean.

Critical Thinking

HAITIAN CANE CUTTERS IN THE DOMINICAN REPUBLIC: A CASE OF STRUCTURE OR HUMAN AGENCY?

The circulation of male labor from villages in Haiti (see Map 16.3, p. 433) to work on sugar estates in the neighboring Dominican Republic is the oldest and perhaps largest continuing population movement within the Caribbean region (Martínez 1996). Beginning in the early twentieth century, Dominican sugar cane growers began to recruit Haitian workers called *braceros*. Between 1852 and 1986, an agreement between the two countries' governments regulated and organized the labor recruitment. Since then, recruitment has become a private matter, with men crossing the border on their own or with recruiters working in Haiti without official approval. Many studies and reports have addressed this system of labor migration. Two competing perspectives exist:

- View 1, the structurist position, says that the bracero system is neo-slavery and a clear violation of human rights.
- View 2, the human agency position, says that braceros are not slaves because they migrate voluntarily.

View 1

Supporters of this position point to interviews with Haitian braceros in the Dominican Republic that indicate, they say, a consistent pattern of labor rights abuses. Haitian recruiters approach poor men, and boys as young as 7 years old, and promise them easy, well-paid employment in the Dominican Republic. Those who agree to go are taken to the frontier on foot and then either transported directly to a sugar estate in the Dominican Republic or turned over to Dominican soldiers for a fee for each recruit and then passed on to the sugar estate. Once there, the workers are given only one option for survival: cutting sugar cane, for which even the most experienced workers can earn only about US$2 a day. Working and living conditions on the estates are bad. The cane cutters are coerced into working even if they are ill, and working hours start before dawn and extend into the night. Many estate owners prevent Haitian laborers from leaving by having armed guards patrol the estate grounds at night. Many of the workers say that they cannot save enough from their meager wages to return home.

View 2

According to this view, reports of coercion are greatly exaggerated and miss the point that most Haitian labor migrants cross the border of their own volition. On the basis of his fieldwork in Haiti, cultural anthropologist Samuel Martínez comments that "Recruitment by force in Haiti seems virtually unheard of. On the contrary, if this is a system of slavery, it may be the first in history to turn away potential recruits" (1996:20). Some recruits have even paid bribes to recruiters in order to be hired. Most people, even young people, are aware of the terrible working conditions in the Dominican Republic, so they are exercising informed choice when they decide to

---

Long-time areas of outmigration of northern, western, and southern Europe are now receiving many immigrants, often refugees from Asia. Hungary, Poland, and Czechoslovakia are now popular destinations for many migrants. International population flows in the Middle East are complex, with some countries, such as Turkey, experiencing substantial movements in both directions. Millions of Turkish people have immigrated to Germany in recent decades. Turkey, in turn, has received many Iraqi and Iranian Kurdish refugees (review Culturama, Chapter 10, p. 276). Several million Palestinian refugees live in Jordan and Lebanon. Israel has attracted Jewish immigrants from Europe, northern Africa, the United States, and Russia.

Transnational Migration

Transnational migration is increasing along with other aspects of globalization. It is important to recall, however, that rising rates of transnational migration are related to the creation of state boundaries in recent centuries. Pastoralists with extensive seasonal herding routes were "transnational" migrants long before state boundaries cut across their pathways.

---

remittance: transfer of money or goods by a migrant to his or her family back home.

migrate. Repeat migration is common and is further evidence of free choice. The major means of maintaining labor discipline and productivity on the sugar estates is not force but wage incentives, especially piece-work. The life histories of braceros show that many of them move from one estate to another, thus discrediting the view that the estates are "concentration camps."

Martínez does, however, raise the issue of how free the "choice" to migrate to the Dominican Republic really is, given the extreme poverty in which many Haitians live. In Haiti, few work opportunities exist, and the prevailing wage for rural workers is US$1 a day. Thus, the poor are not truly free to choose to work in their home country: Labor migration to the Dominican Republic becomes a necessity. What looks like a free choice to participate in the bracero system is actually "illusory" or structured choice. It is based on the unavailability of the option to work for a decent wage in Haiti and on the forced, or structured, choice to work in the Dominican Republic.

A Haitian migrant laborer. It is a matter of debate how much choice such a laborer has in terms of whether he will migrate to the neighboring Dominican Republic for short-term work, cutting cane, given the fact that he cannot find paid work in Haiti. ■ (Source: Edward Keller III)

CRITICAL THINKING QUESTIONS

- What are the comparative strengths of View 1 and View 2?

- What does each perspective support in terms of policy recommendations?

- How does the concept of structured choice change those policy recommendations?

Much contemporary transnational migration is motivated by economic factors. The spread of the global corporate economy is the basis for the growth of one category of transnational migrants nicknamed "astronauts," businesspeople who spend most of their time flying among different cities as investment bankers or corporate executives. At the lower end of the income scale are transnational migrant laborers who spend substantial amounts of time working in different places and whose movements depend on the demand for their labor.

An important feature of transnational migration is how it affects a migrant's identity, sense of citizenship, and entitlements. Constant movement among different places weakens the sense of having one home and promotes instead a sense of belonging to a diffuse community of similar transnational migrants whose lives "in between" locations take on a new transnational cultural reality.

As a response to the increased rate of transnational migration and the growth of overseas diaspora populations (review definition in Chapter 9), many "sending" countries (countries that are the source of emigrants) are redefining themselves as transnational countries (Glick Schiller and Fouron 1999). They include Haiti, Colombia, Mexico, Brazil, the Dominican Republic, Portugal, Greece, and the Philippines. These countries confer continuing citizenship on emigrants and their descendants in order to foster a sense of belonging and willingness to continue to send **remittances,** or transfers of money or goods from migrants to their family back home. Remittances are an increasingly large, though difficult to quantify, proportion of the global economy and often a large part of a country's economy. For example, at least 60 percent of the gross domestic product of the small Pacific island country of Tonga comes from remittances

Turkish people, many of whom are Kurds, migrated to Germany in the 1960s and 1970s as "guest workers" to fill jobs in German factories. German leaders expected them to work, save money, and return to Turkey. Most stayed, and their children are now growing up in Germany, speaking German, and having only a distant relationship with Turkey. Many incidents of violence between so-called neo-Nazis and Turkish people have occurred, including the murder of five Turkish youths in Solingen in 1993. ■ *Do some Web research on the Turkish population of Germany.* (Source: © David Turnley/CORBIS)

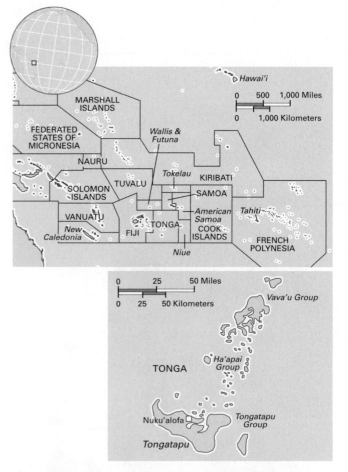

MAP 15.1 Tonga. The Kingdom of Tonga is an archipelago of 169 islands, nicknamed by Captain Cook as the Friendly Islands on the basis of his reception there. A constitutional monarchy, Tonga has great reverence for its king, stemming from a tradition of the sacred paramount chief. The current king, who has reigned since 1965, is Taufa'ahau Tupou IV. Before him, Queen Salote Tupou II reigned from 1918 to 1965. Rural Tongans are small-scale farmers. The manufacturing sector is minor while remittances are a major part of the economy. The population is around 113,000, with two-thirds living on the main island, Tongatapu. Many Tongans have emigrated. Most Tongans are ethnically Polynesian, and Christianity is by far the dominant religion. Languages are Tongan and English.

from members of the Tongan diaspora (Lee 2003:32) (see Map 15.1).

A debate that crosses the social sciences is about the effects of remittances on the welfare of the people and the development of the countries to which they are sent (Binford 2003). The major issue is whether remittances go into long-term investments that raise people's quality of life or are used for short-term consumption purposes. The term *investment* can absorb substantial scholarly thinking in terms of how to define it. Is taking a child to a clinic for a vaccination a short-term expenditure or an investment? Semantic quibbles aside, most experts agree that remittances are important in helping families maintain their health and welfare and in promoting local development through donations to build schools, roads, and clinics.

Categories Based on Reason for Moving

This section reviews categories of migrants based on the reason for relocating. The spatial categories just discussed overlap with these categories. An international migrant, for example, may also be a person who moved for employment reasons. Migrants experience different kinds of spatial change and, at the same time, have various reasons for moving.

circular migration: a regular pattern of population movement between two or more places, either within or between countries.

displaced person: someone who is forced to leave his or her home and community or country.

refugee: someone who is forced to leave his or her home, community, or country.

internally displaced person: someone who is forced to leave his or her home and community but who remains in the same country.

Hakka women of rural southern China are touristically defined by their "lamp shade" hats. Here, a Hakka woman who has migrated to Hong Kong for work wears a traditional Hakka woman's hat as she pursues an urban lifestyle. ■ (Source: Hans Blossey/Das Fotoarchiv/Peter Arnold)

Labor Migrants

Many thousands of people migrate each year to work for a specific period of time. They do not intend to establish permanent residence and are often explicitly barred from doing so. This form of migration, when legally contracted, is called *wage labor migration*. The period of work may be brief or it may last several years, as among rural Egyptian men who go to the Gulf countries to work for an average period of four years (Brink 1991).

Asian women are the fastest-growing category among the world's more than 35 million migrant workers (www.ilo.org). Over 1.5 million Asian women are working abroad. Most are in domestic service jobs, and some work as nurses and teachers. Major sending countries are Indonesia, the Philippines, Sri Lanka, and Thailand. Main receiving countries are Saudi Arabia and Kuwait, and, to a lesser degree, Hong Kong, Japan, Taiwan, Singapore, Malaysia, and Brunei. Such women are usually alone and are not allowed to marry or have a child in the country where they are temporary workers. International migrant workers are sometimes illegally recruited and have no legal protection in their working conditions.

Circular migration is a regular pattern of population movement between two or more places. It may occur within or between countries. Internal circular migrants include, for example, female domestic workers throughout Latin America and the Caribbean. These women have their permanent residence in the rural areas, but they work for long periods of time in the city for better-off people. They may leave their children in the care of grandparents in the country, sending remittances for the children's support.

THINKING OUTSIDE THE BOX

HAVE YOU, with or separately from your family, ever moved for work-related reasons? What kinds of adjustments did you and your family members have to make in the new location?

Displaced Persons

Displaced persons are people who are evicted from their homes, communities, or countries and forced to move elsewhere (Guggenheim and Cernea 1993). Colonialism, slavery, war, persecution, natural disasters, and large-scale mining and dam building are major causes of population displacement.

Refugees are internationally displaced persons. Many refugees are forced to relocate because they are victims or potential victims of persecution on the basis of their race, religion, nationality, ethnicity, gender, or political views (Camino and Krulfeld 1994). Refugees constitute a large and growing category of displaced persons. An accurate count of all categories of refugees globally is unavailable, but it probably exceeds 10 million people. About one of every 500 people are refugees (Lubkemann 2002). One-fourth of the world's refugees are Palestinians.

Women and children form the bulk of refugees and are vulnerable to abuse in refugee camps, including rape and children trading sex for food (Martin 2005). Some case studies shed some more positive light (Burton 2004). Refugee women from El Salvador, for example, learned to read and write in the camps and found positive role models in the "internationalist" workers and their vision of social equality.

Internally displaced persons (IDPs) are people who are forced to leave their home and community but who remain within their country. They are the fastest-growing category of displaced people. Current estimates are that the number of IDPs is double that of refugees, over 20 million people (Cohen 2002). Africa is the continent with the most IDPs, and within Africa, Sudan (see Map 16.7, p. 443) is the country with the highest number (around 4.5 million).

Because IDPs do not cross country boundaries, they do not come under the purview of the United Nations or any other international body. These institutions have limited

Dr. Francis Deng (*right*), former ambassador from Sudan to the United States, was instrumental in gaining international recognition of internally displaced persons as an important category. ■ *Do research on a case of IDPs in your home state or country, and report on it to the class.* (Source: AP/Wide World Photos)

authority over problems within countries. Francis Deng, former Sudanese ambassador to the United States, has taken up the cause of IDPs and is working to raise international awareness of the immensity of the problem. His efforts led to the formal definition of IDPs and to legal recognition of their status. In his former role as UN Secretary-General for Internally Displaced Persons, Deng coordinated a global coalition of institutions (including the UN, governments, and nongovernmental organizations) to provide more timely and effective assistance for internally displaced persons. Many IDPs, like refugees, live for extended periods in camps with miserable conditions and no access to basic supports such as health care and schools.

Development projects (discussed in Chapter 16) often cause people to become IDPs. Large dam construction, mining, and other projects have displaced millions in the past several decades. Dam construction alone is estimated to have displaced around 80 million people since 1950 (Worldwatch Institute 2003). Forced migration due to development projects is called **development-induced displacement (DID)**.

Mega-dam projects are now attracting the attention of concerned people worldwide who support local resistance to massive population displacement. One of the most notorious cases is India's construction of a series of high dams in its Narmada River Valley, which cuts across the middle of the country from the west coast. This massive project involves relocating hundreds of thousands of people. The relocation is against the residents' wishes, and government compensation to the "oustees" for the loss of the homes, land, and livelihood is completely inadequate. Thousands of people in the Narmada Valley have organized protests over the many years of construction, and international environmental organizations have lent support. Celebrated Indian novelist, Arundhati Roy, joined the cause by learning everything she could about the twenty years of government planning for the Narmada dam projects, interviewing people who have been relocated, and writing a passionate statement in opposition to the project called *The Cost of Living* (1999). A man who was displaced and living in a barren resettlement area tells how he used to pick fruit in the forest, forty-eight kinds. In the resettlement area, he and his family have to purchase all their food, and they cannot afford any fruit at all (1999:54–55).

Governments promote mega-dam projects as important to the state's interest. The uncalculated costs, however, are high for the local people who are displaced. The benefits are skewed toward corporate profits, energy for industrial plants, and water for urban consumers who can pay for it.

In China, the Three Gorges Dam project will, when completed, have displaced perhaps 2 million people (McCully 2003). The Chinese government, however, has consulted with cultural anthropologists, notably Michael Cernea of the World Bank, to learn how to lessen the damage caused to the displaced people by improving the relocation process.

The manner in which displaced persons are relocated affects how well they will adjust to their new lives. Displaced persons in general have little choice about when and where they move, and refugees typically have the least choice of all. The Maya people of Guatemala suffered horribly during years of state violence and genocide. Many became refugees, relocating to Mexico and the United States. Others fit in the category of internally displaced persons (see Culturama).

Cultural anthropologists have done substantial research with refugee populations, especially those related to war and other forms of violence and terror (Camino and Krulfeld 1994; Hirschon 1989; Manz 2004). They have helped discover the key factors that ease or increase relocation stresses. One basic factor is the extent to which the new location resembles or differs from the home place in features such as climate, language, and food (Muecke 1987). Generally, the more different the places of origin and destination are, the greater the adaptational demands

development-induced displacement (DID): forced migration due to development projects, such as dam building.

Culturama

The Maya of Guatemala

The term *Maya* refers to a diverse range of indigenous people who share elements of a common culture and speak varieties of the Mayan language. (*Note:* The spelling of the adjective includes a final *n* only when referring to the language.) Most Maya people live in Mexico and Guatemala, with smaller populations in Belize and the western parts of Honduras and El Salvador. Their total population in Mexico and Central America is about six million people.

In Guatemala, the Maya live mainly in the western highlands. The Spanish treated the Maya as subservient, exploited their labor, and took their land. Descendants of a formerly rich and powerful civilization, most Maya now live in poverty and lack basic human rights.

The Maya in Guatemala suffered years of genocide during the 36-year civil war. During the war, about 200,000 Maya "disappeared" and were brutally murdered by government military forces (Manz 2004:3). Many more were forcibly displaced from their homeland, with around 250,000 Maya today living as IDPs (Fitigu 2005). Thousands left the country as refugees, fleeing to Mexico and the United States.

Beatriz Manz tells a chilling story of one group of K'iche' Maya and their struggle to survive during the war (2004). Manz began her fieldwork in 1973 among the Maya living in the rural areas near the highland town of Santa Cruz del Quiché in the province of El Quiché. The Maya farmed small plots, growing maize and other food items, but found it increasingly difficult to grow enough food for their families. An American Catholic priest came to them with an idea for a new settlement, over the mountains to the east, in Santa María Tzejá. The new location was hard to get to, requiring days of hiking through dense jungle.

Several Maya from the highlands decided to establish a new village. They divided land into equal-size plots so that everyone had enough to support their families. Settlers established a democratic form of community organization. Over time, more settlers came from the highland village. They cleared land for houses, farms, workshops, and a school.

In the late 1970s, their lives were increasingly under surveillance by the Guatemalan military who suspected the village of harboring insurgents. In the early 1980s, the military began taking village men away. These men were never seen alive again. In 1982, a brutal attack left the village in flames and survivors fleeing into the jungle. Some went to Mexico, where they lived in exile for years, and others migrated as refugees to the United States. The peace accords of 1996 officially ended the bloodshed (2004:211). Many of the villagers returned and began to rebuild.

Readings

Laurel Bossen. *The Redivision of Labor: Women and Economic Choice in Four Guatemalan Communities.* Albany: State University of New York Press, 1984.

Beatriz Manz. *Paradise in Ashes: A Guatemalan Journey of Courage, Terror, and Hope.* Berkeley: University of California Press, 2004.

Rigoberta Menchú. *I, Rigoberta Menchú: An Indian Woman in Guatemala.* Ann Wright, trans. New York: Verso, 1984.

Websites

Amnesty International Annual Report, http://web.amnesty.org/report NISGUA, Network in Solidarity with the People of Guatemala, www.nisgua.org

Thanks to Beatriz Manz, University of California at Berkeley, for reviewing this material.

Maya women pray in a church fifty-five miles southeast of Guatemala City in 2003 (left). The coffins contain the remains of the victims of a 1982 massacre inside the church. (Source: © Reuters/CORBIS) Maya women are active in market trade, as shown in this scene (right) at the Chichicastenango market. (Source: © Tibor Bogár/CORBIS)

MAP 15.2 *Guatemala. Within the Republic of Guatemala, Maya Indians constitute about 40 percent of the country's population of 14.6 million.*

As construction of the massive Three Gorges Dam project proceeds in China, residents of Wanzhuo, Chongging, collect the belongings from their homes as the bulldozers arrive. ■ *Go to the Web and do research so that you can present a five-minute briefing on the Three Gorges Dam project to the class.* (Source: © Gilles Sabrié/CORBIS)

and stress. Other key factors are the refugee's ability to get a job commensurate with his or her training and experience, the presence of family members, and whether people in the new location are welcoming or hostile to the refugees.

An often overlooked category of involuntary migrants are adopted children. They themselves have no choice in their destination, although their countries of origin may place restrictions on adopters. Adoption occurs within countries as well as internationally. People in the United States are major international adopters, with numbers of international adoptions doubling between 1995 and 2005 (*Washington Post* 2006). More than one-third of the adopted children are from China (see Figure 15.1).

FIGURE 15.1 Immigrant Visas Issued to Orphans Coming to the United States in 2005: Top Countries of Origin

	Number of Visas for Orphans	Country of Origin
1	7,906	China (Mainland)
2	4,639	Russia
3	3,783	Guatemala
4	1,630	South Korea
5	821	Ukraine
6	755	Kazakhstan
7	441	Ethiopia
8	323	India
9	291	Colombia
10	271	Philippines
11	231	Haiti
12	182	Liberia
13	141	China (Taiwan born)
14	98	Mexico
15	73	Poland
16	73	Thailand
17	66	Brazil
18	65	Nigeria
19	63	Jamaica
20	62	Nepal

Source: U.S. Department of State website; http://travel.state.gov/family/adoption/stats/stats_451.html.

Institutional Migrants

Institutional migrants are people who move into a social institution, either voluntarily or involuntarily. They include monks and nuns, the elderly, prisoners, and boarding school or college students. This section considers examples of students and soldiers within the category of institutional migrants.

Student adjustment is similar to many other forms of migration, especially in terms of risks for mental stress (see Everyday Anthropology box). International students face serious challenges of spatial and cultural relocation. They are at greater risk of adjustment stress than are local students. Many international students report mental health problems, depending on age, marital status, and other factors. Spouses who accompany international students also suffer the strains of dislocation.

Soldiers are often sent on long-distance assignments for lengthy periods of time. Their destination may have negative physical and mental health effects on them, in addition to the fact that they may face combat. During the British and French colonial expansion, thousands of soldiers were assigned to tropical countries (Curtin 1989). Colonial soldiers faced new diseases in their destination areas. Their death rates from disease were twice as high as those of soldiers who stayed home, with two exceptions—Tahiti and Hawai'i—where soldiers experienced better health than soldiers at home. Most military personnel were men, but in some colonial contexts, wives accompanied their husbands. In India, mortality rates were higher for women than for men. This finding may be explained by the fact that the men had to pass a physical exam before enlistment, whereas their dependents did not.

As noted in Chapter 11, military anthropology is an emerging specialty in cultural anthropology, but still a small one. Anthropologists have published little about the effects of military migration on people in the military and local people. One matter is clear, however: Military people on assignment need more in-depth training about how to communicate with local people and about the importance of respecting local people's cultures. A pocket-size handbook on Iraqi etiquette used by some U.S. troops in Iraq provides extremely basic guidelines (Lorch 2003). It says, for example, that one should avoid arguments and should not take more than three cups of coffee or tea if one is a guest. Also, one should avoid the "thumbs up" gesture since its meaning is obscene, and one should not sit with one's feet on a desk. Such basics are helpful, but they do little to provide the cultural understanding that is of critical importance in both conflict and postconflict situations.

United States marines wearing gas masks as protection from oil fumes during the 1990–1991 Gulf War. Many poorly understood illnesses afflict veterans of "Desert Storm," including skin conditions, neurological disorders, chronic fatigue, and psychological-cognitive problems. ■ *Do research to learn about current medical thinking on the causes of Gulf War illnesses.* (Source: © David Leeson/The Image Works)

Soldiers during wartime are trained primarily to seek out and destroy the enemy, not to engage in cross-cultural communication. As mentioned in Chapter 11, winning a war in contemporary times often hinges on what the conquerors do following the outright conflict, and that often means keeping troops stationed in foreign contexts for a long time. Such extended assignments take a heavy toll on military personnel's mental health and may be linked to high rates of suicide, interpersonal violence, stress-based acts of violence against people in the occupied country, and serious readjustment problems when returning home.

The New Immigrants to the United States and Canada

The term **new immigrant** refers to a person who moved internationally since the 1960s. The category of new immigrants worldwide includes rapidly increasing proportions of refugees, most of whom are destitute and desperate for asylum. Three trends are apparent in the new international migration that began in the 1990s.

---

institutional migrant: a person who moves into a social institution (such as a school or prison), voluntarily or involuntarily.

new immigrant: international migrant who has moved since the 1960s.

Everyday Anthropology

SCHOOL GIRLS AND STRESS

Ethnographic research conducted among adolescent boarding school children in Ambanja, a town in Madagascar, showed that girls experience more adjustment strains than boys (Sharp 1990). Ambanja is a booming migrant town characterized by rootlessness and anomie. Boarding school children in this town constitute a vulnerable group because they have left their families and come alone to the school.

Many of the boarding school girls, between the ages of 13 and 17, experienced bouts of spirit possession. Local people say that the prettiest girls are the ones who become possessed. The data on possession patterns showed, instead, that possession is correlated with a girl's being unmarried and pregnant. Many of these school girls become the mistresses of older men, who shower them with expensive gifts such as perfume and gold jewelry. Such girls attract the envy of both other girls and school boys, who are being passed over in favor of adult men. Thus, the girls have little peer support among their schoolmates. If a girl becomes pregnant, school policy requires that she be expelled. If the baby's father refuses to help her, she faces severe hardship. Her return home will be a great disappointment to her parents.

Within this context, a girl's spirit possession may be understood as an expression of distress. Through the spirits, girls act out their difficult position between country and city and between girlhood and womanhood.

MAP 15.3 **Madagascar. The Republic of Madagascar includes the main island of Madagascar and several much smaller islands off its coast. It is the home of 5 percent of the world's plant and animal species of which 80 percent are unique to Madagascar. The terrain varies from highlands to lowlands, rainforests, and deserts. The economy is reliant on tourism, especially ecotourism, and mining is increasing. The total population is 18 million. DNA analysis reveals that the population is a mixture of Malay and East African heritage. The primary language is Malagasy which shares about 90 percent of its vocabulary with a language in southern Borneo. About half the people practice traditional religions related to ancestors, and most others are Catholics or Protestants.**

FOOD FOR THOUGHT

- Consider the patterns of psychological stress among college students and their possible gender dimensions. How do these patterns of stress differ from or resemble the situation described here?

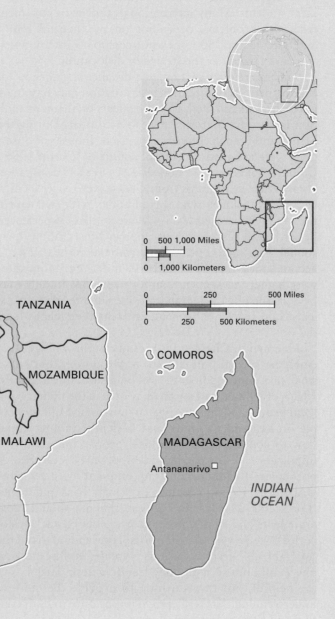

- *Globalization:* More countries are involved in international migration, leading to increased cultural diversity in sending and receiving countries.
- *Acceleration:* Growth in numbers of migrants has occurred worldwide.
- *Feminization:* Women are a growing percentage of international migrants to and from all regions and in all types of migration; some forms exhibit a majority of women.

These three trends raise new challenges for policymakers and international organizations. The cultural practices and beliefs of immigrant groups and those of people in the host countries increasingly come in contact, and sometimes, in conflict, with each other.

In the United States, the category of new immigrants refers to people who arrived following the 1965 amendments to the Immigration and Naturalization Act. This change made it possible for far more people from developing countries to enter, especially if they were professionals or trained in some desired skill. Later, the *family reunification* provision allowed permanent residents and naturalized citizens to bring in close family members. Most of the new immigrants in the United States are from Asia, Latin America, and the Caribbean, although increasing numbers are from Eastern Europe, especially Russia.

The United States offers two kinds of visas for foreigners: immigrant visas (also called residence visas) and nonimmigrant visas for tourists and students (Pessar 1995:6). An immigration visa is usually valid indefinitely and allows its holder to be employed and to apply for citizenship. A nonimmigrant visa is issued for a limited time period and usually bars its holder from paid employment. Some immigrants are granted visas because of their special skills in relation to labor market needs, but most are admitted under the family unification provision.

The New Immigrants from Latin America and the Caribbean

Since the 1960s, substantial movements of the *Latino* population (people who share roots in former Spanish and Portuguese colonies in the Western Hemisphere) have occurred, mainly to the United States. Compared to numbers of legal immigrants in the 1960s, numbers doubled or tripled in the 1980s and then declined in the 1990s. For example, legal immigrants from Central America numbered about 100,000 in the 1960s, nearly 900,000 in the 1980s, and about 270,000 in the 1990s (Parrillo 1997:398). Latinos are about 10 percent of the U.S. population, excluding the population of Puerto Rico.

In the United States as a whole, and in some cities, such as Los Angeles, Miami, San Antonio, and New York, Latinos are the largest minority group. Within the category

Latino immigrants studying English in a program in Virginia. ■ *Besides acquiring new language skills, what other kinds of learning are important for international immigrants?* (Source: © David H. Wells/CORBIS)

of Latino new immigrants, the three largest subgroups are Mexicans, Puerto Ricans, and Cubans. Large streams also come from the Dominican Republic, Colombia, Ecuador, El Salvador, Nicaragua, and Peru.

Mexico is by far the major source of foreign-born immigrants to the United States (www.migrationinformation.org). About 11 million foreign-born Mexicans live in the United States, a number that doubled from 1990 to 2000. Most live in the traditional destination states of California, Texas, and Illinois. Increasing numbers of immigrants from Mexico are settling in new destination states such as Georgia and North Carolina. Mexico is also the major source of unauthorized immigration into the United States. So many people leave Mexico that many rural towns are left with mainly elderly people and their grandchildren until the Christmas holidays when migrant workers return to join their families for a week or two.

THINKING OUTSIDE THE BOX

EXPLORE the website of the Migration Information Source and locate its map of the United States showing foreign-born Mexicans as a percentage of the population by county.

Chain Migration of Dominicans

The Dominican Republic has ranked among the top ten source countries of immigrants to the United States since the 1960s (Pessar 1995) (see Map 16.3, p. 433). Dominicans are one of the fastest-growing immigrant groups in the United States. They live in clusters in a few states, with their highest concentration in New York State. Within New York City, Washington Heights is the heart of the Dominican community. Unlike many other new immigrant streams, the Dominicans are mainly middle and upper class. Most have left their homeland in search of a better life. Many hope to return to the Dominican

A Dominican Day parade in New York City. ■ *Learn about an ethnic festival or event that is being held in the near future. Attend it and observe what signs and symbols of ethnicity are displayed, who attends, and what major messages about identity are conveyed.* (Source: © Stephen Ferry/Getty Images)

Republic, saying that in New York, "there is work but there is no life."

Patricia Pessar conducted fieldwork in the Dominican Republic and with Dominican immigrants living in New York City. She studied the dynamics of departure (such as getting a visa), the process of arrival, and adaptation in New York. Like most anthropologists who work with immigrant groups, she became involved in helping many of her participants: "Along the way I also endeavored to repay people's help by brokering for them with institutions such as the Immigration and Naturalization Service, social service agencies, schools, and hospitals" (1995:xv).

For Dominican immigrants, as for many other immigrant groups, the *cadena*, or chain, links one immigrant to another. **Chain migration** is a form of population movement in which a first wave of migrants comes, which then attracts relatives and friends to join them in the destination place. Most Dominicans who are legal immigrants have sponsored other family members. Thus, many Dominicans have entered the United States through the family unification provision. The policy, however, defines a family as a nuclear unit (review Chapter 8) and excludes important members of Dominican extended families such as cousins and ritual kin (*compadres*). To

overcome this barrier, some Dominicans use a technique called the *business marriage*. In a business marriage, an individual seeking to migrate pays a legal immigrant or citizen a fee, perhaps $2,000, to contract a "marriage." He or she then acquires a visa through the family unification provision. A business marriage does not involve cohabitation or sexual relations; it is meant to be broken.

In New York City, most Dominicans work in manufacturing industries, including the garment industry. They are more concentrated in these industries than any other ethnic group. Recent declines in manufacturing jobs in New York City, and the redefining of better positions into less desirable ones, have therefore disproportionately affected them. Dominicans also work in retail and wholesale trade, another sector that has declined since the late 1960s. Others have established their own retail businesses, or *bodegas*. Many bodegas are located in unsafe areas and some owners have been assaulted or killed. Declining economic opportunities for Dominicans are aggravated by the arrival of even newer immigrants, especially from Mexico and Central America, who are willing to accept lower wages and worse working conditions.

Although many middle-class and upper-class Dominican migrants secured fairly solid employment in the United States on their arrival, they have declined economically since then. Dominicans have the highest poverty rate in New York City of 37 percent, compared with a city average of 17 percent. Poverty is concentrated among women-headed households with young children. The gender gap in wages is high, and women are more likely than men to be on public assistance.

On the other hand, Dominican women in the United States are more often regularly employed than they would be in the Dominican Republic. This pattern upsets a patriarchal norm in which the nuclear family depends on male earnings and female domestic responsibilities. A woman's earning power means that husband–wife decision making is more egalitarian. A working Dominican woman is likely to obtain more assistance from the man in doing household chores. All of these changes help explain why Dominican men are more eager to return to the Dominican Republic than women are. As one man said, "Your country is a country for women; mine is for men" (1995:81).

Salvadorans: Escaping War to Struggle with Poverty

Salvadorans are the fourth largest Latino population in the United States, numbering around 1,200,000 people in 2006 (www.migrationinformation.org). The civil war in El Salvador, which began in 1979 and continued for a

---

chain migration: population movement in which a first wave of migrants comes and then attracts relatives and friends to join them in the destination.

Hillary Clinton visits an orphanage in El Salvador in 1998. Many children were orphaned because their parents were killed during the civil war of the 1980s. Others were abducted by the Salvadoran military and still have not been reunited with their parents, over two decades later. ■ *What can and should governments do to ensure children's safety and rights during war?* (Source: © Yuri Cortez/CORBIS)

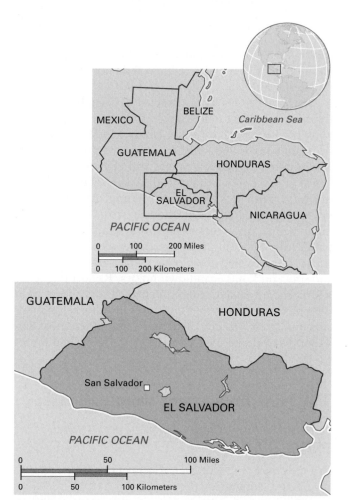

MAP 15.4 El Salvador. The Republic of El Salvador in recent times has tended to emphasize one or two major export crops, with coffee being dominant. Coffee growing requires high-altitude land, and coffee production has displaced many of the indigenous people. The country's total population is nearly 7 million. About 90 percent are mestizo, 9 percent European descent (mostly Spanish), and 1 percent Indigenous. The dominant language is Spanish, although some indigenous people speak Nahuat, a dialect of Nahuatl. Eighty-three percent of the people are Roman Catholic, and Protestants are 15 percent and growing in number.

decade, was the major stimulus for Salvadoran emigration (Mahler 1995) (see Map 15.4). By 1984, one-fourth of its population were either refugees or IDPs (Burton 2004). Most of the refugees came to the United States. About half of all Salvadorans in the United States live in California, especially Los Angeles (Baker-Christales 2004), with another large percentage in the Washington, DC, area. Many also settled around New York City, including some 60,000 who moved to suburban areas of Long Island.

Middle-class and upper-class Salvadorans obtained tourist or even immigration visas relatively easily. The poor, however, were less successful and many entered the United States illegally as *mojados* ("wet-backs"), or undocumented immigrants. Like Mexican illegal immigrants, Salavadorans use the term *mojado* to describe their journey. The Salvadorans, though, had to cross three rivers instead of one. These three crossings are a prominent theme of their escape stories, which are full of physical and psychological hardship, including hunger, arrests, and women being beaten and raped along the way. Once they arrive, things are still not easy, especially in the search for work and housing. Lack of education and marketable skills limit the job search. For undocumented immigrants, getting a decent job is even harder. These factors make it more likely that Salvadorans will work in the informal sector (review Chapter 3), where they are easy targets for economic exploitation.

Salvadorans living on Long Island receive low wages and labor in poor conditions. Their jobs involve providing services to better-off households. Men do outside work, such as gardening, landscaping, construction, and pool cleaning. Women work as nannies, live-in maids, house cleaners, restaurant workers, and caregivers for the elderly. The Salvadorans often hold down more than one job—for example, working at a McDonalds in the morning and cleaning houses in the afternoon. Men's pride prevents them from taking lowly ("female") jobs such as washing dishes. Women are more flexible and hence are more likely than men to find work. For the poorest of Salvadoran refugees, even

THINKING OUTSIDE THE BOX

FIND A detailed map that shows the geography of the United States, Mexico, and Central America, including El Salvador. Trace a possible overland migration route to the United States and find the three rivers that Salvadoran refugees had to cross.

exploitative jobs may be an economic improvement compared to back home, where they could not support their families at all.

The Salvadorans were attracted to Long Island by its thriving informal economy, a sector where checking for visas was less likely to occur. Unfortunately, the cost of living on Long Island is higher than in many other places. The combination of low wages and high costs of living has kept most Salvadorans in the category of the working poor, with few prospects for improvement. They attempt to cope with high housing costs by crowding many people into units meant for a small family. Compared to El Salvador, where most people except for the urban poor owned their own homes, only a few Salvadorans on Long Island own homes. Residential space and costs are shared among extended kin and nonkin who pay rent. This situation causes intrahousehold tension and stress. In spite of all these difficulties, most Salvadorans evaluate their experience in the United States positively.

The New Immigrants from East Asia

Koreans: Economic Achievement and Political Identity

In 1962, the South Korean government began encouraging massive emigration (Yoon 1993). This policy change was motivated by perceived population pressure and an interest in gaining remittances from persons working abroad. Before 1965, most Korean immigrants were wives of U.S. servicemen and children being adopted by American parents. After 1965, most immigrants were members of nuclear families or family members being unified with earlier "pioneer" migrants already in the United States. During the peak years of 1985 and 1987, more than 35,000 Koreans immigrated to the United States annually, making South Korea the largest immigrant source nation after Mexico and the Philippines.

Many of the migrants were displaced North Koreans who had fled their homeland to South Korea to avoid communist rule between 1945 and 1951. They had difficulty gaining an economic foothold in South Korea. When the opportunity arose to emigrate to the United States or South America, they were more willing to do so than many established South Koreans. In 1981, North Koreans constituted only 2 percent of the population of South Korea, but they were 22 percent of the Korean population of Los Angeles. Most of these immigrants were entrepreneurial, Christian, and middle class. In the 1990s, the number of lower-class migrants increased, and many lower-class Korean immigrants moved to Los Angeles (Sonenshein 1996). Whites constitute 47 percent of the population, Latinos account for 47 percent, Blacks 11 percent, and Asian Americans 10 percent (www.laalmanac.com/population).

Korean Americans clean up the debris from attacks on their businesses after the Los Angeles riots of May 1992.
■ *Compare the situation in Los Angeles to that of Baghdad in March 2003 in terms of the social cleavages involved in looting of museums and destruction of other forms of public property.* (Source: © David Young-Wolff/PhotoEdit)

In the area of Los Angeles called South Central—a low-income section of the city shared by Blacks, Latinos, and Korean Americans—Blacks are the most politically active group. Their views are liberal, and they are mainly Democrats. A wide gap separates Black politics from interests of the Korean Americans. Although the Korean Americans are arguably exploited by larger economic interests, especially in their role as small shop owners, within South Central they are seen by other local people as exploitative. One issue over which conflict exists, especially between Blacks and Korean Americans, is liquor store ownership. Over the years, many bank branches, large grocery stores, and movie theaters have left South Central. The gap was filled by stores in which the most valuable commodity sold is liquor. In South Central there are far more liquor licenses per square mile than in the rest of Los Angeles County. Given this background, it is perplexing that no one foresaw the 1992 riots in which thousands of Korean businesses were damaged, including 187 liquor stores. (The Latino population also suffered severe losses. One-third of all deaths resulting from the riot were Latinos.) For the Koreans, one outcome was an increased sense of ethnic unity and political awareness. As of 2006, South Central is becoming increasingly populated by Latinos as members of other ethnic groups move to the suburbs.

Changing Patterns of Consumption among Hong Kong Chinese

Research on how international migrants change their behavior in the new destination have addressed, among other things, the question of whether different consumption patterns emerge and, if so, how, why, and what effects such changes have on other aspects of their culture.

A Canadian study examined consumption patterns among four groups: Anglo-Canadians, new Hong Kong immigrants (who had arrived within the previous seven years), long-time Hong Kong immigrants, and Hong Kong residents (Lee and Tse 1994). Since 1987, Hong Kong has been the single largest source of migrants to Canada. The new immigrant settlement pattern in Canada is one of urban clustering. The Hong Kong Chinese have developed their own shopping centers, television and radio stations, newspapers, and country clubs. Because of generally high incomes, Hong Kong immigrants have greatly boosted Canadian buying power.

For most migrants, however, the move brought a lowered economic situation, reflected in consumption patterns. New immigrants may have to reduce spending on entertainment and expensive items. Primary needs of the new immigrants in the 1990s included items that only about half of all households owned: TVs, car, family house, VCR, carpets, and microwave oven. Items in the second-needs category were dining room set, barbecue stove, deep freezer, and dehumidifier. Long-time immigrants owned more secondary products.

At the same time, businesses in Canada have responded to Hong Kong immigrant tastes by providing Hong Kong style restaurants, Chinese branch banks, and travel agencies. Supermarkets offer specialized Asian sections. Thus, traditional patterns and ties are maintained to some extent. Two characteristics of Hong Kong immigrants distinguish them from other groups discussed in this section: their relatively secure economic status and their high level of education. Still, in Canada, they often have a difficult time finding suitable employment. Some have named Canada "Kan Lan Tai," meaning a difficult place to prosper, a fact that leads many to become astronauts, or transnational migrants.

The New Immigrants from Southeast Asia

Three Patterns of Adaptation among the Vietnamese

Over one and a quarter million refugees left Vietnam during and after the wartime 1970s. Although most relocated to the United States, many went to Canada, Australia, France, Germany, and Britain (Gold 1992). Vietnamese immigrants in the United States constitute the nation's third largest Asian American minority group. Three distinct subgroups are the 1975-era elite, the boat people, and the ethnic Chinese. Although they interact frequently, they have retained distinct patterns of adaptation.

The first group, the 1975-era elite, avoided many of the traumatic elements of flight. They were U.S. employees and members of the South Vietnamese government and military. They left before having to live under the communists, and they spent little time in refugee camps. Most came with intact families and received generous financial assistance from the United States. Using their education and English language skills, most found good jobs quickly and adjusted rapidly.

The boat people began to enter the United States after the outbreak of the Vietnam–China conflict of 1978. Mainly of rural origin, they had lived for three years or more under communism. Their exit, either by overcrowded and leaky boats or on foot through Cambodia, was dangerous and difficult. Over 50 percent died on the way. Those who survived faced many months in refugee camps in Thailand, Malaysia, the Philippines, or Hong Kong before being admitted to the United States. Because many more men than women escaped as boat people, these refugees are less likely to have arrived with intact families. They were less well educated than the earlier wave with half lacking competence in English. They faced the depressed U.S. economy of the 1980s. By the time of their arrival, the U.S. government had severely reduced refugee cash assistance and had canceled other benefits. These refugees had a much more difficult time adjusting to life in the United States than the 1975-era elite.

The ethnic Chinese, a distinct and socially marginalized class of entrepreneurs in Vietnam, arrived mainly as boat people. Following the 1987 outbreak of hostilities between Vietnam and China, the ethnic Chinese were allowed to leave Vietnam. Some, using contacts in the overseas Chinese community, were able to reestablish their roles as entrepreneurs. Most have had a difficult time in the United States because they lacked a Western-style education. They were also sometimes subject to discrimination from other Vietnamese in the United States.

The general picture of Vietnamese adjustment in the United States shows high rates of unemployment, welfare dependency, and poverty, even after several years. Interviews with Vietnamese refugees in southern California reveal generational change and fading traditions among the younger generation. Many Vietnamese teenagers in southern California have adopted the lifestyle of other low-income U.S. teenagers. Their Euro-American friends are of more significance than their Vietnamese heritage in defining their identities. Given social variations and regional differences in adaptation throughout the United States, however, generalizations about "Vietnamese Americans" can be made only with caution.

Hindu worshippers at the Geeta Temple in Elmhurst, Queens, pass their hands over a camphor lamp flame as a blessing. Queens, one of the five boroughs of New York City, is one of the most ethnically diverse communities in the world. ■ (Source: © James Leynse/CORBIS)

Khmer Refugees' Interpretation of Their Suffering

Since the late 1970s, over 150,000 people from Kampuchea (formerly Cambodia) came to the United States as refugees of the Pol Pot regime (Mortland 1994). They survived years of political repression, a difficult escape, and time in refugee camps before arriving in the United States.

Most Khmer refugees were Buddhist when they lived in Kampuchea. They have attempted to understand, within the Buddhist framework of karma (review Chapter 13), why they experienced such disasters. According to their beliefs, good actions bring good to the individual, family, and community; bad actions bring bad. Thus, many Khmer Buddhists blame themselves for the suffering they endured under the Pol Pot regime, thinking that they did something wrong in a previous life. Self-blame and depression characterize many Khmer refugees (Ong 2003). Others feel that Buddhism failed, and so they turn in large numbers to Christianity, the dominant faith of the seemingly successful Americans, including Mormonism.

Recently, a resurgence of Khmer Buddhism has occurred among some refugees from Kampuchea living in North America. Many temples have been constructed, and they sponsor rituals and traditional celebrations that are widely attended. These reviving Buddhists have mixed reactions to Christianity. Some accept it as a complementary religion to Buddhism, whereas others reject it as a threat to Buddhism and their cultural identity.

Changing interpretations of identity, including religion, arise over time with the new generations and altered circumstances. It is difficult to say what the future holds

for either the Kampuchean adults who are still trying to make sense of their suffering or for their children, the new generation (Ong 2003).

The New Immigrants from South Asia

Hindus of New York City Maintain Their Culture

With the 1965 change in legislation in the United States, a first wave of South Asian immigrants dominated by male professionals from India arrived (Bhardwaj and Rao 1990). Members of this first wave settled primarily in eastern and western cities. Subsequent immigrants from India were less well educated and less wealthy. They tend to be concentrated in New York and New Jersey. New York City has the largest population of South Asian Indians in the United States, with about one-eighth of the total number of South Asians in the United States (Mogelonsky 1995).

Members of the highly educated first wave are concentrated in professional fields such as medicine, engineering, and management (Helweg and Helweg 1990). One of the major immigrant groups in Silicon Valley, California, is South Asian Indians. Members of the less educated, later wave find work in family-run businesses or service industries. Indians dominate some trades, such as convenience stores. They have penetrated the ownership of budget hotels and motels and operate nearly half of the total number of establishments in this niche. More than 40 percent of New York City's licensed cab drivers are Indians, Pakistanis, or Bangladeshis (Mogelonsky 1995).

The South Asian Indian population in the United States is one of the better-off immigrant groups and is considered an immigrant success story. They place high value on their children's education and urge them to pursue higher education in fields such as medicine and engineering. They tend to have few children and invest heavily in their schooling and social advancement.

A continuing concern of many members of the first wave is the maintenance of Hindu cultural values in the face of patterns prevalent in mainstream U.S. culture, such as dating, premarital sex, drinking, and drugs (Lessinger 1995). The Hindu population supports the construction of Hindu temples that offer Sunday school classes for young people and cultural events as a way of passing on the Hindu heritage to the next generation. They attempt to appeal to the youth by accommodating to their lifestyles and preferences in terms of things like the kind of food served after rituals. Vegetarian pizza is now a common temple menu item for the young people.

Another challenge for Hinduism in the United States and Canada is to establish temples that offer ritual diversity that speaks to Hindus of many varieties. In New York City, the growth of one temple shows how its ritual flexibility helped it to expand. The Ganesha Temple was founded in 1997 under leadership from Hindus from southern India. Temple rituals at first were the same as those conducted in southern Indian temples. Over the years, though, in order to widen its reach, the temple expanded its rituals to include those that would appeal to Hindus from other regions of India. The congregation has grown, and the physical structure has expanded to provide for this growth. The daily and yearly cycle has become more elaborate and more varied than what one would find at a typical Hindu temple in southern India. The Ganesha temple in New York City is an important pilgrimage destination for Hindus from throughout India.

The New Immigrants from the Former Soviet Union

The breakup of the Soviet Union into fifteen separate countries spurred the movement of over 9 million people throughout Eastern Europe and Central Asia. Many, of Slavic descent, lived in Central Asia during the existence of the Soviet Union and seek to return to their homelands. Another large category includes people who were forcibly relocated to Siberia or Central Asia. Since 1988, refugees from the former Soviet Union have been one of the largest refugee nationalities to enter the United States (Littman 1993, cited in Gold 1995).

Soviet Jews Flee Persecution

Many of the refugees from the former Soviet Union are Soviet Jews. Although most Soviet Jews live in Israel, since the mid-1960s, over 300,000 have settled in the United States, especially in California (Gold 1995). Several features characterize the experience of Soviet Jewish refugees in the United States. First, their origins in the Soviet Union accustomed them to the fact that the government controlled most aspects of life and provided many public services, including jobs, housing, day care, and health care. In their new locations, they had to find ways of meeting these needs in a market economy. Second, Soviet Jews, as "White Europeans,"

In January 2004, more than 50,000 Russian immigrants to Israel returned to Russia. Motivations for the move back include the difficult living conditions for many Russian immigrants in Israel, violence, and the improving economic situation in Russia. Nonetheless, people from Russia continue to migrate to Israel, and they now number over one million people, about 13 percent of the population. ■ *Learn how many people left Russia after the break-up of the Soviet Union in 1989 and where they went.* (Source: © David H. Wells/CORBIS)

Lessons Applied

STUDYING PASTORALISTS' MOVEMENTS FOR RISK ASSESSMENT AND SERVICE DELIVERY

Pastoralists are often vulnerable to malnutrition as a consequence of climate changes, fluctuations in food supply, and war and political upheaval. Because of their spatial mobility, they are difficult to reach with relief aid during a crisis. Cultural anthropologists are devising ways to gather and manage basic information about pastoralists' movements and nutritional needs in order to provide improved service delivery (Watkins and Fleisher 2002). The data required for such proactive planning include the following:

- Information on the number of migrants and the size of their herds in a particular location and at a particular time. Such data can inform planners about the level of services required for public health programs, educational programs, and veterinary services. This information can be used to assess the demand on particular grazing areas and water sources and is therefore important in predicting possible future crises.

- Information on patterns of migratory movements. This information can enable planners to move services to where the people are rather than expecting people to move to the services. Some nongovernmental organizations, for example, are providing mobile banking services and mobile veterinary services. Information

about pastoralist movements can be used as an early warning to prevent social conflicts that might result if several groups arrived in the same place at the same time. And conflict resolution mechanisms can be put in place more effectively if conflict does occur.

The data collection involves interviews with pastoralists, often with one or two key participants, whom the anthropologists select for their specialized knowledge. Interviews cover topics such as the migratory paths followed (both typical and atypical), population levels, herd sizes, and the nutritional and water requirements of people and animals. Given the complex social systems of pastoralists, the data gathering must also include group leadership, decision-making practices, and concepts about land and water rights.

The anthropologists organize this information into a computerized database, linking the ethnographical data with geographic information systems (GIS) data on the environment and climate information from satellites. The anthropologists can then construct various scenarios and assess the relative risks that they pose to the people's health. Impending crises can be foreseen, and warning can be provided to governments and international aid agencies.

---

become members of the "racial" majority group. Their high level of education places them in the elite of new immigrant groups. Third, they have access to established and prosperous communities of American Jews, which provides them with sponsors when they arrive. Most other new immigrant groups do not have these advantages.

Soviet Jewish immigrants, however, face several challenges. Many have a difficult time finding a job commensurate with their education and previous work in the Soviet Union. Throughout the United States, many Soviet Jewish immigrants remain unemployed or work at menial jobs far beneath their qualifications. This pattern is especially true for women. They were employed professionals in the Soviet Union but can find no work in the United States other than house cleaning or babysitting. Another major challenge involves marriage options. Cultural norms promote intraethnic marriage. The number in the U.S. marriage pool is small.

Migration Politics, Policies, and Programs in a Globalizing World

The major questions related to migration politics, policies, and programs concern state and international policies of inclusion and exclusion of particular categories of people. The human rights of various categories of migrants vary dramatically. Migrants of all sorts, including long-standing migratory groups such as pastoralists and horticulturalists, seek to find ways of protecting their lifestyles, maintaining their health, and creating security for future.

Protecting Migrants' Health

Health risks to migrants are many and varied, depending on the wide variety of migrant types and destinations.

In 2006, after three years of drought, two women of eastern Kenya search out pasture for their few remaining goats. As they walk through a dust storm, rain clouds and a rainbow in the distance are signs that rain is coming. Heavy rains did come in the next few days, but most of the pastoralists in the region, like these women, had lost most of their animals during the drought. They are now dependent on food aid and other forms of humanitarian assistance for their survival. Global climate change is linked to increasingly severe swings in climatic conditions in this region. ■ (Source: Gideon Mendel/CORBIS)

FOOD FOR THOUGHT

- The tracking system described here remains outside the control of the pastoralists themselves. How might it be managed so that they participate more meaningfully and gain greater autonomy?

One group of migrants of special concern are those whose livelihoods depend on long-standing economic systems requiring spatial mobility, such as foragers, horticulturalists, and pastoralists. The frequency in recent decades of drought and food shortages in the Sahel region of Africa (see Map 16.6, p. 442) is prompting research by cultural anthropologists to learn how to prevent such situations through better monitoring and enhanced provision of services (see Lessons Applied box).

Inclusion and Exclusion

National policies that set quotas on the quantity and types of immigrants who are welcome and that determine how they are treated are largely dictated by political and economic interests. Even in the cases of seemingly humanitarian quotas, governments undertake a cost–benefit analysis of how much will be gained and how much will be lost. Governments show their political support or dis-

approval of other governments through their immigration policies. One of the most obvious economic factors affecting policy is labor flow. Cheap, including illegal, immigrant labor is used around the world to maintain profits for businesses and services for the better-off. Flows of such labor undermine labor unions and the status of established workers.

In the United States, immigration law specifies who will be allowed entry and what benefits the government will provide. A court case from 1915 presents issues that prevail today (*Gegiow* v. *Uhl*, 1915). The case concerned a number of Russian laborers seeking to enter the United States. Only one member of the group spoke some English, and all had very little money. Their intention was to settle in Portland, Oregon. The acting commissioner of immigration in the port of New York denied them entry on the grounds that they were "likely to become public charges" because employment conditions in Portland were such that they probably would be unable to obtain work. The "aliens" seeking entry obtained legal counsel, and the case eventually went to the Supreme Court, where the decision was handed down by Chief Justice Oliver Wendell Holmes. He focused on "whether an alien can be declared likely to become a public charge on the ground that the labor market in the city of his immediate . . . destination is overstocked." The relevant statute, Holmes declared, deals with admission to the United States, not to a particular city within it. Further, Holmes commented that a commissioner of immigration is not empowered to make decisions about possible overstocking of labor in all of the United States, for that is a matter in the hands of the U.S. president.

State immigration policies are played out in local communities. In some instances, local resentments are associated with a so-called **lifeboat mentality,** a view that seeks to limit enlarging a particular group because of perceived resource constraints. Influxes of immigrants who compete for jobs have led to hostility in many parts of Europe and North America. Some observers have called this *working-class racism* because it emerges out of competition with immigrants for jobs and other benefits (Cole 1996).

The number of immigrants has grown substantially in southern Italy since the early 1980s. In the city of Palermo, Sardegna (see Map 13.4, p. 349), with a total population of one million people, nearly 30,000 immigrants are from Africa, Asia, and elsewhere. Does working-class racism exist among the working class in Palermo? Two conditions seem to predict that it would: large numbers of foreign immigrants and a high rate of unemployment. However, instead of expressing racist condemnation of the immigrants, working-class residents of Palermo accept the immigrants as fellow poor people. One critical factor may be the lack of competition for jobs, which derives from the fact that working Palmeritans and immigrants occupy different niches. Immigrant jobs are less desirable, more stigmatized, and less lucrative. African immigrant men work in bars and restaurants, as building cleaners, or as itinerant street vendors. African and Asian women work as domestic servants in the better-off neighborhoods. Sicilians do refer to immigrants by certain racial/ethnic names, but these seem to be used interchangeably and imprecisely. For example, a common term for all immigrants, Asian or African, is *tuichi*, which means Turks. The word can be applied teasingly to a Sicilian as well and in conversation may connote alarm, as in "Mom, the Turks!" Other loosely applied terms are the Italian words for Moroccans, Blacks, and Tunisians. In a questionnaire given to school children, the great

majority agreed with the statement that "a person's race is not important." The tolerance among Palermo's working class may be only temporary. Nonetheless, it suggests that researchers take a closer look at cases elsewhere that require a loosening up of the theory of working-class racism against immigrants.

Recent politically conservative trends in the United States have succeeded in reversing more progressive policies about immigration and minorities. Police raids in areas thought to have many undocumented migrants have brought mass expulsion. Reversals of affirmative action in college admissions, initiated in California in the late 1990s, gained widespread support among "nativist" Americans. This lifeboat mentality of exclusiveness and privilege is held mainly by the dominant White majority and others who have achieved the "American dream."

Migration and Human Rights

Several questions arise about migration and human rights. One of the most basic is whether migration is forced or voluntary (review the Critical Thinking box, this chapter). Forced migration itself may be considered a violation of a person's human rights. Another issue is whether members of a displaced group have a guaranteed **right of return,** or a person's ability to return to and live in his or her homeland. The right of return has been considered a basic human right in the West since the time of the signing of the Magna Carta. It is included in the United Nations General Assembly Resolution 194 passed in 1948 and was elevated by the UN in 1974 to an "inalienable right."

The right of return is a continuing issue for the hundreds of thousands of Palestinians who fled or were driven from their homes during the 1948 war (Zureik 1994). They went mainly to Jordan, the West Bank/East Jerusalem, Gaza, Lebanon, Syria, and other Arab states. Jordan and Syria have granted Palestinian refugees rights equal to those of their citizens. In Lebanon, where estimates of the number of Palestinian refugees range between 200,000 and 600,000, the government refuses them such rights (Salam 1994). Israel favors the lower number because it makes the problem seem less severe. The Palestinians favor the higher number to highlight the seriousness of their plight. The Lebanese government also favors the higher number to emphasize its burden in hosting so many refugees. Palestinians know that they are not welcome in Lebanon, but they cannot return to Israel because Israel denies them the right of return. Israel

---

lifeboat mentality: local resentment of an immigrant group because of perceived resource constraints.

right of return: United Nations guaranteed right of refugees to repatriation.

responds to the Palestinians' claims by saying that their acceptance of Jewish immigrants from Arab countries constitutes an equal exchange.

The right of return can be considered, just as validly, within states even though most have no policy close to that of the UN. Indigenous people's rights to their ancestral lands are a prominent case in point (to be discussed in Chapter 16). Another stark instance of internal displacement and loss of rights to home comes from the 2005 hurricanes in New Orleans and the coastal counties of Mississippi and Louisiana. The "racial" lines of displacement are nowhere clearer than in the statistics for the city of New Orleans (Lyman 2006). Before Hurricane Katrina, the population of New Orleans was 54 percent White and 36 percent Black, with the other 6 percent Latino. In 2006, the population was 68 percent White and 21 percent Black, with no change in the Latino percentage. The causes for the differential displacement of the Black population are one problem. The fact that many Black people became a "New Orleans diaspora" with little chance of returning to their home city and rebuilding their lives is another.

The Big Questions Revisited

WHAT are the major categories of migration?

Migrants are classified as internal, international, or transnational. Another category is based on the migrants' reason for moving. On this dimension, migrants are classified as labor migrants, institutional migrants, or displaced persons. People's adjustment to their new situations depends on the degree of voluntarism involved in the move, the degree of cultural and environmental difference between the place of origin and the destination, and how closely expectations about the new location are met, especially in terms of making a living and establishing social ties.

Displaced persons are one of the fastest-growing categories of migrants. Refugees fleeing from political persecution or warfare face serious adjustment challenges because they often leave their home countries with few material resources and frequently have experienced much psychological suffering. The number of internally displaced persons is growing even faster than the number of refugees. Dams and other large-scale development projects result in thousands of people becoming IDPs. Internally displaced persons do not fall under the purview of international organizations such as the United Nations, but their situation is attracting the attention of a global consortium of governments and nongovernmental organizations.

WHAT are examples of the new immigrants in the United States and Canada?

Worldwide, the "new immigrants" are contributing to growing transnational connections and to the formation of increasingly multicultural populations within states. In the United States, the new immigrants from Latin America, especially Mexico, are the fastest-growing category. In the United States, members of most refugee immigrant groups tend to have jobs at the lower end of the economic scale. Jewish refugees from the Soviet Union experience a major gap in what their employment was like in Russia versus their limited options in the United States. Immigrants from East and South Asia, who are more likely than others to have immigrated to the United States voluntarily, have achieved greater levels of economic success than most other new immigrant groups.

Immigrant groups throughout the world may face discrimination in their new destinations, although the degree to which it occurs varies with the level of perceived resource competition from residents. Immigrants from India in Canada experience a range of discriminatory practices that differ on the basis of their gender.

HOW do anthropologists contribute to migration policies and programs?

Anthropologists have studied national and international migration policies and practices in terms of social inclusion and exclusion. Fieldwork in particular contexts reveals a range of patterns between local residents and immigrants. Working-class resentment among local people against immigrants is not universal and varies with the overall amount and type of employment available.

Anthropologists examine possible infringements of human rights on migrants, especially in terms of the degree of voluntarism in their move and the conditions they face in the destination area. Another human rights issue related to migration is the right of return. The UN proclaimed the right of return for internationally displaced populations. Most countries, however, have no such policy. Internally displaced persons, including the evacuees from the 2005 hurricanes in the United States, have no guarantee that they can return to their home area.

Cultural anthropologists find many roles in applied work related to migration. Gathering data on migratory movements of traditionally mobile people, such as pastoralists, can help make humanitarian aid programs more timely and effective.

KEY CONCEPTS

chain migration, p. 410
circular migration, p. 403
development-induced displacement
(DID), p. 404
displaced person, p. 403
institutional migrant, p. 407

internal migration, p. 399
internally displaced person (IDP),
p. 403
lifeboat mentality, p. 418
new immigrant, p. 407
push–pull theory, p. 399

refugee, p. 403
remittance, p. 401
right of return, p. 418
transnational migration, p. 399

SUGGESTED READINGS

Rogaia Mustafa Abusharaf. *Wanderings: Sudanese Migrants and Exiles in North America*. Ithaca, NY: Cornell University Press, 2002. Abusharaf provides historical background on the first wave of Sudanese migration to the United States and Canada, information on various Sudanese groups who have migrated, and an interpretation of Sudanese identity in North America.

Beth Baker-Cristales. *Salvadoran Migration to Southern California: Redefining El Hermano Lejano*. Gainesville: University of Florida Press, 2004. This book provides a history of Salvadoran migration to the United States and a detailed description of the lives of Salvadoran migrants in Los Angeles, home to about half of all Salvadorans in the United States.

Linda Basch, Nina Glick Schiller, and Christina Blanc Szanton. *Nations Unbound: Transnational Projects, Postcolonial Predicaments, and Deterritorialized Nation–States*. Langhorne, PA: Gordon and Breach Science Publishers, 1994. Eight chapters explore theoretical issues in transnational migration and present cases of migration from the Caribbean, including St. Vincent, Grenada, and Haiti.

Jeffrey H. Cohen. *The Culture of Migration in Southern Mexico*. Austin: University of Texas Press, 2004. Migration is a way of life for many individuals and entire families in the Mexican state of Oaxaca. Some go to other parts of Mexico and others go to the United States. They send remittances and intend to return to their homes after a few years. Cohen discusses migration patterns in twelve communities and the effects of outmigration on the people who remain.

Sheba Mariam George. *When Women Come First: Gender and Class in Transnational Migration*. Berkeley: University of California Press, 2005. This book traces the experiences of nurses from Kerala, India, who migrate to work in the United States, preceding their husbands. It reveals the adjustments the women make, the effects on their marriage caused by their employment, and their husbands' turn (as trailing spouses) to active involvement in the church.

Farha Ghannam. *Remaking the Modern: Space, Relocation, and the Politics of Identity in a Global Cairo*. Berkeley: University of California Press, 2002. As part of a plan to modernize Cairo, the government relocated low-income residents from what was considered valuable real estate in downtown Cairo to public housing on the city's outskirts. Ghannam explores how the displaced people deal with the loss of social networks and the stigma of living in public housing.

Julianne Hammer. *Palestinians Born in Exile: Diaspora and the Search for a Homeland*. Austin: University of Texas Press, 2004. In the decade following the 1993 Oslo Peace Accords, 100,000 diasporic Palestinians moved to the West Bank and Gaza. This ethnography documents the experiences of young adults between the ages of 16 and 35 years and their adjustment to the move.

Josiah McC. Heyman. *Finding a Moral Heart for U.S. Immigration Policy: An Anthropological Perspective*. Washington, DC: American Ethnological Society, Monograph Series, Number 7, 1998. An applied anthropology perspective inspires this critique of current U.S. immigration policy, finding it to be basically anti-immigrationist. The author suggests steps toward a more inclusive policy and discusses unresolved challenges.

Helen Morton Lee. *Tongans Overseas: Between Two Shores*. Honolulu: University of Hawai'i Press, 2003. This book is about young Tongan migrants in Australia. It is based on fieldwork in Melbourne, analysis of messages on a Tongan Internet forum called Kava Bowl, and email interviews with people who participate in Kava Bowl. Results reveal the varied aspects of young Tongan migrants' identity, ties to family in Tonga, and changing aspirations.

Martin F. Manalansan IV. *Global Divas: Filipino Gay Men in the Diaspora*. Durham, NC: Duke University Press, 2004. This book is based on the life narratives of fifty Filipino gay men in New York City and participant observation in homes, bars, hospitals, Filipino restaurants, and the Gay Pride Parade. It describes how the men negotiate between Filipino and American sexual and gender traditions.

Ann V. Millard and Jorgé Chapa, with others. *Apple Pie and Enchiladas: Latino Newcomers in the Rural Midwest*. Austin: University of Texas Press, 2004. Many Latinos migrate to the rural Midwest in the United States to work in food-processing plants and small factories, doing difficult labor that most local residents avoid. The authors explore interethnic relations, including the opposition of many of the local Anglos to racism and prejudice.

Karen Richman. *Migration and Vodou*. Gainesville: University of Florida Press, 2005. This book and its accompanying CD reveal the innovative ways that Haitian migrants to South Florida maintain their religious traditions and familial connections. It demonstrates the importance of religion in the lives of the migrants and debunks the myths about "primitive" voodoo that many outsiders hold about Haitians.

Archana B. Verma. *The Making of Little Punjab in Canada: Patterns of Immigration*. Thousand Oaks, CA: Sage Publications, 2002. Verma describes the historical connections between Hindu migrants from a village in India's northern state of Punjab, to Vancouver Island, British Columbia. Strong family and kinship ties continue to link the migrants to their home area. Caste group solidarity among the migrants provides support in the face of discrimination on the part of the wider Canadian society.

16

People Defining Development

The Big Questions

- WHAT is development and the approaches to achieving it?

- HOW is development related to indigenous people and women?

- WHAT are urgent issues in development?

A traditional custodian from the Ngarrindjeri nation in South Australia holds a box containing four skulls of Australian Aborigines at a ceremony at Manchester University, England, 2003. The skulls were returned, after 100 years in England, to a sacred keeping place. This repatriation is one result of a worldwide campaign by indigenous peoples to retrieve body parts and artifacts taken from graves during the nineteenth and twentieth centuries. (*Source:* © *Reuters/CORBIS*)

We have had many visitors to Walpole Island since the French "discovered us" in the seventeenth century in our territory, Bkejwanong. In many cases, these visitors failed to recognize who we were and to appreciate our traditions. They tried to place us in their European framework of knowledge, denying that we possessed our indigenous knowledge. They attempted to steal our lands, water, and knowledge. We resisted. They left and never came back. We continued to share our knowledge with the next visitors to our place. . . . It was a long-term strategy that has lasted more than three hundred years. (Dr. Dean Jacobs, Executive Director of Walpole Island First Nation, from his Foreword in VanWynsberghe 2002:ix)

These are the words of a leader of the Walpole Island First Nation, located in southern Ontario, Canada (see Map 16.1). They, along with many other indigenous groups worldwide, have begun to take strong action in recent decades to protect their culture and its natural environment. The Walpole Island First Nation organized itself and successfully fought to control industrial waste that was polluting its water and land. In the process, the people have regained their pride and cultural integrity.

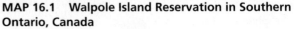

Defining Development and Approaches to It

All cultures go through change, but the causes, processes, and outcomes are varied. Cultural change can be intentional or accidental, forward looking or backward looking, rapid or gradual, obvious or subtle, beneficial or harmful. Biological anthropologists have the longest view. They look back thousands, even millions, of years to learn how humanity originated and evolved biologically. Archaeologists examine remains from human prehistory and history to discover the origins and spread of culture. Linguistic anthropologists study the origin and evolution of communication, the emergence of writing, and the change in contemporary patterns of communication, including the effects of mass media. In contrast to these three fields, cultural anthropology's roots lie in the **synchronic** study of culture, or a "one-time" snapshot view of culture with little attention to the past. This approach led to a static view of culture as unchanging. Cultural anthropologists are now moving toward a **diachronic** approach that includes attention to time and change in studying culture.

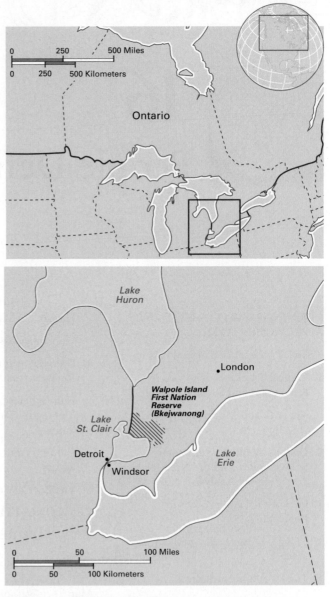

MAP 16.1 Walpole Island Reservation in Southern Ontario, Canada

This chapter focuses on the topic of contemporary cultural change as shaped by **development,** or directed change to improve human welfare usually through poverty reduction. The subfield within cultural anthropology of *development anthropology* is the study of how culture and development interact. It also has a strong applied component.

The chapter's first section considers concepts related to change and development and the approaches to devel-

---

synchronic: a "one-time" view of a culture that devotes little or no attention to its past.
diachronic: the analysis of culture across time.
development: directed change to achieve improved human welfare.
diffusion: the spread of culture through contact.
acculturation: a form of cultural change in which a minority culture becomes more like the dominant culture.
assimilation: a form of culture change in which a culture is thoroughly acculturated, or decultured, and is no longer distinguishable as having a separate identity.

is no longer distinguishable as having a separate identity. In the most extreme cases, the impact on the minority culture is that it becomes extinct. These processes parallel degrees of language change resulting from contact with dominating cultures and languages (review Chapter 12). Such changes have occurred among many indigenous people as the result of globalization and the introduction of new technology (see Lessons Applied box). Other responses to acculturative influences include partial acceptance of something new with localization and syncretism, as in the case of the game of cricket in the Trobriands (Chapter 14), or rejection and resistance.

Theories and Models of Development

This section reviews theories and models of development and the various kinds of institutions involved in development. It then examines development projects. The last section offers insights about special research methods cultural anthropologists use in development work.

No single view of development or how to achieve it exists. Debates about these issues are heated and involve experts from many disciplines, governments, and local people worldwide. Five theories or models of development are presented here. They differ in terms of:

- The definition of development
- The goal of development
- Measures of development
- Attention to environmental and financial sustainability

Modernization

Modernization is a form of change marked by economic growth through industrialization and market expansion, political consolidation through the state, technological innovation, literacy, and options for social mobility. It originated in Western Europe in the beginning of the seventeenth century with the emerging emphasis on secular rationality and scientific thinking as the pathways to progress (Norgaard 1994). Given the insights of rationality and science, modernization is thought to spread inevitably throughout the world and lead to improvement in people's lives everywhere. The major goals of modernization are material progress and individual betterment.

Supporters and critics of modernization are found in both rich and poor countries. Supporters claim that the benefits of modernization (improved transportation, electricity, biomedical health care, and telecommunications) are worth the costs to the environment and society.

Part of the Trans-Alaska Pipeline System (TAPS), also called the Alyeska Pipeline in Alaska. Eight hundred miles long, TAPS connects oil fields in northern Alaska to a port on the southern coast. It accounts for 25 percent of U.S. oil production annually. ■ *Go to the TAPS website, www.alyeska-pipe.com, to see what information the company provides to the public on its operations.* (Source: © Royalty Free/CORBIS)

Others take a critical view and regard modernization as problematic because of its focus on ever-increasing consumption levels and heavy use of nonrenewable resources. Many cultural anthropologists are critical of Westernization and modernization because their research shows how modernization often brings ecological ruin, increases social inequality, destroys indigenous cultures, and reduces global cultural and biological diversity. In spite of strong cautionary critiques from anthropologists, environmentalists, and others about the negative effects of modernization, most countries worldwide have not slowed their attempts to achieve it. Some governments and citizen groups, however, are promoting lifestyles that rely less on nonrenewable resources and include concern for protecting the environment.

---

modernization: a model of change based on belief in the inevitable advance of science and Western secularism and process-es including industrial growth, consolidation of the state, bureaucratization, market economy, technological innovation, literacy, and options for social mobility.

Lessons Applied

THE SAAMI, SNOWMOBILES, AND THE NEED FOR SOCIAL IMPACT ANALYSIS

How might adoption of a new belief or practice benefit or harm a particular culture and its various members? Although often difficult to answer, this question must always be asked. A classic study of the *snowmobile disaster* among a Saami group in Finland offers a careful response to this question in a context of rapid technological diffusion (Pelto 1973). In the 1950s, the Saami of Finland (review Culturama, Chapter 12, p. 333) had an economy based on fishing and reindeer herding, which provided most of their diet.

Besides supplying meat, reindeer had other important economic and social functions. They were used as draft animals, especially hauling wood for fuel. Their hides were made into clothing and their sinews used for sewing. Reindeer were key items of exchange, both in external trade and internal gift giving. Parents gave a child a reindeer to mark the appearance of the child's first tooth. When a couple became engaged, they exchanged a reindeer with each other to mark the commitment. Reindeer were the most important wedding gift. Each summer the herds were let free, and then they were rounded up in the fall, a time of communal festivity.

By the 1960s, all this had changed because of the introduction of the snowmobile. Previously, people herded the reindeer herds on skis. The use of snowmo-

Saami herders follow their reindeer led by a man on a skidoo in Sapmi, Norway. ■ (Source: © Bryan and Cherry Alexander Photography/Alamy)

biles for herd management had several results. The herds were no longer kept domesticated for part of the year, during which they became tame. Instead, they were allowed to roam freely all year and thus became wilder.

Snowmobiles allowed herders to cover larger amounts of territory at round-up time, and sometimes several

Growth-Oriented Development

The concept of *development*, as a kind of "induced" change involving the application of modernization theory in so-called developing countries, emerged after World War II. At that time, the United States began to expand its role as a world leader, and development aid was part of its international policy agenda. International development, as defined by major Western development institutions, is similar to modernization in terms of its goals. The process emphasizes economic growth as the most crucial element.

According to growth-oriented development theory, investments in economic growth will, through the *trickle-down effect*, lead to improved human welfare among the

less well-off. Promoting economic growth in developing countries includes two major strategies:

- Increasing economic productivity and trade through modernized agriculture and manufacturing and participation in world markets.

- Reducing government expenditures on public services such as schools and health in order to reduce debt and reallocate resources to increase productivity. This strategy, called *structural adjustment*, has been promoted by the World Bank since the 1980s.

Measures to assess the achievement of development through this model include the rate of growth of the economy, especially the *gross domestic product*, or *GDP*.

social impact assessment: a study conducted to gauge the potential social costs and benefits of particular innovations before change is undertaken.

round-ups occurred instead of one. Herd size declined dramatically. The reasons for the decline included the stress inflicted on the reindeer by the extra distance traveled during round-ups, the multiple round-ups instead of a single one, and the fear aroused by the noisy snowmobiles. Round-ups were held at a time when the females were near the end of their pregnancy, another factor inducing reproductive stress. As the number of snowmobiles increased, the number of reindeer decreased.

Introduction of snowmobiles for herding also increased young men's dominance in herding (Larsson 2005). Before the snowmobiles, reindeer herding was a family operation. Although men did more of the long-distance herding, women also worked closely with the herd. Since snowmobiles were adopted, parents have steered their sons toward herding and their daughters toward education and a professional career. Two rationales for such gender tracking are that driving a snowmobile is difficult due to its heaviness, and the driver may get stuck somewhere. The use of snowmobiles also changed the age pattern of reindeer herding in favor of youth over age; thus, older herders were squeezed out.

Another change involved a new dependence on the outside through the cash economy. Cash is needed in order to purchase a snowmobile, to buy gasoline, and to pay for parts and repairs. This delocalization of the economy created social inequality, which had not existed before. Other social and economic repercussions include:

- The cash cost of effective participation in herding exceeded the resources of some families, who had to drop out of participation in herding.
- The snowmobile pushed many Saami into debt.
- Dependence on cash and indebtedness forced many Saami to migrate to cities for work.

Pertti Pelto, the anthropologist who first documented this case, calls these transformations a disaster for Saami culture. He offers a recommendation that might be helpful for the future: Communities that are confronting the adoption of new technology should have a chance to weigh evidence on the pros and cons and make an informed judgment. Pelto's work is one of the early warnings from anthropology about the need for **social impact assessments,** studies that gauge the potential social costs and benefits of particular innovations before change is undertaken.

FOOD FOR THOUGHT

- Speculate about what the Saami might have done if they had been able to consider a social impact assessment of the effects of snowmobiles on their culture.

Distributional Development

Distributional development contrasts with growth-oriented development in its emphasis on social equity in benefits, especially in terms of increased income, literacy, and health. It rejects the trickle-down process as ineffective in reaching less well-off people. Its position is based on evidence that growth-oriented strategies, applied without concern for distribution, actually increase social inequality. In this view, the growth model ensures that "the rich get richer and the poor get poorer."

The distributional approach opposes structural adjustment policies because they further undermine the welfare of the poor by removing the few entitlements they had in the form of services. Advocates of the distributional model see the need for benevolent governments to ensure equitable access to crucial resources in order to enhance the ability of the poor to provide for their own needs (Gardner and Lewis 1996).

Conservative ("neo-liberal") economists argue that redistribution is not a realistic or a feasible strategy. Supporters of the distributive approach, including many anthropologists, point to cases in the model that have worked. As one example, anthropological research in Nadur village, central Kerala (see Map 16.2), considered whether redistribution was an effective development strategy (Franke 1993). The findings showed the answer to be positive. Even though Kerala's per capita income is the lowest of any state in India, it has some of the highest social indicators in the country, including health status and literacy.

Government attention to distribution in Kerala came about through democratic channels, including demonstrations and pressure on the government by popular movements and labor unions. These groups forced the state to reallocate land ownership, which alleviated social inequality somewhat. In other instances, people pressured government leaders to improve village conditions

School girls in Bhutan. The government of Bhutan rejects the Western concept of the Gross Domestic Product (GDP) as the best measure of a country's success and instead uses a measure called Gross Domestic Happiness (GDH). ■ *Go to the Internet to learn more about Bhutan and its aspirations for its people.* (Source: Rob Howard/CORBIS)

by providing school lunches for poor children, increasing school attendance by dalit children (review Chapter 9's definition) and investing in school facilities. Through public action, Nadur village became a better place to live for many people.

Human Development

Another alternative to the growth-first model is called *human development*, the strategy that emphasizes investing in human welfare. The United Nations adopted the phrase *human development* to emphasize the need for improvements in human welfare in terms of health, education, and personal security and safety. In this model, investments in improving human welfare will lead to economic development. The reverse is not invariably true: The level of economic growth of a country (or region within a country) is not necessarily correlated with its level of human development, as is clear from the case of Kerala. Thus, in this view, economic growth is neither an end in itself nor even a necessary component of development as measured in human welfare. Economic resources, combined with distributive policies, are a strong basis

for attaining high levels of human development.

Sustainable Development

Sustainable development refers to forms of improvement that do not destroy nonrenewable resources and are financially supportable over time. Advocates of sustainable development argue that the economic growth of wealthy countries has been and still is costly in terms of the natural environment and people whose lives depend on fragile ecosystems. They say that such growth cannot be sustained at even its present level, not to mention projected demands as more countries become industrialized.

FORMULATE YOUR own definition of *development* and sketch out its pros and cons for some different cultures that you have learned about in this book.

THINKING OUTSIDE THE BOX

In 1992, the UN Conference on Environment and Development, better known as the Rio Earth Summit, established goals for global actions to ensure the well-being of the planet and its people. Since then, several follow-up international meetings have occurred, producing more

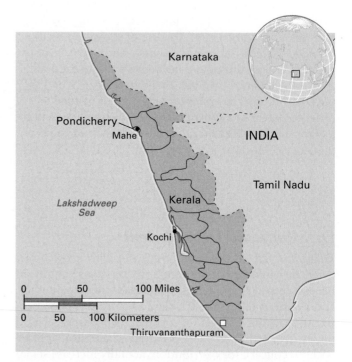

MAP 16.2 Kerala, South India. With a population of 30 million, Kerala's living standard, literacy, and health are high compared to the rest of India. It comprises fourteen districts and three historical regions: Travancore in the south, Kochi in the central part, and Malabar in the north. Long a socialist democracy, Kerala now allows the free market and foreign direct investment to play larger roles. A major tourist destination due to its tropical ecology and cultural features such as dramatic martial arts and theater, Kerala also hosts a growing Ayurvedic health tourism industry along its coast.

agreements and updated plans. Countries vary in terms of how much they support Earth Summit goals, and they differ in the degree to which they implement policies to which they have agreed. In the United States, disregard in the White House for policies to reduce global warming prompted action by city mayors to adopt their own targets and timetables to reduce global warming (Vidal 2006). As of 2006, more than 200 mayors, representing more than 100 million people, have signed on to the Mayors Climate Protection agreement.

Institutional Approaches to Development

Cultural anthropologists are increasingly aware of the importance of examining the institutions, organizations, and specialists involved in development policy making, programs, and projects. With this knowledge, cultural anthropologists are able to have more impact on shaping how development is done. Research includes studying the management systems of large-scale institutions, such as the World Bank, and of small-scale organizations in diverse settings. Topics include behavior within the institutions, social interactions with the "client population," and institutional discourse. This section first describes some large development institutions and then some smaller organizations.

Large-Scale Development Institutions

Two major types of large-scale development institutions exist. First are the *multilateral institutions*—those that include several countries as "donor" members. Second are the *bilateral institutions*—those that involve only two countries: a "donor" and a "recipient."

The largest multilaterals are the United Nations and the World Bank. Each is a vast and complex social system. The United Nations, established in 1945, includes over 160 member states, each contributing money assessed according to its ability and each with one vote in the General Assembly (Fasulo 2003). Several UN agencies exist, fulfilling a range of functions (see Figure 16.1). In all its units combined, the UN employs about 50,000 people.

The World Bank is supported by contributions from over 150 member countries. Founded in 1944, the Bank is dedicated to promoting the concept of economic growth worldwide (Rich 1994). Its main strategy is to promote international investment through loans. The World Bank is guided by a Board of Governors made up of the finance ministers of member countries. The World Bank system assigns each country a number of votes based on the size of its financial commitment. The economic superpowers, therefore, dominate.

The World Bank system includes the International Bank for Reconstruction and Development (IBRD) and the International Development Association (IDA). Both are administered at the World Bank headquarters in Washington, DC. They lend for similar types of projects and often in the same country, but their loan conditions differ. The IBRD provides loans to poor countries that are generally regarded as "bad risks" on the world commercial market. Thus, the IBRD is a source of interest-bearing loans to countries that otherwise would not be able to borrow. The IBRD has recorded a profit every year of its existence. Most of its loans support large infrastructure projects such as roads and dams. The IDA is the "soft-loan" side of the World Bank. It provides interest-free loans (although there is a 0.75 percent annual service charge) and a flexible repayment schedule averaging between thirty-five and forty years (Rich 1994:77). These concessional loans are granted to the poorest countries.

Prominent bilateral institutions include the Japan International Cooperation Agency (JICA), the United States Agency for International Development (USAID), the Canadian International Development Agency (CIDA), Britain's Department for International Development (DfID), the Swedish Agency for International Development (SIDA), and the Danish Organization for International Development (DANIDA). These agencies vary in terms of the total size of their aid programs, the types of

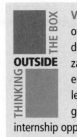

OUTSIDE THINKING THE BOX **VISIT THE** website of one of the multilateral development organizations and one bilateral organization to learn about their goals, programs, and internship opportunities.

The USAID has funded many development projects worldwide, such as this improved road in rural Bangladesh. Proceeds from the toll gate will help pay for maintenance of the road. The rickshaws are parked while their drivers pay their toll. The large white vehicle belongs to USAID and was being used by American researchers. ■ *What kinds of user fees have you paid in the past few months? Did you think the fees were fair?* (Source: Barbara Miller)

FIGURE 16.1 Major Agencies within the United Nations Related to Development

Agency	Headquarters	Mission
The United Nations Development Program, UNDP	New York City, U.S.	Supports countries in planning and managing development, including groundwater and mineral exploration, computer and satellite technology, seed production and agricultural extension, and research. UNDP does not implement projects. Implementation is done through UN "executing agencies," some of which are listed here.
The Food and Agricultural Organization (FAO)	Rome, Italy	Implements agricultural projects that receive funding from the UNDP and host governments.
The World Health Organization (WHO)	Geneva, Switzerland	Disease prevention and control, eradication of major infectious diseases, immunization of all children against major childhood diseases, establishment of primary health-care services.
The United Nations Children's Emergency Fund (UNICEF)	Joint headquarters in New York City and Geneva, Switzerland	Complementary to WHO; promotes children's health and survival, provides support for basic health care and social services for children.
The United Nations Educational, Scientific, and Cultural Organization (UNESCO)	Paris, France	Enhances world peace and security through education, science, and culture, and promotes respect for human rights, the rule of law, and fundamental freedoms.
The United Nations High Commission for Refugees (UNHCR)	New York City, U.S.	Promotes the rights and safety of refugees.
The United Nations International Development Fund for Women (UNIFEM)	New York City, U.S.	Raises the status of women.
The United Nations Fund for Population Activities (UNFPA)	New York City, U.S.	Supports family planning projects.

Source: Adapted from Hancock 1989.

programs they support, and the proportion of aid disbursed as loans that have to be repaid with interest compared to aid disbursed as grants that do not require repayment. The USAID tends to give more loans than grants, compared to other bilaterals.

Loans and grants also differ in terms of whether they are *tied* or *untied*. Tied loans and grants require that a certain percentage of project expenditures go for goods, expertise, and services originating in the donor country. For example, a tied loan to a certain country for road construction would require allocation of a designated percentage of the funds to donor country construction companies, airfare for donor country road experts, and in-country expenses for donor country experts, such as

hotels, food, and local transportation. When loans or grants are untied, the recipient country may decide freely how to use the funds. The USAID offers more tied than untied aid, whereas countries such as Sweden, the Netherlands, and Norway tend to give untied aid.

Another difference among the bilaterals is the proportion of their total aid that goes to the poorest countries. The United Kingdom's DfID sends more than 80 percent of its aid to the poorest countries, whereas most of U.S. foreign aid dollars go to Egypt and Israel. Emphasis on certain types of aid also varies from one bilateral institution to another. Cuba has long played a unique role in bilateral aid. Rather than offering assistance for a wide range of development projects, Cuba has concentrated on aid for training health-care providers and promoting preventive health care (Feinsilver 1993). Cuba's development assistance goes to socialist countries, including many in Africa, and some newly socialist states in Latin America such as Venezuela and Bolivia.

Grassroots Approaches

Many countries have experimented with *grassroots approaches* to development, or locally initiated, small-scale projects. This alternative to the top-down development pursued by the large-scale agencies described in the previous section is more likely to be culturally appropriate, supported through local participation, and successful.

During the 1970s, for example, Kenya (see Map 6.2, p. 158) sponsored a national program whereby the government committed itself to providing teachers if local communities would build schools (Winans and Haugerud 1977). This program was part of Kenya's promotion of *harambee,* or self-help, in improving health, housing, and schooling. Local people's response to the schooling program, especially, was overwhelmingly positive. They turned out in large numbers to build schools, fulfilling their part of the bargain. They built so many schools that the government found it difficult to hold up its end of the bargain: paying the teachers' salaries. This program shows that self-help movements can be highly successful in mobilizing local participation, if the target is valued.

The term **social capital** refers to the intangible resources of social ties, trust, and cooperation. Many local grassroots organizations around the world have existed for several decades, using social capital to provide basic social needs even in the most desperately poor situations (see Culturama, p. 434).

Religious organizations sponsor a wide variety of grassroots development projects. In the Philippines, the Basic Ecclesiastical Community (BEC) movement is based on Christian teachings and follows the model of Jesus as a supporter of the poor and oppressed (Nadeau 2002) (see Map 7.1, p. 174). The BECs seek to follow the general principles of liberation theology, which blends Christian principles of compassion and social justice, political consciousness-raising among the oppressed, and communal activism. In the rural areas, several BECs have successfully built trust among group members and leaders and developed people's awareness of the excesses of global capitalism and the dangers of private greed and accumulation. Part of their success is due to the fact that members were able to pursue new economic strategies

Scavenging for a livelihood in an urban dump in the Philippines. ■ *What kind of an entitlement is this?* (Source: Jeremy Horner/Alamy Images)

outside the constraints of capitalism, such as organic farming, that require little capital input.

A BEC in Cebu City, on the Island of Cebu, the Philippines, however, was unsuccessful. It faced the challenge of organizing people who make a living scavenging in a nearby city dump. Both adults and children scavenge for materials that are then sorted and sold for recycling, such as plastic. They work for fourteen hours a day, seven days a week. It is an organized operation, with district officials monitoring the dump. Customary arrangements among the scavengers regulate their work areas. Scavenging requires no formal education and few tools, just a basket and a steel hook, and a kerosene lantern for nighttime work. Scavengers earn more than other nonskilled laborers in the city. In the BEC meetings, the scavengers found little on which to build solidarity. Instead, they bickered

---

social capital: the intangible resources existing in social ties, trust, and cooperation.
development project: a set of activities designed to put development policies into action.

project cycle: the steps of a development project from initial planning to completion: project identification, project design, project appraisal, project implementation, and project evaluation.

sociocultural fit: a characteristic of informed and effective project design in which planners take local culture into account; opposite of one-size-fits-all project design.

Culturama

The Peyizan yo of Haiti

Haiti and the Dominican Republic share the island of Hispaniola. Following the island's discovery by Columbus in 1492, Spanish colonialists exterminated the island's indigenous Arawak Indians. In 1697, the French took control of what is now Haiti and instituted an exceptionally cruel system of African plantation slavery. In the late 1700s, the half million slaves revolted. In what is the only successful slave revolution in history, they ousted the French and established the first Black republic in the Western Hemisphere.

Haiti's population of over 8 million people occupies a territory somewhat smaller than the state of Maryland in the United States (www.unfpa.org). The land is rugged, hilly, or mountainous. More than 90 percent of the forests have been cleared. Haiti is the poorest country in the Western Hemisphere. Severe inequality exists between the urban elite, who live in the capital city of Port-au-Prince, and everyone else.

The people in the countryside are *peyizan yo* (the plural form of *peyizan*), a Creole term for small farmers who produce for their own use and for the market (Smith 2001). Many also participate in small-scale marketing. Most peyizan yo in Haiti own their own land. They grow vegetables, fruits (especially mangoes), sugarcane, rice, and corn.

Accurate health statistics are not available, but even rough estimates show that Haiti has the highest prevalence level of HIV/AIDS of any country in the region. Medical anthropologist Paul Farmer emphasizes the role of colonialism in the past and global structural inequalities now in causing these high rates (1992).

Colonial plantation owners grew fabulously rich from this island. It produced more wealth for France than all of France's other colonies combined and more than the thirteen colonies in North America produced for Britain. Why is Haiti so poor now? Colonialism launched environmental degradation by clearing forests. After the revolution, the new citizens carried with them the traumatic history of slavery. Now, neo-colonialism and globalization are leaving new scars. For decades, the United States has played, and still plays, a powerful role in supporting conservative political regimes.

In contrast to these structural explanations, some people point to problems with the Haitian people: They cannot work together and they lack a vision of the future. In contrast to these views, Jennie Smith's ethnographic research in southwestern Haiti sheds light on life and perspectives on development of the peyizan yo (2001). She found many active social organizations with functions such as labor sharing to help each member get his or her field planted on time and cost sharing to help pay for health care or funerals. The peyizan yo had clear opinions about their vision for the future, including relative economic equality, political leaders with a sense of social service, *respe* (respect), and access of citizens to basic social services.

Readings

Paul Farmer. *AIDS and Accusation: Haiti and the Geography of Blame*. Berkeley: University of California Press, 1992.

Jennie M. Smith. *When the Hands Are Many: Community Organization and Social Change in Rural Haiti*. Ithaca, NY: Cornell University Press, 2001.

Michel-Rolph Trouillot. *Haiti: State against Nation: The Origins and Legacy of Duvalierism*. New York: Monthly Review Press, 1990.

Video

Désounen: Dialogue with Death (Bullfrog Films).

Thanks to Jeannie Smith-Pariola, Berry College, for reviewing this material.

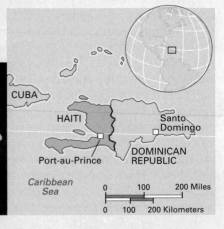

A woman repays her loan at a small-scale savings and loan business in rural Haiti (left). Many of the credit union members use their loans to set up small businesses. ■ *(Source: © Gideon Mendel/CORBIS) At a school in Port-au-Prince, (right), a teacher instructs a class with minimal equipment.* ■ *(Source: © Philip Gould/CORBIS)*

MAP 16.3 *Haiti. The Republic of Haiti occupies one-third of the Caribbean island of Hispaniola.*

with each other and complained about each other to the leaders. Kathleen Nadeau's interpretation is that the sheer poverty of the people was so great that communal values could not compete against their daily economic struggle. In such cases of extreme poverty with highly constrained options for alternative forms of income generation, Nadeau suggests that improving the people's lives may require government programs and support in addition to faith-based, grassroots initiatives.

Beginning with the Reagan administration's push toward privatization in the 1980s in the United States and a similar trend in the United Kingdom, the U.S. government sought to reduce direct support of international development and to encourage privatization of development assistance. Since then, many hundreds of nongovernmental organizations (NGOs) have emerged. A number of NGOs are focused on a particular issue, such as girls' education, HIV/AIDS prevention, human rights, or refugee relief. Some, however, are larger umbrella organizations with substantial projects covering many domains. Others, unfortunately, are only fronts that receive funding from government and nongovernment sources but do no actual work.

The Development Project

Development institutions, whether they are large multilaterals or local NGOs, implement their goals through the **development project,** a set of activities designed to put development policies into action. For example, suppose a government sets a policy of increased agricultural production by a certain percent within a designated period. A development project to achieve the policy goal might be the construction of irrigation canals that would supply water to a targeted number of farmers.

Anthropologists and the Development Project Cycle

Although details vary between organizations, all development projects have a **project cycle,** or the full process of a project from initial planning to completion (Cernea 1985). The project cycle includes five basic steps from beginning to end (see Figure 16.2).

Since the 1970s, applied anthropologists have been involved in development projects. First, they were hired primarily to do project evaluations, to determine whether the project had achieved its goals. Their research often showed that projects were dismal failures (Cochrane 1979). Three of their most frequent findings are:

- The project was inappropriate for the cultural and environmental context.
- The target group, such as the poor or women, had not been reached, but instead project benefits had gone to some other group.

FIGURE 16.2   The Development Project Cycle

Project identification	Selecting a project to fit a particular purpose
Project design	Preparing the details of the project
Project appraisal	Assessing the project's budgetary aspects
Project implementation	Putting the project in place
Project evaluation	Assessing whether the project goals were fulfilled

- The intended beneficiaries were actually worse off after the project than before it.

One reason underlying these failures is poor project design. The projects were all designed by *people-distant* and culturally uninformed bureaucrats, usually Western economists who lived in cities far from the project site with no firsthand experience of the lives of the target population. These experts applied a universal formula ("one size fits all") to all situations (Scott 1998). The cultural anthropologists who evaluated the projects, in contrast, were *people-close,* culturally informed, and therefore shocked by the degree of nonfit between the projects and the people.

Applied anthropologists soon gained a reputation in development circles as troublemakers—people to be avoided by those who favored a move-ahead approach to getting projects funded and implemented. Applied anthropologists are still considered a nuisance by many development policy-makers and planners, but sometimes, at least, a necessary nuisance. On a more positive note, through persistent efforts, they have made progress in gaining a role earlier in the project cycle, at the stages of project identification and design.

Sociocultural Fit

Review of many development projects over the past few decades reveals the importance of **sociocultural fit,** or taking the local culture into account in project design (Kottak 1985). A glaring case of nonfit between a project and its target population is a project intended to improve nutrition and health in some South Pacific islands by promoting increased milk consumption (Cochrane, author's class lecture notes, 1974). The project involved the transfer of large quantities of powdered milk from the United States to an island community. The local people, however, were lactose intolerant (unable to digest raw milk), and they all soon had diarrhea. They stopped drinking the milk and used the powder to white-wash their houses. Beyond wasting resources, inappropriately designed projects result in the exclusion of the intended beneficiaries. Two examples are when a person's signature is required but the people do not know how to write, and when photo identification cards are requested from Muslim women, whose faces may not be shown in public.

One role for applied anthropologists is to provide insights about how to achieve sociocultural fit in order to enhance project success. Gerald Murray played a positive role in redesigning a costly and unsuccessful reforestation project supported by USAID in Haiti (1987). Since the colonial era in Haiti (see Map 16.3, p. 433), deforestation has been dramatic, with an estimated 50 million trees cut annually. Some of the deforestation is driven by the market demand for wood for construction and for charcoal in the capital city of Port-au-Prince. Another reason is that the peyizan yo (small farmers) need cleared land for growing crops and grazing their goats. The ecological consequences of so much clearing, however, are soil erosion and declining fertility of the land.

USAID sent millions of tree seedlings to Haiti, and the Haitian government urged rural people to plant them. The peyizan yo, however, refused to plant the seedlings on their land and instead fed them to their goats. Murray, who had done his doctoral dissertation on rural Haitian land tenure practices, was called on by USAID to diagnose the problem and suggest an alternative approach. He advised that the kind of seedling promoted be changed from fruit trees, in which the peyizan yo saw little benefit because they are not to be cut, to fast-growing trees such as eucalyptus that could be cut as early as four years after planting and sold in Port-au-Prince. The peyizan yo quickly accepted this plan because it would yield profits in the foreseeable future. The cultural non-fit was that USAID wanted trees to stay in place for many years, but the peyizan yo viewed trees as things that were meant to be cut in the short term.

The Anthropological Critique of Development Projects

The early decades of development anthropology were dominated by what I call **traditional development anthropology (TDA)**. In traditional development anthropology, the anthropologist takes on a role of helping to make development policies and programs work better. It is the "add an anthropologist and stir" approach to development. Like good applied anthropology in any domain, TDA does work. For example, an anthropologist familiar with a local culture can provide information about what kinds of consumer goods would be desired by the people or what might persuade people to relocate with less resistance. The anthropologist may act as a cultural broker (review the definition in Chapter 6), using knowledge of both *donor culture* and *recipient culture* to devise a workable plan.

Concern exists among many anthropologists about development projects that have negative effects on local people and their environments (Bodley 1990; Horowitz and Salem-Murdock 1993; Taussig 1978). Comparison of the welfare of local inhabitants of the middle Senegal River valley (see Map 16.4), before and after the construction of a large dam, shows that people's level of food insecurity increased after the dam was built (Horowitz and Salem-Murdock 1993). Before the dam, periodic flooding of the plain supported a dense population supporting itself with agriculture, fishing, forestry, and herding. After the dam was constructed, water was released less often. The people downstream lacked sufficient water for their crops, and fishing was no longer a dependable source of food. At other times, dam managers released a large flood of water, damaging farmers' crops. Many downstream residents have had to leave the area due to the effects of the dam; they are victims of development-induced displacement (review Chapter 15). Downstream people now have high rates of schistosomaisis as a result of the dam construction because the disease spreads in the slow-moving water below the dam (review Figure 7.5., p. 191).

Other "dam stories" document the negative effects of dam construction on local people, including the destruction of their economy, social organization, sacred space, sense of home, and the environment (Loker 2003). Such mega-projects force thousands, even millions, of people in the affected area to cope with the changes in one way or another. Many leave; others stay and try to replace what they have lost by clearing new land and rebuilding. Most end up in situations far worse than where they lived originally.

The growing awareness of the negative effects of many supposedly positive development projects has led to the emergence of what I call **critical development anthropology (CDA)**. In this approach, the anthropologist takes

---

traditional development anthropology: an approach to international development in which the anthropologist accepts the role of helping to make development work better by providing cultural information to planners.

critical development anthropology: an approach to international development in which the anthropologist takes on a critical-thinking role and asks why and to whose benefit particular development policies and programs are pursued.

rapid research method (RRM): fieldwork method designed for use in development anthropology that can yield relevant data in a short period of time.

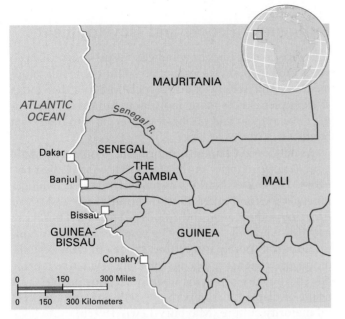

MAP 16.4   Senegal. The Republic of Senegal is mainly rolling sandy plains of the western Sahel. Senegal's economy has been struggling. Social inequality is extreme, and urban unemployment is high. Its population is around 11.7 million of which 70 percent live in rural areas. Of the many ethnic groups, the Wolof are the largest. Islam is the major religion, practiced by 94 percent of the population, with Christians 4 percent. Sufi brotherhoods are the organizing principle of Islam in Senegal.

on a critical-thinking role. The question is not: What can I do to make this project successful? Instead, the anthropologist asks: Is this a good project from the perspective of the local people and their environment? If the answer is yes, then an applied anthropologist can take a supportive role. If the answer is no, then the anthropologist can intervene with this information, taking on the role of either a whistle-blower to stop the project, or as an advocate promoting ideas about how to change the project in order to mitigate harm. In the case of the Senegal River dam project, applied anthropologists worked in collaboration with engineers and local people to devise an alternative management plan for the water flow in which regular and controlled amounts of water were released. In many other cases, the process is less positive with planners ignoring the anthropologist's advice (Loker 2000).

Methods in Development Anthropology

Academic research about development and change relies on long-term fieldwork and standard research methods (described in Chapter 2). A development agency, in contrast, typically needs input from an applied anthropolo-

gist within a few weeks' time. Specialized methods have emerged to respond to the short time frame and provide answers to the specific questions at hand. Compared to standard fieldwork, methods in applied development anthropology are more

- Topically focused, with a less holistic research agenda
- Likely to involve multidisciplinary research teams
- Reliant on rapid research methods
- Likely to involve participatory research methods

The rest of this section describes the last two of these methods.

Rapid Research Methods

Rapid research methods (RRMs) are ways of collecting data that provide focused information in a short time period (Chambers 1983). They include strategies such as going to the field with a checklist of questions, conducting *focus group interviews* (talking to several people at the same time rather than one by one), and conducting *transect observations* (walking through a specific area with key research participants and asking for explanations along the way) (Bernard 1995:139–140). When used correctly, RRMs can provide useful data for assessing the problems and opportunities related to development. Rapid research methods are most effective when several methods are used to complement each other and when researchers work in teams (recall Chapter 2).

An effective mix of rapid research methods was used for project planning in rural Bali, Indonesia (Mitchell 1994) (see Map 1.3, p. 15). The research goal was to identify environmental and social stresses that might be caused by economic development. This information would form the basis of recommendations for the government in preparing its next five-year development plan. Anthropologists and graduate students at the University of Windsor, Canada, and at an Indonesian university designed an eight-village study to provide data on ecological, economic, and social factors. A four-member team was assigned to each village, but each team spent some time in at least two villages. Teams consisted of Indonesian and Canadian researchers, both men and women. All team members could speak Bahasa Indonesian (the official state language), and at least one could also speak Bahasa Bali (the local language).

Researchers lived in the village for four weeks. They employed several methods for data collection. They gathered background data from provincial documents and village records. They conducted interviews with key research participants representing village leaders, religious figures, women, youth, school teachers, health clinic personnel, and agricultural extension workers. They conducted household interviews with fifteen men and fifteen women from different neighborhoods in the village and with a sample of primary schoolchildren. They made observations of the village condition and villagers' daily activities. For each village, they generated a profile of biophysical features, production and marketing, local government, health and welfare, and expressive culture.

After the data collection, researchers gathered to collate their findings and generate a set of recommendations. Their report presented a range of issues for the government's consideration, including a discussion of the environmental and social stresses caused by increasing urbanization and international tourism.

Participatory Research Methods

Building on the RRM approach, another specialized technique is called **participatory research (PR)**, a way of collecting data that includes the involvement of and collaboration with the local people. Participatory research rests heavily on the anthropological assumption that local knowledge should not be bypassed but, rather, should be the foundation of development work. It proceeds by involving key community members at all stages of the research, from data collection to data analysis. This technique responds to the growing awareness that when the target population is involved in a development project, the project is more likely to be successful in the short run and sustainable over the long run (Kabutha, Thomas-Slaytor, and Ford 1993).

Local people, through PR, learn how to collect and analyze data themselves. They gain skills in how to prepare simple maps and charts and to collect and analyze other forms of local data. Once trained, they can continue data collection and analysis on their own. Participatory research increases the likelihood that projects will be maintained over time and will respond to changing local conditions in terms of design and management.

Development and Minority Groups: Indigenous People and Women

This section considers two major categories of people who have been affected by international development in various ways and are increasingly taking an active role in redefining development: indigenous people and women. Although they are overlapping categories, this section presents material about them separately for purposes of illustration.

Indigenous People and Development

This section describes how indigenous peoples have been victimized by many aspects of growth-oriented development, as they were by colonialism before it. It then looks at examples of how many indigenous groups are redefining development and taking development into their own hands.

As defined in Chapter 1, indigenous people are usually a numerical minority in the states that control their territory. The United Nations distinguishes between indigenous peoples and other minority groups such as African Americans, the Roma, and Tamils of Sri Lanka. It is more useful to view all "minority" groups as forming a continuum from purely indigenous groups to minority/ethnic groups that are not geographically original to a place but share many problems with indigenous peoples as a result of displacement and living within a more powerful majority culture (Maybury-Lewis 1997b).

Indigenous peoples differ from most minorities in that they tend to occupy remote areas. Remoteness has, to some extent, protected them from outsiders. Now, however, governments, international business, conservationists, and tourists increasingly recognize that the lands of these people contain valuable natural resources, such as gas in the circumpolar region, gold in Papua New Guinea and the Amazon, sapphires in Madagascar, hydroelectric potential in large rivers throughout the world, and cultural attractions. In different contexts, governments have paid varying degrees of attention to integrating indigenous peoples into "mainstream" culture in the interests of fostering state unity.

Accurate statistics on indigenous populations do not exist. Several reasons account for this lack of information (Kennedy and Perz 2000). First, no one agrees on whom to count as indigenous. Second, some governments do not bother to conduct a census of indigenous people. Third, if they do, they may undercount indigenous people in order to downplay recognition of their existence. Fourth, it is often physically difficult, if not impossible, to carry out census operations in indigenous areas. The indigenous people of North Sentinel Island in India's Andaman Islands remain uncounted because Indian officials cannot land on the island without being shot with arrows (Singh 1994) (see Map 3.2, p. 70). Estimates of the total population of indigenous people worldwide range between 300 million and 500 million people (Hughes 2003). The greatest numbers live in Asia, including Central Asia, South Asia, East Asia, and Southeast Asia. Canada's First Nation population is under two million, whereas that in the United States is around one million. Worldwide, indigenous people are about 5 percent of the global population of around six and a half billion people.

---

participatory research (PR): a method in development anthropology that involves the local people in gathering data relevant to local development projects.

Indigenous People as Victims of Colonialism and Development

Over the past several hundred years, many indigenous groups and their cultures have been exterminated as a result of contact with outsiders. In addition to death and population decline through contagious disease, slavery, warfare, and other forms of violence have threatened their survival. With colonialism, indigenous people have experienced wholesale attacks as outsiders sought to take over their land by force, prevented them from practicing their traditional lifestyle, and integrated them into the colonial state as marginalized subjects. The loss of economic, political, and expressive autonomy have had devastating effects on indigenous peoples (review Chapter 7, pp. 186–187).

Like colonialism, contemporary global and state political and economic interests often involve takeover and control of indigenous people's territory. Reduction in the biodiversity of their natural environment is directly linked to impoverishment, despair, and overall cultural decline (Maffi 2005; Arambiza and Painter 2006). These processes are common worldwide, creating new risks for indigenous people's welfare.

In Southeast Asia, states use policies of "planned resettlement" in order to displace indigenous people, or "hill tribes," in the name of progress (Evrard and Goudineau 2004). Development programs for the hill tribes in Thailand, for example, reveal the links among international interests, state goals, and the well-being of the hill tribes (Kesmanee 1994) (see Map 6.4, p. 163). In Thailand, the hill tribes include groups such as the Karen, Hmong, Mian, Lahu, Lisu, and Akha. They total about half a million people. International pressures are applied to have the hill tribes replace cultivation of opium with other cash crops. International aid agencies therefore sponsor agricultural projects and tourism. The Thai government is concerned with political stability and security in the area, given its strategic location. It promotes development projects such as roads and markets to establish links between the highlands and the lowlands.

Efforts to find viable substitute crops for opium have been unsuccessful, especially among the Hmong, who are most dependent on opium as a cash crop. Alternative crops require heavy use of fertilizers and pesticides, which are costly to the farmers and greatly increase environmental pollution. Alternative crops are less lucrative for the farmers. Logging companies have gained access to the hills and have done far more damage to the forests than the highlanders' horticultural practices. Increased penetration of the hill areas by lowlanders and international tourists have promoted the increase in the highlands of HIV/AIDS rates, illegal trafficking of girls and boys for sex work, and opium addiction.

The Thai government, like neighboring Laos, has attempted to relocate highland horticulturalists to the plains through various resettlement schemes. Highlanders who opt for relocation find the lowland plots to be unproductive due to poor soil quality. Their economic status declined compared to what it had been in the hills. A new risk has emerged for the resettlers in Thailand and Laos. They are now heavy consumers of methamphetamines, or ATS (Lyttleton 2004). Overall, the effects of forty years of "development" have been disastrous for the hill people of Southeast Asia.

In the southern part of Madagascar, there is pressure to grow more rice, which means irrigating more land. The expansion of intensive rice cultivation will bring the death of many baobab trees and threaten the habitats of wild animal species, including lemurs. ■ *Assume you have just been appointed as Madagascar's Minister of People, Nature, and Development. What do you want your research staff to brief you about during your first month of service?* (Source: © Robb Kendrick/Aurora & Quanta Productions)

Throughout their recent history of contact with the outside world, indigenous peoples have actively sought to resist the negative effects of "civilization." Since the 1980s, more effective and highly organized forms of protest have become prominent. Indigenous groups hire lawyers and other experts as consultants in order to reclaim and defend their territorial rights, to gain self-determination, and to secure protection from outside risks. Many indigenous people have themselves become trained as lawyers, researchers, and advocates.

Indigenous People and Territorial Entitlements

The many land and other resource claims being made by indigenous peoples are a direct response to their earlier losses. They can be a basis for conflicts ranging from lawsuits to attempts at secession (Jensen 2004; Plant 1994; Stidsen 2006). The section provides brief notes on the status of indigenous people's territorial rights, especially to land. Within each large world region, country by country variation exists in legal codes and adherence to such codes that may exist.

Few Latin American countries provide legal protection against encroachment on the land of indigenous groups. Nicaragua, Peru, Colombia, Ecuador, Bolivia, and Brazil have taken the lead in enacting policies that legitimize indigenous rights to land and demarcating and titling indigenous territories (Plant 1998; Stocks 2005). A wide gap often exists, however, between policy and actual protection. Despite the efforts, increasing numbers of Indians throughout the entire region of Latin America have been forced off their land in the past few decades, through poverty, violence, and environmental degradation due to encroachment by logging companies, mining operations, ranch developers, and others. In response, many migrate to cities and seek wage labor. Those who remain face extreme poverty, malnutrition, and personal and group insecurity.

A surge of political activism by indigenous people has occurred since the 1990s, sometimes involving physical resistance. Violence continues to erupt between indigenous groups and state-supported power structures, especially in the southern Mexican state of Chiapas (see Map 5.4, p. 128). In November 2005, participants at the First Symposium on Isolated Indigenous Peoples of the Amazon created a group called the International Alliance for the Protection of Isolated Indigenous Peoples (2005). The group seeks to make the relevant state governments aware of the current endangered situation of many indigenous peoples in Amazonia and in the Gran Chaco region to its south. They demand their right to isolation, if that is their choice, and to protection from unwelcome outside contact and encroachment.

In Canada, the law distinguishes between two different types of Native Americans and their land claims (Plant 1994). *Specific claims* concern problems arising from previous agreements or treaties, and *comprehensive claims* are those made by Native Americans who have not been displaced and have made no treaties or agreements. Most of the former claims have led to monetary compensation. In the latter category, interest in oil and mineral exploration has prompted governments to negotiate with indigenous people in an effort to have the latter's native claims either relinquished or redefined. In some provinces, especially British Columbia, claims affect most of the province. The Nunavut land claim was settled, granting about 25,000 Inuit access to a vast tract of land, including subsurface rights (Jensen 2004) (see Map 16.5).

In Asia, most countries have been reluctant to recognize the territorial rights of indigenous people (Plant 1994). In Bangladesh, the Chittagong Hill Tracts in the southeast is being massively encroached upon by settlers from the crowded plains region (see Map 9.2, p. 235). Encroachers now occupy the most fertile land, and the indigenous people are endangered in many ways. A large hydroelectric dam built in 1963 displaced 100,000 hill dwellers because they could no longer practice horticulture in the flooded areas. A few received some financial compensation, but most did not. Tribal opposition groups began emerging, and conflict, although suppressed in the world news, has been ongoing for decades. In Thailand, no legal recognition of hill tribes' land rights exists, whereas in Laos and Vietnam, some land has been allocated to indigenous communities (Jensen 2004:5). Sites of active contestation with the state over land and resources in the Asia-Pacific region include the Moros of the southern Philippines (see Map 7.1, p. 174) and the people of Western Papua, or the western part of the island of New Guinea controlled by Indonesia (see Map 1.4, p. 18). In some cases, indigenous people's fight for secession from the state continues to cost many lives.

In Africa, political interests of state governments in establishing and enforcing territorial boundaries have created difficulties for indigenous peoples, especially mobile populations such as foragers and pastoralists. Many formerly autonomous pastoralists of the Sahel region (see Map 16.6) have been transformed into refugees living in terrible conditions. The Tuareg, for example, have traditionally lived and herded in a territory crossing what are now five different countries: Mali, Niger, Algeria, Burkina Faso, and Libya (Childs and Chelala 1994). Because of political conflict in the region, thousands of Tuareg people live in exile in Mauritania, and their prospects are grim. Resistance movements spring up, but states move quickly to suppress them. The

THINKING OUTSIDE THE BOX

FOR CURRENT information on territorial rights of indigenous peoples, consult the websites of Cultural Survival (www.cs.org) and Survival International (www.survival-international.org).

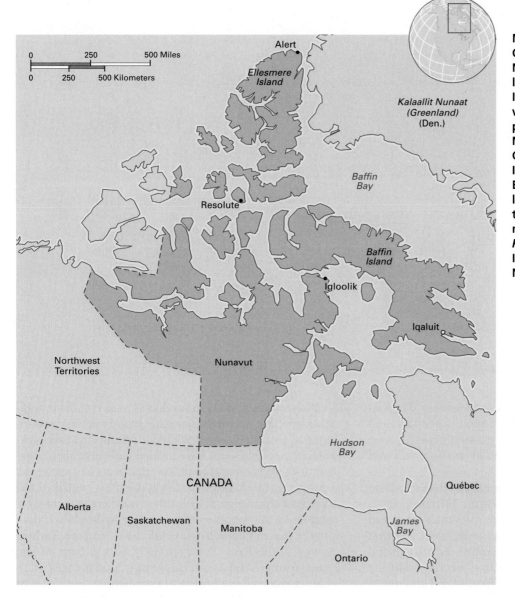

MAP 16.5 Nunavut Province, Canada. Created in 1999, Nunavut is the newest and largest of Canada's provinces. It is also the least populated, with 30,000 people. About 85 percent of the people are First Nations peoples, mainly Inuit. Official languages are Inuktitut, Inuinnagtun, English, and French. The landscape is mainly Arctic tundra. The award-winning movie, *Atanarjuat (The Fast Runner)*, was produced by Inuit filmmakers and filmed in Nunavut.

people of southern Sudan have been living in violence since 1983 (Salih 1999) (see Map 16.7, p. 433). They have been subject to genocide and violent displacement for global and local political and economic reasons, not the least of which involves the rich deposits of oil in the southern part of the country (Warren 2001) As mentioned in the Culturama in Chapter 1 (p. 22), South Africa has established more protective legislation for San peoples than have Namibia or Botswana.

The picture is mixed in Australia and New Zealand, with more progress in Australia in terms of legal recognition of Aboriginal territorial rights. Urban development, expansion of the non-Aboriginal population, road building, mineral extraction, and international tourism are some of the major threats to both livelihood and protection of sacred space. Aboriginal activism has seen some notable successes in achieving what is referred to as *native title* (Colley 2002). A key turning point in Australia occurred

through the efforts of Eddie Koiko Mabo, from the Torres Strait Islands (see Map 4.4, p. 105). He and his group, the Miriam people, took their claim of rights to their traditional land and water to the High Court, contesting the principle of *terra nullius*, or "empty land." Colonialists and neo-colonialist developers use *terra nullius* to justify territorial takeovers. Mabo convinced the High Court of the legitimacy of the Miriams' claim in 1992.

Organizing for Change

Many indigenous peoples have formed organizations for change in order to promote *development from within*. In Ethiopia, for example, many NGOs organized by local people have sprung up since the 1990s (Kassam 2002). One organization in the southern region is especially noteworthy because it seeks to provide a model of development based on the oral traditions of the Oromo peo-

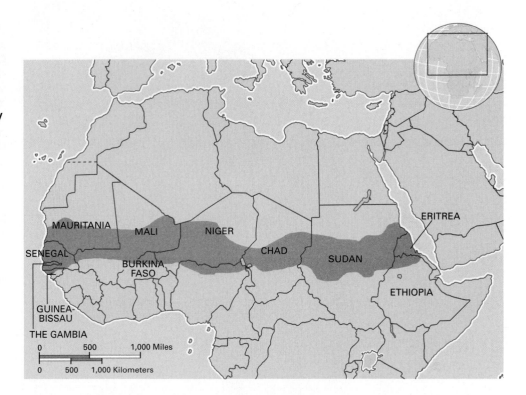

MAP 16.6 Sahel Region. The word *sahel* comes from the Arabic for shore or border, referring in this case to the area between the Sahara desert and the more fertile regions to the south. Primarily savanna, the region has been the home to many rich kingdoms that controlled Saharan trade routes. Most people make their living from pastoralism and semi-sedentary cattle-raising. The region has recently experienced several major droughts, leading to widespread death of herd animals, widespread human starvation and malnutrition, and forced population displacement.

ple. This new model thus combines elements of Western-defined "development" with Oromo values and laws and provides a new approach that is culturally appropriate and goes beyond external notions of development and usual Oromo lifeways.

The indigenous Oromo NGO is called Hundee, which refers to "roots," or the origins of the Oromo people, and, by extension, to all Oromo people, their land, and their culture. Hundee uses a theory of development that is based in Oromo metaphors of fertility and growth and involves gradual transformation like the spirals in the horn of a ram. Hundee relies on Oromo legal and moral principles about the communal use of natural resources and the redistribution of wealth to provide a social welfare system. These are elements of *good development,* as distinguished from the *bad development* that has inflicted hunger and dependency on the Oromo people.

Hundee's long-term goal is to empower Oromo communities to be self-sufficient. It takes the view that the Oromo culture is a positive force for social and economic change, rather than a barrier. Hundee members use a participatory approach in all their endeavors. They consult with traditional legal assemblies to identify needs and then to shape projects to address those needs. Specific activities include the establishment of a credit association and a grain bank to help combat price fluctuations and food shortages.

In many cases, indigenous people's development organizations link formerly separate groups in response to external threats (Perry 1996:245–246). In Australia, several indigenous groups have formed pan-Australian organizations and regional coalitions that have had success in land claim cases. In Canada, the Grand Council of the Cree has collaborated with other northern groups over land issues and opposition to a major hydroelectric dam project (Coon Come 2004; Craik 2004; and see Anthropology in the Real World, p. 309). In southern Africa, many formerly separate San groups joined together to claim a share in the profits of commercial marketing of hoodia as a diet pill (review Culturama, Chapter 1, p. 26). Many indigenous groups are taking advantage of new forms of communication in order to build and maintain links with each other over large areas.

Although it is tempting to see hope in the newly emerging forms of resistance, self-determination, and organizing among indigenous peoples, such hope cannot be generalized to all indigenous groups. Many are making progress and their economic status is improving, but others are suffering extreme political and economic repression.

Women and Development

The category of women contrasts with that of indigenous peoples because women, as a group, do not have a rec-

---

male bias in development: the design and implementation of development projects with men as beneficiaries and without re-gard to their impact on women's roles and status.

ognized territory associated with them. But the effects of colonialism, and now development, on women are similar to their effects on indigenous people: Women have often lost economic entitlements and political power in their communities. Matrilineal kinship, for example, which keeps property in the female line (review Chapter 8), is in decline throughout the world. Westernization and modernization are frequently the cause of this change. Another factor that has had a pervasive negative effect on women's status is the **male bias in development,** or the design and implementation of development projects with men as beneficiaries and without regard to their impact on women's roles and status.

This section presents examples of the male bias in development. It then provides examples in which some

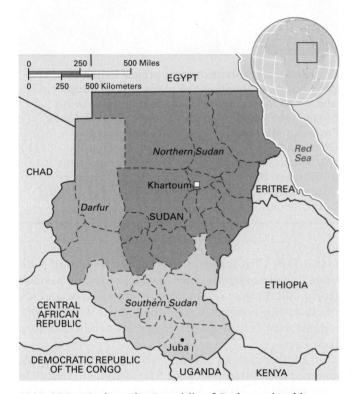

MAP 16.7   Sudan. The Republic of Sudan gained its independence from Britain in 1956 but, unlike other former British colonies, did not join the Commonwealth. The year before independence, a civil war began between the north and south. In 2005, a treaty granted southern Sudan the status of an autonomous region for six years to be followed by a referendum. In 2003, conflict erupted in the Darfur region. Sudan and neighboring Chad are also having conflicts. Most of the economy depends on agriculture, although oil production and trade have increased. The population of 37 million includes two ethnic groups: Arabs with Nubian roots and non-Arab Black Africans. Arabic is the dominant language of the north. Most Sudanese also speak local, tribal languages. Sunni Islam is the dominant religion (70 percent) in the north, with indigenous religions also important (25 percent). Christianity (5 percent) is practiced mainly in the south.

women's groups are redefining development and taking development into their own hands to make it work for their welfare and the welfare of their families.

The Male Bias in Development

In the 1970s, researchers began to notice and write about the fact that development projects were male biased (Boserup 1970; Tinker 1976). Many projects completely bypassed women as beneficiaries, targeting men for such initiatives as growing cash crops and learning about new technology. This male bias in development contributed to increased gender inequality by giving men greater access to new sources of income and by depriving women of their traditional economic roles. The development experts' image of a farmer, for example, was male, not female.

Women's projects were typically focused on the domestic domain—for example, infant feeding practices, child care, and family planning. This emphasis led to the *domestication of women* worldwide, meaning that their lives became more focused on the domestic domain and more removed from the public domain (Rogers 1979). For example, agricultural projects bypassed female horticulturalists who were instead taught to spend more time in the house bathing their babies.

The male bias in development also contributed to project failure. In the West African country of Burkina Faso (see Map 16.6, p. 442), a reforestation project included men as the sole participants, whose tasks would include planting and caring for the trees. Cultural patterns there, however, dictate that men do not water plants; women do. The men planted the seedlings and left them. Excluding women from the project ensured its failure. Exclusion of women from development continues to be a problem, in spite of many years of work attempting to place and keep women's issues on the development agenda.

Inclusion of women's knowledge, concerns, and voices has brought new and important issues to the fore, redefining development to fits women's needs. One such issue is gender-based violence. This issue has gained attention even among the large multilaterals, where experts realize that women cannot participate in a credit program, for example, if they fear that their husbands will beat them for leaving the house. The United Nations Commission on the Status of Women drafted a declaration in opposition of violence against women that was adopted by the General Assembly in 1993 (Heise, Pitanguy, and Germain 1994). Article 1 of the declaration states that violence against women includes "any act of gender-based violence that results in, or is likely to result in, physical, sexual or psychological harm or suffering to women, including threats of such acts, coercion or arbitrary deprivations of liberty, whether occurring in public or private life" (Economic and Social Council 1992). This definition cites women as the focus of concern, but also includes girls (see Figure 16.3).

FIGURE 16.3 Violence against Girls and Women throughout the Life Cycle

Prebirth	Sex-selective abortion, battering during pregnancy, coerced pregnancy
Infancy	Infanticide, emotional and physical abuse, deprivation of food and medical care
Girlhood	Child marriage, genital mutilation, sexual abuse by family members and strangers, rape, deprivation of food and medical care, child prostitution
Adolescence	Dating and courtship violence, forced prostitution, rape, sexual abuse in the workplace, sexual harassment
Adulthood	Rape and partner abuse, partner homicide, sexual abuse in the workplace, sexual harassment
Old Age	Abuse and neglect of widows, elder abuse

Source: Adapted from Heise, Pitanguy, and Germain 1994:5.

Programs that target violence against girls and women tend to deal with their effects rather than the causes, often with disastrous results. For example, programs may seek to increase personal security of women and girls in refugee camps by augmenting the number of guards at the camp when, in fact, the guards are often guilty of abusing refugee women and girls (Martin 2005).

Women's Organizations for Change

In many countries, women have improved their status and welfare through forming organizations, which are sometimes part of their traditional culture and sometimes a response to outside inspiration. These organizations range from mothers' clubs that help provide for communal child care to credit organizations that give women an opportunity to start their own businesses. Some are local and small scale; others are global, such as Women's World Banking, an international organization that grew out of credit programs for poor working women that started in India and Bangladesh.

A community-based credit system in rural Mozambique, southern Africa (see Map 9.5, p. 247), provides loans to help farm women buy seeds, fertilizers, and supplies (Clark 1992). When the loan program began, thirty-two farm families in one village formed themselves into seven solidarity groups, each with an elected leader. The woman-headed farmer groups managed irrigation efficiently and conferred on how to minimize the use of pesticides and chemical fertilizers. Through their efforts, the women quadrupled their harvests and paid off their

Grameen Bank, a development project begun in Bangladesh to provide small loans to poor people, is one of the most successful examples of improving human welfare through micro-credit, or small loans. Professor Mohammed Yunnus (center) founded Grameen Bank and continues to be a source of charismatic leadership for it. ■ *How does the success of Grameen Bank cause you to question your previous image of Bangladesh?* (Source: © Robert Nickelsberg/ Getty Images)

loans. They then turned their attention to getting additional loans to improve their herds and to buy a maize (corn) mill. In spite of poverty, violent military conflict, the lack of government resources, and a drought, the organization helped many women farmers to improve their lives.

In another case, an informal system of social networks emerged to help support poor Maya women vendors in San Cristobal, Chiapas, Mexico (Sullivan 1992) (see Map 5.4, p. 128). Many of the vendors who work in the city square have fled from the highlands because of long-term political conflict there. They manufacture and sell goods to tourists, earning an important portion of household income. In the city, they find social support in an expanded network that helps compensate for the loss of support from the extensive godparenthood system (review Chapter 8) of the highlands. The vendors' new networks include relatives, neighbors, church members, and other vendors, regardless of their religious, political, economic, or social background.

These networks first developed in response to a series of rapes and robberies that began in 1987. Because the offenders were persons of power and influence, the women did not dare to press charges. Mostly single mothers and widows, they adopted a strategy of self-

In the town of San Cristobal de las Casas, the capital city of Chiapas state in Mexico, a Maya vendor sells her goods. The city is located near the Tzotzil Maya communities of Chamula and Zinacantan. ■ *Review the section in Chapter 3 on economic change in Zinacantan.* (Source: © Philippe Giraud/Goodlook/CORBIS)

protection. First, they began to gather during the slow period each afternoon. Second, they always travel in groups. Third, they carry sharpened corset bones and prongs: "If a man insults one of them, the group surrounds him and jabs him in the groin" (39–40). Fourth, if a woman is robbed, the other women surround her, comfort her, and help contribute something toward compensating her for her loss. The mid-afternoon gatherings developed into support groups that provide financial assistance, child care, medical advice, and training in job skills. The groups have publicly demonstrated against city officials' attempts to prevent them from continuing their vending. Through their efforts, they have succeeded in bringing greater security into their lives.

A final example of women's empowerment and personal risk reduction through organized efforts comes from Kazakhstan, Central Asia (see Map 11.4, p. 297). In response to widespread domestic violence of husbands against wives, an NGO called the Society of Muslim Women (SMW) defines domestic violence as a problem that the Islamic faith should address at the grassroots level (Snajdr 2005). The organization declines to work with the police and civic activists who provide secular responses that involve criminalization of the offense, arrest of offenders, and other public procedures. Instead, SMW views domestic violence as a private matter that should be dealt with privately, using Islamic and Kazakhi values to deal with the problem. The SMW thus works completely outside the criminal justice system. Its goal is to provide aid to survivors of domestic abuse. Their three approaches are counseling, shelter, and mediation. Members of SMW are available to and supportive of both abusers and their victims. Their support ranges from simply talking with people to helping move an

abused woman into a safe living situation. The organization's guiding principle is to find a way, if possible, to rebuild the family. This goal may sound conservative, and even dangerous, in a situation where abuse is reported to occur in four out of five marriages. Yet, without funding or professional training, SMW members have provided support for countless women. They help the women overcome isolation (review the Lessons Applied box in Chapter 8, p. 224). They shift blame away from the victims by using Islamic rhetoric of familial commitment and gender equality and nationalist rhetoric that links men's alcoholism with occupation by the Russians. Sheltering abused women is defined as a Kazakhi custom of hospitality and as conforming with the Muslim virtue of patience, giving the spouses time to think about their relationship.

Urgent Issues in Development

This section focuses on some of the most urgent issues and new directions in development as informed by findings of cultural anthropologists and the views and voices of people themselves. The three topics are the redefinition of development projects as more people centered, the relationship between human rights and development, and the role of cultural heritage in development.

From Development Projects to Life Projects

As discussed earlier in this chapter, development projects are the main mechanism through which development

In Colombia, a five-year-old boy, Ever Hernando Salce, has blisters on his face caused by the herbicide sprayed on coca farms from planes working for Plan Colombia, financed by the U.S. war on cocaine *(left).* ■ (Source: © Reuters/ CORBIS) Bolivian security forces confront coca farmers during a protest march to the capital city of La Paz, and they scatter to avoid arrest *(right).* They were protesting the U.S. backed coca eradication plan that affects their livelihoods. This photograph was taken before President Evo Morales was elected. His policy allows coca farmers to grow a small amount of coca for traditional consumption. ■ (Source: © George Philipas/Alamy)

institutions implement their goals. They are typically designed by outsiders, often with little local knowledge, and they follow a universal, one-size-fits-all pattern. They range from mega-projects such as massive dams to small projects, with the former being much more damaging to local people than the latter. The so-called beneficiaries or target population are often not consulted at all about projects that will affect their community. Critics of such externally imposed and often damaging initiatives refer to such actions as **development aggression,** the imposition of development projects and policies without the free, prior, and informed consent of the affected people (Tauli-Corpuz 2005).

Moving beyond critique, indigenous people, women, and others who are victimized by external and mega-development are redefining what should be done to improve their lives or protect them from further decline.

They propose the concept of the life project rather than the development project. A **life project** is local people's vision of the direction they want to take in life, informed by their knowledge, history, and context, and how to achieve that vision.

Human Rights: Global and Local

Life projects, or people-defined and people-centered development, can be considered a human right and thus in accord with the UN's Declaration of Human Rights that was ratified in 1948. Local people around the world are claiming a right to their culture, most basically, under the rubric of cultural rights (Albro and Bauer 2005). Cultural rights protect cultural difference as a basic factor of human identity, dignity, and survival. Cultural rights seek a universal recognition of the right to be different.

development aggression: the imposition of development projects and policies without the free, prior, and informed consent of the affected people.

life project: local people's definition of the direction they want to take in life, informed by their knowledge, history, and context.

As discussed earlier in this chapter, people in developing countries and indigenous people throughout the world have added their voices to discussions of human rights and cultural rights, insisting on group rights to self-determination, locally defined paths of change, and attention to issues such as freedom from hunger (Messer 1993). Local groups are engaging with global definitions of human rights and adapting them to their own interests and needs (Merry 2006). As culturally diverse groups seek to define and claim their rights in an increasingly globalized world, we are all faced with the challenge of considering contending positions (see Everyday Anthropology box).

Human Rights and Development

This section provides two illustrations of how development and human/cultural rights are linked. The first reveals ties between large-scale development institutions and coercive military control. The second considers environmental destruction as a violation of human/cultural rights.

Among the Ifugao, an indigenous people of the highland region of Northern Luzon, the Philippines (see Map 7.1, p. 174), the militarization of everyday life has had serious negative consequences (Kwiatkowski 1998). The military presence is everywhere—in schools, in clinics, and especially at sites of large development projects such as dams. The military is there to ensure that people do not participate in what it considers subversive activities. Military force has been used to suppress local resistance to dams funded by the World Bank, resulting in numerous human rights violations, including torture, killings, imprisonment, and harassment of Ifugao people for suspected subversive activities (Drucker 1988). Members of a local NGO that supports more appropriate, small-scale forms of development that would benefit more people in the area have been harassed by the military. The case of the Ifugao illustrates how the powerful interests of state governments, international development agencies, and corporate interests often promote their plans and projects and violate human rights along the way.

A farmer walks through an oil-soaked field *(left)*. About 500,000 Ogoni people live in Ogoniland, a deltaic region in southern Nigeria. The fertility of the Niger delta has supported farming and fishing populations at high density for many years. Since Shell discovered oil there in 1958, 100 oil wells were constructed in Ogoniland and countless oil spills have occurred. ■ *Do Internet research on the environmental and social effects of massive oil exploitation on the Ogoni people.* (Source: © CORBIS. All Rights Reserved.) **Ogoni author and Nobel prizewinner Ken Saro-Wiwa founded the Movement for Survival of Ogoni People (MOSOP) in 1992 to protest Shell's actions in Ogoniland and the Nigerian government's indifference *(right)*. In 1995, he was arrested, tried for murder under suspicious circumstances, and executed by hanging. His execution brought about an international outcry while Shell's response is largely denial of any problem.** ■ (Source: © CORBIS)

Everyday Anthropology

HUMAN RIGHTS VERSUS ANIMAL RIGHTS

Human rights are sometimes understood to include the right of people, as members of a cultural group, to practice their cultural traditions. This provision extends the notion of human rights from including mainly the right to fulfilling basic physical needs, such as health and personal security, to including practices such as animal sacrifice, female genital cutting, hunting certain animals, and girls wearing headscarves in school—all issues that have received recent attention from European and North American governments and media because they differ from cultural practices in those countries. In the United States, as in many other countries, a debate about some cultural practices is carried out between human rights activists who support cultural rights and those who support animal rights.

In spring 1999, members of the Makah tribe of Washington State undertook a revival of their traditional practice of hunting gray whales (Winthrop 2000). Like that of many other indigenous peoples of the Pacific Northwest, from Canada to the United States, the Makah's traditional economy depended on fish, shellfish, and large marine mammals. A treaty of 1855 acknowledged the Makah's right to hunt whales and seals. The practice died out, however, in the twentieth century because of commercial overhunting and dwindling supplies. In 1982, the International Whaling Commission (IWC) imposed a ban on all commercial whaling but allowed continued whale hunting for "subsistence" pur-

poses. In 1994, the gray whale population had recovered, and the species was taken off the endangered list. The IWC allocated the Makah a quota of twenty whales for the period from 1998 to 2002.

Under this new plan, the Makah killed a whale in May 1999. The Makah watching the event cheered. The animal rights activists at the scene, in contrast, protested and said the occasion should have been one of mourning, not celebration. Although the Makah see the revival of whale hunting as a sign of cultural revitalization, some animal rights activists say that the way the hunt is being carried out is not culturally authentic, since the Makah first harpoon the whale and then shoot it with a rifle to kill it. They say that modern whale hunting does not follow the traditional culture and is not legitimate. Some of the protesters are motivated by ecological concerns for preservation of the species from extinction. Others support the concept of animal (especially mammalian) rights to life.

FOOD FOR THOUGHT

- What other examples of human rights versus animal rights have appeared recently in the media?
- What are the specific issues involved? Where do you stand in these debates and what is the basis for your position?

Development that leads to environmental degradation, including loss of biological diversity, air and water pollution, deforestation, and soil erosion, is another form of human/cultural rights abuse. Slain leader of Nigeria's Ogoni people, Ken Saro-Wiwa, made this point eloquently in a 1992 speech to the United Nations Working Group on Indigenous Populations:

> Environmental degradation has been a lethal weapon in the war against the indigenous Ogoni people. . . . Oil exploration has turned Ogoni into a wasteland: lands, streams, and creeks are totally and continually polluted; the atmosphere has been poisoned, charged as it is with hydrocarbon vapors, methane, carbon monoxide, carbon dioxide, and soot emitted by gas which has been flared 24 hours a day for 33 years in close proximity to human habitation. . . . All one sees and feels around is death (quoted in Sachs 1996:13–16)

Many social scientists agree with Saro-Wiwa, that such forms of development violate human/cultural rights because they undermine a people's way of life and threaten its continued existence (Johnston 1994).

Cultural Heritage and Development: Linking the Past and Present to the Future

Chapter 14 opened the discussion of cultural heritage and its potential for preserving people's heritage, both tangible and nontangible, and creating employment opportunities for local people through cultural tourism. This section goes more deeply into the complicated connections between cultural heritage and improving people's welfare from a life project perspective.

The connection of cultural heritage to development is clearly a double-edged sword (Bauer 2006). In other words, promoting cultural heritage, especially through tourism and expansion of supportive infrastructure such as roads and hotels, can preserve and protect cultural heritage as well as damage and destroy it. An emerging arena for legal involvement with culture is the area of intellectual property rights law, or cultural property rights law. Legal definitions and protections of rights to various forms of knowledge and behavior are another double-edged sword. On one hand, they help people, such as the San of southern Africa, to gain a share of the profits from the hoodia plant (review Culturama, Chapter 1, p. 22). On the other hand, they transform much of everyday life into a legal battle. International and country government laws are one step in seeking to prevent or at least reduce damage and destruction. UNESCO has adopted several guidelines which are just that—they are not binding and have no sanctions in case of violations.

Haitian dancers perform on Discover Miami Day at Miami's Little Haiti Caribbean Marketplace. Haitian culture in Miami is an increasingly popular tourist attraction in North America. ■ (Source: © Jeff Greenberg/Alamy)

At the Shan-Dany museum in Oaxaca, Mexico, indigenous people established a museum to house artifacts from their culture and to promote economic development for the village and the region by strengthening the local weaving industry. The museum provides outreach to schoolchildren and encourages them to learn more about their culture. ■ *Use the Internet to learn about other museum or cultural heritage projects of indigenous peoples.* (Source: Jeffrey Cohen)

Both the preservation of culture and its protection from damage and destruction connect with the reality that culture is always in process, always changing, and thus policies and laws interact with culture awkwardly. Over the next several years, culture—however defined and understood around the world—will be a major factor in international, regional, and local development and change.

Cultural Anthropology and the Future

During the past few decades, cultural anthropologists have defined and exposed many human/cultural rights abuses. Although this "whistle-blowing" can promote positive change, cultural anthropologists need to work harder to collaborate with local people to further their goals and to participate more actively in advocacy work directed toward the protection of human/cultural rights. Another important activity is continued dialogue about culture, cultural diversity, and cultural survival across groups in order to promote greater understanding and tolerance.

Determining how cultural anthropologists can contribute more effectively to a better future for humanity is a challenge for a field with its intellectual roots in studying *what is* rather than *what might be*. But just as local people everywhere are redefining development and reclaiming their culture, so also are they helping to redefine the theory, practice, and application of cultural anthropology. Although we live in a time of war, it is also a time of hope, in which insights and strength often come from those with the least in terms of material wealth but with cultural wealth beyond measure.

The Big Questions Revisited

WHAT is development and the approaches to achieving it?

Several theories or models of development exist, including modernization, growth-oriented development, distributional development, human development, and sustainable development. They differ in terms of how they define development and how to achieve it.

Institutional approaches to development, whether pursued by large-scale or grassroots organizations, tend to rely on the development project as a vehicle of local change. Cultural anthropologists have been hired as consultants on development projects, typically at the end of the project cycle to provide evaluations. Anthropologists have pushed for involvement earlier in the project so that their cultural knowledge can be used in project planning to avoid common errors. A one-size-fits-all project design often results in failed projects because of a lack of sociocultural fit. In traditional development anthropology, anthropological knowledge contributes to development projects by adding insights that will make a project work. In critical development anthropology, anthropological knowledge may suggest that the most socially beneficial path is either to stop the project or to redesign it.

Applied anthropologists involved in development work use several specialized methods for data collection. Rapid research methods (RRMs) provide data in a short time period. Participatory research (PR) is collaborative and involves training local people in how to do applied research such as social mapping and local censuses.

HOW is development related to indigenous people and women?

Indigenous people and women have been affected by international development in various ways, often negatively. They are taking an increasingly active role in redefining development to better suit their vision of the future.

Colonialism, neo-colonialism, and globalization have had serious negative effects on indigenous peoples and women worldwide in terms of declines in their entitlements and standard of living. Often, such losses are tied to environmental degradation and violence. Indigenous peoples throughout the world suffer from lack of secure claim to their ancestral territories. They are seeking legal recognition of territorial claims from state governments and protection from encroachment. Some governments are responding to their claims; others are not. Establishing organizations has been a major source of strength for promoting indigenous people's rights.

Western development planning and projects have long suffered from a male bias in project design. Excluding women from projects serves to domesticate women and often results in failed projects. Women are stating their needs and visions for the future, and thus redefining development in ways that are helpful to them. They have added the issue of violence against women and girls to the policy agenda of development institutions worldwide, including the large multilaterals.

WHAT are urgent issues in development?

Three urgent issues, as informed by cultural anthropology and the views and voices of people themselves, are (1) the redefinition of development projects as life projects or people-centered projects, (2) the relationship between human rights and development, and (3) the role of cultural heritage in development. Indigenous people, women, and others adversely affected by certain forms of development are promoting a new kind of development that is people centered and that enhances the life projects that people define for themselves. The concept of the life project is a human right, and a right to live in one's cultural world without encroachment, threat, and discrimination.

Cultural anthropologists contribute insights from different cultures about perceptions of basic human and cultural rights, and this knowledge, linked to advocacy, may be able to help prevent human/cultural rights abuses in the future. People's cultural heritage can be a path toward improved welfare, but it is a double-edged sword. Promoting cultural tourism can protect culture but also lead to damage and destruction. An emerging area is the legalization of cultural heritage through intellectual property rights law, another double-edged sword.

Culture is a central issue of our time, and local people are working with cultural anthropologists to address the challenges of an increasingly globalized, insecure, but exciting world.

KEY CONCEPTS

acculturation, p. 425
assimilation, p. 425
critical development anthropology
   (CDA), p. 436
development, p. 424
development aggression, p. 446
development project, p. 435

diachronic, p. 424
diffusion, p. 425
life project, p. 446
male bias in development, p. 443
modernization, p. 427
participatory research, (PR), p. 438
project cycle, p. 435

rapid research method (RRM), p. 437
social capital, p. 433
social impact assessment, p. 429
sociocultural fit, p. 435
synchronic, p. 424
traditional development anthropology
   (TDA), p. 436

SUGGESTED READINGS

Robert Albro and Joanne Bauer, eds. Cultural Rights: What They Are, Why They Matter, How They Can Be Realized. Special issue of *Human Rights Dialogue: An International Forum for Debating Human Rights,* Series 2(12), Spring 2005. Articles in this issue address rights to forest resources, languages, marriage practices, and legal issues related to genocide.

Mario Blaser, Harvey A. Feit, and Glenn McRae, eds. *In the Way of Development: Indigenous Peoples, Life Projects and Globalization.* New York: Zed Books, 2004. The authors are indigenous leaders, social activists, and anthropologists. Topics include the environment, women's status, social justice, participation, and dealing with mega-development projects.

Thomas W. Collins and John D. Wingard, eds. *Communities and Capital: Local Struggles against Corporate Power and Privatization.* Athens: University of Georgia Press, 2000. Case studies of local resistance against large capitalist forces include clam farmers of North Carolina, a fishing community in Malaysia, and banana growers in Belize.

Ann Frechette. *Tibetans in Nepal: The Dynamics of International Assistance among a Community in Exile.* New York: Bergahn Books, 2002. This book explores how a long history of international assistance to refugees has affected individual and community identity and values. Focusing on Tibetans in Nepal, Frechette shows how aid complicates exiled Tibetans' attempts to define and maintain a sense of community.

Gil Harper and Asha Moodley, eds. *Gender, Culture, and Rights: Empowering Women for Gender Equity. Agenda Special Focus,* 2005. Articles explore current approaches to gender, rights and culture in South Africa. Authors address law, religion, masculinity, violence, and health. www.agenda.org.za/index.

Dorothy L. Hodgson. *Once Intrepid Warriors: Gender, Ethnicity, and the Cultural Politics of Maasai Development.* Bloomington: Indiana University Press, 2004. This ethnography shows how Maasai identity and gender connect with development and globalization to shape Maasai life today.

Dolores Koenig, Tieman Diarra, Moussa Sow, and Ousmane Diarra. *Innovation and Individuality in African Development: Changing Production Strategies in Rural Mali.* Ann Arbor: University of Michigan Press, 1998. This ethnography covers the history of Malian rural production and how lessons learned contribute to an improved anthropology of development.

Gideon M. Kressel. *Let Shepherding Endure: Applied Anthropology and the Preservation of a Cultural Tradition in Israel and the Middle East.* Albany: SUNY Press, 2003. This book presents a case study of the Bedu of the Negev, southern Israel. It discusses how globalization is encroaching on herders to their great detriment. The author lays out an applied anthropology program for reconstituting and promoting pastoralism.

David H. Lempert, Kim McCarthy, and Craig Mitchell. *A Model Development Plan: New Strategies and Perspectives.* Westport, CT: Praeger, 1995. A group of university students from different disciplines (including one anthropologist, Lempert) spent six weeks in Ecuador, visiting nearly every province and studying development issues as the basis for their development plan for Ecuador.

Mark Moberg. *Citrus, Strategy, and Class: The Politics of Development in Southern Belize.* Iowa City: University of Iowa Press, 1992. Moberg compares the involvement of two villages in Belize in the global citrus market. He describes the formation of a rural class and the increasing dependency of rural Belize on the global market.

David Mosse. *Cultivating Development: An Ethnography of Aid Policy and Practice.* Ann Arbor, MI: Pluto Press, 2005. Mosse uses his experience as a development worker in India to analyze and critique how the structure of aid shapes the actions of development workers. The subject matter is policy making and projects viewed from a critical ethnographic perspective.

Richard J. Perry. *From Time Immemorial: Indigenous Peoples and State Systems.* Austin: University of Texas Press, 1996. Perry provides a comparative review of the history and status of indigenous peoples of Mexico, the United States, Canada, and Australia. Topics covered are state policies, state violence, resistance of the indigenous people, and efforts at self-determination.

Joanne Rappaport. *Intercultural Utopias: Public Intellectuals, Cultural Experimentation, and Ethnography.* Durham, NC: Duke University Press, 2005. The author draws on collaborative research in Colombia with indigenous activists. She documents the country's complex indigenous political movement with a focus on the southwestern Cauca region and its long history of indigenous mobilization and ethnic pluralism.

John Sherry. *Land, Wind and Hard Words: A Story of Navajo Activism.* Albuquerque: University of New Mexico Press, 2002. This book presents the story of the community-based activists of a Navajo environmental organization called Diné CARE that seeks to protect Navajo forests from logging.

Jennie M. Smith. *When the Hands Are Many: Community Organization and Social Change in Rural Haiti.* Ithaca, NY: Cornell University Press, 2001. Fieldwork in southwest Haiti reveals how poor rural people use social organizing and expressive culture to unite in resistance to the larger forces that impoverish them.

John van Willigen. *Anthropology in Action: A Source Book on Anthropological Practice.* Boulder, CO: Westview Press, 1991. This book first provides brief overviews of ethics, publications, and professional organizations in applied anthropology. Case studies follow, arranged alphabetically by topic, from "Agriculture" to "Women in Development."

Glossary

absolute cultural relativism: a perspective that says a person from one culture should not question the rightness or wrongness of behavior or ideas in other cultures because that would be ethnocentric.

acculturation: a form of cultural change in which a minority culture becomes more like the dominant culture.

achieved position: a person's standing in society based on qualities that the person has gained through action.

adolescence: a culturally defined period of maturation from the time of puberty until adulthood.

agency: the ability of humans to make choices and exercise free will.

agriculture: a mode of production that involves growing crops with the use of plowing, irrigation, and fertilizer.

amazon: a person who is biologically female but takes on a male gender role.

ambilineal descent: a kinship system in which a person is said to be descended from both parents but that allows the individual to choose with which descent group to have more affiliation.

animatism: a belief system in which the supernatural is conceived of as an impersonal power.

animism: the belief in souls or "doubles."

anthropology: the study of humanity, including our prehistoric origins and contemporary human diversity.

anthropomorphic: a supernatural in the form of a human.

applied anthropology or **practicing anthropology** or **practical anthropology:** the use of anthropological knowledge to prevent or solve problems or to shape and achieve policy goals.

applied or **clinical medical anthropology:** the application of anthropological knowledge to furthering the goals of health care providers.

archaeology or **prehistory:** the study of past human cultures through their material remains.

art: the application of imagination, skill, and style to matter, movement, and sound that goes beyond what is purely practical.

ascribed position: a person's standing in society based on qualities that the person has gained through birth.

assimilation: a form of culture change in which a culture is thoroughly acculturated, or decultured, and is no longer distinguishable as having a separate identity.

authority: the ability to take action based on a person's achieved or ascribed status or moral reputation.

avunculocality: a kinship rule that defines preferred marital residence with or near the wife's brother.

balanced exchange: a system of transfers in which the goal is either immediate or eventual equality in value.

band: the political organization of foraging groups, with minimal leadership and flexible membership.

banditry: a form of aggressive conflict that involves socially patterned theft, usually practiced by a person or group of persons who are socially marginal and who may gain a mythic status.

basic needs fund: a category of a personal or household budget that includes food, beverages, shelter, clothing, and the tools needed to obtain these items.

below-replacement-level fertility: a situation in which births are fewer than deaths, leading to population decline.

berdache: a blurred gender category, usually referring to a person who is biologically male but who assumes a female gender role.

big-man or big-woman system: a form of political organization midway between tribe and chiefdom involving reliance on the leadership of key individuals who develop a political following through personal ties and redistributive feasts.

bilineal descent: a kinship system in which a child is recognized as being related by descent to both parents.

bilocality: a marital residence pattern that offers a married couple the choice of living near or with the family of either the groom or the bride.

biological anthropology or **physical anthropology:** the study of humans as biological organisms, including their evolution and contemporary variation.

biological determinism: a theory that explains human behavior and ideas mainly as a result of biological features such as genes and hormones.

blood sport: a form of competition that explicitly seeks to bring about a flow of blood, or even death, of human-human contestants, human-animal contestants, or animal-animal contestants.

brideprice or bridewealth: the transfer of cash and goods from the groom's family to the bride's family and to the bride.

bride-service: a form of marriage exchange in which the groom works for his father-in-law for a certain period of time before returning home with the bride.

call system: a form of oral communication among nonhuman primates with a set repertoire of meaningful sounds generated in response to environmental factors.

capital: wealth used to create more wealth.

cargo cult: a form of revitalization movement that emerged in Melanesia and New Zealand in response to Western and Japanese influences.

cash crop: a plant grown primarily for sale rather than own-use.

caste: a ranked group, determined by birth, often linked to a particular occupation and to South Asian cultures.

caste system: a social stratification system linked with Hinduism and based on a person's birth into a particular group.

ceremonial fund: a category of a personal or household budget used for public events such as a potlatch.

chain migration: population movement in which a first wave of migrants comes and then attracts relatives and friends to join them in the destination.

chiefdom: a political unit of permanently allied tribes and villages under one recognized leader.

circular migration: a regular pattern of population movement between two or more places, either within or between countries.

civil society: the collection of interest groups that function outside the government to organize economic and other aspects of life.

clan: a kinship-based group in which people claim descent from a common ancestor, although they may be unable to trace the exact relationship.

class: a way of categorizing people on the basis of their economic position in society, usually measured in terms of income or wealth.

code: a variant within a language that may include a distinct vocabulary, grammar, and intonation, associated with a particular microculture.

collaborative research: an approach to learning about culture that involves anthropologists working with members of the study population as partners and teammates rather than as researchers and "subjects."

communication: the conveying of meaningful messages from one person, animal, or insect to another.

community healing: healing that emphasizes the social context as a key component and is likely to be carried out within the public domain.

consumerism: a mode of consumption in which people's demands are many and infinite and the means of satisfying them are insufficient and become depleted in the effort to satisfy these demands.

consumption fund: a category of a personal or household budget used to provide for consumption demands.

cooperative: an economic group whose members share surpluses and who follow the democratic decision-making principle of one person, one vote.

corporate farm: a large agricultural enterprise that produces goods solely for sale and that is owned and operated by companies that rely entirely on hired labor.

corvee: a labor tax used by the Inca state to finance public works such as roads and monuments and to provide agricultural labor on state lands.

couvade: customs applying to the behavior of fathers during and shortly after the birth of their children.

creole: a language directly descended from a pidgin but possessing its own native speakers and involving linguistic expansion and elaboration.

critical cultural relativism: a perspective that prompts people in all cultures to raise questions about their own and others' cultural practices and ideas, especially regarding who accepts them and why, and whom they might be harming or helping.

critical development anthropology: an approach to international development in which the anthropologist takes on a critical-thinking role and asks why and to whose benefit particular development policies and programs are pursued.

critical discourse analysis (CDA): the study of the relations of power and inequality in language.

critical legal anthropology: an approach within the cross-cultural study of how law and judicial systems serve to maintain and expand dominant power interests rather than protecting marginal and less powerful people.

critical media anthropology: an approach within the cross-cultural study of mass media that examines to what degree media messages are liberating, to what degree they are propagandizing and controlling, and whose interests the media serve.

critical medical anthropology: an approach within the cross-cultural study of health and illness involving the analysis of how economic and political structures shape people's health status, their access to health care, and the prevailing medical systems that exist in relation to them.

critical military anthropology: the study of the military as a power structure in terms of its roles and internal social dynamics.

cross-cousin: offspring of either one's father's sister or one's mother's brother.

cultural anthropology or **social anthropology:** the study of living peoples and their cultures, including variation and change.

cultural broker: a person who is familiar with the practices and beliefs of two cultures and can promote cross-cultural understanding to prevent or mediate conflicts.

cultural configuration: Ruth Benedict's theory that cultures are formed through the unconscious selection of a few cultural traits that interweave to form a cohesive pattern shared by all members of the culture.

cultural constructionism: a theory that explains human behavior and ideas as being mainly the results of learning.

cultural imperialism: a situation in which a dominant culture claims supremacy over minority cultures and makes changes in its culture and the minority culture(s) in its own interests and at the expense of the minority culture(s).

cultural materialism: a theoretical position that takes material features of life, such as the environment, natural resources, and mode of production, as the bases for explaining social organization and ideology.

cultural relativism: the perspective that each culture must be understood in terms of the values and ideas of that culture and should not be judged by the standards of another.

culture: people's learned and shared behaviors and beliefs.

culture of poverty: Oscar Lewis's theory that the personality characteristics of the poor trap them in poverty.

culture shock: persistent feelings of uneasiness, loneliness, and anxiety that often occur when a person has shifted from one culture to a different one.

culture-specific syndrome: a collection of signs and symptoms that is restricted to a particular culture or a limited number of cultures; also called "folk illness."

dalit: the preferred name for the socially defined lowest groups in the Indian caste system, meaning "oppressed" or "ground down."

deductive approach (to research): a research method that involves posing a research question or hypothesis, gathering the empirical data related to the question, and then assessing the findings in relation to the original hypothesis.

demographic transition: the change from the agricultural pattern of high fertility and high mortality to the industrial pattern of low fertility and low mortality.

demography: the study of population dynamics.

descent: the tracing of kinship relationships through parentage.

development: directed change to achieve improved human welfare.

development aggression: the imposition of development projects and policies without the free, prior, and informed consent of the affected people.

development anthropology: the study of how culture and development interact.

development-induced displacement (DID): forced migration due to development projects, such as dam building.

development project: a set of activities designed to put development policies into action.

diachronic: the analysis of culture across time.

dialect: a way of speaking in a particular place or a variety of a language arising from local circumstances.

diaspora population: dispersed group of people living outside their original homeland.

diffusion: the spread of culture through contact.

digital divide: social inequality in access to new and emerging information technology, notably access to up-to-date computers, the Internet, and training related to their use.

direct entitlement: the most secure form of entitlement to providing for one's needs; in an agricultural society, owning land that produces food is a direct entitlement.

direct infanticide: the killing of an infant or child through practices such as beating, smothering, poisoning, or drowning.

discourse: people's talk, stories, and myths.

disease: in the disease/illness dichotomy, a biological health problem that is objective and universal.

disease of development: a health problem caused or increased by economic development activities that affect the environment and people's relationship with it.

disease/illness dichotomy: the distinction between disease as an objective and universal biological pathology, and illness as the culturally specific understandings and experiences of a health problem or other form of suffering; corresponds to the etic/emic distinction.

displaced person: someone who is forced to leave his or her home and community or country.

displacement: a feature of human language that allows people to talk about events in the past and future.

divination: a diagnostic procedure in which a specialist uses techniques to gain supernatural insights.

doctrine: direct and formalized statements about religious beliefs.

domestication: the control and management of plants and animals by humans in terms of both their location and their reproduction.

dominant caste: one caste in a particular locale that controls most of the land and is often numerically preponderant.

dowry: the transfer of cash and goods from the bride's family to the newly married couple and to the groom's family.

ecological/epidemiological approach: an approach within medical anthropology that considers how aspects of the natural environment and social environment interact to cause illness.

emic: what insiders do and perceive about their culture, their perceptions of reality, and their explanations for why they do what they do.

enculturation: the learning of culture through both informal and formal processes.

endogamy: marriage within a particular group or locality.

entertainment fund: a category of a personal or household budget used to provide for leisure activities.

entitlement: a culturally defined right to life-sustaining resources.

ethnicity: a shared sense of identity among a group based on a heritage, language, or culture.

ethnobotany: an area of inquiry exploring knowledge in different cultures of plants and their uses.

ethnocentrism: judging other cultures by the standards of one's own culture rather than by the standards of that particular culture.

ethnocide: the destruction of a culture without physically killing its people.

ethno-esthetics: cultural definitions of what art is.

ethno-etiologies: culturally specific causal explanations for health problems and suffering.

ethnography: a firsthand, detailed description of a living culture, based on personal observation.

ethnology: the study of a particular topic in more than one culture using ethnographic material.

ethnomedicine: the study of cross-cultural health systems.

ethnomusicology: the cross-cultural study of music.

ethno-nosology: the cross-cultural study of culturally specific classifications of health problems.

ethnopsychology: the study of how various cultures define and create personality, identity, and mental health.

ethnosemantics: the study of the meaning of words, phrases, and sentences in particular cultural contexts.

etic: an analytical framework used by outside analysts in studying culture.

euhemerism: the process by which a human who once lived is transformed into a deity; named after the philosopher Euhemerus of Messene.

exogamy: marriage outside a particular group or locality.

expected reciprocity: an exchange of approximately equally valued goods or services, usually between people roughly equal in social status.

expressive culture: behavior and beliefs related to art, leisure, and play.

extended household: a co-residential group that comprises more than one parent-child unit.

extensive strategy: a form of production involving temporary use of large areas of land and a high degree of spatial mobility.

faction: a politically oriented group with strong lateral ties to a leader.

family: a group of people who consider themselves related through a form of kinship, such as descent, marriage, or sharing.

family farming (formerly termed *peasant agriculture*): a form of agriculture in which farmers produce mainly to support themselves but also produce goods for sale in the market system.

female genital cutting: a term used for a range of genital cutting procedures, including the excision of part or all of the clitoris, part or all of the labia, and sometimes infibulation, the stitching together of the vaginal entry.

femicide: the murder of a person based on the fact of her being female.

fertility: the rate of births in a population, or the rate of population increase in general.

feuding: long-term, retributive violence that may be lethal between families, groups of families, or tribes.

fieldwork: research in the field, which is any place where people and culture are found.

focal vocabulary: a cluster of related words referring to important features of a particular culture.

foraging: collecting food that is available in nature, by gathering, fishing, or hunting.

formal sector: salaried or wage-based work registered in official statistics.

frontline anthropology: anthropological research carried out within zones of violent conflict and requiring specialized training and experience.

functionalism: the theory that a culture is similar to a biological organism, in which parts work to support the operation and maintenance of the whole.

gender: culturally constructed and learned behaviors and ideas attributed to males, females, or blended genders.

gender pluralism: the existence within a culture of multiple categories of femininity, masculinity, and androgyny that are tolerated and legitimate.

genealogy: a record of a person's relatives constructed beginning with the earliest ancestors.

generalized reciprocity: exchange involving the least conscious sense of interest in material gain or thought of what might be received in return.

genocide: the destruction of a culture and its people through physical extermination.

globalization: increased and intensified international ties related to the spread of Western, especially United States, capitalism that affects all world cultures.

global language or world language: a language spoken widely throughout the world and in diverse cultural contexts often replacing indigenous languages.

grammar: the rules by which words are organized to make sense in a string.

groomprice: the transfer of cash and goods, often large amounts, from the bride's family to the groom's family.

Hawthorne effect: research bias due to participants changing their behavior to conform to expectations of the researcher.

heterotopia: the creation of an internally varied place by collecting things from diverse cultures and locations.

hijra: term used in India to refer to a blurred gender role in which a person, usually biologically male, takes on female dress and behavior.

historical linguistics: the study of language change using formal methods that compare shifts over time and across space in aspects of language such as phonetics, syntax, and semantics.

historical particularism: the view that individual cultures must be studied and described on their own terms and that cross-cultural comparisons and generalizations ignore cultural specificities and are invalid.

historical trauma: the intergenerational transfer of the negative effects of colonialism from parents to children.

holism: the perspective in anthropology that cultures are complex systems that cannot be fully understood without paying attention to their different components, including economics, social organization, and ideology.

horticulture: a mode of production based on growing domesticated crops in gardens using simple hand tools.

household: a group of people, who may or may not be related by kinship, who share living space.

human development: a model of change promoted by the United Nations that emphasizes improvements in human welfare such as health, education, and personal security.

humoral healing system: healing that emphasizes balance among natural elements within the body.

hypergyny: a marriage in which the groom is of higher status than the bride.

hypogyny: a marriage in which the bride is of higher status than the groom.

illness: in the disease/illness dichotomy, culturally specific perceptions and experiences of a health problem.

image of the limited good: George Foster's theory that in nonindustrial cultures, people have a characteristic worldview of finite resources or wealth such that if someone in the group increases his or her wealth, other people will necessarily lose out.

incest taboo: a strongly held prohibition against marrying or having sex with particular kin.

indigenous knowledge: local knowledge about the environment, including plants, animals, and resources.

indigenous peoples: groups who have a long-standing connection with their home territory that predates colonial or outside societies that prevail in that territory.

indirect entitlement: a way of gaining one's livelihood that depends on exchanging something such as labor or goods.

indirect infanticide: the killing of an infant or child through practices such as food deprivation or failure to seek health care during illness.

inductive approach (to research): a research approach that avoids hypothesis formation in advance of the research and instead takes its lead from the culture being studied.

industrial capital agriculture: a form of agriculture that is capital-intensive, substituting machinery and purchased inputs for human and animal labor.

industrial collectivized agriculture: a form of industrialized agriculture that involves state control of land, technology, and goods produced.

industrialism/informatics: a mode of production in which goods are produced through mass employment in business and commercial operations and through the creation and movement of information through electronic media.

infant mortality rate: the number of deaths of children under the age of one year per 1,000 births.

infanticide: the killing of an infant or child.

influence: the ability to achieve a desired end by exerting social or moral pressure on someone or some group.

informal sector: work that is outside the formal sector, not officially registered, and sometimes illegal.

informed consent: an aspect of fieldwork ethics requiring that the researcher inform the research participants of the intent, scope, and possible effects of the study and seek their consent to be in the study.

infrastructure: in the framework of cultural materialism, the first and most basic level of culture, which includes the material factors of economy and reproduction.

in-kind taxation: a system of mandatory non-cash contributions to the state.

institutional migrant: a person who moves into a social institution (such as a school or prison), voluntarily or involuntarily.

intangible cultural heritage: UNESCO's view of culture as manifested in oral traditions, languages, performing arts, rituals and festive events, knowledge and practices about nature and the universe, and craftmaking. Also called living heritage.

intensive strategy: a form of production that involves continuous use of the same land and resources.

internal migration: population movement within state boundaries.

internally displaced person: someone who is forced to leave his or her home and community but who remains in the same country.

interpretive anthropology or **interpretivism:** the view that cultures can be understood by studying what people think about, their ideas, and the meanings that are important to them.

interview: a research technique that involves gathering of verbal data through questions or guided conversation between at least two people.

isogamy: marriage between status equals.

jajmani system: an exchange system of India in which landholding patrons (jajmans) offer food grains to service providers such as brahman priests, artisans (blacksmiths, potters), and agricultural laborers.

khipu: cords of knotted string used during the Inca empire for keeping accounts and recording events.

kinesics: the study of communication that occurs through body movements, positions, facial expressions, and spatial behavior.

kinship: a sense of being related to another person or persons through descent, sharing, or marriage.

kinship diagram: a schematic way of presenting data on kinship relationships of an individual (called "ego") depicting all of ego's relatives, as remembered by ego and reported to the anthropologist.

kinship system: the predominant form of kin relationships in a culture and the kinds of behavior involved.

kula: a trading network linking many of the Trobriand Islands in which men have long-standing partnerships for the exchange of everyday goods such as food as well as highly valued necklaces and armlets.

language: a form of communication that is a systematic set of learned and shared symbols and signs shared among a group and passed on from generation to generation.

language endangerment: a stage in language decline when a language has fewer than 10,000 speakers.

language extinction: a situation, either gradual or sudden, in which language speakers abandon their native language in favor of a new language to the extent that the native language loses functions and no longer has competent users.

language family: languages descended from a parent language.

language shift or decay: condition of a language in which speakers adopt a new language for most situations, begin to use their native language only in certain contexts, and may be only semi-fluent and have limited vocabulary in their native language.

law: a binding rule created through enactment or custom that defines right and reasonable behavior and is enforceable by threat of punishment.

legal pluralism: a situation in which more than one way exists of defining acceptable and unacceptable behavior and ways to deal with the latter.

leveling mechanism: an unwritten, culturally embedded rule that prevents an individual from becoming wealthier or more powerful than anyone else.

lifeboat mentality: local resentment of an immigrant group because of perceived resource constraints.

life-cycle ritual: a ritual performed to mark a change in status from one life stage to another of an individual or group; also called *rite of passage*.

life history: a qualitative, in-depth portrait of a single life experience of a person as narrated to the anthropologist.

life project: local people's definition of the direction they want to take in life, informed by their knowledge, history, and context.

limited-purpose money: an item or items that can be exchanged only for specified things.

linguistic anthropology: the study of human communication, including its origins, history, and contemporary variation and change.

linguistic determinism: the theory that language determines consciousness of the world and behavior.

linguistic pluralism: the presence of linguistic diversity within a particular context.

linguistic relativism: the position that all languages are equally successful forms of communication.

localization: the transformation of global culture by local cultures into something new.

logograph: a symbol that conveys meaning through a form or picture resembling that to which it refers.

macroculture: a distinct pattern of learned and shared behavior and thinking that crosses local boundaries, such as transnational culture and global culture.

magic: the attempt to compel supernatural forces and beings to act in certain ways.

male bias in development: the design and implementation of development projects with men as beneficiaries and without regard to their impact on women's roles and status.

market exchange: the buying and selling of commodities under competitive conditions in which the forces of supply and demand determine value.

marriage: a union between two people (usually), who are likely to be, but are not necessarily, co-resident, sexually involved with each other, and procreative.

material cultural heritage: sites, monuments, buildings, and movable objects considered to have outstanding value to humanity. Also called cultural heritage.

matrescence: motherhood, or the cultural process of becoming a mother.

matriarchy: a society in which women are dominant in terms of economics, politics, and ideology.

matrifocality: a household system in which a female (or females) is the central, stable figure around whom other members cluster.

matrilineal descent: a kinship system that highlights the importance of women by tracing descent through the female line, favoring marital residence with or near the bride's family, and providing for property to be inherited through the female line.

matrilocality: a kinship rule that defines preferred marital residence with or near the bride's kin.

mechanical solidarity: social bonding among groups that are similar.

medicalization: labeling a particular issue or problem as medical and requiring medical treatment when, in fact, that issue or problem is economic or political.

medical pluralism: the existence of more than one health system in a culture, or a government policy to promote the integration of local healing systems into biomedical practice.

menarche: the onset of menstruation.

menopause: the cessation of menstruation.

microculture: a distinct pattern of learned and shared behavior and thinking found within larger cultures.

migration: the movement of a person or people from one place to another.

minimalism: a mode of consumption that emphasizes simplicity, is characterized by few and finite (limited) consumer demands, and involves an adequate and sustainable means to achieve them.

mode of consumption: the dominant pattern, in a culture, of using things up or spending resources in order to satisfy demands.

mode of exchange: the dominant pattern, in a culture, of transferring goods, services, and other items between and among people and groups.

mode of production: the dominant pattern of making a living in a culture.

mode of reproduction: the dominant pattern of fertility and mortality in a culture.

modernization: a model of change based on belief in the inevitable advance of science and Western secularism and processes including industrial growth, consolidation of the state, bureaucratization, market economy, technological innovation, literacy, and options for social mobility.

moka: a strategy for developing political leadership in highland Papua New Guinea that involves exchanging gifts and favors with individuals and sponsoring large feasts where further gift giving occurs.

money: a medium of exchange that can be used for a variety of goods.

monogamy: marriage between two people.

mortality: deaths in a population, or the rate of population decline in general or from particular causes.

multipurpose money: a medium of exchange that can be used for all goods and services available.

multisited research: fieldwork conducted in more than one location in order to understand the behaviors and ideas of dispersed members of a culture or the relationships among different levels such as state policy and local culture.

museum: an institution that collects, preserves, interprets, and displays objects on a regular basis.

myth: a narrative with a plot that involves the supernaturals.

nation: a group of people who share a language, culture, territorial base, political organization, and history.

national character study: a type of analysis in psychological anthropology that defined basic personality types and core values of entire countries.

neolocality: a kinship rule that defines preferred marital residence in a new location not linked to either the bride's or the groom's parents' residence.

new immigrant: international migrant who has moved since the 1960s.

norm: a generally agreed-upon standard for how people should behave, usually unwritten and learned unconsciously.

nuclear household: a domestic unit containing one adult couple (married or partners), with or without children.

observer's paradox: the logical impossibility of doing research on natural communication events without affecting the naturalness sought.

organic solidarity: social bonding among groups with different abilities and resources.

paralanguage: nonverbal communication such as body posture, voice tone, touch, smells, and eye and facial movements.

parallel cousin: offspring of either one's father's brother or one's mother's sister.

participant observation: basic fieldwork method in cultural anthropology that involves living in a culture for a long period of time while gathering data.

participatory research (PR): a method in development anthropology that involves the local people in gathering data relevant to local development projects.

pastoralism: a mode of production based on keeping domesticated animal herds and using their products, such as meat and milk, for most of the diet.

patrescence: fatherhood, or the cultural process of becoming a father.

patrilineal descent: a kinship system that highlights the importance of men in tracing descent, determining marital residence with or near the groom's family, and providing for inheritance of property through the male line.

patrilocality: a kinship rule that defines preferred marital residence with or near the groom's kin.

personality: an individual's patterned and characteristic way of behaving, thinking, and feeling.

person-centered ethnography: anthropological research that focuses on the individual and how the individual's psychology and subjective experience both shape and are shaped by the wider culture.

phoneme: a sound that makes a difference for meaning in a language.

phonetics: the analysis of phonemes.

phytotherapy: healing through the use of plants.

pidgin: a contact language that blends elements of at least two languages and that emerges when people with different languages need to communicate.

placebo effect or **meaning effect:** in Western science, a positive result from a healing method due to a symbolic or otherwise nonmaterial factor.

policing: the exercise of social control through processes of surveillance and the threat of punishment related to maintaining social order.

political organization: the existence of groups for purposes of public decision making and leadership, maintaining social cohesion and order, protecting group rights, and ensuring safety from external threats.

polyandry: marriage of one wife with more than one husband.

polygamy: marriage involving multiple spouses.

polygyny: marriage of one husband with more than one wife.

postmodernism: a view that questions various aspects of modernism, including the scientific method, human progress through scientific knowledge, urbanization, technological change, and mass communication.

potlatch: a grand feast in which guests are invited to eat and to receive gifts from the hosts.

power: the capacity to take action in the face of resistance, through force if necessary.

priest/priestess: male or female full-time religious specialist whose position is based mainly on abilities gained through formal training.

primary group: a social group in which members meet on a face-to-face basis.

productivity: a feature of human language that offers the ability to communicate many messages efficiently.

project cycle: the steps of a development project from initial planning to completion: project identification, project design, project appraisal, project implementation, and project evaluation.

pronatalism: an ideology promoting many children.

puberty: a time in the human life cycle that occurs universally and involves a set of biological markers and sexual maturation.

public/private dichotomy: gender division in society that emerged with agriculture, whereby men are more involved with the nondomestic domain and women are more involved in activities in or near the home.

pure gift: something given with no expectation or thought of a return.

push–pull theory: an explanation of rural-to-urban migration that emphasizes people's incentives to move based on a lack of opportunity in rural areas (the "push") compared to urban areas (the "pull").

qualitative data: research that emphasizes generating descriptive information.

quantitative data: research that emphasizes gathering and analyzing numeric information and using tables and charts when presenting results.

questionnaire: a formal research instrument containing a pre-set series of questions that the anthropologist asks in a face-to-face setting, by mail, or by email.

race: a classification of people into groups on the basis of supposedly homogeneous biological traits.

rapid research method (RRM): fieldwork method designed for use in development anthropology that can yield relevant data in a short period of time.

rapport: a trusting relationship between the researcher and the study population.

recurrent costs fund: a category of a person's or household's budget used to provide for repair and maintenance of tools, shelter, and other features of one's lifestyle.

redistribution: a form of exchange that involves one person collecting goods or money from many members of a group who then, at a later time and at a public event, "returns" the pooled goods to everyone who contributed.

reflexive anthropology: anthropological research carried out and described with attention to the researcher's presence, role, and influence on the research, research informants, and research results. Also called reflexivity.

refugee: someone who is forced to leave his or her home, community, or country.

religion: beliefs and actions related to supernatural beings and forces.

religious pluralism: when one or more religions co-exist as either complementary to each other or as competitive systems.

remittance: transfer of money or goods by a migrant to his or her family back home.

repatriation: returning art or other objects from museums to the people with whom they originated.

replacement-level fertility: a situation when births equal deaths, leading to maintenance of current population size.

revitalization movement: a religious movement, usually organized by a prophetic leader, that seeks to construct a more satisfying situation by reviving all or parts of a religion that has been threatened by outside forces or by adopting new practices and beliefs.

revolution: a political crisis prompted by illegal and often violent actions of subordinate groups that seek to change the political institutions or social structure of a society.

right of return: United Nations guaranteed right of refugees to repatriation.

ritual: a patterned form of behavior that has to do with the supernatural realm.

ritual of inversion: a ritual in which normal social roles and order are temporarily reversed.

sacrifice: a ritual in which something is offered to the supernaturals.

Sapir-Whorf hypothesis: a theory in linguistic anthropology that says that language determines thought.

secondary group: people who identify with each other on some basis but may never meet with one another personally.

segmentary model: type of political organization in which smaller units unite in the face of external threats and then disunite when the external threat is absent.

sex ratio: the number of males per 100 females in a population.

sex-selective infanticide: the killing an infant or child because of its sex.

shaman/shamanka: male or female part-time religious specialist who gains his or her status through direct relationship with the supernaturals, often by being "called."

sign language: a form of communication that uses mainly hand movements to convey messages.

social capital: the intangible resources existing in social ties, trust, and cooperation.

social control: processes that maintain orderly social life, including informal and formal mechanisms.

social group: a cluster of people beyond the domestic unit who are usually related on grounds other than kinship.

social impact assessment: a study conducted to gauge the potential social costs and benefits of particular innovations before change is undertaken.

social stratification: hierarchical relationships between different groups as though they were arranged in layers or "strata."

sociocultural fit: a characteristic of informed and effective project design in which planners take local culture into account; opposite of one-size-fits-all project design.

sociolinguistics: a theory in linguistic anthropology that says that culture and society and a person's social position determine language.

somatization: the process through which the body absorbs social stress and manifests symptoms of suffering.

state: a centralized political unit encompassing many communities and possessing coercive power.

status: a person's position, or standing, in society.

stem household: a co-residential group that comprises only two married couples related through males, commonly found in East Asian cultures.

structural adjustment: an economic policy that has been pursued by the World Bank since the 1980s requiring that countries receiving World Bank loans pursue privatization of services such as health care and schools and reduce government expenditures in these areas.

structural suffering: human health problems caused by such economic and political situations as war, famine, terrorism, forced migration, and poverty. Also called structural affliction.

structure: within the cultural materialist framework, the second level of culture, which comprises social organization, kinship, and political organization.

structurism: a theoretical position concerning human behavior and ideas that says "free choice" is an illusion since the choices themselves are determined by larger forces such as the economy, social and political organization, and ideological systems.

superstructure: within the cultural materialist framework, the third level of culture, which comprises ideology (communication, religion, and expressive culture).

sustainable development: a directed change that involves forms of development that are not environmentally destructive and are financially supportable by the host country and environmentally supportable by the earth as a whole.

symbol: an object, word, or action with culturally defined meaning that stands for something else; most symbols are arbitrary.

synchronic: a "one-time" view of a culture that devotes little or no attention to its past.

syncretism: the blending of features of two or more cultures, especially used in discussion of religious change.

syntax or grammar: the rules by which words are organized to make sense in a string.

tag question: a question seeking affirmation, placed at the end of a sentence.

tax fund: a category of a person's or household's budget used as payment to a government as part of one's civic responsibilities or to a landlord for use of land or housing.

teknonymy: the practice of naming someone on the basis of his or her relationship to someone else, as in "The Mother of So and So."

theater: a form of enactment, related to other forms such as dance, music, parades, competitive games and sports, and verbal art, that seeks to entertain through acting, movement, and sound.

trade: the formalized exchange of one thing for another according to set standards of value.

traditional development anthropology: an approach to international development in which the anthropologist accepts the role of helping to make development work better by providing cultural information to planners.

transnational migration: a form of population movement in which a person regularly moves between two or more countries and forms a new cultural identity transcending a single geopolitical unit.

trial by ordeal: a way of determining innocence or guilt in which the accused person is put to a test that may be painful, stressful, or fatal.

triangulation: research technique that involves obtaining information on a particular topic from more than one person or perspective.

tribe: a political group that comprises several bands or lineage groups, each with similar language and lifestyle and occupying a distinct territory.

unbalanced exchange: a system of transfers in which one party seeks to make a profit.

unilineal descent: a kinship system that traces descent through only one parent, either the mother or the father.

use rights: a system of property relations in which a person or group has socially recognized priority in access to particular resources such as gathering, hunting, and fishing areas and water holes.

wa: Japanese word meaning discipline and self-sacrifice for the good of the whole.

war: organized and purposeful group action directed against another group and involving lethal force.

Western biomedicine: a healing approach based on modern Western science that emphasizes technology for diagnosing and treating health problems related to the human body.

world religion: a term coined in the nineteenth century to refer to religions that had many followers, that crossed state borders, and that exhibited other features such as a concern with salvation.

worldview: a way of understanding how the world came to be, its design, and people's place in it with or without reference to a supernatural realm.

youth gang: a group of young people, found mainly in urban areas, who are often considered a social problem by adults and law enforcement officials.

zoomorphic: a supernatural in the shape, or partial shape, of an animal.

References

Abélès, Marc. 1991. *Quiet Days in Burgundy: A Study of Local Politics.* Trans. Annella McDermott. New York: Cambridge University Press.

Abbink, Jon. 2003. Love and Death of Cattle: The Paradox in Suri Attitudes toward Livestock. *Ethnos* 68:341–364.

Abu-Lughod, Lila. 1993. *Writing Women's Worlds: Bedouin Stories.* Berkeley: University of California Press.

Adams, Abigail E. 2002. Dyke to Dyke: Ritual Reproduction at a U.S. Men's Military College. In *The Best of Anthropology Today* (pp. 34–42). Jonathan Benthall, ed. New York: Routledge.

Adams, Vincanne. 1988. Modes of Production and Medicine: An Examination of the Theory in Light of Sherpa Traditional Medicine. *Social Science and Medicine* 27:505–513.

———. 1996. *Tigers of the Snow and Other Virtual Sherpas: An Ethnography of Himalayan Encounters.* Princeton, NJ: Princeton University Press.

Afolayan, E. 2000. Bantu Expansion and Its Consequences. In *African History before 1885* (pp. 113–136). T. Falola, ed. Durham, NC: Carolina Academic Press.

Agar, Michael and Heather Schacht Reisinger. 2003. Going for the Global: The Case of Ecstasy. *Human Organization* 62(1):1–11.

Ahern, Laura. 2001. *Invitations to Love: Literacy, Love Letters, and Social Change in Nepal.* Ann Arbor: University of Michigan Press.

Ahmadu, Fuambai. 2000. Rites and Wrongs: An Insider/Outside Reflects on Power and Excision. In *Female "Circumcision" in Africa: Culture, Controversy, and Change* (pp. 283–312). Bettina Shell-Duncan and Ylva Hernlund, eds. Boulder, CO: Lynne Reiner Publishers.

Akinsha, Konstantin. 1992a. Whose Gold? *ARTNews* 91(3):39–40.

———. 1992b. Russia: Whose Art Is It? *ARTNews* 91(5):100–105.

———. 1992c. After the Coup: Art for Art's Sake? *ARTNews* 91(1):108–113.

Albro, Robert and Joanne Bauer. 2005. Introduction. Human Rights Dialogue: An International Forum for Debating Human Rights. Special issue on Cultural Rights: What They Are, Why They Matter, How They Can Be Realized. *Carnegie Journal* 2(12):2–3.

Allen, Catherine J. 2002. *The Hold Life Has: Coca and Cultural Identity in an Andean Community.* Washington, DC: Smithsonian Institution Press.

Allen, Susan. 1994. What Is Media Anthropology? A Personal View and a Suggested Structure. In *Media Anthropology: Informing Global Citizens* (pp. 15–32). Susan L. Allen, ed. Westport, CT: Bergin & Garvey.

Allison, Anne. 1994. *Nightwork: Sexuality, Pleasure, and Corporate Masculinity in a Tokyo Hostess Club.* Chicago: University of Chicago Press.

Alonso, Ana María. 2004. Conforming Disconformity: "Mestizaje," Hybridity, and the Aesthetics of Mexican Nationalism. *Cultural Anthropology* 19:459–490.

Alter, Joseph S. 1992. The Sannyasi and the Indian Wrestler: Anatomy of a Relationship. *American Ethnologist* 19(2):317–336.

Ames, Michael, 1992. *Cannibal Tours and Glass Boxes: The Anthropology of Museums.* Vancouver: University of British Columbia Press.

Amster, Matthew H. 2000. It Takes a Village to Dismantle a Longhouse. *Thresholds* 20:65–71.

Ancrenaz, Marc, Olivier Gimenez, Laurentius Ambu, Karine Ancrenaz, Patrick Andau, Benoît Goossens, John Payne, Azri Sawang, Augustine Tuuga, and Isabelle Lackman-Ancrenaz. 2005. Aerial Surveys Give New Estimates for Orangutans in Sabah, Malaysia. *PloS Biology* 3(1):e3. www.plosbiology.org.

Anderson, Benedict. 1991 [1983]. *Imagined Communities: Reflections on the Origin and Spread of Nationalism.* New York: Verso.

Anderson, Myrdene. 2004. Reflections on the Saami at Loose Ends. In *Cultural Shaping of Violence: Victimization, Escalation, Response* (pp. 285–291). Myrdene Anderson, ed. West Lafayette, IN: Purdue University Press.

———. 2005. The Saami Yoik: Translating Hum, Chant and/or Song. In *Song and Significance: Virtues and Vices of Vocal Translation* (pp. 213–233). Dinda Gorlée, ed. Amsterdam: Rodopi.

Anderson, Richard L. and Karen L. Field. 1993. Chapter Introduction. In *Art in Small-Scale Societies: Contemporary Readings* (p. 247). Richard L. Anderson and Karen L. Fields, eds. Englewood Cliffs, NJ: Prentice-Hall.

Andriolo, Karin. 2002. Murder by Suicide: Episodes from Muslim History. *American Anthropologist* 104:736–742.

Anglin, Mary K. 2002. *Women, Power, and Dissent in the Hills of Carolina.* Chicago: University of Illinois Press.

Appadurai, Arjun. 1986. Introduction: Commodities and the Politics of Value. In *The Social Life of Things: Commodities in Cultural Perspective* (pp. 3–63). Arjun Appadurai, ed. New York: Cambridge University Press.

Applbaum, Kalman D. 1995. Marriage with the Proper Stranger: Arranged Marriage in Metropolitan Japan. *Ethnology* 34(1):37–51.

Arambiza, Evelio and Michael Painter. 2006. Biodiversity Conservation and the Quality of Life of Indigenous People in the Bolivian Chaco. *Human Organization* 65:20–34.

Ariès, Philippe. 1962. *Centuries of Childhood: A Social History of Family Life.* Trans. Robert Baldick. New York: Vintage Books.

Attwood, Donald W. 1992. *Raising Cane: The Political Economy of Sugar in Western India.* Boulder, CO: Westview Press.

Awe, Bolanle. 1977. The Iyalode in the Traditional Yoruba Political System. In *Sexual Stratification: A Cross-Cultural View* (pp. 144–160). Alice Schlegel, ed. New York: Columbia University Press.

Baker, Colin. 1999. Sign Language and the Deaf Community. In *Handbook of Language and Ethnic Identity* (pp. 122–139). Joshua A. Fishman, ed. New York: Oxford University Press.

Baker-Christales, Beth. 2004. *Salvadoran Migration to Southern California: Redefining El Hermano Lejano.* Gainesville: University of Florida Press.

Baptista, Marlyse. 2005. New Directions in Pidgin and Creole Studies. *Annual Review of Anthropology* 34:34–42.

Barfield, Thomas J. 1993. *The Nomadic Alternative.* Englewood Cliffs, NJ: Prentice-Hall.

———. 1994. Prospects for Plural Societies in Central Asia. *Cultural Survival Quarterly* 18 (2&3):48–51.

———. 2001. Pastoral Nomads or Nomadic Pastoralists. In *The Dictionary of Anthropology* (pp. 348–350). Thomas Barfield, ed. Malden, MA: Blackwell Publishers.

Barkey, Nanette, Benjamin C. Campbell, and Paul W. Leslie. 2001. A Comparison of Health Complaints of Settled and Nomadic Turkana Men. *Medical Anthropology Quarterly* 15:391–408.

Barlett, Peggy F. 1980. Reciprocity and the San Juan Fiesta. *Journal of Anthropological Research* 36:116–130.

———. 1989. Industrial Agriculture. In *Economic Anthropology* (pp. 253–292). Stuart Plattner, ed. Stanford, CA: Stanford University Press.

Barnard, Alan. 2000. *History and Theory in Anthropology.* New York: Cambridge University Press.

———. 2004. Coat of Arms and Body Politic: Khoisan Imagery and South African National Identity. *Ethnos* 69:5–22.

Barnard, Alan and Anthony Good. 1984. *Research Practices in the Study of Kinship.* New York: Academic Press.

Barth, Frederik. 1993. *Balinese Worlds.* Chicago: University of Chicago Press.

Basch, Linda, Nina Glick Schiller, and Christina Szanton Blanc. 1994. *Nations Unbound: Transnational Projects, Postcolonial Predicaments, and Deterritorialized Nation-States.* Langhorne, PA: Gordon and Breach Science Publishers.

Basso, Keith. H. 1972 [1970]. "To Give Up on Words": Silence in Apache Culture. In *Language and Social Context* (pp. 67–86). Pier Paolo Giglioni, ed. Baltimore: Penguin Books.

Bauer, Alexander A. 2006. Heritage Preservation in Law and Policy: Handling the Double-Edged Sword of Development. Paper presented at the International Conference on Cultural Heritage and Development, Bibliothèca Alexandrina, Alexandria, Egypt, January.

Beals, Alan R. 1980. *Gopalpur: A South Indian Village. Fieldwork Edition.* New York: Holt, Rinehart and Winston.

Beattie, Andrew. 2002. Changing Places: Relatives and Relativism in Java. *Journal of the Royal Anthropological Institute* 8:469–491.

Beatty, Andrew. 1992. *Society and Exchange in Nias.* New York: Oxford University Press.

Beck, Lois. 1986. *The Qashqa'i of Iran.* New Haven, CT: Yale University Press.

———. 1991. *Nomad: A Year in the Life of a Qashqa'i Tribesman in Iran.* Berkeley: University of California Press.

Beeman, William O. 1993. The Anthropology of Theater and Spectacle. *Annual Review of Anthropology* 22:363–393.

Belikov, Vladimir. 1994. Language Death in Siberia. *UNESCO Courier* 1994(2):32–36.

Bell, Diane. 1998. *Ngarrindjeri Wurruwarrin: A World That Is, Was, and Will Be.* North Melbourne, Australia: Spinifex.

Benedict, Ruth. 1959 [1934]. *Patterns of Culture.* Boston: Houghton Mifflin.

———. 1969 [1946]. *The Chrysanthemum and the Sword: Patterns of Japanese Culture.* Rutland, VT: Charles E. Tuttle.

Bernal, Martin. 1987. *Black Athena: The Afroasiatic Roots of Classical Civilization.* New Brunswick, NJ: Rutgers University Press.

Bernard, H. Russell. 1995. *Research Methods in Anthropology: Qualitative and Quantitative Approaches.* Walnut Creek, CA: Altamira Press/Sage.

Berreman, Gerald D. 1979 [1975]. Race, Caste, and Other Invidious Distinctions in Social Stratification. In *Caste and Other Inequities: Essays on Inequality* (pp. 178–222). Gerald D. Berreman, ed. New Delhi: Manohar.

Best, David. 1986. Culture Consciousness: Understanding the Arts of Other Cultures. *Journal of Art & Design Education* 5(1&2):124–135.

Bestor, Theodore C. 2004. *Tsukiji: The Fish Market at the Center of the World.* Berkeley: University of California Press.

Beyene, Yewoubdar. 1989. *From Menarche to Menopause: Reproductive Lives of Peasant Women in Two Cultures.* Albany: State University of New York Press.

Bhardwaj, Surinder M. and N. Madhusudana Rao. 1990. Asian Indians in the United States: A Geographic Appraisal. In *South Asians Overseas: Migration and Ethnicity* (pp. 197–218). Colin Clarke, Ceri Peach, and Steven Vertovec, eds. New York: Cambridge University Press.

Bhatt, Rakesh M. 2001. World Englishes. *Annual Review of Anthropology* 30:527–550.

Bilharz, Joy. 1995. First among Equals? The Changing Status of Seneca Women. In *Women and Power in Native North America* (pp. 101–112). Laura F. Klein and Lillian A. Ackerman, eds. Norman: University of Oklahoma Press.

Billig, Michael S. 1992. The Marriage Squeeze and the Rise of Groomprice in India's Kerala State. *Journal of Comparative Family Studies* 23:197–216.

Binford, Leigh. 2003. Migrant Remittances and (Under)Development in Mexico. *Critique of Anthropology* 23:305–336.

Bird, Sharon R. 1996. Welcome to the Men's Club: Homosociality and the Maintenance of Hegemonic Masculinity. *Gender & Society* 10(2):120–132.

Blackwood, Evelyn. 1995. Senior Women, Model Mothers, and Dutiful Wives: Managing Gender Contradictions in a Minangkabau Village. In *Bewitching Women: Pious Men: Gender and Body Politics in Southeast Asia* (pp. 124–158). Aihwa Ong and Michael Peletz, eds. Berkeley: University of California Press.

Blaikie, Piers. 1985. *The Political Economy of Soil Erosion in Developing Countries.* New York: Longman.

Blau, Peter M. 1964. *Exchange and Power in Social Life.* New York: Wiley.

Bledsoe, Caroline H. 1983. Stealing Food as a Problem in Demography and Nutrition. Paper presented at the annual meeting of the American Anthropological Association.

Bledsoe, Caroline H. and Helen K. Hirschman. 1989. *Case Studies of Mortality: Anthropological Contributions. Proceedings.* International Union for the Scientific Study of Population, XXIst International Population Conference (pp. 331–348). Liège: International Union for the Scientific Study of Population.

Blim, Michael. 2000. Capitalisms in Late Modernity. *Annual Review of Anthropology* 29:25–38.

Blok, Anton. 1972. The Peasant and the Brigand: Social Banditry Reconsidered. *Comparative Studies in Society and History* 14(4):494–503.

Blommaert, Jan and Chris Bulcaen. 2000. Critical Discourse Analysis. *Annual Review of Anthropology* 29:447–466.

Blood, Robert O. 1967. *Love Match and Arranged Marriage.* New York: Free Press.

Bodenhorn, Barbara. 2000. "He Used to Be My Relative." Exploring the Bases of Relatedness among the Inupiat of Northern Alaska. In *Cultures of Relatedness: New Approaches to the Study of Kinship* (pp. 128–148). Janet Carsten, ed. New York: Cambridge University Press.

Bodley, John H. 1990. *Victims of Progress*, 3rd ed. Mountain View, CA: Mayfield Publishing.

Boellstorff, Tom. 2004. Gay Language and Indonesia: Registering Belonging. *Journal of Linguistic Anthropology* 14:248–268.

Bogin, Barry. 1988. *Patterns of Human Growth.* New York: Cambridge University Press.

Borovoy, Amy. 2005. *The Too-Good Wife: Alcohol, Codependency, and the Politics of Nurturance in Postwar Japan.* Berkeley: University of California Press.

Boserup, Ester. 1970. *Woman's Role in Economic Development.* New York: St. Martin's Press.

Bourdieu, Pierre. 1984. *Distinction: A Social Critique of the Judgement of Taste.* Trans. Richard Nice. Cambridge, MA: Harvard University Press.

Bourgois, Philippe I. 1995. *In Search of Respect: Selling Crack in El Barrio.* New York: Cambridge University Press.

Bowen, John R. 1992. On Scriptural Essentialism and Ritual Variation: Muslim Sacrifice in Sumatra. *American Ethnologist* 19(4):656–671.

———. 1998. *Religions in Practice: An Approach to the Anthropology of Religion.* Boston: Allyn and Bacon.

Bradley, Richard. 2000. *An Archaeology of Natural Places.* New York: Routledge.

Brana-Shute, Rosemary. 1976. Women, Clubs, and Politics: The Case of a Lower-Class Neighborhood in Paramaribo, Suriname. *Urban Anthropology* 5(2):157–185.

Brandes, Stanley H. 1985. *Forty: The Age and the Symbol.* Knoxville: University of Tennessee Press.

———. 2002. *Staying Sober in Mexico City.* Austin: University of Texas Press.

Brave Heart, Mary Yellow Horse. 2004. The Historical Trauma Response among Natives and Its Relationship to Substance Abuse. In *Healing and Mental Health for Native Americans: Speaking in Red* (pp. 7–18). Ethan Nebelkopf and Mary Phillips, eds. Walnut Creek, CA: AltaMira Press.

Bray, Tamara L. 1996. Repatriation, Power Relations and the Politics of the Past. *Antiquity* 70:440–444.

Brewis, Alexandra and Mary Meyer. 2004. Marital Coitus across the Life Course. *Journal of Biosocial Science* 37(4):499–518.

Brink, Judy H. 1991. The Effect of Emigration of Husbands on the Status of Their Wives: An Egyptian Case. *International Journal of Middle East Studies* 23:201–211.

Brodkin, Karen. 2000. Global Capitalism: What's Race Got to Do with It? *American Ethnologist* 27:237–256.

Brookes, Heather. 2004. A Repertoire of South African Quotable Gestures. *Journal of Linguistic Anthropology* 14:186–224.

Brooks, Alison S. and Patricia Draper. 1998 [1991]. Anthropological Perspectives on Aging. In *Anthropology Explored: The Best of AnthroNotes* (pp. 286–297). Ruth Osterweis Selig and Marilyn R. London, eds. Washington, DC: Smithsonian Press.

Broude, Gwen J. 1988. Rethinking the Couvade: Cross-Cultural Evidence. *American Anthropologist* 90(4):902–911.

Brown, Carolyn Henning. 1984. Tourism and Ethnic Competition in a Ritual Form: The Firewalkers of Fiji. *Oceania* 54:223–244.

Brown, Judith K. 1970. A Note on the Division of Labor by Sex. *American Anthropologist* 72(5):1073–1078.

———. 1975. Iroquois Women: An Ethnohistoric Note. In *Toward an Anthropology of Women* (pp. 235–251). Rayna R. Reiter, ed. New York: Monthly Review Press.

———. 1978. The Recruitment of a Female Labor Force. *Anthropos* 73(1/2):41–48.

———. 1999. Introduction: Definitions, Assumptions, Themes, and Issues. In *To Have and To Hit: Cultural Perspectives on Wife Beating,* 2nd ed. (pp. 3–26). Dorothy Ayers Counts, Judith K. Brown, and Jacquelyn C. Campbell, eds. Urbana: University of Illinois Press.

Brown, Nathan. 1990. Brigands and State Building: The Invention of Banditry in Modern Egypt. *Comparative Studies in Society and History* 32(2):258–281.

Browner, Carole H. 1986. The Politics of Reproduction in a Mexican Village. *Signs: Journal of Women in Culture and Society* 11(4):710–724.

Browner, Carole H. and Nancy Ann Press. 1995. The Normalization of Prenatal Diagnostic Screening. In *Conceiving the New World Order: The Global Politics of Reproduction* (pp. 307–322). Faye D. Ginsberg and Rayna Rapp, eds. Berkeley: University of California Press.

———. 1996. The Production of Authoritative Knowledge in American Prenatal Care. *Medical Anthropology Quarterly* 10(2):141–156.

Brownmiller, Susan. 1994. *Seeing Vietnam: Encounters of the Road and Heart.* New York: HarperCollins.

Brumfiel, Elizabeth M. 1994. Introduction. In *Factional Competition and Political Development in the New World* (pp. 3–14). Elizabeth M. Brumfiel and John W. Fox, eds. New York: Cambridge University Press.

Bruner, Edward M. 2005. *Culture on Tour: Ethnographies of Travel.* Chicago: University of Chicago Press.

Bunzel, Ruth. 1972 [1929]. *The Pueblo Potter: A Study of Creative Imagination in Primitive Art.* New York: Dover Publications.

Burdick, John. 2004. *Legacies of Liberation: The Progressive Catholic Church in Brazil at the Turn of a New Century.* Burlington, VT: Ashgate Publishers.

Burton, Barbara. 2004. The Transmigration of Rights: Women, Movement and the Grassroots in Latin American and Caribbean Communities. *Development and Change* 35:773–798.

Buvinic, Mayra and Andrew R. Morrison. 2000. Living in a More Violent World. *Foreign Policy* 118:58–72.

Calhoun, Craig, Donald Light, and Suzanne Keller. 1994. *Sociology,* 6th ed. New York: McGraw-Hill.

Call, Vaughn, Susan Sprecher, and Pepper Schwartz. 1995. The Incidence and Frequency of Marital Sex in a National Sample. *Journal of Marriage and the Family* 57:639–652.

Cameron, Mary M. 1995. Transformations of Gender and Caste Divisions of Labor in Rural Nepal: Land, Hierarchy, and the Case of Women. *Journal of Anthropological Research* 51:215–246.

Camino, Linda A. and Ruth M. Krulfeld, eds. 1994. *Reconstructing Lives, Recapturing Meaning: Refugee Identity, Gender and Culture Change.* Basel: Gordon and Breach Publishers.

Cancian, Frank. 1989. Economic Behavior in Peasant Communities. In *Economic Anthropology* (pp. 127–170). Stuart Plattner, ed. Stanford, CA: Stanford University Press.

Caplan, Pat. 1987. Celibacy as a Solution? Mahatma Gandhi and Brahmacharya. In *The Cultural Construction of Sexuality* (pp. 271–295). Pat Caplan, ed. New York: Tavistock Publications.

———. 2000. "Eating British Beef with Confidence": A Consideration of Consumers' Responses to BSE in Britain. In *Risk Revisited* (pp. 184–203). Pat Caplan, ed. Sterling, VA: Pluto Press.

Carneiro, Robert L. 1994. War and Peace: Alternating Realities in Human History. In *Studying War: Anthropological Perspectives* (pp. 3–27). S. P. Reyna and R. E. Downs, eds. Langhorne, PA: Gordon and Breach Science Publishers.

Carstairs, G. Morris. 1967. *The Twice Born.* Bloomington: Indiana University Press.

Carsten, Janet. 1995. Children in Between: Fostering and the Process of Kinship on Pulau Langkawi, Malaysia. *Man* (n.s.) 26:425–443.

Carsten, Janet, ed. 2000. *Cultures of Relatedness: New Approaches to the Study of Kinship.* New York: Cambridge University Press.

Carter, William E., José V. Morales, and Mauricio P. Mamani. 1981. Medicinal Uses of Coca in Bolivia. In *Health in the Andes* (pp. 119–149). Joseph W. Bastien and John M. Donahue, eds. Washington, DC: American Anthropological Association.

Cassell, Joan. 1991. *Expected Miracles: Surgeons at Work.* Philadelphia: Temple University Press.

Castles, Stephen and Mark J. Miller. 1993. *The Age of Migration: International Population Movements in the Modern World.* New York: Guilford Press.

Cátedra, María. 1992. *This World, Other Worlds: Sickness, Suicide, Death, and the Afterlife among the Vaqueiros de Alzada of Spain.* Chicago: University of Chicago Press.

Caudill, W. and David W. Plath. 1966. Who Sleeps by Whom? Parent-Child Involvement in Urban Japanese Families. *Psychiatry* 29:344–366.

Cernea, Michael M. 1985. Sociological Knowledge for Development Projects. In *Putting People First: Sociological Variables and Rural Development* (pp. 3–22). Michael M. Cernea, ed. New York: Oxford University Press.

———. 2001. *Cultural Heritage and Development: A Framework for Action in the Middle East and North Africa.* Washington, DC: The World Bank.

Chagnon, Napoleon. 1992. *Yanomamö,* 4th ed. New York: Harcourt Brace Jovanovich.

Chalfin, Brenda. 2004. *Shea Butter Republic: State Power, Global Markets, and the Making of an Indigenous Commodity.* New York: Routledge.

Chambers, David L. 2000. Civilizing the Natives: Marriage in Post-Apartheid South Africa. *Daedalus* 129:101–124.

Chambers, Robert. 1983. *Rural Development: Putting the Last First.* Essex, United Kingdom: Longman.

Chanen, Jill Schachner. 1995. Reaching Out to Women of Color. *ABA Journal* 81(May):105.

Charters, Claire. 2006. An Imbalance of Powers: Maori Land Claims and an Unchecked Parliament. *Cultural Survival Quarterly* 30(1): 32–35.

Chavez, Leo R. 1992. *Shadowed Lives: Undocumented Immigrants in American Society.* New York: Harcourt Brace Jovanovich.

Cherlin. Andrew J. 1996. *Public and Private Families: An Introduction.* New York: McGraw-Hill.

Cherlin, Andrew J. and Frank F. Furstenberg Jr. 1992 [1983]. The American Family in the Year 2000. In *One World Many Cultures* (pp. 2–9). Stuart Hirschberg, ed. New York: Macmillan Publishing.

Chernoff, John Miller. 1979. *African Rhythm and African Sensibility: Aesthetics and African Musical Idioms.* Chicago: University of Chicago Press.

Childs, Larry and Celina Chelala. 1994. Drought, Rebellion and Social Change in Northern Mali: The Challenges Facing Tamacheq Herders. *Cultural Survival Quarterly* 18(4):16–19.

Chin, Elizabeth. 2001. *Purchasing Power: Black Kids and American Consumer Culture.* Minneapolis: University of Minnesota Press.

Chiñas, Beverly Newbold. 1992. *The Isthmus Zapotecs: A Matrifocal Culture of Mexico.* New York: Harcourt Brace Jovanovich.

Chowdhury, A. N. 1996. The Definition and Classification of Koro. *Culture, Medicine and Psychiatry* 20(1):41–65.

Churchill, Nancy. 2006. Dignifying Carnival: The Politics of Heritage Recognition in Puebla, Mexico. *International Journal of Cultural Property* 13:1–24.

Clark, Gracia. 1992. Flexibility Equals Survival. *Cultural Survival Quarterly* 16:21–24.

Clarke, Maxine Kumari. 2004. *Mapping Yorùbá Networks: Power and Agency in the Making of Transnational Communities.* Durham, NC: Duke University Press.

Clay, Jason W. 1990. What's a Nation: Latest Thinking. *Mother Jones* 15(7):28–30.

Cleveland, David A. 2000. Globalization and Anthropology: Expanding the Options. *Human Organization* 59:370–374.

Clifford, James, 1988. *The Predicament of Culture: Twentieth Century Ethnography, Literature and Art.* Cambridge, MA: Harvard University Press.

Cochrane, D. Glynn. 1979. *The Cultural Appraisal of Development Projects.* New York: Praeger Publishers.

Cohen, Mark Nathan. 1989. *Health and the Rise of Civilization.* New Haven, CT: Yale University Press.

Cohen, Roberta. 2002. Nowhere to Run, No Place to Hide. *Bulletin of the Atomic Scientists*, November/December:36–45.

Cohn, Bernard S. 1971. *India: The Social Anthropology of a Civilization.* New York: Prentice-Hall.

Cole, Douglas. 1991. *Chiefly Feasts: The Enduring Kwakiutl Potlatch.* Aldona Jonaitis, ed. Seattle: University of Washington Press/New York: American Museum of Natural History.

Cole, Douglas and I. Chaiken. 1990. *An Iron Hand upon the People: The Law against the Potlatch on the Northwest Coast.* Seattle: University of Washington Press.

Cole, Jeffrey. 1996. Working-Class Reactions to the New Immigration in Palermo (Italy). *Critique of Anthropology* 16(2):199–220.

Colley, Sarah. 2002. *Uncovering Australia: Archaeology, Indigenous People and the Public.* Washington, DC: Smithsonian Institution Press.

Colson, Elizabeth. 1995. The Contentiousness of Disputes. In *Understanding Disputes: The Politics of Argument* (pp. 65–82). Pat Caplan, ed. Providence, RI: Berg Publishers.

Comaroff, John L. 1987. Of Totemism and Ethnicity: Consciousness, Practice and Signs of Inequality. *Ethnos* 52(3–4):301–323.

Contreras, Gloria. 1995. Teaching about Vietnamese Culture: Water Puppetry as the Soul of the Rice Fields. *The Social Studies* 86(1): 25–28.

Coon Come, Matthew. 2004. Survival in the Context of Mega-Resource Development: Experiences of the James Bay Crees and the First Nations of Canada. In *In the Way of Development: Indigenous Peoples, Life Projects and Globalization* (pp. 153–165). Mario Blaser, Harvey A. Feit, and Glenn McRae, eds. New York: Zed Books in Association with the International Development Research Centre.

Corbey, Raymond. 2000. *Arts premiers* in the Louvre. *Anthropology Today* 16:3–6.

———. 2003. Destroying the Graven Image: Religious Iconoclasm on the Christian Frontier. *Anthropology Today* 19:10–14.

Cornell, Laurel L. 1989. Gender Differences in Remarriage after Divorce in Japan and the United States. *Journal of Marriage and the Family* 51:45–463.

Cornia, Giovanni Andrea. 1994. Poverty, Food Consumption, and Nutrition During the Transition to the Market Economy in Eastern Europe. *American Economic Review* 84(2):297–302.

Counihan, Carole M. 1985. Transvestism and Gender in a Sardinian Carnival. *Anthropology* 9(1&2):11–24.

Coward, E. Walter, Jr. 1976. Indigenous Organisation, Bureaucracy and Development: The Case of Irrigation. *The Journal of Development Studies* 13(1):92–105.

———. 1979. Principles of Social Organization in an Indigenous Irrigation System. *Human Organization* 38(1):28–36.

Craik, Brian. 2004. The Importance of Working Together: Exclusions, Conflicts and Participation in James Bay, Quebec. In *In the Way of Development: Indigenous Peoples, Life Projects and Globalization* (pp. 166–186). Mario Blaser, Harvey A. Feit, and Glenn McRae, eds. Zed Books in Association with the International Development Research Centre.

Crawford, C. Joanne. 1994. Parenting Practices in the Basque Country: Implications of Infant and Childhood Sleeping Location for Personality Development. *Ethos* 22(1):42–82.

Creighton, Millie R. 1992. The Depāto: Merchandising the West While Selling Japanese Sameness. In *Re-Made in Japan: Everyday Life and Consumer Taste in a Changing Society* (pp. 42–57). Joseph J. Tobin, ed. New Haven, CT: Yale University Press.

Crowe, D. 1996. *A History of the Gypsies of Eastern Europe and Russia.* New York: St. Martin's Press.

Crystal, David. 2000. *Language Death.* New York: Cambridge University Press.

———. 2003. *English as a Global Language,* 2nd ed. New York: Cambridge University Press.

Cunningham, Lawrence S. 1995. Christianity. In *The HarperCollins Dictionary of Religion* (pp. 240–253). Jonathan Z. Smith, ed. New York: HarperCollins.

Curtin, Philip D. 1989. *Death by Migration: Europe's Encounter with the Tropical World in the Nineteenth Century.* New York: Cambridge University Press.

Dalby, Liza Crihfield. 1998. *Geisha,* 2nd ed. New York: Vintage Books.

———. 2001. *Kimono: Fashioning Culture.* Seattle: University of Washington Press.

Danforth, Loring M. 1989. *Firewalking and Religious Healing: The Anestenaria of Greece and the American Firewalking Movement.* Princeton, NJ: Princeton University Press.

Dannhaeuser, Norbert. 1989. Marketing in Developing Urban Areas. In *Economic Anthropology* (pp. 222–252). Stuart Plattner, ed. Stanford, CA: Stanford University Press.

Daugherty, Mary Lee. 1997 [1976]. Serpent-Handling as Sacrament. In *Magic, Witchcraft, and Religion* (pp. 347–352). Arthur C. Lehmann and James E. Myers, eds. Mountain View, CA: Mayfield Publishing.

Dávila, Arlene. 2002. Culture in the Ad World: Producing the Latin Look. In *Media Worlds: Anthropology on New Terrain* (pp. 264–280). Faye D. Ginsburg, Lila Abu-Lughod, and Brian Larkin, eds. Berkeley: University of California Press.

Davis, Susan Schaefer and Douglas A. Davis. 1987. *Adolescence in a Moroccan Town: Making Social Sense.* New Brunswick: Rutgers University Press.

Davis-Floyd, Robbie E. 1987. Obstetric Training as a Rite of Passage. *Medical Anthropology Quarterly* 1:288–318.

———. 1992. *Birth as an American Rite of Passage.* Berkeley: University of California Press.

Daly, Martin and Margo Wilson. 1984. A Sociobiological Analysis of Human Infanticide. In *Infanticide: Comparative and Evolutionary Perspectives* (pp. 487–582). Glen Hausfater and Sarah Blaffer Hrdy, eds. New York: Aldine.

de Athayde Figueiredo, Mariza and Dando Prado. 1989. The Women of Arembepe. *UNESCO Courier* 7:38–41.

de la Cadena, Marisol. 2001. Reconstructing Race: Racism, Culture and Mestizaje in Latin America. *NACLA Report on the Americas* 34:16–23.

de la Pradelle, Michelle. Amy Jacobs, trans. 2006. *Market Day in Provence.* Chicago: University of Chicago Press.

Deitrick, Lynn. 2002. Commentary: Cultural Brokerage in the Newborn Nursery. *Practicing Anthropology* 24:53–54.

Delaney, Carol. 1988. Mortal Flow: Menstruation in Turkish Village Society. In *Blood Magic: The Anthropology of Menstruation* (pp. 75–93). Timothy Buckley and Alma Gottlieb, eds. Berkeley: University of California Press.

Dent, Alexander Sebastian. 2005. Cross-Culture "Countries": Covers, Conjuncture, and the Whiff of Nashville in *Música Sertaneja* (Brazilian Commercial Country Music). *Popular Music and Society* 28:207–227.

Devereaux, George. 1976. *A Typological Study of Abortion in Primitive Societies: A Typological, Distributional, and Dynamic Analysis of the Prevention of Birth in 400 Preindustrial Societies.* New York: International Universities Press.

Diamond, Jared. 1994 [1987]. The Worst Mistake in the History of the Human Race. In *Applying Cultural Anthropology: A Reader* (pp. 105–108). Aaron Podolefsky and Peter J. Brown, eds. Mountain View, CA: Mayfield Publishing.

Dickemann, Mildred. 1975. Demographic Consequences of Infanticide in Man. *Annual Review of Ecology and Systematics* 6:107–137.

DiFerdinando, George. 1999. Emerging Infectious Diseases: Biology and Behavior in the Inner City. In *Urbanism, Health, and Human Biology in Industrialised Countries* (pp. 87–110). Lawrence M. Schell and Stanley J. Ulijaszek, eds. New York: Cambridge University Press.

Dikötter, Frank. 1998. Hairy Barbarians, Furry Primates and Wild Men: Medical Science and Cultural Representations of Hair in China. In *Hair: Its Power and Meaning in Asian Cultures* (pp. 51–74). Alf Hiltebeitel and Barbara D. Miller, eds. Albany: State University of New York Press.

Divale, William T. 1974. Migration, External Warfare, and Matrilocal Residence. *Behavior Science Research* 9:75–133.

Divale, William T. and Marvin Harris. 1976. Population, Warfare and the Male Supremacist Complex. *American Anthropologist* 78:521–538.

Doi, Yaruko and Masami Minowa. 2003. Gender Differences in Excessive Daytime Sleepiness among Japanese Workers. *Social Science and Medicine* 56:883–894.

Donlon, Jon. 1990. Fighting Cocks, Feathered Warriors, and Little Heroes. *Play & Culture* 3:273–285.

Dorgan, Howard. 1989. *The Old Regular Baptists of Central Appalachia: Brothers and Sisters in Hope.* Knoxville: University of Tennessee Press.

Douglas, Mary. 1966. *Purity and Danger: An Analysis of Concepts of Pollution and Taboo.* New York: Penguin Books.

Drake, Susan P. 1991. Local Participation in Ecotourism Projects. In *Nature Tourism: Managing for the Environment* (pp. 132–155). Tensie Whelan, ed. Washington, DC: Island Press.

Dreifus, Claudia. 2000. Saving the Orangutan, Preserving Paradise. *New York Times*, March 21:D3.

Drucker, Charles. 1988. Dam the Chico: Hydropower Development and Tribal Resistance. In *Tribal Peoples and Development Issues: A Global Overview* (pp. 151–165). John H. Bodley, ed. Mountain View, CA: Mayfield Publishing.

Duany, Jorge. 2000. Nation on the Move: The Construction of Cultural Identities in Puerto Rico and the Diaspora. *American Ethnologist* 27:5–30.

Duranti, Alessandro. 1994. *From Grammar to Politics: Linguistic Anthropology in a Western Samoan Village.* Berkeley: University of California Press.

———. 1997a. *Linguistic Anthropology.* New York: Cambridge University Press.

———. 1997b. Universal and Culture-Specific Properties of Greetings. *Journal of Linguistic Anthropology* 7:63–97.

Durkheim, Emile. 1951 [1897]. *Suicide: A Study in Sociology.* New York: Free Press.

———. 1965 [1915]. *The Elementary Forms of the Religious Life.* New York: Free Press.

———. 1966 [1895]. *On the Division of Labor in Society.* Trans. G. Simpson. New York: Free Press.

Durning, Alan Thein. 1993. Are We Happy Yet? How the Pursuit of Happiness Is Failing. *The Futurist* 27(1):20–24.

Durrenberger, E. Paul. 2001. Explorations of Class and Class Consciousness in the U.S. *Journal of Anthropological Research* 57:41–60.

Earle, Timothy. 1991. The Evolution of Chiefdoms. In *Chiefdoms, Power, Economy, and Ideology* (pp. 1–15). Timothy Earle, ed. New York: Cambridge University Press.

Eck, Diana L. 1985. *Darsán: Seeing the Divine Image in India,* 2nd ed. Chambersburg, PA: Anima Books.

Eckel, Malcolm David. 1995. Buddhism. In *The HarperCollins Dictionary of Religion* (pp. 135–150). Jonathan Z. Smith, ed. New York: HarperCollins.

EcoHawk, M. 1997. Suicide: The Scourge of Native American People. *Suicide and Life-Threatening Behavior* 27(1):60–67.

Economic and Social Council. 1992. *Report of the Working Group on Violence against Women.* Vienna: United Nations. E/CN.6/WG.2/1992/L.3.

Eickelman, Dale F. 1981. *The Middle East: An Anthropological Perspective.* Englewood Cliffs, NJ: Prentice-Hall.

Eisler, Kim Isaac. 2001. *Revenge of the Pequots: How a Small Native American Tribe Created the World's Most Profitable Casino.* New York: Simon and Schuster.

Ember, Carol R. 1983. The Relative Decline in Women's Contribution to Agriculture with Intensification. *American Anthropologist* 85(2):285–304.

Englund, Harri. 1998. Death, Trauma and Ritual: Mozambican Refugees in Malawi. *Social Science and Medicine* 46(9):1165–1174.

Ennis-McMillan, Michael C. 2001. Suffering from Water: Social Origins of Bodily Distress in a Mexican Community. *Medical Anthropology Quarterly* 15(3):368–390.

Erickson, Barbra. 1999. Low Dose Radon as Alternative Therapy for Chronic Illness. Paper presented at the WONUC Conference on the Effects of Low Doses of Ionizing Radiation on Health. Versailles, France, June 16–19.

Eriksen, Thomas Hylland. 2001. Between Universalism and Relativism: A Critique of the UNESCO Concept of Culture. In *Culture and Rights: Anthropological Perspectives* (pp. 127–148). Jane K. Cowan, Marie Bénédicte Dembour, and Richard A. Wilson, eds. New York: Cambridge University Press.

Ervin, Alexander M., Antonet T. Kaye, Giselle M. Marcotte, and Randy D. Belon. 1991. *Community Needs, Saskatoon—The 1990's: The Saskatoon Needs Assessment Project.* Saskatoon, Canada: University of Saskatchewan, Department of Anthropology.

Escobar, Arturo. 2002. Gender, Place, and Networks: A Political Ecology of Cyberculture. In *Development: A Cultural Studies Reader* (pp. 239–256). Susan Schech and Jane Haggis, eds. Malden, MA: Blackwell Publishers.

Esman, Milton. 1996. Ethnic Politics. In *The Social Science Encyclopedia* (pp. 259–260). Adam Kuper and Jessica Kuper, eds. New York: Routledge.

Estioko-Griffin, Agnes. 1986. Daughters of the Forest. *Natural History* 95:36–43.

Estrin, Saul. 1996. Co-operatives. In *The Social Science Encyclopedia* (pp. 138–139). Adam Kuper and Jessica Kuper, eds. New York: Routledge.

Etienne, Mona and Eleanor Leacock, eds. 1980. *Women and Colonization: Anthropological Perspectives.* New York: Praeger.

Evans, William and Julie Topoleski. 2002. *The Social and Economic Impact of Native American Casinos.* Cambridge, MA: NBER Working Papers, No. 9198.

Evans-Pritchard, E. E. 1951. *Kinship and Marriage among the Nuer.* Oxford: Clarendon.

———. 1965 [1947]. *The Nuer: A Description of the Modes of Livelihood and Political Institutions of a Nilotic People.* New York: Oxford University Press.

Everett, Daniel L. 1995. Personal communication.

———. 2005. Cultural Constraints on Grammar and Cognition in Pirahã: Another Look at Design Features in Human Language. *Current Anthropology* 46:621–634, 641–646.

Evrard, Olivier and Yves Goudineau. 2004. Planned Resettlement, Unexpected Migrations and Cultural Trauma in Laos. *Development and Change* 35:937–962.

Ewing, Katherine Pratt. 2000 Legislating Religious Freedom: Muslim Challenges to the Relationship between "Church" and "State" in Germany and France. *Daedalus* 29:31–53.

Fabian, Johannes. 1995. Ethnographic Misunderstanding and the Perils of Context. *American Anthropologist* 97(1):41–50.

Fabrega, Horacio, Jr. and Barbara D. Miller. 1995. Adolescent Psychiatry as a Product of Contemporary Anglo-American Society. *Social Science and Medicine* 40(7):881–894.

Fabrega, Horacio, Jr. and Daniel B. Silver. 1973. *Illness and Shamanistic Curing in Zinacantan: An Ethnomedical Analysis.* Stanford, CA: Stanford University Press.

Fadiman, Anne. 1997. *The Spirit Catches You and You Fall Down: A Hmong Child, Her American Doctors, and the Collision of Two Cultures.* New York: Farrar, Straus and Giroux.

Faiola, Anthony. 2005. Sick of Their Husbands in Graying Japan: Stress Disorder Diagnosed in Many Women after Spouses Retire. *Washington Post*, October 10: A1, A16.

Farmer, Paul. 1992. *AIDS and Accusation: Haiti and the Geography of Blame.* Berkeley: University of California Press.

———. 2005. *Pathologies of Power: Health, Human Rights and the New War on the Poor.* Berkeley: University of California Press.

Fasulo, Linda. 2003. *An Insider's Guide to the UN.* New Haven, CT: Yale University Press.

Feinsilver, Julie M. 1993. *Healing the Masses: Cuban Health Politics at Home and Abroad.* Berkeley: University of California Press.

Feldman, Gregory. 2003. Breaking Our Silence on NATO. *Anthropology Today* 19:1–2.

Ferguson, R. Brian. 1990. Blood of the Leviathan: Western Contact and Amazonian Warfare. *American Ethnologist* 17(1):237–257.

Ferguson, James. 1994. *The Anti-Politics Machine: "Development," Depoliticization, and Bureaucratic Power in Lesotho.* Minneapolis: University of Minnesota Press.

Fields, Jason and Lynne M. Casper. 2000. *America's Families and Living Arrangements: Population Characteristics.* Washington, DC: United States Census Bureau. Current Population Reports P20-537.

Fischer, Edward F. 2001. *Cultural Logics and Global Economies: Maya Identity in Thought and Practice.* Austin: University of Texas Press.

Fisher, James. 1990. *Sherpas: Reflections on Change in Himalayan Nepal.* Berkeley: University of California Press.

Fishman, Joshua A. 1991. *Reversing Language Shift: Theoretical and Empirical Foundations of Assistance to Threatened Languages.* Clevedon, UK: Multilingual Matters Ltd.

Fishman, Joshua A., ed. 2001. *Can Threatened Languages Be Saved? Reversing Language Shift, Revisited: A 21st Century Perspective.* Buffalo, NY: Multilingual Matters Ltd.

Fiske, John. 1994. Radical Shopping in Los Angeles: Race, Media and the Sphere of Consumption. *Media, Culture & Society* 16:469–486.

Fitchen, Janet M. 1990. How Do You Know If You Haven't Listened First?: Using Anthropological Methods to Prepare for Survey Research. *The Rural Sociologist* 10(2):15–22.

Fitigu, Yodit. 2005. Forgotten People: Internally Displaced Persons in Guatemala. www.refugeesinternational.org/content/article/detail/6344.

Foley, Kathy. 2001. The Metonymy of Art: Vietnamese Water Puppetry as Representation of Modern Vietnam. *The Drama Review* 45(4): 129–141.

Foley, William A. 2000. The Languages of New Guinea. *Annual Review of Anthropology* 29:357–404.

Foster, George. 1965. Peasant Society and the Image of the Limited Good. *American Anthropologist* 67:293–315.

Foster, George M. and Barbara Gallatin Anderson. 1978. *Medical Anthropology.* New York: Alfred A. Knopf.

Foster, Helen Bradley and Donald Clay Johnson, eds. 2003. *Wedding Dress across Cultures.* New York: Berg.

Foster, Robert J. 2002. *Materializing the Nation: Commodities, Consumption, and Media in Papua New Guinea.* Bloomington: Indiana University Press.

———. 2006. From Trobriand Cricket to Rugby Nation: The Mission of Sport in Papua New Guinea. *The International Journal of the History of Sport* 23(5):739–758.

Foucault, Michel. 1970. *The Order of Things: An Archaeology of the Human Sciences.* New York: Random House.

———. 1977. *Discipline and Punish: The Birth of the Prison.* New York: Pantheon Books.

Fox, Richard G. and Andre Gingrich. 2002. Comparison and Anthropology's Public Responsibility. In *Anthropology, By Comparison* (pp. 1–24). Andre Gingrich and Richard G. Fox, eds. New York: Routledge.

Fox, Robin. 1995 [1978]. *The Tory Islanders: A People of the Celtic Fringe.* Notre Dame: University of Notre Dame Press.

Frake, Charles O. 1961. The Diagnosis of Disease among the Subanun of Mindanao. *American Anthropologist* 63:113–132.

Franke, Richard W. 1993. *Life is a Little Better: Redistribution as a Development Strategy in Nadur Village, Kerala.* Boulder, CO: Westview Press.

Frankel, Francine R. 1971. *India's Green Revolution: Economic Gains and Political Costs.* Princeton, NJ: Princeton University Press.

Fratkin, Elliot. 1998. *Ariaal Pastoralists of Kenya: Surviving Drought and Development in Africa's Arid Lands.* Boston: Allyn and Bacon.

Fratkin, Elliot, Kathleen Galvin, and Eric A. Roth, eds. 1994. *African Pastoralist Systems: An Integrated Approach.* Boulder, CO: Westview Press.

Frazer, Sir James. 1978 [1890]. *The Golden Bough: A Study in Magic and Religion.* New York: Macmillan.

Freedman, Diane C. 1986. Wife, Widow, Woman: Roles of an Anthropologist in a Transylvanian Village. In *Women in the Field: Anthropological Experiences* (pp. 333–358). Peggy Golde, ed. Berkeley: University of California Press.

Freeman, Derek. 1983. *Margaret Mead and Samoa: The Making and Unmaking of an Anthropological Myth.* Cambridge, MA: Harvard University Press.

Freeman, James A. 1981. A Firewalking Ceremony that Failed. In *Social and Cultural Context of Medicine in India* (pp. 308–336). Giri Raj Gupta, ed. New Delhi: Vikas Publishing.

———. 1989. *Hearts of Sorrow: Vietnamese-American Lives.* Stanford, CA: Stanford University Press.

French, Howard W. 2006. In a Richer China, Billionaires Put Money on Marriage. *The New York Times,* January 24:A4.

Frieze, Irene et al. 1978. *Women and Sex Roles: A Social Psychological Perspective.* New York: W. W. Norton.

Furst, Peter T. 1989. The Water of Life: Symbolism and Natural History on the Northwest Coast. *Dialectical Anthropology* 14:95–115.

Gable, Eric. 1995. The Decolonization of Consciousness: Local Skeptics and the "Will to Be Modern" in a West African Village. *American Ethnologist* 22(2):242–257.

Gage-Brandon, Anastasia J. 1992. The Polygyny-Divorce Relationship: A Case Study of Nigeria. *Journal of Marriage and the Family* 54: 282–292.

Galdikas, Biruté. 1995. *Reflections of Eden: My Years with the Orangutans of Borneo.* Boston: Little, Brown.

Gale, Faye, Rebecca Bailey-Harris, and Joy Wundersitz. 1990. *Aboriginal Youth and the Criminal Justice System: The Injustice of Justice?* New York: Cambridge University Press.

Gardner, Katy and David Lewis. 1996. *Anthropology, Development and the Post-Modern Challenge.* Sterling, VA: Pluto Press.

Garland, David. 1996. Social Control. In *The Social Science Encyclopedia* (pp. 780–783). Adam Kuper and Jessica Kuper, eds. Routledge: New York.

Gaski, Harald. 1993. The Sami People: The "White Indians" of Scandinavia. *American Indian Culture and Research Journal* 17:115–128.

———. 1997. Introduction: Sami Culture in a New Era. In *Sami Culture in a New Era: The Norwegian Sami Experience* (pp. 9–28). Harald Gaski, ed. Seattle: University of Washington Press.

Geertz, Clifford. 1966. Religion as a Cultural System. In *Anthropological Approaches to the Study of Religion* (pp. 1–46). Michael Banton, ed. London: Tavistock.

Geronimus, Arline T. 2003. Damned If You Do: Culture, Identity, Privilege and Teenage Childbearing in the United States. *Social Science and Medicine* 57:881–893.

Gifford-Gonzalez, Diane. 1993. You Can Hide, But You Can't Run: Representation of Women's Work in Illustrations of Palaeolithic Life. *Visual Anthropology Review* 9(1):23–41.

Gill, Lesley. 1997. Creating Citizens, Making Men: The Military and Masculinity in Bolivia. *Cultural Anthropology* 12:527–550.

———. 2006. Personal communication.

Gillette, Maris Boyd. 2000. *Between Mecca and Beijing: Modernization and Consumption among Urban Chinese Families.* Stanford: Stanford University Press.

Gilman, Antonio. 1991. Trajectories towards Social Complexity in the Later Prehistory of the Mediterranean. In *Chiefdoms: Power, Economy and Ideology* (pp. 146–168). Timothy Earle, ed. New York: Cambridge University Press.

Ginsberg, Faye D. and Rayna Rapp. 1991. The Politics of Reproduction. *Annual Review of Anthropology* 20:311–343.

Glick Schiller, Nina and Georges E. Fouron. 1999. Terrains of Blood and Nation: Haitian Transnational Social Fields. *Ethnic and Racial Studies* 22:340–365.

Glínski, Piotr. 1994 Environmentalism among Polish Youth: A Maturing Social Movement? *Communist and Post-Communist Studies* 27(2):145–159.

Gliotto, Tom. 1995. Paradise Lost. *People Weekly,* 43(17):70–76.

Gmelch, George. 1997 [1971]. Baseball Magic. In *Magic, Witchcraft, and Religion* (pp. 276–282). Arthur C. Lehmann and James E. Myers, eds. Mountain View, CA: Mayfield Publishing.

Godelier, Maurice. 1971. "Salt Currency" and the Circulation of Commodities among the Baruya of New Guinea. In *Studies in Economic Anthropology* (pp. 52–73). George Dalton, ed. Anthropological Studies No. 7. Washington, DC: American Anthropological Association.

Godoy, Ricardo, Victoria Reyes-García, Tomás Huanca, William R. Leonard, Vincent Valdez, Cynthia Valdés-Galicia, and Dakun Zhao. 2005. Why Do Subsistence-Level People Join the Market Economy? Testing Hypotheses of Push and Pull Determinants in Bolivian Amazonia. *Journal of Anthropological Research* 61:157–178.

Gold, Stevan J. 1992. *Refugee Communities: A Comparative Field Study.* Newbury Park: Sage Publications.

———. 1995. *From the Workers' State to the Golden State: Jews from the Former Soviet Union in California.* Boston: Allyn and Bacon.

Goldstein, Melvyn C. and Cynthia M. Beall. 1994. *The Changing World of Mongolia's Nomads.* Berkeley: University of California Press.

Goldstein-Gidoni, Ofra. 2003. Producers of "Japan" in Israel: Cultural Appropriation in a Non-Colonial Context. *Ethnos* 68(3):365–390.

Goldstone, Jack. 1996. Revolutions. In *The Social Science Encyclopedia* (pp. 740–743). Adam Kuper and Jessica Kuper, eds. New York: Routledge.

González, Nancie L. 1970. Toward a Definition of Matrifocality. In *Afro-American Anthropology: Contemporary Perspectives* (pp. 231–244). Norman E. Whitten, Jr. and John F. Szwed, eds. New York: Free Press.

Goodman, Marjorie H. 1990. *He-Said-She-Said: Talk as Social Organization among Black Children.* Bloomington: Indiana University Press.

Goodwin, Marjorie Harness. 1990. *He-Said-She-Said: Talk as Social Organization among Black Children.* Bloomington: Indiana University Press.

Goody, Jack. 1976. *Production and Reproduction: A Comparative Study of the Domestic Domain.* New York: Cambridge University Press.

———. 1993. *The Culture of Flowers.* New York: Cambridge University Press.

Goossens, Benoît, Lounès Chikhi, Marc Ancrenaz, Isabelle Lackman-Ancrenaz, Patrick Andau, and Michael W. Bruford. 2006. Genetic Signature of Anthropogenic Population Collapse in Orangutans. *PloS Biology* 4(2):e25. www.plosbiology.org.

Graburn, Nelson H. H., ed. 1976. *Ethnic and Tourist Arts: Cultural Expressions from the Fourth World.* Berkeley: University of California Press.

Graeber, David. 2004. Fragments of an Anarchist Anthropology. *Paradigm* 14. Chicago: Prickly Paradigm Press.

Greenhalgh, Susan. 2003. Science, Modernity, and the Making of China's One-Child Policy. *Population and Development Review* 29:163–196.

Gregg, Jessica L. 2003. *Virtually Virgins: Sexual Strategies and Cervical Cancer in Recife, Brazil.* Stanford: Stanford University Press.

Gregor, Thomas. 1982. No Girls Allowed. *Science* 82.

Gremillion, Helen. 1992. Psychiatry as Social Ordering: Anorexia Nervosa, a Paradigm. *Social Science and Medicine* 35(1):57–71.

Grenier, Guillermo J., Alex Stepick, Debbie Draznin, Aileen LaBorwit, and Steve Morris. 1992. On Machines and Bureaucracy: Controlling Ethnic Interaction in Miami's Apparel and Construction Industries. In *Structuring Diversity: Ethnographic Perspectives on the New Immigration* (pp. 65–94). Louise Lamphere, ed. Chicago: University of Chicago Press.

Grinker, Roy Richard. 1994. *Houses in the Rainforest: Ethnicity and Inequality among Farmers and Foragers in Central Africa*. Berkeley: University of California Press.

Gross, Daniel R. 1984. Time Allocation: A Tool for the Study of Cultural Behavior. *Annual Review of Anthropology* 13:519–558.

Gruenbaum, Ellen. 2001. *The Female Circumcision Controversy: An Anthropological Perspective*. Philadelphia: University of Pennsylvania Press.

Guggenheim, Scott E. and Michael M. Cernea. 1993. Anthropological Approaches to Involuntary Resettlement: Policy, Practice, and Theory. In *Anthropological Approaches to Resettlement: Policy, Practice, and Theory* (pp. 1–12). Michael M. Cernea and Scott E. Guggenheim, eds. Boulder, CO: Westview Press.

Gugler, Josef. 1988. The Urban Character of Contemporary Revolutions. In *The Urbanization of the Third World* (pp. 399–412). Josef Gugler, ed. New York: Oxford University Press.

Guidoni, Enrico. 1987. *Primitive Architecture*. Trans. Robert Erich Wolf. New York: Rizzoli.

Günes-Ayata, Ayse. 1995. Women's Participation in Politics in Turkey. In *Women in Modern Turkish Society: A Reader* (pp. 235–249). Sirin Tekeli, ed. London: Zed Books.

Hackenberg, Robert A. 2000. Advancing Applied Anthropology: Joe Hill in Cyberspace—Steps Toward Creating "One Big Union." *Human Organization* 59:365–369.

Hackenberg, Robert A. et al. 1983. Migration, Modernization and Hypertension: Blood Pressure Levels in Four Philippine Communities. *Medical Anthropology* 7(1):45–71.

Hacker, Andrew. 1992. *Two Nations: Black and White, Separate, Hostile, Unequal*. New York: Ballantine Books.

Haddix McCay, Kimber. 2001. Leaving Your Wife and Your Brothers: When Polyandrous Marriages Fall Apart. *Evolution and Human Behavior* 22:47–60.

Hakamies-Blomqvist, Liisa. 1994. Aging and Fatal Accidents in Male and Female Drivers. *Journal of Gerontology [Social Sciences]* 49(6): 5286–5290.

Hamabata, Matthews Masayuki. 1990. *Crested Kimono: Power and Love in the Japanese Business Family*. Ithaca, NY: Cornell University Press.

Hammond, Peter B. 1966. *Yatenga: Technology in the Culture of a West African Kingdom*. New York: Free Press.

Hancock, Graham. 1989. *Lords of Poverty: The Power, Prestige, and Corruption of the International Aid Business*. New York: Atlantic Monthly Press.

Handler, Richard. 2003. Cultural Property and Cultural Theory. *Journal of Social Archaeology* 3:353–365.

Hardman, Charlotte E. 2000. *Other Worlds: Notions of Self and Emotion among the Lohorung Rai*. New York: Berg.

Harner, Michael. 1977. The Ecological Basis of Aztec Sacrifice. *American Ethnologist* 4:117–135.

Harragin, Simon. 2004. Relief and Understanding of Local Knowledge: The Case of Southern Sudan. In *Culture and Public Action* (pp. 307–327). Vijayendra Rao and Michael Walton, eds. Stanford, CA: Stanford University Press.

Harris, Marvin. 1974. *Cows, Pigs, Wars and Witches: The Riddles of Culture*. New York: Random House.

———. 1975. *Culture, People, Nature: An Introduction to General Anthropology*, 2nd ed. New York: Thomas Y. Crowell.

———. 1977. *Cannibals and Kings: The Origins of Culture*. New York: Random House.

———. 1984. Animal Capture and Yanomamo Warfare: Retrospect and New Evidence. *Journal of Anthropological Research* 40(10):183–201.

———. 1989. *Our Kind: The Evolution of Human Life and Culture*. New York: Harper & Row Publishers.

———. 1992. Distinguished Lecture: Anthropology and the Theoretical and Paradigmatic Significance of the Collapse of Soviet and East European Communism. *American Anthropologist* 94:295–305.

———. 1993. The Evolution of Human Gender Hierarchies. In *Sex and Gender Hierarchies* (pp. 57–80). Barbara D. Miller, ed. New York: Cambridge University Press.

Hart, C. W. M., Arnold R. Pilling, and Jane C. Goodale. 1988. *The Tiwi of North Australia*. New York: Holt, Rinehart and Winston.

Hart, Gillian. 2002. *Disabling Globalization: Places of Power in Post-Apartheid South Africa*. Berkeley: University of California Press.

Hartmann, Betsy. 1987. *Reproductive Rights and Wrongs: The Global Politics of Population Control and Reproductive Choice*. New York: Harper & Row.

Hastrup, Kirsten. 1992 Anthropological Visions: Some Notes on Visual and Textual Authority. In *Film as Ethnography* (pp. 8–25). Peter Ian Crawford and David Turton, eds. Manchester: University of Manchester Press.

Hawkes, K., J. F. O'Connell, and N. G. Blurton Jones. 2001. Hadza Meat Sharing. *Evolution and Human Behavior* 22:113–142.

Hawn, Carleen. 2002. Please Feedback the Animals. *Forbes* 170(9):168–169.

Hefner, Robert W. 1998. Multiple Modernities: Christianity, Islam, and Hinduism in a Globalizing Age. *Annual Review of Anthropology* 27:83–104.

Heise, Lori L., Jacqueline Pitanguy, and Adrienne Germain. 1994. Violence against Women: The Hidden Health Burden. *World Bank Discussion Papers No. 255*. Washington, DC: The World Bank.

Helweg, Arthur W. and Usha M. Helweg. 1990. *An Immigrant Success Story: East Indians in America*. Philadelphia: University of Pennsylvania Press.

Herdt, Gilbert. 1987. *The Sambia: Ritual and Gender in New Guinea*. New York: Holt, Rinehart and Winston.

Herrnstein, Richard J. and Charles A. Murray. 1994. *The Bell Curve: Intelligence and Class Structure in American Life*. New York: Free Press.

Herzfeld, Michael. 1985. *The Poetics of Manhood: Contest and Identity in a Cretan Mountain Village*. Princeton, NJ: Princeton University Press.

Hewlett, Barry S. 1991. *Intimate Fathers: The Nature and Context of Aka Pygmy Paternal Care*. Ann Arbor: University of Michigan Press.

Hiatt, Betty. 1970. Woman the Gatherer. In *Woman's Role in Aboriginal Society* (pp. 2–28). Fay Gale, ed. Canberra: Australian Institute of Aboriginal Studies.

Hill, Jane H. 2001. Dimensions of Attrition in Language Death. In *On Biocultural Diversity: Linking Language, Knowledge, and the Environment* (pp. 175–189). Luisa Maffi, ed. Washington, DC: Smithsonian Institution Press.

Hill, Jane H. and Bruce Mannheim. 1992. Language and World View. *Annual Review of Anthropology* 21:381–406.

Hiltebeitel, Alf. 1988. *The Cult of Draupadi: Mythologies from Gingee to Kuruksetra*. Chicago: University of Chicago Press.

Hirschon, Renee. 1989. *Heirs of the Catastrophe: The Social Life of Asia Minor Refugees in Piraeus*. New York: Oxford University Press.

Hobsbawm, Eric J. 1969. *Bandits*, 2nd ed. New York: Delacorte Press.

Hodge, Robert W. and Naohiro Ogawa. 1991. *Fertility Change in Contemporary Japan*. Chicago: University of Chicago Press.

Hodgson, Dorothy L. 2004. *Once Intrepid Warriors: Gender, Ethnicity, and the Cultural Politics of Maasai Development*. Bloomington: Indiana University Press.

Hoffman, Danny. 2003. Frontline Anthropology: Research in a Time of War. *Anthropology Today* 19:9–12.

Hoffman, Danny and Stephen Lubkemann. 2005. Warscape Ethnography in West Africa and the Anthropology of "Events." *Anthropological Quarterly* 78:315–327.

Hollan, Douglas. 2001. Developments in Person-Centered Ethnography. In *The Psychology of Cultural Experience* (pp. 48–67). Carmella C. Moore and Holly F. Mathews, eds. New York: Cambridge University Press.

Holland, Dorothy C. and Margaret A. Eisenhart. 1990. *Educated in Romance: Women, Achievement, and College Culture.* Chicago: University of Chicago Press.

Hopkins, Nicholas S. and Sohair R. Mehanna. 2000. Social Action against Everyday Pollution in Egypt. *Human Organization* 59:245–254.

Hornbein, George and Marie Hornbein. 1992. *Salamanders: A Night at the Phi Delt House.* Video. College Park: Documentary Resource Center.

Horowitz, Irving L. 1967. *The Rise and Fall of Project Camelot: Studies in the Relationship between Social Science and Practical Politics.* Boston: MIT Press.

Horowitz, Michael M. and Muneera Salem-Murdock. 1993. Development-Induced Food Insecurity in the Middle Senegal Valley. *GeoJournal* 30(2):179–184.

Horst, Heather and Daniel Miller. 2005. From Kinship to Link-up: Cell Phones and Social Networking in Jamaica. *Current Anthropology* 46:755–764, 773–778.

Hostetler, John A. and Gertrude Enders Huntington. 1992. *Amish Children: Education in the Family, School, and Community.* New York: Harcourt Brace Jovanovich.

Howell, Nancy. 1979. *Demography of the Dobe !Kung.* New York: Academic Press.

———. 1986. Feedbacks and Buffers in Relation to Scarcity and Abundance: Studies of Hunter-Gatherer Populations. In *The State of Population Theory: Forward from Malthus* (pp. 156–187). David Coleman and Roger Schofield, eds. New York: Basil Blackwell.

———. 1990. *Surviving Fieldwork: A Report of the Advisory Panel on Health and Safety in Fieldwork.* Washington, DC: American Anthropological Association.

Hughes, Charles C. and John M. Hunter. 1970. Disease and "Development" in Africa. *Social Science and Medicine* 3:443–493.

Hughes, Lotte. 2003. *The No-Nonsense Guide to Indigenous Peoples.* London: Verso.

Humphrey, Caroline. 1978. Women, Taboo and the Suppression of Attention. In *Defining Females: The Nature of Women in Society* (pp. 89–108). Shirley Ardener, ed. New York: John Wiley and Sons.

Hunte, Pamela A. 1985. Indigenous Methods of Fertility Regulation in Afghanistan. In *Women's Medicine: A Cross-Cultural Study of Indigenous Fertility Regulation* (pp. 44–75). Lucile F. Newman, ed. New Brunswick, NJ: Rutgers University Press.

Hutchinson, Sharon E. 1996. *Nuer Dilemmas: Coping with Money, War, and the State.* Berkeley: University of California Press.

Hutter, Michael. 1996. The Value of Play. In *The Value of Culture: On the Relationship between Economics and the Arts* (pp. 122–137). Arjo Klamer, ed. Amsterdam: Amsterdam University Press.

Illo, Jeanne Frances I. 1985. Who Heads the Household? Women in Households in the Philippines. Paper presented at the Women and Household Regional Conference for Asia, New Delhi.

Ingham, John M. 1996. *Psychological Anthropology Reconsidered.* New York: Cambridge University Press.

Inhorn, Marcia C. 2003. Global Infertility and the Globalization of New Reproductive Technologies: Illustrations from Egypt. *Social Science and Medicine* 56:1837–1851.

———. 2004. Middle Eastern Masculinities in the Age of New Reproductive Technologies: Male Infertility and Stigma in Egypt and Lebanon. *Medical Anthropology Quarterly* 18(2):162–182.

International Alliance for the Protection of Isolated Indigenous Peoples. 2005. *Belém Declaration on Isolated Indigenous Peoples.* Adopted at the First International Symposium on Isolated Indigenous Peoples of the Amazon, Belém, Brazil, November.

IUCN/SSC Conservation Breeding Specialist Group. 2004. *Orangutan: Population and Habitat Viability Assessment: Final Report.* Apple Valley, MN: IUCN/SSC Conservation Breeding Specialist Group. www.cbsg.org.

Jacobs-Huey, Lanita. 1997. Is There an Authentic African American Speech Community: Carla Revisited. *University of Pennsylvania Working Papers in Linguistics* 4(1):331–370.

———. 2002. The Natives Are Gazing and Talking Back: Reviewing the Problematics of Positionality, Voice, and Accountability among "Native" Anthropologists. *American Anthropologist* 104:791–804.

———. 2006. *From the Kitchen to the Parlor: Language and Becoming in African American Women's Hair Care.* New York: Oxford University Press.

Janes, Craig R. 1990. *Migration, Social Change, and Health: A Samoan Community in Urban California.* Stanford, CA: Stanford University Press.

———. 1995. The Transformations of Tibetan Medicine. *Medical Anthropology Quarterly* 9(1):6–39.

Janes, Craig R. and Oyuntsetseg Chuluundorj. 2004. Free Markets and Dead Mothers: The Social Ecology of Maternal Mortality in Post-Socialist Mongolia. *Medical Anthropology Quarterly* 18(2):230–257.

Jankowski, Martín Sánchez. 1991. *Islands in the Street: Gangs and American Urban Society.* Berkeley: University of California Press.

Jeffrey, Leslie Ann. 2002. *Sex and Borders: Gender, National Identity, and Prostitution Policy in Thailand.* Vancouver: UBC Press.

Jenkins, Gwynne. 2003. Burning Bridges: Policy, Practice, and the Destruction of Midwifery in Rural Costa Rica. *Social Science and Medicine* 56:1893–1909.

Jenkins, Gwynne L. and Marcia C. Inhorn. 2003. Reproduction Gone Awry: Medical Anthropology Perspectives. *Social Science and Medicine* 56:1831–1836.

Jensen, Marianne Wiben, ed. Elaine Bolton, trans. 2004. Land Rights: A Key Issue. *Indigenous Affairs* 4.

Jernsletten, Nils. 1997. Sami Traditional Terminology: Professional Terms Concerning Salmon, Reindeer and Snow. In *Sami Culture in a New Era: The Norwegian Sami Experience* (pp. 86–108). Harald Gaski, ed. Seattle: University of Washington Press.

Jet. 1995. Baseball Team Members Who Used KKK Symbol Will Receive Multi-Cultural Training. *Jet* 88(18):39–40, September 11.

Jeter, Jon. 2004. Young Brazilians Find Suicide Only Way Out. *The Washington Post*, April 13, p. A22.

Jiang, David W. 1994. Shanghai Revisited: Chinese Theatre and the Forces of the Market. *The Drama Review* 38(2):72–80.

Jinadu, L. Adele. 1994. The Dialectics of Theory and Research on Race and Ethnicity in Nigeria. In *"Race," Ethnicity and Nation: International Perspectives on Social Conflict* (pp. 163–178). Peter Ratcliffe, ed. London: University College of London Press.

Johnson, Walter R. 1994. *Dismantling Apartheid: A South African Town in Transition.* Ithaca, NY: Cornell University Press.

Johnson-Hanks, Jennifer. 2002. On the Limits of Life Stages in Ethnography: Toward a Theory of Vital Conjectures. *American Anthropologist* 104:865–880.

Johnston, Barbara Rose. 1994. Environmental Degradation and Human Rights Abuse. In *Who Pays the Price?: The Sociocultural Context of Environmental Crisis* (pp. 7–16). Barbara Rose Johnston, ed. Washington, DC: Island Press.

Jonaitis, Aldona. 1995. *A Wealth of Thought: Franz Boas on Native American Art.* Seattle: University of Washington Press.

Jones, Anna Laura. 1993. Exploding Canons: The Anthropology of Museums. *Annual Review of Anthropology* 22:201–220.

Joralemon, Donald. 1982. New World Depopulation and the Case of Disease. *Journal of Anthropological Research* 38:108–127.

Jordan, Brigitte. 1983. *Birth in Four Cultures,* 3rd ed. Montreal: Eden Press.

Jordan, Mark. 1998. Japan Takes Dim View of Fertility Treatments. *New York Times,* July 5:A13.

Joseph, Suad. 1994. Brother/Sister Relationships: Connectivity, Love, and Power in the Reproduction of Patriarchy in Lebanon. *American Ethnologist* 21:50–73.

Jourdan, Christine. 1995. Masta Liu. In *Youth Cultures: A Cross-Cultural Perspective* (pp. 202–222). Vered Amit-Talai and Helena Wulff, eds. New York: Routledge.

Judd, Ellen. 2002. *The Chinese Women's Movement: Between State and Market.* Stanford, CA: Stanford University Press.

Kaberry, Phyllis. 1952. *Women of the Grassfields: A Study of the Economic Position of Women in Bamenda, British Cameroons.* London: Her Majesty's Stationery Office.

Kabutha, Charity, Barbara P. Thomas-Slaytor, and Richard Ford. 1993. Participatory Rural Appraisal: A Case Study from Kenya. In *Rapid Appraisal Methods* (pp. 176–211). Krishna Kumar, ed. Washington, DC: The World Bank.

Kahn, Miriam. 1995. Heterotopic Dissonance in the Museum Representation of Pacific Island Cultures. *American Anthropologist* 97(2): 324–338.

Kanaaneh, Rhoda. 2005. Boys or Men? Duped or "Made"? Palestinian Soldiers in the Israeli Military. *American Ethnologist* 32:260–275.

Kapchan, Deborah A. 1994. Moroccan Female Performers Defining the Social Body. *Journal of American Folklore* 107(423):82–105.

Karan, P. P. and Cotton Mather. 1985. Tourism and Environment in the Mount Everest Region. *Geographical Review* 75(1):93–95.

Kassam, Aneesa. 2002. Ethnodevelopment in the Oromia Regional State of Ethiopia. In *Participating in Development: Approaches to Indigenous Knowledge* (pp. 65–81). Paul Sillitoe, Alan Bicker, and Johan Pottier, eds. ASA Monographs No. 39. New York: Routledge.

Katz, Nathan and Ellen S. Goldberg. 1989. Asceticism and Caste in the Passover Observances of the Cochin Jews. *Journal of the American Academy of Religion* 57(1):53–81.

Katz, Richard. 1982. *Boiling Energy: Community Healing among the Kalahari Kung.* Cambridge, MA: Harvard University Press.

Katz, Richard, Megan Biesele, and Verna St. Denis. 1997. *Healing Makes Our Hearts Happy: Spirituality and Cultural Transformation among the Kalahari Ju/'hoansi.* Rochester, VT: Inner Traditions.

Kaul, Adam. 2004. The Anthropologist as Barman and Tour-guide: Reflections on Fieldwork in a Touristed Destination. *Durham Anthropology Journal* 12:22–36.

Kawanishi, Y. 2004. Japanese Youth: The Other Half of the Crisis? *Asian Affairs* 35:22–32.

Kearney, Robert N. and Barbara D. Miller. 1985. The Spiral of Suicide and Social Change in Sri Lanka. *Journal of Asian Studies* 48:81–101.

Kehoe, Alice Beck. 1989. *The Ghost Dance: History and Revitalization.* Philadelphia: Holt.

Keiser, R. Lincoln. 1986. Death Enmity in Thull: Organized Vengeance and Social Change in a Kohistani Community. *American Ethnologist* 13(3):489–505.

Kelley, Heidi. 1991. Unwed Mothers and Household Reputation in a Spanish Galician Community. *American Ethnologist* 18:565–580.

Kelley, Heidi, Monika Abels, Bettina Lamm, Relindis D. Yovsi, Susanne Voelker, and Aruna Lakhani. 2005. Ecocultural Effects on Early Infant Care: A Study in Cameroon, India, and Germany. *Ethos* 33(4): 512–541.

Kendall, Carl, Aimee Afable-Munsuz, Ilene Speizer, Alexis Avery, Norine Schmidt, and John Santelli. 2005. Understanding Pregnancy in a Population of Inner-City Women in New Orleans: Results of Qualitative Research. *Social Science and Medicine* 60:297–311.

Kendon, A. 1998. Parallels and Divergences between Warlpiri Sign Language and Spoken Warlpiri: Analyses of Spoken and Signed Discourse. *Oceania* 58:239–254.

Kennedy, David P. and Stephen G. Perz. 2000. Who Are Brazil's Indígenas? Contributions of Census Data Analysis to Anthropological Demography of Indigenous Populations. *Human Organization* 59: 311–324.

Kerns, Virginia. 1999. Preventing Violence against Women: A Central American Case. In *To Have and To Hit: Cultural Perspectives on Wife Beating,* 2nd ed. (pp. 153–168). Dorothy Ayers Counts, Judith K. Brown, and Jacquelyn C. Campbell, eds. Urbana: University of Illinois Press.

Keskitalo, Jan Henry. 1997. Sami Post-Secondary Education: Ideals and Realities. In *Sami Culture in a New Era: The Norwegian Sami Experience* (pp. 155–171). Harald Gaski, ed. Seattle: University of Washington Press.

Kesmanee, Chupinit. 1994. Dubious Development Concepts in the Thai Highlands: The Chao Khao in Transition. *Law & Society Review* 28:673–683.

Khanaaneh, Rhoda. 2005. Boys or Men? Duped or "Made"? Palestinian Soldiers in the Israeli Military. *American Ethnologist* 32:250–275.

Kideckel, David A. 1993. *The Solitude of Collectivism: Romanian Villagers to the Revolution and Beyond.* Ithaca, NY: Cornell University Press.

Kirsch, Stuart. 2002. Anthropology and Advocacy: A Case Study of the Campaign against the Ok Tedi Mine. *Critique of Anthropology* 22: 175–200.

Kleinman, Arthur. 1995. *Writing at the Margin: Discourse between Anthropology and Medicine.* Berkeley: University of California Press.

Klima, Alan. 2002. *The Funeral Casino: Meditation, Massacre, and Exchange with the Dead in Thailand.* Princeton: Princeton University Press.

Knott, Kim. 1996. Hindu Women, Destiny and Stridharma. *Religion* 26:15–35.

Kolenda, Pauline M. 1978. *Caste in Contemporary India: Beyond Organic Solidarity.* Prospect Heights, IL: Waveland Press.

Kondo, Dorinne. 1997. *About Face: Performing "Race" in Fashion and Theater.* New York: Routledge.

Konner, Melvin. 1989. Homosexuality: Who and Why? *New York Times Magazine.* April 2:60–61.

Kottak, Conrad Phillip. 1985. When People Don't Come First: Some Sociological Lessons from Completed Projects. In *Putting People First: Sociological Variables and Rural Development* (pp. 325–356). Michael M. Cernea, ed. New York: Oxford University Press.

———. 1992. *Assault on Paradise: Social Change in a Brazilian Village.* New York: McGraw-Hill.

Kovats-Bernat, J. Christopher. 2002. Negotiating Dangerous Fields: Pragmatic Strategies for Fieldwork amid Violence and Terror. *American Anthropologist* 104:1–15.

Kramer, Jennifer. 2005. Personal communication.

Krantzler, Nora J. 1987. Traditional Medicine as "Medical Neglect": Dilemmas in the Case Management of a Samoan Teenager with Diabetes. In *Child Survival: Cultural Perspectives on the Treatment and Maltreatment of Children* (pp. 325–337). Nancy Scheper-Hughes, ed. Boston: D. Reidel.

Kroeber, A. L. and Clyde Kluckhohn. 1952. *Culture: A Critical Review of Concepts and Definitions.* New York: Vintage Books.

Kuipers, Joel C. 1990. *Power in Performance: The Creation of Textual Authority in Weyéwa Ritual Speech.* Philadelphia: University of Pennsylvania Press.

———. 1991. Matters of Taste in Weyéwa. In *The Varieties of Sensory Experience: A Sourcebook in the Anthropology of the Senses* (pp. 111–127). David Howes, ed. Toronto: University of Toronto Press.

———. 2004. Ethnography of Language in the Age of Video: "Voices" in Context of Religious and Clinical Authority. In *Discourse and Technology: Multimodal Discourse Analysis* (pp. 167–183). Philip LeVine and Ron Scollon, eds. Washington, DC: Georgetown University Press.

Kuipers, Joel C. and Ray McDermott. 1996. Insular Southeast Asian Scripts. In *The World's Writing Systems* (pp. 474–484). Peter T. Daniels and William Bright, eds. New York: Oxford University Press.

Kumar, Krishna. 1996. Civil Society. In *The Social Science Encyclopedia* (pp. 88–90). Adam Kuper and Jessica Kuper, eds. New York: Routledge.

Kurin, Richard. 1980. Doctor, Lawyer, Indian Chief. *Natural History* 89(11):6–24.

Kuwayama, Takami. 2004. *Native Anthropology: The Japanese Challenge to Western Academic Hegemony*. Melbourne: Trans Pacific Press.

Kwiatkowski, Lynn M. 1998. *Struggling with Development: The Politics of Hunger and Gender in the Philippines*. Boulder, CO: Westview Press.

Labov, William. 1966. *The Social Stratification of English in New York City*. Washington, DC: Center for Applied Linguistics.

Lacey, Marc. 2002. Where 9/11 News Is Late, But Aid Is Swift. *New York Times,* June 3:A1, A7.

Ladányi, János. 1993. Patterns of Residential Segregation and the Gypsy Minority in Budapest. *International Journal of Urban and Regional Research* 17(1):30–41.

Laderman, Carol. 1988. A Welcoming Soil: Islamic Humoralism on the Malay Peninsula. In *Paths to Asian Medical Knowledge* (pp. 272–288). Charles Leslie and Allan Young, eds. Berkeley: University of California Press.

LaFleur, William. 1992. *Liquid Life: Abortion and Buddhism in Japan*. Princeton, NJ: Princeton University Press.

Lake, Amy and Steven Deller, 1996. *The Socioeconomic Impacts of a Native American Casino*. Madison: Department of Agricultural and Applied Economics, University of Wisconsin.

Lakoff, Robin. 1973. Language and Woman's Place. *Language in Society* 2:45–79.

———. 1990. *Talking Power: The Politics of Language in Our Lives*. New York: Basic Books.

LaLone, Mary B. 2003. Walking the Line between Alternative Interpretations in Heritage Education and Tourism: A Demonstration of the Complexities with an Appalachian Coal Mining Example. In *Signifying Serpents and Mardi Gras Runners: Representing Identity in Selected Souths* (pp. 72–92). Southern Anthropological Proceedings, No. 36. Celeste Ray and Luke Eric Lassiter, eds. Athens: University of Georgia Press.

Lamphere, Louise. 1992. Introduction: The Shaping of Diversity. In *Structuring Diversity: Ethnographic Perspectives on the New Immigration* (pp. 1–34). Lousie Lamphere, ed. Chicago: University of Chicago Press.

Lane, Sandra D., Robert H. Keefe, Robert A. Rubenstein, Brooke A. Levandowski, Michael Freedman, Alan Rosenthal, Donald A. Cibula, and Maria Czerwinski. 2004. Marriage Promotion and Missing Men: African American Women in a Demographic Double Bind. *Medical Anthropology Quarterly* 18:405–428.

Lanehart, Sonja L. 1999. African American Vernacular English. In *Handbook of Language and Ethnic Identity* (pp. 211–225). Joshua A. Fishman, ed. New York: Oxford University Press.

Larsen, Ulla and Marida Hollos. 2003. Women's Empowerment and Fertility Decline among the Pare of Kilimanjaro Region, Northern Tanzania. *Social Science and Medicine* 57:1099–1115.

Larsen, Ulla and Sharon Yan. 2000. Does Female Circumcision Affect Infertility and Fertility? A Study of the Central African Republic, Côte d'Ivoire, and Tanzania. *Demography* 37:313–321.

Larsson, Sara. 2005. Legislating Gender Equality: In Saami Land, Women Are Encouraged to Become Lawyers—But Many Would Rather Be Reindeer Herders. *Cultural Survival Quarterly* 28(4):28–29.

Lassiter, Luke Eric, Hurley Goodall, Elizabeth Campbell, and Michelle Natasya Johnson. 2004. *The Other Side of Middletown: Exploring Muncie's African American Community*. Walnut Creek, CA: AltaMira Press.

Leach, Jerry W. 1975. *Trobriand Cricket: An Ingenious Response to Colonialism*. Video.

Lebra, Takie. 1976. *Japanese Patterns of Behavior*. Honolulu: University of Hawaii Press.

Lederer, Edith. 2006. Record Number of Women in Politics. *Guardian Weekly,* March 10–15:9.

Lee, Gary R. and Mindy Kezis. 1979. Family Structure and the Status of the Elderly. *Journal of Comparative Family Studies* 10:429–443.

Lee, Helen Morton. 2003. *Tongans Overseas: Between Two Shores*. Honolulu: University of Hawai'i Press.

Lee, Richard B. 1969. Eating Christmas in the Kalahari. *Natural History,* December 14–22, 60–63.

Lee, Richard Borshay. 1979. *The !Kung San: Men, Women, and Work in a Foraging Society*. New York: Cambridge University Press.

Lee, Wai-Na and David K. Tse. 1994. Becoming Canadian: Understanding How Hong Kong Immigrants Change Their Consumption. *Pacific Affairs* 67(1):70–95.

Lempert, David. 1996. *Daily Life in a Crumbling Empire*. 2 volumes. New York: Columbia University Press.

Lepowsky, Maria. 1990. Big Men, Big Women, and Cultural Autonomy. *Ethnology* 29(10):35–50.

———. 1993. *Fruit of the Motherland: Gender in an Egalitarian Society*. New York: Columbia University Press.

Lessinger, Johanna. 1995. *From the Ganges to the Hudson: Indian Immigrants in New York City*. Boston: Allyn and Bacon.

Levinson, David. 1989. *Family Violence in Cross-Cultural Perspective*. Newbury Park, CA: Sage Publications.

Lévi-Strauss, Claude. 1967. *Structural Anthropology*. New York: Anchor Books.

———. 1968. *Tristes Tropiques: An Anthropological Study of Primitive Societies in Brazil*. New York: Atheneum.

———. 1969 [1949]. *The Elementary Structures of Kinship*. Boston: Beacon Press.

Levy, Jerrold E., Eric B. Henderson, and Tracy J. Andrews. 1989. The Effects of Regional Variation and Temporal Change in Matrilineal Elements of Navajo Social Organization. *Journal of Anthropological Research* 45(4):351–377.

Lew, Irvina. 1994. Bathing as Science: Ancient Sea Cures Gain Support from New Research. *Condé Nast Traveler* 29(12):86–90.

Lewis, Oscar. 1966. The Culture of Poverty. *Scientific American* 215:19–25.

Leynaud, Emile. 1961. Fraternités d'âge et sociétés de culture dans la Haute-Vallée du Niger. *Cahiers d'Etudes Africaines* 6:41–68.

Lightfoot, David. 2006. *How New Languages Emerge*. New York: Cambridge University Press.

Lincoln, Kenneth. 1993. *Indi'n Humor: Bicultural Play in Native America*. New York: Oxford University Press.

Lindenbaum, Shirley. 1979. *Kuru Sorcery: Disease and Danger in the New Guinea Highlands*. Mountain View, CA: Mayfield Publishing.

Linnekan, Jocelyn. 1990. *Sacred Queens and Women of Consequence: Rank, Gender, and Colonialism in the Hawaiian Islands*. Ann Arbor: University of Michigan Press.

Lipka, Jerry, Maureen P. Hogan, Joan Parker Webster, Evelyn Yanez, Barbara Adams, Stacy Clark, and Doreen Lacy. 2005. Math in a Cultural Context: Two Case Studies of a Successful Culturally Based Math Project. *Anthropology and Education Quarterly* 36(4):367–385.

Lloyd, Cynthia B. 1995. *Household Structure and Poverty: What Are the Connections?* Working Papers, No. 74. New York: The Population Council.

Lock, Margaret. 1993. *Encounters with Aging: Mythologies of Menopause in Japan and North America*. Berkeley: University of California Press.

Loker, William. 1993. Human Ecology of Cattle-Raising in the Peruvian Amazon: The View from the Farm. *Human Organization* 52(1): 14–24.

———. 2000. Sowing Discord, Planting Doubts: Rhetoric and Reality in an Environment and Development Project in Honduras. *Human Organization* 59:300–310.

———. 2003. Dam Impacts in a Time of Globalization: Using Multiple Methods to Document Social and Environmental Change in Rural Honduras. *Current Anthropology* 44(supplement):S112–S121.

Long, Susan Orpett. 2005. *Final Days: Japanese Culture and Choice at the End of Life.* Honolulu: University of Hawai'i Press.

Lorch, Donatella. 2003. Do Read This for War. *Newsweek* 141(11):13.

Low, Setha M. 1995. Indigenous Architecture and the Spanish American Plaza in Mesoamerica and the Caribbean. *American Anthropologist* 97(4):748–762.

Lubkemann, Stephen C. 2002. Refugees. In *World at Risk: A Global Issues Sourcebook* (pp. 522–544). Washington, DC: CQ Press.

———. 2005. Migratory Coping in Wartime Mozambique: An Anthropology of Violence and Displacement in "Fragmented Wars." *Journal of Peace Research* 42:493–508.

Lutz, Catherine. 2002. Making War at Home in the United States: Militarization and the Current Crisis. *American Anthropologist* 104: 723–735.

Lutz, Ellen L. 2005. The Many Meanings of Technology: A Message from our Executive Editor. *Cultural Survival Quarterly* 29(2):5.

Lyman, Rick. 2006. Reports Reveal Hurricanes' Impact on Human Landscape. *New York Times,* May 6, p. A16.

Lyttleton, Chris. 2004. Relative Pleasures: Drugs, Development and Modern Dependencies in Asia's Golden Triangle. *Development and Change* 35:909–935.

Maclachlan, Morgan. 1983. *Why They Did Not Starve: Biocultural Adaptation in a South Indian Village.* Philadelphia: Institute for the Study of Human Issues.

MacLeod, Arlene Elowe. 1992. Hegemonic Relations and Gender Resistance: The New Veiling as Accommodating Protest in Cairo. *Signs: The Journal of Women in Culture and Society* 17(3):533–557.

Macnair, Peter. 1995. From Kwakiutl to Kwakwa ka̲'wakw. In *Native Peoples: The Canadian Experience,* 2nd ed. (pp. 586–605). R. Bruce Morrison and C. Roderick Wilson, eds. Toronto: McClelland & Stewart.

Maffi, Luisa. 2003. The "Business" of Language Endangerment: Saving Language or Helping People Keep Them Alive? In *Language in the Twenty-First Century: Selected Papers of the Millenial Conference of the Center for Research and Documentation on World Language Problems* (pp. 67–86). H. Tonkin and T. Reagan, eds. Amsterdam: John Benjamins.

———. 2005. Linguistic, Cultural, and Biological Diversity. *Annual Review of Anthropology* 34:599–617.

Magga, Ole Henrik and Tove Skutnabb-Kangas. 2001. The Saami Languages: The Present and the Future. *Cultural Survival Quarterly* 25(2):26–31.

Magliocco, Sabina. 2004. *Witching Culture: Folklore and Neo-Paganism in America.* Philadelphia: University of Pennsylvania Press.

Mahler, Sarah J. 1995. *Salvadorans in Suburbia: Symbiosis and Conflict.* Boston: Allyn and Bacon.

Major, Marc R. 1996. No Friends but the Mountains: A Simulation on Kurdistan. *Social Education* 60(3):C1–C8.

Makepeace, James M. 1997. Courtship Violence as Process: A Developmental Theory. In *Violence between Intimate Partners: Patterns, Causes, and Effects* (pp. 29–47). Albert P. Cardarelli, ed. Boston: Allyn and Bacon.

Malinowski, Bronislaw. 1929. *The Sexual Life of Savages.* New York: Harcourt, Brace & World.

———. 1961 [1922]. *Argonauts of the Western Pacific.* New York: E. P. Dutton & Co.

———. 1962 [1926]. *Crime and Custom in Savage Society.* Paterson, NJ: Littlefield, Adams & Co.

Mamdani, Mahmoud. 1972. *The Myth of Population Control: Family, Caste, and Class in an Indian Village.* New York: Monthly Review Press.

———. 2002. Good Muslim, Bad Muslim: A Political Perspective on Culture and Terrorism. *American Anthropologist* 104:766–775.

Manuelito, Katheryn. 2005. The Role of Education in American Indian Self-Determination: Lessons from the Ramah Community School. *Anthropology and Education Quarterly* 36:73–87.

Manz, Beatriz. 2004. *Paradise in Ashes: A Guatemalan Journey of Courage, Terror, and Hope.* Berkeley: University of California Press.

March, Kathryn S. and Rachell L. Taqqu. 1986. *Women's Informal Associations in Developing Countries: Catalysts for Change?* Boulder, CO: Westview Press.

Marcoux, Alan. 2000. *The Feminization of Poverty: Facts, Hypotheses, and the Art of Advocacy.* www.undp.org.popin.fao.womnpoor.htm.

Marcus, George. 1995. Ethnography in/of the World System: The Emergence of Multi-Sited Ethnography. *Annual Review of Anthropology* 24:95–117.

Margolis, Maxine. 1994. *Little Brazil: An Ethnography of Brazilian Immigrants in New York City.* Princeton, NJ: Princeton University Press.

Margolis, Maxine L. and Marigene Arnold. 1993. Turning the Tables? Male Strippers and the Gender Hierarchy in America. In *Sex and Gender Hierarchies* (pp. 334–350). Barbara D. Miller, ed. New York: Cambridge University Press.

Marshall, Robert C. 1985. Giving a Gift to the Hamlet: Rank, Solidarity and Productive Exchange in Rural Japan. *Ethnology* 24:167–182.

Martin, Richard C. 1995. Islam. In *The HarperCollins Dictionary of Religion* (pp. 498–513). Jonathan Z. Smith, ed. New York: HarperCollins.

Martin, Sarah. 2005. *Must Boys Be Boys?: Ending Sexual Exploitation and Abuse in UN Peacekeeping Missions.* Washington, DC: Refugees International.

Martínez, Samuel. 1996. Indifference with Indignation: Anthropology, Human Rights, and the Haitian Bracero. *American Anthropologist* 98(1):17–25.

Masquelier, Adeline. 2005. The Scorpion's Sting: Youth, Marriage and the Struggle for Social Maturity in Niger. *Journal of the Royal Anthropological Institute* 11:59–83.

Massiah, Joycelin. 1983. *Women as Heads of Households in the Caribbean: Family Structure and Feminine Status.* Paris: UNESCO.

May, Ann. 2003. *Masai Migrations: Implications for HIV/AIDS and Social Change in Tanzania.* Boulder: University of Colorado at Boulder, Institute of Behavioral Science, Population Aging Center, Working Paper PAC2003-0001.

Maybury-Lewis, David. 1997a. Museums and Indigenous Cultures. *Cultural Survival Quarterly* 21(1):3.

———. 1997b. *Indigenous Peoples, Ethnic Groups, and the State.* Boston: Allyn and Bacon.

———. 2002. Genocide against Indigenous Peoples. In *Annihilating Difference: The Anthropology of Genocide* (pp. 43–53). Alexander Laban Hinton, ed. Berkeley: University of California Press.

McCallum, Cecilia. 2005. Explaining Caesarean Section in Salvador da Bahia, Brazil. *Sociology of Health and Illness* 27(2):215–242.

McCallum, Cecilia and Ana Paula dos Reis. 2005. Childbirth as Ritual in Brazil: Young Mothers' Experiences. *Ethnos* 70(3):335–360.

McCully, Patrick. 2003. Big Dams, Big Trouble. *New Internationalist* 354:14–15.

McDonald, James H. 2005. The Narcoeconomy in Small-town, Rural Mexico. *Human Organization* 64:115–125.

McElroy, Ann and Patricia K. Townsend. 1996. *Medical Anthropology in Ecological Perspective,* 3rd ed. Boulder, CO: Westview Press.

McMahon, April M. S. 1994. *Understanding Language Change.* New York: Cambridge University Press.

Mead, Margaret. 1928 [1961]. *Coming of Age in Samoa: A Psychological Study of Primitive Youth for Western Civilization.* New York: Dell Publishing.

———. 1963 [1935]. *Sex and Temperament in Three Primitive Societies.* New York: William Morrow.

———. 1986. Field Work in the Pacific Islands, 1925–1967. In *Women in the Field: Anthropological Experiences* (pp. 293–331). Peggy Golde, ed. Berkeley: University of California Press.

Meador, Elizabeth. 2005. The Making of Marginality: Schooling for Mexican Immigrants in the Rural Southwest. *Anthropology and Education Quarterly* 36(2):149–164.

Meigs, Anna S. 1984. *Food, Sex, and Pollution: A New Guinea Religion.* New Brunswick, NJ: Rutgers University Press.

Mencher, Joan P. 1974. The Caste System Upside Down, or The Not-So-Mysterious East. *Current Anthropology* 15(4):469–493.

Mernissi, Fatima. 1987. *Beyond the Veil: Male-Female Dynamics in Modern Muslim Society.* Revised edition. Bloomington: Indiana University Press.

Merry, Sally Engle. 1992. Anthropology, Law, and Transnational Processes. *Annual Review of Anthropology* 21:357–379.

———. 2006. *Human Rights and Gender Violence: Translating International Law into Local Justice.* Chicago: University of Chicago Press.

Messer, Ellen. 1993. Anthropology and Human Rights. *Annual Review of Anthropology* 22:221–249.

Michaelson, Evelyn Jacobson and Walter Goldschmidt. 1971. Female Roles and Male Dominance among Peasants. *Southwestern Journal of Anthropology* 27:330–352.

Michaud, Catherine M., W. Scott Gordon, and Michael R. Reich. 2005. *The Global Burden of Disease Due to Schistosomiasis.* Cambridge: Harvard School of Public Health, Harvard Center for Population and Development Studies, Schistosomiasis Research Program Working Paper Series. Volume 14, Number 1.

Migration Information Source. 2003. *Global Data.* www.migrationinformation.org/GlobalData/countrydata.

Miller, Barbara D. 1997 [1981]. *The Endangered Sex: Neglect of Female Children in Rural North India,* 2nd ed. New Delhi: Oxford University Press.

———. 1993. Surveying the Anthropology of Sex and Gender Hierarchies. In *Sex and Gender Hierarchies* (pp. 3–31). Barbara D. Miller, ed. New York: Cambridge University Press.

———. 2005. Putting People First to Strengthen Cultural Heritage Advocacy: Rationale, Results, and an Advocacy Tool. Paper presented at the Workshop on Preserving the World's Heritage, Cumberland, SC, October.

Miller, Barbara D. and Carl Stone. 1983. *The Low-Income Household Expenditure Survey: Description and Analysis.* Jamaica Tax Structure Examination Project, Staff Paper No. 25. Syracuse, NY: Metropolitan Studies Program, Syracuse University.

Miller, Barbara D. and Showkat Hayat Khan. 1986. Incorporating Voluntarism into Rural Development in Bangladesh. *Third World Planning Review* 8(2):139–152.

Miller, Bruce G. 1994. Contemporary Native Women: Role Flexibility and Politics. *Anthropologica* 36:57–72.

Miller, Daniel, ed. 2001. *Car Cultures.* New York: Berg.

Miller, Daniel. 2003. Could the Internet Defetishise the Commodity? *Environment and Planning D: Society and Space* 21:359–372.

Miller, Laura. 2004. Those Naughty Teenage Girls: Japanese Kogals, Slang, and Media Assessments. *Journal of Linguistic Anthropology* 14:225–247.

Mills, Mary Beth. 1995. Attack of the Widow Ghosts: Gender, Death, and Modernity in Northeast Thailand. In *Bewitching Women, Pious Men: Gender and Body Politics in Southeast Asia* (pp. 44–273).

Aihwa Ong and Michael G. Peletz, eds. Berkeley: University of California Press.

Milton, Katherine. 1992. Civilization and Its Discontents. *Natural History* 3(92):37–92.

Miner, Horace. 1965 [1956]. Body Ritual among the Nacirema. In *Reader in Comparative Religion: An Anthropological Approach* (pp. 414–418). William A. Lessa and Evon Z. Vogt, eds. New York: Harper & Row.

Mines, Mattison. 1994. *Public Faces, Private Voices: Community and Individuality in South India.* Berkeley: University of California Press.

Mintz, Sidney. 1985. *Sweetness and Power: The Place of Sugar in Modern History.* New York: Viking.

Mitchell, Bruce. 1994. Sustainable Development at the Village Level in Bali, Indonesia. *Human Ecology* 22(2):189–211.

Mitter, Partha. 1977. *Much Maligned Monsters: A History of European Reactions to Indian Art.* Chicago: University of Chicago Press.

Miyazawa, Setsuo. 1992. *Policing in Japan: A Study on Making Crime.* Frank G. Bennett, Jr. with John O. Haley, trans. Albany: State University of New York Press.

Moberg, Mark. 1991. Citrus and the State: Factions and Class Formation in Rural Belize. *American Ethnologist* 18(20):215–233.

Modell, Judith S. 1994. *Kinship with Strangers: Adoption and Interpretations of Kinship in American Culture.* Berkeley: University of California Press.

Moerman, Daniel. 2002. *Meaning, Medicine and the "Placebo" Effect.* New York: Cambridge University Press.

Mogelonsky, Marcia. 1995. Asian-Indian Americans. *American Demographics* 17(8):32–39.

Montesquieu, Charles. 1949 [1748]. *The Spirit of the Laws.* Trans. T. Nugent. New York: Hafner.

Montgomery, Heather. 2001. *Modern Babylon: Prostituting Children in Thailand.* New York: Bergahn Books.

Moore, Carmella C. and Holly F. Mathews. 2001. Introduction: The Psychology of Cultural Experience. In *The Psychology of Cultural Experience* (pp. 1–18). Carmella C. Moore and Holly F. Mathews, eds. New York: Macmillan.

Moore, John H. 1999. *The Cheyenne.* Malden, MA: Blackwell Publishers.

Morris, Brian. 1998. *The Power of Animals: An Ethnography.* New York: Berg.

Morris, Rosalind. 1994. Three Sexes and Four Sexualities: Redressing the Discourses on Gender and Sexuality in Contemporary Thailand. *Positions* 2:15–43.

Mortland, Carol A. 1994. Khmer Buddhism in the United States: Ultimate Questions. In *Cambodian Culture Since 1975: Homeland and Exile* (pp. 72–90). May M. Ebihara, Carol A. Mortland, and Judy Ledgerwood, eds. Ithaca, NY: Cornell University Press.

Muecke, Marjorie A. 1987. Resettled Refugees: Reconstruction of Identity of Lao in Seattle. *Urban Anthropology* 16(3–4):273–289.

Mukerjee, Madhusree. 2005. Lessons on Island Living. Samar: South Asian Magazine for Action and Reflection. www.samarmagazine.org/archive/article

Mulk, Inga-Maria. 1994. Sacrificial Places and Their Meaning in Saami Society. In *Sacred Sites, Sacred Places* (pp. 121–131). David L. Carmichael, Jane Hubert, Brian Reeves, and Audhild Schanche, eds. New York: Routledge.

Mull, Dorothy S. and J. Dennis Mull. 1987. Infanticide among the Tarahumara of the Mexican Sierra Madre. In *Child Survival: Anthropological Perspectives on the Treatment and Maltreatment of Children* (pp. 113–132). Nancy Scheper-Hughes, ed. Boston: D. Reidel Publishing.

Mullings, Leith. 2005. Towards an Anti-Racist Anthropology: Interrogating Racism. *Annual Review of Anthropology* 34:667–693.

Murdock, George Peter. 1965 [1949]. *Social Structure.* New York: Free Press.

Murphy, Yolanda and Robert F. Murphy. 1985. *Women of the Forest*. New York: Columbia University Press.

Murray, Gerald F. 1987. The Domestication of Wood in Haiti: A Case Study of Applied Evolution. In *Anthropological Praxis: Translating Knowledge into Action* (pp. 233–240). Robert M. Wulff and Shirley J. Fiske, eds. Boulder, CO: Westview Press.

Myerhoff, Barbara. 1978. *Number Our Days*. New York: Simon and Schuster.

Myers, James. 1992. Nonmainstream Body Modification: Genital Piercing, Branding, Burning, and Cutting. *Journal of Contemporary Ethnography* 21(3):267–306.

Myers, Norman. 2000. Sustainable Consumption. *Science* 287 (March 31):2419.

Nadeau, Kathleen M. 2002. *Liberation Theology in the Philippines: Faith in a Revolution*. Westport: Praeger.

Nader, Laura. 1972. Up the Anthropologist—Perspectives Gained from Studying Up. In *Reinventing Anthropology* (pp. 284–311). Dell Hymes, ed. New York: Vintage Books.

———. 1995. Civilization and Its Negotiations. In *Understanding Disputes: The Politics of Argument* (pp. 39–64). Pat Caplan, ed. Providence, RI: Berg Publishers.

———. 2001. Harmony Coerced Is Freedom Denied. *The Chronicle of Higher Education*. July 13:B1.

Nag, Moni. 1972. Sex, Culture and Human Fertility: India and the United States. *Current Anthropology* 13:231–238.

———. 1983. Modernization Affects Fertility. *Populi* 10:56–77.

Nag, Moni, Benjamin N. F. White, and R. Creighton Peet. 1978. An Anthropological Approach to the Study of the Economic Value of Children in Java and Nepal. *Current Anthropology* 19(2):293–301.

Nanda, Serena. 1990. *Neither Man nor Woman: The Hijras of India*. Belmont, CA: Wadsworth.

———. 1994. *Cultural Anthropology*. Wadsworth, CA: Wadsworth.

Natcher, David C., Susan Davis, and Clifford G. Hickey. 2005. Co-Management: Managing Relationships, Not Resources. *Human Organization* 64:240–250.

National Park Service. 2005. *Low Country Gullah Culture: Special Resource Study and Final Environmental Impact Statement*. Atlanta: NPS Southeast Regional Office. www.nps.gov.

Neff, Deborah L. 1994. The Social Construction of Infertility: The Case of the Matrilineal Nayars in South India. *Social Science and Medicine* 39(4):475–485.

Nettle, Daniel and Suzanne Romaine. 2000. *Vanishing Voices: The Extinction of the World's Languages*. New York: Oxford University Press.

Neusner, Jacob. 1995. Judaism. In *The HarperCollins Dictionary of Religion* (pp. 598–607). Jonathan Z. Smith, ed. New York: HarperCollins.

Nevins, M. Eleanor. 2004. Learning to Listen: Confronting Two Meanings of Language Loss in the Contemporary White Mountain Apache Speech Community. *Journal of Linguistic Anthropology* 14:269–288.

Newman, Katherine. 1998. Place and Race: Midlife Experiences in Harlem. In *Welcome to Middle Age! (And Other Fictions)* (pp. 259–293). Richard A. Shweder, ed. Chicago: University of Chicago Press.

Newman, Lucile. 1972. *Birth Control: An Anthropological View*. Module No. 27. Reading, MA: Addison-Wesley.

Newman, Lucile, ed. 1985. *Women's Medicine: A Cross-Cultural Study of Indigenous Fertility Regulation*. New Brunswick: Rutgers University Pres.

Ngokwey, Ndolamb. 1988. Pluralistic Etiological Systems in Their Social Context: A Brazilian Case Study. *Social Science and Medicine* 26:793–802.

Nichter, Mark. 1992. Of Ticks, Kings, Spirits and the Promise of Vaccines. In *Paths to Asian Medical Knowledge* (pp. 224–253). Charles Leslie and Allan Young, eds. Berkeley: University of California Press.

———. 1996. Vaccinations in the Third World: A Consideration of Community Demand. In *Anthropology and International Health: Asian Case Studies* (pp. 329–365). Mark Nichter and Mimi Nichter, eds. Amsterdam: Gordon and Breach Publishers.

Nichter, Mimi. 2000. *Fat Talk: What Girls and Their Parents Say about Dieting*. Cambridge, MA: Harvard University Press.

Nodwell, Evelyn and Neil Guppy. 1992. The Effects of Publicly Displayed Ethnicity on Interpersonal Discrimination: Indo-Canadians in Vancouver. *The Canadian Review of Sociology and Anthropology* 29(1):87–99.

Nordstrom, Carolyn. 1997. *A Different Kind of War Story*. Philadelphia: University of Pennsylvania Press.

Norgaard, Richard B. 1994. *Development Betrayed: The End of Progress and the Coevolutionary Revisioning of the Future*. New York: Routledge.

Nyambedha, Erick Otieno, Simiyu Wandibba, and Jens Aagaard-Hansen. 2003. Changing Patterns of Orphan Care Due to the HIV Epidemic in Western Kenya. *Social Science and Medicine* 57:301–311.

Obeyesekere, Gananath. 1981. *Medusa's Hair: An Essay on Personal Symbols and Religious Experience*. Chicago: University of Chicago Press.

Ochs, Elinor. 1993. Indexing Gender. In *Sex and Gender Hierarchies* (pp. 146–169). Barbara D. Miller, ed. New York: Cambridge University Press.

Ohnuki-Tierney, Emiko. 1980. Shamans and Imu: Among Two Ainu Groups. In *The Culture-Bound Syndromes* (pp. 91–110). Ronald C. Simons and Charles C. Hughes, eds. Dordrecht: D. Reidel Publishing.

———. 1994. Brain Death and Organ Transplantation: Cultural Bases of Medical Technology. *Current Anthropology* 35(3):233–242.

Oinas, Felix J. 1993. Couvade in Estonia. *Slavic & East European Journal* 37(3):339–345.

Oliver-Smith, Anthony. 2002. Theorizing Disasters: Nature, Power, and Culture. In *Catastrophe and Culture: The Anthropology of Disaster* (pp. 23–47). Anthony Oliver-Smith and Susannah Hoffman, eds. Sante Fe, NM: School of American Research Press.

Oloi-Dapash, Meitamei. 2002. Mau Forest Destruction: Human and Ecological Disaster in the Making. *Cultural Survival Voices* 1(3):1, 9.

Olsen, Teresa, Gabrielle M. Maxwell, and Allison Morris. 1995. Maori and Youth Justice in New Zealand. In *Popular Justice and Community Regeneration: Pathways of Indigenous Reform* (pp. 45–65). Kayleen M. Hazlehurst, ed. Westport, CT: Praeger.

Ong, Aihwa. 1987. *Spirits of Resistance and Capitalist Discipline: Factory Women in Malaysia*. Albany: State University of New York Press.

———. 1995. State versus Islam: Malay Families, Women's Bodies, and the Body Politic in Malaysia. In *Bewitching Women, Pious Men: Gender and Body Politics in Southeast Asia* (pp. 159–194). Aihwa Ong and Michael G. Peletz, eds. Berkeley: University of California Press.

———. 2003. *Buddha Is Hiding: Refugees, Citizenship, the New America*. Berkeley: University of California Press.

Ongley, Patrick. 1995. Post–1945 International Migration: New Zealand, Australia and Canada Compared. *International Migration Review* 29(3):765–793.

Ortner, Sherry. 1999. *Life and Death on Mt. Everest: Sherpas and Himalayan Mountaineering*. Princeton, NJ: Princeton University Press.

Paine, Robert. 2004. Saami Reindeer Pastoralism: Quo Vadis? *Ethnos* 69:23–42.

Painter, Andrew A. 1996. The Telerepresentation of Gender. In *Re-Imaging Japanese Women* (pp. 46–72). Anne E. Imamura, ed. Berkeley: University of California Press.

Paley, Julia. 2002. Toward an Anthropology of Democracy. *Annual Review of Anthropology* 31:469–496.

Pang, Keum Young Chung. 1994. Understanding Depression among Elderly Korean Immigrants through Their Folk Illnesses. *Medical Anthropology Quarterly* 8(2):209–216.

Panter-Brick, Catherine and Malcolm T. Smith, eds. 2000. *Abandoned Children*. New York: Cambridge University Press.

Pappas, Gregory. 1989. *The Magic City: Unemployment in a Working-Class Community*. Ithaca, NY: Cornell University Press.

Parker, Richard G. 1991. *Bodies, Pleasures, and Passions: Sexual Culture in Contemporary Brazil*. Boston: Beacon Press.

Parrillo, Vincent N. 1997. *Strangers to These Shores: Race and Ethnic Relations in the United States*. Boston: Allyn and Bacon.

Parry, Jonathan P. 1996. Caste. In *The Social Science Encyclopedia* (pp. 76–77). Adam Kuper and Jessica Kuper, eds. New York: Routledge.

Pasquino, Gianfranco. 1996. Democratization. In *The Social Science Encyclopedia* (pp. 173–174). Adam Kuper and Jessica Kuper, eds. Routledge: New York.

Patterson, Thomas C. 2001. *A Social History of Anthropology in the United States*. New York: Berg.

Paxson, Heather. 2003. With or Against Nature: IVF, Gender and Reproductive Agency in Athens, Greece. *Social Science and Medicine* 56:1853–1866.

Peacock, James L. and Dorothy C. Holland. 1993. The Narrated Self: Life Stories in Process. *Ethos* 21(4):367–383.

Pedelty, Mark. 1995. *War Stories: The Culture of Foreign Correspondents*. New York: Routledge.

Peletz, Michael. 1987. The Exchange of Men in 19th-Century Negeri Sembilan (Malaya). *American Ethnologist* 14(3):449–469.

———. 2006. Transgenderism and Gender Pluralism in Southeast Asia since Early Modern Times. *Current Anthropology* 47(2):309–325, 333–340.

Pelto, Pertti. 1973. *The Snowmobile Revolution: Technology and Social Change in the Arctic*. Menlo Park, CA: Cummings.

Pelto, Pertti, Maria Roman, and Nelson Liriano. 1982. Family Structures in An Urban Puerto Rican Community. *Urban Anthropology* 11:39–58.

Peng Xizhe. 1991. *Demographic Transition in China: Fertility Trends Since the 1950s*. New York: Oxford University Press.

People's Daily. 2003. Xi'an Protects Oldest Residential Area. April 9.

Perin, Constance. 1988. *Belonging in America: Reading between the Lines*. Madison: University of Wisconsin Press.

Perry, Richard J. 1996. *From Time Immemorial: Indigenous Peoples and State Systems*. Austin: University of Texas Press.

Pessar, Patricia R. 1995. *A Visa for a Dream: Dominicans in the United States*. Boston: Allyn and Bacon.

Petras, James and Tienchai Wongchaisuwan. 1993. Free Markets, AIDS and Child Prostitution. *Economic and Political Weekly*, March 13: 440–442.

Pfeiffer, James. 2004. Condom Social Marketing, Pentecostalism, and Structural Adjustment in Mozambique: A Clash of AIDS Prevention Messages. *Medical Anthropology Quarterly* 18:77–103.

Pieterse, Jan Nederveen. 2004. *Globalization and Culture*. Global Mélange. New York: Rowman and Littlefield.

Pillsbury, Barbara. 1990. The Politics of Family Planning: Sterilization and Human Rights in Bangladesh. In *Births and Power: Social Change and the Politics of Reproduction* (pp. 165–196). W. Penn Handwerker, ed. Boulder, CO: Westview Press.

Plant, Roger. 1994. *Land Rights and Minorities*. London: Minority Rights Group.

———. 1998. *Issues in Indigenous Poverty*. Washington, DC: Inter-american Development Bank. No. IND-105.

Plattner, Stuart. 1989. Markets and Marketplaces. In *Economic Anthropology* (pp. 171–208). Stuart Plattner, ed. Stanford, CA: Stanford University Press.

Poirier, Sylvie. 1992. "Nomadic" Rituals: Networks of Ritual Exchange between Women of the Australian Western Desert. *Man* 27:757–776.

Population Reference Bureau. 2005. *2005 World Population Data Sheet*. Washington, DC: Population Reference Bureau.

Posey, Darrell Addison. 1990. Intellectual Property Rights: What Is the Position of Ethnobiology? *Journal of Ethnobiology* 10:93–98.

Postgate, Nicholas, Tao Wang, and Toby Wilkinson. 1995. The Evidence for Early Writing: Utilitarian or Ceremonial? *Antiquity* 69: 459–480.

Potter, Jack M. 1976. *Thai Peasant Social Structure*. Chicago: University of Chicago Press.

Potter, Sulamith Heins. 1977. *Family Life in a Northern Thai Village: A Study in the Structural Significance of Women*. Berkeley: University of California Press.

Price, David. 2003. Personal communication, response to "Six Questions Survey," author's files, Washington, DC.

Price, David H. 1995. Water Theft in Egypt's Fayoum Oasis: Emics, Etics, and the Illegal. In *Science, Materialism, and the Study of Culture* (pp. 96–110). Martin F. Murphy and Maxine L. Margolis, eds. Gainesville: University of Florida Press.

———. 2004. *Threatening Anthropology: McCarthyism and the FBI's Surveillance of Activist Anthropologists*. Durham, NC: Duke University Press.

Purdum, Elizabeth D. and J. Anthony Paredes. 1989. *Facing the Death Penalty: Essays on Cruel and Unusual Punishment*. Philadelphia: Temple University Press.

Radcliffe-Brown, A. R. 1964 [1922]. *The Andaman Islanders*. New York: Free Press.

Raheja, Gloria Goodwin. 1988. *The Poison in the Gift: Ritual, Presentation, and the Dominant Caste in a North Indian Village*. Chicago: University of Chicago Press.

Ramesh, A., C. R. Srikumari, and S. Sukumar. 1989. Parallel Cousin Marriages in Madras, Tamil Nadu: New Trends in Dravidian Kinship. *Social Biology* 36(3/4):248–254.

Ramphele, Mamphela. 1996. Political Widowhood in South Africa: The Embodiment of Ambiguity. *Daedalus* 125(1):99–17.

Raphael, Dana. 1975. Matrescence: Becoming a Mother: A "New/Old" *Rite de Passage*. In *Being Female: Reproduction, Power and Change* (pp. 65–72). Dana Raphael, ed. The Hague: Mouton Publishers.

Rapoport, Tamar, Yoni Garb, and Anat Penso. 1995. Religious Socialization and Female Subjectivity: Religious-Zionist Adolescent Girls in Israel. *Sociology of Education* 68:48–61.

Rapp, Rayna. 1993. Reproduction and Gender Hierarchy: Amniocentesis in America. In *Sex and Gender Hierarchies* (pp. 108–126). Barbara D. Miller, ed. New York: Cambridge University Press.

Rathje, William and Cullen Murphy. 1992. *Rubbish! The Archaeology of Garbage*. New York: Harper & Row.

Ravaillon, Martin. 2003. The Debate on Globalization, Poverty and Inequality: Why Income Measurement Matters. *International Affairs* 79:739–753.

Rehbun, L. A. 1994. Swallowing Frogs: Anger and Illness in Northeast Brazil. *Medical Anthropology Quarterly* 8:360–382.

Reid, Russell M. 1992. Cultural and Medical Perspectives on Geophagia. *Medical Anthropology* 13:337–351.

Reiner, R. 1996. Police. In *The Social Science Encyclopedia* (pp. 619–621). Adam Kuper and Jessica Kuper, eds. New York: Routledge.

Rende Taylor, Lisa. 2005. Dangerous Trade-Offs: The Behavioral Ecology of Child Labor and Prostitution in Rural Northern Thailand. *Current Anthropology* 46:411–423, 428–431.

Reyna, Stephen P. 1994. A Mode of Domination Approach to Organized Violence. In *Studying War: Anthropological Perspectives* (pp. 29–65). S. P. Reyna and R. E. Downs, eds. Langhorne, PA: Gordon and Breach Science Publishers.

Rhodes, Lorna A. 2001. Toward an Anthropology of Prisons. *Annual Review of Anthropology* 30:65–83.

Rich, Bruce. 1994. *Mortgaging the Earth: The World Bank, Environmental Impoverishment, and the Crisis of Development*. Boston: Beacon Press.

Rickford, John. 1997. Unequal Partnership: Sociolinguistics and the African American Speech Community. *Language in Society* 26:161–198.

Robertson, Jennifer. 1991. *Native and Newcomer: Making and Remaking a Japanese City*. Berkeley: University of California Press.

Robins, Kevin. 1996. Globalization. In *The Social Science Encyclopedia*, 2nd ed. (pp. 345–346). Adam Kuper and Jessica Kuper, eds. New York: Routledge.

Robson, Colin. 1993. *Real World Research: A Resource for Social Scientists and Practitioner-Researchers*. Cambridge, MA: Blackwell Publishers.

Rogers, Barbara. 1979. *The Domestication of Women: Discrimination in Developing Societies*. New York: St. Martin's Press.

Rosaldo, Renato. 1980. *Ilongot Headhunting 1883–1974: A Study in Society and History*. Stanford, CA: Stanford University Press.

Roscoe, Will. 1991. *The Zuni Man-Woman*. Albuquerque: University of New Mexico Press.

Rose, Jerome C., Thomas J. Green, and Victoria D. Green. 1996. NAGPRA is Forever: Osteology and the Repatriation of Skeletons. *Annual Review of Anthropology* 25:81–103.

Roseman, Marina. 1987. Inversion and Conjuncture: Male and Female Performance among the Temiar of Peninsular Malaysia. In *Women and Music in Cross-Cultural Perspective* (pp. 131–149). Ellen Koskoff, ed. New York: Greenwood Press.

Rosenberger, Nancy. 1992. Images of the West: Home Style in Japanese Magazines. In *Re-made in Japan: Everyday Life and Consumer Taste in a Changing Society* (pp. 106–125). James J. Tobin, ed. New Haven, CT: Yale University Press.

Rosenblatt, Paul C., Patricia R. Walsh, and Douglas A. Jackson. 1976. *Grief and Mourning in Cross-Cultural Perspective*. New Haven, CT: HRAF Press.

Ross, Marc Howard. 1993. *The Culture of Conflict: Interpretations and Interests in Comparative Perspective*. New Haven, CT: Yale University Press.

Roy, Arundhati. 1999. *The Cost of Living*. New York: Modern Library.

Rubel, Arthur J., Carl W. O'Nell, and Rolando Collado-Ardon. 1984. *Susto: A Folk Illness*. Berkeley: University of California Press.

Rubin, Gayle. 1975. The Traffic in Women: Notes on the "Political Economy" of Sex. In *Toward an Anthropology of Women* (pp. 157–210). Rayna R, Rapp, ed. New York: Monthly Review Press.

Rylko-Bauer, Barbara, Merrill Singer, and John van Willigen. 2006. Reclaiming Applied Anthropology: Its Past, Present, and Future. *American Anthropologist* 108:178–190.

Sachs, Aaron. 1996. Dying for Oil. *WorldWatch,* June:10–21.

Sahlins, Marshall. 1963. Poor Man, Rich Man, Big Man, Chief. *Comparative Studies in Society and History* 5:285–303.

Saitoti, Tepilit Ole. 1986. *The Worlds of a Maasai Warrior*. New York: Random House.

Salam, Nawaf A. 1994. Between Repatriation and Resettlement: Palestinian Refugees in Lebanon. *Journal of Palestine Studies* 24:18–27.

Salamandra, Christa. 2004. *A New Old Damascus: Authenticity and Distinction in Urban Syria*. Bloomington: Indiana University Press.

Salih, M. A. Mohamed. 1999. Land Alienation and Genocide in the Nuba Mountains, Sudan. *Cultural Survival Quarterly* 22(4):36–38.

Sanday, Peggy Reeves. 1973. Toward a Theory of the Status of Women. *American Anthropologist* 75:1682–1700.

———. 1986. *Divine Hunger: Cannibalism as a Cultural System*. New York: Cambridge University Press.

———. 1990. *Fraternity Gang Rape: Sex, Brotherhood, and Privilege on Campus*. New York: New York University Press.

———. 1996. *A Woman Scorned: Date Rape on Trial*. New York: Doubleday.

———. 2002. *Women at the Center: Life in a Modern Matriarchy*. Ithaca, NY: Cornell University Press.

Sanders, Douglas E. 1999. Indigenous Peoples: Issues of Definition. *International Journal of Cultural Property* 8:4–13.

Sanders, William B. 1994. *Gangbangs and Drive-Bys: Grounded Culture and Juvenile Gang Violence*. New York: Aldine de Gruyter.

Sanjek, Roger. 1990. A Vocabulary for Fieldnotes. In *Fieldnotes: The Making of Anthropology* (pp. 92–138). Roger Sanjek, ed. Ithaca, NY: Cornell University Press.

———. 1994. The Enduring Inequalities of Race. In *Race* (pp. 1–17). Steven Gregory and Roger Sanjek, eds. New Brunswick, NJ: Rutgers University Press.

———. 2000. Keeping Ethnography Alive in an Urbanizing World. *Human Organization* 53:280–288.

Sant Cassia, Paul. 1993. Banditry, Myth, and Terror in Cyprus and Other Mediterranean Societies. *Comparative Studies in Society and History* 35(4):773–795.

Sargent, Carolyn F. 1989. *Maternity, Medicine, and Power: Reproductive Decisions in Urban Benin*. Berkeley: University of California Press.

———. 2005. Counselling Contraception for Malian Migrants in Paris: Global, State and Personal Politics. *Human Organization* 64:147–156.

Saugestad, Sidsel. 2001. *The Inconvenient Indigenous: Remote Area Development in Botswana, Donor Assistance, and the First People of the Kalahari*. Uppsala, Sweden: The Nordic Afrika Institute.

Sault, Nicole L. 1985. Baptismal Sponsorship as a Source of Power for Zapotec Women of Oaxaca, Mexico. *Journal of Latin American Lore* 11(2):225–243.

———. 1994. How the Body Shapes Parenthood: "Surrogate" Mothers in the United States and Godmothers in Mexico. In *Many Mirrors: Body Image and Social Relations* (pp. 292–318). Nicole Sault, ed. Brunswick, NJ: Rutgers University Press.

Savishinsky, Joel S. 1974. *The Trail of the Hare: Life and Stress in an Arctic Community*. New York: Gordon and Breach.

———. 1991. *The Ends of Time: Life and Work in a Nursing Home*. New York: Bergin & Garvey.

Schaft, Kai and David L. Brown. 2000. Social Capital and Grassroots Development: The Case of Roma Self-Governance in Hungary. *Social Problems* 47(2):201–219.

Scheper-Hughes, Nancy. 1990. Three Propositions for a Critically Applied Medical Anthropology. *Social Science and Medicine* 30(2):189–197.

———. 1992. *Death without Weeping: The Violence of Everyday Life in Brazil*. Berkeley: University of California Press.

Schlegel, Alice. 1995. A Cross-Cultural Approach to Adolescence. *Ethos* 23(1):15–32.

Schlegel, Alice and Herbert Barry III. 1991. *Adolescence: An Anthropological Inquiry*. New York: Free Press.

Schmid, Thomas J. and Richard S. Jones. 1993. Ambivalent Actions: Prison Adaptation Strategies of First-time, Short-term Inmates. *Journal of Contemporary Ethnography* 21(4):439–463.

Schneider, David M. 1968. *American Kinship: A Cultural Account*. Englewood Cliffs, NJ: Prentice-Hall.

Scott, James C. 1985. *Weapons of the Weak: Everyday Forms of Peasant Resistance*. New Haven, CT: Yale University Press.

———. 1998. *Seeing Like a State: How Certain Schemes to Improve the Human Condition Have Failed*. New Haven, CT: Yale University Press.

Scrimshaw, Susan. 1984. Infanticide in Human Populations: Societal and Individual Concerns. In *Infanticide: Comparative and Evolutionary Perspectives* (pp. 463–486). Glenn Hausfater and Sarah Blaffer Hrdy, eds. New York: Aldine.

Scudder, Thayer. 1973. The Human Ecology of Big Dam Projects: River Basin Development and Resettlement. *Annual Review of Anthropology* 2:45–55.

Sen, Amartya. 1981. *Poverty and Famines: An Essay on Entitlement and Deprivation*. New York: Oxford University Press.

Senghas, Richard J. and Leila Monaghan. 2002. Signs of Their Times: Deaf Communities and the Culture of Language. *Annual Review of Anthropology* 31:69–97.

Sentumbwe, Nayinda. 1995. Sighted Lovers and Blind Husbands: Experience of Blind Women in Uganda. In *Disability and Culture* (pp. 159–173). Benedicte Ingstad and Susan Reynolds, eds. Berkeley: University of California Press.

Shahrani, Nazif M. 2002. War, Factionalism, and the State in Afghanistan. *American Anthropologist* 104:715–722.

Shanklin, Eugenia. 2000. Representations of Race and Racism in American Anthropology. *Current Anthropology* 41(1):99–103.

Shapiro, Thomas M. 2004. *The Hidden Cost of Being African American*. New York: Oxford University Press.

Sharff, Jagna Wojcicka. 1995. "We Are All Chickens for the Colonel": A Cultural Materialist View of Prisons. In *Science, Materialism, and the Study of Culture* (pp. 132–158). Martin F. Murphy and Maxine L. Margolis, eds. Gainesville: University of Florida Press.

Sharp, Lesley. 1990. Possessed and Dispossessed Youth: Spirit Possession of School Children in Northwest Madagascar. *Culture, Medicine and Psychiatry* 14:339–364.

Shenhav-Keller, Shelly. 1993. The Israeli Souvenir: Its Text and Context. *Annals of Tourism Research* 20:182–196.

Sheriff, Robin E. 2000. Exposing Silence as Cultural Censorship: A Brazilian Case. *American Anthropologist* 102:114–132.

Shibamoto, Janet. 1987. The Womanly Woman: Manipulation of Stereotypical and Nonstereotypical Features of Japanese Female Speech. In *Language, Gender, and Sex in Comparative Perspective* (pp. 26–49). Susan U. Philips, Susan Steel, and Christine Tanz, eds. New York: Cambridge University Press.

Shipton, Parker. 2001. Money. In *The Dictionary of Anthropology* (pp. 327–329). Malden, MA: Blackwell Thomas Barfield, ed.

Shore, Bradd. 1998. Status Reversal: The Coming of Age in Samoa. In *Welcome to Middle Age! (And Other Cultural Fictions)* (pp. 101–138). Richard A. Shweder, ed. Chicago: University of Chicago Press.

Short, James F. 1996. Gangs. In *The Social Science Encyclopedia* (pp. 325–326). Adam Kuper and Jessica Kuper, eds. New York: Routledge.

Shostak, Marjorie. 1981. *Nisa: The Life and Times of a !Kung Woman*. Cambridge, MA: Harvard University Press.

Shu-Min, Huang. 1993. A Cross-Cultural Experience: A Chinese Anthropologist in the United States. In *Distance Mirrors: America as a Foreign Culture* (pp. 39–45). Philip R. DeVita and James D. Armstrong, eds. Belmont, CA: Wadsworth.

Shweder, Richard A. 1998. Preface. In *Welcome to Middle Age! (And Other Cultural Fictions)* (pp. vii–viii). Chicago: University of Chicago Press.

———. 2003. *Why Do Men Barbecue? Recipes for Cultural Psychology*. Cambridge, MA: Harvard University Press.

Sidnell, Jack. 2000. *Primus inter pares*: Storytelling and Male Peer Groups in an Indo-Guyanese Rumshop. *American Ethnologist* 27:72–99.

Silva, Noenoe K. 2004. *Aloha Betrayed: Native Hawaiian Resistance to American Colonialism*. Durham, NC: Duke University Press.

Silver, Ira. 1993. Marketing Authenticity in Third World Countries. *Annals of Tourism Research* 20:302–318.

Silverstein, Michael. 1997. Encountering Language and Languages of Encounter in North American Ethnohistory. *Journal of Linguistic Anthropology* 6:126–144.

Singer, Merrill, Tom Stopka, Susan Shaw, Cludia Santelices, David Buchanan, Wei Tang, Kaveh Khooshnood, and Robert Heimer. 2005. Lessons from the Field: From Research to Application in the Fight Against AIDS among Injection Drug Users in Three New England Cities. *Human Organization* 64(2):179–191.

Singh, K. S. 1994. *The Scheduled Tribes. Anthropological Survey of India, People of India, National Series Volume III*. Delhi: Oxford University Press.

Siskind, Janet. 1992. The Invention of Thanksgiving: A Ritual of American Nationality. *Critique of Anthropology* 12(2):167–191.

Skinner, G. William. 1993. Conjugal Power in Tokugawa Japanese Families: A Matter of Life or Death. In *Sex and Gender Hierarchies* (pp. 236–270). Barbara D. Miller, ed. New York: Cambridge University Press.

Skocpol, Theda. 1979. *States and Social Revolutions: A Comparative Analysis of France, Russia, and China*. New York: Cambridge University Press.

Slocum, Sally. 1975. Woman the Gatherer: Male Bias in Anthropology. In *Toward an Anthropology of Women* (pp. 36–50). Rayna R. Reiter, ed. New York: Monthly Review Press.

Smith, Jennie M. 2001. *When the Hands Are Many: Community Organization and Change in Rural Haiti*. Ithaca, NY: Cornell University Press.

Smith, Jonathan Z., ed. 1995. *The HarperCollins Dictionary of Religion*. New York: HarperCollins.

Smith, Laurajane, Anna Morgan, and Anita van der Meer. 2003. Community-driven Research in Cultural Heritage Management: The Waanyi Women's History Project. *International Journal of Heritage Studies* 9(1):65–80.

Smitherman, Geneva. 1997. "The Chain Remain the Same": Communicative Practices in the Hip Hop Nation. *Black Studies* 28(1):3–25.

Snajdr, Edward. 2005. Gender, Power, and the Performance of Justice: Muslim Women's Responses to Domestic Violence in Kazakhstan. *American Ethnologist* 32:294–311.

Sobel, Elizabeth and Gordon Bettles. 2000. Winter Hunger, Winter Myths: Subsistence Risk and Mythology among the Klamath and Modoc. *Journal of Anthropological Archaeology* 19:276–316.

Soh, Chunghee Sarah. 1993. *Women in Korean Politics*, 2nd ed. Boulder, CO: Westview Press.

Solomon, Maui and Leo Watson. 2001. The Waitungi Tribunal and the Māori Claim to the Cultural and Intellectual Heritage Rights Property. *Cultural Survival Quarterly* 24(4):46–50.

Sonenshein, Raphael J. 1996. The Battle over Liquor Stores in South Central Los Angeles: The Management of an Interminority Conflict. *Urban Affairs Review* 31(6):710–737.

Spatig, Linda, Kathy Seelinger, Amy Dillon, Laurel Parrott, and Kate Conrad. 2005. From an Ethnographic Team to a Feminist Learning Community: A Reflective Tale. *Human Organization* 64(1):103–113.

Sperber, Dan. 1985. *On Anthropological Knowledge: Three Essays*. New York: Cambridge University Press.

Spilde Contreras, Kate. 2006. Indian Gaming in California Brings Jobs and Income to Areas that Need It Most. Indian Gaming. www.indiangaming.com/regulatory/view/?id=35.

Spiro, Melford. 1967. *Burmese Supernaturalism: A Study in the Explanation and Reduction of Suffering*. Englewood Cliffs, NJ: Prentice-Hall.

———. 1990. On the Strange and the Familiar in Recent Anthropological Thought. In *Cultural Psychology: Essays on Comparative Human Development* (pp. 47–61). James W. Stigler, Richard A. Shweder, and Gilbert Herdt, eds. Chicago: University of Chicago Press.

Spitulnik, Deborah. 1993. Anthropology and Mass Media. *Annual Review of Anthropology* 22:293–315.

Srinivas, M. N. 1959. The Dominant Caste in Rampura. *American Anthropologist* 1:1–16.

Staats, Valerie. 1994. Ritual, Strategy or Convention: Social Meaning in Traditional Women's Baths in Morocco. *Frontiers: A Journal of Women's Studies* 14(3):1–18.

Stack, Carol. 1974. *All Our Kin: Strategies for Survival in a Black Community*. New York: Harper & Row.

Stanford, Craig B. 1999. *The Hunting Apes: Meat Eating and the Origins of Human Behavior*. Princeton: Princeton University Press.

Stanlaw, James. 1992. "For Beautiful Hjman Life": The Use of English in Japan. In *Re-Made in Japan: Everyday Life and Consumer Taste in a Changing Society* (pp. 58–76). Joseph J. Tobin, ed. New Haven, CT: Yale University Press.

Stein, Gertrude. 1948. *Picasso*. Boston: Beacon Press.

Stephen, Lynn. 1995. Women's Rights Are Human Rights: The Merging of Feminine and Feminist Interests among El Salvador's Mothers of the Disappeared (CO-MADRES). *American Ethnologist* 22(4): 807–827.

Stidsen, Sille, comp. and ed. Elaine Bolton, trans. 2006. *The Indigenous World 2006*. Rutger, NJ: Transaction Books.

Stillman, Amy Ku'uleialoha. 1996. Hawaiian Hula Competitions: Event, Repertoire, Performance and Tradition. *Journal of American Folklore* 109(434):357–380.

Stivens, Maila, Cecelia Ng, and Jomo K. S., with Jahara Bee. 1994. *Malay Peasant Women and the Land*. Atlantic Highlands, NJ: Zed Books.

Stocks, Anthony. 2005. Too Much for Too Few: Problems of Indigenous Land Rights in Latin America. *Annual Review of Anthropology* 34:85–104.

Stoler, Ann Laura. 1985. *Capitalism and Confrontation in Sumatra's Plantation Belt, 1870–1979*. New Haven, CT: Yale University Press.

Storper-Perez, Danielle and Harvey E. Goldberg. 1994. The Kotel: Toward an Ethnographic Portrait. *Religion* 24:309–332.

Strathern, Andrew. 1971. *The Rope of Moka: Big-Men and Ceremonial Exchange in Mount Hagen, New Guinea*. London: Cambridge University Press.

Stringer, Martin D. 1999. Rethinking Animism: Thoughts from the Infancy of Our Discipline. *Journal of the Royal Anthropological Institute* 5:541–556.

Stronza, Amanda. 2001. Anthropology of Tourism: Forging New Ground for Ecotourism and Other Alternatives. *Annual Review of Anthropology* 30:261–283.

Sullivan, Kathleen. 1992. Protagonists of Change: Indigenous Street Vendors in San Cristobal, Mexico, Are Adapting Tradition and Customs to Fit New Life Styles. *Cultural Survival Quarterly* 16:38–40.

Sundar Rao, P. S. S. 1983. Religion and Intensity of In-breeding in Tamil Nadu, South India. *Social Biology* 30(4):413–422.

Suttles, Wayne. 1991. The Traditional Kwakiutl Potlatch. In *Chiefly Feasts: The Enduring Kwakiutl Potlatch* (pp. 71–134). Aldona Jonaitis, ed. Washington, DC: American Museum of Natural History.

Tannen, Deborah. 1990. *You Just Don't Understand: Women and Men in Conversation*. New York: Morrow.

Tannenbaum, Nicola B. 1987. Tattoos: Invulnerability and Power in Shan Cosmology. *American Ethnologist* 14:693–711.

Tauli-Corpuz, Victoria. 2005. Indigenous Peoples and the Millenium Development Goals. Paper submitted to the Fourth Session of the UN Permanent Forum on Indigenous Issues, New York City, May 16–27. www.tebtebba.org.

Taussig, Michael. 2004. *My Cocaine Museum*. Chicago: University of Chicago Press.

Te Pareake Mead, Aroha. 2004. He Paua, He Korowai, me Nga Waahi Tapu. *Cultural Survival Quarterly* 28(1):61–64.

Tester, Frank James and Paule McNicoll. 2004. Isumagijaksaq: Mindful of the State: Social Constructions of Inuit Suicide. *Social Science and Medicine* 58:2625–2636.

Thomas, Frédéric, Francois Renaud, Eric Benefice, Thierry de Meeüs, and Jean-François Guegan. 2001. International Variability of Ages at Menarche and Menopause: Patterns and Main Determinants. *Human Biology* 73(2):271–290.

Thompson, Nile R. and C. Dale Sloat. 2004. The Use of Oral Literature to Provide Community Health Education on the Southern Northwest Coast. *American Indian Culture and Research Journal* 28(3):1–28.

Thompson, Robert Farris. 1971. Aesthetics in Traditional Africa. In *Art and Aesthetics in Primitive Societies* (pp. 374–381). Carol F. Jopling, ed. New York: E. P. Dutton.

Tice, Karin E. 1995. *Kuna Crafts, Gender, and the Global Economy*. Austin: University of Texas Press.

Tidball, Keith G. and Christopher P. Toumey. 2003. Signifying Serpents: Hermeneutic Change in Appalachian Pentecostal Serpent Handling. In *Signifying Serpents and Mardi Gras Runners: Representing Identity in Selected Souths* (pp. 1–18). Southern Anthropological Society Proceedings, No. 36. Celeste Ray and Luke Eric Lassiter, eds. Athens: University of Georgia Press.

Tierney, Patrick. 2000. *Darkness in El Dorado: How Scientists and Journalists Devastated the Amazon*. New York: W. W. Norton.

Tiffany, Walter W. 1979. New Directions in Political Anthropology: The Use of Corporate Models for the Analysis of Political Organizations. In *Political Anthropology: The State of the Art* (pp. 63–75). S. Lee Seaton and Henri J. M. Claessen, eds. New York: Mouton.

Tinker, Irene. 1976. The Adverse Impact of Development on Women. In *Women and World Development* (pp. 22–34). Irene Tinker and Michele Bo Bramsen, eds. Washington, DC: Overseas Development Council.

Tooker, Elisabeth. 1992. Lewis H. Morgan and His Contemporaries. *American Anthropologist* 94(2):357–375.

Toren, Christina. 1988. Making the Present, Revealing the Past: The Mutability and Continuity of Tradition as Process. *Man* (n.s.) 23: 696–717.

Traphagan, John W. 2000. The Liminal Family: Return Migration and Intergenerational Conflict in Japan. *Journal of Anthropological Research* 56:365–385.

Trawick, Margaret. 1988. Death and Nurturance in Indian Systems of Healing. In *Paths to Asian Medical Knowledge* (pp. 129–159). Charles Leslie and Allan Young, eds. Berkeley: University of California Press.

Trelease, Murray L. 1975. Dying among Alaskan Indians: A Matter of Choice. In *Death: The Final Stage of Growth* (pp. 33–37). Elisabeth Kübler-Ross, ed. Englewood Cliffs, NJ: Prentice-Hall.

Trigger, Bruce G. 1996. State, Origins of. In *The Social Science Encyclopedia* (pp. 837–838). Adam Kuper and Jessica Kuper, eds. New York: Routledge.

Trosset, Carol and Douglas Caulkins. 2001. Triangulation and Confirmation in the Study of Welsh Concepts of Personhood. *Journal of Anthropological Research* 57:61–81.

Trotter, Robert T. II. 1987. A Case of Lead Poisoning from Folk Remedies in Mexican American Communities. In *Anthropological Praxis: Translating Knowledge into Action* (pp. 146–159). Robert M. Wulff and Shirley J. Fiske, eds. Boulder, CO: Westview Press.

Trouillot, Michel-Rolph. 1990. *Haiti: State against Nation: The Origins and Legacy of Duvalierism*. New York: Monthly Review Press.

———. 2001. The Anthropology of the State in the Age of Globalization. *Current Anthropology* 42:125–133, 135–138.

Turner, Terrence. 2002. Representation, Politics, and Cultural Imagination in Indigenous Video: General Points and Kayapo Examples. In *Media Worlds: Anthropology on New Terrain* (pp. 75–89). Faye D. Ginsburg and Lila Abu-Lughod, eds. Berkeley: University of California Press.

Turner, Victor W. 1969. *The Ritual Process: Structure and Anti-Structure*. Chicago: Aldine.

Tylor, Edward Burnett. 1871. *Primitive Culture: Researchers into the Development of Mythology, Philosophy, Religion, Art, and Custom*. 2 volumes. London: J. Murray.

Uhl, Sarah. 1991. Forbidden Friends: Cultural Veils of Female Friendship in Andalusia. *American Ethnologist* 18(1):90–105.

UNFPA. Accessed June 15, 2006. www.unfpa.org.

United Nations Development Programme. 1995. *Human Development Report 1994.* New York: Oxford University Press.

United Nations Environment Programme. 2002. *Impact of Global Warming on Mountain Areas Confirmed by UNEP-Backed Mountaineers.* News Release.

Uphoff, Norman T. and Milton J. Esman. 1984. *Local Organizations: Intermediaries in Rural Development.* Ithaca, NY: Cornell University Press.

Ury, William L. 1990. Dispute Resolution Notes from the Kalahari. *Negotiation Journal* 63:229–238.

van der Geest, Sjaak, Susan Reynolds Whyte, and Anita Hardon. 1996. The Anthropology of Pharmaceuticals: A Biographical Approach. *Annual Review of Anthropology* 25:153–178.

Van Gennep, Arnold. 1960 [1908]. *The Rites of Passage.* Chicago: University of Chicago Press.

VanWynsberghe, Robert M. 2002. *AlterNatives: Community, Identity, and Environmental Justice on Walpole Island.* Boston: Allyn and Bacon.

Veltmeyer, Henry and James Petras. 2002. The Social Dynamics of Brazil's Rural Landless Workers' Movement: Ten Hypotheses on Successful Leadership. *Canadian Review of Sociology and Anthropology* 39:79–96.

Vickers, Jeanne. 1993. *Women and War.* Atlantic Highlands, NJ: Zed Books.

Vidal, John. 2006. Seizing the Sustainability Agenda. *Guardian Weekly,* April 28–May 4: 3.

Vincent, Joan. 1996. Political Anthropology. In *The Social Science Encyclopedia* (p. 624). Adam Kuper and Jessica Kuper, eds. New York: Routledge.

Wainwright, Elsina. 2003. Responding to State Failure: The Case of Australia and the Solomon Islands. *Australian Journal of International Affairs* 57:485–498.

Wallerstein, Immanuel. 1979. *The Capitalist World-Economy.* New York: Cambridge University Press.

Walsh, Michael. 2005. Will Indigenous Languages Survive? *Annual Review of Anthropology* 34:293–315.

Ward, Martha C. 1989. Once Upon a Time. In *Nest in the Wind: Adventures in Anthropology on a Tropical Island* (pp. 1–22). Martha C. Ward, ed. Prospect Heights, IL: Waveland Press.

Warren, Carol A. B. 1988. *Gender Issues in Field Research. Qualitative Research Methods, Volume 9.* Newbury Park, CA: Sage Publications.

Warren, D. Michael. 2001. The Role of the Global Network of Indigenous Knowledge Resource Centers in the Conservation of Cultural and Biological Diversity. In *Biocultural Diversity: Linking Language, Knowledge and the Environment* (pp. 446–461). Washington, DC: Smithsonian Institution Press.

Warren, Seth. 2001. Oil and Human Rights in Sudan. *Cultural Survival Quarterly* 25(3):20.

Washington Post. 2006. Hidden in Plain View: It Takes a Global Village, March 10, p. A2.

Watkins, Ben and Michael L. Fleisher. 2002. Tracking Pastoralist Migration: Lessons from the Ethiopian Somali National Regional State. *Human Organization* 61:328–338.

Watson, James, L., ed. 1997. *Golden Arches East: McDonald's in East Asia.* Stanford, CA: Stanford University Press.

Watson, Rubie S. 1986. The Named and the Nameless: Gender and Person in Chinese Society. *American Ethnologist* 13(4):619–631.

———. 1997. Museums and Indigenous Cultures: The Power of Local Knowledge. *Cultural Survival Quarterly* 21(1):24–25.

Weatherford, J. 1981. *Tribes on the Hill.* New York: Random House.

Weber, Linda R., Andrew Miracle, and Tom Skehan. 1994. Interviewing Early Adolescents: Some Methodological Considerations. *Human Organization* 53(1):42–47.

Websdale, Neil. 1995. An Ethnographic Assessment of the Policing of Domestic Violence in Rural Eastern Kentucky. *Social Justice* 22(1): 102–122.

Webster, Gloria Cranmer. 1991. The Contemporary Potlatch. In *Chiefly Feasts: The Enduring Kwakiutl Potlatch* (pp. 227–250). Aldona Jonaitis, ed. Washington, DC: American Museum of Natural History.

Weine, Stevan M. et al. 1995. Psychiatric Consequences of "Ethnic Cleansing": Clinical Assessments and Trauma Testimonies of Newly Resettled Bosnian Refugees. *American Journal of Psychiatry* 152(4): 536–542.

Weiner, Annette B. 1976. *Women of Value, Men of Renown: New Perspectives in Trobriand Exchange.* Austin: University of Texas Press.

———. 1988. *The Trobrianders of Papua New Guinea.* New York: Holt, Rinehart and Winston.

Werbner, Pnina. 1988. "Sealing the Koran": Offering and Sacrifice among Pakistani Labour Migrants. *Cultural Dynamics* 1:77–97.

White, Douglas R. and Michael L. Burton. 1988. Causes of Polygyny: Ecology, Economy, Kinship, and Warfare. *American Anthropologist* 90(4):871–887.

Whitehead, Tony Larry. 1986. Breakdown, Resolution, and Coherence: The Fieldwork Experience of a Big, Brown, Pretty-talking Man in a West Indian Community. In *Self, Sex, and Gender in Cross-Cultural Fieldwork* (pp. 213–239). Tony Larry Whitehead and Mary Ellen Conway, eds. Chicago: University of Illinois Press.

Whiting, Beatrice B. and John W. M. Whiting. 1975. *Children of Six Cultures: A Psycho-Cultural Analysis.* Cambridge, MA: Harvard University Press.

Whiting, Robert, 1979. You've Gotta Have "Wa." *Sports Illustrated,* September 24:60–71.

Wikan, Unni. 1977. Man Becomes Woman: Transsexualism in Oman as a Key to Gender Roles. *Man* 12(2):304–319.

———. 1982. *Behind the Veil in Arabia: Women in Oman.* Chicago: University of Chicago Press.

———. 2000. Citizenship on Trial: Nadia's Case. *Daedalus* 129:55–76.

Williams, Brett. 1984. Why Migrant Women Feed Their Husbands Tamales: Foodways as a Basis for a Revisionist View of Tejano Family Life. In *Ethnic and Regional Foodways in the United States: The Performance of Group Identity* (pp. 113–126). Linda Keller Brown and Kay Mussell, eds. Knoxville: University of Tennessee Press.

———. 1991. Good Guys and Bad Toys: The Paradoxical World of Children's Cartoons. In *The Politics of Culture* (pp. 109–132). Brett Williams, ed. Washington, DC: Smithsonian Institution Press.

———. 1994. Babies and Banks: The "Reproductive Underclass" and the Raced, Gendered Masking of Debt. In *Race* (pp. 348–365). Steven Gregory and Roger Sanjek, eds. Ithaca, NY: Cornell University Press.

Williams, Walter. 1992. *The Spirit and the Flesh: Sexual Diversity in American Indian Cultures,* 2nd ed. Boston: Beacon Press.

Williamson, Nancy. 1976. *Sons or Daughters: A Cross-Cultural Study of Parental Preferences.* Beverly Hills, CA: Sage Publications.

Wilson, Richard. 1995. *Maya Resurgence in Guatemala: Q'eqchi' Experiences.* Norman: University of Oklahoma Press.

Wilson, Thomas M. 2000. The Obstacles to European Union Regional Policy in the Northern Ireland Borderlands. *Human Organization* 59:1–10.

Winans, Edgar V. and Angelique Haugerud. 1977. Rural Self-Help in Kenya: The Harambee Movement. *Human Organization* 36:334–351.

Winthrop, Robert. 2000. The Real World: Cultural Rights/Animal Rights. *Practicing Anthropology* 22:44–45.

Wolf, Charlotte. 1996. Status. In *The Social Science Encyclopedia* (pp. 842–843). Adam Kuper and Jessica Kuper, eds. New York: Routledge.

Wolf, Eric R. 1966. *Peasants.* Englewood Cliffs, NJ: Prentice-Hall.

———. 1969. *Peasant Wars of the Twentieth Century.* New York: Harper & Row.

Wolf, Margery. 1968. *The House of Lim: A Study of a Chinese Farm Family.* New York: Appleton-Century-Crofts.

Woolfson, Peter, Virginia Hood, Roger Secker-Walker, and Ann C. Macaulay. 1995. Mohawk English in the Medical Interview. *Medical Anthropology Quarterly* 9(4):503–509.

World Bank. 2003. *Roma Poverty Remains Key Hurdle to Shared Prosperity in Central and Eastern Europe.* Washington, DC: The World Bank. www.worldbank.org/roma.

Worldwatch Institute. 2003. *Vital Signs 2003: The Trends That Are Shaping Our Future.* Washington, DC: Worldwatch Institute/W.W. Norton.

Wormald, Tom. 2005. Visions of the Future: Technology and the Imagination in Hungarian Civil Society. *Anthropology Matters* 7(1):1–10. http://www.anthropologymatters.com.

Wright, Sue. 1998. The Politicization of "Culture." *Anthropology Today* 14:1, 7–15.

Wu, David Y. H. 1990. Chinese Minority Policy and the Meaning of Minority Culture: The Example of Bai in Yunnan, China. *Human Organization* 49(1):1–13.

www.greatapetrust.org/bonobo/meet/kanzi.php.

www.npr.org.

Xizhe, Peng. 1991. *Demographic Transition in China: Fertility Trends since the 1980s.* New York: Oxford University Press.

Yoon, In-Jin. 1993. *The Social Origins of Korean Immigration to the United States from 1965 to the Present.* Papers of the Program on Population, Number 121. Honolulu: East-West Center.

Young, Michael W. 1983. "Our Name is Women; We are Bought with Limesticks and Limepots": An Analysis of the Autobiographical Narrative of a Kalauna Woman. *Man* 18:478–501.

Zabusky, Stacia E. 1995. *Launching Europe: An Ethnography of European Cooperation in Space Science.* Princeton, NJ: Princeton University Press.

Zaidi, S. Akbar. 1988. Poverty and Disease: Need for Structural Change. *Social Science and Medicine* 27:119–127.

Zarrilli, Phillip B. 1990. Kathakali. In *Indian Theatre: Traditions of Performance* (pp. 315–357). Farley P. Richmond, Darius L. Swann, and Phillip B. Zarrilli, eds. Honolulu: University of Hawaii Press.

Zureik, Elia. 1994. Palestinian Refugees and Peace. *Journal of Palestine Studies* 24(1):5–17.

Sources for "Anthropology in the Real World"

Part I: Susan Squires

American Breakfast & the Mother-in-Law: How an Anthropologist Created Go-Gurt. National Association for the Practice of Anthropology. (2003–2004). www.practicinganthropology.org/learn/index.cfm?print=1storyid=4.

Boss, Shira J. (2 January 2001). Anthropologists on the Job. *The Christian Science Monitor.* http://csmonitor.com/cgi-bin/durableRedirect.pl?/durable/2001/01/02/fp9sl-csm.shtml.

Squires, Susan. Ph.D., Research Director, Tactics LLC. (2004). Southwestern Anthropological Association. www2.sjsu.edu/depts/anthropology/swaa/pages/PgSquares.html.

Walsh, Sharon. (23 May 2001). Corporate Anthropology: Dirt-Free Research. CNN.com/CAREER. www.cnn.com/2001/CAREER/dayonthejob/05/23/corp.anthropologist.idg/.

Part II: Lara Tabac

Lara Tabac. (29 September 2003). Slate. http://slate.msn.com/id/2088748/entry/2088987/.

Part III: Fredy Peccerelli

AAAS Human Rights Action Network. American Association for the Advancement of Science. (21 March 2002). http://shr.aaas.org/news/050204_peccerelli.html.

Black, Richard. Guatemala Rights Scientist Honoured. BBC. (15 February 2004). http://news.bbc.co.uk/go/pr/fr/-/2/hi/science/nature/3489743.stm.

Digging for Truth in Guatemala. American Association for the Advancement of Science Public Release. (14 February 2004). www.eurekalert.org/pub_releases/2004-02/aaft-dft020504.php.

Elton, Catherine. (27 March 2002). Despite Threats, Guatemalan Scientists Dig for the Truth. *The Christian Science Monitor.* www.csmonitor.com/2002/0327/pO8s01-woam.html.

Peccerelli, Fredy. (2004). Executive Director of the Guatemalan Forensic Anthropology Foundation Speaks at AAAS. American Association for the Advancement of Science. http://shr.aaas.org/news/050204_peccerelli.html.

Part IV: Brian Craik

Craik, Brian. (n.d.). The Importance of Working Together: Exclusions, Conflicts and Participation in James Bay, Quebec. IDRC Books Online. www.idrc.ca/en/ev-64530-201-1-DO_TOPIC.html.

Grand Council of the Crees website. (7 August 2006). www.gcc.ca/gcc/fedrelations.php.

Preston, Richard J. (12 May 2006). Reflections on Becoming an Applied Anthropologist. The 2006 Weaver-Tremblay Lecture, presented at the Canadian Anthropology Section/Société Canadien Anthropologie, Concordia University, Montreal. www.socsci.mcmaster.ca/anthro/emplibrary/prestonawardreflection.

Part V: Mamphela Ramphele

Across Boundaries. (21 April 1997). Online NewsHour: Zair: End of an Era. 1999, MacNeil-Lehrer Productions. www.pbs.org/newshur/bb/africa/april97/ramph_4-21.html.

New Vice-Chancellor Appointed. (10 December 1996). University of Capetown Department of Development and Public Affairs. web.uct.ac.za/depts/dpa/news/ramphele.html.

Ramphele, Mamphela. Dr. Mamphela Ramphele's Biography. www.sahistory.org.za/pages/people/ramphele-m.html.

Index

Words in boldface type indicate key concepts; italicized page numbers indicate photos, figures, or maps.

The Bell Curve: Intelligence and Class Structure in American Life (Herrnstein-Murray), 5

Below-replacement-level fertility, 123, *123*

Bemba of northern Zambia, 348

Bemessi people, Cameroon, West Africa, 241–242

Benally, Steven, Jr., 171

Benedict, Ruth, 11, 146–147

Benin, West Africa, 53, 221

Beoku-Betts, Josephine, 387

Berber people, 107, 374

Berdache, 162

Bernal, Martin, 328

Bernard, H. Russell, 437

Berreman, Gerald D., 245

Best, David, 381

Bestor, Theodore C., 46, 108

Beti people of Southern Cameroon, 164

Bettles, Gordon, 343

Beverages, 99, 104. *See also* Alcoholic beverages

  drinking patterns, 16

Beyene, Yewoubdar, 166

Bhardwaj, Surinder M., 414

Bhatt, Rakesh M., 332

Bhutan, *430*

Bhutto, Benazir, 273

Bible, 101, 204

Biesele, Megan, 22

Big Foot, 363

Big-man or big-woman system, 264–266

Bikers, *239*

Bilateral institutions, 431

Bilharz, Joy, 279

Bilineal descent, 204, 209–210

Bilingualism, 331, *331*

Billig, Michael S., 218

Biodiversity, indigenous peoples as victims of loss of, 439

Biological anthropology, 4–5, 8–9, 424. *See also* Biological determinism

Biological determinism

  adolescence and, 26, 157

  Boas on, 21

  versus cultural constructionism, 27

  defined, 27

  gender identity and, 161–162

  race and, 26

  role of romantic love in spouse selection, 216

  warfare and, 300

Biological diversity, 427, 448

Biological evolution. *See* Evolution

Bird, Sharon R., 238

Birth and infancy

  baby talk and, 324

  bonding, 150

  caregiver-infant proximity, 152

  gender in infancy, 153

  Maya women in Mexico, 150

  sleeping patterns and personality, 152–153

  Western medical model of, 150, 164

Black Hills, South Dakota, 141

Blackwood, Evelyn, 208

Blaikie, Piers, 73

Blau, Peter M., 102

Bledsoe, Caroline H., 110, 133

Blim, Michael, 84

Blok, Anton, 294

Blommaert, Jan, 323

Blood, Robert O., 221

Blood brotherhood, 210

Blood as metaphor for kinship relations, 203

Blood sports, 384

Boas, Franz

  on art, 371, 373

  on potlatching, 102, 114

  on race, 21, 246

  research methods, 47–48

  theoretical concepts, 11–*12*

Bodenhorn, Barbara, 203

Bodh Gaya, India, 348

Bodley, John H., 436

Body language, 317–319

Body modification, 240, *241*, 317

Boellstorff, Tom, 326

Bogin, Barry, 150

Boine, Marie, *333*

Bolivia

  aid from Cuba to, 434

  coca use in, 182

  location and description, *303*

  military in, 302–303

  rights of indigenous peoples of, *274*, *275*, 440

Bonding, 151

Borneo

  Kelabit household formation, 227–228

  orangutan conservation, 8–9

Borovoy, Amy, 221

Borzu Qermezi, 264

Bosa, Sardegna (Sardinia), Italy, 348–349

Boserup, Ester, 225, 443

Bosnia, 298–299

Boston, Massachusetts, street gangs in, 239

Botswana, *22*, *57*, 441

Bourdieu, Pierre, 98

Bourgois, Philippe, 53, 56

Bowen, John R., 343, 361

Boys

  leisure patterns in Yemen, 211

  relationships with sisters in Lebanon, 223

  son preference, 129, 132, 135, 136

  work patterns, 72, 75, 79, 83–84, 154

Bradley, Richard, 345

Brana-Shute, Rosemary, 238

Brandes, Stanley, 165, 244

Brando, Cheyenne, 138

Brando, Marlon, 138

Brando, Tarita, 138

Brave Heart, Mary Yellow Horse, 141, 185

Bray, Tamara L., 381

Brazil

  abortion and, 132

  African diaspora religions in, 362

  carnaval in, 40

  childbirth and, 151, 164, 173

  country music and globalization in, 369, 376

  emigrants from, 401

  ethno-etiologies in, 176

  friendship patterns among urban poor, 237

godparenting in Bahia, 212

indirect infanticide among, 134

industrial capital agriculture in, 79

Kayopo people of, *113*, 263

medicalization and, 187

men as heads of households in, 220

Mundurucu of, 85

NSM (Rural Landless Workers' Movement), 279–280

nutrition in, 73

perceptions of the body in, 172–173

protection of indigenous peoples' rights in, 440

skin color diversity in, *247*

Umbanda in, 180

Yanomami region in, *73*

Breast feeding

  as fertility control, 120, 131

  and the incest rule, 210

  infant death and, 134

  of other women's babies, in South Pacific, 165

  personality and, 146

  sleeping and, 16

  son preference and, 136

Brewis, Alexandra, 221

Brideprice (bridewealth), 136, *217*, 218, 291

Bride-service, 216, *217*

Brink, Judy H., 403

British colonialism, 294, 407

British Columbia, Canada, 440

British English, 332

Brodkin, Karen, 246

Brooks, Alison S., 22, 166

Broude, Gwen, 164

Brown, Carolyn Henning, 352

Brown, David L., 250

Brown, Judith K., 72, 77, 159, 223, 267, 347

Brown, Nathan, 294

Browner, Carole H., 125, 128, 164

Brumfiel, Elizabeth M., 270

Brunei, 403

Brunelleschi, Filippo, 379

Bruner, Edward M., 384–385

Bryne, Brian, 1

Buddha, 347, 353, 354

Buddhism

  abortion and, 132

  blending with local religions, 354

  healing therapies and, 192

  initiation into monkhood, *145*

  Khmer refugees and, 414

  Lao Buddhist temple in Virginia, *342*

  in mainland Southeast Asia, *163*

  in Nepal, 193

  overview, 353–354

  periodic ritual in, 347

  pilgrimages to Bodh Gaya, 348

  population distribution of, *351*

  suicide and, 135

  in Tibet, 248

Bulgaria, 113

Bulimia, 176

Bunzel, Ruth, 373

Burdick, John, 362

Bureaucracy, 427, 435

Childs, Larry, 440
Chile, 121, 273
Chin, Elizabeth, 100
China. *See also* Hong Kong
  adopted children from, *405*
  arranged marriages in, 217
  the arts since 1949, 391
Chinese women's movement, 253
Coca
  eradication campaign in Bolivia, *446*
  herbicides and child health in Colombia, *446*
  traditional use of in Bolivia, 182
Coca Cola promotion in, 36
  demographic transition and, 124
  dowries in, 218
  ethnic cleansing and, 23
  female infanticide in, 132
  food preferences in, 14
  genocide and, 140
  geophagia in, 183
  Great Wall of, 268
  historical data collection in, 49
  hookworm in rice cultivators, 183, *185*
  humoral healing systems in, 179
  industrial capital agriculture in, 79
  industrial collectivized agriculture, 79–80
  Mahayana Buddhism in, 354
  market exchange in, *108*
  Muslims of Xi'an, 360, *360*
  One-Child-per-Couple Policy, 131–132, 220
  orphanages in, *213*
  population growth rate in, 120
  racial classification in, *21*
  and restrictions on research by foreigners, 37
  revolution in, 297, 298
  Shanghai World Financial Trade Center, *379*
  son preference in, 135
  state political organization and, 268
  stem households in, *220*
  Three Gorges Dam Project, *405*
  Tibet and, 274, *364*
  women marketeers, *108*
  women's political roles and, 273
  women's reproductive rights in, 132
  as a world leader, 280
  written language in, 329
  Xi'an, *360*
Chiñas, Beverly, 78
Chinese Canadians, *398*
Chirac, Jacques, 370
Chittagong Hill Tracts in Bangladesh, 440
Choctaw Indians, 163
Chowdhury, A. N., 175
Christianity. *See also* Amish communities;
    Catholicism; Protestantism
  animism in, 342
  Appalachian protestantism, 358–359
  Bible, 101, 204
  birth control and, 129
  branches of, 358
  Church of England, 345
  fertility rates of European-descent
      Christians, 121
  genital cutting and, 159

  in Ghana, *211*
  godparenting and, 212
  in Hong Kong, *206*
  Hutterites, 120, 121
  images of the Last Supper in Fiji, *359*
  Jesus Christ, 358, 359, 434
  Judaism and, 358
  Khmer refugees and, 414
  in mainland Southeast Asia, *163*
  Mennonites, 120, 121, 286
  missionaries and, 333, 345, 351
  pilgrimages to Jerusalem, 348
  population distribution of, *351, 358*
  Presbyterian Church of Wales, *148*
  proselytizing and, 352
  Protestantism, 135, 357–358
  ritual of communion and, 345
  sacred sites and, 364
The Chrysanthemum and the Sword, 147
Chuluundorj, Oyunsetseg, 141
Churchill, Nancy, 349
Church of England, 345
CIDA (Canadian International Development
    Agency), 431
Circular migration, 402, 403
Circumpolar regions
  consumerism and, 95
  female infanticide and, 135
  foraging and, 66, 67, 68, 74, 95
  gardens of, 379
  natural resources in, 438
Citizenship, 269, 271, 401, 409
Civil disobedience, 304
Civilization, 11, 13–14, 19
Civil society
  activist groups, 253
  Chinese women's movement, 253
  CO-MADRES, 253, 255
  definition, 252
  new social movements and cyberpower, 255
Clans, 262–263
Clark, Gracia, 20, 444
Clarke, Kumari Maxone, 362
Clash of civilizations, 19
Class
  achieved status and, 245
  characteristics, 20–21
  consumption and, 98–99
  defined, 20
  entitlements and, 98
  fertility and, 121
  fieldwork and, 42–43
  formal schooling and, 155–156
  genetic testing and, 132–133
  health problems and, 184
  language and, 323
  modernization and, 427
  personality shaping and, 147–148
  sexual activity and, 126
  son preference and, 136–137
Class struggle, 20. *See also* Marxism
Clay, Jason W., 273, 297
Cleveland, David A., 10
Clifford, James, 375, 381
Clinical medical anthropology, 194–195
Clinton, Bill, 109
Clinton, Hillary, 273, *411*

Clothing. *See* Dress
Clubs and fraternities, 238
Coat of arms and symbols, *275*
Coca, 182
Coca Cola promotion in China, 36
Cochrane, D. Glynn, 435
Code of Ethics of the American
    Anthropological Association, *55*
Coercive harmony, 289
Cognitive regression, 189
Cohen, Mark Nathan, 183
Cohen, Roberta, 403
Cohn, Bernard, 249
Cole, Douglas, 114, 115
Cole, Jeffrey, 418
Collaborative research, 54, 56, *56*
Collado-Ardón, Rolando, 175
Collateral extended household, 219
Colley, Sarah, 441
Colombia, 401, 409, 440, 446
Colonialism
  in Africa, 158, 247, 259, 267
  Andaman Islanders and, 70
  art and, *381, 386–388*
  banditry and, 291
  British, 294, 407
  Canadian, 139
  caste system and, 249
  in Central America, 177
  changes in kinship and household
      dynamics, 225–229
  Christianity and, 351
  consumerism and, 92
  disease and, 184–185
  Dutch, 48, 225
  European, 24, 177, 220, 266
  First Nations of Canada and, 69, 139
  French, 407
  Gandhi and, 304
  in Haiti, 433
  in Hawai'i, 389
  headhunting and, 19
  heterotopia and, 380
  historical trauma and, 184
  humoral healing system and, 179
  imperial gardens and, 380
  indigenous legal systems and, 291–292
  indigenous peoples and, 23, 84, 439
  institutional migrants and, 407
  in Java, 48
  language and, 331, 338
  in Mexico, 65, *120, 275*
  missionaries and, 19, 351, 359
  Native Americans and, 73, 141, 186, 278
  politics and, 260
  population displacement and, 403
  Puerto Rican ancestry and, 278
  race and ethnicity and, 43
  repatriation and, 381
  in Samoa, 26
  San peoples and, 22, 23
  slavery and, 105
  syncretism and expressive culture and,
      386–388
  and *terra nullius,* 441
  tourism and, 385
  women's status and, 267, 278, 443

migration and, 416
nutritional effects of Western contact in the Brazilian Amazon, 112
Hearts of Sorrow (Freeman), 47
Hecht, Tobias, *44*
Hefner, Robert W., 351
Hegel, 252
Height hypergyny, 216
Heimer, Robert, 482
Heise, Lori L., 443, 444
Helweg, Arthur W., 414
Helweg, Usha M., 414
Henderson, Eric B., 225
Herding, 23, 74–75, 85–86, 333, 428–429. *See also* Pastoralism
Herdt, Gilbert, 11, 157
Heritage. *See* Cultural heritage
Herod, King, 356
Herodotus, 10
Herrnstein, Richard J., 5
Herzegovina, *299*
Herzfeld, Michael, *295*
Heterotopia, 380
Hiatt, Betty, 67
Hiawatha, *73*
Hickey, Clifford G., 386
Hierarchy, 20. *See also* Social control; Social stratification
Hijira, 162, 163
Hikikomori, 175
Hill, Charlie, 304
Hill, Jane H., 323, 334
Hiltebeitel, Alf, 352, 468
Himalayan region, 218–219
Hindi, 18, 314–315
Hinduism
    abortion and, 132
    Brahman priests, *251*
    Buddhism as a protest against, 354
    caste system and, 249
    celebration of Holi and, *353*
    conflict with Muslims, 364
    epics in, 376
    and flowers as ritual offerings, 380
    food and, 27
    and Jews of the Kochi area, 357
    karma beliefs in England, 353
    lost semen complex among men, 127, 304
    Mahabharata, 352
    matrilateral parallel-cousin marriages and, 214
    matrilineal kinship and Nayar fertility ritual, 353
    menarche and, 161
    pilgrimage to Varanasi, 348
    population distribution of, *351, 353*
    population growth rate and, 120
    Ramayama, 352
    relationship of sexual intercourse to fertility, 126–127
    sacred sites and, 364
    sexual abstinence and, 127
    Sri Lankan life histories, 47–*48*
    suicide and, 138
    Vedas, 452
    village endogamy and exogamy among, 215

worshippers in Queens, New York, *414*
Hin-mah-too-yah-lat-kekt, 266
Hip-hop, 375
Hirschman, Helen K., 133
Hirschon, Renee, 404
Hispanics. *See* Latinos of the United States
Historical archaeology, 6
Historical data, 49
Historical linguistics, 6, 328–329
Historical particularism, 11, 13, 146
Historical trauma, 184–185
Hitler, Adolf, 21
HIV/AIDS
    among hill tribes of Thailand, 439
    among Maasai of Kenya, 158
    children in Tanzania and, *189*
    cultural contexts and, 14
    female genital cutting and, 160
    in Haiti, 433
    mortality and, 139
    orphan care in Kenya, 140
    in Papua New Guinea, *18*
    selecting fieldwork projects and, 36
    sex workers and, 83
    study of sexuality and, 125
    Treatment Action Campaign (TAC) in South Africa, *247*
    tuberculosis and, 184
Hmong people of Thailand, 439
Hobsbawm, Eric J., 294
Hodge, Robert W., 125
Hodgson, Dorothy L., 158
Holism
    cultural anthropology in the business world and, 1
    definition, 10
    early research methods and, 1
    functionalism and, 11
    internal cultural integration and, 19
Hollan, Douglas, 149
Holland. *See* The Netherlands
Holland, Dorothy C., 47, 217
Hollos, Marida, 121
Holmes, Oliver Wendell, 418
Holocaust, 25
Homo sapiens, 6
Homosexuality. *See also* Gay and lesbian anthropology
    carnaval in Brazil, 40
    fieldwork and, 43
    language in Indonesia and, 326
    as a sensitive research issue, 37
Hong Kong
    culture-specific syndromes and, 176
    location and description, *206*
    migrants to Canada, 413
    naming system in Ha Tsuen, 206–207
    son preference in, 135
    wage labor immigration and, 403
Hoodia plant, *22, 442, 449*
Hopkins, Nicholas S., 255
Hornbein, George, 16
Hornbein, Marie, 16
Horowitz, Irving L., 54
Horst, Heather, 236
Horticulture
    adolescence in, 157

architecture in, 378
    changing economies of, 85
    definition, 71
    extended households in, 219
    female infanticide and, 135
    five stages of, 72
    leveling mechanisms in, 94
    matrilineal descent and, 206
    as a mode of production, 71–72
    mortality and, 139
    property relations and, 73
    shifting cultivation as synonym for, 71
    social control and, 287–288
    sustainability of, 73
    tribes in, 262
    unilineal descent and, 205
    warfare and, 139
    work groups in, 241
Hospitality, in the Middle East, 102
Household
    changes in everyday life in, 228–229
    definition, 218
    divorce and, 225
    domestic violence and, 223, 292
    versus family, 219
    forms of, 219–220
    globalization and, 227
    head of, 220–221
    international migration and, 227–228
    multigenerational, 228
    sibling relationships, 221, 223
    spouse/partner relationships, 221
    widow(er)hood, 225
    women as heads of, *222*
The House of Lim (Wolf), 205
Howell, Nancy, 57, 71, 120
HTA (Hungarian Telecottage Association), 320
Hughes, Charles C., 190, 438
Hughes, Lotte, 438
Hui Muslims of Xi'an, China
    Culturama, 360
    location, *360*
    men cooking noodles, *360*
    as a religious minority, 361
    women's commemorative ritual, *360*
Huizinga, Johan, 382
Hula of Hawai'i, 389
Human rights. *See also* Cultural rights; Use rights
    activist groups and, *233*, 253, 254, 363
    versus animal rights, 448
    apartheid and, 395
    Boas and, 12
    in Burma, *278*
    in Chechnya, *290*
    children and war, *411*
    cross-cultural analysis and, 24, 25
    development and, 446–448
    of Kurds, 275
    labor migration and, 400
    legal anthropology and, 286
    legal issues and, 286, 292
    Maya people of Guatemala, 400
    microcultures and, 20, 23
    migration and, 416, 418–419
    nonviolent conflict and, 304

Malaysia. *See also specific regions and
    peoples*
    humoral healing systems in, 179
    location, *163*
    orangutan regions in, *8*
    sharing-based kinship in, 210
    wage labor immigration and, 403
Malden, M. A., 341
Male bias in development, 442, 443–444
Male dominance. *See also* Masculinity; Men;
    Patriarchy
    in agricultural societies, 77, 78, 79, 123
    domestic violence and, 223
    entitlements and, 98
    in foraging societies, 67
    gang rape and, 238
    of men as heads of households, 220
    naming system in Ha Tsuen, Hong Kong,
        206
    in pastoralist societies, 74, 75
    patrilineal descent and, 205
    in political organizations, 272
    Romanian socialism and, 80
    use rights and, 75
Male strip dancing, 374
Mali
    fertility in, 121
    immigrants from, 125
    sexual activity in, 221
    Tuareg people in, 440
Malinowski, Bronislaw
    on communication, 321
    on men's trading systems, *38–39*, *53*, 102
    on myth, 342
    on participant observation, 35
    on sexuality, 125
    on social control, 286, 288
    theoretical concepts, 11, 260
Mamani, Mauricio P., 182
Mamdani, Mahmoud, 123, 365
Mandela, Nelson, 395
Mannheim, Bruce, 323
Man the Hunter model, 67
Manuelito, Katheryn, 157
Manufacturing, 87
Manz, Beatriz, 404, 406
Māori of New Zealand
    cargo cults, 363
    Culturama, 293
    indigenous norms and laws, 203
    political activism, *293*
    relationships with nature, 293
    social inequality compared to Paheka, 293
    traditional religion, *293*
    Treaty of Waitungi, 293
March, Kathryn S., 234
Marco Polo, 10
Marcoux, Alan, 222
Marcus, George, 11, 35
Mardi Gras, 348
Margolis, Maxine L., 374, 398
Market exchange, 106, 107
Markets, 107–109
Marriage. *See also* **Brideprice (bridewealth);
    Divorce; Dowry; Groomprice; the
    Household**
    age and, 216

among Lese and Efe people of the
    Democratic Republic of Congo, 111
bride-service and, 216
business marriages and immigration, 410
caste system and, 252
changing forms of, 226–227
of cousins, *214*
crisis in among the Hausa of Niger and
    among African Americans of Syracuse,
    New York, 226–227
definitions, 212, 213
descent and residence rules and, 209–210
European colonialism and indigenous
    systems, 291–292
forms of, 218–219
gifts associated with, 217–218, *217*
hypergyny, 215–216
hypogyny, 215
in Ha Tsuen, Hong Kong, 206–207
incest taboos and, 213–214
isogamy, 215
items of exchange and, *103*
monogamy, 85
physical disabilities and, 216
polyandry, 218–219, *219*
polygamy, 85, 218
polygyny, 218
preference rules for spouses, 214–218
role of romantic love in spouse selection
    and, 216–217
status and, 215–216
weddings, changes in, 227
Marshall, Robert C., 269
Marsh Arab people of Iraq, *397*
Martial arts, 383
Martin, Mungo, 114
Martin, Richard C., *359*
Martin, Sarah, 403, 444
Martínez, Samuel, 400–401
Martyrdom, 138
Marx, Karl, 87, 245, 252, 342
Marxism, 20, 245, 268, 342
Masculinity. *See also* Adolescent males,
    Boys, Gender, Men
    alcoholism in Mexico and, 244
    in vitro fertilization and, 133
    military in Bolivia and, 302–303
Maskit, souvenirs and, 375
Masquelier, Adeline, 226
Mass communication, 13
Massiah, Joycelin, 222
Material cultural heritage, 388–389
Material goods, as items of exchange, *103*
Materialism. *See* Cultural materialism
Maternal mortality rate, 141
Maternity, Medicine, and Power (Sargent),
    53
Matrescence, 164
Matriarchy, 266
Matrifocality, 209, 220
Matrilineal descent
    and lack of understanding of "God the
        father" concept in Christianity, 352
    cultures following, 206
    decline of, 225, 443
    definitions, 204, 205
    extended households and, 219

matrilocality and, 210
Minangkabau people and, 208, 209, 225
Navajo people and, 225
and Nayar fertility rituals, 352–353
recognized public leadership and, 209
Trobriand Islanders and, 39
Matrilocality, 210
Mauritania, 440
Maxwell, Gabrielle M., 293
May, Ann, 158
Maya people
    art and, 374
    as IDPs in Guatemala, 404
    of Chiapas, Mexico, 86–87, 440, 444–445
    civil war in Guatemala and, 405
    Culturama, 405
    forensic anthropology and, 6
    horticulture and, 72
    menopause and women of Mexico, 166
    as migrant laborers, 79
    as a nation-state, 274
    political activism in Guatemala, 53
    prevention of illness, 177
    socialization of children in Oaxaca, 154
Maybury-Lewis, David, 23, 273, 380, 438
Mayors Climate Protection Agreement, 431
McCallum, Cecilia, 132, 164, 173
McCoy clan, 296
McCully, Patrick, 404
McDermott, Ray, 330
McDonald, James H., 83
McDonaldization model, 19
McElroy, Ann, 179
McLary, Kathleen, 122
McMahon, April M. S., 322
McNicoll, Paule, 139
MDRTB (multi-drug resistant tuberculosis),
    184
Mead, Margaret
    on adolescence, 26, 159
    child studies in Sicily, *147*
    on fieldwork, 44
    gender studies, 146
    theoretical concepts, 11–12
Meador, Elizabeth, 24
Meaning effect, 185–186
Mecca, Saudi Arabia, 348, 361
Mechanical solidarity, 244, 245
Media
    advertising for Latinos in the U.S., 320
    digital divide in Hungary, 320–321
    influence on Euro-American children, 155
    journalism *versus* cultural anthropology
        research goals, 246
    politics of journalism, 319–320
    religion and television, 351
    shaping of culture by, 13
    state unity and, 274
    television programming in Japan, 320
Media anthropology, 319
Medical anthropology. *See also*
    Ethnomedicine
    applied, 194–195
    critical medical anthropology approach,
        186–189
    ecological/epidemiological approach, 182–
        185

Miyazawa, Setsuo, 288
Moberg, Mark, 270
Modell, Judith S., 211
Modernization, 135, 427
Mode of consumption, 92–94. *See also*
  Consumerism; Consumption;
  Minimalism
  changing patterns, 111–115
  consumption funds, 95–96
  consumption microcultures, 98–100
  entitlements and, 97–98
  overview, 92–93, *93*
  responsible consumption, 96
Mode of exchange, 92, 106–111. *See also*
  Balanced exchange; Exchange;
  Unbalanced exchange
  changing patterns, 111–115
  items of exchange, 102–106
  overview, 92, *93*
Mode of production. *See also* Agriculture;
  Foraging; Horticulture;
  Industrialism/Informatics; Pastoralism
  access to healing roles and,
  changes in, 84–87
  child personality formation and,
  compared to modes of reproduction, *121*
  Culture of Poverty theory and, 148
  groups and, *235*
  Image of the Limited Good and, 148
  kinship systems and, 202, *203*, 219
  male personality formation in Japan,
  overview, 64–65, *65*
Mode of reproduction
  agricultural, 121, 122
  compared to modes of production, *121*
  overview, 120, *121*
  foraging, 120–121
  industrialism/informatics, 123–125
  kinship systems and, 202, 203
Mode of social organization in relation to
  production, *235*
Moerman, Daniel, 185
Mogelonsky, Marcia, 414
Moka, 264
Mola,
Monaghan, Leila, 316
Money, 102, 104, 105
Mongolia, 75, 141, 248
Monogamy, 85, 218
Monotheism, 341–342, 355
Montana, radon spas in, 182
Monterrey, Mexico, *65*
Montesquieu, Charles, 10
Montgomery, Heather, 83
Monuments, 274, 359, 378.
Moore, John H., 94, 341
Moral economy, 104
Morales, Evo, *275*, 446
Morales, José V., 182
Morgan, Anna, 390
Morgan, Lewis Henry, 11, 34
Mormonism, Khmer refugees and, 414
Morocco
  Islam Feast of Sacrifice in, 361
  location and overview, *127*
  markets and, 107
  shikhat performers in, 374

wedding clothing in, *127*, 227
Moros people of the Philippines, 440
Morris, Allison, 293
Morris, Brian, 72
Morris, Kevin R., 145
Morris, Rosalind, 163
Morrison, Andrew R., 138
Mortality. *See also* Death
  causes of, 134, 160
  cross-cultural aspects of, 167
  epidemics, 139
  HIV/AIDS and, 139
  on Indian reservations, 141
  infanticide, 134–135
  infant mortality rate, 135
  maternal mortality rate, 141
  research on, 133–134
  suicide, 135, 137–139
  violence, public and private, 139–141
Mortland, Carol A., 414
Moser, Stephanie, *56*
Moses, 354
MOSOP (Movement for Survival of Ogoni
  People), 447
Motherese, 324
Mothers of the Disappeared, 255
Movement for Survival of Ogoni People
  (MOSOP), 447
Mozambique, 298, 444
Mt. Hagen, Papua New Guinea, 265–266
Mubarak, Hosni, 271, 431
Muecke, Marjorie A., 404
Muhammad, 135–136, 343, 359, 361
Mukerjee, Madhusree, 70
Mulk, Inga-Maria, 345
Mull, Dorothy S., 134
Mull, J. Dennis, 134
Mullings, Leith, 11, 13
Multiculturalism, in the business world, 1
Multidisciplinary teams, 49, 50, *56*
Multilateral institutions, 431
Multimedia resources, 49, 51
Multinational corporations, 95, 96
Multisited research, 34, 35, 148, 398, 405
Multisourcing, 95, 96
Muncie, Indiana, 54, *56*
Mundugumor people of Papua New Guinea,
  146
Mundurucu people of the Brazilian Amazon,
  85
Murdock, George Peter, 209, 218, 219
Murphy, Cullen, 6
Murphy, Robert F., 85
Murphy, Yolanda, 85
Murray, Charles A., 5
Murray, Gerald F., 436
Museums
  definition, 380
  origins of, 380–381
  politics of exhibits in, 381–382
  repatriation and, 381–382
  tribal art and the Louvre, 370
Music, 375, *376*
Muslims. *See also particular regions and
  peoples*; Islam
  adolescence as recent life-cycle stage for
    females, 157

Bosnian refugees, 298
  conflict with Hindus in India, 364
  cultural relativism and, 292
  ethnic cleansing, 23
  female genital cutting, 159
  gardens and, 379
  Hui people in China, 360
  immigrant issues and, 228
  marriage crisis in Niger, 226
  Minangkabau culture, 208
  patrilateral parallel-cousin marriage and,
    214
  pilgrimage of, 348
  population distribution of, 361
  Qu'ran and, 345
  September 11, 2001 attacks on the U.S.
    and, 365
  sociocultural fit and, 436
  village endogamy and, 215
  women's political roles and, 273
Mwadha, James, *316*
Myanmar, *70, 163,* 354
Multi-drug resistant tuberculosis (MDRTB),
  184
Myerhoff, Barbara, 44
Myers, James, 240
Myers, Norman, 94
Myth, 342–343, *353*

Nacirema, 10
Nadeau, Kathleen M., 434–435
Nader, Laura, 11, 43, 281, 289, 305
Nadur village, Kerala, 429
NAFTA (North American Free Trade
  Agreement), 66
Nag, Moni, 79, 127, 128
NAGPRA (Native American Graves
  Protection and Repatriation Act), 381
Naidu, Sarojini, *304*
Naiyomeh, Kimeli, 286
Namibia, San peoples and, *22,* 441
Naming systems, *204, 205,* 206–207
Nanda, Serena, 163, 370
Narcoeconomies, 83
Narhitao, Crown Prince, 172
Narrative therapy, 298
NASCAR racing, *383*
Natcher, David C., 386
National archives, 48–49
National character, 146–147
Nation
  definitions, 272, 273–274
  failed states, 275, 277
  globalization and, 275
  migration and, 275, 277
  nation-states, 274–275
Native American Graves Protection and
  Repatriation Act (NAGRPA), 381
Native Americans. *See also specific
  countries, tribes, and peoples*
  alcoholism among, 141
  ancestor cults and, 344
  as anthropologists, 13
  collaborative project with, 54
  cultural configuration and, 147
  elimination practices, 18
  ethnicity and, 23

Stoler, Ann Laura, 48, 260
Stone, Carl, 222
Stories. *See also* Life histories
   friendship, 236
   narrative therapy, 298
   performance, 330
   as qualitative data, 51–52
   symbolic analysis of, 146
   symbolic archaeology and, 13
   textual material, 48
Storper-Perez, Danielle, 357
Strathern, Andrew, 265
Stratified reproduction, 124
Street gang, 239–240
Stress
   adolescent, 26, 27
   among Hare Indians, 68
   of boarding school girls, 408
   culture-specific, 175
   hazing and, 189
   migration and, 399, 404–405, 407, 412
   post-traumatic stress syndrome, 298
   somatization and, 174, 175
   unemployment and, 87
   urban, 184
   war-related, 407
Stringer, Martin D., 342
Stronza, Amanda, 386
Structural adjustment, 428
Structural linguistics, 6
Structural suffering, 176
Structured/unstructured interviews, 46
Structurism
   adolescence and, 157
   versus agency, 28, 110, 160
   class differences in child-bearing, 126
   defined, 12
   gender identity and, 161–164
   government policies as instruments of
     indirect violence, 141
   labor migration and, 400
   medicalization and, 186
   politics, 260
   postmodernism and, 13
   poverty in Haiti and, 433
   power of economic class position and, 245
   push-pull theory of migration and, 399
   snakehandling in Appalachia and, 358–
     359
   structural suffering, 176–177
   urban youth gangs and, 240
Students. *See* Adolescent females; Adolescent
   Males; Education; Schools
Subanun people of the Philippines, 174, 314
Sub-Saharan Africa. *See also specific*
   countries and peoples
   Bantu migrations, 330, *330*
   child fostering in, 211
   horticulture in, 71
   matrilineal descent and, 205
   Sahel region, *442*
   schistosomiasis in, 190
Substance abuse, 141. *See also* Alcoholism
Sudan. *See also* Nuer people of
   Darfur, 141
   as a failed state, 275
   famine in, 98

internally displaced persons (IDPs) in,
   403, 440
   selecting fieldwork projects and, 36
Sufism, 361
Sugar, consumption of, *93*
Sugita, Eriko, 325
Suicide
   among Native Americans, 141
   European colonialism and, 185
   overview, 135, 137–139
   sexual orientation and, 162
   as a terrorist tactic, 135
Sukumar, S., 214
Sullivan, Kathleen, 444
Sumatra, Indonesia
   Minangkabau homeland, *208*
   orangutan regions in, *8*
Sumba, Indonesia, 14, *15*, 287, *373*
Summerfield, Anne, 208
Summerfield, John, 208
Sundar Rao, P. S. S., 215
Sunni Islam, *103*, *127*, 276, 348, 359, 360
Supernaturals, 344–345, 354
Superstructure, 27
Supply and demand, 92
Suriname, *237*, 238, 332
Suri people of Ethiopia, 74
Sustainability
   of agriculture, 81
   and development, 430
   of foraging, 71
   of horticulture,
   pastoralism and, 75–76
Suttles, Wayne, 92
Sweden
   aid to development projects and, 432
   birth practices in, 151
   income taxes in, 96
   women's political roles in, 273
Swedish Agency for International
   Development (SIDA), 431
Symbolic anthropology, 13, 101, 342
Symbol
   definition, 18
   exchanging symbolic goods, 104
   food taboos and, 101
   language as, 312
   to promote state unity, 274, *275*
   religious, 341, 342
   youth gangs and, 239
Synchronic approach, 424
Syncretism
   African diaspora religions and, 362
   art and expressive culture, 386–388
   definition, 350, 351
   Our Lady of Guadaloupe in Mexico, *352*
   passover in Kerala, India, 357
   snakes in the Caribbean and St. Patrick in
     Ireland, 351
Syntax, 314
Syria, 41, *42*, 181, 418
Szanton Blanc, Christina, 398

Tabac, Lara, applied medical anthropologist,
   61
Taboos
   food, 100–101

incest, 105, 210, 212
Tag question, 322, 323
Tahiti, tattoos and status in, 138, *241*
Taiwan
   Lim family, *207*
   Mahayana Buddhism in, 354
   patrilineal descent and, 205
   Taiwanese businesses in South Africa, 87
   wage labor immigration and, 403
Tajikistan, 129, *297*
Taj Mahal, *216*, 379
Tamales, and gender roles among Tejanos,
   17
Tamils of Sri Lanka, 23, 274
Tannen, Deborah, 323
Tannenbaum, Nicola B., 354–355
Tanz, C., 325
Tanzania
   female genital cutting and fertility, 160
   fertility in, 121, 123, 160
   HIV/AIDS and, *189*
   industrial collectivized agriculture and, 80
   location and description, *123*
Taoism, 351
Tape recording, 49, 51, 321, 372
TAPS (Trans-Alaska Pipeline System), *427*
Taqqu, Rachelle L., 234
Tarahumara people of northern Mexico,
   119, 134, *135*
Tarong people of the Philippines, 154
Tasmania, 140
Tattoos, *241*, 355
Tauli-Corpuz, Victoria, 446
Tuareg people of North Africa, 440
Taussig, Michael, 36, 436
Taxation, *269*
Tchambuli people of Papua New Guinea,
   146
Teamwork, in fieldwork, 49, 50, *56. See also*
   Collaborative research
Technology
   cultural change and, 19
   digital divide and, 320–321
   improvement of fertility, in
     industrial/informatics societies, 125
   industrial collectivized agriculture and, *80*
   inventions and, 425
   modernization and, 427
   modern weapons of war, 304
   new reproductive techniques, 132
   postmodernism and, 13
   western biomedicine and, 188–189
Teenage pregnancy, 126
Tejano migrant farm workers in the United
   States, 17
Telecommunications, cultural change and,
   19
Television, influence on Euro-American
   children, 155
Temiar people in Malaysia, gender
   differences in performance, 376
Temperate-climate foraging, 67
Temple Mount, 356
Tenochtitlan, Mexico, 268
Te Pareake Mead, Aroha, 293
Territorial entitlements, 440–441. *See also*
   Indigenous peoples; Use rights

Wodziwob, 363
Wolf, Charlotte, 244
Wolf, Eric R., 77, 298
Wolf, Margery, 205
Woman the Gatherer model, 67–68
Women. *See also* Gender; Matriarchy;
    Matrilineal descent
  abortion and, 129, 131
  adolescence and, 157, 159–160, 161
  African American, 35, 43
  Bariba women and childbirth, 53
  biased treatment of Mexicana girls in a
    U.S. school, 24
  colonialism and, 443
  in contemporary politics, 278–279
  development and, 442–445
  domestication of, 443
  domestic workers and circular migration,
    403
  Egyptian Bedu women, 52
  employment and immigrant Dominican
    women, 410
  empowerment through Muslim social
    groups in Kazakhstan, 444–445
  entitlements and, 98
  exchange networks in Balgo Hill region of
    Australia, 104
  exchange networks in the Trobriand
    Islands, 38, 39
  female farming systems, 78–79
  female genital cutting and, 159, 160
  foraging and, 67–68
  formal schooling and gender roles, 156–
    157
  growing percentage as international
    migrants, 409
  gynophobic clubs and, 238
  as household heads, 220–221, 222
  as healers, 179
  high status of Maya women, 212–213
  hospitality in Oman, 102
  inheritance rules, 79
  as law and order professionals, 288
  Maasai property rights and, 158
  marketers, *108*, *405*, 444–445, *445*
  marriage costs and, 136
  marriage crisis among African American, 226

matriarchy, 266
matrifocality, 266
matrilineal extended households, 219
matrilocality, 210
mortality and, 134
new reproductive technology and, 132–
  133
as objects of exchange in marriage, 105–
  106
in pastoralist societies, 74–75
pregnancy and African Americans, 126
refugees, 403
reproductive rights in Bangladesh, 130
reproductive rights in China, 132
role as caretakers of infants and children,
  165
selecting grooms for daughters, 106
sororities, 238
violence against, as a development issue,
  443–444, *444*
widowhood and, 225
women and child care hypothesis, 77
women and food processing hypothesis,
  78
Women of Value, Men of Renown (Weiner),
  38
Women's World Banking, 444
Wongchaisuwan, Tienchai, 83
Woolfson, Peter, 326
Work groups, 241–242
Working Group of Indigenous Minorities in
  Southern Africa (WIMSA), 22
World Bank, 389, 395, 428, 431
World Court, The Hague, Netherlands, 305
World economy, 65. *See* Global economy
World Health Organization (WHO), 195
World Heritage List, 388
World order, 304–305
World religion, 350. *See also* African
  Religions; Buddhism; Christianity;
  Hinduism; Islam; Judaism
World Trade Organization (WTO), 66
Worldview, 340
World War II, 280
Wormald, Tom, 320
Wounded Knee, 363
Wovoka, 363

Wrestling, *383–384*
Wright, Sue, 281
Writing systems, 329
Writing Women's Worlds (Abu-Lughod), 52
WTO (World Trade Organization), 66
Wu, David Y. H., 248
Wundersitz, Joy, 291

Xenophanes, 344
Xi'an, China, *360*
Xizhe, Peng, 124

Yan, Sharon, 160
Yanomami people of Brazil and Venezuela
  division of labor among, 72
  Iroquois naming system of, 205
  location of, *73*
  Napoleon Chagnon and, 300–301, *301*
  socialization of children and, 154–155,
    155
  warfare and, 139
  Yanomami region, *73*
Yemen, 159, *210, 211*
Yoga, 384
Yonggom people of Papua New Guinea,
  254
Yoon, In-Jin, 412
Yorùbá people of West Africa
  art of, 371, *372*
  religion, 362
  women of, 267
You Just Don't Understand (Tannen), 323
Young, Michael W., 48
Youth gang, 238–240
Youth work group, 242
Yugoslavia (former), 23, 25, 36
Yunnus, Mohammed, 444
Yup'ik people of Alaska, 157

Zabusky, Stacia, 280
Zaiki, S. Akbar, 187
Zambia, *294*
Zapotec people of Mexico, 78
Zarrilli, Phillip B., 377, 485
Zoomorphism, 344
Zuni people of the United States, 162, 373
Zureik, Elia, 418